Time Out

Barcelona

timeout.com/barcelona

Penguin Books

PENGUIN BOOKS

Published by the Penguin Group
Penguin Books Ltd, 27 Wrights Lane, London W8 5TZ, England
Penguin Books USA Inc., 375 Hudson Street, New York, New York 10014, USA
Penguin Books Australia Ltd, Ringwood, Victoria, Australia
Penguin Books Canada Ltd, 10 Alcorn Avenue, Toronto, Ontario, Canada M4V 3B2
Penguin Books (NZ) Ltd, 182-190 Wairau Road, Auckland 10, New Zealand

Penguin Books Ltd, Registered Offices: Harmondsworth, Middlesex, England

First published 1996
Second edition 1998
Third edition 2000
Fourth edition 2001
10 9 8 7 6 5 4 3 2 1

Colour reprographics by Icon, Crown House, 56-58 Southwark Street, London SE1
and Precise Litho, 34-35 Great Sutton Street, London EC1
Printed and bound by Cayfosa-Quebecor, Ctra. de Caldes, Km 3 08 130 Sta, Perpètua de Mogoda, Barcelona, Spain

Edited and designed by
Time Out Guides Limited
Universal House
251 Tottenham Court Road
London W1T 7AB
Tel + 44 (0) 20 7813 3000
Fax + 44 (0) 20 7813 6001
Email guides@timeout.com
www.timeout.com

Editorial

Editor William Truini
Deputy Editor Sally Davies
Consultant Editor Nick Rider
Listings Researcher Aitziber de la Quintana
Proofreader Gill Harvey
Indexer Selena Cox

Editorial Director Peter Fiennes
Series Editor Ruth Jarvis
Deputy Series Editor Jonathan Cox
Editorial Assistant Jenny Noden

Design

Art Director John Oakey
Art Editor Mandy Martin
Senior Designer Scott Moore
Designers Benjamin de Lotz, Lucy Grant,
Scanning/Imaging Dan Conway
Picture Editor Kerri Miles
Deputy Picture Editor Olivia Duncan-Jones
Ad Make-up Glen Impey

Advertising

Group Advertisement Director Lesley Gill
Sales Director Mark Phillips
Advertisement Sales (Barcelona) Barcelona Metropolitan
International Sales Co-ordinator Ross Canadé
Advertising Assistant Catherine Shepherd

Administration

Publisher Tony Elliott
Managing Director Mike Hardwick
Financial Director Kevin Ellis
Marketing Director Christine Cort
Marketing Manager Mandy Martinez
General Manager Nichola Coulthard
Production Manager Mark Lamond
Production Controller Samantha Furniss
Accountant Sarah Bostock

Features in this guide were written and researched by:
Introduction William Truini. **History** EM Butterfield, Nick Rider, Jeffrey Swartz. **Barcelona Today** Jeffrey Swartz (**Power in the City** Matthew Tree). **Architecture** David Howel Evans, Jane Opher, Nick Rider. **Accommodation** Anne Heverin.
Sightseeing Jonathan Bennett, EM Butterfield, Nick Rider, Jeffrey Swartz, William Truini. **Museums** Jeffrey Swartz.
Restaurants Cynthia Wong, William Truini. **Cafés & Bars** Amber Ockrassa. **Shops & Services** Anne Heverin, Katrin Vogel.
By Season Jonathan Bennett. **Children** Juliet King. **Dance** Juliet King. **Film** Jonathan Bennett. **Galleries** Jeffrey Swartz. **Gay & Lesbian** Eric Goode. **Music: Classical & Opera** Jonathan Bennett. **Music: Rock, Roots & Jazz** Jack Recasens. **Nightlife** Sheri Ahmed, Nick Chapman. **Sport & Fitness** Juliet King, Gavin Pierce. **Theatre** Jeffrey Swartz. **Trips Out of Town** Matthew Tree. **Directory** Robert Southon.

The editors would like to thank the following: the staff of the Arxiu Fotogràfic de la Ciutat, Maria Lluïsa Albacar and the rest of the staff of Turisme de Barcelona, Esther Jones and all at Metropolitan, the staff of the Palau Robert, Andreu Alsius, Alfons Blanco at Transports Metropolitans de Barcelona, Josep Maria Blasi, Tom Bowden-Green, Sarah Curran, Fundació Miró, Eddie Fox, John David Harmon, Museu Picasso, John O'Donovan, Amaia de la Quintana, RENFE, Ros Sales.

With thanks to Go, the low-cost airline from British Airways, which flies to Barcelona from London Stansted three times a day. To book, call 0845 6054321 or visit the website at www.gofly.com.

Maps by Mapworld.

Photography by Ingrid Morato except: page 211 Oriol Alev; page 25 Stephan Savoia/Associated Press; page 264 Jordi Pareto; page 265 William Truini; page 268 top, 275 World Pictures; page 268 middle and bottom, 272 Neil Setchfield; page 285 Bettina Marten.

The following pictures were supplied by the featured establishments: 110, 111, 118, 274, 202.

Contents

Contents

Introduction

Few places on the planet can match Barcelona's appeal these days. It seems like everyone either knows someone who's been here, is about to make a visit themselves, or can't wait to come back. In the case of the truly stricken, life just doesn't seem worth living without actually moving here to stay.

On the face of it, the allure of Barcelona seems obvious enough. Colourful, vibrant and with the Mediterranean shimmering at its doorstep, the city is also just about perfect in size. Contained by the hills of Tibidabo and Montjuïc, it has been spared the horrors of urban sprawl and yet is large enough to have the feel of a true metropolis.

However, when compared to other world-famous cities, the reasons for Barcelona's staggering popularity can seem less evident. The city's fame, for one thing, is not based on a stack of great monuments. Many first-time visitors will of course make a beeline straight for the Sagrada Familia and other works of wonder by Gaudí, but apart from these, fresh arrivals are unlikely to show up with a headful of postcards or an arm-long list of obligatory visits.

Furthermore, in a world apparently under the spell of globalisation, Barcelona persists as an outpost of local identity as the capital of Catalonia, a small country that has witnessed a remarkable resurgence of its own language and culture in the nearly 25 years since democracy was restored in Spain. Or another contradiction: on a planet that grows more overpopulated by the second and where a bit of breathing space is what you'd expect most people to hunt for, Barcelona is a tremendously crowded place.

Of course, the fascination with Barcelona probably has much to do precisely with these qualities. For starters, the city's contagious, non-stop buzz is a direct product of its density. And a lack of obvious monuments means the stage, the focus of attention, is the city itself. This means anyone and everyone who sets foot in Barcelona becomes a part of the play. The Rambla is a striking example. Glimpsed through a post-modern lens, perhaps the Rambla is in fact one long, horizontal monument, a homage to the flow of humanity that is made tangible and real, *alive*, by the fact that any one of us can join it.

The city's rejoicing in its own identity, its Catalan-ness, must also touch a nerve in our modern sense of loss and longing for local roots. Sure, the city is under bombardment by fast-food chains and American-style mega-malls, but what most appeals about the place are its myriad tiny shops, its restaurants run by people who treat you like people, who serve up their *xai amb all i oli* and delectable *crema catalana* with love, or its unique, entirely engaging festivals.

This resistance by the city to becoming one more cliché on the tourist circuit helps explain why it is so tantalisingly attractive. For all its visitors, Barcelona is still tinged with an aura of the unknown; you may be told about the narrow, winding streets of the Old City, but until you're actually on them, you won't know where they lead. Barcelona, in short, is still very much a place to be discovered.

ABOUT THE TIME OUT CITY GUIDES

The *Time Out Barcelona Guide* is one of an expanding series of *Time Out* City Guides, now numbering over 30, produced by the people behind London and New York's successful listings magazines. Our guides are all written and updated by resident experts who have striven to provide you with all the most up-to-date information you'll need to explore the city or read up on its background, whether you're a local or a first-time visitor.

THE LOWDOWN ON THE LISTINGS

Above all, we've tried to make this book as useful as possible. Addresses, telephone numbers, websites, transport information, opening times, admission prices and credit card details are all included in our listings. And, as far as possible, we've given details of facilities, services and events, all checked and correct as we went to press. However, owners and managers can change their arrangements at any time. Also, in Barcelona, small shops and bars often do not keep precise opening hours, and may close earlier or later than stated according to the level of trade. Similarly, arts programmes are often finalised very late. Before you go out of your way, we'd advise you whenever

> There is an online version of this guide, as well as weekly events listings for over 30 international cities, at www.timeout.com.

possible to phone and check opening times, ticket prices, and other particulars. While every effort has been made to ensure the accuracy of the information in this guide, the publishers cannot accept responsibility for any errors it may contain.

PRICES AND PAYMENT

The prices we have listed should be treated as guidelines, not gospel; fluctuating exchange rates and inflation can cause prices to change rapidly. We have noted where venues such as shops, hotels and restaurants accept the following credit cards: American Express (**AmEx**), Diners Club (**DC**), MasterCard (**MC**), and Visa (**V**). Many businesses also accept other cards, including Switch, Delta and JCB. In addition, some shops, restaurants and attractions take travellers' cheques issued by major financial insitutions.

THE LIE OF THE LAND

We have divided the city into areas – simplified, for convenience, from the full complexity of Barcelona's geography – and the relevant area name is given with each venue listed in this guide. For most places listed we also give a map reference, which indicates the page and square on which an address will be found on our street maps at the back of the book (starting on page 319).

TELEPHONE NUMBERS

It is necessary to dial provincial area codes with all numbers in Spain, even for local calls. Hence all normal Barcelona numbers begin with 93, whether or not you're calling from outside the city. From abroad, you must dial 34 (the international dialling code for Spain) followed by the number given in the book – which includes the initial 93.

ESSENTIAL INFORMATION

For all the practical information you might need for visiting the city, including emergency phone numbers and details of local transport, turn to the **Directory** chapter at the back of the guide. It starts on page 287.

MAPS

The map section at the back of this book includes an overview of the city; detailed street maps of the Eixample, the Raval, Gràcia and other districts, and a small-scale map of the Old City, with a comprehensive street index; a large-scale locality map for planning trips out of town and maps of the local rail and Metro networks. It begins on page 317.

LET US KNOW WHAT YOU THINK

We hope you enjoy the *Time Out Barcelona Guide*, and we'd like to know what you think of it. We welcome tips for places that you consider we should include in future editions and take note of your criticism of our choices. There's a reader's reply card at the back of this book for your feedback – or you can email us at barcelonaguide@timeout.com.

Advertisers

In Context

Feature boxes

History

Roman backwater, centre of empire, bourgeois paradise, hotbed of revolution and modern style mecca – Barcelona has lived many lives.

THE ORIGINS

The Romans founded Barcelona, in about 15 BC, on the Mons Taber, a small hill between two streams that had a good view of the Mediterranean, and which today is crowned by the cathedral. The plain around it was sparsely inhabited by the Laetani, an agrarian Iberian people known for producing grain and honey and gathering oysters. Named Barcino, the town was much smaller than the capital of the Roman province of Hispania Citerior, Tarraco (Tarragona), but had the only harbour, albeit a poor one, between there and Narbonne.

Like virtually every other Roman new town in Europe it was a fortified rectangle with a crossroads at its centre, where the Plaça Sant Jaume is today. It was a decidedly unimportant, provincial town, but nonetheless the rich plain provided it with a produce garden, and the sea gave it an incipient maritime trade. It acquired a Jewish community very soon after its

foundation, and was associated with some Christian martyrs, notably Barcelona's first patron saint Santa Eulàlia. She was supposedly executed at the end of the third century via a series of revolting tortures, including being rolled naked in a sealed barrel full of glass shards down the alley now called Baixada (descent) de Santa Eulàlia.

Nevertheless, Barcelona accepted Christianity shortly afterwards, in 312 AD, together with the rest of the Roman Empire, which by then was under growing threat of invasion. In the fourth century Barcino's rough defences were replaced with massive stone walls, many sections of which can still be seen today. It was these ramparts that ensured Barcelona's continuity, making it a stronghold much desired by later warlords (for more on relics of Roman Barcelona, see p72).

These and other defences did not prevent the empire's disintegration. In 415, Barcelona

The streets of Roman Barcino, beneath the **Plaça del Rei**. *See p75.*

briefly became capital of the kingdom of the Visigoths, under their chieftain Ataülf. He brought with him as a prisoner Gala Placidia, the 20-year-old daughter of a Roman emperor, whom he forced to marry him. She is famous, though, as a woman of strong character, and is credited with converting the barbarian king to Christianity. She was also perhaps fortunate in that Ataülf died shortly afterwards, whereupon Gala Placidia left, married her relative the Emperor Constantius I, and for a time became the most powerful figure in the court of Byzantium. Back in Barcelona, meanwhile, the Visigoths soon moved on southwards to extend their control over the whole of the Iberian peninsula, and for the next 400 years the town was a neglected backwater.

It was in this state when the Muslims swept across the peninsula after 711, easily crushing Goth resistance. They made little attempt to settle Catalonia, but much of the Christian population retreated into the Pyrenees, the first Catalan heartland. Then, at the end of the eighth century, the Franks began to drive southwards against the Muslims from across the mountains. In 801 Charlemagne's son Louis the Pious took Barcelona and made it a bastion of the Marca Hispanica, or 'Spanish March', the southern buffer of his father's empire. This gave Catalonia a trans-Pyrenean origin entirely different from that of the other Christian states in Spain; equally, it is for this reason that the closest relative of the Catalan language is Provençal, not Castilian.

When the Frankish princes returned to their main business further north, loyal counts were left behind with sections of the Catalan lands to rule, charged in exchange with defending the frontier against the Saracens. Towards the end of the ninth century one of these, Count Guifré el Pilós, Wilfred 'the Hairy' (c860-98), succeeded in gaining title to several of the Catalan territories from his base in the Pyrenean valleys around Ripoll. He united them under his rule, creating the basis for a future Catalan state and founding the dynasty of Counts of Barcelona that would reign in an unbroken line until 1410. His successors made Barcelona their capital, and so set the seal on the city's future.

'The Quatre Barres is the oldest national flag in Europe.'

As a founding patriarch Wilfred is a semi-mythical figure, surrounded by legends, not the least of them that he was the source of the Catalan national flag, the Quatre Barres (Four Bars) of red on a yellow background, also known as La Senyera. The story goes that he was fighting against the Saracens alongside his lord, the Frankish emperor, when he was mortally wounded; in recognition of Wilfred's heroism, the emperor dipped his fingers into his friend's bloody wounds and ran them down the Count's golden shield. Whatever its mythical origins, the four-red-stripes-on-yellow symbol is first reliably recorded on the tomb of Count Ramon Berenguer II in 1082, making the Quatre Barres the oldest national flag in Europe, predating its nearest competitor, that of Denmark, by a hundred years. What is not known is in what way Wilfred was so hairy, although he could perhaps be imagined as the prototype of every deep-voiced, barrel-chested Catalan man with a beard.

A century after Wilfred, in 985, a Muslim army attacked and sacked Barcelona. The hairy Count's great-grandson, Count Borrell II, requested aid from his theoretical feudal lord, the Frankish king. He received no reply, and so repudiated all Frankish sovereignty over Catalonia. From then on – although the name was not yet in use – Catalonia was effectively independent, and the Counts of Barcelona were free to forge its destiny.

A MEDIEVAL GOLDEN AGE
In the first century of the new millennium Catalonia was consolidated as a political entity. The Catalan counties retained from their Frankish origins a French system of aristocratic feudalism – another difference from the rest of Iberia – but also had a peasantry who were notably independent and resistant to noble demands. In the 1060s the Usatges ('Usages') were established, the country's distinctive legal code.

The Counts of Barcelona and lesser nobles also endowed monasteries throughout Catalonia. This provided the background to the years of glory of Romanesque art, with the building of the great monasteries and churches of northern Catalonia, such as **Sant Pere de Rodes** near Figueres, and the painting of the superb murals now in the **Museu Nacional** on Montjuïc. There was also a flowering of scholarship, reflecting Catalan contacts with both Islamic and Carolingian cultures. In Barcelona, shipbuilding and commerce in grain and wine all expanded, and a new trade developed in textiles. The city grew both inside its old Roman walls and outside them, where *vilanoves* or 'new towns' appeared at Sant Pere and La Ribera.

Catalonia – a name that gained currency in Latin in the 11th century – was also gaining more territory from the Muslims to the south, beyond the Penedès. For a long time, though, the realm of the Counts of Barcelona continued to look just as much to the north, across the Pyrenees, where the Provençal-speaking Languedoc was then the most sophisticated society in western Europe. After 1035, during the reigns of the four Counts Ramon Berenguer, large areas of what is now southern France were acquired, either through marriage or with Arab booty. In 1112 the union of Ramon

Berenguer III 'the Great' (1093-1131) with Princess Dolça of Provence extended his authority as far as the Rhône.

A more significant marriage occurred in 1137, when Ramon Berenguer IV (1131-62) wed Petronella, heir to the throne of Aragon. This would, in the long term, bind Catalonia into Iberia. The uniting of the two dynasties created a powerful entity known as the 'Crown of Aragon', each element retaining its separate institutions, and ruled by monarchs known as the 'Count-Kings'. Since Aragon was already a kingdom, it was given precedence and its name was often used to refer to the state, but the court language was Catalan and the centre of government remained in Barcelona.

Ramon Berenguer IV also extended Catalan territory to its current frontiers in the Ebro valley. At the beginning of the next century, however, the dynasty lost virtually all of its lands north of the Pyrenees to France, when Count-King Pere I 'the Catholic' was killed at the battle of Muret in 1213. This was a blessing in disguise. In future, the Catalan-Aragonese state would be oriented decisively towards the Mediterranean and the south, and was able to embark on two centuries of imperialism equalled in vigour only by Barcelona's burgeoning commercial enterprise.

MEDITERRANEAN EMPIRE
Pere I's successor was the most expansionist of the Count-Kings. Jaume I 'the Conqueror' (1213-76) abandoned any idea of further adventures in Provence and joined decisively in the campaign against the Muslims to the south, taking Mallorca in 1229, Ibiza in 1235 and then, at much greater cost, Valencia in 1238. He made it another separate kingdom, the third part of the 'Crown of Aragon'.

Barcelona became the centre of an empire extending across the Mediterranean. The city grew tremendously under Jaume I, and in mid-century he ordered the building of a new, second wall, along the line of the Rambla and roughly encircling the area between there and the modern Parc de la Ciutadella, thus bringing La Ribera and the other *vilanoves* within the city. In 1274 he also gave Barcelona a form of representative self-government, the Consell de Cent, council of 100 chosen citizens, an institution that would last for over 400 years. In Catalonia as a whole, royal powers were limited by a parliament, the Corts, with a permanent standing committee, known as the Generalitat.

Catalan imperialism advanced by conquest and marriage well beyond the Balearic Islands. The Count-Kings commanded a powerful fleet and a mercenary army, the 'Catalan Companies' (Almogàvers). For decades they were led by two great commanders, the fleet by Roger de Llúria and the army by Roger de Flor. The stuff of another set of heroic legends – such as their sword-in-hand battle cry '*Desperta ferro!*' ('Awaken, iron!') – the Almogàvers made themselves feared equally by Christians and Muslims as they travelled the Mediterranean conquering, plundering and enslaving in the name of God and the Crown of Aragon.

In 1282 Pere II 'the Great' annexed Sicily, and Catalan domination over the island would last for nearly 150 years. The Catalan empire reached its greatest strength under Jaume II 'the Just' (1291-1327). Corsica (1323) and Sardinia (1324) were added to the possessions of the Crown of Aragon, although the latter would never submit to Catalan rule and would be a constant focus of revolt.

THE CITY OF THE GOLDEN AGE

The Crown of Aragon was often at war with Arab rulers, but its capital flourished through commerce with every part of the Mediterranean, Christian and Muslim. Catalan ships also sailed into the Atlantic, to England and Flanders. Their ventures were actively supported by the Count-Kings and burghers of Barcelona, and regulated by the first-ever code of maritime law, the 'Llibre del Consolat de Mar' (written 1258-72), an early example of the Catalans' tendency to legalism, the influence of which extended far beyond their own territories. By the late 13th century nearly 130 consulates ringed the Mediterranean, engaged in a complex system of trade that involved spices, coral, grain, slaves, metals, wool and other textiles, olive oil, salt fish and leather goods.

Not surprisingly, this age of power and prestige was also the great era of building in medieval Barcelona. The Catalan Gothic style reached its peak between the reigns of Jaume the Just and Pere III 'the Ceremonious' (1336-87). The Count-Kings' imperial conquests may have been ephemeral, but their talent for permanence in building can still be admired today. Between 1290 and 1340 the construction of most of Barcelona's major Gothic buildings was initiated. Religious edifices such as the **cathedral**, **Santa Maria del Mar** and **Santa Maria del Pi** were matched by civil buildings such as the **Saló de Tinell** and the **Llotja** (lodge), the old market and stock exchange. As a result, Barcelona today contains the most important nucleus of Gothic civil architecture anywhere in Europe.

The ships of the Catalan navy were built in the monumental **Drassanes** (shipyards), begun by Pere II and completed under Pere III, in 1378. In 1359 Pere III also built the third, final city wall, along the line of the modern

Jaume I, the Conqueror

Paral.lel, Ronda Sant Pau and Ronda Sant Antoni. This gave the 'old city' of Barcelona its definitive shape.

La Ribera, 'the waterfront', was the centre of trade and industry in 14th-century Barcelona. Once unloaded at the beach, wares were taken to the Llotja. Just inland, the Carrer Montcada was the street *par excellence* where newly enriched merchants could display their wealth in opulent Gothic palaces. All around were the workers of the various craft guilds, grouped together in their own streets (*see p82* **Walk 2: La Ribera**).

'Catalonia was one of the first areas in Europe to use its vernacular language in written form.'

Women's domains in this Barcelona were initially limited to home, market, convent or brothel, although in 1249 they won the right to inherit property, and women were at one time the main textile workers. At the very top of society some women became very powerful, as it was quite common – unusually for that era – for

Catalan Count-Kings to delegate their authority to their queens when they went on campaigns, as happened with Eleonor of Sicily, wife of Pere III.

The Catalan 'Golden Age' was also an era of cultural greatness. Catalonia was one of the first areas in Europe to use its vernacular language, as well as Latin, in written form and as a language of culture. The oldest written

texts in Catalan are the *Homilies d'Organyà*, translations from the Bible dating from the 12th century. Not just monks, but also the court and the aristocracy seem very early to have attained an unusual level of literacy, and Jaume I wrote his own autobiography, the *Llibre dels Feits* or 'Book of Deeds', dramatically recounting his achievements and conquests.

Jewish Barcelona: the *Call*

The placid streets of Barcelona's former *Call*, or Jewish quarter, reveal little at first sight of its splendid past. Founded by immigrants to Barcino in the second century, the *Call* predates Christianisation, something the city's tiny present-day Jewish community likes to draw to locals' attention. Thriving for 1100 years, it fostered one of Spain's most important medieval Jewish populations, its fate shifting with the vicissitudes of each political moment. Alhough the Visigoths decreed all Jews to be slaves in 694, under the Count-Kings their status improved, and they eventually gained the right to be civil servants. Missionising pressure from Christian orders, however, lead to a law of King Jaume I of 1243 requiring them to wear identifiable clothing.

The Barcelona *Call* came to be highly reputed for its learning. Rabbi Benjamin of Tudela, a famous 12th-century travel chronicler, wrote of the 'wise and learned men among the Jewish community in Barcelona'. Its early inhabitants were mostly artisans and farmers, yet soon many became known as able fiscal agents and traders, and as doctors, Arabic translators and even Catalan language poets. Others served the Catalan nobility and advised the counts of Barcelona; in the archive of the Crown of Aragon one surprisingly finds Catalan documents drafted in Hebrew lettering. Such prestige lead Jaume I to sponsor the famous 'Disputation of Barcelona' in 1263, with Moses ben Nahman (Nahmanides, known locally as Bonastruc da Porta), the mystical scholar from Girona, defending his faith for three days against the radical Dominican Friar Paul Christian, a converted Jew turned proselytising monk.

By that time the community was shut in at nightfall behind the arches that once lined the Carrer del Call, the quarter's eastern limit, and between the streets where the current Palau de la Generalitat is to the north and curving Banys Nous to the south-west. Eventually the Dominicans had their way; the

Call was sacked in a wave of pogroms of 6-8 August 1391, which affected every Jewish quarter in Catalonia, Valencia and Mallorca. A fanatical mob, incited by the monks, massacred scores of its inhabitants. The *Call* never recovered, and few Jews were left in Barcelona when the official ban was signed in 1424, a prelude to the expulsion of all Jews from Spain in 1492.

Today a meander through these winding streets still stirs the imagination. Recently uncovered documents identify the south-west corner of the intersection between Carrer Marlet and Carrer Sant Domènec del Call as the site of the Sinagoga Major; the dank half basement seen through the low windows corresponds to the maximum size of a synagogue (some 100sq m/300 sq ft) permitted under the Crown of Aragon. A private project to convert the space into a *Call* information point seems to have stalled. A separate water fountain for the *Call* was located in the centre of C/Sant Honorat where C/Fruita meets it, while a smaller synagogue (the Sinagoga Poca) sat where the Gothic Sant Jordi chapel inside the Generalitat now stands. Arc de Sant Ramon del Call housed a girl's school, and at C/Marlet, 1, we can read a twelfth-century Hebrew inscription from a long-demolished house, on a stone which was placed there in the 1820s.

After 1391 the Jewish cemetery on Montjuïc was desecrated and headstones were used for new construction. Hebrew inscriptions can be seen on stones set into the eastern wall of Plaça Sant Iu, across from the Cathedral, and at ankle level in the south-west corner of the Plaça del Rei. Larger Jewish tombstones can be seen in the **Museu Militar** on Montjuïc and in the Gothic section of the **Museu Nacional d'Art** de Catalunya (see chapter **Museums**). The city's history museums fail to deal adequately with Jewish history, with the Museu de l'Història de Catalunya unpatriotically ignoring Nahmanides, certainly one of medieval Catalonia's most illustrious figures.

Incipient Catalan literature was given a vital thrust by the unique figure of Ramon Llull (1235-1316). After a debauched youth, he turned to more serious pursuits after he experienced a series of religious visions, and became the first man in post-Roman Europe to write philosophy in a vernacular language. Steeped in Arabic and Hebrew writings, he brought together Christian, Islamic, Jewish and classical ideas, and also wrote a vast amount on other subjects – from theories of chivalry to poetry and visionary tales. In doing so he effectively created Catalan as a literary language. Catalan translations from Greek and Latin were also undertaken at this time. In the very twilight of the Golden Age, in 1490, the Valencian Joanot Martorell published *Tirant Lo Blanc*, the bawdy story that is considered the first true European novel.

CRISIS & DECLINE

Barcelona was not, though, a peaceful and harmonious place during its Golden Age, especially as the 14th century wore on. Social unrest and violence in the streets were common: grain riots, popular uprisings, attacks on Jews and gang warfare. An ongoing struggle took place between two political factions, the *Biga* (roughly representing the most established merchants) and the *Busca* (roughly composed of smaller tradesmen).

The extraordinary prosperity of the medieval period was not to last. The Count-Kings had overextended Barcelona's resources, and overinvested in far-off ports. By 1400 the effort to maintain their conquests by force, especially Sardinia, had exhausted the spirit and the coffers of the Catalan imperialist drive. The Black Death, which had arrived in the 1340s, had also had a devastating impact on Catalonia. This only intensified the bitterness of social conflicts between the aristocracy, merchants, peasants and the urban poor.

In 1410 Martí I 'the Humane' died without an heir, bringing to an end the line of Counts of Barcelona unbroken since Guifré el Pilós. After much deliberation between church and aristocracy the Crown of Aragon was passed to a member of a Castilian noble family, the Trastámaras: Fernando de Antequera (1410-16).

His son, Alfons V 'the Magnanimous' (1416-58), undertook one more conquest, of Naples, but the empire was under ever greater pressure, and Barcelona merchants were unable to compete with the Genoese and Venetians. At home, in the 1460s, the effects of war and catastrophic famine led to a collapse into civil war and peasant revolt. The population was depleted to such an extent that Barcelona would not regain the numbers it had had in 1400 (40,000) until the 18th century.

THE FALL OF BARCELONA

In 1469 an important union for Spain initiated a woeful period in Barcelona's history, dubbed by some Catalan historians the *Decadència*, which would lead to the end of Catalonia as a separate entity. In that year Ferdinand of Aragon (reigned 1479-1516) married Isabella of Castile (1476-1506), and so united the different Spanish kingdoms, even though they would retain their separate institutions for another two centuries.

As Catalonia's fortunes had declined, so those of Castile had risen. While Catalonia was impoverished and in chaos, Castile had become larger, richer, had a bigger population and was on the crest of a wave of expansion. In 1492 Granada, last Muslim foothold in Spain, was conquered, Isabella decreed the expulsion of all Jews from Castile and Aragon, and Columbus discovered America.

It was Castile's seafaring orientation toward the Atlantic, rather than the Mediterranean, that confirmed Catalonia's decline. The discovery of the New World was a disaster for Catalan commerce: trade shifted decisively away from the Mediterranean, and Catalans were officially barred from participating in the exploitation of the new empire until the 1770s. The weight of Castile within the monarchy was increased, and it very soon became the clear seat of government.

In 1516 the Spanish crown passed to the House of Habsburg, in the shape of Ferdinand and Isabella's grandson the Emperor Charles V. His son Philip II of Spain established Madrid as the capital of all his dominions in 1561. Catalonia was managed by appointed Viceroys, the power of its institutions increasingly restricted, with a down-at-heel aristocracy and a meagre cultural life.

THE GREAT DEFEATS

While Castilian Spain went through its 'Golden Century', Catalonia was left more and more on the margins. Worse was to come, however, in the following century, with the two national revolts, both heroic defeats, that have since acquired a central role in Catalan nationalist mythology.

'In 1640 a mass of peasants surged into the city and murdered the Viceroy.'

The problem for the Spanish monarchy was that, whereas Castile was an absolute monarchy and so could be taxed at will, in the former Aragonese territories, and especially Catalonia, royal authority kept coming up against a mass of local rights and privileges. As the

Habsburgs' empire became bogged down in endless wars and expenses that not even American gold could meet, the Count-Duke of Olivares, the formidable great minister of King Philip IV (1621-65), resolved to extract more money and troops from the non-Castilian dominions of the crown. The Catalans, however, felt they were taxed quite enough already.

In 1640 a mass of peasants, later dubbed Els Segadors, 'the Reapers', gathered on the Rambla in Barcelona, outside the Porta Ferrissa or 'Iron Gate' in the second wall. They rioted against royal authority, surged into the city and seized and murdered the Viceroy, the Marqués de Santa Coloma. This began the general uprising known as the Guerra dels Segadors, the 'Reapers' War'. The authorities of the Generalitat, led by its President Pau Claris, were fearful of the violence of the poor and, lacking the confidence to declare Catalonia independent, appealed for protection from Louis XIII of France. French armies, however, were unable to defend Catalonia adequately, and in 1652 a destitute Barcelona capitulated to the equally exhausted army of Philip IV. Later, in 1659, France and Spain made peace with a treaty under which the Catalan territory of Roussillon, around Perpignan, was given to

France. After the revolt, Philip IV and his ministers were surprisingly magnanimous, allowing the Catalans to retain what was left of their institutions despite their disloyalty. This war, however, provided the Catalan national anthem, *Els Segadors*.

Fifty years later came the second of the great national rebellions, in the War of the Spanish Succession, the last time Catalonia sought to regain its national freedoms by force. In 1700 Charles II of Spain died without an heir. Castile accepted the grandson of Louis XIV of France, Philip of Anjou, as King Philip V of Spain (1700-46). However, the alternative candidate, the Archduke Charles of Austria, promised to restore the traditional rights of the former Aragonese territories, and so won their allegiance. He also had the support, in his fight against France, of Britain, Holland and Austria. Once again, though, Catalonia backed the wrong horse, and was let down in its choice of allies. In 1713 Britain and the Dutch made a separate peace with France and withdrew their aid, leaving the Catalans stranded with no possibility of victory. After a 13-month siege in which every citizen was called to arms, Barcelona fell to the French and Spanish armies on 11 September 1714.

Grim reapers seize Barcelona, 1640.

The most heroic defeat of all, this date marked the most decisive political reverse in Barcelona's history, and is now commemorated as Catalan National Day, the Diada. Some of Barcelona's resisters were buried next to the church of Santa Maria del Mar in La Ribera in the **Fossar de les Moreres** ('Mulberry Graveyard'), now a memorial (*see p81*).

In 1715 Philip V issued his decree of 'Nova Planta', abolishing all the remaining separate institutions of the Crown of Aragon and so, in effect, creating 'Spain' as a single, unitary state. Large-scale 'Castilianisation' of the country was initiated, and Castilian replaced the Catalan language in all official documents.

In Barcelona, extra measures were taken to keep the city under firm control. The crumbling medieval walls and the castle on Montjuïc were refurbished with new ramparts, and a massive new citadel was built on the eastern side of the old city, where the Parc de la Ciutadella is today. To make space for it, thousands of people had to be expelled from La Ribera and forcibly rehoused in the Barceloneta, Barcelona's first-ever planned housing scheme, with its barrack-like street plan unmistakably provided by French military engineers. This citadel became the most hated symbol of the city's subordination.

BARCELONA BOUNCES BACK
Politically subjugated and without much of a native ruling class following the departure of many of its remaining aristocrats to serve the monarchy in Madrid, Catalonia nevertheless revived in the 18th century. Catalans continued speaking their language, and developed independent commercial initiatives.

Ironically, the Bourbons, by abolishing legal differences between Catalonia and the rest of Spain, also removed the earlier restrictions on Catalan trade, especially with the colonies. The strength of Barcelona's guilds had enabled it to maintain its artisan industries, and the city revived particularly following the official authorisation to trade with the Americas by King Charles III in 1778.

Shipping picked up again, and in the last years of the 18th century Barcelona had a booming export trade to the New World in wines and spirits from Catalan vineyards and textiles, wool and silk. In 1780 a merchant called Erasme de Gómina opened Barcelona's first true factory, a hand-powered weaving mill in C/Riera Alta with 800 workers. In the next decade Catalan trade with Spanish America quadrupled; Barcelona's population had grown from around 30,000 in 1720 to close to 100,000 by the end of the century.

This prosperity was reflected in a new wave of building in the city. Neo-classical mansions

appeared, notably on C/Ample and the Rambla. The greatest transformation, though, was in the Rambla itself. Until the 1770s it had been no more than a dusty, dry riverbed where country people came to sell their produce, lined on the Raval side mostly with giant religious houses and on the other with Jaume I's second wall. In 1775 the Captain-General, the Marqués de la Mina, embarked on an ambitious scheme to demolish the wall and turn the Rambla into a paved promenade. Beyond the Rambla, the previously semi-rural Raval was becoming densely populated.

Barcelona's expansion was briefly interrupted by the French invasion of 1808. Napoleon sought to appeal to Catalans by offering them national recognition within his empire, but, curiously, met with very little response. After six years of turmoil, Barcelona's growing business class resumed their projects in 1814, with the restoration of the Bourbon monarchy in the shape of Ferdinand VII.

FACTORIES, POETS & BARRICADES
The upheaval of the Napoleonic occupation ushered in 60 years of conflict and political disorder in Spain, as new and traditional forces in society – reactionaries, conservatives, reformists and revolutionaries – struggled with each other to establish a viable system of government. Even so, during this same era Barcelona was still able to embark upon the transformations of the industrial revolution, Catalonia, with Lombardy, being one of only two areas in southern Europe to do so before the end of the 19th century.

On his restoration, Ferdinand VII (1808-33) attempted to reinstate the absolute monarchy of his youth and reimpose his authority over Spain's American colonies, and failed to do either. On his death he was succeeded by his three-year-old daughter Isabel II (1833-68), but the throne was also claimed by his brother Carlos, who was backed by the most reactionary sectors in the country. To defend Isabel's rights the Regent, Ferdinand's widow Queen Maria Cristina, was obliged to seek the support of liberals, and so granted a very limited form of constitution. Thus began Spain's Carlist Wars, which had a powerful impact in conservative rural Catalonia, where Don Carlos' faction won a considerable following, in part because of its support for traditional local rights and customs.

INDUSTRIAL REVOLUTION
While this see-saw struggle went on around the country, in Barcelona a liberal-minded local administration, freed from subordination to the military, was able to engage in some city planning, opening up the soon-to-be fashionable

Cerdà: Getting it straight

Once Barcelona's walls came down (see p16), a plan was needed to develop the land beyond them and connect the city with Gràcia and the outlying towns. The Ajuntament held a competition for projects in 1859. The councillors actually preferred a scheme presented by the prestigious architect Antoni Rovira i Trias, for long straight streets radiating fan-like from Plaça Catalunya. Controversially, however, and for reasons that have never been explained, orders came from Madrid that the plan to be adopted was that of another Catalan engineer, Ildefons Cerdà (1815-75).

Cerdà had surveyed and drawn the city's first accurate plans in 1855. He was also a radical influenced by utopian socialist ideas, concerned with the cramped, unhealthy conditions of workers' housing in the old city. With its love of straight lines and uniform grid, Cerdà's plan is very much related to visionary rationalist ideas of its time, as was the idea of placing two of its main avenues along a geographic parallel and a meridian. His central aim was to alleviate overpopulation problems while encouraging social equality by using quadrangular blocks of a standard size, with strict building controls to ensure that they were built up on only two sides, to a limited height, leaving a garden in between. Each district would be of 20 blocks, containing all community necessities.

In the event, though, this idealised use of urban space was scarcely ever achieved, for the private developers who actually built the Eixample regarded Cerdà's restrictions on their property as pointless interference. Buildings went up to much more than the planned heights, and in practice all the blocks from Plaça Catalunya to the Diagonal have been enclosed, with very few inner gardens withstanding the onslaught of construction.

The Ajuntament had disliked the scheme because it seemed to disregard the old centre of the city, and *Modernista* architects, in love with curves, initially railed against the project as a horror. Nevertheless, it would become the primary showcase for their imaginative feats, and an essential part of Barcelona's identity.

C/Ferran and Plaça Sant Jaume in the 1820s, and later adding the Plaça Reial. A fundamental change came in 1836, when a liberal government in Madrid decreed the *Desamortización*, or disentailment, of Spain's monasteries. In Barcelona, where convents and religious houses still took up great sections of the Raval and the Rambla, a huge area was freed for development.

The Rambla took on the appearance it roughly retains today, while the Raval, the main district for new industry in a Barcelona still contained within its walls, rapidly filled up with tenements and textile mills several storeys high. In 1832 the first steam-driven factory in Spain was built on C/Tallers, sparking resistance from hand-spinners and weavers.

> ## 'Barcelona's people were rebellious, and liberal, republican, free-thinking and utopian socialist groups proliferated.'

Most of the city's factories, though, were still relatively small, and Catalan manufacturers were very aware that they were at a disadvantage in any competition with the industries of Britain and other countries to the north. For decades, their political motto would not be anything to do with nationalism but protectionism, as they incessantly demanded of Madrid that the textile markets of Spain and its remaining colonies be sealed against all foreign competition.

Also, they did not have the city to themselves. Not only did the anti-industrial Carlists threaten from the countryside, but Barcelona soon became a centre of radical ideas. Its people were notably rebellious, and liberal, republican, free-thinking and even utopian socialist groups proliferated between sporadic bursts of repression. In 1842 a liberal revolt, the *Jamancia*, took over Barcelona, and barricades went up around the city. This was the last occasion Barcelona was bombarded from the castle on Montjuïc, as the army struggled to regain control.

The Catalan language, by this time, had been relegated to secondary status, spoken in every street but rarely written or used in cultured discourse. Then, in 1833 Bonaventura Carles Aribau published his *Oda a la Pàtria*, a romantic eulogy in Catalan of the country, its language and its past. This poem had an extraordinary impact, and is traditionally credited with initiating the *Renaixença* (rebirth) of Catalan heritage and culture. The year 1848 was a high point for Barcelona and Catalonia, with the inauguration of the first railway in Spain, from Barcelona to Mataró, and the opening of the Liceu opera.

BARCELONA BREAKS ITS BANKS

The optimism of Barcelona's new middle class was counterpointed by two persistent obstacles: the weakness of the Spanish economy as a whole, and the instability of their own society, reflected in atrocious labour relations. No consideration was given to the manpower behind the industrial surge: the underpaid, overworked men, women and children who lived in increasingly appalling conditions in high-rise slums within the cramped city. In 1855 the first general strike took place in Barcelona. The Captain-General, Zapatero, inaugurating a long cycle of conflict, refused to permit any workers' organisations, and bloodily suppressed all resistance.

One response to the city's problems that had almost universal support in Barcelona was the demolition of the city walls, which had imposed a stifling restriction on its growth. For years, however, the Spanish state refused to relinquish this hold on the city. To find space, larger factories were established in villages around Barcelona, such as Sants and Poble Nou. In 1854 permission finally came for the demolition of the citadel and the walls. The work began with enthusiastic popular participation, crowds of volunteers joining in at weekends. Barcelona at last broke out of the space it had occupied since the 14th century and spread outward into its new *eixample*, 'extension', to a plan by Ildefons Cerdà (*see p15*).

In 1868 Isabel II, once a symbol of liberalism, was overthrown by a progressive revolt. During the six years of upheaval that followed, power in Madrid would be held by a provisional government, a constitutional monarchy under an Italian prince and then a federal republic. Workers were free to organise, and in November 1868 Giuseppe Fanelli, an Italian emissary of Bakunin, brought the ideas of anarchism to Madrid and Barcelona, encountering a ready response in Catalonia. In 1870 the first-ever Spanish workers' congress was held, in Barcelona. The radical forces, however, were divided between multiple factions, while the established classes of society, increasingly threatened, called for the restoration of order. The Republic proclaimed in 1873 was unable to establish its authority, and succumbed to a military coup.

THE YANKEES OF EUROPE

In 1874 the Bourbon dynasty was restored to the Spanish throne in the shape of Alfonso XII, son of Isabel II. Workers' organisations were again suppressed. The middle classes, however, felt their confidence renewed. The 1870s saw a frenzied boom in stock speculation, the *febre d'or* or 'gold fever', and the real take-off of building in the Eixample. From the 1880s *Modernisme* (*see pp36-7*) became the preferred style of the new district, the perfect expression for the self-confidence, romanticism and impetus of the industrial class. The first modern Catalanist political movement was founded by Valentí Almirall.

Barcelona felt it needed to show the world all that it had achieved, and that it was more than just a 'second city'. In 1885 an exhibition promoter named Eugenio Serrano de Casanova proposed to the city council the holding of an international exhibition, such as had been held successfully in London, Paris and Vienna. Serrano was actually a highly dubious character, who eventually made off with large amounts of public funds, but by the time this became clear the city fathers had fully committed themselves. The Universal Exhibition of 1888 was used as a pretext for the final conversion of the **Ciutadella** into a park; giant efforts had to be made to get everything ready in time, a feat that led the mayor, Francesc Rius i Taulet, to exclaim that 'the Catalan people are the yankees of Europe'. The first of Barcelona's three great efforts to demonstrate its status to the world, the 1888 Exhibition signified the consecration of the *Modernista* style, and the end of provincial, dowdy Barcelona and its establishment as a modern-day city on the international map.

THE CITY OF THE NEW CENTURY

The 1888 Exhibition left Barcelona with huge debts, a new look and reasons to believe in itself as a paradigm of progress. As the year 1900 approached, there were few cities where the new century was regarded with greater anticipation than in Barcelona.

The Catalan *Renaixença* continued, and acquired a more political tone. In 1892 the 'Bases de Manresa' were drawn up, a first draft plan for Catalan autonomy. Middle-class opinion was becoming more sympathetic to political Catalanism. A decisive moment came in 1898, when the underlying weakness of the Spanish state was abruptly made plain, despite the superficial prosperity of the first years of the Bourbon restoration.

Spain was manœuvred into a short war with the United States, in which it very quickly lost its remaining empire in Cuba, the Philippines and Puerto Rico. Catalan industrialists, horrified at losing the lucrative Cuban market, despaired of the ability of the state ever to reform itself. Many swung behind a conservative nationalist movement founded in 1901, the Lliga Regionalista or 'Regionalist League', led by Enric Prat de la Riba and the politician-financier Francesc Cambó. It promised both national revival and modern, efficient government.

Barcelona continued to grow, fuelling Catalanist optimism. The city officially incorporated most of the surrounding smaller communities in 1897, reaching a population of over half a million, and in 1907 initiated the 'internal reform' of the old city with the cutting through it of the Via Laietana, intended to allow in more air and so make the streets less unhealthy.

Catalan letters were thriving: the Institut d'Estudis Catalans (Institute of Catalan Studies) was founded in 1906, and Pompeu Fabra set out to create the first Catalan dictionary. Literature had acquired a new maturity, and in 1905 Víctor Català (a pseudonym for a woman, Caterina Albert) shocked the country with *Solitud*, a darkly modern novel of a woman's sexual awakening. Above all, Barcelona had a vibrant artistic community, centred on *Modernisme*, consisting of great architects and established, wealthy painters like Rusiñol and Casas, and the penniless bohemians who gathered round them, like the young Picasso.

Barcelona's bohemians were also drawn to the increasingly wild nightlife of the Raval. The area had already been known for very downmarket entertainments in the 1740s, but cabarets, bars and brothels multiplied at the end of the 19th century (*see pp18-19*).

Around the cabarets, though, there were also the poorest of the working class, whose conditions had continued to decline. Barcelona had some of the worst overcrowding and highest mortality rates of any city in Europe.

One of the (unexploded) bombs thrown into the Liceu opera in 1893. *See p18*.

Most exploited were women and children, toiling for a pittance 15 hours a day. A respectable feminist movement undertook philanthropic projects aimed at educating the female masses. Barcelona, however, was more associated internationally with revolutionary politics and violence than gradual reform.

In 1893 over 20 people were killed in a series of anarchist bombings, the most renowned of them when a bomb was thrown down into the stalls of the Liceu during a performance of *William Tell*. The perpetrators were individuals acting alone, but the authorities took the opportunity to carry out a general round-up of anarchists and radicals, several of whom were tortured and executed in the castle above Barcelona. In retaliation, in 1906 a Catalan anarchist tried to assassinate King Alfonso XIII on his wedding day in Madrid.

Anarchism was still only a minority current among workers in Barcelona during the 1900s, but in general rebellious attitudes, growing republican sentiment and a fierce hatred of the Catholic Church united the underclasses and

Streets of vanished vice

Barcelona has been famous for many things: Gaudí, the Rambla – and the Barrio Chino, for decades one of the legendary centres of low-life in Europe. The French in particular romanticised the *Chino* – Jean Genet's *The Thief's Journal* and André Pieyre de Mandiargues' *La Marge* are two classics of *Chino* literature – and right up until very recently visiting French literati, when asked what most impressed them in Barcelona, regularly used to say the *Chino*, with its Felliniesque whores and smell of piss.

Barcelona without its *Chino* used to be inconceivable, but there is no preservation order on it, and today only lipstick traces of this lost world can be seen. This was a harsh, often overwhelming, desperate place, certainly; it was also one of the planet's rarer environments, and before it vanishes entirely it can be thought-provoking to take a last look.

Unless otherwise indicated, all the places mentioned here have disappeared. Another leap of imagination is required to populate these streets with massed crowds of people, for photos from the '30s, when the *Chino* was at its peak, show its alleys packed from one side to the other 24 hours a day. There were brothels, gambling dens, *tavernas*, pawnshops, music halls, drifters, ordinary workers and the very poor, all coexisting side by side, equally dedicated to the business of surviving. Today, although the streets may be far quieter, this is still a hard area, and this walk is not one to try after dark (it is shown in **orange** on the map on p324).

Near the bottom of the Rambla, at the corner of C/Portal de Santa Madrona and Avda Drassanes, it's impossible not to see a 1960s skyscraper, the **Edifici Colom**, the product of Franco-era attempt at modernisation. It stands on the site of a celebrated brothel of the 1930s, **Can Manco** ('House of the One-Armed Man'),

famous for specialising in cheap and quick *flautes* (flutes) or blow-jobs. Around the corner at C/Montserrat 20 stood the **Teatro Circo Barcelonés**, known for its *transformistas* or drag-queens. This street maintains its traditions, and the **Cangrejo** at No.9 is perhaps the most authentic survivor of old *Chino* nightlife.

Turning left into **C/Cervelló** and then right and across at Avda Drassanes you enter **C/del Cid. C/Peracamps**, on the left, was known as a street of ultra-cheap doss-houses. In the 1930s C/del Cid was the epicentre of the *Chino*: No.10, now a more recent block of flats, was the site of **La Criolla**, most celebrated cabaret of the era, renowned for its drag and female performers and patronised by high and low society. Lesbians also met here in relative safety. It was a gambling joint too, and a centre for drugs and arms dealing; the owner, Pepe el de la Criolla, was shot down in the doorway in one of the *Chino*'s most famous murders, in April 1936.

A turn right into the Paral.lel and right again takes you to **C/Arc de Teatre** (pictured, right, in the 1930s). On the site of the present **Mercat del Carme** was **La Mina**, a *taverna* that had – shades of Dickens – an *academia de lladres* (school for thieves) in its basement. At the junction with Avda Drassanes is Barcelona's memorial to its most famous rent boy, the tiny **Plaça Jean Genet**. Genet came to the *Chino* in the '30s, selling sex, thieving and begging. He robbed clients after servicing them, stole from churches and earned three pesetas a night in La Criolla, dressed as a girl. C/Arc de Teatre 6, now demolished, was the site of **Madame Petit**, an internationally famous brothel known for answering every need, including sado-masochism and necrophilia.

Turn left into the Rambla and left again into **C/Nou de la Rambla**. This was the more public main avenue of the *Chino*, especially in the predisposed them to take to the barricades with little provocation. In 1909 came the explosive outburst of the Setmana Tràgica, the Tragic Week. It began as a protest against the conscription of troops for the colonial war in Morocco, but degenerated into a general riot, with the destruction of churches by excited mobs. Suspected culprits were summarily executed, as was anarchist educationalist Francesc Ferrer, accused of 'moral responsibility' even though he had not even been in Barcelona at the time.

These events dented the optimism of the Catalanists of the Lliga, but in 1914 they secured from Madrid the Mancomunitat, or administrative union, of the four Catalan provinces, the first joint government of any kind in Catalonia in 200 years. Its first President was Prat de la Riba, who would be succeeded on his death in 1917 by the architect Puig i Cadafalch. However, the Lliga's many other projects for respectable Catalonia were to be obstructed by a further inflammation of social tensions.

boom years of World War I. The **Hotel Gaudí** at No.12 – opposite the **Palau Güell** – occupies the site of the **Eden Concert**, Barcelona's most opulent *café concierto*, a combination of music hall, high-class restaurant, gambling den and strip club. Here textile millionaires and their mistresses rubbed shoulders with *pinxos* – the *Chino*'s hard men, part pimps, part bouncers, part gang members.

On the left is **C/Lancaster**, where at No.2 the sign can still be read of the **Bar Bohemia**, a legendary venue where very aged performers of the old cabarets used to keep their acts going, and which only finally closed in 1997. On the right at C/Nou 34 is the 1910 **London Bar**, last of the *cafés concierto*, and now a foreigner's favourite (*see chapter* **Nightlife**). Further along C/Nou is C/Estel, which had at No.2 **La Suerte Loca**, a 1900s brothel frequented by Picasso. At the very end of C/Nou (No.103), was **El Pompeya**, a cheap cabaret for workers and students. It is now the **Bagdad**, where live porn is available and which currently offers 'inter-active sex' by Internet.

If you loop back onto C/Tapies after passing the old **Arnau** music hall on Paral.lel, and carry on along it back toward the Rambla, then turn left at C/Sant Oleguer, go right at C/Marqués de Barberà and left again at C/Sant Ramon you will enter an area where street prostitution and squalor are still very visible. In the middle of the area, on the corner of C/Sant Ramon and C/Sant Pau, there is the **Bar Marsella**, a bar that has survived all of the district's renovations, and so continues to fascinate young foreigners. Almost opposite it is the **Plaça Salvador Seguí**: he was the greatest of Barcelona's CNT union leaders, and was murdered in 1923 by a gunman hired by employers, at the nearby corner of C/Cadena (now one border of the new Rambla del Raval) and C/Sant Rafael. Along **C/Robador**, across the shabby square, there are still a few *bares de camareras*, shabby 'girly bars' used for prostitution. This last vestige of the *Chino*, though, is doomed, for these old, decrepit blocks will soon be swept away, and new apartments, as it were, erected.

MAD YEARS, BAD YEARS, RED YEARS

Spain's neutral status during World War I gave a huge boost to the Spanish, and especially Catalan, economy. Exports soared as Catalonia's manufacturers made millions supplying uniforms to the French army. Barcelona's industry was at last able to diversify from textiles into engineering, chemicals and other more modern sectors.

Barcelona also became the most amenable place of refuge for anyone in Europe who wished to avoid the war. It acquired an international refugee community, among them avant-garde artists Sonia and Robert Delaunay, Francis Picabia, Marie Laurencin and Albert Gleizes, and was a bolt-hole for all kinds of low-life from around Europe. The Raval area would shortly be dubbed the Barrio Chino, 'Chinatown', definitively identifying it as an area of sin and perdition, and the city acquired a reputation similar to that of Marseille in the 1970s, as the primary centre of drug trafficking and about every other kind of illegal trade in the Mediterranean.

Some of the most regular patrons of the lavish new cabarets were industrialists, for many of the war profits were spent immediately in very conspicuous consumption. The war also set off massive inflation, driving people in their thousands from rural Spain into the cities. Barcelona doubled in size in 20 years to become the largest city in Spain, and the fulcrum of Spanish politics.

Workers' wages, meanwhile, had lost half their real value. The chief channel of protest in Barcelona was the anarchist workers' union, the CNT, constituted in 1910, which gained half a million members in Catalonia by 1919. The CNT and the socialist UGT launched a joint general strike in 1917, roughly co-ordinated

City of anarchy

One of Barcelona's many distinctions is that of being the only city in western Europe to have experienced a thoroughgoing social revolution within living memory. Another is that this revolution was to a very large extent inspired by anarchists. Anarchism arrived in the city in the 1860s, and attained greater influence here than anywhere else in the world. Over the next 70 years the Catalan anarchist movement hit the depths and scaled the heights, from crude violence to the highest idealism, from euphoria to defeat.

The individual terrorist attacks of the 1890s were very untypical of Catalan anarchism. Rather, anarchists believed that an entirely self-managed society could be achieved through constant collective organisation, and a pugnacious intransigence before the ruling classes and the law. Anarchists set up co-operatives and workers' societies, schools and social centres, and were among the first to introduce progressive ideas on education and sexuality into Spain. During the 1930s, anarchist housing campaigns ensured that many of the poorest of the poor paid no rent, a feminist group, Mujeres Libres (Free Women), gained momentum, and a group called the 'Practical Idealists' planned a self-managed health service.

Anarchism gained its greatest strength in the 1910s and 1930s, after the creation of the union confederation, the CNT. If the Passeig de Gràcia was the heart of the respectable city, the centre of anarchist

Barcelona was the Paral.lel. On a corner of the small plaça by Paral.lel Metro a Caixa bank office now occupies the site of the bar La Tranquilidad, which, as one veteran remembers, 'had nothing tranquil about it' – a meeting place of legendary militants such as Durruti and Ascaso, and frequently raided by the police. Nearby in Avda Mistral (at No.17) was the base of the Agrupación Faros, largest of the anarchist clubs of the 1930s, which at one time had over 2,000 members.

In the first months of the Civil War, factories, public services, cinemas, the phone system and food distribution were all collectivised. Some of the collectives, such as those that took over public transport, worked very well; others met with more and more difficulties, especially as the war ground on, and morale was steadily worn down. Today the CNT continues to keep the flame alive in union affairs, but this world can often seem to be just so many ghosts, less commemorated in modern Barcelona than events of the 1640s.

with a campaign by the Lliga and other liberal politicians for political reform. However, the politicians quickly withdrew at the prospect of serious social unrest. Inflation continued to intensify, and in 1919 Barcelona was paralysed for two months by a CNT general strike over union recognition. Employers refused to recognise the CNT, and the most intransigent among them hired gunmen to get rid of union leaders, often using a gang organised by an ex-German spy known as the 'Baron de Koening'. Union activists replied in kind, and virtual guerrilla warfare developed between the CNT, the employers and the state. Over 800 people were killed on the city's streets in the space of five years.

In 1923, in response both to the chaos in Barcelona and a crisis in the war in Morocco, the Captain-General of Barcelona, Miguel Primo de Rivera, staged a coup and established a military dictatorship under King Alfonso XIII. The CNT, already exhausted, was suppressed. Conservative Catalanists, longing for an end to disorder and the revolutionary threat, initially supported the coup, but were rewarded by the abolition of the Mancomunitat and a vindictive campaign by the Primo regime against the Catalan language and national symbols.

> **'By 1930, Barcelona was very different from the place it had been in 1910; it had over a million people, and sprawled over into Hospitalet and Santa Coloma.'**

This, however, achieved the contrary of the desired effect, helping to radicalise and popularise Catalan nationalism. After the terrible struggles of the previous years, the 1920s were actually a time of notable prosperity for many in Barcelona, as some of the wealth recently accumulated filtered through the economy. This was also, though, a highly politicised society, in which new magazines and forums for discussion – despite the restrictions of the dictatorship – found a ready audience.

A prime motor of Barcelona's prosperity during the 1920s was the International Exhibition of 1929, the second of the city's great showcase events. It had been proposed by Cambó and Catalan business groups, but Primo de Rivera saw that it could also serve as a propaganda event for his regime. A huge number of public projects were undertaken in association with the main event, including the post office in Via Laietana, the Estació de França

and Barcelona's first Metro line, from Plaça Catalunya to Plaça d'Espanya. Thousands of migrant workers came from southern Spain to build them, many living in decrepit housing or shanties on the city fringes. By 1930, Barcelona was very different from the place it had been in 1910; it had over a million people, and its urban sprawl had crossed into neighbouring towns such as Hospitalet and Santa Coloma.

For the Exhibition itself Montjuïc and Plaça d'Espanya were comprehensively redeveloped, with grand halls by Puig i Cadafalch and other local architects in the style of the Catalan neo-classical movement *Noucentisme*, a backward-looking reaction to the excesses of *Modernisme*. They contrasted strikingly, though, with the German pavilion by Mies van der Rohe (the **Pavelló Barcelona**), emphatically announcing the international trend toward rationalism.

THE REPUBLIC

Despite the Exhibition's success, in January 1930 Primo de Rivera resigned, exhausted. The King appointed another soldier, General Berenguer, as Prime Minister with the mission of restoring stability. The dictatorship, though, had fatally discredited the old regime, and a protest movement spread across Catalonia against the monarchy. In early 1931 Berenguer called local elections, as a first step towards a restoration of constitutional rule. The outcome was a complete surprise, for republicans were elected in all of Spain's cities. Ecstatic crowds poured into the streets, and Alfonso XIII abdicated. On 14 April 1931, the Second Spanish Republic was proclaimed.

The Republic came in amid real euphoria. It was especially so in Catalonia, where it was associated with hopes for both social change and national reaffirmation. The clear winner of the elections in the country had been the Esquerra Republicana, a leftist Catalanist group led by Francesc Macià. A raffish, elderly figure, Macià was one of the first politicians in Spain to win genuine affection from ordinary people. He declared Catalonia independent, but later agreed to accept autonomy within the Spanish Republic.

The Generalitat was re-established as a government that would, potentially, acquire wide powers. All aspects of Catalan culture were then in expansion, and a popular press in Catalan achieved a wide readership. Barcelona was a small but notable centre of the avant-garde. Miró and Dalí had already made their mark in painting; under the Republic, the Amics de l'Art Nou (ADLAN, 'Friends of New Art'), group worked to promote contemporary art, while the GATCPAC architectural collective sought to work with the new authorities to bring rationalist architecture to Barcelona.

In Madrid, the Republic's first government was a coalition of republicans and socialists led by Manuel Azaña. Its overrriding goal was to modernise Spanish society through liberal-democratic reforms, but as social tensions intensified the coalition collapsed, and a conservative republican party, with support from the traditional Spanish right, secured power after new elections in 1933. For Catalonia, the prospect of a return to right-wing rule prompted fears that it would immediately abrogate the Generalitat's hard-won powers. On 6 October 1934, while a general strike was launched against the central government in Asturias and some other parts of Spain, Lluís Companys, leader of the Generalitat since Macià's death the previous year, declared Catalonia independent. This 'uprising', however, turned out to be something of a farce, for the Generalitat had no means of resisting the army, and the 'Catalan Republic' was rapidly suppressed.

The Generalitat was suspended, its leaders imprisoned. Over the next year fascism seemed to become a real threat for the left, as political positions became polarised throughout Spain. Then, in February 1936, fresh Spain-wide elections were won by the Popular Front of the left. The Generalitat was reinstated, and in Catalonia the next few months were, surprisingly, relatively peaceful. In the rest of Spain, though, tensions were reaching bursting point, and right-wing politicians, refusing to accept the loss of power, talked openly of the need for the military to intervene. In July, the 1929 stadium on Montjuïc was to be the site of the Popular Olympics, a leftist alternative to the main Olympics of that year in Nazi Germany. On the day of their inauguration, however, 18 July, army generals launched a coup against the Republic and its left-wing governments, expecting no resistance.

REVOLUTIONARY BARCELONA

In Barcelona, militants of the unions and leftist parties, on alert for weeks, poured into the streets to oppose the troops in fierce fighting. Over the course of 19 July the military were gradually worn down, and finally surrendered in the Hotel Colón on Plaça Catalunya (by the corner with Passeig de Gràcia, the site of which is now occupied by the Radio Nacional de España building). Opinions have always differed as to who could claim most credit for this remarkable popular victory: workers' militants have claimed it was the 'people in arms' who defeated the army, while others stress the importance of the police having remained loyal to the Generalitat. A likely answer is that they actually encouraged each other.

Tension released, the city was taken over by the revolution. People's militias of the revived CNT, different Marxist parties and other left-wing factions marched off to Aragon, led by streetfighters such as the anarchists Durruti and García Oliver, to continue the battle. The army rising had failed in Spain's major cities but won footholds in Castile, Aragon and the south, although in the heady atmosphere of Barcelona in July 1936 it was often assumed that their resistance could not last long, and that the people's victory was near-inevitable.

Far from the front, Barcelona was the chief centre of the revolution in republican Spain, the only truly proletarian city. Its middle class avoided the streets, where, as Orwell recorded in his *Homage to Catalonia*, workers' clothing was all there was to be seen. Barcelona became a magnet for leftists from around the world, including writers such as Malraux, Hemingway and Octavio Paz. Industries and public services were collectivised. Ad-hoc 'control patrols' of the revolutionary militias roamed the streets supposedly checking for suspected right-wing

The militias leave for the front...

...and women protest against bombing, 1937.

agents and sometimes carrying out summary executions, a practice that was condemned by many leftist leaders.

The alliance between the different left-wing groups was unstable and riddled with tensions. The Communists, who had extra leverage because the Soviet Union was the only country prepared to give the Spanish Republic arms, demanded the integration of the loosely-organised militias into a conventional army under a strong central authority. The following months saw continual political infighting between the discontented CNT, the radical-Marxist party POUM, and the Communists. Co-operation broke down completely in May 1937, when republican and Communist troops seized the telephone building in Plaça Catalunya (on the corner of Portal de l'Angel) from a CNT committee, sparking off the confused war-within-the-civil-war witnessed by Orwell from the roof of the Teatre Poliorama. A temporary agreement was patched up, but shortly afterwards the POUM was banned, and the CNT excluded from power. A new republican central government was formed under Dr Juan Negrín, a Socialist allied to the Communists.

The war became more of a conventional conflict. This did little, however, to improve the Republic's position, for the Nationalists under General Francisco Franco and their German and Italian allies had been continually gaining ground. Madrid was under siege, and the capital of the Republic was moved to Valencia, and then to Barcelona, in November 1937.

Catalonia received thousands of refugees, and food shortages and the lack of armaments ground down morale. Barcelona also had the sad distinction of being the first major city in Europe to be subjected to sustained intensive bombing, to an extent that has rarely been appreciated, with heavy raids throughout 1938, especially by Italian bombers based in Mallorca. The Basque Country and Asturias had already fallen to Franco, and in March 1938 his troops reached the Mediterranean near Castellón, cutting the main Republican zone in two. The Republic had one last throw of the dice, in the Battle of the Ebro in summer 1938, when for months the Popular Army struggled to retake control of the river. After that, the Republic was exhausted. Barcelona fell to the Francoist army on 26 January 1939. Half a million refugees fled to France, to be interned in barbed-wire camps along the beaches.

GREY YEARS

In Catalonia the Franco regime was iron-fisted and especially vengeful. Thousands of Catalan republicans and leftists were executed, Generalitat President Lluís Companys among them; exile and deportation were the fate of thousands more. Publishing, teaching and any other public cultural expression in Catalan, including even speaking it in the street, were prohibited, and every Catalanist monument in the city was dismantled. All independent political activity was suspended: censorship and the secret police were a constant presence, and the resulting atmosphere of fear and suspicion was to mark many who lived through it. The entire political and cultural development of the country during the previous century and a half was thus brought to an abrupt halt.

'Barcelona is recorded as a grimy, pinched city full of the smell of drains and casual cruelty.'

The epic of the Spanish Civil War is known worldwide; more present in the collective memory of Barcelona, though, is the long *posguerra* or post-war period, which lasted nearly two decades after 1939. The Barcelona of these years is best recorded in the novels of Juan Marsé, a grimy, pinched city full of the smell of drains and casual cruelty, in which any high idealistic expectations had given way to a fatalistic concern for getting by from one day to the next.

Barcelona was impoverished, and would not regain its standard of living of 1936 until the mid-1950s; food and electricity were rationed. Nevertheless, migrants in flight from the still more brutal poverty of the south flowed into the city, occupying precarious shanty towns around Montjuïc and other areas in the outskirts. Reconstruction of the nearly 2,000 buildings destroyed by bombing was slow, for the regime built little during its first few years in power other than monumental showpieces and the vulgarly ornate basilica on top of Tibidabo, completed to expiate Barcelona's 'sinful' role during the war.

Some underground political movements were able to operate. Anarchist urban guerrillas such as the Sabaté brothers attempted to carry on armed resistance, and March 1951 saw the last gasp of the pre-war labour movement in a general tram strike, the only major strike during the harshest years of the regime. It was fiercely repressed, but also achieved some of its goals. Clandestine Catalanist groups undertook small acts of resistance and rebellion – underground publications, secret theatre performances. Some Catalan high culture was tolerated: the poet Salvador Espriu promoted a certain resurgence of Catalan literature, and the young Antoni Tàpies held his first solo exhibition in 1949. For a great many people, though, the only remaining public focus of national sentiment – of any collective excitement – was Barcelona football club, which took on an extraordinary importance at this time, above all in its biannual meetings with the 'team of the regime', Real Madrid.

As a fascist survivor, the Franco regime was subject to a UN embargo after World War II. Years of international isolation and attempted self-sufficiency came to an end in 1953, when the United States and the Vatican saw to it that this anti-communist state was at least partially readmitted to the Western fold. Even a limited opening to the outside world meant that foreign money began to enter the country, and the regime relaxed some control over its population. In 1959 the 'Plan de Estabilización' (Stabilisation Plan), drawn up by Catholic technocrats of the Opus Dei, brought Spain definitively within the Western economy, throwing its doors wide open to tourism and foreign investment.

Two years earlier, in 1957, José María de Porcioles was appointed Mayor of Barcelona, a post he would retain until 1973. Porcioles has since been regarded as the personification of the damage inflicted on the city by the Franco regime during its 1960s boom, accused of covering it with drab high-rises and road schemes without any concern for its character. Many valuable historic buildings – such as the grand cafés of the Plaça Catalunya – were torn down to make way for bland modern business blocks, and minimal attention was paid to collective amenities.

After the years of repression and the years of development, 1966 marked the beginning of what became known as *tardofranquisme*, 'late Francoism'. Having made its opening to the outside world, the regime was losing its grip, and labour, youth and student movements began to emerge from beneath the shroud of repression. Nevertheless, the Franco regime never hesitated to show its strength. Strikes and demonstrations were dealt with savagely, and just months before the dictator's death the last person to be executed in Spain by the traditional method of the garrotte, a Catalan anarchist named Puig Antich, went to his death in Barcelona.

In 1973, however, Franco's closest follower, Admiral Carrero Blanco, had been blown into the sky by a bomb planted by the Basque terrorist group ETA, leaving no one to guard over the core values of the regime. Change was in the air.

THE NEW ERA

When Franco died on 20 November 1975, the people of Barcelona took to the streets in celebration, and not a bottle of cava was left in the city by evening. However, no one knew

quite what was about to happen. The Bourbon monarchy was restored, under King Juan Carlos, but his attitudes and intentions were not clear. In 1976 he made a little-known Francoist bureaucrat, Adolfo Suárez, Prime Minister, charged with leading the country to democracy.

The first months and years of Spain's 'transition' were still a difficult period. Nationalist and other demonstrations continued to be repressed by the police with considerable brutality, and far-right groups threatened less open violence. However, political parties were legalised, and June 1977 saw the first democratic elections since 1936. They were won across Spain by Suárez' own new party, the UCD, and in Catalonia by a mixture of Socialists, Communists and nationalist groups.

'New freedoms were explored, newly released energies expressed in a multitude of ways.'

It was, again, not clear how Suárez expected to deal with the demands of Catalonia, but shortly after the elections he surprised everyone by going to visit the President of the Generalitat in exile, a veteran pre-Civil War politician, Josep Tarradellas. His office was the only institution of the old Republic to be so recognised, perhaps because Suárez astutely identified in the old man a fellow conservative. Tarradellas was invited to return as provisional President of a restored Generalitat, and arrived amid huge crowds in October 1977.

The following year the first free local elections took place, won by the Socialist Party, with Narcís Serra as Mayor. They have retained control of the Barcelona Ajuntament ever since. The year 1980 saw yet another set of elections, to the restored Generalitat, won by Jordi Pujol and his party Convergència i Unió. Again, they have kept power throughout the '80s and '90s. Imprisoned for Catalanist activities in 1960, Pujol represents a strain of conservative nationalism that goes back to Prat de la Riba. Facing each other across Plaça Sant Jaume, Generalitat and Ajuntament are the two constants of modern Catalan politics.

STYLE CITY

Inseparable from the restoration of democracy was a complete change in the city's atmosphere in the late 1970s. New freedoms – in culture, in sexuality, in work – were explored, newly released energies expressed in a multitude of ways. Barcelona soon began to look different too, as the inherent dowdiness of the Franco years was swept away by a new Catalan style

The spectacular image of Barcelona '92.

for the new Catalonia: postmodern, high-tech, punkish, comic strip, minimalist and tautly fashionable. For a time, street culture was still highly politicised, but simultaneously it was also increasingly hedonistic. In the 1980s design mania struck the city, a product of unbottled energies and a rebirth of Barcelona's artistic, artisan and architectural traditions.

This emphasis on slick, fresh style began on a street and underground level, but the special feature of Barcelona was the extent to which it was taken up by public authorities, and above all the Ajuntament, as a central part of their drive to reverse the policies of the previous regime. The highly-educated technocrats who led the Socialist city administration began, gradually at first, to 'recover' the city from its neglected state, and in doing so enlisted the elite of the Catalan intellectual and artistic community in their support. No one epitomises this more than Oriol Bohigas, the architect and writer who was long the city's head of culture and chief planner. A rolling programme of urban renewal was initiated, beginning with the open spaces and public art programme (*see chapter* **Museums**) and low-level initiatives such as the campaign in which hundreds of historic façades were given an overdue facelift.

This ambitious, emphatically modern approach to urban problems acquired much greater focus after Barcelona's bid to host the 1992 Olympic Games was accepted, in 1986. Far more than just a sports event, the Games were to be Barcelona's third great effort to cast aside suggestions of second-city status and show the world its wares. The exhibitions of 1888 and 1929 had seen developments in the Ciutadella and on and around Montjuïc; the Olympics provided an opening for work on a city-wide scale. Taking advantage of the public and private investment they would attract, Barcelona planned an all-new orientation of itself toward the sea, in a programme of urban renovation of a scope unseen in Europe since the years of reconstruction after World War II.

Along with the creation of the new Barcelona in bricks and mortar went the city-sponsored promotion of Barcelona-as-concept, a seductive cocktail of architecture, imagination, tradition, style, nightlife and primary colours. This was perhaps the most spectacular – certainly the most deliberate – of Barcelona's many reinventions of itself; it also succeeded in good part because this image of creativity and vivacity fitted an idea many of Barcelona's citizens had always had of their town, as if the drab decades had been just a bad dream.

Inseparable from all this was Pascual Maragall, mayor of Barcelona from 1982 to 1997, a tireless 'Mr Barcelona' who appeared in every possible forum to expound his vision of the role of cities, and intervened personally to set the guidelines for projects or secure the participation of major international architects. In the process Barcelona, like all Spanish cities a byword for modern blight only a few years before, became an international reference point in urban affairs. Maragall also established a personal popularity well beyond that of his Catalan Socialist Party.

BARCELON-AAH
When the Games were finally held in July-August 1992, everyone agreed they were a great success. Once the parade had gone by, however, the city held its breath to see what would happen next, and 1993 was a difficult year.

From 1994 onwards, however, confidence picked up again, the city's relentless self-promotion seemed actually to be working in attracting investment, and Barcelona and Catalonia rode out Spain's post-1992 recession better than any other part of the country. The Ajuntament announced still more large-scale projects, this time in areas little touched in the run-up to 1992, such as the Old Port and the Raval. Maragall's own popularity was such that he was able to stand aside from the corruption scandals that dragged down his Socialist allies in the central government of Felipe González after 13 years in office, and enabled the right-wing Partido Popular to take power in Madrid after the elections of 1996.

From 1993 to 1999, the support of the Catalan nationalists in the Madrid parliament was essential to keep minority Socialist (till 1996) and then Partido Popular central governments in power, a situation that enabled Jordi Pujol and his Convergència party to build up a pivotal role in all-Spanish affairs. In return for this support Pujol won more and more concessions for the Generalitat, and a reputation for being the most artful operator in Spanish politics. Though this political agility reinforced his popularity among his core support in Catalonia, it intensified the aversion felt towards him in many other parts of Spain. Since the spectacular absolute majority won

Key Events

ORIGINS
c15 BC Barcino founded by Roman soldiers.
c350 AD Roman stone city walls built.
415 Barcelona briefly capital of Visigoths under Ataülf.
719 Muslims attack and seize Barcelona.
801 Barcelona taken by Franks, under Louis the Pious.
878 Guifré el Pilós becomes Count of Barcelona.
985 Muslims sack Barcelona; Count Borrell II renounces Frankish sovereignty.

A MEDIEVAL GOLDEN AGE
1035-76 Count Ramon Berenguer I of Barcelona extends his possessions into southern France.
1064-8 First Catalan 'Usatges', or legal code, written.
1137 Count Ramon Berenguer IV marries Petronella of Aragon, uniting the two states in the 'Crown of Aragon'.
1148-9 Lleida and Tortosa taken from the Muslims.
c1160 *Homílies d'Organyà*, first Catalan texts, written.
1213 Battle of Muret: Pere I is killed and virtually all his lands north of the Pyrenees are seized by France.
1229 Jaume I conquers Mallorca, then Ibiza (1235) and Valencia (1238); second city wall built in Barcelona.
1265 Ramon Llull devotes himself to thought and writing.
1274 Consell de Cent (Council of 100), municipal government of Barcelona, established.
1282 Pere II conquers Sicily.
1298 Gothic cathedral begun. Population of city c40,000.
1323-4 Conquest of Corsica and Sardinia.
1347-8 Black Death cuts population by half.
1391 Hundreds of Jews massacred in Barcelona *Call.*

1412 Crown of Aragon given to Fernando de Antequera.
1462-72 Catalan civil war.
1474 First book printed in Catalan, in Valencia.

THE FALL OF BARCELONA
1479 Ferran II (Ferdinand) inherits Crown of Aragon, and with his wife Isabella unites the Spanish kingdoms.
1492 Final expulsion of Jews, and discovery of America.
1516 Charles of Habsburg (Charles V), King of Spain.
1522 Catalans refused permission to trade in America.
1640 Catalan national revolt, the Guerra dels Segadors.
1652 Barcelona falls to Spanish army.
1659 Catalan territory of Roussillon is given to France.
1702 War of Spanish Succession begins.
1714 Barcelona falls to Franco-Spanish army after siege.
1715 'Nova Planta' decree abolishes Catalan institutions; new ramparts and citadel built around Barcelona. Population of the city c33,000.
1775 Paving of the Barcelona Rambla begun.
1808-13 French occupation.

FACTORIES, POETS & BARRICADES
1814 Restoration of Ferdinand VII.
1832 First steam-driven factory in Spain, in Barcelona.
1833 Aribau publishes *Oda a la Pàtria*, beginning of Catalan cultural renaissance. Carlist wars begin.
1836-7 Dissolution of most monasteries in Barcelona.
1839 First workers' associations formed in Barcelona.
1842-4 Barcelona bombarded for the last time from Montjuïc, to suppress a liberal revolt, the Jamancia.

by the PP in national elections in 2000, though, Pujol has been forced to retreat, somewhat ignominiously, from his power-broker status.

In the Barcelona Ajuntament, Pasqual Maragall caused general surprise by standing down in 1997, after winning a fifth term. He was succeeded as Mayor by his deputy Joan Clos, a previously rather anonymous figure who, however, held on to the post with an increased majority in the next city elections in June 1999. Maragall declared his intention to stand as the next Socialist candidate for President of the Generalitat and big changes seemed on the cards: then, in the October '99 elections the Socialists won more votes than Convergència, but fewer seats in the Catalan Parliament. To stay in power Pujol was obliged to call on the local PP to return the favour he had done their government in Madrid. Change was coming, but not fast enough to deny Jordi Pujol the 20th year of his reign.

1848 First railway line in Spain, between Barcelona and Mataró; Liceu opera house inaugurated.

1854 Demolition of Barcelona city walls begins.

1855 First general strike is violently suppressed.

1859 Cerdà plan for the Barcelona Eixample approved.

1868 September: revolution overthrows Isabel II. November: first anarchist meetings held in Barcelona.

1873 First Spanish Republic.

1874 Bourbon monarchy restored under Alfonso XII.

1882 Work begins on the Sagrada Família.

1888 Barcelona Universal Exhibition.

THE CITY OF THE NEW CENTURY

1892 'Bases de Manresa', demands for Catalan autonomy.

1897 Gràcia and Sants incorporated into Barcelona.

1898 Spain loses Cuba and Philippines in war with USA.

1899 FC Barcelona founded; first electric trams.

1900 Population of Barcelona 537,354.

1907 Via Laietana cut through old city of Barcelona.

1909 Setmana Tràgica, anti-church and anti-army riots.

1910 CNT anarchist workers' union founded.

1919 CNT general strike paralyses Barcelona.

1920 Spiral of violence in labour conflicts in Catalonia.

1921 First Barcelona Metro line opened.

1923 Primo de Rivera establishes dictatorship in Spain.

1929 Barcelona International Exhibition held on Montjuïc.

1930 Population 1,005, 565. Fall of Primo de Rivera.

1931 14 April: Second Spanish Republic. Francesc Macià declares Catalan independence, then accepts autonomy within the Republic.

1934 October: Generalitat attempts revolt against new right-wing government in Madrid, and is then suspended.

1936 February: Popular Front wins Spanish elections; Catalan Generalitat restored. 19 July: military uprising against left-wing government is defeated in Barcelona.

1937 May: fighting within the republican camp in Barcelona, mainly between anarchists and Communists.

1939 26 January: Barcelona taken by Franco's army.

GREY YEARS

1951 Barcelona tram strike.

1953 Co-operation treaty between Spain and the USA.

1959 Stabilisation Plan opens up Spanish economy.

1975 20 November: death of Franco.

THE NEW ERA

1977 First democratic general elections in Spain since 1936; provisional Catalan Generalitat re-established.

1978 First democratic local elections in Barcelona won by Socialists.

1980 Generalitat fully re-established under Jordi Pujol.

1982 Pasqual Maragall becomes Mayor; urban spaces programme gains momentum.

1986 Barcelona awarded 1992 Olympic Games.

1992 Barcelona Olympics.

1996 Partido Popular wins Spanish national elections.

1997 Joan Clos replaces Pasqual Maragall as Mayor.

1999 Jordi Pujol wins sixth term as President of the Generalitat.

2000 Partido Popular wins absolute majority in the Madrid parliament.

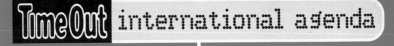

Barcelona Today

As a triumphant Barcelona sails into the 21st century, the city relentlessly proceeds to push the limits of design.

Not long ago a columnist for the *El País* newspaper overheard a conversation between a tour guide and her group, as they pressed her to explain why Barcelona was so filthy. The visitors could not understand how a city with such a strong visual culture and refined taste in just about everything could allow the streets around La Rambla or in the Barri Gòtic to accumulate unsightly residues from shops and restaurants, along with piles of litter and construction rubble.

In her studied reply, the guide explained that the city had decided to deliberately let rubbish have its way in certain tourist areas as a way of cultivating an image of urban decadence. Eager to please those hopping in for an on-the-edge weekend, the city had relaxed its street-cleaning services, adding freshly squeezed trash to a cocktail already spiked with an ounce of bar, an ounce of beach, and a pinch of petty street crime.

City hall officials must have cringed when they read the journalist's note, not least because the town has just spent a huge sum on a spanking smart fleet of electric buggies driven around the narrow lanes of the old quarters by a very stylishly uniformed sanitary patrol. Indeed most Barcelonans, so attuned to the

praise of outsiders when it comes to anything concerning their hometown, are afflicted by momentary deafness upon the slightest insinuation that the city's rougher spots could have a modicum of charm. What is fine for literature – seedy low-life settings have abounded from Jean Genet's *The Thief's Journal* in the '20s to the ongoing Carvalho detective series by Raval-born writer Manuel Vázquez Montalban – in real life is sneered upon as an impediment to progress.

It has been that way for some time now. The promise of an optimistic, hygienic, Brussels-like Barcelona was postulated 150 years ago, when the walls around the old quarters were joyfully torn down and the new city begun. Dreamt up by engineer Ildefons Cerdà in the 1850s, the Eixample (or Expansion) plan, with its neat grid pattern and trademark cut corners, still has a tremendous influence on how the city aspires to see itself: egalitarian, orderly, and rational. Much of the growth of Barcelona since the 1992 Olympics has stubbornly gone about fulfilling aspects of Cerdà's vision that were never completed, such as the new town centre near Plaça de les Glòries, with its concert hall and national theatre; the extension of Diagonal to

Power in the City

Barcelona's postmodern politics, as told by English-born writer published in Catalan, Matthew Tree.

As a rule, there is no reason why short-term visitors should feel a need to wade into the sticky morass of Catalan politics which fills the pages of the Barcelona press and vies with football as a favourite topic of local conversation. However, a quick glance at the city's power structure can help to explain the significance of plenty of its buildings and institutions (not to mention the four different varieties of policemen who patrol its streets).

The best place for politician-spotting is the Plaça Sant Jaume. Here, the two centres of local power glower – and occasionally wink – at each other across a cobbled square. On the right-hand side (if you walk up C/Ferran from the Rambla) is the Ajuntament, or City Council. To your left is the Generalitat or Catalan Autonomous Government.

The Ajuntament is responsible for trade and social security, the arts, tourism, and some public transport, all within Barcelona. It runs a municipal police force, the Guàrdia Urbana (who wear caps with a check band). The Generalitat – which has its own bunch of rozzers, the *Mossos d'Esquadra* (caps with red bands) – is responsible for the same things as the Ajuntament, but over the whole

of Catalonia, which includes Barcelona, resulting in a baffling duplication of certain services within the city. If you want to check out who runs what, simply take a butcher's at the logo on the door of the building you happen to have wandered into: the oval with four stripes means it belongs to the Generalitat; the lozenge with four stripes and a cross, to the Ajuntament.

To understand the various parties that run these institutions, a simple political classification (left, right or centre) is not enough: the degree of their allegiance to either Spain or Catalonia, respectively, is just as important. For example, a majority of the Ajuntament's 41 *regidors* or town councillors belong to the PSC – *Partit Socialista de Catalunya* – led by Mayor Joan Clos; this is a moderate left of centre grouping, affiliated to the 'mother' Spanish socialist party. It believes that Spain ought to be federalised (like Germany, say) and its Constitution changed accordingly. It rules in alliance with ERC – *Esquerra Republicana de Catalunya* – a non-Marxist left-wing party that aims to create an independent Catalan republic within the European Union. The other ruling party in the

the sea near the mouth of the Besòs River; or the just-opened Rambla del Raval (*see p78*).

Back in the 19th century, Barcelona's only way of 'putting itself on the map' was literal, with streets like Meridiana (pointing exactly North–South) and Paral.lel (running along parallel 41° 22'34) fitting the city into a cartographic web of longitudes and latitudes. Successive socialist administrations running Barcelona in post-Franco democracy have been more ambitious, striving for an economic, social and cultural place in the pantheon of great world cities as well. To achieve this goal, local planners and architects have taken a downright militant attitude towards any vestige of grunge romanticism (ruling out the otherwise fascinating prospect of designer garbage, tour guides notwithstanding). After warming up with a few snappy squares and parks in outlying parts of the city, the Olympic designation in 1986 set off a monumental face-lifting operation affecting entire districts, transforming contemporary Barcelona into the

face to launch a thousand ships – no doubt of the Mediterranean cruise variety, as the city has become a top-ranked port of destination for leisure sea travellers.

BEYOND THE MASTER PLAN

The 1992 Olympics left a sports legacy, and even more so an image of Barcelona as a dynamic trendsetter in anything visual. The city has played the design card so well that its name is now synonymous with excellence in the eye-pleasing presentation of architecture and public space, not to mention furniture, fashion, food and even music (as anyone who has grooved at the Sonar techno festival will attest). Years of visionary planning and earnest self-promotion have paid off, as record-breaking tourism and dynamic foreign investment stroke Barcelona's collective ego while buoying the local economy. This success story owes a lot to the city's special kind of beauty, quaint and sophisticated, richly layered by past and present.

Yet the Barcelona miracle is a double-edged sword. A good part of the Olympic triumph

Ajuntament is IC – *Iniciativa per Catalunya* – a coalition of (mainly) ex-communist groups, which also supports eventual Catalan sovereignty. Over in the Generalitat, the roost is ruled by *CiU*, itself a coalition of a liberal party (Catalan president Jordi Pujol's *Convergència*) and a smaller conservative party (*Unió*) led by a man who looks like an ageing, intellectual skinhead, called Josep-Antoni Duran i Lleida. Neither Pujol nor Duran i Lleida have ever demanded independence for Catalonia and prefer to spend most of their political time pleading (in vain) for a lessening of the heavy tax quota imposed on the area. Over in the Catalan parliament (located in the Parc de la Ciutadella), many of the policies of CiU's Generalitat are hotly contested by the opposition, which consists of all the previously mentioned parties together with the local branch of the PP, the Popular Party, which rules mightily in Spain but comes a poor fourth in Catalonia (where it has just 12 seats out of 135); this is a Madrid-based, Spanish nationalist, jingoistic party which believes Catalonia should shed some of its current autonomy in order to 'integrate' better with the rest of Spain.

In a nutshell: Barcelona, the capital of Catalonia and the second most important city in Spain, is run by a left-wing coalition of Catalan federalists and independentists. Whereas the Catalan government, in charge of one of the most densely populated and heavily industrialised areas of Spain, is run by a centre-right coalition which – although usually described as nationalist in the international press – has always stuck, in practice, to a strictly regionalist line.

However, lurking conspicuously in the background is a third political force with no elected representatives at all. The *Delegación del Gobierno* is located in a resplendent 1790s building next to the Estació de França; the heir to an institution closely associated with the Franco period, it houses a shadow regional government which takes direct orders from Madrid. Its members not only keep an eye on their opposite numbers in the Generalitat, but also handle all those parcels of power which Madrid refuses to cede to Catalonia in general or, indeed, to Barcelona (such as the port and the airport). It controls two police forces, the Policia Nacional (navy blue uniforms) and the Guàrdia Civil (machine guns), whose excessive use of force when dealing with certain pro-Catalan demonstrations serves, in effect, as a taste of what both the Ajuntament and the Generalitat can expect, should they ever get too big for their boots.

depended on the complicity (or just plain passivity) of citizens, business, labour unions and the cultural and intellectual elites, who accepted the sacrifices involved – including widespread evictions, or the razing of beloved parts of the city, like the beach restaurants in Barceloneta – without excessive resistance or criticism. It was as if the sentiments of the entire population had been brought into line by a great master plan, dictated from on high.

Such docile yea-saying could not have been expected to continue once the rallying cry of the Games was over. As the high standards set in 1992 have spread out into the general populace, citizens now demand as much from city administrators as town hall once required of them. Ardent letters to the editor complain about everything imaginable, from brusque bus driving to dog mess, while neighbourhood associations, once allies of local politicians, are independent and vociferous. The squatters' movement, which grew in response to the increased cost of housing in the '90s, now

spearheads radical anti-globalisation protests. Even immigrant communities (including Moroccans, Pakistanis, Filipinos, and Eastern Europeans), once just concerned with getting their papers in order, have begun to voice grievances and express themselves culturally.

Outsiders are making a dent on Barcelona's urban landscape in more ways than one. A stroll down the Pakistani strip on C/Sant Pau or the Dominican zone along C/Carders reveals a degree of visual tackiness that both fascinates and irritates typically high-brow Catalan tastes. Curiously enough, Barcelonan uptowners and Catalan suburbanites have taken to visiting the ebullient old city as if they were tourists as well, making up the most loyal clientele for a panorama of Irish pubs, falafel stands, Dunkin' Donuts, and endless cappuccinos. Perhaps there will come a day when, tired of complaining about the inevitable side effects of trash, kitsch and petty crime, even locals will see them as part of some typically ingenious Barcelona design.

Architecture

Barcelona's buildings reflect the city's soul: a unique mix of genius, solidity, and unrestrained creativity.

Architecture has had a very special importance among all the arts in Catalonia. It has frequently taken on the role of most appropriate medium – ahead of painting, music or any other art form – through which to express national identity. Periods when architecture flourished have paralleled eras of increased Catalan freedom of action and self-expression, greater wealth and a reinforcement of collective civic pride.

A clear line of continuity, of recurring characteristics, can be traced between generations of Catalan architects. Ideas, attitudes and trends are taken in from abroad, but are assimilated into this strong local culture. Catalan builders have always shown interest in decorating surfaces, and a concern with texture and the use of fine materials and finishes. This is combined with a simplicity of line and sense of sobriety often seen as distinguishing Catalan character from that of

the rest of Spain. Other common elements are references to the traditional architecture of rural Catalonia – the large *masia* farmhouses, with chalet-type tile roofs, massive stone walls and round-arched doorways, a style maintained by anonymous builders for centuries – and to the powerful constructions of Catalan Romanesque and Gothic. There has also long been a close relationship between architects and craftsmen in the production of buildings, especially in the working of metal and wood.

> **'Catalans have a sense of contributing to their architectural heritage, rather than preserving it as a relic.'**

The revival and renewed vigour of Catalan culture and the city of Barcelona since 1975 have once again been accompanied by dynamic expansion in architecture, as is now world-

> ▶ For details of buildings mentioned in this chapter, *see section* **Sightseeing**.

famous. Modern Catalans have a sense of contributing to their architectural heritage in the present day, rather than preserving it as a relic. Contemporary buildings are daringly constructed alongside (or even within) old ones, and this mix of old and new is a major characteristic of many spectacular projects seen in Barcelona over the last two decades.

The importance of architecture is also reflected in public attitudes. Barcelona's citizens cherish their buildings, and form a critical audience. A range of architectural guides is available, some in English (*see p309* **Further Reference**). Informative leaflets on different styles are also provided (in English) at tourist offices (*see p304*).

The old city

The old city of Barcelona, confined within its successive rings of walls, had by 1850 become one of the densest urban areas in Europe. With open space at a premium, small squares and paved areas feel almost sculpted out of a solid mass of buildings. The Mediterranean sun, which rarely reaches some streets, fills other, often modest, unannounced spaces with light, giving an unequalled sense of drama. The spaces within buildings also sometimes seem hollowed out from the city fabric. The breathtaking beauty of **Santa Maria del Mar** or the sweeping scale of the **Saló del Tinell** contrast strikingly with the tightly packed streets around them. This gives a feeling of luxury to even the simplest square or church.

ROMAN TO ROMANESQUE

The Roman citadel of Barcino was founded on the hill of Mons Taber, just behind the cathedral, which to this day remains the religious and civic heart of the city. It left an important legacy in the shape of the fourth-century city wall, fragments of which are visible at many points around the old city (*see pp72-3*).

Barcelona's next occupiers, the Visigoths, left little in the city, although a trio of fine Visigothic churches survives nearby in **Terrassa**. When the Catalan state began to form under the Counts of Barcelona from the ninth century, the dominant architecture of this new community was massive, simple Romanesque. In the Pyrenean valleys there are

The elegance of **Santa Maria del Mar.**

hundreds of fine Romanesque buildings, notably at **Sant Pere de Rodes**, **Ripoll**, **Sant Joan de les Abadesses** and **Besalú** (*see chapter* **Trips Out of Town**). There is, however, relatively little in Barcelona. On the right-hand side of the cathedral, looking at the main façade, is the 13th-century chapel of **Santa Llúcia**, incorporated into the later building; tucked away near Plaça Catalunya is the church of **Santa Anna**; and in La Ribera there is the tiny travellers' chapel, the **Capella d'en Marcús**. The city's greatest Romanesque monument, though, is the beautifully plain 12th-century church and cloister of **Sant Pau del Camp**, built as part of a larger monastery.

CATALAN GOTHIC

By the 13th century, Barcelona was the capital of a trading empire, and was growing rapidly. The settlements called *ravals* or *vilanoves* that had sprung up outside the Roman walls were brought within the city by the building of Jaume I's second set of walls, which extended Barcelona west to the Rambla, then just an (often dry) riverbed.

This commercial growth and political eminence formed the background to the great flowering of Catalan Gothic, and the construction of many of Barcelona's most important civic and religious buildings to replace Romanesque equivalents. The **cathedral** was begun in 1298, in place of an 11th-century building. Work commenced on the **Ajuntament** (Casa de la Ciutat) and **Palau de la Generalitat** – later subject to extensive alteration – in 1372 and 1403 respectively. Major additions were made to the **Palau Reial** of the Catalan-Aragonese kings, especially the **Saló del Tinell** of 1359-62, and the great hall of the **Llotja** or trading exchange was finished in 1380-92. Many of Barcelona's finest buildings were built or completed in these years, in the midst of the crisis that followed the Black Death.

Catalan Gothic has very particular characteristics that distinguish it clearly from more northern, classic Gothic. It is simpler, and gives more prominence to solid, plain walls between towers and columns rather than the empty spaces between intricate flying buttresses of the great French cathedrals. Buildings thus appear much more massive. In façades, as much emphasis is given to horizontals as to verticals; and in the latter, octagonal towers end in cornices and flat roofs, not spires. Decorative intricacies are mainly confined to windows, portals, arches and gargoyles. Many churches have no aisles but only a single nave, the classic example of this design being the beautiful **Santa Maria del Pi** in Plaça del Pi, which was built between 1322 and 1453.

This style has ever since provided the historic benchmark for Catalan architecture. It is simple and robust, yet elegant and practical.

Gaudí, the hermit-genius

Seen as the genius of the *Modernista* movement, Antoni Gaudí was really a one-off, an unclassifiable figure. His work was a product of the social and cultural context of the time, but also of his own unique perception of the world, together with a typically Catalan devotion to anything specifically Catalan. His two great colleagues in Modernism, Domènech and Puig, were public figures who took an active part in politics and many other fields; Gaudí, after being fairly sociable as a youth, became increasingly eccentric, leading a semi-monastic existence enclosed in his own obsessions.

Born in Reus in 1852, he qualified as an architect in 1878. His first architectural work was as assistant to Josep Fontseré on the building of the **Parc de la Ciutadella** during the 1870s. The gates and fountain of the park are attributed to him, and around the same time he also designed the lamp-posts in the **Plaça Reial**. His first major commission was for the **Casa Vicens**, built between 1883 and 1888. An orientalist fantasy, it is structurally fairly conventional, but his control of the use of surface material already stands out in the building's exuberant neo-Moorish decoration, the multi-coloured tiling and superbly elaborate ironwork on the gates (*see p100*). The **Col.legi de les Teresianes** convent school, undertaken in 1888-9, is more restrained still, but the clarity and fluidity of the building, with its simple finishes and use of light, is very appealing.

An event of crucial importance in Gaudí's life came in 1878, when he met Eusebi Güell, heir to one of the largest industrial fortunes in Catalonia. Güell had been impressed by some of Gaudí's early furniture, and they also discovered they shared many religious ideas, on the socially redemptive role of architecture and (for Güell) philanthropy. Güell placed such utter confidence in his architect that he was able to work with complete liberty. He produced several buildings for his patron, beginning with the **Palau Güell** (1886-8), a

darkly impressive, historicist building that established Gaudí's reputation, and also including the crypt at **Colònia Güell** outside Barcelona, one of his most structurally experimental and surprising buildings.

In 1883 Gaudí first became involved in the design of the temple of the **Sagrada Família**, begun the previous year. He would eventually devote himself entirely to this work. Gaudí was profoundly religious, and an extreme Catholic conservative; part of his obsession with the building was a belief that it would help redeem Barcelona from the sins of secularism and the modern era (some conservative Catalan Catholics are currently campaigning for him to be made a saint). From 1908 until his death he worked on no other projects, often sleeping on site, a shabby, white-haired hermit, producing visionary ideas that his assistants had to 'interpret' into drawings (on show in the museum alongside).

The Sagrada Família became the testing ground for his ideas on structure and form. However, he would see the completion of only the crypt, apse and nativity façade, with its representation of 30 different species of plants. As his work matured he abandoned historicism and developed free-flowing, sinuous expressionist forms. His boyhood interest in nature began to take over from more architectural references, and what had previously provided external decorative motifs became the inspiration for the actual structure of his buildings.

Innovative, sophisticated techniques were developed: the use of transverse arches supporting timber roofs allowed the spanning of great halls uninterrupted by columns, a system used in the Saló del Tinell. Designed by Pere III's court architect Guillem Carbonell, it has some of the largest pure masonry arches in

Europe, the elegance and sheer scale of which give the space tremendous splendour. The **Drassanes**, built from 1378 as the royal shipyards (and now the **Museu Marítim**), is really just a very beautiful shed, but the enormous parallel aisles make it one of the most exciting spaces in the city.

In his greatest years, Gaudí combined other commissions with his cathedral. **La Pedrera** or **Casa Milà**, begun in 1905, was his most complete project (pictured below). In a prime location on a corner of Passeig de Gràcia, it has an aquatic feel about it: the balconies resemble seaweed, and the undulating façade the sea, or rocks washed by it. Interior patios are in blues and greens, and the roof is like an imaginary landscape inhabited by mysterious figures. The **Casa Batlló**, across Passeig de Gràcia, was an existing building remodelled by Gaudí in 1905-7, with a roof resembling a reptilian creature perched high above the street. An essential contribution was made by Gaudí's assistant Josep Maria Jujol, himself a very original *Modernista* architect, and more skilled than his master as a mosaicist.

Gaudí's later work has a dreamlike quality, making it unique and personal. His fascination with natural forms found full expression in the **Parc Güell** of 1900-14. Here he blurs the distinction between natural and built form in a series of colonnades winding up the hill. These seemingly informal paths lead up to the surprisingly large central terrace projecting over the hall below, a forest of distorted Doric columns planned as the marketplace for Güell's proposed 'garden city' (pictured left). The benches of the terrace are covered in some of the finest examples of *trencadís* or broken mosaic work, again mostly by Jujol.

In June 1926, Antoni Gaudí was run over by a tram on the Gran Via. Nobody recognised the down-at-heel old man, and he was taken

to a public ward in the old Hospital de Santa Creu in the Raval. When it was discovered who he was, however, Barcelona gave its most famous architect almost a state funeral.

Gaudí in Barcelona

Gaudí left ten buildings in Barcelona. There are also buildings by him nearby at the **Colònia Güell** in Santa Coloma de Cervelló (now closed indefinitely for restoration) and **Garraf** (*see p263*).

Casa Batlló *See p96.*

Casa Calvet *C/Casp 48. Metro Urquinaona/bus all routes to Plaça Urquinaona.* **Map** *p326 B-C1.*
An apartment block from 1898-1900, relatively conventional from the outside, but with a more radical interior and fine details typical of Gaudí. There's a first-rate restaurant on the first floor (*see p147*).

Casa Vicens *C/Carolines 22. Metro Fontana/ 22, 24, 28, N4 bus.* **Map** *p320 D2.*
Not open to the public, but the exterior is very visible from the street.

Col.legi de les Teresianes *C/Ganduxer 85-105 (93 212 33 54). FGC Bonanova/14, 16, 70, 72, 74 bus.* **Open** (by appointment only) *Sept-June* 11am-1pm *Sat.* **Admission** free. **Map** *p320 B-C2.*

Palau Güell *See p78.*

Parc Güell *See p100.*

Pavellons de la Finca Güell *Avda. Pedralbes 7. Metro Palau Reial/7, 33, 67, 68, 75, N12 bus.* **Map** *p319 A2.*
The spectacular dragon gates in wrought iron from 1884-7 and the gatehouses on either side were the only parts of the Güell estate built by Gaudí.

La Pedrera *See p96.*

Temple Expiatori de la Sagrada Família *See pp96-98.*

Torre Bellesguard *C/Bellesguard 16-20, Zona Alta. Bus 22, 60, 64, 75.* A more than usually Gothic-looking fantasy house built in 1900-2, not open to visitors but visible from the street. To find it, follow C/Sant Joan de la Salle straight up from the Plaça Bonanova.

Catalan Gothic: the **Saló del Tinell**. *See p33.*

La Ribera, the *Vilanova del Mar*, was the commercial centre of the city, and gained the great masterpiece of Catalan Gothic, **Santa Maria del Mar**, built between 1329 and 1384. Its superb proportions are based on a series of squares imposed on one another, with three aisles of, unusually, almost equal height. The interior is staggering in its austerity and spareness of structure.

The domestic architecture of medieval Barcelona, at least that of its noble and merchant residences, can be seen at its best in the line of palaces along **Carrer Montcada**, next to Santa Maria. Built by the city's merchant élite at the height of their confidence and wealth, they all conform to a very Mediterranean style of urban palace, making maximum use of space. A plain exterior is presented to the street, with heavy doors opening into an imposing patio, on one side of which a grand external staircase leads to the main rooms on the first floor (*planta noble*), which often have elegant open loggias. Many of these palaces now house some of Barcelona's most visited cultural institutions.

FORGOTTEN CENTURIES

By the beginning of the 16th century, political and economic decline meant there were far fewer patrons for new building in the city. In the next 300 years a good deal was still built in Barcelona, but rarely in any distinctively Catalan style, with the result that these structures have often been disregarded.

In the 1550s the **Palau del Lloctinent** was built for the royal viceroys on one side of Plaça del Rei, and in 1596 the present main façade was added to the **Generalitat**, in an Italian Renaissance style. The Church built lavishly, with baroque convents and churches along La Rambla, of which the **Betlem** (from 1680-1729), at the corner of C/Carme, is the most important survivor. Later baroque churches include **Sant Felip Neri** (1721-52) and **La Mercè** (1765-75).

Another addition, after the siege of Barcelona in 1714, was new military architecture, since the city was encased in ramparts and fortresses. Examples remain in the **Castell de Montjuïc**, the buildings in the **Ciutadella** – one, curiously, the Catalan parliament – and the **Barceloneta**.

A more positive 18th-century alteration was the conversion of the Rambla into an urbanised promenade, begun in 1775 with the demolition of Jaume I's second wall. Neo-classical palaces were built alongside: **La Virreina** and the **Palau Moja** (at the corner of Portaferrisa) both date from the 1770s. Also from that time but in a less classical style is the Gremial dels Velers (Candlemakers' Guild) at Via Laietana 50, with its two-coloured stucco decoration.

It was not, however, until the closure of the monasteries in the 1820s and 1830s that major rebuilding on the Rambla could begin. Most of the first constructions that replaced them were still in international, neo-classical styles. The site that is now the **Mercat de la Boqueria** was first remodelled in 1836-40 as Plaça Sant Josep to a design by Francesc Daniel Molina, based on the English Regency style of John Nash. It is now buried beneath the 1870s market building, but its Doric colonnade can still be detected.

Molina also designed the **Plaça Reial**, begun in 1848. Other fine examples from the same era are the collonaded Porxos d'en Xifré, the 1836 blocks opposite the Llotja on Passeig Isabel II, by the Port Vell.

The Eixample & the new city

In the 1850s, Barcelona was able to expand physically, with the demolition of the walls, and psychologically, with economic expansion and the cultural reawakening of the Catalan *Renaixença*. The stage was set for it to spread into the great grid of Ildefons Cerdà's **Eixample** (*see also p15*).

Cerdà's most visionary ideas were largely lost; however, the construction of the Eixample saw the refinement of a specific type of building: the apartment block, with giant flats on the *principal* floor (first above the ground), often with large glassed-in galleries for the drawing room, and smaller flats above. The area's growth also provided perfect conditions for the pre-eminence of the most famous of Catalan architectural styles, *Modernisme*.

MODERNISME

The late 19th century was a time of uncertainty in the arts and architecture across Europe. The huge expansion of cities, dramatic social upheavals and new political pressures all created special tensions, while the introduction of new materials such as iron and steel demanded a new architectural language. As the end of the century approached, the movement that is known in French and English as art nouveau emerged, encompassing some of these concerns and contradictions.

International interest in Gaudí has often eclipsed the fact that the branch of art nouveau that developed so vigorously in Catalonia, *Modernisme* (always confusing, since 'modernism' in English usually refers to 20th-century functional styles), was quite distinct in its ideas and its products, and also that the style was perhaps more widely accepted in Barcelona than in any other European city.

It developed out of the general renaissance of Catalan culture. Influenced, like other forms of art nouveau, by Ruskin, William Morris and the Arts and Crafts movement, French Symbolism and other international currents, *Modernisme* was also a self-consciously indigenous expression that made use of its own Catalan traditions of design and craftwork. *Modernista* architects, as the name suggests, sought to function entirely within the modern world – hence their experimental use of iron and glass – but also to revalue distinctly Catalan traditions, and so showed enormous interest in the Gothic of the Catalan Golden Age.

Modernisme was also a very wide-ranging and flexible movement. It admitted the coexistence of Gothic revivalism, floralising and decoration to the point of delirium, as well as rationalist machine worship and the most advanced, revolutionary expressionism. *Modernistes* also sought to integrate fine and decorative arts, and so gave as much weight to furniture or glasswork as to painting, sculpture or architecture.

Modernista architecture was given a decisive boost by the buildings commissioned for the Universal Exhibition of 1888, most of which were by Lluís Domènech i Montaner (1850-1923). Most of them no longer exist, notably the 'International Hotel' on the Moll de la Fusta, which was built in under 100 days and demolished even more rapidly once the exhibition closed, but one that remains is the 'Castle of the Three Dragons' in the Ciutadella, designed to be the exhibition restaurant and now the **Museu de Zoologia**. It already demonstrated many key features of Modernist style: the use of structural ironwork allowed greater freedom in the creation of openings, arches and windows, and plain brick, instead of the stucco previously applied to most buildings in Barcelona, was used in an exuberantly decorative manner.

Domènech was one of the first Modernist architects to develop the idea of the 'total work', working closely with craftsmen and designers on every aspect of a building – ornament, lighting, glass. His greatest creations are the

Hospital de Sant Pau, built as small 'pavilions' within a garden to avoid the usual effect of a monolithic hospital, and the fabulous **Palau de la Música Catalana**, an extraordinary display of outrageous decoration.

'The Eixample has the greatest concentration of art nouveau in Europe.'

After Domènech and Gaudí, third in the trio of leading Modernist architects was Josep Puig i Cadafalch (1867-1957), who showed a strong neo-Gothic influence in such buildings as his Casa de les Punxes ('House of Spikes', officially the **Casa Terrades**) in the Diagonal, combined with many traditional Catalan touches.

These are the famous names of *Modernista* architecture, but there were many others, for the style caught on with extraordinary vigour throughout Catalonia. Some of the most engaging are the least known internationally, such as Gaudí's assistant Josep Maria Jujol, who in his own name built some remarkable, sinuous buildings in Sant Joan Despí, to the west of Barcelona.

Catalan *Modernista* creativity was at its peak for about 20 years, from 1888 to 1908, during which time an enormous amount of work was produced, large and small. The Eixample is the style's foremost display case, with the greatest concentration of art nouveau in Europe (the Ajuntament's *Quadrat d'Or* book is a good architectural guide), but *Modernista* buildings and details can be found in innumerable other locations around Barcelona and Catalonia: in streets behind the Paral.lel or villas on Tibidabo, in shop interiors or dark hallways, in country town halls or the cava cellars of the Penedès. For a walk taking in some of the lesser-known features of the *Modernista* **Eixample**, *see pp94-5.*

The 20th century

By the 1900s *Modernisme* had become too extreme for the Barcelona middle class, and the later buildings of Gaudí, for example, were met with derision. The new 'proper' style for Catalan architecture was *Noucentisme*, which stressed the importance of classical proportions. However, it failed to produce anything of much note: the main buildings that survive are those of the 1929 Exhibition – also the excuse for the bizarre neo-baroque **Palau Nacional**.

The 1929 Exhibition also brought to Barcelona, though, one of the most important buildings of the century: Mies van der Rohe's German Pavilion, the **Pavelló Barcelona**.

Even today it is modern in its challenge to conventional ideas of space, and its impact at the time was extraordinary. The famous Barcelona chair was designed for this building, which was rebuilt to its original design in 1986.

Mies had a strong influence on the main new trend in Catalan architecture of the 1930s, which, reacting against *Modernisme* and nearly all earlier Catalan styles, was emphatically functionalist. Its leading figures were Josep Lluís Sert and the GATCPAC collective, who struggled to introduce the ideas of their friend Le Corbusier and the 'International Style'. Under the Republic, Sert built a sanatorium off C/Tallers, and the **Casa Bloc**, a workers' housing project at Passeig Torres i Bages 91-105 in Sant Andreu. In 1937 he also built the Spanish Republic's pavilion for that year's Paris Exhibition, since rebuilt in Barcelona as the **Pavelló de la República** in Vall d'Hebron. Sert's finest work, however, came much later, in the **Fundació Joan Miró**, built in the 1970s after he had spent years in exile in the USA.

BARCELONA'S THIRD STYLE

The Franco years had an enormous impact on the city: as the economy expanded at breakneck pace in the 1960s, Barcelona received a massive influx of migrants, in a context of unchecked property speculation and minimal planning controls. The city was thus surrounded by endless high-rise suburbs. Another legacy of the era are some ostentatiously tall office blocks, especially on the Diagonal and around Plaça Francesc Macià.

Hence, when an all-new democratic city administration finally took over the reins of Barcelona at the end of the 1970s, there was a great deal for them to do. Budgets were limited, so it was decided that resources should initially be concentrated not on buildings as such, but on the gaps in between them, the public spaces, with a string of fresh, contemporary parks and squares, many of them incorporating original artwork (*see chapter* **Museums**). From this beginning, Barcelona placed itself in the forefront of international urban design.

Barcelona's renewal programme took on a far more ambitious shape with the award of the 1992 Olympics, helped by a booming economy in the late 1980s. The Barcelona Games were intended to be stylish and innovative, but most of all to provide a focus for a sweeping renovation of the city, with emblematic new buildings and infrastructure projects linked by clear strategic planning.

The three main Olympic sites – Vila Olímpica, Montjuïc and Vall d'Hebron – are quite different. The **Vila Olímpica** had the most comprehensive masterplan, which sought to extend Cerdà's grid down to the seafront. The main project on **Montjuïc** was the transformation of the existing 1929 stadium, but alongside it there is also Arata Isozaki's **Palau Sant Jordi**, with its space-frame roof. **Vall d'Hebron** is the least successful of the three sites, but Esteve Bonell's **Velòdrom** is one of the finest (and earliest) of the sports buildings, built before the Olympic bid in 1984.

Not content with all the projects completed up to 1992, the city has continued to expand its modern architecture collection ever since, as one major scheme has followed another. Post-1992 the main focus of activity shifted to the **Raval** and the **Port Vell** (old port), and is now moving on to the Diagonal-Mar area in the north of the city. Many striking buildings are by local architects such as Helio Piñón and Albert Viaplana, whose work combines fluid, elegant lines with a strikingly modern use of materials, from the controversial 1983 **Plaça dels Països Catalans** through daring transformations of historic buildings such as the Casa de la Caritat, now the **Centre de Cultura Contemporània**, and on to all-new projects like **Maremàgnum** in the port. Others are by international names: Richard Meier's bold white **MACBA**, or Norman Foster's **Torre de Collserola** on Tibidabo, which, with the skyscrapers in the Vila Olímpica, has provided new emblems for Barcelona's skyline. One of the latest major acquisitions, the giant boxlike **Auditori**, is by a Madrid-based Spanish architect (a rare thing in Barcelona), Rafael Moneo. Barcelona's dynamic modern architecture has come to represent a 'third style' incorporated into the city's identity, alongside Gothic and *Modernisme* – but far more diffuse and eclectic than either.

The city's audacious approach to urban renewal has also won it unprecedented international praise, not least with the award of the Royal Institute of British Architects' Gold Medal in 1999. With all this acclaim, though, it's perhaps time to point out that amid the work carried out with real imagination and panache, Barcelona also acquired mediocre architecture in the 1990s. Recently, especially, there has been a growing tendency to rely on an up-and-down 'beige-block' style – quick to build, with no expensive details, but easily forgettable. This has been the style for many lesser-profile projects: the tourist police station on the Rambla, health centres, new hotels and many of the new housing blocks in the Raval. Beige blocks also now loom over the Plaça Catalunya – stubbornly despite all efforts by planners to displace it – with the dull 1999 **Triangle** mall facing the 1994 façade of the **Corte Inglés**. It could be time to draw breath.

Accommodation

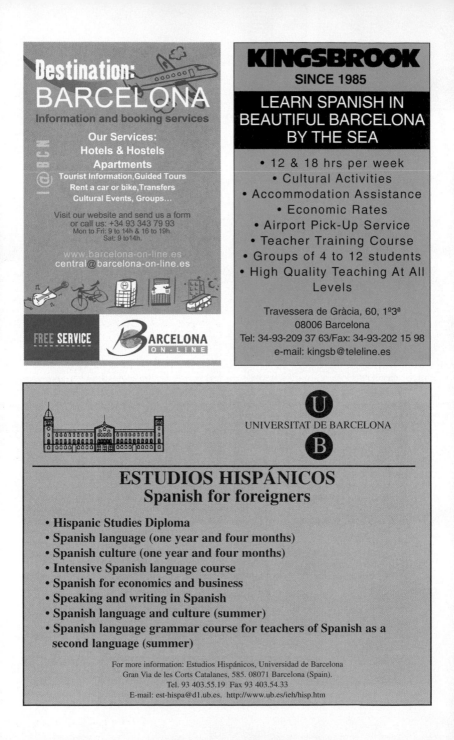

Accommodation

Rooms, rooms everywhere, but hardly a place to sleep.

The 1992 Olympic Games provided the first big catalyst for recent hotel building in Barcelona, with some 30 all-new places opening in just a couple of years. New construction and improvements, modernisations or complete makeovers of older hotels have not ceased ever since, as Barcelona has grown massively – above all in the late '90s – in popularity as a city to visit. Even with all this building activity, demand has moved still faster. Barcelona no longer has a true low season as such (although January and February are perhaps relatively slack), and since 1999 it has actually become hard to find a room of any kind in the city at some times of the year, especially in midsummer or when there are trade fairs.

This unprecedented worldwide exposure may do much for Barcelonese pride, but to the rest of us it means that **it is always advisable to book a room well in advance** where possible; many of the cheaper hotels will not take reservations. This rapid growth in numbers has also pushed up prices

very noticeably: mid-range hotel rates, especially, shot up, and there has been an almost total disappearance of the once-traditional cheaper weekend rates.

Barcelona's first real hotels were all built along the Rambla, and a great many places are still concentrated in the old city, which is also still the best area to find cheaper accommodation. Hotels on or very near the Rambla itself are naturally convenient, but have tended to bring in the most swingeing price hikes; they're also often noisy, and this is where you most need to be streetwise about petty crime. The other main hotel area is the Eixample, with many mid-range places and some good-value *hostals*. As the centre has filled up, mid-range and budget hotels have also been opening up in districts a bit further afield such as Poble Sec or Vall d'Hebron, which are worth considering: they offer greater tranquility, and thanks to Barcelona's compactness and good transport links, are never more than 20 minutes or so from the centre of the city.

Check in and check out the stars at **Hotel Le Meridien Barcelona**. *See p43.*

STARS, HOTELS, *HOSTALS*, PRICES

All accommodation in Catalonia is regulated by the regional government, the Generalitat. There are now only two official categories, hotels (H) and *hostals* (HS), although many places still use older names (*fondes, residències, pensions*), which can be confusing. To be a hotel, star-rated one to five, a place must have bathrooms in every room. Ratings are given on the basis of general quality and services rather than price. *Hostals*, rated one to three and usually cheaper, do not have to have en suite bathrooms throughout, nor do many have restaurants. Most, though, have also been renovated in the last few years, and many now have bathrooms in at least some rooms. In short, star ratings are not an automatic guide to cost or facilities.

All hotel bills are subject to seven per cent IVA (value added tax) on top of the basic price, which is normally quoted separately on bills. Hotels and *hostals* listed here are divided according to the basic price of a double room without IVA, according to the official weekday rates in high season. They should be taken as guidelines only, though, for prices can still vary by sizeable amounts at different times of year. Also, although far fewer hotels now offer weekend and other short-term discounts, it's still worth asking whether any such deals may be available. Breakfast is not included in rates given below unless stated. Hotel breakfasts are often poor and overpriced, and you frequently do better to go to a café. If you make use of a hotel car park this will also add to the bill, and you should reserve a space when booking the room.

BOOKING A ROOM

If you arrive in Barcelona without a room, the **tourist offices** in Plaça Catalunya and Plaça Sant Jaume have hotel booking desks that can usually find somewhere. There's no commission, but a deposit is requested against the bill. Two private services are listed below. None of their lists covers all accommodation in Barcelona, but tourist offices can provide a complete local hotel booklet. When booking, to be sure of light or a view, ask for an outside room (*habitación exterior*); many Barcelona buildings are built around a central patio or air shaft, which can be gloomy. Inside (*interior*) rooms, though, often gain in quietness what they lack in light. For flat rental agencies, *see p61*; for student and youth accommodation services, *see p303*.

Halcón Viajes

C/Aribau 34, Eixample (93 454 59 95/902 30 06 00/ www.alcon-viajes.es). Metro Universitat/bus all routes to Plaça Universitat. **Open** 9.30am-1.30pm, 4.30-8pm Mon-Fri; 10am-1.30pm Sat; closed Sun. **Credit** AmEx, DC, MC, V. **Map** p324 C5.
This giant travel agency with 500 offices across Spain can also book rooms in many hotels (often with car rental deals included). Commission is charged.

Ultramar Express

Vestibule, Estació de Sants, Sants (93 491 44 63/ www.uex.es). Metro Sants Estació/bus all routes to Estació de Sants. **Open** 8am-9.30pm daily. **Credit** MC, V. **Map** p323 A4.
An office in the hall at Sants train station: when booking you will be asked to pay a deposit (around 2,000ptas), which will be incorporated into your final hotel bill, plus a small fee of about 100ptas. You will be given a map and directions to the hotel.

Deluxe (40,000ptas+)

Barcelona Hilton

Avda Diagonal 589-591, Eixample (93 495 77 77/ fax 93 495 77 00/hilton@lix.intercom.es/ www.hilton.com). Metro Maria Cristina/6, 7, 33, 34, 63, 66, 67, 68, N12 bus. **Rates** 40,000-48,000ptas single; 44,000-52,000ptas double; 50,000-62,000ptas suite. **Credit** AmEx, DC, MC, V. **Map** p319 B2-3.
Opened in 1990, the steel-and-glass 286-room Hilton lacks the range of facilities of some of its competi-

---

The best Hotels for kids

Hotel Arts
Expensive, but there's all-day child-minding, a ground-level pool and the beach. *See p43.*

Hotel Balmes
A safe, ground-level pool and a small garden patio. *See p45.*

Hotel Mesón Castilla
Big family rooms, well-protected terraces and a delightful breakfast patio. *See p50.*

Aparthotel Bertran
Spacious apartments with balconies, a large rooftop terrace, a small rooftop pool and a nearby park offer breathing space for children. *See p61.*

Pensió 2000
Orlando and Manuela's friendly pension is probably the only place in this price range that offers cot facilities and extra-large rooms adaptable for families. *See p55.*

tors, but its rooms are a little more intimate. Located in the heart of Barcelona's modern business district, the Hilton concentrates on providing a comprehensive range of business services.
Hotel services *Air-conditioning. Babysitting. Bar. Conference facilities. Car park. Disabled: rooms (4) adapted for the disabled, toilets, wheelchair access. Email. Fax. Gym. Interpreters. Laundry. Limousine. Multilingual staff. Non-smoking rooms. Restaurants. Safe. Terrace.* **Room services** *Hairdryer. Minibar. Radio. Room service (24hrs). Telephone. TV (satellite).*

Hotel Arts

C/Marina 19-21, Vila Olímpic (93 221 10 00/fax 93 221 10 70/from UK freephone 0800 234 0000/from US freephone 0800 2241 3333/info@harts.es/ www.ritzcarlton.com). Metro Ciutadella/10, 36, 71, 92, N6, N8 bus. **Rates** *50,000-70,000ptas standard room; 62,000-87,000ptas suite.* **Credit** AmEx, DC, MC, V. **Map** p325 F7.

Designed by US architects Skidmore, Owings and Merrill, the first Ritz-Carlton hotel in Europe towers 44 storeys above the beachfront and Port Olímpic. Fountains play by the entrance, and palm-fringed gardens surround modern sculptures and the city's only beach-front pool. The Arts offers matchless service, stunning interiors – specially commissioned artwork is scattered throughout the building – and staggering views, and the hotel has impressed even seasoned world travellers. Three upper floors form 'The Club' for guests desiring still more comfort and service, and the top six floors house magnificent luxury duplex apartments with contemporary décor by Catalan designer Jaume Treserra.
Hotel services *Air-conditioning. Babysitting. Bar. Beauty salon. Car park. Conference facilities. Disabled: rooms (3) adapted for the disabled, toilets, wheelchair access. Email. Fax. Fitness centre (gym/sauna/massage). Garden. Hairdresser. Interpreters. Laundry. Lifts. Limousine. Multilingual staff. Non-smoking floor. Restaurants. Shops. Swimming pool (outdoor). Ticket agency.* **Room services** *CD player. Hairdryer. Minibar. Radio. Room service (24hrs). Safe. Telephone. TV (satellite).*

Views and interiors to die for at **Hotel Arts**.

Hotel Claris: ancient art, modern comforts.

Hotel Claris

C/Pau Claris 150, Eixample (93 487 62 62/fax 93 215 79 70/claris@derbyhotels.es/info@dervihotels.es/ www.derbyhotels.es). Metro Passeig de Gràcia/7, 16, 17, 20, 22, 24, 28, 43, 44, N6, N7 bus. **Rates** *44,500-49,500ptas single; 49,500-55,000ptas double; 65,000ptas suites; 75,000ptas duplex.* **Credit** AmEx, DC, MC, V. **Map** p320 D4.

This discreet, refined 120-room Eixample hotel is the perfect place for lovers of ancient art, modern design, new technology and *la dolce vita* to rest their heads. The Claris reflects the archaeological interests of owner Jordi Clos, who maintains the private Museu Egipci of Egyptian relics artefacts from his wide-ranging collections (Roman, Egyptian, Asian and American) are distributed around the hotel, some in a small museum, others in the public areas and bedrooms. The Egyptian relics formerly to be found in the hotel were all transferred to the museum in 2000, and were replaced by Pre-Columbian American art.
Hotel services *Air-conditioning. Bar. Business services. Car park. Child-minding service. Conference facilities. Disabled: rooms (4) adapted for the disabled, wheelchair access. Email. Fax. Fitness centre (gym/sauna). Interpreters. Laundry. Lifts. Limousine. Multilingual staff. Non-smoking floor. Restaurants. Swimming pool (outdoor). Ticket agency.* **Room services** *Hairdryer. Minibar. Room service (24hrs). Safe. Telephone. TV (satellite). Video (on request).*

Hotel Le Meridien Barcelona

La Rambla 111, Rambla (93 318 62 00/fax 93 301 77 76/www.meridienbarcelona.com). Metro Liceu/14, 38, 59, 91, N9, N12 bus. **Rates** *48,000-60,000ptas single; 52,000-64,000ptas double; 78,000-140,000ptas suite.* **Credit** AmEx, DC, MC, V. **Map** p326 A2.

Gaze out at the cathedral from the gracious **Hotel Colón**. *See p48.*

An ultra-central location right on the Rambla and luxurious accommodation have often made this 206-room hotel a first choice for celebs such as Bruce Springsteen, Michael Jackson, the Stones and Oasis (although lately the Arts has stolen its thunder). It has a fine restaurant, Le Patio, with Mediterranean cuisine. Good rates have been available December-February and July-August.
Hotel services *Air-conditioning. Babysitting. Bar. Car park. Conference facilities. Disabled: rooms (4) adapted for the disabled, toilets, wheelchair access. Email. Fax. Fitness centre (gym). Interpreters. Laundry. Lifts. Limousine. Multilingual staff. Non-smoking rooms. Restaurant. Safe. Ticket agency.* **Room services** *Hairdryer. Minibar. Radio. Room service (24hrs). Telephone. TV (satellite). Video.*

Ritz Hotel

Gran Via de les Corts Catalanes 668, Eixample (93 318 52 00/fax 93 317 36 40/ritz@ritzbcn.com). Metro Passeig de Gràcia/7, 39, 45, 47, 50, 54, 56, 62 bus. **Rates** *46,000ptas single; 49,500ptas double; 65,000-175,000ptas suite.* **Credit** AmEx, DC, MC, V. **Map** D5.

After an interlude as the Husa Palace, Barcelona's Ritz has once again regained its original emblematic title. The 19th-century building has been finely renovated, and it still qualifies as the most elegant hotel in town, offering old-fashioned style in quantities its rivals can only envy. The celebrity guest list has included Woody Allen, Orson Welles and especially Salvador Dali, who spent months here at a stretch; suite 108 is the one to go for. The sumptuous restaurant is open to non-guests.
Hotel services *Air-conditioning. Babysitting. Bar. Conference facilities. Email. Fax. Garden. Interpreters. Laundry. Lifts. Limousine. Multilingual staff. Non-smoking floor. Restaurant. Ticket agency.* **Room services** *Hairdryer. Minibar. Room service (24hrs). Safe. Telephone. TV.*

Expensive (20-40,000ptas)

Barcelona Plaza Hotel

Plaça Espanya 6-8, Sants (93 426 26 00/fax 93 426 04 00/plaza@hoteles-catalonia.es). Metro Plaça Espanya/bus all routes to Plaça Espanya. **Rates** *21,900-32,900ptas single; 27,500-37,900ptas double; 40,000-50,000ptas suite.* **Credit** AmEx, DC, MC, V. **Map** p323 A5.

The bunker-like façade of this 347-room hotel, looming up like a great monolith beside the Plaça d'Espanya, hides a splendid and charming interior. Guest rooms at the front – although not very spacious – and the nine tower suites have breathtaking views over the *plaça* and Montjuïc and its fountains; the ornate breakfast room is magnificently over-the-top, and its many leisure facilities include a truly stunning rooftop pool. The Plaza is often booked up, with business and holiday travellers; November-December and July-August are the easiest times to get in, when lower rates may be available.
Hotel services *Air-conditioning. Babysitting. Bar. Car park. Conference facilities. Disabled: rooms (4) adapted for the disabled, wheelchair access. Email. Fax. Fitness centre (gym/massage/sauna). Interpreters. Laundry. Lifts. Limousine. Multilingual staff. Restaurant. Swimming pool (outdoor). Terrace.* **Room services** *Hairdryer. Minibar. Room service (24hrs). Safe. Telephone. TV (satellite).*

Hotel Alimara

C/Berruguete 126, Horta-Guinardó (tel/fax 93 427 00 00/fax 93 427 92 92/ hotel.alimara@cett.es/www.cett.es). Metro Montbau/10, 27, 60, 73, 76, 85, 173, N4 bus. **Rates** (incl buffet breakfast) *20,800ptas single; 23,950ptas double; 31,900ptas suite. Weekend rates 12,000ptas single; 14,300ptas double; 23,300ptas suite.* **Credit** AmEx, DC, V.

In an unusual location in the hills of Vall d'Hebron, the Alimara is still only 15 minutes from Passeig de

Gràcia. It was built in 1992 near the Olympic velo-drome and tennis courts, but, unlike many hotels of the same vintage, has elegant decoration and a comfortable, airy atmosphere to go with its modern exterior. The junior suites on the third floor have large terraces with wonderful views; more spectacular still are those from the glass lift, and La Ronda restaurant. Good weekend rates are offered, and it's also handy for anyone coming to Barcelona by car.
Hotel services *Air-conditioning. Bar. Business services. Car park. Conference facilities. Disabled: rooms (3) adapted for the disabled, toilets, wheelchair access. Fax. Garden. Interpreters. Laundry. Lift. Multilingual staff. Non-smoking rooms. Restaurant. Ticket agency.* **Room services** *Hairdryer. Minibar. Radio. Room service (24hrs). Safe. Telephone. TV. Video.*

Hotel Allegro
Avda Portal de l'Angel 17, Barri Gòtic (93 318 41 41/ fax 93 301 26 31/cataloni@hoteles-catalonia.es). Metro Catalunya/bus all routes to Plaça Catalunya. **Rates** 23,900ptas single; 26,900ptas double; 29,000ptas triple. **Credit** AmEx, DC, MC, V. **Map** p326 B2.
This very elegant 74-room hotel opened in 1998. Built in 1872, the former mansion of the Rocamora family retains a great deal of its original structure. The spacious and comfortable guest rooms are completely new; several have terraces over the gracious courtyard, or balconies overlooking a pedestrian street. Breakfast is served in a marquee structure (with heat or air-con) in the courtyard. A treat.
Hotel services *Air-conditioning. Bar. Disabled: rooms (2) adapted for the disabled, toilets, wheelchair access. Fax. Garden. Interpreters. Laundry. Lift. Multilingual staff. Ticket agency.* **Room services** *Hairdryer. Minibar. Room service. Safe. Telephone. TV (satellite).*

Hotel Ambassador
C/Pintor Fortuny 13, Raval (93 412 05 30/ reservations 93 301 34 75/fax 93 302 79 77/ rivoli@alba.mssl.es/www.rivolihotels.com). Metro Liceu/14, 38, 59, 91, N9, N12 bus. **Rates** 27,000ptas single, 32,500ptas double; 49,000ptas suite. **Credit** AmEx, DC, MC, V. **Map** p326 A2.
The slightly shabby street off the Rambla gives no clue to the smart, stylish interior of this modern hotel. Drinks are served from a turn-of-the-century newspaper kiosk in the lounge bar; other highlights include a rooftop pool, Jacuzzi and sun lounge with panoramic views. Upper-floor rooms at the back benefit from direct sunlight, but others lower down can be a bit gloomy. Prices vary accordingly.
Hotel services *Air-conditioning. Bar. Car park. Conference facilities. Disabled: rooms (4) adapted for the disabled, toilets, wheelchair access. Email. Fax. Fitness centre (gym/massage/sauna). Interpreters. Laundry. Lifts. Limousine. Multilingual staff. Non-smoking rooms. Restaurant. Swimming pool (outdoor). Terrace. Ticket agency.* **Room services** *Hairdryer. Minibar. Room service (7am-11pm daily). Safe. Telephone. TV (satellite).*

Hotel Balmes
C/Mallorca 216, Eixample (93 451 19 14/fax 93 451 00 49/balmes@derbyhotels.es/www.derbyhotels.es). FGC Provença/7, 16, 17, 20, 43, 44, 67, 68, N7 bus. **Rates** 13,500ptas single; 22,200ptas double; 25,000ptas suite. **Credit** AmEx, DC, MC, V. **Map** p320 C4.
A pleasant 1990-vintage 100-room hotel in the middle of the Eixample offering all-round comfort and a high standard of service. Rooms at the rear get the morning sun, and look onto the interior garden, solarium and pool; some ground-floor rooms have outside terraces. The peace of the patio contrasts greatly with the bustle of the street outside.
Hotel services *Air-conditioning. Babysitting (24hrs' notice). Bar (Mon-Fri). Car park. Conference facilities. Email. Fax. Garden. Interpreters. Laundry. Lifts. Limousine. Multilingual staff. Restaurant (Mon-Fri). Swimming pool (outdoor). Ticket agency.* **Room services** *Hairdryer (some rooms). Minibar. Radio. Room service (8am-11pm Mon-Fri). Safe. Telephone. TV (satellite).*

Hotel Caledonian
Gran Via de les Corts Catalanes 574, Eixample (93 453 02 00/fax 93 451 77 03/www.hotel-caledonian.com). Metro Universitat/9, 14, 50, 56, 59, N1, N2, N13, N14, N15 bus. **Rates** 13,500ptas single; 25,000ptas double. *Weekend rates* 19,100ptas (when available). **Credit** AmEx, DC, MC, V. **Map** p314 C5.

The **Hotel Duques de Bergara**. *See p48.*

Yet another classic hotel which, although modernised for the 1992 Olympic Games, maintains style with warmth. The Caledonian is centrally located yet sufficiently away from the crowds of the Plaça Catalunya/Rambla area to give it a relatively peaceful feel.
Hotel services *Air-conditioning. Bar. Laundry.Lift.* **Room services** *Hairdryer. Minibar. Room service. Safe. Telephone. TV (satellite).*

Hotel Colón

Avda de la Catedral 7, Barri Gòtic (93 301 14 04/fax 93 317 29 15/www.hotelcolon.es/colon@nexus.es).
Metro Jaume I/17, 19, 40, 45 bus. **Rates** 18,000-21,500ptas single; 27,000-40,000ptas double; 47,500ptas suite. **Credit** AmEx, DC, MC, V.
Map p326 B2.
With touches of old-world luxury, this 147-room hotel has a superb location opposite the cathedral, with matchless views of the Sunday sardana dancing or Thursday's antique market. There's a relaxing piano bar and good restaurant; staff are friendly and efficient. Guests at a sister hotel around the corner, the cheaper **Regencia Colón** (14,500ptas double), can use the Colón's facilities.
Hotel services *Air-conditioning. Babysitting. Bar. Conference facilities. Disabled: rooms (2) adapted for the disabled, wheelchair access. Email. Fax. Laundry. Lifts. Limousine. Multilingual staff. Restaurant.* **Room services** *Hairdryer. Minibar. Radio. Room service (24hrs). Safe. Telephone. TV (satellite).*
Branch: Hotel Regencia Colón C/Sagristans 13-17, Barri Gòtic (93 318 98 58/fax 93 317 28 22).

Hotel Duques de Bergara

C/Bergara 11, Eixample (93 301 51 51/fax 93 317 34 42/cataloni@hoteles-catalonia.es/www.hoteles-catalonia.es). Metro Catalunya/bus all routes to Plaça Catalunya. **Rates** 21,900-29,900ptas single; 26,900-34,900ptas double; 29,900-37,900ptas triple; 42,500ptas suite. **Credit** AmEx, DC, MC, V.
Map p326 A1.
An opulent hotel just off Plaça Catalunya, created in the 1980s within an 1898 Modernist edifice by Gaudí's professor Emili Sala. The original style remains in the hall and stairways, while the communal areas and 151 guest rooms are modern, spacious and well furnished. In the courtyard there is a medium-sized swimming pool. Check when booking to avoid the hotel's few dark rooms.
Hotel services *Air-conditioning. Babysitting. Conference facilities. Disabled: rooms (7) adapted for the disabled, toilets, wheelchair access. Fax. Laundry. Lifts. Limousine. Multilingual staff. Restaurant. Swimming pool (outdoor). Terrace. Ticket agency. Pay TV.* **Room services** *Hairdryer. Minibar. Radio. Room service (24hrs). Safe 500ptas. Telephone. TV (satellite).*

Hotel Inglaterra

C/Pelai 14, Eixample (93 505 11 00/fax 93 505 11 09/hi@hotelinglaterra.com/www.hotelmagestic.es). Metro Universitat/bus all routes to Plaça Universitat. **Rates** 26,000ptas single; 30,000ptas double; 36,000ptas. **Credit** AmEx, DC, MC, V. **Map** p326 A1.

Barcelona Plaza Hotel

Wake up to a hot and cold buffet breakfast in an over-the-top atmosphere. *See p44.*

Guillem Hotel

Varied, generous, both hot & cold. *See p49.*

Hotel Granvía

Century-old glitter and a generous buffet of cold-cuts. *See p49.*

Hotel Mesón Castilla

Tuck in to all you want, either indoors or on the patio. *See p50.*

Hotel Splendid

Get off to a good start before getting down to business. *See p51.*

Pensió 2000

Six breakfast menus, including macrobiotic, for 450ptas. *See p55.*

The Inglaterra opened only in 1999, and everything in the building except the façade and tiled staircase is entirely new. It's aimed mainly at a business clientele, but the hotel couldn't be better located for seeing the major sights. The rooms offer an impressive level of refined comfort, and, as well as a rooftop terrace, the sixth floor contains a very large guest room that is ideal for anyone looking for extra space and privacy.
Hotel services *Air-conditioning. Bar. Conference facilities. Disabled: room (1) adapted for the disabled, toilets, wheelchair access. Fax. Interpreters. Laundry. Lifts. Multilingual staff. Safe. Ticket agency.* **Room services** *Hairdryer. Minibar. Room service. Telephone. TV (satellite).*

Hotel Podium

C/Bailèn 4, Eixample (93 265 02 02/reservations 902 115 116/fax 93 265 05 06/nhpodium@nh-hoteles.es). Metro Arc de Triomf/19, 39, 40, 41, 42, 55, 141, N4, N11 bus. **Rates** 19,500ptas single; 23,100ptas double; 40,000pts suite. **Credit** AmEx, DC, MC, V. **Map** p315 E5.
Part of the NH chain, this 145-room hotel housed in a refurbished turn-of-the-century building offers all the comforts of an upmarket hotel. Decorated with modern art works throughout, it also has a pleasant rooftop pool.
Hotel services *Air-conditioning. Babysitting. Bar. Car park. Disabled: rooms adapted for the disabled, toilets, wheelchair access. Gym. Interpreters. Laundry. Limousine. Lifts. Multilingual staff. Pool. Restaurant. Safe. Sauna.* **Room services** *Hairdryer. Minibar. Radio. Room service. Telephone. TV (satellite).*

Hotel Regente

Rambla Catalunya 76, Eixample (93 487 59 89/fax 93 487 32 27/regente@inf.entorno.es/www.hoteles-centro-ciudad.es). Metro Passeig de Gràcia, FGC Provença/7, 16, 17, 22, 24, 28, N4 bus. **Rates** 18,000-22,900ptas single; 24,900-32,000ptas double. **Credit** AmEx, DC, MC, V. **Map** p320 D4.

The Regente occupies a renovated 1913 Evarist Juncosa Modernista mansion with a finely restored façade. Stained-glass decoration imparts distinctive charm, while double glazing shields guests from the Eixample's street noise; sixth- and seventh-floor rooms have terraces with stunning views, many lower rooms open onto grand wrought-iron balconies, and there's a rooftop pool that's a perfect place to enjoy the sunset.
Hotel services *Air-conditioning. Babysitting. Bar. Conference facilities. Disabled: rooms (2) adapted for the disabled, wheelchair access. Fax. Fitness facilities. Interpreters. Laundry. Lifts. Limousine. Multilingual staff. Swimming pool (outdoor). Ticket agency.* **Room services** *Fitness cycles (in some rooms). Hairdryer. Minibar. Radio. Room service (7am-11pm daily). Safe. Telephone. TV (satellite).*

Hotel Rivoli Ramblas

La Rambla 128, Rambla (93 302 66 43/reservations 93 412 09 88/fax 93 317 50 53/rivoli@mssl.es/www.rivolihotels.com). Metro Catalunya or Liceu/bus all routes la Plaça Catalunya. **Rates** 19,500-31,000ptas single; 23,000-37,000ptas double; 55,000-99,000ptas suite. **Credit** AmEx, DC, MC, V. **Map** p326 A2.

Rebuilt in the early '90s, the Rivoli is a world apart from the bustle on the Rambla outside. The 89 rooms have interesting colour schemes, and the Blue Moon piano bar is a relaxing place to end the evening. A popular choice for tourists and business people.
Hotel services *Air-conditioning. Babysitting. Bar. Car park. Conference facilities. Email. Fax. Fitness centre (gym/sauna/solarium). Interpreters. Laundry. Lifts. Limousine. Multilingual staff. Restaurant. Terrace. Ticket agency.* **Room services** *Hairdryer. Minibar. Room service (7am-11pm). Safe. Telephone. TV (satellite).*

Upper-mid (14-25,000ptas)

Guillem Hotel

C/Guillem Tell 49, Gràcia (93 415 40 00/fax 93 217 34 65). Metro Fontana or Lesseps/FGC Plaça Molina/16, 17, 27, 31, 32 bus. **Rates** 15,000-17,000ptas single; 19,000-22,800ptas double. **Credit** MC, V. **Map** p320 D2.

A year 2000-vintage hotel, the independently owned Guillem is located in a residential part of upper Barcelona near Plaça Molina, but still just three metro stops from Plaça Catalunya. The small 61-room hotel has warm, colonial-style furnishings, good hot and cold buffet breakfasts and personal service. All rooms have exterior windows; those looking on to c/Guillem Tell are more spacious than those on the side of c/Lincoln.
Hotel services *Air-conditioning. Bar. Car park. Conference facilities. Disabled: rooms adapted for the*

Hotel Oriente, from the Rambla. *See p50.*

disabled. Laundry. Lift. Restaurant. Safe. **Room services** *Hairdryer. Minibar. Room service. Telephone. TV.*

Hotel Gaudí

C/Nou de la Rambla 12, Raval (93 317 90 32/fax 93 412 26 36/gaudi@hotelgaudi.es/www.hotelgaudi.es). Metro Liceu/14, 38, 59, 91, N9, N12 bus. **Rates** 14,500ptas single; 19,000ptas double; 24,500ptas triple; 27,500ptas quad. **Credit** AmEx, DC, MC, V. **Map** p327 A3.

The Gaudí's great selling point is its convenience as the main mid-level hotel in a central, much-visited area, directly opposite Gaudí's Palau Güell (*see p63*). True to its name, it has a Gaudí-inspired lobby; the 73 rooms contrast with the shabbiness of the surrounding Barrio Chino and are good for the area, but staff make little effort to be welcoming.
Hotel services *Air-conditioning. Babysitting. Bar (noon-midnight). Car park. Conference facilities. Disabled: rooms (2) adapted for the disabled, wheelchair access. Email. Fax. Fitness centre (gym). Interpreters. Lifts. Multilingual staff. Restaurant.* **Room services** *Hairdryer. Radio. Room service (noon-midnight). Safe (for hire). Telephone. TV (satellite).*

Hotel Granvía

Gran Via de les Corts Catalanes 642, Eixample (93 318 19 00/fax 93 318 99 97/hgranvia@nnhoteles.es). Metro Passeig de Gràcia/7, 16, 17, 22, 24, 28, 42, 47, 50, 54, 56, 62, N1, N2, N3, N9 bus. **Rates** 10,000-12,000ptas single; 15,000ptas double; 21,000ptas triple. **Credit** AmEx, DC, MC, V. **Map** p324 D5.

Amid the renovation fever of '90s Barcelona, the Granvía with its splendid Victorian-rococo interiors counts as a remarkable survivor. The mansion was built for a wealthy banker in 1873, and has been a hotel since 1936. The bedrooms have now been modernised, but no changes have marred the lounge area and mirrored breakfast room with their paintings, chandeliers and gilt frames. To go with this look of fading grandeur the atmosphere is suitably old-fashioned and sedate, but the hotel has real charm. There's also a pleasant outdoor patio with its fountain and plants.
Hotel services *Air-conditioning. Conference facilities. Garden. Lift.* **Room services** *Minibar. Room service. Safe. Telephone. TV (cable, satellite).*

Accommodation

The **Hotel San Agustín**. *See p51.*

Hotel Mesón Castilla

C/Valldonzella 5, Raval (93 318 21 82/fax 93 412 40 20/hmesoncastilla@teleline.es). Metro Universitat/ bus all routes to Plaça Catalunya, Plaça Universitat. **Rates** (incl breakfast) 11,600ptas single; 14,800ptas double; 20,000ptas triple. **Credit** AmEx, DC, MC, V. **Map** p326 A1.

A favourite with British and North American visitors, who enjoy the hearty buffet breakfasts served in the cosy dining room or on the patio terrace. This old-world-style hotel has 56 impeccably clean, quiet rooms, some furnished with antiques, and some rear rooms have balconies. Three large rooms with up to four beds are great for families with children. **Hotel services** *Air-conditioning. Car park. Disabled: wheelchair access. Fax. Laundry. Lifts. Multilingual staff. Safe. Terrace.* **Room services** *Minibar (most rooms). Telephone. TV (satellite).*

Hotel Metropol

C/Ample 31, Barri Gòtic (93 310 51 00/ fax 93 319 12 76/www.hoteles-hesperia.es). Metro Jaume I/14, 17, 19, 36, 40, 45, 57, 59, 64, 157, N6, N8 bus. **Rates** 15,000ptas single; 16,500ptas double; 18,500ptas triple. **Credit** AmEx, DC, MC, V. **Map** p323 B4.

Another 19th-century hotel that was given a makeover in 1992, although the reception area still has its old charm. Half the 71 rooms look on to C/Ample, which is surprisingly quiet and tranquil for an old-city street very near the port. Location-wise, the place is ideal for nightlife. **Hotel services** *Air-conditioning. Disabled: rooms currently being adapted, toilets, wheelchair access. Fax. Laundry. Lifts. Multilingual staff.* **Room services** *Minibar. Safe. Telephone. TV (satellite).*

Hotel Onix

C/Llançà 30, Sants (93 426 00 87/fax 93 426 19 81). Metro Espanya/bus all routes to Plaça d'Espanya. **Rates** 13,600-16,400ptas single; 17,000-20,500ptas double; 18,500-25,000ptas triple. **Credit** AmEx, DC, MC, V. **Map** p323 B5.

A comfortable if functional business hotel off Plaça d'Espanya, close to Sants rail station and with easy access to the airport. The quiet outside rooms have views of the old Arenas bullring on one side, and Parc Joan Miró on the other. All rooms have balconies. The Onix also has a tiny rooftop pool and sun deck and underground parking. **Hotel services** *Air-conditioning. Bar. Babysitting (24hrs' notice). Conference facilities. Car park. Disabled: rooms (3) adapted for the disabled, wheelchair access. Fax. Laundry. Lifts. Multilingual staff. Restaurant (for groups only). Swimming pool*

(outdoor). Ticket agency. **Room services** *Hairdryer. Minibar. Radio. Refrigerator. Room service (8am-11pm). Safe. Telephone. TV (satellite).*

Hotel Oriente

La Rambla 45-47, Rambla (93 302 25 58/fax 93 412 38 19/horiente@husa.es/www.husa.es). Metro Drassanes/14, 38, 59, 91, N9, N12 bus. **Rates** 12,000ptas single; 16,900ptas double; 21,000ptas triple. **Credit** AmEx, DC, MC, V. **Map** p327 A3.

Inaugurated in 1842 as Barcelona's first ever 'grand hotel', the Oriente is undeniably atmospheric. It was built incorporating parts of an old Franciscan monastery – remnants of the pillars of which are just visible in the ballroom – and long played host to the illustrious musicians – Toscanini, Maria Callas and others – who performed in the Liceu next door. Hans Christian Andersen, General Grant and Errol Flynn also put up here. The old-world dining room and elegant ballroom (now a lounge) are a reminder of this glorious past, but the hotel is now a far cry from the glamour of its heyday. Its 142 rooms are spacious but rather spartan, and those with a view of the Rambla are quite noisy. Service is also distinctly patchy. **Hotel services** *Bar. Conference facilities. Fax. Lifts. Multilingual staff. Restaurant.* **Room services** *Room service (7am-10pm). Safe. Telephone. TV.*

Hotel Roma

Avda. de Roma 31, Eixample (93 410 66 33/fax 93 410 13 52). Metro Entença or Sants/27, 30, 32, 43, 44, 78, 215, N7 bus. **Rates** 16,900ptas single; 19,900ptas double. **Credit** AmEx, DC, MC, V. **Map** p323 B4.

Located near the main Sants station and Plaça Espanya, the Roma is a warm, comfortable hotel, elegantly decorated, with some rooms with antique furniture, while others are modern. There is a pleasant patio off the dining room. **Hotel services** *Air-conditioning. Bar. Car park. Disabled: rooms adapted for the disabled. Laundry. Lift. Restaurant. Safe.* **Room services** *Hairdryer. Minibar. Room service. Telephone. TV.*

Hotel Rubens

Passeig de la Mare de Déu del Coll 10, Gràcia (93 219 12 04/fax 93 219 12 69/cataloni@hoteles-catalonia.es/www.hoteles-catalonia.es). Metro Lesseps/bus 24, 31, 32, 74, 87 bus. **Rates** 16,900ptas single; 19,900ptas double; 22,900ptas triple; 23,900ptas quad; 25,900ptas quintuple. **Credit** AmEx, DC, MC, V.

The three-star, modern Rubens stands in a hilly residential area above Gràcia, between the Parc Güell and the Crueta del Coll park. As an alternative to city centre hotels, it offers cleaner air, panoramic views, and the chance to go walking in the parks nearby. Upper-floor rooms have private terraces, and there is a large sun deck on the sixth floor. The city centre is ten minutes away by Metro. **Hotel services** *Air-conditioning. Bar. Car park. Conference facilities. Disabled: rooms (2) adapted for the disabled, toilets, wheelchair access. Fax. Laundry. Lifts. Restaurant.* **Room services** *Radio. Safe. Telephone. TV (satellite).*

Hotel San Agustín

Plaça Sant Agustí 3, Raval (93 318 16 58/fax 93 317 29 28/www.hotelsa.com). Metro Liceu/14, 38, 59, 91, N9, N12 bus. **Rates** (incl buffet breakfast) 12,500-14,000ptas single; 17,500-18,500ptas double; 23,000ptas triple. **Credit** AmEx, DC, MC, V.
Map p327 A3.

One of the oldest continually functioning hotels in Barcelona, the San Agustín has been welcoming guests for well over 100 years, but has had two major facelifts in the last decade. It now offers an all-new reception, lifts, modern bathrooms, air-con and TVs in every room. Some say it's lost its character, but the rooms are comfortable, and retain a bit of old-world charm: top-floor rooms have oak-beamed ceilings and romantic views. Three big rooms (with two bathrooms each) sleep up to six. The hotel also has a very pleasant lounge bar, and it remains one of the most attractive options in the Rambla area.
Hotel services *Air-conditioning. Babysitting. Bar. Conference facilities. Disabled: rooms (2) adapted for the disabled, wheelchair access. Fax. Laundry. Lifts. Multilingual staff. Restaurant (dinner only).* **Room services** *Hairdryer. Safe. Telephone. TV (satellite).*

Hotel Sant'Ángelo

C/Consell de Cent, 74, Eixample (93 423 46 47/fax 93 423 88 10/www.nh-hoteles.es). Metro Rocafort or Turragona/27, 109, N0 bus. **Rates** 16,500ptas single; 19,400ptas double; 25,000ptas junior suite. **Credit** AmEx, DC, MC, V. **Map** p323 B5.

A member of the NH chain, the Sant'Ángelo is located in the Eixample beside the Joan Miró park. The small 48-room hotel offers all the comforts of more expensive places. A notable feature is the lounge area which gives on to an interior garden.
Hotel services *Air-conditioning. Bar. Car park. Disabled: rooms adapted for the disabled. Laundry.Lifts. Restaurant. Safe.* **Room services** *Hairdryer. Minibar. Radio. Room service. Telephone. TV (satellite).*

Hotel Splendid

C/Muntaner 2, Eixample (93 451 21 42/fax 93 323 16/splendid@smc.es/www.hotel-splendid.com). Metro Universitat/24, 41, 55, 64, 91, 141, N6 bus. **Rates** 14,000/17,000ptas single; 20,000ptas double; 23,000ptas triple; 23,000ptas junior suite.
Credit AmEx, DC, MC, V. **Map** p324 C5.

Small and functional, this brand new hotel just beside Plaça Universitat opened in 1999. It's been created with the business world in mind, but its central location is also ideal for sightseeing. Each room has a minibar, desk and direct Net access, and a very generous hot buffet breakfast is served for 1,500ptas.
Hotel services *Air-conditioning. Bar. Car park. Conference facilities. Disabled: room (1) adapted for the disabled, toilet, wheelchair access. Fax. Interpreters. Laundry. Lift. Multilingual staff. Non-smoking rooms.* **Room services** *Hairdryer. Minibar. Modem points. Room service. Safe. Telephone. TV (satellite). Video.*

The best Locations

Hostal Jardí
Plaça del Pí, with its bohemian atmosphere, street painters, musicians... *See p57.*

Hostal Layetana
So you want to be right beside the Roman wall and the cathedral... *See p57.*

Hostal-Residencia Barcelona
For the theatres and nightlife of the Paral.lel area. *See p52.*

Hotel Internacional
An institution for living the Rambla experience. *See p53.*

Pensión Ambos Mundos
For the Plaça Reial nightlife scene. *See p60.*

Pensió 2000
It's the next best thing to a box in the Palau de la Musica. *See p55.*

Hotel Internacional. *See p53.*

Accommodation

Ramblas Hotel

La Rambla 33, Rambla (93 301 57 00/fax 93 412 25 07/www.ramblashotels.com). Metro Liceu/14, 38, 59, 91, N9, N12 bus. **Rates** (incl breakfast) 14,000-20,500ptas single; 15,000-22,000ptas double; 19,000-26,000ptas triple; 20,000-30,000ptas quad. **Credit** AmEx, MC, V. **Map** p327 A3-4.

The simply named Ramblas occupies an attractive 18th-century building with tiled *Modernista* façade, but is another very recent conversion. Rooms are spacious and comfortable; those on the eighth and ninth floors have large terraces, and while front rooms have views of the Rambla and the port, those at the back have an outlook taking in Montjuïc and the roof of Gaudí's Palau Güell. If you stay here, though, be prepared to be in the busiest part of the Rambla.

Hotel services *Air-conditioning. Bar. Laundry. Lift.* **Room services** *Hairdryer. Minibar. Room service (breakfast only). Safe. Telephone. TV (satellite).*

Enjoy breakfast on the terrace of the **Hotel Mesón Castilla.** *See p50.*

Lower-mid (7-14,000ptas)

Hostal Ciudad Condal

C/Mallorca 255, pral, Eixample (93 215 10 40/fax.93 487 04 59). Metro Passeig de Gràcia/FGC Provença/20, 21, 28, 43, 44, N7 bus. **Rates** 6,000ptas single; 9,500ptas double. **Credit** MC, V. **Map** p320 D4.

The Ciudad Condal occupies part of the Casa Angel Batlló, an 1891 Modernista block of three houses with one single façade that was designed by Josep Vilaseca i Casanovas (not, though, the same building as Gaudí's Casa Batlló). The 15 rooms are a little spartan, but those on the outside have high ceilings and balconies.

Hotel services *Bar. Car park . Fax. Hairdryer. Laundry. Safe.* **Room services** *Room service. Telephone. TV*

Hostal Girona

C/Girona 24, 1° 1ª, Eixample (93 265 02 59/fax 93 265 85 32). Metro Urquinaona/19, 39, 40, 41, 42, 55, 141, N4, N11 bus. **Rates** 3,000ptas single; 7,000ptas double. **Credit** MC, V. **Map** p326 C1.

A white marble stairway leads up to this cosy, family-run eight-room *pensión* in the Eixample. All bedrooms have central heating and TV; the four doubles also boast new en suite bathrooms. Refreshments are served in a tiny breakfast area. In the reception area there is some grand original *Modernista* furniture, and the streets nearby, off any of the main tourist routes, are full of fine Modernist architecture.

Hotel services *Telephone.* **Room services** *TV.*

Hostal Plaza

C/Fontanella 18, Eixample (tel/fax 93 301 01 39/plazahostal@mx3.redestb.es). Metro Urquinaona or Plaça Catalunya/bus all routes to Plaça Catalunya, Plaça Urquinaona. **Rates** 4,500-5,000ptas single; 7,000-8,000ptas double. **Credit** AmEx, DC, MC, V. **Map** p326 B1.

Run by eager-to-please Hispanic Americans, the Plaza is an unusual, fun hotel. It offers a glut of services rarely found in lower-bracket Spanish hotels, including laundry, TV room, fridge, freezer and microwave, loads of information on the city and even, they say, discounts at local restaurants and clubs. All 14 rooms have showers and fans.

Hotel services *Email. Fax. Laundry. Lift. Microwave. Multilingual staff. Safe. TV room (satellite). Vending machine.* **Room services** *Fan. Radio (some).*

Hostal-Residencia Barcelona

C/Roser 40, Poble Sec (tel/fax 93 443 27 06). Metro Paral.lel/20, 57, 64, 91, 157, N6 bus. **Rates** 3,800ptas single; 7,000ptas double; 9,000ptas triple; 12,000ptas quad. **Credit** AmEx, MC, V. **Map** p323 B6.

A *hostal* in the pleasant *barri* of Poble Sec, just off the Paral.lel – still only a walk from the centre. Its 60 rooms are basic but clean; most have bathrooms. Guests have use of a fridge in the reception area.

Hotel services *Lift. Multilingual staff. Safe. Ticket agency.* **Room services** *Air-conditioning (some). TV.*

Hostal-Residencia Ramos

C/Hospital 36, Raval (93 302 07 23/fax 93 302 04 30). Metro Liceu/14, 38, 59, 91, N9, N12 bus. **Rates** 4,000-5,000ptas single; 7,000-8,000ptas double; 9,600-10,500ptas triple. **Credit** AmEx, DC, MC, V. **Map** p326-7 A2-3.

Another off-Rambla hotel, the Ramos occupies the first and second floors of a charming old building with a tiled entrance and elegant wide staircase. All rooms have bathrooms; those at the front overlook the church and trees of Plaça San Agustí.

Hotel services *Air-conditioning. Fax. Lift. Multilingual staff. Refreshments available. Safe. Terrace.* **Room services** *(10am-6pm). Telephone. TV.*

Hostal Rey Don Jaime I

C/Jaume I 11, Barri Gòtic (tel/fax 93 310 62 08/
r.d.jaime@atriumhotels.com/www.atriumhotels.com).
Metro Jaume I/bus 17, 19, 40, 45, N8. **Rates**
5,800ptas single; 8,500ptas double; 12,000ptas triple.
Credit AmEx, DC, MC, V. **Map** p327 B3.
The Don Jaime sits on the noisy main artery through
the centre of the old city, but is therefore handy for
both the Barri Gòtic and La Ribera, and it's popular
with a mostly young clientele. Basic but clean, the
30 rooms all have balconies and bathrooms.
Hotel services *Disabled: toilets. Fax. Lift.*
Lounge. Multilingual staff. Safe. TV.
Room services *Telephone.*

Hotel Call

C/Arc de Sant Ramon del Call 4, Barri Gòtic (93 302
11 23/fax 93 301 34 86). Metro Liceu, Jaume I/
14, 38, 59, 91, N9, N12 bus. **Rates** 5,600ptas
single; 8,200ptas double; 10,270ptas triple.
Credit MC, V. **Map** p327 B3.
On a spectacularly narrow street in what was the
medieval Jewish quarter – the Call – around the corner from Plaça Sant Jaume, this hotel (rebuilt in 1992)
is clean and modern, though rather functional in
design. Rooms overlook quiet pedestrian streets or a
darkish interior patio. All have modern bathrooms.
Hotel services *Air-conditioning. Fax. Lift. Lounge.*
Multilingual staff. TV. **Room services** *Telephone.*

Hotel Cisneros

C/Aribau 54, Eixample (93 454 18 00/fax 93 451 39
08). Metro Universitat, FCG Provença/54, 58, 63,
64, 66, 67, 68, N3, N8 bus. **Rates** (incl breakfast)
5,300-6,300ptas single; 7,400ptas-8,400ptas double;
11,500ptas triple. **Credit** DC, MC, V. **Map** p320 C4.
Located in the Eixample, four blocks from Plaça
Universitat, all rooms have TV, telephone and central heating, and most have en suite bathrooms. A
generous self-service breakfast is served.
Hotel services *Restaurant (buffet).*
Room services *Telephone. TV.*

Hotel España

C/Sant Pau 9-11, Raval (93 318 17 58/fax 93 317
11 34/hotelespanya@tresnet.com). Metro Liceu/14,
38, 59, 91, N9, N12 bus. **Rates** 5,600ptas single;
10,700ptas double; 14,600ptas triple. **Credit** AmEx,
DC, MC, V. **Map** p327 A3.
The España is a *Modernista* landmark, with lower
floors designed by Domènech i Montaner in 1902.
The main restaurant (good for lunch) is decorated
with floral motifs in tile and elaborate woodwork, the
larger dining room beyond it features extravagant
tiled murals of river-nymphs by Ramon Casas, and
the huge fireplace in the bar was sculpted by Eusebi
Arnau. After all this, the more modern guest rooms
can come as a disappointment, but several open onto
a bright interior patio. Book well in advance; prices
have risen less than at many nearby hotels.
Hotel services *Air-conditioning. Conference*
facilities. Email. Fax. Lifts. Multilingual staff.
Restaurant. Safe. TV lounge. **Room services** *Safe*
(some). Telephone. TV.

Hotel Ginebra

Rambla Catalunya 1, 3º 1ª, Eixample (93 317 10 63/
fax 93 317 55 65). Metro Catalunya/all buses to
Plaça Catalunya. **Rates** 5,200ptas single; 8,500ptas
double; 10,000ptas triple. **Credit** V. **Map** p326 B1.
As centrally located as can be, this small hotel
housed on the third floor of a gracious old building
overlooking Plaça Catalunya is pleasant and cosy.
All rooms have TV, telephone, air-conditioning and
private baths, and the double-glazed windows help
keep the noise out. A few rooms have balconies with
views of the *plaça.*
Hotel services *Air-conditioning. Cafeteria*
(snack bar). Car park. Hairdryer. Lift. Safe.
Room services *Telephone. TV*

Hotel Internacional

La Rambla 78-80, Rambla (93 302 25 66/fax 93 317
61 90/www.husa.es). Metro Liceu/14, 38, 59, 91, N9,
N12 bus. **Rates** (incl breakfast) 7,500ptas single;
13,800ptas double; 17,500ptas triple. **Credit** AmEx,
DC, MC, V. **Map** p327 A3.
An institution on the Rambla, presiding over the Pla
de la Boqueria, and popular with visiting foreign
football fans, who drape their colours along the balconies. Built in 1894, the 60-room hotel has been fully
refurbished. It's always full, so book way ahead; it's
also noisy, and note that this hotel has brought in
some of the biggest recent price hikes of any
Barcelona hotel.
Hotel services *Bar. Fax. Lift (from 1st floor).*
Meals for groups. Multilingual staff. TV.
Room services *Safe (for hire). Telephone.*

Hotel Oasis

Pla del Palau 17, La Ribera (93 319 43 96/fax 93
310 48 74). Metro Barceloneta/14, 17, 36, 40, 45,
57, 59, 64 157 bus. **Rates** 6,400-6,950ptas single;
7,800-8,400ptas double; 10,700ptas triple.
Credit AmEx, DC, MC, V. **Map** p327 C4.
This unusually well-equipped near-budget hotel is
handily located between La Ribera and the Port Vell.
All rooms have bathrooms and TVs; exterior rooms
also have balconies, but can be noisy. On the ground
floor, there's also a handy bar-restaurant.
Hotel services *Bar. Lift (from first floor).*
Multilingual staff. Restaurant. Safe. **Room services**
Air-conditioning (some rooms). Safe (some rooms).
Telephone. TV.

Hostal Orleans

Avda Marquès de L'Argentera 13, La Ribera (93
319 73 82/fax 93 319 22 19). Metro Barceloneta/14,
39, 51 bus. **Rates** 3,000-4,500ptas single; 7,400-8,400
double. **Credit** AmEx, DC, MC, V. **Map** p320 C4.
This family-run *hostal* near the Port and the
Ciutadella has 17 good-sized rooms with en suite
facilities, and some have balconies (which can be
noisy). All are clean, but upper-floor rooms are more
modern. There are special rates for triple or quadru-
ple occupancy; weekly rates can also be negotiated.
Hotel services *Fax. Laundry. Multilingual staff.*
Telephone. Vending machine. **Room services**
Telephone (some). TV.

Hotel Paseo de Gracia

Passeig de Gràcia 102, Eixample (93 215 58 24/fax 93 215 06 03). Metro Diagonal/ 22, 24, 28, 100, 101, N4 bus. **Rates** 7,100/8,400ptas single; 9,400ptas double. **Credit** V. **Map** p320 D4.

This pleasant 33-room hotel is proof that not everything on Passeig de Gràcia is necessarily expensive. All room have TV and telephone. Ideally located for shopping, visiting nearby Gaudi buildings or just sitting at the many terrace cafés in the area and watching the world go by.

Hotel services *Air-conditioning. Lifts. Safe.*
Room services *Telephone. TV*

Hotel Pelayo

C/Pelai 9, Eixample (93 302 37 27/fax 93 412 31 68). Metro Universitat/bus all routes to Plaça Universitat. **Rates** (incl small breakfast) 7,500ptas single; 10,500ptas double; 14,000ptas triple; 6,500ptas quad; 18,000ptas quintuple. **Credit** MC, V. **Map** p326 A1.

The Pelayo occupies the first and second floors of a building in an ultra-central location by Plaça Universitat. Personal touches in the decoration give it warmth and character, and the owner appreciates it if her guests respond with equal courtesy. All 15 rooms have bathrooms, air-con and central heating.

Hotel services *Air-conditioning. Laundry. Lift. Multilingual staff. Safe.* **Room services** *Safe. Telephone. TV.*

Hotel Peninsular

C/Sant Pau 34-6, Raval (93 302 31 38/fax 93 412 36 99). Metro Liceu/14, 38, 59, 91, N9, N12 bus. **Rates** (incl IVA and breakfast) 7,000ptas single; 9,000ptas double; 12,000ptas triple; 14,000ptas quad; 16,000ptas quintuple. **Credit** MC, V. **Map** p326 A3.

Like the Oriente, the Peninsular was built inside the shell of a former monastery, and the semi-subterranean room that's now the TV lounge once had a passageway connecting it to Sant Agusti church. The hotel was modernised in the early '90s, but wicker furniture imparts a colonial feel to its plant-lined patio. All 85 rooms are clean and comfortable, and most have en suite baths or showers, and air-conditioning.

Hotel services *Air-conditioning. Fax. Lift. Multilingual staff. Patio. Safe. TV lounge.*
Room services *Telephone.*

Hotel Principal

C/Junta de Comerç 8, Raval (93 318 89 74/ fax 93 412 08 19/hotel@hotelprincipal.es/ www.hotelprincipal.es). Metro Liceu/14, 38, 59, 91, N9, N12 bus. **Rates** (incl breakfast) 9,000 single; 11,300ptas double; 14,900ptas triple; 18,200ptas quad. **Credit** AmEx, DC, MC, V. **Map** p327 A3.

One of a few hotels and *hostals* on this quiet street near the Rambla, the Principal is distinguished by the ornate furniture in its 60 bedrooms, all of which have modernised bathrooms. The same owners also have the slightly cheaper Joventut, along the street, which has been thoroughly renovated.

Hotel services *Air-conditioning. Babysitting. Bar. Disabled: rooms (3) adapted for the disabled, toilets. Email. Fax. Lifts. Multilingual staff. Restaurant.*
Room services *Safe. Telephone. TV.*
Branch: Hotel Joventut C/Junta de Comerç 12, Raval (93 301 84 99).

Hotel Triunfo

Passeig Picasso 22, La Ribera (tel/fax 93 315 08 60). Metro Arc de Triomf/39, 40, 41, 42, 51, 141 bus. **Rates** 6,500ptas single; 10,500ptas double; 15,000ptas triple. **Credit** MC, V. **Map** p325 E6.

Located in a very central but quiet area of the Born beside the Ciutadela Park, this hotel offers impeccably clean rooms with bath, telephone, TV, and air-conditioning. There's lots of nightlife in the Born area, but if healthy bicycle rides are your thing, the park is yours. Plans are to open a sister hotel – **Nuevo Triunfo** – in C/Cabanyes 34 in Poble Sec in the spring of 2001.

Hotel services *Air-conditioning. Lifts. Safe.*
Room services *Telephone. TV.*

Hotel Urquinaona

Ronda de Sant Pere 24, La Ribera (93 268 13 36/fax 93 295 41 37/www.barcelonahotel.com/urquinaona). Metro Urquinaona/19, 39, 40, 41, 45, 55, 141 bus. **Rates** 9,400ptas single; 12,900ptas double; 16,800ptas triple. **Credit** MC, V. **Map** p326 B1.

A former old-style *hostal* very recently transformed by enterprising management into a spic and span modern hotel, offering comforts that normally cost more – air-con, satellite TV, phones, minibars and safes in all rooms – plus a small breakfast room, and Internet access. A welcome departure from the norm in Barcelona hotels. Book early.

Hotel services *Air-conditioning. Disabled: wheelchair access. Email. Fax. Interpreting service. Laundry service. Multilingual staff.* **Room services** *Hairdryer. Minibar. Refrigerator. Room service (breakfast only). Safe. Telephone. TV (satellite).*

Hotel Via Augusta

Via Augusta 63, Zona Alta (93 217 92 50/fax 93 237 77 14). Metro Fontana, FGC Gràcia/16,17, 22, 24, 25, 28, 31, 32, N4 bus. **Rates** 8,500-10,000ptas single; 12,600ptas double; 13,000ptas triple; cot 1,500ptas. **Credit** AmEx, DC, MC, V. **Map** p320 D3.

A pleasant hotel with superior facilities in an elegant building in Sant Gervasi, on the edge of Gràcia and well-communicated with the centre. The atmosphere is friendly, and the 56 rooms modern and bright, all with bathrooms; those facing Via Augusta can be a bit noisy. Generous buffet breakfasts.

Hotel services *Air-conditioning. Disabled: room (1) adapted for the disabled. Interpreting services. Laundry. Lift. Multilingual staff. Safe. Ticket agency.*
Room services *Telephone. TV(satellite).*

Pensió 2000

C/Sant Pere Més Alt 6, Sant Pere (93 310 74 66/fax 93 319 42 50). Metro Urquinaona/17, 19, 40, 45, N8 bus. **Rates**: 4,800-6,400ptas single; 6,000-8,000ptas double; 8,500-10,500ptas triple; 10,500-12,500ptas quad. **Credit** MC, V. **Map** p326 B2.

The grand white marble stairway leading up to the family-run **Hostal Girona**. *See p52.*

Opened in the spring of 2000 by the friendly Orlando and Manuela, this small pension is located directly in front of the Palau de la Mùsica. Three rooms have en suite bathrooms, while the other three – those which face the Palau – share one large bathroom, but who would complain? They offer six different breakfast menus, including a macrobiotic menu, all served in the rooms (which have large pine tables) or on the outdoor patio.
Hotel services *Laundry. Safe. TV.*
Room services *Room service.*

Budget (under 7,000ptas)

The Barri Gòtic (particularly in and around the Plaça Reial) and the Raval, on the opposite side of the Rambla are still the best spots for cheap beds. The Eixample also has some more tranquil, good-value accommodation, and, again, it's also worth considering areas a little further from the centre. Some budget hotels do not have someone on the door 24-hours a day.

Hostal Béjar

C/Béjar 36-38, 1°-3a , Sants (93 325 59 53). Metro Espanya, Tarragona, Sants Est/27, 127, 109 bus. **Rates** 3,500ptas single; 6,000-7,000ptas double. **Credit** MC, V. **Map** p323 A4.
In the Hostafrancs district, the Béjar is only a five-minute walk from Sants station and the Plaça d'Espanya. Its 22 rooms are in two buildings, with one reception area; six have bathrooms, and guests have use of a fridge. The owners speak English.
Hotel services *Laundry. Lift.*

Hostal Eden

C/Balmes 55, Eixample (93 454 73 63/fax 93 452 66 21/www.barcelona-on-line.es/hostaleden/ hostaleden@hotmail.com). Metro Passeig de Gràcia/ 7, 16, 17, 63, 67, 68 bus. **Rates** 4,500-5,500ptas single; 6,500-8,000ptas double; 8,000-10,000ptas triple. **Credit** MC, V. **Map** p320 D4.
One of the most interesting places in this price slot, the Eden occupies two floors of an old Eixample building. José and Dani, who run it, speak four languages and have a good idea of what budget travellers want. Recently expanded from 15 to 25 rooms, and with plans for further additions in mid 2001, all rooms are pleasant, but some enjoy unusual added facilities such as whirlpool baths and fridges, and still more extras are planned. Guests also have (coin-operated) Net access, and there's a 24-hour porter.
Hotel services *Currency exchange. Fax. Internet access. Multilingual staff. Telephone. Ticket agency.*
Room services *Fan. Safe. TV.*

Hostal Fontanella

Via Laietana 71, 2n, Eixample (tel/fax 93 317 59 43). Metro Urquinaona/bus all routes to Plaça Urquinaona. **Rates** 3,000-4,000ptas single; 5,000-6,900ptas double; 6,700-9,650ptas triple; 5,800-10,150ptas quad. **Credit** AmEx, DC, MC, V. **Map** p319 B1.
This *hostal* benefits from the personal touches of its owner, Encarna, who supervises everything down to the dried flower arrangements and 'weekend kits' (comb, soap and toothpaste) in each room. The Fontanella is clean, cosy and centrally located, and is particularly popular with young women.
Hotel services *Laundry. Lift. Safe.*

Hostal Goya

C/Pau Claris, 74, Eixample (93 302 25 65/fax 93 412 04 35). Metro Urquinaona/41, 55, 141, N4, N8 bus. **Rates** 3,500pts single; 6,000-6,800pts double. **Credit** V. **Map** p314 D5.

Just off Plaça Urquinaona in an Eixample building, this old *hostal* is a bit ramshackle, but it couldn't be better located for visiting the sites and getting some shopping done. Angeles, the young owner, is welcoming and friendly.
Hotel services *Lift. Safe. TV room.*

Hostal Jardí

Plaça Sant Josep Oriol 1, Barri Gòtic (93 301 59 00/ fax 93 318 36 64). Metro Liceu/14, 38, 59, 91, N9, N12 bus. **Rates** (incl IVA) 4,000/7,500ptas single; 5,500/7,500ptas double. **Credit** AmEx, DC, MC, V. **Map** p327 A3.

Always one of the most popular budget options in Barcelona, the Jardí has a wonderful situation overlooking the leafy Plaça del Pi; central but peaceful. The rooms to go for are those with an outside view; cheaper, interior rooms are more basic, and the patio can be noisy. All rooms have bathrooms, but facilities vary. To get in here, book well in advance.
Hotel services *Drink dispenser. Safety deposit box.*
Room services *Telephone. TV (some).*

Hostal Lausanne

Avda Portal de l'Àngel 24, Barri Gòtic (93 302 11 39). Metro Catalunya/bus all routes to Plaça Catalunya. **Rates** 4,000-5,500 single; 5,500-7,500ptas double; 6,500-9,600ptas triple. **No credit cards.** **Map** p326 B2.

This 17-room family-run *hostal* is on the first floor of a fine old building with high ceilings and ample rooms, some with balconies overlooking the wide, pedestrian Portal de l'Angel street. It's clean and bright, with a big sitting room, and the owners are helpful and friendly.
Hotel services *24hr reception. Lift. Lounge. Multilingual staff. Safe. Telephone. TV. Terrace.*

Hostal Layetana

Plaça Ramon Berenguer el Gran 2, Barri Gòtic (tel/fax 93 319 20 12). Metro Jaume I/17, 19, 40, 45, N8 bus. **Rates** 3,150ptas single; 5,250-6,700ptas double; 7,300-9,350ptas triple. **Credit** MC, V. **Map** p327 B3.

A view right along the Roman wall and a stunning hall give this *hostal* loads of character. Service is friendly, most of its 20 rooms have bathrooms, and the communal areas are well-kept. Noise from Via Laietana is the major drawback.
Hotel services *Drinks machine. Lift. Reception (24hrs). Safe. Terrace. TV.*

Hostal Malda

C/del Pi 5, 1°1ª, Barri Gòtic (93 317 30 02). Metro Liceu/14, 38, 59, 91, N9, N12 bus. **Rates** 1,500ptas single; 2,500-3,000ptas double; 3,500ptas triple. **No credit cards.** **Map** p326 B2.

This small, bright, comfortable hostal in the heart of the Barri Gòtic is a find in every sense: access is through one of the entrances to the Galeries Maldà shopping arcade, but even the hike up the stairs (no lift) is forgotten when you meet the friendly lady who runs it. No en suite facilities, but the communal bathrooms are impeccably clean. The entrance to the Galeries is open until 12.30am, when a porter comes on duty. A great bargain.
Hotel services *Laundry. Lounge. Refrigerator. Telephone. TV (satellite).*

Hostal Noya

La Rambla 133, 1°, Rambla (93 301 48 31). Metro Catalunya/bus all routes to Plaça Catalunya. **Rates** 2,500ptas single; 4,800ptas double. **No credit cards.** **Map** p326 A2.

This modest *hostal* is in an excellent position on the Rambla, and is decent value for its location. All 15 rooms have balconies overlooking the crowds, but bathrooms are communal. No breakfast either, but there is a good café-restaurant below.
Hotel services *Telephone.*

Hostal Opera

C/Sant Pau 20, Raval (93 318 82 01). Metro Liceu/14, 38, 59, 91, N9, N12 bus. **Rates** 3,500-5,000ptas single; 6,000-7,500ptas double; 9,000ptas triple. **No credit cards.** **Map** p327 A3.

As the name hints this *hostal* is right beside the Liceu opera house, just off the Rambla. All 69 rooms are newly decorated, and most have new bathrooms and air-conditioning. However, a promised makeover of the reception area is still pending.
Hotel services *Disabled: rooms (6) adapted for the disabled. Lift. Multilingual staff. Safe.*
Room services *Air-conditioning (some).*

Hostal Palermo

C/Boqueria 21, Barri Gòtic (tel/fax 93 302 40 02). Metro Liceu/14, 38, 59, 91, N9, N12 bus. **Rates** 4,200-6,000ptas single; 6,500-7,500ptas double; 10,800ptas triple. **Credit** DC, MC, V. **Map** p327 A3.

A cheerful place with 34 impeccably clean, recently refurbished rooms. Some have baths, some don't. English-speaking staff.
Hotel services *Lounge. Safe. Telephone. TV.*

Hostal Paris

C/Cardenal Casañas 4, Barri Gòtic (93 301 37 85/ fax 93 412 70 96). Metro Liceu/14, 38, 59, 91, N9, N12 bus. **Rates** 3,000ptas single; 5,800ptas-8,000ptas double. **Credit** DC, MC, V. **Map** p327 A3.

This 45-room *hostal* has a pleasant reception area and large sitting room looking onto the Pla de la Boqueria. The exterior rooms are fine, but the interior ones, while quieter, face a narrow air shaft – not for claustrophobics.
Hotel services *Multilingual staff. Telephone. TV.*
Room services *Safe (some). TV.*

Hostal Parisien

La Rambla 114, Rambla (tel/fax 93 301 62 83). Metro Liceu/14, 38, 59, 91, N9, N12 bus. **Rates** 3,500ptas single; 5,500-7,000ptas double. **No credit cards.** **Map** p326 A2.

Run by a friendly young couple, the Parisien has a great mid-Rambla location opposite the Virreina. The 12 rooms at this student favourite are well-kept; eight have bathrooms. Those above the Rambla are noisy but atmospheric; others are darker but quieter. **Hotel services** *Lounge. Multilingual staff. Safe. Telephone. TV (satellite).*

Hostal Rembrandt

C/Portaferrissa 23, Barri Gòtic (tel/fax 93 318 10 11). Metro Liceu/14, 38, 59, 91, N9, N12 bus. **Rates** (incl IVA) 3,200-4,300ptas single; 5,000-7,000 double; 7,000-10,000ptas triple. **No credit cards.** **Map** p326 B2.
Popular with backpackers, the cheerful 29-room Rembrandt is spotlessly clean with pleasantly decorated rooms, and the foyer opens onto a pleasant communal patio. The owners will accommodate up to five people in a room at reasonable prices. **Hotel services** *Multilingual staff. Safe. Telephone. TV.*

Hostal-Residencia Oliva

Passeig de Gràcia 32, 4°, Eixample (93 488 01 62/ fax 93 487 04 97). Metro Passeig de Gràcia/7, 16, 17, 22, 24, 28, N1, N4, N6 bus. **Rates** 3,200ptas single; 6,000-7,000ptas double. **No credit cards.** **Map** p324 D5.
The relaxed, family-run Oliva occupies the fourth floor of an old Eixample apartment block with two lifts – one a museum piece, much photographed by Japanese guests. Most rooms are light and well-aired, and doubles with bathrooms are especially comfortable. The six rooms facing Passeig de Gràcia have splendid views, but can be noisy in summer. **Hotel services** *Lounge. Lifts. Telephone.* **Room services** *TV (some).*

Hostal de Ribagorza

C/Trafalgar 39/Méndez Núñez 17, Eixample (93 319 19 68/fax 93 319 12 47) Metro Urquinaona/ 19, 39, 40, 41, 42, 55, 141, N4 bus. **Rates** 5,000-6,500ptas double; 7,000 ptas triple. **Credit** AmEx, MC, V. **Map** p326 C2.
A family-run *hostal* located in a central but quiet area near the Palau de la Música and the Arc de Triomf. Rooms vary in size and facilities, some have baths, others not, but all have TV. **Hotel services** *Lift.* **Room services** *Telephone. TV.*

Hostal San Remo

C/Ausiàs Marc 19-C/Bruc 20, 1° 2ª, Eixample (93 302 19 89/fax 93 301 07 74). Metro Urquinaona/ bus all routes to Plaça Urquinaona. **Rates** 4,000-6,000ptas single; 6,000-8,000ptas double; 8,000-10,000ptas triple. **Credit** MC, V. **Map** p326 C1.
This friendly, family-run *hostal* on the first floor of an Eixample building offers pleasant rooms with new bathrooms en suite; outside rooms have sunny balconies. Guests are given front-door keys. The attentive owner and her son speak some English. **Hotel services** *Air-conditioning. Lift. Safe. Telephone. TV.*

Hostal Sofia

Avda de Roma 1-3, Eixample (93 419 50 40/fax 93 430 69 43). Metro Sants Estació/27, 30, 32, 43, 44, 78, 215, N7 bus. **Rates** 4,000-6,000ptas single; 6,000-8,000ptas double; 8,000-9,000ptas triple. **Credit** MC, V. **Map** p323 B4.
The *pensión*, located beside the Sants railway station and with two underground lines to take you just about everywhere, is clean and functional and a good base from which to explore the Plaça Espanya/Montjuïc area, site of the Olympic games and several museums, as well as famous fountains. All 18 rooms have baths. **Hotel services** *Lift. Telephone.* **Room services** *TV (some).*

Hostal La Terrassa

C/Junta de Comerç 11, Raval (93 302 51 74/fax 93 301 21 88). Metro Liceu/14, 38, 59, 91, N9, N12 bus. **Rates** 2,400ptas single; 3,600-4,600ptas double; 5,100-6,000ptas triple. **Credit** DC, MC, V. **Map** p327 A3.
Under the same ownership as the hugely popular Jardí (*see p57*), La Terrassa is one of Barcelona's most likeable cheap *hostals*, and great value. About half the rooms have bathrooms, and the best have balconies overlooking the street or an attractive interior patio, where breakfast is served in summer. **Hotel services** *Lounge. Multilingual staff. Safe. Telephone. Terrace. TV.*

Hostal Victòria

C/Comtal 9, 1° 1ª, Barri Gòtic (93 318 07 60/93 317 45 97). Metro Catalunya, Urquinaona/bus all routes to Plaça Catalunya. **Rates** 3,000-3,500ptas single; 5,000-5,500ptas double. **No credit cards.** **Map** p326 B2.
This spacious 30-room *hostal* in the heart of the old city offers communal cooking and washing facilities. The owner is a bit authoritarian and rooms are basic, but they're clean and light, and most have balconies. Another feature is that discounts are available in winter (Nov-Mar) for stays of over a month. **Hotel services** *Dining room. Drink Machine. Kitchen. Laundry. Lift. Lounge. Telephone. Terrace. TV.*

The **Hotel Call**. *See p53.*

Hosteria Grau

C/Ramelleres 27, Raval (93 301 81 35/fax 93 317 68 25/www.intercom.es/grau/hgrau@lix.intercom.es). Metro Catalunya/bus all routes to Plaça Catalunya. **Rates** 4,500ptas single; 6,500-8,500ptas double; 9,500-11,500ptas triple. **Credit** AmEx, DC, MC, V. **Map** p326 A1.

This pleasant *hostal* has a charming café downstairs (open until 9pm), and serves breakfast until noon in the tiny first-floor sitting room. Rooms are clean and pleasant, but inside singles are dark. City information is provided in reception.

Hotel services *24-hour reception. Bar. Fax. Multilingual staff. Telephone. TV lounge.*

Hotel Toledano

La Rambla 138, Rambla (93 301 08 72/fax 93 412 31 42). Metro Catalunya/bus all routes to Plaça Catalunya. **Rates** 2,500-3,000ptas single; 4,500-6,000ptas double. **Credit** AmEx, DC, MC, V. **Map** p326 A2.

Very near Plaça Catalunya, the Toledano may be handily placed, but it can be rather noisy – interior rooms, with views of the cathedral, are the quietest. Its 28 rooms are basic but all have bathrooms, and there is a chintzy lounge area overlooking the Rambla.

Hotel services *Lift. Multilingual staff. Safe.*
Room services *Telephone. TV (satellite).*

Pensión Ambos Mundos

Plaça Reial 10, Barri Gòtic (93 318 79 70/fax 93 412 23 63). Metro Drassanes/14, 38, 59, 91, N9, N12 bus. **Rates** 4,000ptas single; 6,000ptas double; 2,000ptas extra bed. **Credit** AmEx, DC, MC, V. **Map** p327 A3.

A very popular Plaça Reial *hostal*, the Ambos Mundos is located above a bar of the same name. The 12 simple tiled rooms all have baths; the outside rooms have balconies overlooking the street action. Guests can play pool or watch TV in the cavernous reception.

Hotel services *Bar-restaurant. Safe.*
Room services *Telephone.*

Pensión Cortés

Gran Vía de les Corts Catalanes 540, Eixample (93 454 84 83). Metro Urgell/9, 20, 50, 56, N1, N2, N13, N14, N15 bus. **Rates** 2,500ptas. single; 5,600-6,400ptas. **Credit** V. **Map** p324 C5.

Housed in what was once the mansion of the Condes de Rocamora, this typically ornate Eixample construction has been declared of historical/artistic interest by city authorities. The entrance is magnificent but the part occupied by this simple pension has seen better days. The Metro is on the doorstep and the airport bus stop is nearby.

Hotel services *Lift.*

Pensión-Hostal Mari-Luz

Plaça Reial 10, Barri Gòtic (93 318 79 70/fax 93 412 23 63). Metro Drassanes/14, 38, 59, 91, N9, N12 bus. **Rates** 4,000ptas single; 6,000ptas double; 2,000ptas extra bed. **Credit** AmEx, DC, MC, V. **Map** p327 A3.

The friendly **Pensión-Hostal Mari-Luz**.

Mari-Luz takes great care of her lodgers in this spotlessly clean *hostal*, a few streets' walk from the main Plaça Reial drag. The 15 rooms, five of which have showers, are plain but quiet, and the old building is atmospheric and affordable. The family also own the similarly cheap Fernando nearby.

Hotel services *Bar-restaurant. Safe.*
Room services *Telephone.*
Branch: Pensión Fernando C/Ferran 31 (93 301 79 93).

Pensión Rondas

C/Girona 4, Eixample (tel/fax 93 232 51 02). Metro Urquinaona/19, 39, 40, 41, 42, 55, 141, N4, N11 bus. **Rates** 2,500-3,000ptas single; 4,500-6,000ptas double. **No credit cards. Map** p326 C1.

Nine basic, clean rooms, on the third floor of an old Eixample building in a central but unusually quiet location. The young sister and brother who run it are exceptionally friendly and helpful, and the atmosphere is pleasantly relaxed. The lift looks like a museum piece and is actually under an official preservation order, but it's recently been overhauled.

Hotel services *Lift.*

Pensión Sants

C/Antoni de Campmany 82, Sants (93 331 37 00/ fax 93 421 68 64). Metro Plaça de Sants/ 30, 215, N7 bus. **Rates:** 2,900-3,500ptas single; 4,600-5,500ptas double. **Credit** MC, V. **Map** p323 A4.

This large, recently renovated *pensión* (76 rooms) occupies a seven-floor building just a stone's throw from the Sants station and on the corner of the busy shopping street of C/de Sants. The rooms are bright – even those to the rear – and impeccably clean. Almost all have en suite baths, some have balconies. To avoid street noise and get a spectacular view, ask for one on the upper floors (all singles are on 7th floor), preferably with a balcony.

Hotel services *Drink dispenser. Lift. Safe. TV.*
Room services *Telephone.*

Pensión Vitoria

C/de la Palla 8, pral, Barri Gòtic (tel/fax 93 302 08 34). Metro Liceu/14, 38, 59, 91, N9, N12 bus. **Rates** 1,500-2,000ptas single; 3,500-5,000ptas double; 4,000ptas triple. **Credit** MC, V. **Map** p326 B2.

Close to Plaça del Pi, the Vitoria has 11 clean, light, airy rooms, with balconies. Nine rooms share one bathroom, while two doubles have en suite showers and toilets. Despite the basic facilities, the *pensión* has a loyal bunch of repeat guests, so book early. **Hotel services** *Multilingual staff. Telephone. TV.*

Apartment hotels

Apartment hotels are made up of self-contained small flats, with kitchen facilities, plus maid service. They are good for slightly longer stays, and usually offer reduced monthly or longer-term rates.

Apartaments Calàbria

C/Calàbria 129, Eixample (93 426 42 28/fax 93 426 76 40). Metro Rocafort/9, 41, 50, 56, N1, N2, N13, N14, N15 bus. **Rates** *Per night* 14,000ptas one person; 16,000ptas two people; 4,000ptas each additional person. *Per month* 195,000ptas. *Two months or more* 175,000ptas per month. **Credit** AmEx, MC, TC, V. **Map** p323 B5.

This Eixample apartment block houses 72 functional short-term apartments with good kitchen and bathroom facilities and separate lounge areas. Office services are available. Rates are competitive, so apartments need to be booked well in advance. **Hotel services** *Air-conditioning. Disabled: wheelchair access. Fax. Laundry. Lifts. Multilingual staff.* **Room services** *Room service (not 24-hr). Safe. Telephone. TV (satellite).*

Aparthotel Bertran

C/Bertran 150, Zona Alta (93 212 75 50/fax 93 418 71 03). Metro Vallcarca, FGC Tibidabo/16, 17, 74 bus. **Rates** *Per night* 10,400ptas single; 13,000ptas double. **Credit** AmEx, DC, MC, V.

In the residential Putxet area, near Tibidabo and with good vehicle access to the *rondes*, these 30 apartments are spacious and bright, with good facilities. Most have balconies, some have larger terraces, and there are extras than at most aparthotels: a gym, cycle rental, rooftop terrace and a pool. **Hotel services** *Air-conditioning. Car park. Conference facilities. Gym. Interpreters. Laundry. Lifts. Multilingual staff. Safe. Swimming pool (outdoor). Ticket agency.* **Room services** *Radio. Telephone. TV (satellite). Video (on request).*

Aparthotel El Saüc

C/de l'Olivera 35 , Poble Sec (93 325 83 73/fax 93 325 27 75). Metro Poble Sec/38, 55, 57, 157, N0 bus. **Rates** from 9,075pts double to 23,715ptas 7-person apartment. **Credit** AmEx, DC, MC, V.

Housed in two nearby buildings in Poble Sec close to Plaça Espanya, El Saüc offers the conveniences of apartment living at more reasonable than usual prices. The larger apartments are located in the quiet C/Olivera, while those for two persons are three blocks away on the corner with C/Lleida, which can be noisy. **Hotel services** *Air-conditioning. Daily cleaning & towel change. Lift. Telephone. TV.*

Aparthotel Senator

Via Augusta 167, Zona Alta (93 201 14 05/fax 93 202 00 97/senator@city-hotels.es). FGC Muntaner/ 58, 64, N8 bus. **Rates** *Per night* 15,500ptas one person; 17,500ptas two people; 19,500ptas three people; 21,500ptas four people. *Per month* 245,000ptas one person; 275,000ptas two people; 280,000ptas three people. **Credit** AmEx, DC, MC, V. **Map** p320 C2.

Straightforward but comfortable apartments, with a few individual touches such as bamboo furniture and plants in each flat, in the Sant Gervasi district. There is no restaurant or bar, but the apartment kitchens are fine for preparing light meals. **Hotel services** *Air-conditioning. Fax. Laundry. Lift. Multilingual staff. Safe.* **Room services** *Minibar. Telephone. TV.*

Atenea Aparthotel

C/Joan Güell 207-11, Zona Alta (93 490 66 40/fax 93 490 64 20/atenea@city-hotels.es). Metro Les Corts/bus all routes to Plaça Maria Cristina. **Rates** *Per night* 25,000ptas single studio or apt; 28,000ptas double studio or apartment; 4,000ptas third person supplement; group discounts. *Per month* 480,000ptas. **Credit** AmEx, DC, MC, V. **Map** p319 A3.

A big (105 apartments) 1990s aparthotel offering four-star facilities including bar, restaurant and conference rooms, in the heart of the business district. Apartments are highly efficiently organised with first-rate technology, without having any great character. If you're really busy, a food shopping service is available on request. **Hotel services** *Air-conditioning. Bar. Car park. Conference facilities. Disabled: rooms (4) adapted for the disabled, wheelchair access. Email. Fax. Lift. Multilingual staff. Photocopiers. Restaurant.* **Room services** *Hairdryer. Room service (7am-11pm). Safe. Telephone. TV (satellite). Video (on request).*

Apartment/room rentals

Barcelona Allotjament

C/Pelai 12, pral B, Eixample (tel/fax 93 268 43 57/ bcnacom@ibernet.com/www.barcelona-allotjament. com). Metro Universitat, Catalunya/bus all routes to Plaça Universitat, Plaça Catalunya. **Open** 10am-2pm, 5-7pm Mon-Thur; 10am-2pm Fri; closed Aug. **No credit cards. Map** p326 A1.

Rooms with local families (B&B, half-board or full-board), in shared student flats, in aparthotels and hotels or whole apartments can be booked through this agency, aimed at student, business and individual travellers. Short-term rates from 2,800ptas per day, B&B; long-term (course-length) stays cost around 50,000ptas per month, B&B, plus a 15,000ptas agency fee. Courses (in languages, dance, cookery) are also offered.

B&B Norma Agency

C/Ali Bei 11, 3° 2ª, Eixample (tel/fax 93 232 37 66).
Metro Arc de Triomf/19, 39, 40, 41, 42, 55, 141
bus. **Open** 24-hr answerphone. **Map** p326 C1.
Rooms booked on a B&B basis in private homes, or
whole apartments, in Barcelona and along the coast,
for short or longer-term stays. B&B rates begin at
around 5,000ptas per night for a single room, or
7,500-10,000ptas for doubles.

Habit Servei

C/Muntaner 200, 2n 3a, Eixample (93 209 50 45/
fax 93 414 54 25/www.bbs.seker.es/~habit_servei).
FGC Provença/bus 58, 64, 66, 67, 68.
Open 9am-8pm Mon-Fri; closed Sat, Sun.
Credit DC, MC, V. **Map** p320 C3.
This agency can find rooms in flats for anyone staying in Barcelona for at least two weeks. Rates are
about 50,000ptas a month for a flat-share, or
40,000ptas for a room in a private house. Whole
flats are also available. The agency fee (17,400ptas)
is payable only when a suitable place is found, and
a 40,000ptas deposit is returned at the end of the
stay. English is spoken, and it's popular with
Erasmus students.

Youth hostels

Rates can vary by season. For student and
youth services and websites that can take
reservations for hostels, *see p297.*

Alberg Mare de Déu de Montserrat

Passeig de la Mare de Déu del Coll 41-51, Horta (93
210 51 51/fax 93 210 07 98/www.tujuca.com).
Metro Vallcarca/25, 28, 87, N4 bus. **Open** *Hostel*
8am-midnight (ring for entry after hours). *Reception*
8am-4pm, 4.30-11pm daily. **Rates** 2,000ptas under-
25s; 2,700ptas over-25s. *Sheet hire* 350ptas.
Towel purchase 650pts. **Credit** MC,V.
This 183-bed hostel in a pleasant old house with garden is some way from the centre, but not far from a
Metro station. Rooms sleep two to eight people, and
there are lots of facilities. IYHF cards are required.
Hotel services *Auditorium. Car park. Dining*
room. Disabled: room (1) adapted for the disabled,
toilets, wheelchair access. Fax & copy service. Internet
access. Laundry. Multilingual staff. Refreshments
available. Safe. TV (satellite)/video room.

Alberg Pere Tarres

C/Numància 149-151, Zona Alta (93 410 23 09/
fax 93 419 62 68/alberg@peretarres.org/
www.peretarres.org). Metro Les Corts/bus all routes
to C/Numància. **Rates** (incl breakfast) 1,600ptas.
Sheet hire 350ptas. **Credit** MC, V. **Map** p319 B3.
This hostel has 94 places, five shared bathrooms and
an attractive roof terrace. Regulations are strict: no
cigarettes or alcohol in dorms; no eating or drinking
outside the dining room. IYHF cards are required,
and you need to book in summer.
Hotel services *Car park. Kitchen. Laundry. Meals*
cooked for groups. Multilingual staff. Patio.
Refreshments. TV lounge.

Albergue Kabul

Plaça Reial 17, Barri Gòtic (93 318 51 90/fax 93
301 40 34/kabul@kabul-hostel.com/www.kabul-
hostel.com). **Open** 24hrs daily. **Rates** (per person) 1,200-
2,500ptas. **No credit cards. Map** p327 A3.
Rooms in this welcoming private hostel vary from
cramped dormitories with mattresses on the floor to
airy doubles with views of Plaça Reial. No private
bathrooms, but communal facilities are clean.
Hotel services *Billiard table. Kitchen. Laundry.*
Lift. Lounge. Multilingual staff. Refreshments. Safe.
Telephone. TV (satellite). Video.

Hostal Hedy Holiday

C/Buenaventura Muñoz, 4, Eixample (93 300 57 85/
fax 93 300 94 44). Metro Arc de Triomf/ 39, 41, 51
bus. **Rates**: 2,000ptas in dorms of up to 6 or 8 beds.
No credit cards.
Located beside the Ciutadela Park, this spacious,
luminous place is new. All rooms have central heating, with individual locker/wardrobes. There is an
Internet room as well as a large bar/cafeteria.
Hotel services *Bar. Cafeteria (with snacks, meals*
prepared on request). Multilingual staff.

Campsites

For more information on the 13 campsites not
far from the city, get the Catalunya Campings
brochure from the Palau Robert (*see p295*).

Cala Gogó

Carretera de la Platja, El Prat de Llobregat,
Outer Limits (93 379 46 00/fax 93 379 47 11/
www.campingcalagogoprat.com). Bus 65 from Plaça
d'Espanya/by car C246 to Castelldefels, then Airport
exit to Prat beach. **Open** *Reception* Easter, 1June-30
Sept 9am-10pm daily. **Rates** (per person per night)
Easter, 1 June-6 July, mid-Aug-30 Sept 650ptas;
under-10s 490ptas; plus plot 1,675-2,150ptas. *7 July-19*
Aug 715ptas; under-10s 540ptas; plus plot 1,840-
2,365ptas. Lower rates for single tents. **Credit** MC, V.
The nearest campsite to Barcelona, 7km (4 miles) to
the south near the beach and the airport, Cala Gogó
is large and well-equipped, with a supermarket,
restaurant, bar and swimming pool on-site.

Masnou

Carretera N2, km 633, 08320 El Masnou, Outer
Limits (tel/fax 93 555 15 03). Bus CASAS from
Passeig Sant Joan/by car N11 to Masnou (11km/
7 miles)/by train RENFE to Masnou from Plaça
Catalunya. **Open** *Reception* 9am-1pm, 2.30-7pm daily
winter; 8am-1pm, 2.30pm-10pm daily summer.
Campsite 7am-11.30pm daily. **Rates** (per person)
725ptas; under-10s 585ptas; plus extra charges for cars,
motorbikes, caravans, tents, & light. **No credit cards.**
Near the coast north of Barcelona, this small site has
a bar, restaurant and supermarket (open June-Sept),
kids' playground and pools. There's a sandy beach
nearby, with diving and sailing facilities. Bungalows
(2,500ptas per person per day) and rooms (4,100ptas,
double) can also be rented.

Sightseeing

Feature boxes

Introduction

Barcelona is a sight to be seen.

Once upon a time, Barcelona was a tourist backwater, visited mostly by businessmen in town for annual trade fairs, or day trippers in on a rainy day from the nearby beaches. Two decades of intense urban renewal – most dramatically with the preparations for the 1992 Olympics – and a massive self-promotion blitz have changed all that, and visitors stream in from around the planet to pay homage.

In truth, it's not hard to see why Barcelona has become such a worldwide draw, with its incomparable mix of tradition, modernity and style, unique architecture and vivid streetlife. Along with its seaside location and agreeable climate, the city has a compactness that makes it easy to explore, with many sights within enjoyable walking distance of each other. When places are further afield, an excellent transport system makes them easy to reach (*see p289*).

Pick up any map of Barcelona and you will see a tightly-packed mass of narrow streets bordered by Avda Paral.lel, the Ciutadella park, Plaça Catalunya and the sea. This is the area that fell within the medieval walls and, until 150 years ago, made up the entire city. At its heart is the **Barri Gòtic** (Gothic Quarter), a body of interconnecting streets and buildings from Barcelona's Golden Age. Its twisting streets grew inside the original Roman wall; then, as Barcelona grew wealthy in the Middle Ages, new communities developed around the Roman perimeter. These areas, **La Mercè**, **Sant Pere** and **La Ribera**, were brought within the city with the building of the second wall in the 13th century. The area south of this wall, on the other side of the riverbed later to become the Rambla, was the **Raval**, enclosed within a third city wall built in the 14th century.

Tourist tickets & discounts

Barcelona offers a variety of tour facilities and discount schemes for admission to many attractions. Where discounts apply this is indicated in the listings below and throughout the guide with the abbreviations **BC**, **BT**, **RM** and **Articket** (for Articket, a joint entry ticket for seven major art centres, *see pp107-8*).

For tourist offices, *see pp304-5*, and for regular city transport, *see pp289-90*.

Barcelona Card
Rates 2,500ptas 24 hours; 3,000ptas 48 hours; 3,500ptas 72 hours. **Concessions** 2,000ptas 24 hours; 2,500ptas 48 hours; 3,000ptas 72 hours.

Discount scheme run by the city tourist authority: for the time stipulated the card gives you unlimited transport on Metro and buses, and discounts on the airport bus, as well as entry to a wide variety of attractions and at some shops and restaurants (a current list comes with the card). It is sold at city tourist offices (*see p304*) or via Tel-entrada (*see p196*). When Barcelona Card discounts are available at museums or other attractions this is indicated in this guide with the letters BC. Another scheme,

the Barcelona Pass, must be ordered via travel agents. Enquire when booking.

Bus Turístic (Tourist Bus)
Dates Mar-Jan; not Feb. **Frequency** Mar-June, Oct-Jan every 30min, July-Sept every 10min. **Tickets** from tourist office or on board the bus. **Tickets** *One day* 2,000 ptas; 1,200ptas 4-12s. *Two days* 2,500ptas; free under-4s. **No credit cards.**

A special sightseeing bus service with two circular routes, both running through Plaça Catalunya: the northern (red) route passes La Pedrera, Sagrada Família, Parc Güell, Tibidabo and Pedralbes; the southern (blue) route takes in Montjuïc, Port Vell, Vila Olímpica and the Barri Gòtic. With one ticket you can get on and off buses on either route as many times as you like the same day. Buses have multilingual guides, and most are adapted for wheelchairs. Tickets are bought at city tourist offices (*see p289*), transport offices or on the buses themselves. Ticket-holders have discount vouchers for another big range of attractions (which need not be used the same day). Where these discounts apply this is shown in this guide with the letters BT.

All of Barcelona's great medieval buildings are within this old walled city, except for a very few – most notably the superb Gothic monastery of **Pedralbes** (*see p102*) – which when built were in open countryside.

Barcelona grew little between 1450 and 1800. The old walls remained standing, and the city's first modern industries developed inside them. Factories also appeared in small towns on the surrounding plain such as **Gràcia**, **Sants**, **Sant Martí** and **Sant Andreu**. The walls finally came down in the 1850s, and Barcelona extended across the plain following Ildefons Cerdà's plan for the **Eixample** (*see p15*). With its long, straight streets, this became the city's second great characteristic district, and the location for many of the greatest works of *Modernista* creativity between 1880 and 1914 – although there are others to be found in many parts of the city. Beyond that lie the green mountains of **Montjuïc** and, at the centre of the great ridge of the Serra de Collserola, **Tibidabo**, both towering above Barcelona and providing wonderful views.

Each of Barcelona's traditional districts (*barris*) has its own resilient, often idiosyncratic character. However, since the 1970s the city has undergone an unprecedented physical transformation, in a burst of urban renovation unequalled in Europe. Areas such as Montjuïc – with the main stadium – the **Port Olímpic** and the **beach** were rebuilt or created from next to nothing for the 1992 Olympics; since then the pace of renovation has not let up, with the spectacular reinvention of the old harbour or **Port Vell**, the dramatic urban surgery performed in the Raval, and attention now moving on to the Diagonal-Mar project, in the very north of the city. In the process the identities of individual *barris* have been altered, pushed and pulled in many directions, and sometimes changed beyond recognition.

Barcelona has entered squarely into the post-industrial age, as a city with big ambitions. Most of its factories are now in the **Zona Franca**, the industrial zone between Montjuïc and the airport. Within the city, old factories that had still not moved out have been encouraged to, while the shells of those that did have become art spaces, sports centres, studios, clubs or restaurants. The ultimate aim, according to former Mayor Maragall, has been 'for Barcelona to become a city of services'. Time will tell if it does.

Rodamolls

Dates & times Apr-Oct 11am-9.30pm Sat, Sun. *Mid June-mid Sept* 11am-9.30pm daily. **Tickets** 300ptas. **Concessions** 180ptas; free under-3s. **Discounts** BT. **No credit cards**.

The 'quay-wanderer' is another special bus service that follows a route around the port area, from Colom to Port Olímpic and back.

Barcelona by Bicycle

C/Esparteria 3, La Ribera (93 268 21 05). Metro Barceloneta/14, 17, 39, 40, 45, 51 bus. **Tours** 10am Sat, Sun; 8.30pm Tue, Sat. Group tours also available daily. **Prices** Day tours 2,800ptas. Evening tours 6,500ptas. **No credit cards. Map** p327 C3-4.

Un Cotxe Menys cycle shop (*see p292*) offers tours of the city, bike hire included, day tours (snack included) last 22 hours, evening trips (meal included) 32 hours. Booking essential.

Museu d'Història tours

Information: Museu d'Història de la Ciutat C/Veguer 2, Barri Gòtic (93 315 11 11/ www.bcn.es/icub). Metro Jaume I/17, 19, 40, 45 bus. **Tours** Nit al Museu (June-Sept) 9pm Tue, Wed. Ruta del Gòtic (phone to confirm) 10am Sat. **Tickets** Nit al Museu 1,000ptas; Ruta del Gòtic 1,000ptas; various concessions. **Advance tickets** Servi-Caixa. **No credit cards. Map** p327 B3.

One of the most enterprising of Barcelona museums is the focus for several interesting tours, especially Una Nit al Museu, a great night tour around the buildings of Plaça del Rei. Always check timings and programmes.

Ruta del Modernisme

Information: Centre del Modernisme, Casa Amatller, Passeig de Gràcia 41, Eixample (93 488 01 39/www.bcn.es). Metro Passeig de Gràcia/7, 16, 17 22, 24, 28 bus. **Open** 10am-7pm Mon-Sat; 10am-2pm Sun. **Tickets** 600ptas; 400ptas concessions; free under-10s. **Discount** 50% all buildings. **No credit cards. Map** p324 D5.

Multi-access ticket giving discounts on entry to *Modernista* buildings (and at some restaurants); a guidebook is available, and guided tours are often included. Tickets valid 30 days and where discounts apply this is shown in this guide with the letters RM.

Walking tours

Information: tourist offices, Plaça Catalunya 17, C/Ciutat 2 (906 301 282/ www.barcelonaturisme.com). **Tours** 10am (English), noon (Catalan/Spanish), Sat, Sun. **Tickets** 1,000ptas; 500ptas 4-12s. **Discounts** BC, BT. **No credit cards. Map** p326 B1.

Professional English-speaking guides take visitors around the Barri Gòtic on foot in an informative tour of about two hours. Numbers are limited, so booking is necessary.

Sightseeing

Hubs of the City

Key spots to help you locate yourself on the map.

Like every city, Barcelona has its essential reference points. First and foremost is **La Rambla**, which divides the old city in two and ends at the harbour. Should you arrive by boat, this remarkable, tree-lined walkway will most likely be your first contact with the city. La Rambla begins at **Plaça Catalunya**, the city's centre. The airport bus begins and ends here and RENFE's train from the plane also makes a stop. Out along Gran Via de les Corts Catalanes in the direction of the airport is **Plaça Espanya**, not so much a square as an ornate traffic roundabout. The airport bus also makes a stop here and the city's main train station, Sants Estació, is a five-minute walk away. Practically at the other end of Gran Via, heading north up the coast, is **Plaça de les Glòries**, a hub of increasing importance as development plans for the area take off.

La Rambla

One of the first things any visitor to Barcelona does – it's all but inevitable – is to stroll along La Rambla, the magnificent mile-long walkway that cuts through the middle of the old city and leads down to the port. This is perhaps Barcelona's most original contribution to urban design, although there has never been anything planned about it. Neatly reversing the modern urban relationship between pedestrian and vehicle, it has often been described as the world's greatest street, and is certainly the definitive stroller's boulevard.

A *rambla* is an urban feature virtually unique to Catalonia, and there is one in most towns in this part of the country. Originally, the Rambla of Barcelona, like most of its smaller equivalents, was a seasonal riverbed, running along the western edge of the 13th-century city, the name deriving from an Arabic word for riverbed, *ramla*. From the Middle Ages to the baroque era a great many churches and convents were built on the other side of this riverbed, some of which have given their names to sections of it: as one descends from Plaça Catalunya, it is successively called Rambla de Canaletes, Rambla dels Estudis (or dels Ocells), Rambla de Sant Josep (or de les Flors), Rambla dels Caputxins and Rambla de Santa Mònica. Hence, the plural is often used – Rambles in Catalan, or Ramblas in Spanish and English.

The Rambla also served as the meeting ground for city and country dwellers, for on the other side of these church buildings lay the still scarcely built-up Raval, 'the city outside the walls', and rural Catalonia. At the fountain on the corner with C/Portaferrissa, once a city gateway, there is an artist's impression in tiles of this space beside the wall, which became a natural market-place. From these beginnings sprang **La Boqueria**, the city's largest market, still on the Rambla today.

The Rambla took on its recognisable present form roughly between 1770 and 1860. The second city wall came down in 1775, and the Rambla was gradually paved and turned into a boulevard. Seats were available to strollers for rent in the late 18th century. The avenue acquired its definitive shape after the closure of the monasteries in the 1830s, which made swathes of land available for new building. No longer on the city's edge, the Rambla became a wide path through its heart.

It used to be said it was an obligation for every true Barcelona citizen to walk down the Rambla and back at least once a day. Nowadays, many locals are blasé about the place, and it could well do with fewer multinational fast-food outlets. The growth in tourist numbers has been met by a positive overdose of human statues – Julius Caesars, Chinese warriors – working at turning the Rambla into a cliché (another growth area has been in pickpockets, so that you need to be at least a little streetwise, and not wander along with open bags dangling at your back). Nevertheless, the avenue remains one of Barcelona's essential attractions. There are many ways of *ramblejant*, a specific verb for going along the Rambla, from a saunter to a purposeful stride, but the best way to get a feel for the place is to take a seat at one of the newly installed public benches at the top of the avenue or, more expensively, in a café, and watch the parade go by. An eternal feature of the Rambla is eye contact: people look you in the eye, see what's what, and glance away. It may be personal, or it may not.

As well as having five names, the Rambla is divided into territories. The first part – at the top, by Plaça Catalunya – has belonged by unwritten agreement to groups of men perpetually engaged in a *tertulia*, a classic Iberian half-conversation, half-argument about

Miró's mosaic on La Rambla.

anything from politics to football. The **Font de Canaletes** drinking fountain is beside them; if you drink from it, the legend goes, you'll return to Barcelona. Here too is where Barça fans converge to celebrate their triumphs.

Below this, heading downhill, there are kiosks divided between those selling fauna and those selling flora. Keep walking, past the Poliorama theatre, and on the left is C/Portaferrissa, now a fashionable shopping street, which leads to the cathedral and the Barri Gòtic; to the right, C/Bonsuccès or C/Carme will take you towards the **MACBA** and other attractions of the Raval.

Next comes perhaps the best-loved section of the boulevard, known as Rambla de les Flors for its line of magnificent flower-stalls, open into the night. To the right is **La Virreina** exhibition and information centre, and the superb Boqueria market. A little further is the **Pla de l'Os** (or **Pla de la Boqueria**), centre-point of the Rambla, with a pavement mosaic created in 1976 by Joan Miró. On the left, where more streets run off into the Barri Gòtic, is the extraordinary **Bruno Quadros** building (1883), with umbrellas on the wall and a Chinese dragon protruding over the street. Almost opposite is the **Liceu** opera, reopened in 1999 after its 1994 fire. Behind it lies the Barrio Chino, traditional home of Barcelona low-life, but now much changed (*see pp77-8*).

The Rambla de Caputxins is lined with mostly expensive cafés. The **Café de l'Opera**, opposite the Liceu, is the best (*see p155*). Further down on the left are C/Ferran, the most direct route to **Plaça Sant Jaume**, and the **Plaça Reial**, with its cafés, restaurants, budget hotels and drunks. A detour to the right on C/Nou de la Rambla will take you to Gaudí's **Palau Güell**, before the promenade widens into the Rambla de Santa Mònica. Here you hit

the stretch that for years was a thriving prostitution belt. You may still see a few lycra-and-furred transvestites, but official clean-up efforts have greatly reduced the visibility (if not the existence) of street soliciting. A series of renovations, including a 1980s arts centre (the **Centre d'Art Santa Mònica**), have diluted the sleaziness of this part of the Rambla, although this is still one of the areas where you need to be most wary of pickpockets and bag-snatchers. Further towards the port and the Colom column are the **Museu de Cera** wax museum and, at weekends, stalls selling bric-a-brac and craftwork, alongside fortune-tellers and tarot-readers catering to an incorrigible local interest in all things astrological.

Other 'sights' of the Rambla are the 24-hour newsstands, offering the Spanish and world press and huge amounts of porn. As well as the human statues there will be buskers, clowns, puppeteers, dancers and musicians. There's street theatre of another kind in the shape of the three-card sharpers or hustlers with three walnut shells and a pea under one of them, challenging you to a bet. There's the portrait painter and the caricature painter and the poet selling his wares. In short, all human life is there – along what García Lorca called 'the very spirit of a city'.

Three squares

Plaça Catalunya & Passeig de Gràcia

Map p326 B1. The Plaça Catalunya is the city's centre – despite many plans to replace it – and the point at which the old, once-walled city meets Cerdà's 19th-century **Eixample**, the 525 square blocks above it. Most of the Plaça's statues and fountains date from the 1920s, but since the 1980s the square has been repeatedly dug up and relaid to accommodate new traffic patterns. Of late it has also begun to be surrounded by rather monolithic beige-block buildings such as the early '90s façade of the **El Corte Inglés** department store and, opposite, a big new mall, **El Triangle**, opened in 1999. On the Rambla side there is also a giant **Marks & Spencer's** store, installed in a former bank. The Plaça Catalunya is an obvious city focal point, in that it's a transport hub: many bus routes stop here, including the airport bus; two Metro lines meet; the FGC lines to Tibidabo, Sarrià and the suburbs begin; and it has a mainline (RENFE) railway station serving the airport, the coast to the north and the Montseny and Pyrenees mountains. **Bus Turístic** routes start here (*see p64*), and the *plaça* contains (underground) the very useful main city **tourist office** (*see p304*), on the Corte Inglés side and identified by large red signs with a white i on them. Around the *plaça* are plenty of pavement cafés, with their attendant buskers. The most strategically-sited is the Cafè Zurich, at the top of the Rambla in one corner of the Triangle building. Built within the new mall and a magnet for tourists and locals, it's really a simulation of the historic café that until 1997 stood on this site.

Stretching away from the square down towards the sea are Barcelona's most famous avenue, **La Rambla**, and the **Portal de l'Angel**, a popular shopping street and another gateway to the **Barri Gòtic**. On the inland side is the **Passeig de Gràcia**, main thoroughfare of the Eixample. Along it are two of Gaudí's greatest works, **La Pedrera** and the **Casa Batlló**, and on either side the long, straight streets are full of *Modernista* gems. Parallel to Passeig de Gràcia is **Rambla Catalunya**, the Rambla of the Eixample, with more cafés. Back on the Passeig itself, halfway up, is Passeig de Gràcia RENFE station, stopping-point for long-distance trains and services to Castelldefels and Sitges. At the top, Passeig de Gràcia crosses the great avenue of the **Diagonal** to disappear into

the attractive old town of **Gràcia**. From here the Diagonal, longest single street in Europe, runs left up to **Plaça Francesc Macià**, the modern business centre of Barcelona and a fashionable shopping area, and to the right down to Plaça de les Glòries and the sea.

Plaça d'Espanya

Map p323 A-B5. The Plaça d'Espanya is the main entrance route to the park of **Montjuïc** and the **Palau Nacional**, home of the **Museu Nacional d'Art de Catalunya (MNAC)** (*see pp118-9*). Like the Palau the *plaça* itself was created for Barcelona's last great international jamboree before the Games of 1992, the Exhibition of 1929. Today most of the original Exhibition area is occupied by the **Fira de Barcelona**, the city's Trade Fair. Montjuïc also provided the most important of the Olympic sites for 1992, the **'Olympic Ring'**, with the **Estadi Olímpic** and **Palau Sant Jordi** indoor sports hall, and is the location of several more museums and cultural venues. From Plaça d'Espanya a 61 bus will take you up the hill to the Olympic Ring, the **Fundació Miró**, or, nearer the bottom, the **Poble Espanyol** and the **Casaramona**, a *Modernista* factory from 1911 under conversion into a cultural centre. Giant escalators have also been installed alongside the steps up to the Palau Nacional, giving easy access to the top of the hill, and another way up is to take the **Funicular** from another side of Montjuïc, by Paral.lel Metro. Not to be missed is a summer evening visit, when the **Font Màgica**, the giant illuminated fountain, dances elegantly to sometimes cheesy music (*see p90*).

The Plaça d'Espanya also has a train station, for the FGC line to western Catalonia and Montserrat, and the airport bus stops here. Along the foot of Montjuïc, Avda Paral.lel leads back to the port area, while on the opposite side of the *plaça*, C/Tarragona – with, on one side, the **Parc de l'Escorxador**, containing an obelisk by Miró (*see p98*) – runs up to Barcelona's main rail station in Sants, and C/Creu Coberta leads straight into the *barri* of Sants.

Plaça de les Glòries

Map p325 F5. In Ildefons Cerdà's original 1859 plan for the Eixample it was intended that this square should eventually become the centre of Barcelona. For most of the time since then it's been merely an unlovely traffic junction; only in the last few years, almost semi-accidentally, have some of Cerdà's ideas for it finally begun to take shape. Next to it there are now several recently built major cultural projects, the **Teatre Nacional**, the **Auditori** concert hall and a historical archive, the Arxiu de la Corona d'Aragó; there is also the vast **Barcelona Glòries** shopping mall. The extension of the Diagonal to the sea and development of the Diagonal-Mar area will increase this area's importance in the future. More traditionally, Glòries is the location of **Els Encants** flea market, and is already of interest to drivers, as the site of the Metro-Park park-and-ride (*see p292*).

Stilt life on **La Rambla**.

The Old City

With medieval squares, lively pedestrian streets and a changing population, the old city is rich with history and life.

Patio of the **Museu Frederic Marès**.

The old city, or *'ciutat vella'*, appears on the map like a six-sided gem, the outline left by the city's third and final wall, built in the 14th-century. Contained within this hexagon are a series of neighbourhoods, each with its own distinctive history and character. Ancient as they are, these neighbourhoods also brim with life in the present, with some *barris* (quarters) now home to thriving immigrant populations and whole areas converted into very popular pedestrian-only zones.

Barri Gòtic

In the first century BC Roman soldiers established a colony on a small hill called the Mons Taber, the precise centre of which was long believed to have been marked by a round millstone set into the paving of the Carrer Paradís, between the cathedral and the Plaça Sant Jaume. The real centre of the Roman city, however, was a road junction that occupied one part of the modern Plaça Sant Jaume. Large sections of the Roman wall can still be seen (*see p72-3* **Walk 1: Barcino**).

When Barcelona began to revive under the Catalan Counts, its social and political core stayed where it had been under the Romans. As a result, it became the site of what is now one of the most complete surviving ensembles of medieval buildings – from churches to private residences – in Europe.

The Gothic **cathedral** is the third one to be built on the same site; the first was in the sixth century. Many buildings around here represent history written in stone. In C/Santa Llúcia, just in front of the cathedral, is **Ca de l'Ardiaca**, an originally 15th-century residence, with a superb tiled patio which now houses the city archives. It was renovated recently, and before that in the 1870s, when it acquired its curious letterbox by the *Modernista* architect Domènech i Montaner showing swallows and a tortoise, said to symbolise the contrast between the swiftness of truth and 'the law's delay'. On the north side of the cathedral, in Plaça Sant Iu, is the **Museu Frederic Marès** (*see p118*), with a Gothic courtyard hosting a café in summer that's one of the best places in the city

> ►Though Barcelona's streets are by no means dangerous, thieves and pickpockets are increasingly a problem. For more information, *see p302-3*.

Visit us at the Palau Robert,
the best place in Barcelona
for getting to know **Catalonia**

Exhibitions, bookshop, interactive information terminals, staffed information desk, etc.

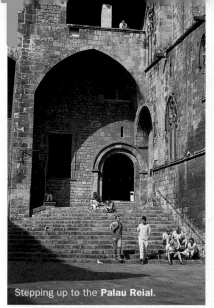

Stepping up to the **Palau Reial**.

on a hot day, the massive stone having a
wonderfully cooling effect.

Alongside the cathedral the Catalan
monarchs built the various sections of the Palau
Reial, Royal Palace, clustered around the **Plaça
del Rei**. Most of them now form part of the
Museu d'Història de la Ciutat. Even after
Catalonia lost its indigenous monarchy in the
15th century, this complex was still the seat of
the Viceroys who then governed the country.
Local civil administration, meanwhile, was
centred in the nearby **Generalitat** and
Ajuntament, which before the opening up of
the **Plaça Sant Jaume** in the 1820s had faced
onto the Carrers Bisbe and Ciutat.

The district's ancientness is very genuine,
but the idea of it as a 'Gothic Quarter' is a fairly
recent invention, from the 1920s. To help the
image stick, a few touches were made to
enhance the area's 'Gothicness'. One of the most
photographed features of the Barri Gòtic, the
'Bridge of Sighs' across C/Bisbe from the
Generalitat, was actually a completely new
addition, from 1928.

A great part of the charm of the Barri Gòtic
and areas around it lies in the way in which you
can discover some of their ancient corners
almost by accident, apparently half-forgotten
amid later building. Right next to the noise of
Plaça Catalunya is the marvellous little
Romanesque church of **Santa Anna**, begun in
1141 as part of a monastery then outside the
walls, and with an exquisite 14th-century
cloister; nearby, in the sorely mistreated **Plaça
Vila de Madrid**, there are some excavated
Roman tombs. If you walk from Plaça Sant

Jaume up C/Ciutat, to the left of the Ajuntament,
and turn down the narrow alley of C/Hércules
you will come to **Plaça Sant Just**, a
fascinating old square with a Gothic water
fountain from 1367 and the grand church of
Sants Just i Pastor, built in the 14th century
on the site of a chapel founded by
Charlemagne's son Louis the Pious.

The narrow streets bounded by Carrers
Banys Nous, Call and Bisbe once housed a rich
Jewish **Call** or ghetto (*see p11*). Today the area
is best known for its antique shops. To walk
around this area is to delight in what is perhaps
the most satisfying and peaceful part of the
Barri Gòtic. Near the centre of the Call is the
beautiful little square of **Sant Felip Neri**, with
a fine baroque church and a soothing fountain
in the centre.

Close by are the leafily attractive **Plaça del
Pi** and **Plaça Sant Josep Oriol**, where there
are some great pavement bars, and painters
exhibit work at weekends. The squares are
separated by **Santa Maria del Pi**, one of
Barcelona's most distinguished – but least
visited – Gothic churches, with a magnificent
rose window. Another attraction of the streets
between the Rambla and Via Laietana is the
wonderful variety of their shops, from the
oldest in Barcelona to smart modern arcades.
The **C/Portaferrissa** is one of the city's most
popular shopping streets, with trendy shops in
places like the **Gralla Hall** mini-mall.

Despite the expansion of Barcelona into the
Eixample, the old centre has remained a hub of

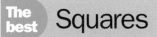

The best Squares

For street life
The **Plaça Reial** is bursting with all walks of
life; keep an eye out for fellow easyJet
passengers and pickpockets. *See p73*.

For skateboarders
The **Plaça dels Angels** in front of the MACBA
is skateboard heaven.*See p79*.

For buying art
The **Plaça Sant Josep Oriol** by Santa Maria
del Pi is home to an outdoor art market one
weekend every month.

For a quiet drink
Plaça de les Olles in the Born has cafés
with tranquil outdoor tables. *See p81*.

For students on a binge
Plaça George Orwell is the scene students
in party mode. *See p75*.

Sightseeing

A different slant on the **Plaça Reial**.

Walk 1: Barcino

Medieval Barcelona and all subsequent
buildings in the Barri Gòtic were constructed
on top of Roman Barcino, founded in 15 BC,
and many a local resident has set out to
makeover a bathroom and turned up a bit of
ancient masonry. The original Roman city
was only a second-rank outpost, covering
just 10 hectares (24 acres). Some of its
street plan can be seen in the extraordinary
remains (*pictured*) beneath the **Museu
d'Història de la Ciutat** (*see p75* and *p118*),
the largest underground excavation of a
Roman site in Europe. Barcino has had an
unappreciated impact on every subsequent
era: many of Barcelona's most familiar
streets – C/Hospital, even Passeig de
Gràcia – follow the line of Roman roads. The
best way to get an idea of the Roman town
is to walk the line of its walls. Along the
route all kinds of Roman remains can be
found, poking out from where they were re-
used or built over by medieval and later
builders (this walk is marked in pink on
pages 326-7).

Barcino's central axis was the junction of
C/Llibreteria and C/Bisbe, now a corner of
Plaça Sant Jaume. **Llibreteria** began life as
the Cardus Maximus, the main road to Rome;
walk down it, and at **C/Tapineria** turn left to

reach **Plaça Ramon Berenguer el Gran** and
the largest surviving stretch of ancient wall,
incorporated into the medieval Palau Reial.
Continue on along Tapineria, where there are
many sections of Roman building, to **Avda
Catedral**. The massive twin-drum gate on
C/Bisbe, while often retouched, in its basic
shape has not changed since it was the main
gate of the Roman town. To its left are
fragments of aqueduct. If you take a detour
up C/Capellans to **C/Duran i Bas**, you can
see another four arches of an aqueduct;
nearby in **Plaça Vila de Madrid** are tombs
from the ancient cemetery, which in
accordance with Roman custom had to be
outside the city walls.

Returning to the cathedral, turn right into
C/de la Palla. A little way along a large
chunk of wall is visible, only discovered when
a building was demolished in the 1980s.
Palla runs into **C/Banys Nous**, where at
No.16 there is a centre for disabled children
that has inside it a piece of wall with a relief
of legs and feet (try to phone ahead, 93 318
14 81, for a viewing time). Beyond there is
the junction with **C/Call**, the other end of the
Cardus, and so the opposite side of the
Roman town from Llibreteria-Tapineria. The
owners of the shoe shop at C/Call 1 are

cultural, social and political life. In a narrow street off Portal de l'Angel, C/Montsió, is the **Els Quatre Gats** café, legendary haunt of Picasso and other artists and bohemians. Between C/Portaferrissa and Plaça del Pi lies C/Petritxol, one of the most charming streets of the Barri Gòtic, known for its traditional *granges* offering coffee and cakes (*see p160*), but which also has the **Sala Parés**, the city's oldest art gallery, where Rusiñol, Casas and the young Picasso all exhibited.

Properly called **La Mercè**, the area between C/Ferran and the port has a different atmosphere from the Barri Gòtic proper, shabbier and with less prosperous shops. Its heart is the **Plaça Reial**, known for its bars and cheap hotels, and a favourite spot for a drink or an outdoor meal, provided you don't mind the odd drunk or other strange human fauna who might also be around. An addition from the 1840s, the *plaça* has the **Tres Gràcies** fountain in the centre and lamp-posts designed by the young Gaudí. On Sunday mornings a coin and stamp market is held here. Plaça Reial has had a dangerous reputation in the past, but

has been made safer by heavy policing, and its revival in popularity can be seen in the opening or revamping of restaurants such as the **Taxidermista** and clubs like the **Jamboree**. Such are the fickle ways of Barcelona fashion that **C/Escudellers**, the next street towards the port, once a deeply dubious and shabby prostitutes' alley, is now a trendy place for grungy, hip socialising, with a string of cheap, studenty bars.

It's hard to imagine, but the streets nearest the port, particularly C/Ample, were until the building of the Eixample the most fashionable in the city. The grand porticoes of some buildings – once wealthy merchants' mansions – still give evidence of former glories. Here too is the church of the **Mercè**, home of Barcelona's patron Virgin, where Barça football club has to come to properly dedicate its victories. There are also the lively *tasca* tapas bars on C/de la Mercè. Most of this area, however, became steadily more run down throughout the 20th century. The city authorities, as elsewhere, have been making efforts to change the district's character, opening up new squares: **Plaça**

used to people wandering in to examine their piece of Roman tower.

Carry on across C/Ferran and down **C/Avinyó**, next continuation of the perimeter. At the back of the Pakistani restaurant at No.19 there is a cave-like space that once again incorporates portions of Roman wall. At Plaça Milans, turn left onto **C/Gignás**: by the junction with **C/Regomir** there are remains of the fourth sea gate of the town, which would have faced the beach, and the Roman shipyard. On C/Regomir there is also one of the most important relics of Barcino, the **Pati Llimona**. After visiting there, walk up **C/Correu Vell**, where there are more fragments of wall, to reach one of the most impressive relics of Roman Barcelona in the small, shady **Plaça Traginers** – a Roman tower, one corner of the ancient wall, in a remarkable state of preservation, despite having had a medieval house built on top of it. Turn up **C/Sots-Tinent Navarro** – with a massive stretch of Roman rampart – to complete the circuit back at Llibreteria, and maybe head back to Barcino's centre and the **Temple of Augustus**.

Pati Llimona

*C/Regomir 3 (93 268 47 00).
Metro Jaume I/17, 40, 45
bus.* **Open** *8am-10pm Mon-Fri;
10am-2pm Sat, Sun.
Exhibitions 10am-2pm, 4-8pm,
Mon-Fri; 10am-2pm Sat, Sun.
Closed Aug.* **Admission** *free.*
Map *p324 D5.*
One of the oldest continually occupied sites in Barcelona, incorporating part of a round tower that dates from the first Roman settlement, and later Roman baths. The excavated foundations are visible from the street. Most of the building above is a 15th-century residence, converted into a social centre in 1988.

Temple d'August (Temple of Augustus)

C/Paradís 10 (Information Museu d'Història de la Ciutat, 93 315 11 11). Metro Jaume I/17, 19, 40, 45 bus. **Open** *10am-2pm, 4-8pm Tue-Sat; 10am-2pm Sun; closed Mon.* **Admission** *free.* **Map** *p324 D5.*
The Centre Excursionista de Catalunya (a hiking club) contains four fluted Corinthian columns that formed the rear corner of this temple, built in the first century BC as the hub of the town's Forum.

The day is Mare. Have a coffee. Unwind. This is a place to take in the sea and enjoy shopping in a relaxed, informal atmosphere for everything you can buy. And everything you can eat. And everything you can look at.

SHOPS   GAMES

MAREMAGNUM ®

RESTAURANTS   CINEMAS   DRINKS

The night is Magnum. Have a drink. This is a place where you can ponder which film you are going to see. And what you will eat for dinner. And choose which music you will dance to.

George Orwell on Escudellers, known as the 'Plaça del Trippy' by the youthful crowd that hangs out there, and **Plaça Joaquim Xirau**, off the Rambla. Another tactic is the siting of parts of the Universitat Pompeu Fabra on the lower Rambla, using students as guinea pigs in urban renewal. Flats in run-down areas of the old city are also popular with young foreigners, who don't object to their condition as much as local families do.

Beyond C/Ample and the Mercè you emerge from narrow alleys onto the Passeig de Colom, where a few shipping offices and ships' chandlers still recall the dockside atmosphere of former decades (*see also p85*). **Plaça Medinaceli**, where Almodóvar shot some scenes in his *Todo Sobre Mi Madre*, has in the **Paulino** one of the oldest bars in the city. Monolithic on Passeig de Colom is the army headquarters, the **Capitanía General**, with a façade that has the distinction of being the one construction in Barcelona directly attributable to the Dictatorship of Primo de Rivera.

Catedral de Barcelona

Pla de la Seu (93 315 15 54). Metro Jaume I/17, 19, 40, 45 bus. **Open** 8am-1.30pm, 4-7.30pm Mon-Fri; 8am-1.30pm, 5-7.30pm Sat, Sun. *Cloister* 9am-1.15pm, 4-7pm daily. *Museum* 10am-1pm daily. **Admission** cathedral/cloister free; choir 125ptas. **No credit cards**. Map p327 B3.

The first cathedral on this site was founded in the sixth century, but the present one dates from between 1298 and 1430, except for its façade, only completed in a rather un-Catalan Gothic-revival style in 1913 during the 'rediscovery' of medieval Barcelona. Not all is Gothic: in the far right corner of the cathedral, looking at the façade, is the older and simpler Romanesque chapel of **Santa Llúcia**. The most striking aspect of the cathedral is its volume: it has three naves of near-equal width. It contains many images, paintings and sculptures, and an intricately-carved choir built in the 1390s. The cathedral museum, in the 17th-century Chapter House, has paintings and sculptures with works by the Gothic masters Jaume Huguet, Bernat Martorell and Bartolomé Bermejo. In the crypt is the alabaster tomb of Santa Eulàlia, local Christian martyr and first patron saint of Barcelona. The cloister, bathed in light filtered through arches, palms and fountains, is the most attractive section of the cathedral, and an atmospheric retreat from the city. It contains some white geese, said to represent the purity of Santa Eulàlia. Inside there is also a lift to the roof, for a magnificent view of the old city.

Plaça del Rei & Museu d'Història de la Ciutat

Plaça del Rei 1, Metro Jaume I/17, 19, 40, 45 bus. **Museum** *(93 315 11 11)* **Open** *Oct-May* 10am-2pm, 4-8pm Tue-Sat; 10am-2pm Sun, public holidays. *June-Sept* 10am-8pm Tue-Sat; 10am-2pm Sun, public

holidays. *Guided tours* by appointment. **Admission** 700ptas; 500ptas concessions; free under-12s & first Sat of month. **Discounts** BC. **No credit cards**. Map p327 B3.

This wholly-preserved medieval square is flanked on two sides by the **Palau Reial** (Royal Palace), most of which was built in the 13th and 14th centuries for the Catalano-Aragonese 'Count-Kings', and is now part of the Museu d'Història de la Ciutat. With additions from different periods piled on top of each other, the *plaça* gives a vivid impression of the nature of life in the medieval city, particularly since the square, as well as receiving all the traffic of the court, also served as the main flour and fodder market. It has been fairly well established that Ferdinand and Isabella received Columbus on his first return from America either on the palace steps or in the **Saló del Tinell** behind, although miserable sceptics still place the story in doubt. To the left, looking into the *plaça*, is the 16th-century Viceroys' palace, with its five-tiered watchtower, the Mirador del Rei Martí. The square, magnificently floodlit, is an important venue for summer concerts in the **Grec** festival (*see p203*).

The interest of the City History Museum lies as much in the buildings it occupies as in the collections it holds. The basements of the 15th-century main building contain excavations of a huge area of the Roman city, which extend like a giant, complex cavern under the adjoining square (*see also p72* **Walk 1: Barcino**). The main sections of the Palau Reial are the chapel of **Santa Agata** and the extraordinary Great Hall or Saló del Tinell – its massive, unadorned arches a classic example of Catalan Gothic. The chapel has a 15th-century altarpiece by Jaume Huguet, one of the greatest Catalan medieval paintings. From the upper floors, there is access to the inside of the **Roman wall**, and from the chapel you can climb up the **Mirador del Rei Martí** watchtower. Another section, the Casa Padellàs, houses excellent temporary exhibitions. The museum has added to its attractions Barcelona: Una Història Virtual, an impressive state-of-the-art virtual reality presentation on the city's history (with English commentary; shows last approx 30min; book for a time when you arrive at the museum). There's a well-stocked bookshop and information centre with informative leaflets in English, and the museum is also a jumping-off point for city tours, and opens for special late-night visits (*see p65*). *See also chapter* **Museums**.

Plaça Sant Jaume

The main square of the old city and still the administrative centre of modern Barcelona, the Plaça Sant Jaume contains both the City Hall (**Ajuntament**) and the seat of the Catalan regional government (**Palau de la Generalitat**), standing opposite each other in occasional rivalry. They have not always done so: the square was only opened up in 1823, after which the present neo-classical façade was added to the Ajuntament. That of the Generalitat is older, from 1598-1602. The greater part of both buildings, however, was built in the early 15th century, and both of their original main entrances open onto the street now called Bisbe Irurita on one side of the *plaça*, and Ciutat on the other.

Ajuntament de Barcelona

Plaça Sant Jaume (93 402 70 00/special visits 93 402 73 64/www.bcn.es). Metro Liceu, Jaume I/14, 17, 19, 38, 40, 45, 59 bus. **Open** *Office* 8.30am-2.30pm Mon-Fri. *Visits* 10am-2pm Sat, Sun. **Admission** free. **Map** p327 B3.

Contrasting completely with the main façade, the old C/Ciutat entrance to the City Hall is entirely a work of Catalan Gothic. The centrepiece of the Ajuntament is the 15th-century **Saló de Cent** (Hall of One Hundred), site of all major municipal ceremonies. Visitors can see the main rooms at weekends. The entrance to the tourist information office and gift shop is on the C/Ciutat side.

Palau de la Generalitat

Plaça Sant Jaume (93 402 46 00/www.gencat.es). Metro Liceu, Jaume I/14, 17, 19, 38, 40, 45, 59 bus.

Open *guided tours* 10.30am-1.30pm 2nd & 4th Sun of each month. **Admission** free. **Map** p327 B3.

Like the City Hall, the Generalitat has a Gothic side entrance, with above it a beautiful relief of Saint George, patron saint of Catalonia, made by master carver Pere Johan in 1418. Inside, the finest features are the raised patio the **Pati de Tarongers** ('orange tree patio'), and the magnificent chapel of **Sant Jordi** of 1432-4, the masterpiece of Catalan architect Marc Safont. The Generalitat is traditionally open to the public on Sant Jordi, 23 April, when its patios are spectacularly decorated with red roses (and queues are huge); it also opens its doors on 11 September (Catalan National Day) and 24 September (La Mercè) and on some other holidays each year (*see chapter* **By Season**). Tours are also run on two Sundays each month, and on other Saturdays and Sundays can be booked by prior reservation.

The Raval

If, from the Rambla, instead of going into the Barri Gòtic you turn right, looking towards the sea, you will enter the Raval. This is the name currently used for the area bounded by the Rambla, Paral.lel, Ronda Sant Pau and Ronda

Barcelona's cultural paella pan

Things are changing in Barcelona. Over the last few years there has been a sharp rise in the number of immigrants coming in to the city from both EU and non-EU countries, and while it has a long way to go before it reaches the multicultural mix of London or Paris, Barcelona is home to more cultural and ethnic variety than ever before.

The change is particularly obvious in the *ciutat vella*, on the margins of the Barri Gòtic. Before the Olympics, these were areas of considerable social neglect, and with housing correspondingly cheap, they became an immediate magnet for low-income immigrants. In the space of a few years these groups have established robust communities and spearheaded a certain degree of social and economic regeneration in these areas.

While not compact enough to form ghettos, the main immigrant communities are strongly identified with certain zones: Pakistani in the lower part of the Raval, Philippine in the upper part, Dominican along Carrer Carders and Maghrebi, particularly Moroccan, around Sant Pere. The Pakistani and Dominican communities in particular have contributed to the changing nature of the Ciutat Vella, setting up supermarkets, restaurants and call

centres for phoning and sending money home, as well as contributing to the energy and atmosphere of the area: Carrer Carders in La Ribera and the Plaça de les Angels in front of the MACBA come alive in the late afternoon/early evening, and on Sunday mornings it is not unusual to see a large group of Pakistani men playing cricket in the park at the end of Carrer Sant Pau.

Inevitably there are problems, both in the form of sporadic racist attacks and a certain level of police harassment. Spain's right-wing central government is trying to tighten up recently revised immigration laws, and non-legal immigration continues to be a contentious issue. At the same time, small groups of mostly Maghrebi delinquents have made life difficult for others, inducing the Pakistani population to set up their own local vigilante patrols.

In general, though, the changes of the last decade have been relatively smooth. Immigration in Barcelona as a whole amounts to less than 5 per cent of the total population, increasing to up to 20 per cent in the Ciutat Vella. It's not so much a melting pot, as a paella pan – a homogenous base dotted with occasional bits of colour.

La Rambla del Raval, making a name for itself. *See p78.*

Sant Antoni, but it has been known by many different names in the past. 'Raval' is the original medieval name, referring to the part of the city outside the walls. The trades and institutions then confined here were those too dangerous or noxious to be allowed inside the city, such as brickmaking or slaughtering, or the huge **Antic Hospital de la Santa Creu**, which served the needs of the city from the 15th century until it finally closed in 1926. Other institutions located here were those that demanded too much space, such as the line of monasteries that once ran down one side of the Rambla. In the corner of the Raval next to the sea were the **Drassanes** or shipyards, now the **Museu Marítim**.

On the Paral.lel, near the port, there is still a large section of Barcelona's third city wall: the one which brought the Raval within the city in the 14th century. However, Barcelona largely stagnated in the following centuries, and, as late as 1800, much of the Raval had still not been built up, but consisted of small fruit and vegetable gardens, or sometimes even vineyards. A trace of this earlier Raval can still be seen in the name of one of the most beautiful pockets of peace in the district, the ancient Romanesque church of **Sant Pau del Camp** ('Saint Paul in the Field').

Hence, when industry began to develop, it was in this area that most land was available. A great deal more land also came into use when liberal governments dissolved the monasteries in 1836, especially in the area around one of the great hubs of the district, the **Boqueria** market, built on the site of the former convent of Sant Josep. Barcelona's first industry, mainly textile mills, thus had to grow within the cramped confines of the still-walled Raval, making use of every particle of space. Some of the strange, barrack-like factories from that time can still be seen in places, despite recent demolitions. Their workers lived alongside them, often in appalling conditions.

Then known to most people as the *Quinto* or 'Fifth District', this was the area where the dangerous classes of society took refuge, and it became the great centre of revolutionary Barcelona, a perennial breeding ground for anarchist and other radical groups. Conspiracies galore were hatched here, riots and revolts began on innumerable occasions, and whole streets became no-go areas for the police after dark.

The other aspect of the area (or of that part of it between C/Sant Pau and the port) that made it notorious was its situation as a centre of low-life, drug trafficking and the sex industry, with high-class brothels for the rich and cheap dives for the poor in the so-called *Barrio Chino* (*Xino*, in Catalan) or Chinatown. This label was given to the area (which had no Chinese connections) in the 1920s by a journalist, Francesc Madrid, after he saw a film about vice in San Francisco's Chinatown, and swiftly caught on. Barcelona had always had an underworld, centred in the

Raval, but it really took off during World War I (*see p20*). The heyday of the Barrio Chino was in the '20s and '30s, but it managed to survive to a certain extent under Franco. Hundreds of bars and cheap hostals lined streets like Nou de la Rambla, catering to a floating population (for a walk around some relics of the area, *see pp18-9*).

Today the whole district has changed enormously, perhaps more comprehensively than anywhere else in Barcelona. Its surviving industry consists of a dwindling number of old-fashioned workshops in trades like printing, bookbinding, furniture repair or building supplies. The hospital now houses cultural and academic institutions. The former hotbed of radical politics is but a shadow of its pre-Franco self. The biggest change of all has been in the Chino, a prime target of the Ajuntament's urban renewal schemes.

In the late 1970s serious problems were caused in the Chino by the arrival of heroin. The old, semi-tolerated petty criminality became much more threatening, affecting the morale of Barcelona residents and the tourist trade. The authorities set about the problem with their customary clean-sweep approach. Between 1988 and 1992 the cheapest *hostals* were closed, and whole blocks associated with drug dealers or prostitution demolished to make way for new squares. The people displaced were often transferred to newer flats on the outskirts of town, out of sight and so perhaps out of mind. Another element in the *esponjament* (mopping up) of the Raval has been gentrification, with the construction of a students' residence, a new police station and office blocks. Most dramatic of all has been the plan to create a '*Raval obert al cel*' – 'a Raval open to the sky', with far more open space. The most tangible result so far is the Rambla del Raval, completed in 2000, which now ranks as one of the city's most sweeping pedestrian spaces. Just below the new *rambla*, Avinguda Drassanes, by Colom, was actually created in an earlier attempt to 'open up' the Raval, under Franco's mayor Porcioles in the '60s (one thing Franco's administrators and modern planners could agree on is that the Chino must go), but only got as far as C/Nou de la Rambla. The new Rambla now extends the effort far into the district, bulldozing all before it up to C/Hospital. Entire streets – once densely populated but rotten with neglect – have vanished in its wake.

Some of these changes have undeniably been for the best, but their cumulative effect has been to leave one of the more unique parts of the city looking rather empty. It still has a hard edge, though, and it's an area where it's advisable to be wary of thieves and avoid acting the dumb tourist, especially between Sant Pau and the

port. Another, unpredicted change in the Raval has been the appearance of a sizeable Muslim community, mostly from Pakistan and the Maghreb countries, who have taken over flats no longer wanted by Spaniards. This is now one of the city's most multicultural areas, where Muslim halal butcher shops serving North Africans sit alongside *carnisseries* selling every part of the pig to Catalans.

The main thoroughfare of the lower Raval, **C/Nou de la Rambla**, today has only a fraction of its earlier animation, but retains a sometimes surreal selection of shops. It also contains a peculiar addition from the 1880s, the **Palau Güell**, built by Gaudí for Eusebi Güell. It was a very eccentric decision of Güell's to have his new residence located in what was then a deeply unfashionable area, and he often had trouble persuading reluctant dinner guests to take up his invitations. Nearby, in C/Sant Pau, is another *Modernista* landmark, the **Hotel España** (*see p53*).

The upper Raval, towards Plaça Catalunya, has seen large-scale official projects for the rejuvenation of the area in the giant cultural complex that includes the Museu d'Art Contemporani (**MACBA**) and the Centre de Cultura Contemporània (**CCCB**), built in what was once the workhouse, the Casa de la Caritat. A clutch of galleries has sprung up around them, although a failure to attract wealthier art-buyers has led to some moving back to more traditional gallery areas in the Eixample (*see chapter* **Galleries**). C/Riera Baixa is now Barcelona's liveliest street for innovative club and street fashion.

Alongside the new association with sophisticated culture, parts of the old Raval are also enjoying a new lease of life thanks to their being (re)discovered as hip places to be. There are laid-back restaurants like **Silenus**, cool bars like **Muebles Navarro** or **Rita Blue** on Plaça Sant Agustí, and open-air bars like the **Kasparo** on Plaça Vicenç Martorell. At one end of the Raval the **Pastis** on C/Santa Mònica remains interestingly French, and a great night out can be had in **La Paloma** on C/Tigre.

Antic Hospital de la Santa Creu

C/Carme 47- C/Hospital 56 (no phone). Metro Liceu/14, 18, 38, 59 bus. **Open** 9am-8pm Mon-Fri; 9am-2pm Sat; closed Sun. **Admission** free. **Map** p326 A2,

A hospital was founded on this site in 1024: the buildings combine a 15th-century Gothic core – including a beautifully shady colonnaded courtyard – with baroque and classical additions. It remained the city's main hospital until 1926, and Gaudí died here. Today it houses Catalonia's main library, an arts school and the La Capella exhibition space, in the chapel (*see p113*).

Antic Hospital de la Santa Creu. *See p78.*

Palau Güell

C/Nou de la Rambla 3-5 (93 317 39 74). Metro Liceu/14, 18, 59, 91 bus. **Open** *guided tours only* 10am-1pm, 4-7pm Mon-Sat; closed Sun (hours are subject to change). **Admission** 400ptas; 200ptas concessions; free under-6s. **Discount** RM. **No credit cards. Map** p327 A3.

This vaguely medievalist palace was built in 1886-8 as a residence for Gaudí's patron Eusebi Güell. It was Gaudí's first major commission for Güell, and one of the first buildings in which he revealed the originality of his ideas. Once past the fortress-like façade, one finds an interior in impeccable condition, with lavish wooden ceilings, dozens of snake-eye stone pillars, and original furniture. The roof terrace is a garden of decorated chimneys, each one different from the other. Queues are often long for the guided tours, so try to get there early; mornings are better than afternoons.

Sant Pau del Camp.

C/Sant Pau 101 (93 441 00 01). Metro Paral.lel/ 20, 36, 57, 64, 91 bus. **Open** 11.30am-1pm, 6-7.30pm Mon, Wed-Sun; 11.30am-12.30pm Tue. **Admission** free. **Map** p324 C6.

Barcelona's oldest surviving church was built in the 12th century, when the surrounding Raval was just open fields, as part of a monastery. The Romanesque structure has none of the towering grandeur of the cathedral or Santa Maria del Mar: it is a squat, hulking building, rounded in on itself to give a sense of intimacy and protection to worshippers. On either side of the portal are columns made of material from seventh- and eighth-century buildings.

Sant Pere, La Ribera & Born

Back on the east side of the Rambla, the Barri Gòtic is now effectively limited on its eastern flank by the long, straight Via Laietana. This is a 20th-century addition, cut through the old city in 1907. The *barris* to the right of it on the map were contained, like the Barri Gòtic, within the second, thirteenth-century city wall, and include some of the most fascinating parts of the medieval city.

Below Plaça Urquinaona lies the district of Sant Pere, originally centred around the monastery of **Sant Pere de les Puelles**, which still stands, if greatly altered, in Plaça de Sant Pere. This was Barcelona's main centre of textile production for centuries, and to this day streets like Sant Pere Més Baix and Sant Pere Més Alt contain many textile wholesalers and retailers. The area may be medieval in origin, but its finest monument is one of the most extraordinary works of *Modernisme*, the **Palau de la Música Catalana**, facing C/Sant Pere Més Alt. Less noticed on the same street is a curious feature, unique in Barcelona, the **Passatge de la Indústria**, a long narrow arcade between C/ Sant Pere Més Alt and C/Ortigosa.

Like other parts of the old city Sant Pere looks very run down in places, but as elsewhere is undergoing renovation. The district market, **Mercat de Santa Caterina** – one of Barcelona's oldest – is being completely rebuilt, and in the meantime its stallholders have been relocated along Passeig Lluís Companys, by the park. As with the Raval, the district's neglected state is an obvious explanation of why it has become home to many recent immigrants, the most prominent of whom are black Latin Americans from the Dominican Republic – you can often hear salsa or merengue wafting out across medieval alleys like C/Fonollar.

The name of the area below Sant Pere, La Ribera (the waterfront), recalls the time before permanent quays were built, when the shoreline reached much further inland. One of the most engaging districts of the old city, it has, though, fallen victim to two historic acts of urban vandalism. The first took place after the 1714 siege, when the victors razed one whole corner of the Ribera in order to construct the fortress of the Ciutadella, now the **Parc de la Ciutadella**. The second occurred when the Via Laietana was struck through the *barri* in the 1900s, in line with the contemporary theory of 'ventilating' insanitary city districts by driving wide avenues through them.

In Barcelona's Golden Age, from the 12th century onwards, La Ribera was both the favourite residential area of the city's merchant elite and the principal centre of commerce and trade. The **Plaça de l'Àngel**, now a rather nondescript space on Via Laietana by Jaume I Metro station, is all that remains of the Plaça del Blat, the 'wheat square', where all grain brought into the city was traded. If the Royal Palace, Generalitat and Ajuntament were the 'official' centre of the medieval city, this was its commercial and popular heart, where virtually

Sightseeing

Palau de la Música Catalana.

everybody had to come at least once a day. The main street of La Ribera is still **Carrer Montcada**, one of the unmissable parts of old Barcelona. It is lined with an extraordinary succession of medieval palaces, the greatest of which house museums such as the **Museu Tèxtil**, the **Museu Barbier-Mueller** of Pre-Columbian art and, above all, the **Museu Picasso** (for all, see chapter **Museums**). Montcada also has a unique selection of bars for settling into (see pp164-6). The surrounding streets were once filled with workshops supplying anything the merchant owners might need (see pp82-3 **Walk 2: La Ribera**).

On the corner of Montcada and C/Assaonadors is the small chapel the **Capella d'en Marcús**, which when built, in the 12th century, was surrounded by fields and gardens. Close by was the main route through the district, along Carrers Corders and Carders. C/Princesa is a much more recent addition, created in the 1850s.

From C/Carders, C/Montcada leads across C/Princesa to the centre of the Ribera, the **Passeig del Born**. 'Born' originally meant 'joust' or 'list', and in the Middle Ages and for many centuries thereafter this was the centre for the city's festivals, processions, tournaments, carnivals and the burning of heretics by the Inquisition. At one end of the square is the old **Born** market, a magnificent 1870s wrought-iron structure that used to be Barcelona's main wholesale food market. It closed in the 1970s, when the market was transferred to the other side of Montjuïc. The building was saved from demolition, and current plans are that it should house a library and arts centre.

At the other end of the Passeig from the market stands the greatest of all Catalan Gothic buildings, the magnificent church of **Santa Maria del Mar**. On one side of it a rather ugly new square was opened in 1989 on the site where it is believed the last defenders of the city were executed after the fall of Barcelona to the Spanish army in 1714. Called the **Fossar de les Moreres**, the 'mulberry graveyard', the square is inscribed with emphatic patriotic

poetry, and nationalist demonstrations converge here every year on Catalan National Day, 11 September.

The closure of the Born market led initially to a certain decline in this area, but it has survived as the home of an old-established community, and thanks to its inherent attractions for tourism and nightlife. As a nightlife haunt the Born tends to go in and out of fashion, with booms and slumps every few years; currently it is starting the millennium on a roll, as the once quiet Passeig and its bars are packed with wandering crowds on weekend nights. The area is full of great bars, and has an ever-expanding number of restaurants. Since the 1980s it has also been a hub of the city's alternative art scene. Around C/Banys Vells, parallel to Montcada, there is now an interesting selection of independent textile and craft workshops, set up by young designers (see chapter **Shopping**).

From the Born and Santa Maria, tiny streets lead through centuries-old arches and the little **Plaça de les Olles** to the harbourside avenue and another symbol of the Ribera, the **Llotja** (Exchange). Its outer shell is neo-classical, added in the 18th century, but its core is a superb 1380s Gothic hall which, until the exchange moved to Passeig de Gràcia in 1994, was the oldest continuously functioning stock exchange in Europe. It once housed the Consolat del Mar, the 'Consulate of the Sea', established to arbitrate in commercial disputes throughout the Mediterranean, and since then has accommodated a Customs Post and a School of Fine Arts, at which Picasso studied. Unfortunately it can (usually) only be visited if you attend a function organised through its owners, the Chamber of Commerce (see p293).

Palau de la Música Catalana

C/Sant Françesc de Paula 2 (93 295 72 00/ www.palaumusica.org). Metro Urquinaona/17, 19, 40, 45 bus. **Guided tours** 10am-3.30pm daily.

Born, yesterday.

Walk 2: La Ribera

Centuries of Barcelona life, work and wealth are reflected in the medieval streets of La Ribera. This walk is marked in green on pages 326-7; it begins, like that around the Roman city (*see p72-3*), on Plaça Sant Jaume. From there, walk down **C/Llibreteria**, as important in the Middle Ages as it had been as the Roman Cardus, and still the main north road. Cross **Plaça de l'Angel**, site of the Plaça del Blat, the grain market. The continuation of the Roman road across Via Laietana is **C/Bòria**, a name that probably means 'outskirts' or 'suburbs', since it was outside the original city.

C/Bòria continues into the extraordinarily evocative **Plaça de la Llana** ('wool'), old centre of wool trading in the city, now with a clutch of Dominican-owned bars. Alleys to the left were associated with food trades: **C/Mercaders** ('traders', probably in grain), **C/de l'Oli** ('olive oil'); **C/Semoleres**, where semolina was made. To the right on Bòria is **C/Pou de la Cadena** ('well with a chain'), a reminder that water was essential for textile working.

After Plaça de la Llana the Roman road's name becomes **C/Corders** ('rope-makers'), and then **C/Carders** ('carders', or combers of wool). Where the name changes there is a tiny square, Placeta Marcús, with a smaller Romanesque chapel, the **Capella d'en Marcús**, built in the early 12th century to give shelter to travellers on the road who arrived after the city gates had closed for the night. Bernat Marcús, who paid for it, is also said to have organised the first postal service in Europe, and it was from here that his riders set off north. The chapel is rarely open (and then for worship only).

Carry on a little way along C/Carders to **Plaça Sant Agustí Vell**, different bits of which hail from many centuries, from medieval to 19th: in **C/Basses de Sant Pere**, leading away to the left, there is an intact 14th-century house.

Retrace your steps down C/Carders, to turn left into **C/Blanqueria** ('bleaching'). Here wool was fulled and washed before being spun. Inside its giant doorways are smaller versions of the patios seen on C/Montcada. At **C/Assaonadors** ('tanners'), turn right. At the end of this street, behind the Marcús chapel, is a statue of Saint John the Baptist, patron saint of the tanners' guild.

Here you are at the top of **C/Montcada**. In La Ribera's Golden Age this beautiful street was the broadest thoroughfare in the district, and its busiest. Its merchant residences conform to a typical style of Mediterranean urban palace – elegant entrance patios with the main rooms on the first floor – and are closely packed together. Most have features from several periods. Today this is one of

---

Admission 700ptas; 600ptas concessions. **Advance tickets** box office 10am-9pm daily. **Credit** MC, V (groups over 10 only). **Map** p326 B-C2.

Gaudí may be the best-known of Barcelona's *Modernista* architects, but the building that most truly represents the style is Domènech i Montaner's 'Palace of Catalan Music'. Built in 1905-8, it's still the most prestigious concert hall in the city, despite the inauguration of the all-modern **Auditori**. The façade, with its combination of bare brick, busts and mosaic friezes representing Catalan musical traditions alongside the great composers, is impressive enough, but it is surpassed by the building's staggering interior. Decoration erupts everywhere: the ceiling centrepiece is of multi-coloured stained glass; 18 half-mosaic, half-relief figures representing the musical muses appear out of the back of the stage; and on one side, massive Wagnerian carved horses ride out to accompany a bust of Beethoven. The old Palau has been bursting under the pressure of the musical activity going on inside it, and an extension and renovation programme by Oscar Tusquets in the 1980s is being followed by yet more alterations by the same architect.

The best way to see the Palau is to go to a concert, but now that the opening of the Auditori and re-opening of the **Liceu** have relieved concert pressure in the hall it is easier to visit it with a guided tour. Tours are available in English, Catalan or Spanish, last 50 minutes and leave every half-hour or so. They begin with a 20-minute video, which can make the remaining tour a bit rushed, and parts of the building (such as the exterior decoration) are not touched upon. Don't feel shy about asking questions: it's the best way to get to interesting information beyond the basics. Photography and filming are forbidden during tours. The Palau also has an attractive shop, **Les Muses del Palau**. *See also chapter* **Music: Classical & Opera**.

Parc de la Ciutadella

Pg Picasso. Metro Arc de Triomf, Barceloneta/14, 39, 40, 41, 42, 51, 100, 141 bus. **Open** *Nov-Feb* 10am-6pm daily. *Mar, Oct* 10am-7pm daily. *Apr, Sept* 10am-8pm daily. *May-Aug* 10am-9pm daily. **Map** p325 E6.

Barcelona's most historic park, the Parc de la Ciutadella occupies the site of the 18th-century

Montcada ends at **Passeig del Born**, a hub of the city's trades for 400 years. Turn left, and on the left there is **C/Flassaders** ('blanket makers'), and to the right **C/del Rec**, the irrigation canal. Go down Rec to turn right into **C/Esparteria**, where *espart* (hemp) was woven. Turnings off it include **C/Calders**, where smelting furnaces would have been found, and **C/Formatgeria**, where one would have gone to buy cheese. After that is **C/Vidrieria**, where glass was stored and sold; **Vidrieria Grau** at No.6 is the last survivor of this centuries-old trade in the street.

Esparteria runs into C/Ases, which crosses **C/Malcuinat** ('badly-cooked'), so there must have been evil smells nearby. Turn left into **C/Espaseria** ('sword-making') to emerge out of ancient alleys onto the open space of Pla del Palau. Turn right, and then right again into **C/Canvis Vells** ('old exchange'). A tiny street to the left, **C/Panses**, has an archway above it, with a stone sculpture of a face over the second floor. This face, called a *carabassa*, indicated the existence of a legalised brothel. At the end of Canvis Vells you come to **Plaça Santa Maria** and La Ribera's superb parish church: on the left-hand side is **C/Abaixadors** ('unloaders'), where porters would unload goods, and from the square **C/Argenteria** ('silverware') leads back to the Plaça de l'Angel.

Barcelona's great museum centres. The first palace you reach after crossing C/Princesa is the **Palau Berenguer d'Aguilar**, home of the **Museu Picasso**, which has also taken over four more palaces (*see pp110-3*). Opposite is one of the finest and largest palaces, the **Palau dels Marquesos de Llió**, now the **Museu Tèxtil**, with a fine café (pictured); nearby is another great Montcada feature, the **Xampanyet** cava bar. A relative newcomer is the bar in the 17th-century **Palau Dalmases**.

To the right is **C/Sombrerers**, where hat makers wrought their craft; opposite it is Barcelona's narrowest street, **Carrer de les Mosques** ('street of flies'), not even wide enough for an adult to lie across. It has since been closed off because too many people were pissing in it at night.

citadel (*see p14*). It was created as the site of the 1888 Exhibition, and just outside it is the **Arc de Triomf** ('triumphal arch'), which formed the main entrance to the Exhibition. In the middle of the park there is a lake where boats can be hired (200ptas per person, per half-hour). Beside the lake is the *Cascade*, or ornamental fountain, on which the young Gaudí worked as assistant to Josep Fontseré, the architect of the park.

Although formally laid out, the Ciutadella makes an attractive change from the surrounding streets. Surprisingly extensive, it also has specific attractions: the **Museu d'Art Modern**, sharing the surviving buildings of the Citadel with the Catalan Parliament, the **Museu de Geologia** and **Museu de Zoologia**. The Zoo, due to move to the Diagonal-Mar area by 2004, currently takes up over half the park's space. Not to be missed are the *umbracle* or greenhouse, also from the 1880s, beautifully restored to provide a mysterious pocket of tropical forest in the city, and the *hivernacle* or winter garden, with a fine café (*see p164*). Near the Ciutadella bikes can be hired to ride in the park.

Santa Maria del Mar

Plaça de Santa Maria (93 310 23 90). Metro Jaume I/17, 19, 40, 45 bus. **Open** 9am-1.30pm, 4.30-8pm daily. **Admission** free. **Map** p327 C3.

The cathedral may attract more attention, but Santa Maria del Mar, known as 'the people's cathedral' because of its traditionally greater popularity, is undoubtedly the city's finest church, the summit of Catalan Gothic. Built, remarkably quickly for a medieval building, between 1329 and 1384, it has an unusual unity of style. Inside, two ranks of slim, perfectly proportioned columns soar up to fan vaults, creating a wonderful atmosphere of space and peace. It's not so much a historical artefact as simply a marvellous building. There's also superb stained glass, particularly the great 15th-century rose window above the main door. Our ability to appreciate it is helped greatly by the fact that revolutionaries set fire to it in 1936, clearing out the wooden baroque images that clutter so many Spanish churches, and allowing the simplicity of its lines to emerge. From the outside, especially from Plaça Santa Maria with its delightful pavement cafés (*see pp164-6*), the church is equally impressive.

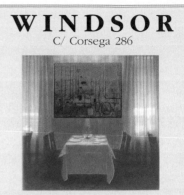

The Port & Shoreline

Mega-ports, daring new projects and hot fun under the sun.

Step right up to the **Moll d'Espanya**.

The Port Vell

At the foot of the Rambla, Columbus (Colom in Catalan) points out to sea from atop his column, confusingly enough towards Italy. To his right are the 14th-century shipyards or **Drassanes**, now the **Museu Marítim**, and from near the foot of his column you can cross the harbour on the **Golondrines** boat trips (*see p86*). These are features that have been in place for years. However, had you made the ride up to the crown at Columbus' feet in, say, 1980, you would have seen the harbour beneath you thronged with cargo ships waiting to load or unload. Today, they have disappeared, and the scene has changed utterly. Commercial traffic has moved away to container terminals outside the main port, in the Zona Franca. Simultaneously, Barcelona's inner harbour, rechristened the **Port Vell** or old port, has undergone an extraordinary overhaul to turn it into a waterside leisure area, so much so that 20 years on a visitor simply would not know it. In just a few years since the mid-1990s, the former dockside has become one of Barcelona's foremost party zones.

At the end of the Rambla, if you make your way through the traffic of the Passeig de Colom to the waterfront, you will come to the **Rambla de Mar**, a swivel-section wooden footbridge (which opens to let boats enter and leave) that leads to the **Moll d'Espanya** quay. The quay is dominated by the **Maremàgnum** complex, a trademark work by ever-active architects Helio Piñón and Albert Viaplana (*see also chapters* **Nightlife** and **Shopping**). As much an entertainment as a shopping centre, it contains 50 shops, 25 restaurants and a dozen clubs and bars and on weekend evenings the place is packed with young crowds. Further along the same quay there's also an eight-screen cinema, the **IMAX** giant-format movie-house and Barcelona's **Aquàrium**, one of the best of its kind in the world.

If you've had enough of Maremàgnum and come back across the footbridge and turn right, you will come to the **Moll de la Fusta** or wood quay, which was the first part of the port to be redeveloped. When it was inaugurated in 1987 it contained a string of pavement bars and restaurants. Among them was Gambrinus, topped by a giant fibreglass lobster by designer Javier Mariscal that became a real symbol of 1980s, pre-Olympic Barcelona. Today Gambrinus, along with the rest of the bars and restaurants, has closed – even though the lobster's still there – as the city rethinks its plans for the strip. Impossible to miss at the north end of the Moll de la Fusta, by the borders of La Ribera, is the impressive 14-metre (46-foot) high mosaic sculpture *Barcelona Head*, by the late Roy Lichtenstein.

If you carry on round the port to the right, you will reach the marina – with some very luxurious yachts – and a line of waterside restaurants. The *tinglados*, the huge dock storage sheds that once dominated Passeig Joan de Borbó, have nearly all been pulled down to open up an entirely new, positively gracious harbourside promenade on this side of Barceloneta. One exception is the **Palau de Mar**, a converted warehouse that now hosts a clutch of restaurants and the **Museu d'Història de Catalunya**. The only remaining commercial section is a small area for fishermen. Beyond there, if you continue walking you can go through the Barceloneta district to the Port Olímpic and the city's beaches.

Returning to Columbus' feet, if, instead of walking across to Maremàgnum or along the Moll de la Fusta you head to the right, looking out to sea, you will come to the **Moll de Barcelona**. This is a working quay, the departure point for Balearics ferries (*see p271*). At the end of the quay, though, there is another giant new building scheme labelled (in English) the **World Trade Center (WTC)**, which opened in July 1999. Looking like a vast docked oceanliner, the WTC has 130,000 square metres/400,000 square feet of floor space, between offices, an exhibition hall, a conference centre, and shops. On either side of it are cruise terminals, which will round off Barcelona's – already hugely successful – drive to become the dominant cruise port of the Mediterranean. To serve the cruise passengers there will be a giant hotel making up the landward side of the complex, due to open its doors by early 2002.

South of Montjuïc work is under way on extending the Zona Franca industrial area to create a new 'Logistics Park' with optimum port, road, rail and air links. To facilitate this plan, the port has been divided in two, with the strictly commercial zone to be located south of the WTC, while cruise ships and pleasure craft will have their own new harbour entry across from the WTC, due to be open by late 2001. The latest completed link in this grand design is the immense drawbridge inaugurated in 2000, the Porta d'Europa, the widest bridge of its type in the world – one metre or so more than Rotterdam's – that connects the old breakwater with the land. The objective of all this is to consolidate Barcelona as the foremost freight port and distribution centre in the western Mediterranean, ahead of eternal rivals Marseilles and Genoa. The strategy is evidently working, as multinationals have stampeded to set up their Mediterranean headquarters in the now almost entirely filled WTC.

Colom (Columbus monument)
Plaça Portal de la Pau (93 302 52 24). Metro Drassanes/14, 20, 36, 38, 57, 59, 64, 91, 157 bus. **Open** *Late Sept-Mar* 10am-1.30pm, 3.30-6.30pm Mon-Fri; 10am-6.30pm Sat, Sun. *April, May* 10am-1.30pm, 3.30-7.30pm Mon-Fri; 10am-7.30pm Sat, Sun. *June-late Sept* 9am-8.30pm daily. **Admission** 250ptas; 150ptas concessions; free under-4s; group discounts. **Discounts** BT, BC. **No credit cards Map** p327 A4.
Ride to the top of the Columbus column, which was built for the Exhibition of 1888, to get a panoramic view of the old city and the port from within the crown at the explorer's feet. The lift only holds four people and the attendant at any one time, so there's often quite a queue.

Golondrines (Swallow Boats)
Moll de la Fusta (93 442 31 06/ www.lasgolondrines.com). Metro Drassanes/ 14, 36, 38, 57, 59, 64,157 bus.
Drassanes-breakwater & return (35min) *Late-Sept-June* (no stop at the breakwater) hourly 11.45am-5pm Mon-Fri; every 35mins (phone to check times) Sat-Sun. *July-Sept* every 35-45mins 11am-8pm daily. **Tickets** 525ptas; 275ptas concessions; free under-4s.
Drassanes-Port Olímpic & return (1½hrs): *Oct-Mar* two daily. *Apr-June* three daily. *July-Sept* every 30-45min. **Tickets** 1,325ptas; 950-575ptas concessions; free under-4s.
Discounts Groups, BC, BT. **Credit** MC, V. **Map** p324 C7. All outings are subject to weather conditions.

Port Vell: Fish 'n' ships.

Barceloneta's beach.

The double-decker 'Swallow Boats' take you around the harbour to the end of the breakwater, where you can eat out, take in the sea air, go fishing, or come straight back. More solid, sea-going boats run on a longer trip round to the Port Olímpic.

Transbordador Aeri (cable-cars)
Miramar, Parc de Montjuïc–Torre de Jaume I, Port Vell–Torre de Sant Sebastià, Barceloneta (93 441 48 20). Metro Paral.lel & Funicular de Montjuïc/61 bus, or 17, 64 bus to Barceloneta. **Open** (daily) *Mid Oct-Feb* 10.30am-5.30pm. *Mar-mid June, mid Sept-mid Oct* 10.30am-7pm. *Mid June-mid Sept* 10.30am-8pm.
Tickets 1,200ptas round trip; 1,000ptas one way; 1,000ptas round trip Barceloneta–Jaume I or Jaume I–Miramar. **No credit cards. Map** p324 C-D7.
The 1929 cable-car rattles its way across the harbour from Miramar on Montjuïc to Barceloneta, with a stop in the middle by the World Trade Center. Views of Barceloneta and the Port are spectacular; however, the WTC project will likely lead to its closure, so catch it while you can.

Barceloneta

The triangular district known as Barceloneta ('Little Barcelona'), the part of the city between the harbour and the sea, was the product of an early example of authoritarian town planning. When after 1714 a large section of the Ribera (*see p20 and p65*) was razed to the ground to make way for the new Citadel, the people displaced lived for many years in makeshift shelters on the beach, until in the 1750s the authorities decided to rehouse them in line with a plan drawn up by a French army engineer, Prosper Verboom.

The new district was built on land reclaimed from the sea. The street plan of Barceloneta, with long, narrow blocks, reveals its military origins. In the 19th century this became the dockers' and fishermen's district, and a massive road and rail barrier was built cutting

Barceloneta off from the rest of the city right up until the transformations of the 1990s. This helped the area retain a distinctive atmosphere and identity; the local **Festa Major** in September is a riot of colour (*see p204*).

Barceloneta has also traditionally been the city's gateway to the beach. Until not so long ago this was of interest only to a few devotees of sunbathing rather than seabathing. Some may cavil at the water quality even today, but since the comprehensive reconstruction of the city's beaches it has become far cleaner and more pleasant. Consequently Barceloneta has become still more crowded on summer weekends, as throngs make their way through its streets for a meal or a swim.

Away from the beach and the city, at its 'tip' Barceloneta leads into Passeig de l'Escullera, the road along the breakwater which will now be truncated by the new harbour entry for pleasure craft just beyond where the beaches end. Plans for this area, by the often-controversial Ricard Bofill, involve the creation of yet more leisure area on reclaimed land, and most spectacularly, the building of a 150-metre/450-foot-high, sail-shaped hotel; the exact dimensions of the project, however, have yet to meet with final approval from City Hall.

A famous feature of Barceloneta was that it used to be possible to combine the district's two pleasures in the traditional paella and seafood restaurants that lined the beach. These basic *chiringuitos* were closed down by city edict in 1991, but have (slightly) revived in smarter

The best Beaches

For volleyball
The **Platja de la Nova Icària**, just beyond the Port Olímpic, is the scene for smacking balls over the net. Map p325 F7.

For renting sea kayaks
The **Base Nàutica at the Mar Bella** beach has kayaks, windsurfing boards and catamarans. See p244 and p255.

For nudists
The **Platja de la Mar Bella,** north of the **Base Nàutica**, located behind a large dune, is home of the city's official nudist beach.

For night-time parties
The **Platja de la Nova Mar Bella**, the last beach heading north, hosts occasional all-night parties in summer; look for Punta Negra flyers for details.

form. For Barceloneta, the city's massive reworking of the old port – and the transformation of **Passeig Joan de Borbó** from dockyard service road to waterside promenade – has in effect meant a complete re-orientation of the area through 180°, from looking out to sea to overlooking the port. Some former *chiringuito* owners have therefore gradually been encouraged to reopen, alongside smart all-new restaurants, on the new harbourside *passeig* and in the **Palau de Mar**, while other dock buildings have been torn down to open up a view of the harbour and Montjuïc that most Barceloneta residents had been unaware of all their lives.

The Vila Olímpica

In 1986 Barcelona was elected Olympic City for 1992, and the whole population seemed to pour into the streets to celebrate. Then the job began of preparing to build what would soon be called the city's newest *barri*, the Olympic Village, most ambitious of all the 1992 projects. It was a local cliché to say that Barcelona had turned its back to the sea, with barriers of railways, factories and dirty industrial roads that since the 1850s had cut its citizens off from their abandoned, refuse-strewn beaches. Now, the plan was to open out.

Not since Cerdà or Gaudí has anyone had such an impact on the face of Barcelona as the architects Oriol Bohigas, Josep Martorell, long-time English resident David Mackay and Albert Puigdomènech, who were entrusted with the overall design of the all-new district, to be built on reclaimed industrial land. Constructed in just two years, it was initially named Nova Icària to recall the utopian socialist community that briefly existed in this area in the last century, but the name has never stuck. As well as a range of services some 2,000 apartments were built, which it was hoped would provide low-cost housing once the athletes had vacated them after the Games. However, economic realities have since dictated otherwise.

Those who have paid the relatively high prices and acquired flats in the village have at their disposal an impressive range of new leisure areas and seafront parks. Taken as a whole the project is spectacular, even by Barcelona's standards. By far the most successful part of the Vila is the **Port Olímpic**, the 743-mooring space leisure marina built from nothing since 1988, now lined with bars and restaurants packed with crowds of all ages every weekend night of the year (*see chapters* **Restaurants** and **Nightlife**). By day, the Port Olímpic is also the place to go to hire sailing boats (*see chapter* **Sport & Fitness**).

Further inland, Ildefons Cerdà's original concept for the Eixample was taken as an inspiration, with semi-open blocks built around services and garden areas. Every stop had to be pulled out to get things ready for July 1992 – some sections, such as the skyscraper **Hotel Arts**, missed the date and were not inaugurated until a good while later.

The final effect, however, is of a rather cold, un-Mediterranean suburb, although the waterway parallel to C/Moscou and the red brick of **Plaça Tirant lo Blanc** soften the harshness. The glass and stone gateway buildings to the *barri* create a forbidding impression; there are few corner shops or cafés; the spiky metal pergolas on Avda Icària look like a grim parody of trees. Even the jokey sculpture in Parc de Carles I, *David i Goliat*, leaves one with the feeling that this is a world in which the Goliaths usually slay the Davids. However a touch of humour can be found in the same park, in the enormous six-metre (20-foot) sculpture of the lower half of a human body. By Basque artist Eduardo Úrculo, it has inevitably become known as *el culo de Úrculo*, Úrculo's arse. And, as in many suburbs, the Vila's open spaces are colonised by cyclists and rollerbladers at weekends.

Globus Tùristic

Passeig de Circumval.lació corner C/de Wellington (93 597 11 40/www.globusbcn.es). Metro Ciutadella-Vila Olímpica/14 bus. **Open** *Oct-May* 10.30am-7.30pm Mon-Thur; 10.30am-9.30pm Sat; 10.30am-8.30pm Sun. *June-Sept* 10am-9pm Mon-Fri; 10am-11pm Sat, Sun. **Admission** 1,900ptas; 1,100 concessions; free under-3s. **Credit** MC, V. **Map** p325 E7.

For those who have been unable to book a top floor room at the Hotel Arts, this child-safe balloon ride – located behind the Arts near the Zoo – offers stunning views of the city and sea. The only drawback is the all-too-short duration of the trip – a mere 15 minutes.

Frank Gehry's *Fish* at the **Vila Olimpica**.

Montjuïc

Barcelona's magic mountain has unique parks, Olympic installations and stunning views of the city.

Whether the name means 'mountain of the Jews' or 'mountain of Jupiter', the huge, sprawling mass of Montjuïc, rising over the city from beside the port, is one of Barcelona's most loved features. This hill of 200 hectares (494 acres) is a world of its own, encompassing any number of quite different areas. It's not a district, for hardly anyone lives there, but it is a delightful place for a stroll. From all over the hill you get wonderful views: they're particularly spectacular by the **Palau Nacional** and at **Miramar**, overlooking the harbour.

According to one legend of the origins of Barcelona, it was founded by Hercules and populated by the crew of the ninth ship (*barca nona*) that went with him on his labours. Hercules then sat on Montjuïc to admire his creation. But it also has other associations. The **Castell de Montjuïc**, built in the 17th century, became a symbol of the suppression of Catalan liberties after 1714. As a prison and torture centre for rebels and radicals – or those deemed as such – it inspired fear and loathing for two centuries. The castle was finally handed over to Barcelona by the army in 1960, but it still houses the **Museu Militar**.

The military refused to allow much building on the mountain until well into the 20th century, and it was not until the run-up to the 1929 Exhibition that Montjuïc was landscaped. Today Montjuïc, like so many parts of Barcelona, has been earmarked for some big changes, especially on its still semi-wild, mysterious southern flank. A 'macropark', with lake included, is projected between Miramar and the vast cemetery on the mountain's south side. The old Montjuïc funfair has already closed, perhaps because it was a bit vulgar and shabby for the planners. As in Poble Nou, it is hoped everything will be ready for the new magical year, 2004.

Despite all the activity on the mountain, and its proximity to the city centre, it's surprisingly easy to find peaceful, shaded places among the many park areas. Below the castle, on the steep flank nearest the port, are the **Jardins Costa i Llobera**, which abound in exotic plants such as a Mexican cactus popularly known as *el seient de la sogra*, 'mother-in-law's seat'. Not far above, on the Montjuïc road, Avda Miramar, are the **Jardins del Mirador**, from where there is

a spectacular view over the harbour. Carry on along this road away from the sea and you will reach the **Jardins Cinto Verdaguer**, with a beautiful pond, flowers and more views; a little further on are the municipal swimming pool, spectacularly rebuilt for the 1992 diving events, and the **Fundació Miró**. Continue uphill to reach the **Anella Olímpica**, with the main Olympic buildings and the **Bernat Picornell** swimming pool. If you want to cut the walk short, Montjuïc has several fun means of transport to help you up the hill (*see pp90-1*).

If you turn right from the Fundació Joan Miró and head downhill you will come upon a veritable orgy of monumentalist and *Noucentista* architecture from 1929, which now contains the area's other main cultural centres. There are museums (the **MNAC**, the **Museu d'Arqueologia**, the **Museu Etnològic** – for all, *see chapter* **Museums**), and the **Mercat de les Flors** and **Teatre Grec** theatres. Plans are under way to integrate these venues into a Ciutat del Teatre, a complete theatre complex (*see chapter* **Theatre**). Further down are the **Mies van der Rohe Pavilion** and the ineffable **Poble Espanyol**, and next to Plaça d'Espanya are the Trade Fair buildings (the **Fira**). Across the road from the Mies Pavilion, a *Modernista* factory, the **Casaramona**, is being made into yet another new cultural centre, by the Fundació la Caixa (*see p114-5*). As you approach Plaça d'Espanya, Carles Buigas' water-and-light spectacular the **Font Màgica**, however corny, never fails to round off a memorable walk.

L'Anella Olímpica (The Olympic Ring)

Passeig Olímpic, Montjuïc (93 426 20 89). Metro Espanya, or Paral.lel, then Funicular de Montjuïc/50 bus. **Information** *Estadi Olímpic (93 426 20 89); Palau Sant Jordi (93 481 11 92); Palau d'Esports (93 481 10 93/ 93 423 15 41).* **Map** p323 A6.
The core area from the 1992 Games consists of a compact hub of buildings in contrasting styles. The **Estadi Olímpic** – now home to the city's 'second' football team, Espanyol – although entirely new, was built within the façade of an existing 1929 stadium by a design team led by Federico Correa and Alfonso Milà. Next to it is the most original and attractive of the Olympic facilities, Arata Isozaki's **Palau Sant Jordi** indoor hall, with a vast metal

roof built on the ground and raised into place by hydraulic jacks. It now regularly serves as a concert venue. In the *plaça* in front locals gather on Sundays for family walks and picnics, next to Santiago Calatrava's remarkable bow-like **Telefònica tower**; further along is Barcelona's best swimming pool, the **Bernat Picornell** – predating the Games, but rebuilt for them – and the Sports University, designed by Ricard Bofill and Peter Hodgkinson in their neo-classical style. At the foot of the hill by Plaça d'Espanya is another sports hall, the Palau d'Esports, built in the 1960s but rebuilt for 1992.

Font Màgica de Montjuïc

Plaça d'Espanya. Metro Espanya/bus all routes to Plaça d'Espanya. **Fountains** *23 June-23 Sept* 8pm-midnight; *music* 9.30-11.30pm Thur-Sun, public holidays. **Map** p323 A5.

Outrageously over-the-top but not to be missed, the 1929 'magic fountain' swells and dances to Tchaikovsky's *Nutcracker*, Abba hits and other favourites, showing off its kaleidoscope of pastel colours, while searchlights play in a giant fan pattern over the palace dome. Fantastic.

Funicular de Montjuïc

Metro Paral.lel-Avda Miramar (93 443 08 59/ www.tmd.net). Metro Paral.lel/20, 36, 57, 64, 91, 157 bus. **Open** *Nov-Apr* 10.45am-8pm Sat, Sun. *Apr-June* 10.45am-8pm daily. *June-Oct* 11am-10pm daily. **Tickets** single 250ptas; return 400ptas. **Discounts** BT. **No credit cards.** **Map** p323-4 B-C6.

Mostly underground, so not much sightseeing, but the fast, cog-wheel train brings you out well placed for the Fundació Joan Miró and Miramar. It connects with the Telefèric.

Galeria Olímpica

Estadi Olímpic, Parc de Montjuïc (93 426 06 60). Metro Paral.lel, then Funicular de Montjuïc/61 bus. **Open** *Oct-Mar* 10am-1pm, 4-6pm Mon-Fri; 10am-2pm Sat, Sun. *Apr-June* 10am-2pm, 4-7pm, Mon-Sat; 10am-2pm Sun. *July-Sept* 10am-2pm, 4-8pm, Mon-Sat; 10am-2pm Sun. **Admission** 400ptas; 170-350ptas concessions. **Discounts** Groups, BC, BT. **Credit** AmEx, MC, V. **Map** p323 A6.

The small space is chock-full of photos and video fragments, and a lot of peripheral paraphernalia, such as a huge inflatable Cobi mascot and designer volleyball holders. There is a large video library, but it's open only to researchers. The best part is a section of costumes, props and scenery – some by the atre group La Fura dels Baus – from the opening and closing ceremonies. A spectacular big-screen film on the Games is uninformative but gives you some feel of the event.

Montjuïc Tourist Train

Plaça d'Espanya. Metro Espanya/bus all routes to Plaça d'Espanya. **Dates** *June-Sept* every 30min, 11am-8.30pm daily. **Tickets** 300ptas; 225ptas concessions; all-day ticket 500ptas, 400ptas concessions. **Discounts** BT. **No credit cards.** **Map** p323 A-B5.

Riding high above the **Jardins Cinto Verdaguer**. *See p89.*

Not a train but an open trolley pulled by a truck, which goes up Montjuïc to Miramar.

Pavelló Barcelona (Pavelló Mies van der Rohe)

Avda. Marqués de Comillas (93 423 40 16/ www.miesbcn.com). Metro Espanya/bus all routes to Plaça Espanya. **Open** *Nov-Mar* 10am-8pm daily. **Admission** 500ptas; 250pts concessions; free under-18s. **Credit** (shop only) MC, V. **Map** p323 A5.

The German Pavilion for the 1929 Exhibition, by Ludwig Mies van der Rohe, was also home to the 'Barcelona chair', copied in millions of office waiting rooms across the world. The pavilion was a founding monument of modern rationalist architecture, with a revolutionary use of stone, glass and space. It was demolished after the Exhibition, but in 1986 a replica was built on the same site. Purists may think of it as a synthetic inferior of the original pavilion, but the elegance and simplicity of the design are still a striking demonstration of what rationalist architecture could do before it was reduced to production-line clichés.

Poble Espanyol

*Avda. Marqués de Comillas (93 325 78 66/
www.poble-espanyol.com). Metro Espanya/bus all
routes to Plaça Espanya* . **Open** *Sep-June* 9am-8pm
Mon; 9am-2am Tue-Sat; 9am-midnight Sun. *July, Aug*
9am-8pm Mon; 9am-2am Tue-Thur; 9am-4am Fri;
9am-midnight Sun. **Admission** 975ptas; 550-
775ptas concessions; free under-7s; group discounts.
Discounts BC, BT. **Credit** MC, V. **Map** p323 A5.
As part of the preparations for the 1929 Exhibition,
someone had the bright idea of building, in one
enclosed area, examples of traditional architecture
from every region in Spain. The result was the Poble
Espanyol, or 'Spanish village'. Inside it, a Castilian
square leads to an Andalusian church, then to repli-
cas of village houses from Aragon, and so on. There
are bars and restaurants of every kind, including
vegetarian, and over 60 shops. Many of its businesses are workshops in which craftspeople make
and sell Spanish folk artefacts – ceramics, embroidery, fans, metalwork, candles and so on. Some of
the work is quite attractive, some tacky, and prices
are generally high. Outside, street performers recre-
ate bits of Catalan and Spanish folklore; there are
special children's shows, and the 'Barcelona
Experience', an audio-visual history presentation
(available in English).

The Poble has an unmistakeable tourist-trap air,
but it does have its fun side, and many of its buildings and squares are genuinely attractive. It also
tries hard to promote itself as a night-spot, with
karaoke bars, Cuban dinner-and-dance restaurants,
discos and a flamenco show, and dance bands and
music groups perform regularly in the main square.
Attached to the village is the bar that was once the
pinnacle of Barcelona design-bardom, **Torres de
Avila**, and lately one of the city's most hip clubs,
La Terrrazza/Discothèque, is now located at the
back of the Poble (*see chapter* **Nightlife**).

Telefèric de Montjuïc (cable cars)

*Estació Funicular, Avda Miramar (93 443 08 59/
www.tmd.net). Metro Paral.lel, Funicular de
Montjuic/61 bus.* **Open** *Nov-Mar* 11.30am-7.15pm,
Sat, Sun. *April-May, mid Sept-Oct* 11.30am-7.15pm
daily. *June-mid Sept* 11.15am-8pm Mon-Fri; 11.15am-
9pm Sat, Sun. **Tickets** single 475ptas; return
675ptas, 550ptas concessions. **Discounts** BT.
No credit cards. Map p323 B6.
From outside the funicular station, the Montjuïc
cable cars run up to the castle at the top. Vertigo suf-
ferers might not enjoy the trip, but there are superb
views over Montjuïc and the port.

Paral.lel & Poble Sec

Back in the old city, on the south side of the
Raval near the Drassanes, if you stand by the
surviving stretch of 14th-century city wall at
Santa Madrona and look across the broad street
towards Montjuïc, you will see a *barri* lining the
side of the hill. The street is Avinguda Paral.lel,
a curious name that derives from the fact that it
coincides exactly with 41° 44' latitude north,
one of Ildefons Cerdà's more eccentric conceits.
The district is called Poble Sec. The avenue was
the prime centre of Barcelona nightlife – often
called its 'Montmartre' – in the first half of
the 20th century, and was full of theatres,
nightclubs and music halls. A statue on the
corner with C/Nou de la Rambla commemorates
Raquel Meller, a legendary star of the street
who went on to equal celebrity around the
world. She stands outside Barcelona's notorious
modern live-porn venue, the Bagdad. Apart
from this, while there are still theatres and
cinemas along the Paral.lel, most of its cabarets
have disappeared. A real end of an era came in
1997 when El Molino, most celebrated of the
avenue's traditional, ultra-vulgar old music
halls, suddenly shut up shop.

The name Poble Sec means 'dry village',
fitting testimony to the fact that as late as 1894
the poor workers of the *barri* celebrated with
dancing the installation of the area's first street
fountain, which still stands, in C/Margarit. By
1914 some 5,000 people lived in shanty towns
up where the district meets Montjuïc. During
the riots of the Setmana Tràgica, 'tragic
week', in 1909, more religious buildings
were destroyed here than in any other part
of Barcelona (*see p19*).

On the stretch of the Paral.lel opposite the
city walls three tall chimneys stand
incongruously in the middle of modern office
blocks. They are all that remains of the Anglo-
Canadian-owned power station known locally
as *La Canadença* ('The Canadian'), centre of the
city's largest general strike, in 1919. Beside the
chimneys an open space has been created – the
Parc de les Tres Xemeneies, now popular
with rollerbladers.

Today Poble Sec remains a friendly, working
class area of quiet, relaxed streets and squares.
It has plenty of cheap bars, some more eccentric
bars (*see p167*) and several reasonable
restaurants (*see pp145-6*). Towards the Paral.lel
there are some distinguished *Modernista*
buildings, which local legend has maintained
were built for *artistas* from the cabarets by rich
sugar-daddies. At No.12 on C/Tapioles there is
a beautiful, extremely narrow wooden
Modernista door with typically writhing
ironwork, while at C/Elkano 4 don't miss **La
Casa de les Rajoles**, which has a strange
white mosaic façade that gives an impression
of weightlessness. Poble Sec is also one of the
most characterful access points to Montjuïc,
and as you penetrate further into the densely
populated *barri* the streets grow steeper, some
becoming narrow lanes of steps climbing up
the mountain that eventually provide a
superb view of the city.

Sightseeing

You haven't seen anything yet

The Eixample

Barcelona's economic and commercial core is a treasure-trove of *Modernista* gems.

Modernisme: a retrospective.

A fateful decision was taken in the 1850s when, after Barcelona was finally given permission to expand beyond its medieval walls, the plan chosen (by the government in Madrid) was the regular gridiron of Ildefons Cerdà. Opinion in Barcelona was much more favourable to the fan-shaped design of the municipal architect Antoni Rovira i Trias, a reproduction of which can be seen at the foot of a sculpture of the man in Plaça Rovira i Trias, in Gràcia (*see p15*).

With time, though, the 'Extension' (*Eixample/Ensanche*) has become as much – if not more – of a distinctive feature of Barcelona as the medieval city. With its love of straight lines, parallels, diagonals and meridians, Cerdà's plan is a monumental example of 19th-century rationalism. The more utopian features of the plan, however – building on only two sides of each block, height limits of just two or three storeys, and gardens in the middle of the blocks – were quickly discarded. Today, most of the interior courtyards are car parks, workshops or shopping centres. The garden around the **Torre de les Aigües** water tower at C/Llúria 56 is one of the few courtyards where one can get a glimpse of how attractive Cerdà's plan could have been.

The Eixample was built up between 1860 and the 1920s, mostly after 1890. This coincided with – and vitally encouraged – the great flowering of *Modernisme*, the distinctive Catalan variant of art nouveau. The equal weight *Modernistes* gave to decorative and fine arts is reflected throughout the district, in countless shop fronts, hallways, and small gems of panelling or stained glass.

The Eixample is the economic and commercial core of Barcelona, with banks and insurance companies, fashion shops and arcades, any number of restaurants, good cinemas and the best art galleries and bookshops, as well as its world-famous architecture. However, the fabric is showing its age, to the extent that people have been killed in the last ten years by crumbling pieces of façades falling into the streets. Over 3,000 buildings have undergone face-lifts, but just under a tenth of all the façades in the Eixample still require urgent repairs. As a residential area the district also has an ageing population. Traffic, which has become more and more dominant in the long one-way streets, is a major source of problems. The city council has set up a Pro-Eixample project to revitalise the area,

Walk 3: The details of *Modernisme*

The grander (or more outrageous) *Modernista* buildings are easy to find; however, one of the most striking things about the style is the way it appears at so many points in the city's fabric, often in unexpected places. This route (shown in blue on *pp320-1, 324-5*) covers a selection of lesser-known *Modernista* creations. The buildings are nearly all private, but it's often possible to look in the entrances; however, most also require repair work, so there's always a risk they may be under scaffolding.

The walk begins at Plaça Urquinaona (Map D5). From there, go along C/Ausiàs Marc. At No.20 is **Casa Manuel Felip**, designed by a little-known architect, Telmo Fernández, in 1901, with tall graceful galleries to the left and right which connect the first and second floors. At No.31 is the **Farmàcia Nordbeck** (1905), with a rich dark wood exterior. *Modernisme* and pharmacies were peculiarly closely associated in the Eixample.

At the next corner, with C/Girona, is **Casa Antoni Roger** (1890), at C/Ausiàs Marc 33-5, by one of the more prominent (and bombastic) *Modernista* architects, Enric Sagnier. Further along Ausiàs Marc, on the next block at Nos.42-6, is **Casa Antonia Burés** (1906), a truly extraordinary building by another forgotten architect, Juli Batllevell. Two magnificent stone columns in the shape of trees seem to be holding up the building, anticipating the same motif in the Parc Güell.

Turn left at C/Bailen, then left again into C/Casp, and walk back two blocks. At No.48 is **Casa Calvet** (1900), Gaudí's first commissioned apartment block, which now contains an excellent restaurant of the same name (*see p147*). The symmetrical façade seems very un-Gaudí-like, but the interlacing wrought iron strips around the gallery – with mushroom motifs – and immense iron door-knockers betray the 'master's touch'. On the next block, still on C/Casp at No.22, is **Casa Llorenç Camprubí** (1901). The long, narrow windows in its (huge) first-floor gallery and very neo-Gothic windows give a superb impression of verticality.

Turn right up C/Pau Claris, past **Laie** bookshop. On the next corner, at Gran Via 650, is another extravagant *Modernista* pharmacy, **Farmàcia Vilardell** (1914). From there, walk along Gran Via three blocks, cross over and turn left into C/Girona. **Casa Jacinta Ruiz**, designed by Ramon Viñolas in 1909, is at No.54. Glassed-in *galeries* characterise most *Modernista* houses, but here the spectacular four-storey gallery takes up the entire façade, and is almost modern rather than *Modernista* in the cleanness of its lines. The wrought iron of the balconies is also especially delicate.

Another block up, at the corner of C/Consell de Cent, is **Forn Serrat**, C/Girona 73. This bakery looks a little rundown;

one aim of which is to re-humanise its streets by recovering for communal use the inner courtyard of each block.

When the Eixample was first built and until the 1920s the rail line to Sarrià (now the FGC) went above ground up C/Balmes, effectively cutting the district in two. Ever since then, the grid has been regarded as having two halves. The Dreta ('right' – to the right of C/Balmes as you are looking uphill) contains the most distinguished *Modernista* architecture, the main museums and the main shopping avenues. The Esquerra ('left' – to the left of C/Balmes) was built slightly later, and now contains some great markets. Together they have formed the centre of Catalan middle-class life for most of the last hundred years, and to some extent, despite considerable migration to quieter areas out of town, they still do. To those unused to such straight lines they can be disorientating, but they form a very special urban environment, with an atmosphere all of its own.

The Dreta

The great avenue of the **Passeig de Gràcia** is the centre of the district. It is famous for its architectural masterpieces, built as elegant residences, such as Gaudí's **La Pedrera** and the **Mansana de la Discòrdia**, with buildings by Gaudí, Puig i Cadafalch and Domènech i Montaner. The Passeig de Gràcia and parallel Rambla Catalunya are fashionable shopping streets, a centre for both stylish arcades like **Bulevard Rosa** and design emporia like **Vinçon**. Window shopping for art has traditionally been concentrated close by in C/Consell de Cent between Balmes and Rambla Catalunya, and nearby there is too one of the most impressive of all Barcelona's art spaces, the **Fundació Tàpies**.

The cafés on Rambla Catalunya are pleasant, but pricey, and a favourite meeting place for affluent local residents on summer evenings. Cheaper possibilities for a stopover on a walk

Casa Comalat. *See p95.*

outside, though, it has curving woodwork framing a picture of a girl with bales of wheat and ears of corn – a classic example of the *Modernista* tendency to round off work with a grand flourish.

At C/Girona 86, in the next block, is **Casa Isabel Pomar** (1906), an almost bizarrely narrow building by Joan Rubió i Bellver. Its neo-Gothic roof and pinnacle, like a church in the sky, may have been an architect's joke. Cross C/Aragó, and continue to C/València. Turn right to go to the next corner (C/Bailen) and the marvellous **Casa Manuel Llopis** (1902), No.339, by Antoni Gallissà and Gaudí's collaborator Josep Maria Jujol. It has angular galleries running almost the whole height of the building, together with very elaborate thin brickwork and lovely inlaid tilework.

If you retrace your steps along C/València and continue for another three blocks, at the corner with C/Roger de Llúria you will come upon a veritable explosion of *Modernista* architecture. At No.312 (Llúria 80) is **Casa Villanueva** (1909), with graceful thin columns, elaborate glass galleries and a needle-topped tower. Opposite at No.285, **Casa Jaume Forn** (1909) has beautiful stained glass and a magnificent carved door. Also on this crossing is **Queviures Murrià** grocery, with its tiled advertising posters, created from designs by Ramon Casas, still in place (*see p188*), and down the street at C/Roger de Llúria 74 is one more pharmacy, **Farmàcia Argelaguet** (1904), which has fine stained glass and floral decoration on the walls.

At the next junction uphill, C/Roger de Llúria–C/Mallorca, there are two major buildings by Domènech i Montaner. To the left, at Mallorca 278, is the **Palau Montaner** (1893), built for his own family and now government offices. Close by at Mallorca 291 is **Casa Thomas** (1905), now, fittingly, home to the **BD** design company and store (*see chapter* **Shopping**). Much less known is the elegant **Casa Dolors Xiró** (1913), C/Mallorca 302, by Josep Barenys. To finish, go up just another block and a half to Puig i Cadafalch's neo-Gothic fantasy house the **Casa Terrades**, or *Casa de les Punxes* (*see below*).

around the area are **La Bodegueta** and the **Bracafé** (*see chapter* **Cafés & Bars**). This part of the Eixample is also the place to find some of the city's celebrated 1980s design bars and clubs, which, after a long slide down from the pinnacle of fashion, now seem to be on the way up again. Notable from a design point of view is **Nick Havanna** – currently known as **Row** on weekend nights – near the corner of C/Balmes and C/Rosselló.

As well as the most renowned *Modernista* buildings, the streets around Passeig de Gràcia are full of other extraordinary examples of work from that period, in the shape of whole buildings or just in small details. The section of the Eixample between C/Muntaner and C/Roger de Flor has been labelled the Quadrat d'Or or 'Golden Square' of *Modernisme*, and plaques have been placed on 150 protected buildings. A guide to them is available (with an English edition) from most city bookshops.

Particularly of note are the hallway and exuberant decoration of **Casa Comalat**, designed by Salvador Valeri in 1906 (Avda Diagonal 442-C/Còrsega 316). On Avda Diagonal are two characteristic buildings by Puig i Cadafalch, the **Casa Vidal Quadras** (No.373), now the **Museu de la Música**, and the **Casa Terrades** (No.416-420), an extraordinary neo-Gothic fantasy with pointed towers that gained it the alternative name of *Casa de les Punxes* ('house of spikes'). Not far away – in the block on the corner of C/València and C/Bruc – there is a market by Rovira i Trias, the **Mercat de la Concepció** reopened after extensive repair work that has saved the lovely tilework of its roof. This is the market where it is possible to buy flowers 24 hours a day, although its flower stalls are now inside the building, rather than in the street.

The outer Eixample above the Diagonal is a mainly residential area, for the most part built after 1910, but with some striking Modernist

Sightseeing

buildings such as Puig i Cadafalch's 1901 **Casa Macaya**, now the cultural centre of the **Fundació La Caixa** (*see pp114-5*). The area is dominated, though, by the towering mass of the Sagrada Família. Not far away is another great *Modernista* project, Domènech i Montaner's **Hospital de Sant Pau**. It and Gaudí's creation stand at opposite ends of Avda Gaudí, made into a pleasant walkway in 1985.

Hospital de la Santa Creu i Sant Pau

C/Sant Antoni María Claret 167 (93 291 90 00). Metro Hospital de Sant Pau/15, 19, 20, 35, 45, 47, 50, 51, 92, N1, N4 bus. **Map** p321 F4.
Influenced by garden-city ideas, Domènech's hospital became the most useful of *Modernista* projects, as well as one of the most beautiful. Begun in 1901 as a long-overdue replacement for the old hospital in the Raval, it was not finished until 1930, by the architect's son. It consists of 48 pavilions, separated by gardens and linked by underground tunnels. A wealth of sculptures, murals and mosaics strikes the eye everywhere, each pavilion having its own ornamental identity. As a place for a patient suffering from a not-too-distressing illness, it really is wonderful – though not, alas, for much longer: Domènech's design is considered unsuitable for modern medicine, and plans are currently afoot to move some of its services elsewhere. While it is a working hospital visitors are free to wander through the courtyards and gardens.

La 'Mansana de la Discòrdia'

Passeig de Gràcia 35-45 (93 488 01 39). Metro Passeig de Gràcia/bus all routes to Passeig de Gràcia. Façades explained in English at 10am, 12pm, 1pm, 3pm, 4pm and 6pm. **Admission** 200ptas; free with **RM**. **Map** p320 D4.
The 'Block of Discord', on Passeig de Gràcia between Carrers Consell de Cent and Aragó, is so-called because on it, almost alongside each other, stand buildings by the three greatest figures of Catalan Modernist architecture, all constructed between 1900 and 1907 in wildly clashing styles. On the corner of C/Consell de Cent at number 35 is Domènech i Muntaner's **Casa Lleó Morera**, a classic *Modernista* building of exuberantly convoluted, decorative forms. Three doors up the street at No. 41 is Puig i Cadafalch's Gothic-influenced **Casa Amatller**, and next to that is Gaudí's **Casa Batlló**, rising like a giant fish out of the pavement (*see also chapter* **Architecture**). The Casa Lleó Morera is now a **Centre del Modernisme**, with a small exhibition on the style, and the hub of the **Ruta del Modernisme** tour (*see p65*). Visitors to the centre also get to see the first floor of the building, which has a superb *Modernista* interior, and fabulous stained glass.

Parc de l'Estació del Nord

C/Nàpols. Metro Arc de Triomf/40, 42, 54, 141 bus. **Open** (daily) *Nov-Feb* 10am-6pm. *Mar, Oct* 10am-7pm. *Apr, Sept* 10am-8pm. *May-Aug* 10am-9pm. **Map** p325 E-F5-6.
Behind the Estació de Nord bus station is this very striking park created in 1988. It's an open, grassy crescent with very few trees or benches, just flat ceramic forms in turquoise and cobalt, swooping and curving through the park: an earthwork sculpture by Beverly Pepper.

La Pedrera

Passeig de Gràcia 92, C/Provença 261-265 (93 484 59 00/www.caixacat.es/fund_cat.html). Metro Diagonal/7, 16, 17, 22, 24, 28 bus. **Open** 10am-8pm daily (*mid June-mid Sept* also 9pm-1am Fri, Sat). *Guided tours* (English) 6pm Mon-Fri; 11am Sat, Sun, public holidays. **Admission** 600ptas; 350ptas concessions; free under-12s. **Discounts** BC, BT, RM, Airticket. **Credit** MC, V. **Map** p320 D4.
The last non-religious building Gaudí worked on represents his most radical departure from a recognisably *Modernista* style. Built entirely using columns and parabolic arches, with no supporting walls, and supposedly without a single straight line or right-angled corner, this curving, globular apartment block, also known as the **Casa Milà**, contrasts strikingly with the angularity of much of the Eixample. Its revolutionary features were not appreciated by the Milà family – who paid for it – nor by contemporary opinion, which christened it La Pedrera ('The Stone Quarry') as a joke.
It is now owned by the Fundació Caixa de Catalunya, which has restored the building beautifully. One floor is an exhibition space, while in another is a permanent exhibition, the **Espai Gaudí** (*see pp108-9*), and the fourth floor contains the **Pis de la Pedrera**, a reconstruction of a *Modernista* apartment interior of the 1900s. Informative guided tours (in English, Catalan or Spanish) allow you to see more of the Pedrera's main features and especially the roof, with its extraordinary semi-abstract sculptures (actually ventilation shafts and chimneys). In winter tours may not continue after dark, even though the exhibition space stays open; in summer, however, the roof is opened as **La Pedrera de Nit**, a very special terrace bar (*see p247*).

Temple Expiatori de la Sagrada Família

Plaça Sagrada Família, C/Mallorca 401 (93 207 30 31). Metro Sagrada Família/10, 19, 33, 34, 43, 44, 50, 51, 101 bus. **Open** (daily) *Nov-Feb* 9am-6pm. *Mar, Sep-Oct* 9am-7pm. *Apr-Aug* 9am-8pm. **Admission** 800ptas; 600ptas concessions; free under-10s. Lifts to the spires 200ptas. **Discounts** BC, BT. **Credit** (groups only) MC, V. **Map** p321 F4.
It is a supreme irony what has become the emblematic symbol of the city and Gaudí's masterpiece (or monsterpiece, depending on your point of view) was neither begun nor finished by the great man. The project was initiated in 1882 by another architect, Francisco del Villar, and Gaudí's involvement did not begin until 1891. He did, however, transform the design completely and dedicate over 40 years of his

Sagrada Família.

Sightseeing

Not a lot of bull

Plaza de Toros Monumental

Gran Via de les Corts Catalanes 749,
Eixample (93 215 95 70 main office).
Metro Monumental/6, 7, 18, 56, 62 bus.
Open (Apr-Sept) *Museum* 10.30am-2pm,
4-7pm, Mon-Sat; 10.30am-1pm Sun.
Bullfights 5-6pm Sun. **Admission** *Museum*
375ptas. *Bullfights* 2,600-14,000ptas.
No credit cards. Map p325 F5.
This archetypal Spanish activity has never
had a very strong following in Barcelona,
and one of the city's two bullrings has
closed. The other, the Monumental, still
holds fights on Sundays in season, and
has a small museum. Also, the Catalan
government dislikes bullfighting, and
among new restrictive regulations on
the *corrida* is a minimum age limit of
14 for seeing a bullfight.

life to the building – the last 18 years exclusively –
often sleeping on the site. Only the crypt, the apse
and the four towers of the Façade of the Nativity,
along C/Marina, were completed in his lifetime.
Every element in the decoration, much of it carved
from life, was conceived by Gaudí as having a precise symbolic meaning, and he was deeply opposed
to the idea of anyone appreciating the building outside its religious context. An essential part of any
visit to the Sagrada Família is an attempt to climb
the towers beyond the level that can be reached by
lift: this gives an extraordinary sensation of walking out into space. Descent via the spiral staircase,
however, is definitely not recommended for those
suffering from vertigo.

The **museum** in the crypt contains models and a
history of the project and other information on Gaudí
(*see p109*). The architect himself is buried beneath
the nave of the basilica, and steps towards his canon-
isation have been taken by Catalan bishops. Work
on the temple was resumed in 1952 by some of
Gaudí's assistants, who drew up plans based on
some of his sketches and on what they remembered
of the great man's ideas (he never used detailed
plans). The work has accelerated considerably since
the 1980s. Josep Maria Subirachs has completed the
new towers of the Façade of the Passion along
C/Sardenya – with sculptures that horrify many
Gaudí admirers – and is now sculpting the apostles
on the bronze entrance to the cathedral.

The second sculptor working on the building is
Japanese, Etsuro Sotoo, who seems to be adhering
more faithfully to Gaudí's intentions, with six flowing, modest musicians, at the rear of the temple.
Among the next parts due for completion are the
vaults of the principal nave, which would for the

first time give the Sagrada Família a substantial
roof, but (as is often the case) work has been
nowhere near advanced enough to meet the ambitious schedule. Work has also begun on the construction of four massive columns made of porphyry
– the hardest stone in existence – to support the
great dome, which will make the temple once again
the tallest building in Barcelona. No one is prepared
to hazard a guess as to when it will be finished.

The Esquerra

This side of the Eixample quickly became the
new area for some activities of the city that the
middle classes did not want to see on their
doorsteps. A huge slaughterhouse was built in
the extreme left of the area, knocked down and
replaced by the **Parc Joan Miró** in 1979. The
functional **Hospital Clínic** was sited on two
blocks between C/Còrsega and C/Provença, and
further out still on C/Entença is the city's 1905
Modelo prison, the relocation of which outside
the city is currently undergoing negotiation.
There are two great markets, the **Ninot**, by the
hospital, and the **Mercat de Sant Antoni**, on
the edge of the Raval, which is taken over by a
great second-hand **book market** every
Sunday morning. This is also an area for
academic institutions, from the vast **Escola
Industrial** on C/Comte d'Urgell to the original
Universitat central building on Plaça
Universitat, constructed in 1842.

Modernista architecture does extend over
into the Esquerra (as the Quadrat d'Or concept
recognises), with superb examples such as the
Casa Societat Torres Germans (C/Paris 180-2)
from 1905. The area also has Barcelona's
biggest concentration of gay nightlife in the
streets around the crossing of C/Consell de Cent
and C/Muntaner. Beyond the hospital the outer
Eixample has no great sights, but leads up to
Plaça Francesc Macià, developed since the
1960s as the centre of the new business district,
and the main crossroads of affluent Barcelona.
Beyond the office blocks of the plaça lie the
fashionable business, shopping and residential
areas of the Zona Alta.

Parc Joan Miró (Parc de l'Escorxador)

C/Tarragona, Eixample. Metro Tarragona, Espanya/
bus all routes to Plaça d'Espanya. **Open** (daily) *Nov-*
Feb 10am-6pm. *Mar, Oct* 10am-7pm. *Apr, Sept*
10am-8pm. *May-Aug* 10am-9pm. **Map** p323 B4-5.
This park takes up four blocks of the city but feels
like much more. Built on the site of a huge slaughterhouse, it mainly comprises stubby *palmera* trees.
There is, however, a surprising tranquillity to the
large dirt space, which is helped by Miró's huge
phallic sculpture *Dona i Ocell* (Woman and Bird) rising out of the pool for which it was designed.

Gràcia & Other Districts

Just a little way off the beaten track await tranquil squares, great mountain views, and the hum of daily life in charming neighbourhoods.

Gràcia

'Gràcia – independència' and even 'Freedom for Gràcia' can sometimes be seen on T-shirts here. This isn't a demand for the district to become one of the smallest states in the world but rather a half-serious petition to be separated from Barcelona, to which it was annexed in 1897. Fiercely protective of their own identity, *graciencs* still sometimes refer to outsiders from other parts of town as '*barcelonins*', as if they did not really belong here.

Little more than a village in 1820, with about 2,500 inhabitants, Gràcia had become the ninth-largest city in Spain by 1897, when it had 61,000 people. It was also known as a radical centre of Catalanism, republicanism, anarchism and, to a certain extent, feminism. Place names such as Mercat de la Llibertat, Plaça de la Revolució and C/Fraternitat tell their own story.

As you enter the district, and the rigid blocks of Cerdà's grid give way to narrow streets arranged haphazardly, the change in atmosphere is striking. Some streets consist of small, two-storey buildings, and a series of attractive small squares provide space to pause and talk. The most important of them are

Plaça Rius i Taulet, site of the pre-1897 town hall and a magnificent clock tower designed by Rovira i Trias, **Plaça de la Virreina**, with its village-like church, the peaceful and relaxing **Plaça Rovira i Trias**, with an appealing bronze statue of this great-but-unappreciated architect himself, and **Plaça del Sol**. In **Plaça del Diamant**, the setting of one of the most popular of modern Catalan novels, a Civil War air-raid shelter has recently been discovered, which it is hoped will be made into a peace museum. Gràcia also acquired a new square in 1993, not elegant but unpretentious and designed for kids, the **Plaça John Lennon**.

Gràcia contains one of Gaudí's earliest and most fascinating works, the **Casa Vicens** of 1883-8, hidden away in C/Carolines (not open to visitors, but the exterior is impressive enough). And of course the most visited place in the whole municipal district is his **Parc Güell**, on the Tibidabo side of the area above Plaça Lesseps, across the busy Travessera de Dalt. *Modernisme* is also represented by Domènech's **Can Fuster** (1908-11) at C/Gran de Gràcia 2-4, and above all by the work of Francesc Berenguer, one of Gaudí's assistants, who designed the **Mercat de la Llibertat**.

Catching the rays in the **Café del Sol**. *See p100*.

Gaudí's **Casa Vicens**. *See p99*.

Gràcia's independent attitude is also reflected in a strong attachment to traditions like the **Festa Major**, the biggest in Barcelona, which for a few days in August makes the *barri* a centre for the whole city (*see p203*). The district contains many small factories and workshops, and has a sizeable Catalan-speaking gypsy community. Gràcia is also home to a large number of students, and a substantial creative community of artists, actors, musicians, photographers and designers, all of whom contribute to its bohemian flavour.

Coffee in Plaça del Sol is a relaxing alternative to busier places in the centre of the city, though the area is at its best after dark. The **Café del Sol** itself is an old favourite but the streets below are full of other cafés. Gràcia had its turn as the city's most in-vogue area for night-time wandering during the 1980s, when many bars opened; since then it's settled into a comfortable position neither at the top nor at the bottom of the fashion league, but remaining enduringly popular.

The educated nature of local residents is seen in the number of cultural venues in the district, such as the **Centre Artesà Tradicionarius** for folk music and dance, theatres such as the innovative **Sala Beckett** and two of the most enterprising cinemas in the city, the **Verdi** and **Verdi Park** (*see chapter* **Film**). The district is also home to the **Gràcia Territori Sonor** experimental music collective, who perform at Sonar and other festivals.

Parc Güell

C/d'Olot. Metro Vallcarca/22, 24, 25, 28 bus. **Open** (daily) *Nov-Feb* 10am-6pm. *Mar, Oct* 10am-7pm. *Apr, Sept* 10am-8pm. *May-Aug* 10am-9pm. **Map** p321 E2.

In 1900 Gaudí's patron Eusebi Güell commissioned him to oversee the design of a garden city development on a hill on the edge of the city, which he envisaged would become a fashionable residential area. Gaudí was to design the basic structure and main public areas; the houses were to be designed by other architects. The wealthy families of the time, however, did not appreciate Gaudí's wilder ideas, scarcely any plots were sold, and eventually the estate was taken over by the city as a park. Its most complete part is the entrance, with its Disneylandish gatehouses and the mosaic dragon that's become another of Barcelona's favourite symbols. The park has a wonderfully playful quality, with its twisted pathways and avenues of columns intertwined with the natural structure of the hillside. At the centre is the great esplanade, with an undulating bench covered in *trencadís*, broken mosaic – much of it not the work of Gaudí but of his assistant Josep Maria Jujol. Gaudí lived for several years in one of the two houses built on the site (not designed by himself); it is now the **Casa-Museu Gaudí** (*see p108*). The park stretches well beyond the area designed by Gaudí, away into the wooded hillside. Guided tours are available, sometimes in English. Note: the best way to get to the park is on the 24 bus; if you go via Lesseps Metro, be ready for a steep uphill walk.

Sants

The official city district of Sants, meaning 'Saints', includes three *barris*, Sants proper, La Bordeta and Hostafrancs. In the days when Barcelona's gates shut at 9pm every night, hostels, inns and smithies grew up around the city to cater for latecomers. Such was the origin of Sants, but by the 1850s it had also become a major industrial centre.

Centred around an old Roman road called for centuries Camí d'Espanya ('the road to Spain') and now C/Creu Coberta-C/de Sants, Sants became the site for giant textile factories such as Joan Güell's **Vapor Vell**, the Muntades brothers' **L'Espanya Industrial** and Can Batlló. Few of the people who admire Gaudí's work in the Casa Batlló, the Palau Güell or Parc Güell give much attention to the fact that it was these factories and the workers in them that produced the wealth necessary to support such projects. It was also a centre of labour militancy, and in 1855 the first ever general strike in Catalonia broke out there.

Today Sants remains, like Gràcia, one of the areas of Barcelona with a strong sense of its own identity, and like Gràcia also has a large Catalan-speaking gypsy community. Practically all its industrial centres, however, have disappeared. The huge Espanya Industrial site became a futuristic park in 1985 after a long neighbourhood campaign for more open spaces; and after a 20-year struggle by residents, El Vapor Vell, inaugurated in 2000, has finally been converted into one of the city's biggest libraries.

The **Estació de Sants**, alongside the Espanya Industrial, also dominates the *barri*. In front of it is the **Plaça dels Països Catalans**, a square of granite and grim metal as much loathed by local residents as it is admired by design critics. On the other side of the station are the more appealing places of **Sants** and **Peiró**. In the latter the first-ever Catalan film was shot, *Baralla en un café* (Cafe Brawl), in 1898. Near the Plaça de Sants is a complex called **Les Cotxeres**, an old tram depot, now converted into a multifunctional community and arts centre. From there, C/Creu Coberta runs to Plaça d'Espanya, where C/Tarragona, to the left, sharply marks the end of Sants and the beginning of the Eixample. This street has been changed totally by pre- and post-Olympic projects, with high-rise office towers that have led it to be dubbed – perhaps in hope – the 'Wall Street' of Barcelona.

Parc de l'Espanya Industrial & Plaça dels Països Catalans

Pg. de Antoni, Metro Sants-Estació/bus all routes to Sants-Estació. **Open** (daily) *Nov-Feb* 10am-6pm. *Mar, Oct* 10am-7pm. *Apr, Sept* 10am-8pm. *May-Aug* 10am-9pm. **Map** p323 A4.

The Espanya Industrial, by Basque architect Luis Peña Ganchegui, is the most postmodern of Barcelona's new parks. Ten watchtowers, like ship superstructures, look out over the boating lake: at night, lit up, they create the impression that some strange warship has managed to dock by Sants rail station. This is one of the 1980s parks most liked by the public: boats can be hired on the lake, and kids play on Andrés Nagel's Gran Drac de Sant Jordi dragon sculpture. Another sculpture is by Anthony Caro. On the other side of the station is the ferociously modern Plaça dels Països Catalans, created by Helio Piñón and Albert Viaplana in 1983 on a site where, they claimed, nothing could be planted due to the amount of industrial detritus in the soil. It's an open, concreted space, with shelter provided not by trees but steel ramps and canopies, the kind of architecture you either find totally hostile or consider to have great monumental strength.

Tibidabo & the Zona Alta

Local dignitaries have customarily taken official visitors to the top of **Tibidabo**, the giant peak towering up behind the city, for an overview of Barcelona. The name comes from the Latin, *tibi dabo,* 'to thee I shall give', the words used by the Devil during his temptation of Christ. The view is certainly magnificent, even when there's smog down below, and the clean air is a welcome change. Since it was made accessible by the building of the rail line to Avinguda Tibidabo and the wonderful **Tramvia Blau**, 'blue tram', *(see p104)* in the 1900s, Tibidabo has joined Montjuïc as one of Barcelona's two 'pleasure mountains', visited at least a few times each year by just about everyone in town.

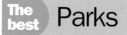

The best Parks

For hiring a boat
Parc de la Ciutadella has a boat pond where Sunday rowers compete with ducks and geese for a stretch of open water (*see p82-3*).

For Gaudí
Parc Güell is a veritable orgy of organic forms, where nature and the master's mind begin to blur (*see p100*).

For swimming
Parc de la Creueta del Coll, once a quarry, now has a lake fit for swimming as well as an artificial beach (*see p103*).

For dragons
Parc de l'Espanya Industrial features a huge metal dragon by the artist Andrés Nagel, with a slide for kids (*see p101*).

For getting lost
Parc del Laberint, in the refined gardens of a former mansion, is the perfect spot to wander around aimlessly (*see p106*).

Sightseeing

Getting there, by train, Tramvia Blau and **funicular**, is part of the fun (*see p103*). The square between the tram and the funicular is one of the best places in the city for an alfresco drink or meal: try the Mirablau or La Venta (*see chapters* **Restaurants** and **Cafés & Bars**). From the square, the tracks along the city side of the Serra de Collserola are great for jogging. Further down the flanks of the hill there are more elegant, airy bars (*see chapter* **Nightlife**), and the **Museu de la Ciència**. At the very top of the funicular is a great **funfair** (*see p208*), and, for a completely limitless view, the giant needle of Norman Foster's **Torre de Collserola**. Next to the funfair is a church, built in an extravagantly bombastic style and completed in 1940 to 'atone' for Barcelona's revolutionary role in the Spanish Civil War. To the left of it, on the other side of the ridge, there are stunning views over the Vallès to the north, while down the hillside are tracks into the Parc de Collserola where you can easily lose yourself for an afternoon among near-virgin pinewoods.

Below Tibidabo are the districts of the **Zona Alta** (literally 'upper zone', or simply 'uptown'). This is the name collectively given to a series of *barris* including Sant Gervasi, Sarrià, Pedralbes and Putxet that fan out across the area above the Diagonal and to the left of Gràcia on the

map. They are 'upper' both literally (in that they are at a higher elevation than most of the city and so enjoy cleaner air) and in social standing (these are the most expensive residential areas of Barcelona).

These areas have few major sights other than the remarkable **Museu-Monestir de Pedralbes**, now home of the Barcelona branch of the **Col.lecció Thyssen**. However, the centre of **Sarrià** and the web of streets of old **Pedralbes** around the monastery still retain an appreciable flavour of what were quite sleepy country towns until well into the 20th century.

The Zona Alta has dotted around it several interesting works by Gaudí. From wealthy Pedralbes a walk down Avda de Pedralbes leads to his wonderful gatehouse and gates, the **Pavellons de la Finca Güell** at No.15, with a bizarre wrought iron dragon. In the garden of the **Palau de Pedralbes** on Avda Diagonal, a former Güell residence, there is a delightful Gaudí fountain, and back on the other side of the Zona Alta off the Plaça Bonanova, near Tibidabo FGC station, is the remarkable Gothic-influenced **Torre Figueres**, or **Bellesguard**. Further into town near Putxet is one of Gaudí's larger but more sober designs, the **Col.legi de les Teresianes** (C/Ganduxer 85-105) from 1888-9.

Exploring Collserola

With the exception of Tibidabo, for decades Barcelona cold-shouldered the long Collserola mountain chain to its north and west. Now, though, things have changed. **Tibidabo**, with its funfair, tram, bars, restaurants and fabulous views, especially from the huge **Torre de Collserola**, is at the centre of the ridge. The 6,550-hectare (16,000-acre) park of the Serra de Collserola proper is, however, more easily reached by FGC trains on the Terrassa-Sabadell line from Plaça Catalunya, getting off at **Baixador de Vallvidrera** station.

A 10-minute walk from the station up into the woods along Carretera de l'Església will take you to the **Museu Verdaguer** (*see p125*) and the park's **Centre d'Informació** (93 280 35 52, open 9.30am-3pm daily) where maps can be bought. This very helpful centre also has an exhibition area and bar. There are five suggested itineraries, ranging from an easy walk of a mere 20 minutes to an excursion to the Serra d'en Cardona of two hours plus. The great thing, however, is to explore for oneself, because the Collserola is a

wonderful natural reserve, with the trees providing delicious shade on a hot day. Walking is easy, as paths and climbs are well maintained. Holm oak and pines predominate among the trees, squirrels and rabbits are everywhere, and the scents and colours of herbs and wild flowers are exhilarating. For bird-watchers there is scarcely a better place in Catalonia, and it's also an excellent place for mountain-biking.

One easy itinerary is to walk the 2km (1.2 miles) from the Information Centre to the quiet hilltop town of **Vallvidrera**, stopping on the way at the **Font de la Budellera**, a spring and picnic site. In Vallvidrera's main *plaça* there are two bar-restaurants to provide rest and refreshment for the traveller, **Can Trampa** and **Can Josean** – the latter has a superb view down over Barcelona. The Torre de Collserola is just a short walk away, or a ride down the funicular – with another panoramic view – will take you to **Peu del Funicular** station, from where FGC trains run back to Plaça Catalunya.

Funicular de Tibidabo

Plaça Doctor Andreu–Plaça Tibidabo (93 211 79 42). FGC Avda Tibidabo/17, 22, 58, 73, N8 bus, then Tramvia Blau. **Open** *End Sept-early June* 10.30am-7.30pm Sat, Sun, public holidays (plus May 10am-6pm Thur, Fri). *June-Aug* 10.30am-10.30pm Mon-Fri, 10.30am-1.30pm Sat, Sun. **Tickets** single 300ptas; return 400ptas. **No credit cards.**

The funicular that takes you from the end of the tramline to the very top of the mountain is art deco-esque, like much of the funfair. Each train has two halves, one pointing down and one up, and from the 'down' end you get a panoramic view of the city.

Monestir de Pedralbes (Col.lecció Thyssen-Bornemisza)

Baixada del Monestir 9 (93 280 14 34). FGC Reina Elisenda/22, 63, 64, 75, 78 bus. **Open** 10am-2pm Tue-Sun. Closed Mon. **Admission** Free first Sun of each month. *Monastery only* 400ptas; 250ptas concessions; free under-12s. *Col.lección Thyssen only* 400ptas; 250ptas concessions; free under 12s. *Monastery & Col.lección Thyssen* 700ptas; 400ptas concessions; free under-12s. **Discounts** BC, BT. **Credit** (shop only) DC, AmEx, MC, V. **Map** p319 A1.

Founded in 1326 by Queen Elisenda, wife of Jaume II of Aragon, this monastery is still home to a community of 24 nuns. With the installation of the Thyssen-Bornemisza art collection in part of the cloister, the rest of the monastery that is on view has also been thoroughly reorganised. A tour of the building now provides a fascinating glimpse of life in a medieval cloister: visitors can see the pharmacy, the kitchens, and the huge refectory with its vaulted ceiling. The main attraction, though, is the convent itself, and above all its magnificent, entirely intact three-storey Gothic cloister. To one side is the tiny chapel of Sant Miquel, covered with striking murals from 1343 by Ferrer Bassa, a Catalan painter who was a student of Giotto. The Thyssen collection occupies an all-white former nuns' dormitory on one of the upper floors (*see also p116*).

Parc de la Creueta del Coll

C/Mare de Déu del Coll, Zona Alta. Metro Penitents/19, 25, 28, 87 bus. **Open** *(daily) Nov-Feb* 10am-6pm. *Mar, Oct* 10am-7pm. *Apr, Sept* 10am-8pm. *May-Aug* 10am-9pm.

An impressive park created from an old quarry by Josep Martorell and David Mackay in 1987. At its centre is a large lake with artificial beach, and like other '80s parks it has modern sculpture: an Ellsworth Kelly, and a monumental piece by Eduardo Chillida, *In Praise of Water*, hanging from cables. In 1998 one snapped and the massive block came crashing down, injuring three people. It has been restored, but people tend to give it a wide berth.

Torre de Collserola

Parc de Collserola (93 406 93 54/ www.parccollserola.amb.es). FCG Peu Funicular and then the Funicular. **Open** *Sept-May* 11am-2.30pm, 3.30-7pm Wed-Fri; 11am-7pm Sat, Sun; closed Mon, Tue. *June-Aug* 11am-2.30pm, 3.30-8pm Wed-Fri; 11am-

Norman Foster's **Torre de Collserola**.

The Palau de Pedralbes contains two interesting museums, the **Museu de Ceràmica** and **Museu de les Arts Decoratives** (*see pp119-20*). Around it, stretching out on either side of the Diagonal, is the bleakly functional Zona Universitària, chosen as the area for the expansion of Barcelona's main university in the 1950s. On the very fringes of the city, at the very end of the Diagonal, is the pretty **Parc de Cervantes** with a magnificent rose garden.

From there, a turn back along the Diagonal toward Plaça Maria Cristina and Plaça Francesc Macià will take you to Barcelona's fastest-growing modern business district. It is growing just as rapidly as a shopping area, with stores, fashion malls and the 'horizontal skyscraper', **L'Illa**. Close to Plaça Francesc Macià itself there is a small, popular park, the **Turó Parc**, which is currently being redesigned. To the right of it on the map is **Sant Gervasi**. This area had its moment of glory as the most fashionable night-time meeting-point in early '90s Barcelona, especially the streets around the junction of C/Marià Cubí and C/Santaló, site of bars and clubs such as **Mas i Mas** and **Universal**. Also in Sant Gervasi, but closer to Gràcia, is one of the great survivors of the Barcelona club scene, the Otto Zutz.

8pm Sat, Sun; closed Mon, Tue. **Admission** 500 ptas; free under-7s; group discounts. **Credit** MC, V.

Norman Foster's 288-metre (800-ft) communications tower, built to take TV signals to the world in 1992, stands atop Collserola like some mutant insect poised to swoop on the city. A glass lift takes you to an observation deck 115m (377ft) up, which means you are 560m (1,838ft) above sea level. On a decent day, there 's a staggering eagle's-eye view of Barcelona: a couple of times a year, it's also clear enough to see Mallorca; at other times, you might just see an endless haze.

Tramvia Blau (Blue Tram)

Avda Tibidabo–Plaça Doctor Andreu (93 318 70 74). FGC Avda Tibidabo/17, 22, 58, 73, N8 bus. **Services** *Mid Sept-end May* 9am-9.30pm Sat, Sun; (bus 9am-9.30pm Mon-Fri). *End June-mid Sept* 10am-9pm daily. **Tickets** single 275ptas; return 400ptas; one mth 3,100ptas. **Frequency** 30min Mon-Fri; 15min Sat-Sun. **No credit cards**.

The Blue Trams, beautiful old machines in service since 1902, clank their way up Avda Tibidabo between the FGC station and Plaça Doctor Andreu. Once there, you can take in the view, have a meal or a drink, or catch the funicular to the funfair. Except in summer there's a plain bus service on weekdays.

Les Corts

The rural origin of this *barri* can still be heard in the name, 'the farmsheds', although there rarely seems much that's rustic in it any more. In among its apartment blocks, though, there is **Plaça del Carme**, the surviving core of the old village of Les Corts, which was annexed to Barcelona in 1867 and still evokes the atmosphere of a very different era.

For most Barcelona residents, though, Les Corts is synonymous with **Fútbol Club Barcelona**, whose massive sports complex takes up a great deal of the district's space. Curiously, at night the surrounding area becomes the haunt of prostitutes, transvestites and cruising drivers. Barça, though, like every other institution in Barcelona, has development plans, and has proposed the construction of a vast all-purpose leisure complex called **Barça 2000** around the existing stadium. However, the plan has been severely criticised by architects and locals alike, and so far has not won approval from the Ajuntament.

Nou Camp – FC Barcelona

Avda Aristides Maillol, access 7&9 (93 496 36 00/ www.fcbarcelona.com). Metro Collblanc/15, 54, 56, 57, 75, 101, 157 bus. **Open** *Museum* 10am-6.30pm Mon-Sat, 10am-2pm Sun. **Admission** 550ptas; 425ptas concessions. **Discounts** BC, BT. **No credit cards. Map** p319 A3.

The largest football stadium in Europe, and a shrine to Barcelona FC. First built in 1954, the Nou Camp has since been extended to accommodate nearly all of the club's 100,000-plus members. It also contains the club museum – visitors to the museum also get to tour the stadium (*see also pp124-5 and chapter* **Sport & Fitness**).

Poble Nou, Clot, Sagrera

These three districts, north of the old city along the coast, once formed part of one large independent municipality, **Sant Martí de Provençals**. Originally a farming and fishing community, it was, like Sants, one of the areas chosen by manufacturers as they sought to expand, and became the great centre of heavy industry in Barcelona, disputing with Sabadell the title of la Manchester Catalana. This brought the usual problems – child labour, diseases, overcrowding, noise, smells, smoke – and the usual responses: co-operatives, unions, strikes and other conflicts. In 1897 it was absorbed into Barcelona, and split into three districts, Poble Nou, Clot and La Sagrera.

Poble Nou contained the greater part of Sant Martí's industry, and so continued to be a centre of radicalism and conflict. As a result it would pay dearly after 1939. Then, in the 1960s, the *barri* began to change its character as entire factories folded, moved to the Zona Franca or got out of the city altogether. The departure of the most historic, Can Girona, in 1992, marked the end of an epoch.

Today Poble Nou has become a laboratory for post-industrial experiments. Old factories are now schools, civic centres, workshops and open spaces. In the early '90s many artists moved in, drawn by greater working space and lower rents compared with Ciutat Vella. For a while Poble Nou gained a reputation as a new centre for contemporary artistic activity, but more recently many artists have moved out again, as the cheap old buildings they occupied have been replaced by new blocks of flats.

One entire section of the *barri* is now the Vila Olímpica; once a hive of dirty industry, it is now one of the gateways to the beach. In the middle of the district there are still parts of the old Poble Nou, and even earlier Sant Martí: lovely **Rambla del Poble Nou** compares favourably with the one in the city centre, and the area around **Plaça Prim** has kept its village atmosphere. And Poble Nou still has (looking odd amid recent developments) Barcelona's oldest, most atmospheric cemetery, the **Cementiri de l'Est**, with the extraordinary sculpture *El bes de la mort* (Kiss of Death) to remind us of the brevity of human existence.

Clot and **La Sagrera**, both small *barris*, experienced much the same history as Poble Nou. Clot boasts a very intimate and friendly food market in the **Plaça Font i Sagué**, and a striking piece of urban design, the **Parc del Clot**. Nearby is **Plaça de les Glòries** (*see p68*), centrepiece of plans to upgrade this incorrigibly shabby area.

In La Sagrera, meanwhile, the huge Pegaso truck factory has been recycled into a school and the **Parc Pegaso**, with a boating lake, and the area has one of the finest pieces of recent architecture in Barcelona, the supremely elegant **Pont de Calatrava** bridge, linking it to Poble Nou via C/Bac de Roda. This is about the only new construction in the city to be popularly known by the name of its architect, Santiago Calatrava.

Parc del Clot

C/Escultors Claperós. Metro Glóries/7, 56, 60, 92, N2 bus. **Open** (daily) *Nov-Feb* 10am-6pm. *Mar, Oct* 10am-7pm. *Apr, Sept* 10am-8pm. *May-Aug* 10am-9pm.
A few streets from the flea market at Glóries, a park built on the site of an old RENFE warehouse, full of palms and pines. Curving sections of the old brick walls are imaginatively integrated into the space.

Diagonal-Mar

It is, however, the area on the north side of Poble Nou along the coast that is undergoing the greatest changes, for this is the part of Barcelona that, with the transformation of the Port Vell complete, has become the latest focus of attention of the city planners. Starting point of the scheme, carried out in 1999, has been the extension all the way to the sea of Avda Diagonal, which – contrary to the Cerdà plan – used to fizzle out just east of Glòries. The area where the avenue now meets the sea by the mouth of the Besòs, previously known as a Franco-era slum, has been rechristened Diagonal-Mar; and work is well under way on reshaping it into an all-new, landscaped district, with more new beaches, a lake, a multimedia business park and a new site for Barcelona's zoo, removing it from its cramped location in the Ciutadella. The site is already used as a venue for the **Feria de Abril** (*see p199*).

As in 1929 and 1992, though, Barcelona hopes to underpin its infrastructural schemes with an attention-grabbing international event, in this case the highly controversial **Fòrum Universal de les Cultures** or 'Universal Forum of Cultures', scheduled for 2004. This was actually conceived entirely in Barcelona (and with Barcelona's own ends in mind), and how much interest (and so money) it will ultimately generate internationally is a very open question. If it all comes to fruition, this will be one more part of Barcelona changed out of all recognition.

Guinardó, Horta, Vall d'Hebron

The area north of Gràcia, above and to the right of it on the map, is made up of contrasting districts, traditionally of rich and poor, the former in valleys and the latter perched on hillsides. Until the building of the **Túnel de la Rovira**, which begins near the Plaça d'Alfons el Savi, many of these areas were relatively isolated from the city.

Joined to Gràcia by the long Avda Mare de Déu de Montserrat, **Guinardó** above all consists of two big parks. One, the **Parc de les Aigües**, contains a fun sculpture of a buried submarine by Josep Maria Riera, and Barcelona's most eccentrically beautiful municipal district headquarters, the **Casa de les Altures**, a neo-Arabic fantasy from 1890. The other, **Parc del Guinardó**, is one of the city's older parks, opened in 1920. The *barri* of **El Carmel** has its own **Parc del Carmel**, but also the extraordinary **Parc de la Creueta del Coll**, an old quarry turned into a swimming pool. Escalators have been installed in some of the district's (very) steep streets to make climbing easier.

Incorporated into Barcelona in 1904, the aptly named **Horta**, 'market garden', has retained many rural features, including some very well-preserved *masies,* traditional farmhouses. The medieval **Can Cortada**, in C/Campoamor, shows at a glance that these houses also served as fortresses, while **Can Mariner** in C/d'Horta is said to date back to 1050. Another now houses a great restaurant, **Can Travi Nou**. Horta's abundant water supply once made it the laundry centre for respectable Barcelona, with a whole community of *bugaderes* or washerwomen, as the open-air stone tanks along the lovely C/Aiguafreda attest.

The **Vall d'Hebron**, just above Horta along the Ronda de Dalt ring road on the flanks of Collserola, was one of the city's four main venues for Olympic events, and so has inherited centres for tennis, archery and cycling, at the Velòdrom. Around the sports venues there are very striking examples of street sculpture, such as Claes Oldenburg's spectacular *Matches*, near the tennis centre, and Joan Brossa's *Visual Poem*, by the **Velòdrom**. There is also a reconstruction of the **Pavelló de la República**. One of the area's most distinctive assets is much older, the delightful, semi-concealed **Parc del Laberint** from 1791 (*see p106*) – testimony to this hillside's much earlier role as a site for aristocratic country residences. For many locals, though, the Vall d'Hebron means above all the **Ciutat Sanitària**, largest hospital in the city and the place where many first saw the light of day.

Parc del Laberint

C/Germans Desvalls, Passeig Vall d'Hebron. Metro Montbau/27, 60, 73, 76, 85, 173 bus. **Open** (daily) *Nov-Feb* 10am-6pm. *Mar, Oct* 10am-7pm. *Apr, Sept* 10am-8pm. *May-Aug* 10am-9pm. **Admission** 275ptas Mon, Tue, Thur-Sat; free under-6s, over-65s. Wed, Sun free.

One of the most atmospheric (and leafiest) parks is also the most out of the way, in Vall d'Hebron. Originally the grounds of a mansion (long demolished), it is densely wooded with pines, and in the centre there is an 18th-century formal garden with a deliberately picturesque fantasy element, including a romantic stream and waterfall. The maze that gives the park its name has often proved a match for cynics who thought it was only for children.

Pavelló de la República

Avda Cardenal Vidal y Barraquer (93 428 54 57). Metro Montbau/10, 27, 60, 73, 76, 85, 173 bus. **Open** 9am-8pm Mon-Fri; closed Sat, Sun. **Admission** free.

The Spanish Republic's pavilion for the 1937 Paris Exhibition, designed by Josep Lluís Sert, was the building in which Picasso's *Guernica* was first exhibited, and an emblematic work of rationalist architecture. It was demolished after the exhibition, but in 1992, following the recreation of that other flagship building the **Pavelló Barcelona** (*see p90*), the controversial decision was taken to create a facsimile of Sert's building, even though it had no direct connection with Barcelona. Austerely functionalist, it forms a curious pair with Oldenberg's Matches across the street. It houses a research library, but visitors can see most of the building.

Sant Andreu & Nou Barris

On the way out of Barcelona along the Meridiana, which like the Paral.lel derives its name from solar co-ordinates, Sant Andreu is to the right, and **Nou Barris** to the left. **Sant Andreu** was another of the industrial and working class hubs of the city. Much altered in the 1960s, it has seen some recent renovations: on Passeig Torres i Bages, at Nos. 91-105, Sert's **Casa Bloc**, a rationalist block of flats that was one of the main contributions of the brief republican era to Barcelona, has been restored, and, just off the Meridiana, a lovely wine press has been installed in Plaça d'en Xandri. A more spectacular recent addition is La Maquinista, the city's newest, biggest shopping mall, built on the grounds of a long-defunct train station.

Nou Barris (nine neighbourhoods) has a different make-up. In the 1950s, when the flow of migration into the city was at its height, ramshackle settlements were built here, followed by tower blocks. The price is now being paid, as flats scarcely 40 years old have fallen into ruins and are being demolished. Services of all kinds are deficient: **Vallbona**

does not have a single pharmacy; in **Roquetas** some streets are still dirt tracks. The city has now provided parks, sculptures and services – the **Can Dragó** sports complex has the biggest public swimming pool in Barcelona, and a new **Parc Central** was completed in 1999 – but overall these areas represent very much the 'other side' of the new Barcelona.

The outer limits

As well as Barcelona proper, the city's Area Metropolitana is made up of a ring of smaller cities. Until the 20th century, all were still rural, but since the 1920s they have increasingly acquired industrial estates and large migrant populations from the rest of Spain, and in many cases they have become virtual dormitory towns for Barcelona.

Due north of the city and spanning both banks of the Besòs river, **Sant Adrià del Besòs** is famous for two things. The first is the district of **La Mina**, notorious as a hotbed of crime and poverty, although it is hoped it will benefit from the Fòrum 2004 to be staged nearby. The second is that for the next few years the **Feria de Abril** is likely to be held nearby, in the Diagonal-Mar development zone (*see p199*). North of Sant Adrià, **Badalona** is famous for its basketball team, **Joventut Badalona**, which has won the European Basketball Cup, something its rival FC Barcelona has never managed. It also has its own traditions, with a great **Festa Major** in May, climaxing with the Cremada del Dimoni, when a huge devil is burnt on the beach.

On some cars in Barcelona you may see the sticker 'L'H'. This assertion of identity is a reminder that **L'Hospitalet de Llobregat**, just southwest, is the second city of Catalonia, even though it is completely integrated into Barcelona's transport network. With a big Andalusian-born population, it is also Catalonia's main centre for flamenco. There are several flamenco *peñas*, or clubs, in the town, among them **ACA**, C/Clavells 2-4 (93 437 55 02), for dancing, and **Tertulia Flamenca**, C/Calderon de la Barca 12 (93 437 20 44), which also runs guitar classes. A special flamenco festival is held on the Saturday before Christmas at **Teatre Joventut**, C/Joventut 10, Hospitalet (93 448 12 10), when *villancicos*, strange flamenco carols, are sung. Equally, Hospitalet has plenty of bars and restaurants with good Andalusian specialities – try **Andalucía Chiquita**, Avda Isabel la Catòlica 89 (93 438 12 67). In summer, the area around C/Severo Ochoa becomes a huge outdoor café, offering tapas of all types at much more reasonable prices than in Barcelona itself.

Museums

Fascinating, eclectic, at times downright eccentric – Barcelona's museums are a reflection of the city's unique character.

Barcelona's museums and exhibition spaces are above all a song to the city itself, a eulogy to its idiosyncratic identity and indeed that of all Catalonia. In a city of shopkeepers, where gathering, ordering and displaying are the bread and butter of street level commerce, filling beautiful spaces with equally precious collections comes altogether naturally. Their essentially bourgeois character is chiefly historical. Unlike in major capitals such as London, Paris or Madrid, where museums have benefited from monarchic vanities and imperialist booties, Barcelona's museums are the fruit of private initiatives and individual energies; they tend to be more partial than comprehensive, more locally specific than universal, full of wonderful objects, but with only a handful of recognised masterworks.

Only in art and architecture, where illustrious locals – Picasso, Miró, Dalí in Figueres, Gaudí – are equally celebrated internationally, does Barcelona dare represent the entire world along with itself. Only in art is Barcelona outright uppity, offering international quality exhibits in a dozen or so spaces. In contrast, most of Barcelona's museums are celebrations of the rich specificity of the city, its otherness, which is after all what makes the town so beloved to visitors and residents alike.

Barcelona's first public museum – now the **Museu de Geologia** (*see p124*) – was set up just before the 1888 Universal Exhibition, and more were born following the 1929 Exhibition on Montjuïc. Only since the recent restoration of the Catalan government – the Generalitat – in 1980 has there been a drive to create 'national' museums, with the aim of representing historical and contemporary art (the **MNAC** and **MACBA** respectively), Catalan history (the **Museu d'Història de Catalunya**, *see p122*) or Catalonia's scientific legacy, in the **Museu Nacional de la Ciència i la Tècnica in Terrassa** (*see p273*).

Barcelona has had the good sense to house its exhibits and collections in the best of its architecture, from the **Museu d'Història de la Ciutat,** the city history museum (*see pp122-3*) literally within the ruins of the Roman city and a medieval royal palace, to the **Museu Picasso** with its Gothic patio, and the **Museu Marítim** in the inspiring 14th-century

shipyard of the Drassanes. Purpose-built and equally impressive are Josep Lluís Sert's impeccable **Fundació Miró**, and the luminous **MACBA**, by Richard Meier.

In contrast to these more spectacular examples, there's a rambling selection of private, small museums hidden away in the oddest of places, like the scrumptious new **Museu de la Xocolata** 'chocolate museum' (*see p125*) the **Museu del Perfum** (*see p125*) with its thousands of scent bottles, the **Museu de Carrosses Fúnebres** (see *p124*) with its old hearses or the **Museu del Calçat**, the shoe museum (*see p120*). Vroom-crazy Catalonia will soon have its very own motorcycle museum in a renovated Poble Nou factory.

Rounding off the local cultural scene are public exhibition spaces, such as the **CCCB** or the **Virreina**, which seek, ever more actively, to bring contemporary art to the general public. Likewise, certain savings banks, such as omnipresent 'la Caixa', fund important cultural foundations which are major players in the arts.

OPENING DAYS AND INFORMATION

Most museums, and all public ones except the MACBA, are closed on Mondays. They are open, with Sunday hours, on most public holidays, but there are days when virtually all museums close: Christmas Day; 26 December; New Year's Day; 6 January. When it comes to working out what is being shown, most labelling is in Catalan, Spanish or both. A small (if slowly growing) number of museums now provide some labelling in English, or offer free brochures or translations to be consulted while touring the galleries. Some museums also offer guided tours, but, again, they are rarely in English.

THE ARTICKET AND OTHER DISCOUNTS

The Articket is a joint entry ticket for seven major arts centres – **MNAC** (which includes the **Museu d'Art Modern**), **MACBA**, the **Fundació Miró**, **Espai Gaudí/La Pedrera**, the **Fundació Tàpies** and the **CCCB** (for the last two, *see chapter* **Galleries**). It has the distinction of being the first product in Barcelona priced from the outset in euros: 15 euros, or an awkward 1,997ptas (so each centre is roughly half-price). You can visit them at any time within three months of the date of purchase; the ticket is available from participating venues and via **Tel-entrada** (*see p196*). Many museums also give discounts to holders of the **Barcelona Card** and/or **Bus Turístic** tickets (*see p64*); where this is so, it is indicated in listings with the letters **BC** and **BT**.

Gaudí, Miró & Picasso

Gaudí

Casa-Museu Gaudí

Parc Güell, Zona Alta (93 219 38 11). Bus 24, 25. **Open** *Nov-Feb* 10am-6pm; *Mar, Apr, Oct* 10am-7pm. *May-Sept* 10am-8pm daily. **Admission** 400ptas; 200ptas over-65s from EC; free under-10s. **Credit** (shop only) MC, V. **Map** *p321 E2.*

One of only a few houses completed in the Parc Güell, this modest residence was actually designed by Gaudí's colleague Francesc Berenguer. Gaudí conceived the graceful pergola in the garden, and lived here from 1906 to 1926 – although in the years leading up to his untimely death he mostly slept in the workshop at the Sagrada Família. The simple interior, in tune with Gaudí's spartan religiosity, offers examples of the beautiful and outlandish furniture designed by him and by his disciples, such as Josep Maria Jujol. Also on show are memorabilia of Gaudí and his collaborators, and drawings for some of his wilder, unfinished projects.

Espai Gaudí – La Pedrera

Passeig de Gràcia 92-C/Provença 261-5, Eixample (93 484 59 95/93 489 59 00/ www.caixacat.es/fundcat.html). Metro Diagonal/7, 16, 17, 22, 24, 28 bus. **Open** 10am-8pm daily (mid June-mid Sept also 9pm-1am Fri, Sat). **Admission** 600ptas; 350ptas concessions; free under-12s; exhibitions free. **Guided tours** (English) 6pm Mon-Fri; 11am Sat, Sun. **Credit** (shop only) MC, V. **Discounts** Articket, BC, BT, RM. **Map** p320 D4.

The cultural foundation of the Caixa Catalunya savings bank owns Gaudí's masterpiece the Casa Milà (La Pedrera, *see pp96,98*), which has been restored as a cultural centre. Access to the no-charge exhibition space is via the spectacular main entrance and staircase. The gallery itself is an excellent example of a Gaudí interior: fabulous plaster ceiling reliefs recall the building's marine-

Street art

Barcelona's urban revival has its roots in the early '80s, when architect and planning guru Oriol Bohigas came up with the catchy idea to 'monumentalise the periphery'. The idea was to create spatial and visual landmarks in outlying neighbourhoods that had sprung up chaotically in the 1950s and 1960s. Beginning well before the Olympics were even a vague project, the city embarked on an ambitious programme to develop transitional space in the city, with nearly 100 entirely new squares and parks.

Typified by hard surfaces and creatively designed furnishings and lamp-posts, these squares were also conceived to incorporate dozens of public sculptures specially commissioned by the city, in what was then the largest programme of its kind in the world. Artists were offered a modest flat fee, with costs borne by the Ajuntament; many major Spanish and international artists – Joan Miró, Antoni Tàpies, Eduardo Chillida, Richard Serra, Roy Lichtenstein, Jannis Kounellis, Rebecca Horn – responded. The result is truly impressive, even though the initiative has died down since 1993, leaving Barcelona with a quality public sculpture landscape.

The few post-Olympics works feature Lawrence Weiner's homage to Provençal writer and revivalist Frédéric Mistral (Avinguda Mistral Metro Rocafort); Joseph Kosuth is currently preparing a piece for the Nou Barris neighbourhood. Artistically treated facades include a fascinating mural on the history of photography by Arranz-Bravo and Bartolozzi (Aurora 11 bis, Metro Paral.lel), and the balconies of the building called the Casa de los Toros, near the Monumental bullring, wonderfully adorned by Francesc Català-Roca photos (Gran Via 798-812, Metro Glòries). The following are some of the major examples to be found around the city.

Barceloneta, Port Vell & La Ribera

Metro Barceloneta or Drassanes/14, 17, 36, 39, 45, 57, 59, 64, 157 bus. **Map** D-E7. Sculptures on maritime themes by Rebecca Horn (Barceloneta beach), Jannis Kounellis (C/Almirall Cervera), Lothar Baumgarten (the names of the winds of the Catalan coast, set into the paving of Passeig Joan de Borbó), and Juan Muñoz (end of Passeig Joan de Borbó). Commissioned at the same time, James Turrell's wonderful intervention of light volumes in architecture is in the entrance to the cloister at Centre Cívic Convent de Sant Agustí (C/Comerç) in La Ribera. Roy Lichtenstein's unmissable *Barcelona Head* is on Passeig de Colom at Via Laietana.

life themes, and none of the walls is straight. The gallery habitually programmes exhibits of top-tier international 20th-century art, such as a 2001 show of new American art (*Humour and Rage*). The *Pis de la Pedrera*, on the fourth floor, is a fine-tuned reconstruction of a *Modernista* flat interior (not by Gaudí) from the first decades of the 20th century. Notable is the bedroom suite by famed furniture designer Gaspar Homar, along with art by Modest Urgell and Ramon Casas, and the antique dolls in the kids' room, from the toy museum in Figueres. A complementary gallery describing everyday life during the same period rounds off the Pis de la Pedrera. The Espai Gaudí is higher up in the large attic, once used to hang residents' washing but now appropriately enclosed. Beneath Gaudí's inspiring sequence of flat brick catenary arches, the Espai offers the city's only systematic overview of the architect's œuvre. Drawings, photographs, models and audio-visual displays give a brief yet clear idea of each of the master's important buildings, with special emphasis on La Pedrera itself. Above it is the building's marvellous roof terrace. La Pedrera is preparing special activities for 2002, proclaimed International Gaudí Year.

Museu del Temple Expiatori de la Sagrada Família

C/Mallorca 401, Eixample (93 207 30 31/ www.sagradafamilia.org). Metro Sagrada Família/10, 19, 33, 34, 43, 44, 50, 51, 101 bus. **Open** *Nov-Feb* 9am-6pm daily. *Mar, Sept, Oct* 9am-7pm daily. *Apr-Aug* 9am-8pm daily. **Admission** 800ptas; 600ptas concessions; free under-10s. Lifts to spires 200ptas. **Discounts** BC, BT, RM. **Credit** (groups & shop only) MC, V. **Map** p321 F4.

In the bowels of the Sagrada Família itself is a somewhat piecemeal display on the design and the ongoing construction of Gaudí's interminable cathedral. Perhaps the most fascinating discovery is that, perhaps unfortunately for later collaborators, Gaudí's drawings for the project were largely creative expressions of his ideas, rather than any kind of detailed plan that could be followed. Another piece of interest is the imaginary drawing and model of the finished cathedral, showing the immense height projected for the imposing centre spire. Photos trace the long and difficult history of the Sagrada Família, while models and decorative details bring the construction process closer. There are also images from other Gaudí buildings.

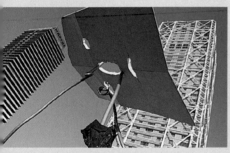

Antoni Llena's *David*.

Parc de la Creueta del Coll

Metro Penitents/19, 25, 28, 87 bus.
Giant sculptures by Ellsworth Kelly and Eduardo Chillida. Chillida also has a strong small piece in the Plaça del Rei (Metro Jaume I), while the mural beside the MACBA is a good example of what public art should not be. *See p103.*

Parc de l'Espanya Industrial

Metro Sants-Estació/bus all routes to Estació Sants. **Map** p323 A4.
Small sculptures by Anthony Caro, Pablo Palazuelo and others. *See p101.*

Parc de l'Estació del Nord

Metro Arc de Triomf/40, 42, 141 bus. **Map** p325 E-F5-6.

A large contoured landscape by Beverly Pepper. *See p96.*

Plaça de les Palmeres

Metro La Pau/11, 12, 34, 35, 36, 40 bus.
Richard Serra's brilliantly conceived white concrete double-wall does what *Titled Arc* would not: let people through.

Vall d'Hebron

Metro Montbau/27, 60, 73, 76, 85, 173 bus.
Near the former Olympic tennis site are works by Susana Solano and Claes Oldenburg (his marvellous giant *Matches*). Joan Brossa's disintegrating *Visual Poem* is nearby, by the Horta Velodrome. Further up is the older, but equally fascinating (and challenging) maze of the Parc del Laberint *(see p106)*.

Via Júlia

Metro Roquetes/11, 32, 50, 51, 76, 81 bus.
Sculptures by Sergi Aguilar and Jaume Plensa.

Vila Olímpica

Metro Ciutadella-Vila Olímpica/36, 41 bus. **Map** p325 F7.
Sculptures including Frank Gehry's enormous copper *Fish* (at the Hotel Arts) and Antoni Llena's kite-like *David* in the Parc de les Cascades.

Sightseeing

Miró.

Miró

Fundació Joan Miró

Parc de Montjuïc, Montjuïc (93 329 19 08/
fjmiro@bcn.fjmiro.es/www.bcn.fjmiro.es). Metro
Paral.lel, then Funicular de Montjuïc/bus 61. **Open**
10am-7pm (*July-Sept* 10am-8pm) Tue, Wed, Fri, Sat;
10am-9.30pm Thur; 10am-2.30pm Sun; closed Mon.
Guided tours 12.30pm Sat, Sun. **Admission**
800ptas; 450ptas concessions; free under-14s; group
discounts. **Discounts** Articket, BC, BT. **Credit**
(shop only) MC, V. **Map** p323 B6.

Conceived by Miró in his final years, the foundation
celebrates its 25th anniversary in 2001 with the
spring opening of the Sala K, designed to show 23
first-class Miró paintings ceded by Japanese collector Kazumasa Katsuta. Like all expansions to the
building, the new wing is inspired by the original
architecture of Miró's friend Josep Lluís Sert, who
came up with one of the world's great museums:
white walls, rustic tile floors, open airy galleries, and
an elegant system of roof arches to let in natural
light. It houses a collection of over 225 paintings, 150
sculptures and all of Miró's graphic work, plus a
huge legacy of some 5,000 drawings, notebooks and
other material. The permanent collection occupies
the second half of the exhibition space. It begins with
large paintings from Miró's late period, giving an
idea of his trademark use of primary colours and
simplified organic forms symbolising stars, the
moon and women. On the way to the sculpture
gallery is the reconstructed *Mercury Fountain* by

Alexander Calder, originally created for the Spanish
Republic's pavilion at the 1937 Paris Exhibition.
Next is a gallery of Miró sculptures, made with great
technical virtuosity, such as the bronze *Man and
Woman in the Night* (1969). His transition from
youth to maturity is seen in donations from his wife,
Pilar Juncosa, and his dealer, Joan Prats. The Sala
Joan Prats shows Miró as a cubist (*Street in
Pedralbes*, 1917), naïve (*Portrait of a Young Girl*,
1919) or surrealist (*Man and Woman in Front of a
Pile of Excrements,* 1935).

From mid 2001, the Sala Pilar Juncosa will connect
to the Sala K, with paintings ranging from early
depictions of Montroig, where Miró summered, to
unusual late pieces like *Wing of the Lark Haloed in
Golden Blue Touching the Heart of the Sleeping
Poppy on the Meadow Adorned with Diamonds*, a
mouthful from 1967. A ramp over the sculptures
leads to the simpler, black-outlined paintings from
the final period, like *Catalan Peasant by Moonlight*
(1968). The large *Sunbird* (1968) is of Carrara marble, and more sculpture is found on the roof terrace.
Donated works by other 20th-century masters –
Moore, Léger, Balthus, Ernst, Oldenburg – will be
moved downstairs. The Miró is an important venue
for temporary shows, which in 2001 will include a
retrospective of Catalan visual poet Joan Brossa, and
an exhibition on the women-bird-star triad in Miró
iconography. The Espai 13 in the basement features
young contemporary artists. The Foundation hosts
other activities, especially contemporary music (*see
p229*), and has a fine research library.

Picasso.

Picasso

Museu Picasso

C/Montcada 15-23, La Ribera (93 319 63 10/ www.museupicasso.bcn.es). Metro Jaume I/17, 19, 40, 45 bus. **Open** 10am-8pm Tue-Sat; 10am-3pm Sun; closed Mon. **Admission** *Museum only* 725ptas; 400ptas concessions; 300ptas student groups (by appointment); free 1st Sun of mth. *Temporary exhibitions* 800ptas; 400ptas concessions; free under-12s. **Discounts** BC. **Credit** (shop only) AmEx, MC, V. **Map** p327 C3.

When his father José Ruiz Blasco was hired to teach at Barcelona's art school in 1895, 13-year-old Pablo Ruíz Picasso was a budding young artist whose drawings suggested a firm academic training. By the time of his definitive move to Paris in 1904 he had already painted his greatest Blue Period works, and was on his way to becoming the most acclaimed artist of the century. Barcelona's Picasso Museum is testimony to these vital formative years, spent in the company of Catalonia's nascent avant-garde. The Picasso Museum does not show off the 20th century's most lauded artist at his peak; rather it is a fascinating window into the formation of a genius.

The museum arose out of a donation to the city by Picasso's secretary and life-long friend Jaume Sabartès (seen in a Blue Period painting from 1901) complemented by holdings from the artist's family. It graces a tight row of medieval courtyard-palaces on C/Montcada, beginning with the mostly 15th-century Palau Berenguer d'Aguilar, with a court-

yard probably by Marc Safont, architect of the Generalitat patios. Since opening in 1963, it has expanded to incorporate adjacent mansions: the later but also impressive Palaus Meca and Castellet, and in 1999 into the baroque Casa Mauri and early Gothic Casa Finestres (Nos.21 and 23). A courtyard behind them now hosts the restaurant. All of this now shows as much of the collection of over 3,000 paintings, drawings and other work as possible, together with temporary shows housed in the newly-acquired spaces (featuring a late 2001 exhibition on Picasso's unflagging eroticism).

Two things stand out in the museum. The seamless presentation of Picasso's development from 1890 to 1904, from schoolboy doodling to art school copies to intense innovations in blue, is unbeatable. Then, in a flash, one jumps to a gallery of mature cubist paintings from 1917, and completes the hopscotch with a leap to oils from the late 1950s, based on Velázquez' famous *Las Meninas* in the Prado in Madrid. This *vistus interruptus* could leave the visitor itching for more. The culmination of Picasso's early genius in *Les Demoiselles d'Avignon* (1907) and the first cubist paintings from the time (many of them done in Catalonia) are completely absent.

After some wonderful ceramics – donated by his widow Jacqueline – the chronological galleries begin in 1890, when young Pablo still lived in his native Málaga, sketching pigeons like his father (who bred and painted them incessantly). Already at the age of nine his drawing was sure and inventive. Work from his student years includes academic life drawings,

ARticKET

Visit **6** **art centers** in Barcelona for **15€**

M**N**A**A**IC — MUSEU NACIONAL D'ART DE CATALUNYA

MAC BA — Museu d'Art Contemporani de Barcelona

Fundació Joan Miró

FUNDACIÓ ANTONI TÀPIES — BARCELONA

Centre de Cultura Contemporània de Barcelona

Centre Cultural CAIXA CATALUNYA

Ticket valid for three months
www.telentrada.com
From abroad (+34) 933 262 945
Ticket offices at the art centers.

902 10 12 12 TEL·ENTRADA CAIXA CATALUNYA

portraits of his family and himself (a sombre oil from 1896) and sketchier landscapes, including some of Barceloneta beach. Under pressure from his father to attract patrons, he did some large realist oils, one of which, *Science and Charity* (1897), won a prize in Madrid. Only in the late 1890s, now in a studio away from home, did he begin to sign his bawdy nightlife scenes with 'Picasso', his mother's last name. There are fascinating sketches of art scene buddies Casagemas and Raventós, letters-in-cartoons from his first trip to Paris, and his menu cover from Els Quatre Gats, his first paid commission (*see p160*).

As he gained in artistic independence, Picasso's taste for marginal types – like the prostitute *La Chata* (1899) – intensified, with perversely beautiful paintings of Margot and the midget *La Nana* (1901). The intense Blue Period is represented by *Dead Woman* (1903) and *El Loco* (1904), as well as the azure *Rooftops of Barcelona* (1902-03), donated to the museum by his heirs. The chronology is broken with the mature cubism of 1917 – the last extended period Picasso spent in Barcelona – before coming to the Velázquez-inspired works, a series done in Cannes in 1957, and later portraits including one of Jacqueline (from 1963). The museum has an extensive collection of his limited-edition lithographs and linocuts.

Contemporary art

La Capella (Capella de l'Antic Hospital de la Santa Creu)

C/Hospital 56, Raval (93 442 71 71/ www.bcn.es/icub). Metro Liceu/14, 38, 59, 91 bus. **Open** noon-2pm, 4-8pm Tue-Sat; 11am-2pm Sun; closed Mon. **Admission** free. **Map** p326 A2.

An attractive exhibition space run by the city, La Capella accepts contemporary projects from young Barcelona-based artists, as well as commissioning innovative work able to give a social dimension to the gallery. The impressive Gothic building used to be the church of the medieval hospital beside it, and the choir balcony and side chapels are still visible, adding character to the shows. In the summer of 2001 Chicano artist Guillermo Gómez Peña will be holding a workshop with local artists using La Capella as a base.

Centre d'Art Santa Mònica

La Rambla 7, Rambla (93 316 28 10/ www.cultura.gencat.es/casm/index.htm). Metro Drassanes/14, 38, 59, 91 bus. **Open** 11am-2pm, 5-8pm Mon-Sat; 11am-3pm Sun. **Admission** normally free. **Map** p327 A4.

The Catalan government renovated this 17th-century monastery as a centre for contemporary art back in the 1980s. The controversial result, designed by Maremàgnum architects Piñón and Viaplana, is difficult for installation artists to work with, and is equally ill-conceived when it comes to showing paintings (observe, for example, the extravagantly tiled lower cloister, or the narrow corridors that pass for galleries upstairs). The centre regularly revives work by important Catalan *Modernistes*. During 2001 it will continue a series of exhibitions of the work of contemporary Spaniards (including Pedro G Romero and Marcelo Expósito) on the theme of urban social space.

Sightseeing

The imposing façade of the **CCCB**. *See p114.*

Centre de Cultura Contemporània de Barcelona (CCCB)

C/Montalegre 5, Raval (93 306 41 00/www.cccb.org).
Metro Catalunya/bus all routes to Plaça Catalunya.
Open *Mid June-mid Sept* 11am-8pm Tue-Sat; 11am-
3pm Sun; closed Mon. *Mid Sept-mid June* 11am-2pm,
4-8pm Tue, Thur, Fri; 11am-8pm Wed, Sat; 11am-
7pm Sun; closed Mon. **Admission** (prices vary)
1 exhibition 600ptas, 400ptas concessions; 2
exhibitions 800ptas, 600ptas concessions; 3
exhibitions 1,000ptas, 700ptas concessions;
free under-16s. **Discounts** Articket, BC, BT.
Credit MC, V. **Map** p326 A1.
This multi-use centre teams up with the adjacent
MACBA to form a culture front in the Raval. It occupies part of the Casa de la Caritat, built in 1802 on
the site of a medieval monastery to serve as the city's
main workhouse. The massive façade and part of
the courtyard remain from the old building, while
the rest was rebuilt by Piñón and Viaplana, resulting in a dramatic combination of original elements
with the imposing curtain wall in the cloister. Its def-
inition as a contemporary culture centre means pick-
ing up on whatever falls through the cracks
elsewhere in Barcelona, including urban culture
(architecture, but also linking writers with their
cities – Joyce's Dublin, Kafka's Prague), early 20th
century art, and thematic shows on television or cinema. In 2001, there will be a Canaletto exhibit in
spring, a show on the Pegaso sports car, produced
in Spain amid the poverty of the 1950s, and another of contemporary African art over the summer.
The CCCB offers a whole gamut of other activities
as well: a festival of video art, an alternative cinema
festival, the Sonar music festival (*see p202*), dance,
concerts, and oddities like an online flyer project
(www.cccb.org/flyercenter). There is also a particularly good bookshop specialising in a vast range of
urban-related topics.

Col.legi d'Arquitectes

Plaça Nova 5, Barri Gòtic (93 301 50 00/
www.coac.net). Metro Jaume I/17, 19, 40, 45 bus.
Open 10am-9pm Mon-Fri; 10am-2pm Sat; closed
Sun. **Admission** free. **Map** p326 B2.
The College of Architects, opposite the Cathedral,
hosts interesting exhibitions on 20th-century architecture. The façade murals were designed by Picasso
in the 1950s, but executed by other artists, since he
was not then able to enter Spain.

Fundació Antoni Tàpies

C/Aragó 255, Eixample (93 487 03 15/
museu@ftapies.com). Metro Passeig de Gràcia/7, 16,
17, 22, 24, 28 bus. **Open** 10am-8pm Tue-Sun; closed
Mon. **Admission** 700ptas; 350ptas concessions;
under-16s free. **Discounts** Articket, BC, RM. **No**
credit cards. Map p320 D4.
Antoni Tàpies is Catalonia's best-known living
painter, and his foundation in the Eixample is worth
a visit, if not for obvious reasons. Rather than create a shrine to himself, Tàpies had the sense to
approve a line of programming not overtly related
to his style. The idiosyncratic three-floor gallery

takes up a renovated early *Modernista* industrial
building from the 1880s by Domènech i Muntaner.
In 2001 there is a major installation by Catalan
Eulàlia Valldosera, with a show of Victor Burgin's
work in the spring, followed by *Architectures of*
Discourse, curated by Ute Meta Bauer (opening in
September), and exhibits of Hans Peter Feldmann
and Asger Jorn. A selection of Tàpies' own work is
often shown on the upper floor, and sometimes
throughout the entire space. The winding tube
sculpture on the roof, titled *Núvol i Cadira* ('cloud
and chair'), reflects his fascination with eastern mys-
ticism. The library contains a fine collection of material on oriental art.

Fundació la Caixa

Centre Cultural de la Fundació la Caixa, Passeig
de Sant Joan 108, Eixample (93 476 86 00/
www.fundacio.lacaixa.es). Metro Verdaguer/6,
15, 19, 33, 34, 43, 44, 50, 51, 55 bus. **Open** 11am-
8pm Tue-Sat; 11am-3pm Sun; closed Mon. Closed
Aug. **Admission** free. **Credit** AmEx, DC, MC, V.
Map p321 E4.
Spain's largest savings bank, 'la Caixa' has a very
high profile cultural foundation with an excellent
collection of international contemporary art and a
Spain-wide exhibitions programme, which touches on ethnology and archaeology as well as art and
photography. The main cultural centre in

Fundació Tàpies gets its wires crossed.

The wide-open spaces of the **MACBA**.

Museums

Barcelona has long been at the Palau Macaya, a magnificent *Modernista* building by Puig i Cadafalch that creatively draws from Moorish and Gothic styles. At present the Caixa is converting another Puig i Cadafalch edifice – the Casaramona factory near Plaça d'Espanya – into a still larger centre to be called CaixaForum, with room to show part of the collection at all times. It is due to open in late 2001 with an exhibit of the collection occupying the entire space.

For 2001, the Caixa has organised exhibits of Arman, a spring show on the artistic image of the desert, as well as taking in a travelling show on art and childhood (*Almost Warm and Fuzzy*), opening in April. There will also be a retrospective of Dutch photographer Ed van der Elsken. The Caixa runs a library with Barcelona's best documentation of video and media art, and has an excellent bookshop. The Caixa also runs one of Barcelona's finest spaces for more daring contemporary art, the Sala Montcada by the Picasso Museum, including 2001 exhibits of Sergio Prego's video performances, and the films of Finnish artist Eija-Liisa Ahtila.
Branches: CaixaForum, Avda Marquès de Comillas s/n, Montjuïc (93 484 5165); Sala Montcada C/Montcada 14, La Ribera (93 310 06 99).

Museu d'Art Contemporani de Barcelona (MACBA)

Plaça dels Àngels 1, Raval (93 412 08 10/group enquiries 93 412 14 13/fax 93 412 46 02/ macba@macba.es/www.macba.es). Metro Catalunya/bus all routes to Plaça Catalunya. **Open** *26 Sept-24 June* 11am-7.30pm Mon, Wed-Fri; 10am-8pm Sat; 10am-3pm Sun; closed Tue. *25 June-25 Sept* 11am-8pm Mon, Wed, Fri; 11am-9.30pm Thur; 10am-8pm Sat; 10am-3pm Sun; closed Tue. **Guided tours** (26 Sept-24 June only) 6pm Wed, Sat; noon Sun; group tours by appointment. **Admission** 800ptas; 550ptas concessions; 550ptas 1 exhibition; 400ptas Wed; free under-16s. **Discounts** Articket, BC, BT. **Credit** AmEx (shop only), MC, V. **Map** p326 A1.
When Richard Meier's bone-white MACBA abruptly landed in the working class Raval neighbourhood in late 1995, before a single artwork had been installed, streams of Barcelonans dutifully shuffled through the empty galleries wagging their chins in

approval. With its perky external geometry and airy transitional spaces, including never-ending ramps between floors, MACBA was sure to shine as Barcelona's calling card to humanity. However, five years and three directors later, citizens and denizens morosely consent that Frank Gehry's spectacular Guggenheim in Bilbao has utterly upstaged it, at least when it comes to press fawning and architectural kudos. Even the paved square in front, meant to be a mecca for culturite posing (after the passé model of the Centre Pompidou in Paris) has instead become the city's nucleus for skateboarding and trick-biking as Filipino immigrants gaze on.

There is just one solace to this humbling landscape; under current director Manuel Borja-Villel, MACBA is now doing what no Barcelona museum has ever done: showing contemporary art and collecting it with certain criteria. Hired on the basis of a successful stint at the Tàpies Foundation, where he organised the best exhibitions in town, Borja-Villel has silenced years of criticism and artworld infighting. He is intelligent, but also shrewd. A Tàpies scholar, he has tried to demonstrate that Catalonia's most prestigious living artist is not merely an abstract painter but in fact a modern alchemist, in the spirit of Joseph Beuys and the Italian *arte povera*, a current he admires. Borja is allied as well to the reinterpretation of socio-political art of the '60s and '70s seen at Documenta X in 1997. In just two years he has regurgitated a handful of artists featured at that event, including Gerhard Richter, Pistoletto, South African William Kentridge and Swedish-Brazilian Öyvind Fahlström, often with admirable results. MACBA is thus a successful branch plant for contemporary art's most recent official alternative. *Art as Service*, a group show recurring to a very 70s way of thinking (opening in June 2001), reiterates this line of programming. The MACBA has been less fortunate in its treatment of Spanish art, where Borja is not as comfortable, though 2001 will include an exhibit of post-surrealist Zush and another on filmmaker Pere Portabella, who produced many of Buñuel's films (both until March). This year will also see solo shows by Dieter Roth (April-June) and Blinky Palermo (opening in October), as well as an autumn selection from

Sightseeing

Berlin's Onnasch Collection, a trade-off for its permanent loan of some excellent works (like a 1987 Dan Graham) to the museum.

MACBA shows a part of its permanent collection at all times. Since the MNAC and Museu d'Art Modern are supposed to take us up to the Civil War, the MACBA begins with the 1940s, although earlier works by Paul Klee, Alexander Calder and Catalan sculptor Leandre Cristòfol can be seen. The work from the 1940s to the 1960s is mostly painting, with Spanish expressionists like Saura, Tàpies, and Millares, and Basque abstract sculptors Jorge Oteiza and Eduardo Chillida. Holdings from the last 30 years feature more international artists, with work by Rauschenberg, Beuys, Anselm Kiefer, Mario Merz, and Christian Boltanski, along with recent acquisitions of Hans Haacke, Bruce Naumann and Raymond Hains. A copy of Richter's extraordinary 48 Portraits has been donated by the Miarnau Foundation. The Spanish collection includes a review of Catalan painting (Ràfols Casamada, Xavier Grau, Miquel Barceló) and Spanish sculpture (Miquel Navarro, Susana Solano, Sergi Aguilar), as well as conceptual artists Muntadas, Francesc Torres and the unclassifiable ZAJ.

Palau de la Virreina

La Rambla 99 (93 301 77 75) Metro Liceu/14, 38, 59, 91 bus. **Open** 11am-8.30pm Tue-Sat; 11am-2.30pm Sun, closed Mon. **Admission** 500ptas; 250ptas concessions; free under-16s. **No credit cards. Map** p326 A2.

This neo-classical palace takes its name from the wife of a Viceroy of Peru, who lived in it after its completion in the 1770s. Once the city council's main exhibition space, the Virreina handed over all significant programming to the MACBA during the late '90s. Now, under the direction of Cuban critic Iván de la Nuez, Virreina has come back strong, with the upstairs dedicated to international group shows (such as *You Are Here*, coinciding with the summer Triennial, *see p216*) and the smaller downstairs gallery focused on historical and contemporary photography (an exhibition of Mexican writer Juan Rulfo's mid 20th-century photos opens in April 2001).

Tecla Sala Centre Cultural

Avda Josep Tarradellas 44, Hospitalet de Llobregat, Outer Limits (93 338 57 71). Metro La Torrassa/bus L12 from Plaça Maria Cristina. **Open** 11am-2pm, 5-8pm Tue-Sat; 11am-2pm Sun. Closed sometimes Aug. **Admission** normally free.

Barcelona's magnetism tends to condemn all suburban museums to anonymity, even when shows are top notch. In l'Hospitalet, Tecla Sala is an attractive space doing exhibitions of international contemporary art. For spring of 2001 there is a show of British art, 'The Other Britannia', including work by David Bachelor, Grayson Perry, and Chad McCail. An expanded gallery will open in October 2001 with an exhibition of the collection of Rafael Tous (founder/director of the Metrònom gallery).

Historical art

Col.lecció Thyssen-Bornemisza – Museu Monestir de Pedralbes

Baixada del Monestir 9 (93 280 14 34). FGC Reina Elisenda/22, 63, 64, 75, 78 bus. **Open** 10am-2pm Tue-Sun; closed Mon. **Admission** *Monastery only* 400ptas; 250ptas concessions; free under-12s. *Col.lecció Thyssen only* 400ptas; 250ptas concessions; free under-12s. *Combined ticket* 700ptas; 400ptas concessions; free under-12s. Group discounts to monastery & museum. **Discounts** BC, BT. **Credit** (shop only) AmEx, DC, MC, V. **Map** p319 A1.

The Pedralbes convent was a fascinating place to visit even before the Thyssen Collection moved in, and together they make medieval religious life all the more vivid. While most of Baron Hans-Heinrich von Thyssen-Bornemisza's remarkable art collection, acquired for Spain in 1993, is in his namesake museum in Madrid, the 90 works in Barcelona harmonise with the setting, with religious images such as the Virgin predominant.

Occupying a former dormitory on one side of the noble 14th-century cloister, the collection specialises in Italian painting from the 13th to the 17th centuries – an important influence in Catalonia – and European baroque works. There is one true masterpiece, Fra Angelico's Madonna of Humility (c1430s), with her tender round cheeks and gentle demeanour. Notable paintings include a small Nativity (c1325) by Taddeo Gaddi, a subtle Madonna and Child (1545) by Titian, and a Zurbaran crucifixion. Other highlights are the Lucas Cranach the Elder portraits of saints and Tiepolo's Way to Golgotha (c1728). The Velázquez portrait of Queen Maria Anna of Austria (1655-7) is magnificent. Occasionally paintings from the Madrid museum are brought to complement the works on permanent display. Still a convent of the 'Poor Clares', the convent, with its three-level cloister, is one of the best preserved in Europe. In place until September 2001, the exhibition Petras Albas traces its history from its foundation by Queen Elisenda of Montcada to the 17th century, with special emphasis on the evolution of the architecture and the everyday life of the nuns. In the irregular Saint Michael's chapel off the cloister there are extraordinary mural paintings (1346) by Catalan master Ferrer Bassa, influenced by the school of Sienna. It is also possible to visit the old infirmary and kitchen, the downstairs stables and cistern, as well as many curious day cells built along the cloister walls (see p103).

Fundació Francisco Godia

C/Valencia 284 pral, Eixample (93 272 31 80/ www.fundaciofgodia.org). Metro Passeig de Gràcia/20, 22, 24, 28, 43, 44 bus. **Open** 10am-8pm Mon, Wed-Sun; closed Tue. **Admission** 700ptas; 350ptas concessions; free under-6s. **Credit** MC, V.

Francisco Godia united two apparently incongruous passions: he was a Formula I racing car driver (for Maserati) and an avid art collector. This cosy private museum indicates his three principal interests:

Museu Frederic Marès. *See p118.*

medieval religious art, historical ceramics, and modern painting. Medieval standouts include Alejo de Vahía's Pietà sculptural group. The modern collection has works by Ramon Casas, Julio González and Manolo Hugúe, to whom a temporary show will be dedicated in early 2001. The collection continues to expand through purchases, including foreign contemporary artists. The Godia and the Museu Egipci, located next door, share a joint entry ticket.

Museu d'Art Modern

Edifici del Parlament, Parc de la Ciutadella, La Ribera/Port Olímpic (93 319 57 28). Metro Ciutadella/14, 39, 40, 41, 42, 51, 100, 141 bus. **Open** 10am-7pm Tue-Sat; 10am-2.30pm Sun; closed Mon. **Guided tours** noon Sat, Sun. **Admission** 500ptas; 350ptas concessions; free under-7s; group discounts. **Discounts** Articket, BC. **Credit** (shop only) V. **Map** p325 F6.

Sharing one of the 18th-century citadel buildings in the Parc de la Ciutadella with the Catalan Parliament, this museum is not a 'museum of modern art' as understood elsewhere. Its theme is not 20th-century art, but Catalan art from the mid 19th century to the 1930s. It is therefore the main showcase for the great burst of creativity – including design – associated with *Modernisme*, Catalan art nouveau. Administratively part of the MNAC (*see pp118-9*), it is destined to move to the Palau Nacional when the upper floors of the Montjuïc museum are completed in 2003.

The galleries begin with the Romantic painter Marià Fortuny, whose liking for oriental exoticism and ostentatious detail led to his *Odalisque* (1861). After the realism of the Olot school (the Vayreda brothers) there is some impressionist-influenced work by the main *Modernista* painters, Ramon

Casas and Santiago Rusiñol. Casas' beloved image painted for the Els Quatre Gats café (*see p160*), of himself and the café's owner Pere Romeu riding a tandem, gives a vivid sense of the vibrant spirit of the close of the 19th century. There is a large related collection of drawings and graphic work as well. *Modernisme* refused to discriminate between fine and decorative arts, and a major attraction here is the superb selection of furniture and decorative. There is masterful work by Gaudí and Puig i Cadafalch, and exquisite marquetry tables and other pieces by talented furniture-maker Gaspar Homar. Josep Llimona and the neo-classicist Josep Clarà represent figurative sculpture. In painting, the collection carries on with the dark, intense gypsy portraits by Isidre Nonell, which influenced Picasso's Blue Period, the blurry, lavishly coloured landscapes of Joaquim Mir, and the eerie tones of Josep de Togores. The collection trickles off at the end with just two paintings by Dalí – one a 1925 portrait of his father – and work by two avant-garde sculptors from the 1930s, Julio González and Pau Gargallo. González' welded head (*The Tunnel*, 1932-3) points to the origins of contemporary abstract sculpture.

Museu Diocesà

Avda de la Catedral, Pla de la Seu 4, Barri Gòtic (93 315 22 13). Metro Jaume I/17, 19, 40, 45 bus. **Open** 10am-2pm, 5-8pm Tue-Sat; 11am-2pm Sun; closed Mon. **Admission** 300ptas. **Credit** (shop only) V. **Map** p326 B2.

The best of Catalan religious art is in the MNAC on Montjuïc, but this space run by the Diocese of Barcelona has a few strong works, such as a group of sculpted virgins on the top floor, altarpieces by the Gothic master Bernat Martorell and the murals from Polinyà. The display is rather confusing and disorganised, but the visit is interesting for the building itself, which includes the Pia Almoina, a former almshouse, stuck on to a Renaissance canon's residence, which in turn was built inside a Roman tower. The effects of recent renovation top off this architectural mishmash so typical of Barcelona.

Museu Frederic Marès

Plaça Sant Iu 5-6, Barri Gòtic (93 310 58 00). Metro Jaume I/17, 19, 40, 45 bus. **Open** 10am-5pm Tue, Thur; 10am-7pm Wed, Fri, Sat; 10am-3pm Sun; closed Mon. **Admission** 500ptas; 400ptas groups (by appointment); 300ptas concessions; free under-12s and for all from 4pm Wed, 1st Sun of month. **Guided tours** 11.30pm Sun. **Discounts** BC. **Credit** (shop only) AmEx, MC, V. **Map** p327 B3.

The son of a customs agent in Port Bou on the French border, Frederic Marès possibly learnt his trade by observing how valuable objects were 'collected' from travellers unable to pay import duties in cash. Trained as a sculptor (his figurative bronzes and marbles are found all over Barcelona), Marès dedicated his 97-year-long life to gathering every imaginable type of object. Created for him by the city in the 1940s, his museum contains his personal collection of religious sculpture, and the stunning 'Sentimental Museum'. Legions of sculpted virgins, crucifixions and saints on the lower floors testify to an intense interest in the history of his profession. Marès even collected clothing for saints. The Museu Sentimental on the top floor contains his more extraordinary collections: everything from iron keys, ceramics and tobacco pipes to pocket watches, early daguerreotypes, and Torah pointers. Especially beautiful is the Sala Femenina, in a room once belonging to the medieval royal palace: fans, sewing scissors, nutcrackers and perfume flasks give a charming image of 19th-century bourgeois taste. The museum has completed the first part of a well-tempered renovation programme, which is bringing some coherence to Marès' kleptomaniac collecting and making it possible to appreciate the real quality of the pieces. When the basement is completed, religious sculpture from different periods will be more clearly organised (Romanesque, Gothic, Renaissance, baroque); the renovation has also included the opening of Marès' own study and library upstairs. The Marès also hosts an interesting and unusual range of temporary shows; other pluses include unusually good labelling in English for a Barcelona museum, and the fact that the handsome patio contains a great open-air café in summer, the Cafè d'Estiu (*see p158*).

Museu Nacional d'Art de Catalunya (MNAC)

Palau Nacional, Parc de Montjuïc (93 325 57 73/ www.gencat.es/mnac). Metro Espanya/bus all routes to Plaça d'Espanya, then escalator. **Open** 10am-7pm Tue, Wed, Fri, Sat; 10am-9pm Thur; 10am-2.30pm Sun; closed Mon. **Admission** 800ptas; temporary exhibitions 500ptas; combined ticket 900ptas; 30% discount concessions, after 6pm Thur; group, family

By Jaume Huguet, from the **MNAC**.

discounts; free under-7s. *Romanesque & Gothic* free 1st Thur of month. **Discounts** Articket, BC, BT. **Credit** (shop only) V. **Map** p323 A6.

In the first decades of the 20th century a handful of art historians realised that scores of solitary churches in the Pyrenees were falling into ruin, and with them the extraordinary Romanesque mural paintings that adorned their interiors. Entire chunks of buildings were 'saved' by private collectors to be set up elsewhere (as in The Cloisters in New York), but in Catalonia the laborious task was begun of removing murals intact from church apses and remounting them on new supports. Since the 1930s, the Palau Nacional has been the haven for this rare legacy, unique in the world, now shown in an updated installation. Looking down from a regal perch on Montjuïc, the Palau may look like the baroque palace of some absolute monarch, although it was actually built as a 'temporary pavilion' for the 1929 Exhibition. If that clash of times and styles does not make it enough of a pastiche, then its renovation under the architect Gae Aulenti, famous for the Musée d'Orsay in Paris, helps provide the ultimate postmodern touch.

The MNAC makes no attempt to represent major international tendencies in art as truly great art museums do. The Gothic section, however superb, presents exclusively Catalan art and its influences. Not even the large private collection left to Catalonia by the Cambó family can make up for this. Stalled construction work has finally got going again, and in 2003 the collection from the Museu d'Art Modern in the Ciutadella park will be moved into upstairs galleries, yet even this will not turn the MNAC into anything more than an excellent showcase for the history of art in Catalonia.

The undisputed star of the MNAC is the Romanesque, a style long disdained as rough and primitive. As 11th-century Christendom pushed the Moors out of Catalonia, small churches and monasteries were founded, serving as beacons for the beleaguered pilgrims and monks. Inside, unsophisticated depictions of the Pantocrator (Christ in Majesty), the Virgin, biblical stories and the sufferings of the saints served to instruct doubting villagers in the basics of the faith. The result is a series of images of extraordinary and timeless power. The display comprises 21 sections in loose chronological order, with the murals set into freestanding wood supports or reconstructed church interiors. One of the highlights is the tremendous Crist de Taüll, from the 12th-century church of Sant Climent de Taüll in the Pyrenean valley of Boí, in section five. The massive figure of the Pantocrator holds a book with the words *Ego Sum Lux Mundi*, 'I am the Light of the World'. Section seven reveals another treasure, from the church of Santa Maria de Taüll (in the same village as Sant Climent), with an apse of the Epiphany and Three Kings and a wall of the Last Judgement, packed with images of Purgatory. On some columns original 'graffiti' has been preserved, scratchings – probably by monks – of animals, crosses and labyrinths. Other sections, including carvings and sculptures, focus thematically on dramatic angels, strange seraphim with wings covered in eyes (from the apse of Santa Maria d'Aneu), or the transition from the expressionless early figures of the Virgin to the more tender renderings that emerged later.

The Gothic collection is also impressive. Visitors can follow the evolution of Catalan Gothic painting, including altarpieces on wood panels and alabaster sculptures pulled out of parish churches in Barcelona itself. The highlights are the works of the indisputable Catalan masters from the Golden Age, Bernat Martorell (section 11), and the tremendously subtle Jaume Huguet (section 12), including a series on Saint Vincent and a lovely *Saint George Escorting a Princess*. The MNAC's Renaissance and baroque holdings come predominantly from the personal collection of early 20th-century politician-financier Francesc Cambó, and are an international mix of works from the 15th to the 18th centuries, with a few non-Spanish masters (Tintoretto, Rubens, De la Tour) mixed in with national figures (Zurbarán and Goya). High-quality temporary shows presented at the MNAC in 2001 include a spring retrospective of *Modernista* painter Ramon Casas, an autumn exhibit of Italian painting from the Hermitage, and a review of photography from the Spanish Civil War late in the year. The MNAC has good English labelling, and a helpful English guidebook.

Decorative & performing arts

Museu de Ceràmica/Museu de les Arts Decoratives

*Palau Reial de Pedralbes, Avda Diagonal 686, Zona Alta (*Ceràmica *93 280 16 21/*Arts Decoratives *93 280 50 24/www.bcn.es/icub).*
Metro Palau Reial/7, 33, 67, 68, 74, 75 bus.
Open 10am-6pm Tue-Sat; 10am-3pm Sun; closed Mon. **Guided tours** by appointment 10am-1pm Tue-Fri. **Admission** *Both museums* 700ptas; 400ptas concessions; free under-12s. *One museum only* 400ptas; 250ptas concessions. **Discounts** BC, BT. **No credit cards. Map** p319 A2.

The Palau Reial on the Diagonal was originally built as a residence for the family of Gaudí's patron Eusebi Güell, and in one corner of the gardens is a famous iron gate designed by Gaudí. It became a royal palace and was greatly expanded in the 1920s, when it was given to King Alfonso XIII. It now houses two separate museums, both accessible on the same ticket.

The Ceramics Museum, another museum that has been attractively refurbished, has an exceptionally fine collection of Spanish ceramics stretching back several centuries. These are expertly organised by sharply varying regional and historical styles. Especially beautiful are the medieval dishes, mostly for everyday use, like those from Manises near Valencia. Catalan holdings feature two popular tile murals from the 18th century: *La Xocolatada* depicts chocolate-drinking at a garden party, while the other gives a graphic image of a chaotic baroque bullfight. An entire section is dedicated to the famous Valencia manufactory of Alcora, which from 1727 to 1895 satisfied the tastes of the world's aristocracies.

Upstairs there is a refined selection of 20th-century Spanish work – highlights are the refined simplicity of Catalan master Josep Llorens Artigas, and pieces by Picasso and Miró – and a space for excellent temporary exhibits of contemporary ceramics. The Decorative Arts Museum occupies the other wing of the building. The palace's original painted walls provide a warm setting for furniture and decorative objects from the Middle Ages onward, with styles from Gothic through to romanticism and Catalan *Modernisme*, moving to art deco and into our era. Quality is high, although only a small portion of the first-class holdings of decorative clocks, Catalan glasswork and other artefacts are shown at any one time. Visitors can also look down into the palace's sumptuously decorated oval throne room. The final section is normally dedicated to 20th-century Catalan industrial design in changing temporary shows. Until the biennial Design Spring in 2001 there will be an exhibition by Standby, an online platform for innovative design, while throughout the year there is a show of modern jewellery from some 30 designers.

Sightseeing

Museu de les Arts Decoratives.

Museu del Calçat (Shoe Museum)

*Plaça Sant Felip Neri 5, Barri Gòtic (93 301 45 33).
Metro Liceu, Jaume I/17, 19, 40, 45 bus.*
Open 11am-2pm Tue-Sun; closed Mon. **Admission**
200ptas; 100ptas concessions; free under-7s; group
discounts. **No credit cards. Map** p327 B3.

Run by a shoemakers' guild founded in 1203, this
museum is in a tiny building on one of the city's
most enigmatic squares. On view is only a small part
of a collection that begins with original Roman sandals and goes up to present-day footwear: especially fine are the women's embroidered satin dress
shoes from the last century. Shoes worn by the
famous include pairs donated by cellist Pau Casals
and celebrated Catalan clown Charlie Rivel, or the
boots of the first Catalan to climb Everest. There is
also seamless footwear, baby booties, traditional
shepherds' shoes, and an enormous shoe made from
the mould for the Columbus statue at the foot (where
else) of La Rambla.

Museu de la Música

*Avda Diagonal 373, Eixample (93 416 11 57).
Metro Diagonal/6, 15, 33, 34 bus.* **Open** *Mid June-
mid Sept* 10am-2pm Tue-Sun. *Mid Sept-mid June*
10am-2pm Tue, Thur-Sun; 10am-8pm Wed; closed
Mon. **Admission** 400ptas; 200ptas concessions;
free under-12s. **Discounts** BC. **No credit cards.
Map** p320 D4.

The museum now occupies the beautiful *Modernista*
Casa Quadras, reformed by the *Modernista* architect
Puig i Cadafalch in 1902, though it is destined to
move to the Auditori music hall. Its collection of historic guitars, tracing the instrument from its origins
200 years ago in Andalusia, is one of the best in the
world, and the museum does a good job of contrasting European instruments with parallel versions from other continents. An excellent example
is a display linking African percussion with jazz
drumming, while the cross-cultural mix of instruments as diverse as wooden flutes, bagpipes and
sitars is fascinating. The collection testifies to an
ebullient instrument industry in Barcelona dating
back to the 18th century. Small temporary shows are
held on the top floor.

Museu Tèxtil i de la Indumentària (Textile & Fashion Museum)

*C/Montcada 12, La Ribera (93 319 76 03/93 310 45
16). Metro Jaume I/17, 19, 40, 45 bus.* **Open** 10am-
6pm Tue-Sat; 10am-3pm Sun; closed Mon. **Guided
tours** by appointment. **Admission** 400ptas; 300ptas
groups; 200ptas concessions; free under-12s, 3-6pm
1st Sat of mth, student groups (by appointment) on
3rd Wed of mth. *Combined ticket with Museu
Barbier-Mueller* 700ptas; 400ptas concessions.
Discounts BC. **Credit** (shop only) AmEx, MC, V.
Map p327 C3.

Even if clothing is not your thing, the sight of café
tables might draw you into the handsome courtyard
of this C/Montcada palace, across from the Picasso
Museum. It occupies two adjacent buildings, the

Palau Nadal and Palau dels Marquesos de LIió; the latter retains some of its 13th-century wooden ceilings. It brings together items from a number of collections, including medieval Hispano-Arab textiles and the city's lace and embroidery collection. The real highlight is the collection of historic fashions – from baroque to 20th-century – that Manuel Rocamora donated in the 1960s, one of the finest anywhere. Recently the museum has also benefited from some important donations, including one from Spanish designer Cristóbal Balenciaga, famous for the 1958 'baby doll' dress; a related temporary exhibit of tailored women's suits from the same period will last until June 2001. Contemporary textile art is the theme of small temporary shows, and the museum has an excellent shop (see p185). For the very popular café, see p166.

History & archaeology

Museu d'Arqueologia de Catalunya
Passeig de Santa Madrona 39-41, Montjuïc (93 423 21 49/www.mac.es). Metro Poble Sec/55 bus. **Open** 9.30am-7pm Tue-Sat; 10am-2.30pm Sun; closed Mon. **Admission** 400ptas; 300ptas concessions; free under-16s; group discounts. **No credit cards. Map** p323 B6.

In the Palace of Decorative Arts, built for the 1929 Exhibition on Montjuïc, this is one of the city's better scientific museums, and the art deco centre section has been imaginatively spruced up. Its artefacts come mostly from digs in Catalonia and Mediterranean Spain, starting with the Palaeolithic period and moving on through subsequent eras, with relics of Greek, Punic, Roman and Visigoth colonisers, taking us up to the early Middle Ages. There are curious objects related to early metallurgy, along with models of Neolithic and Iron Age burial sites.

A few galleries are dedicated to the Majorcan Talaiotic cave culture, and there is a very good display (expanded with the results of several digs-in-progress) on the Iberians, the pre-Hellenic, pre-Roman inhabitants of Southeastern Spain, whose level of decorative sophistication has been re-evaluated in recent years. Lovely terracotta goddesses and some beautiful jewellery taken from a dig on Ibiza recall the Carthaginian presence in the Balearics, and a large gallery is wholly dedicated to Greek Empúries, a source of extensive holdings (for Empúries itself, *see pp271-2*). Roman work includes original floor mosaics, actually set into the floor, and a reconstructed Pompeian palace room. The centre section has monumental Greek and Roman pieces, including a sarcophagus showing the rape of Proserpina (Persephone), and upstairs there are Roman funerary *steles* and fine mosaics, one of a woman wearing a grotesque comic mask. For some reason an enormous statue of a sexually charged Priapus cannot be visited up close (formerly hidden from view completely, it is still an embarrassment to curators). The museum also hosts the odd temporary show.

Museu Barbier-Mueller d'Art Precolombí
C/Montcada 14, La Ribera (93 319 76 03/ museubarbie@mail.bcn.es). Metro Jaume I/17, 19, 40, 45 bus. **Open** 10am-6pm Tue-Sat; 10am-3pm Sun; closed Mon. **Admission** 500ptas; 350ptas concessions; group discounts; free under-12s, 3-6pm 1st Sat of mth, student groups (by appointment) on 3rd Wed of mth. *Combined ticket with Museu Tèxtil* 700ptas; 400ptas concessions. **Discounts** BC. **Credit** (shop only) AmEx, MC, V. **Map** p327 C3.

Though Columbus' famed voyage took place in 1492, this museum demonstrates how the 'pre-Columbian' era extended well beyond that date, as the subjugation of indigenous cultures by the *conquistadores* lasted for decades. In 1996 the Barbier-Mueller museum in Geneva agreed to show pieces from its collection of New World art in Barcelona, carefully selected and displayed on a rotating basis. To house them, the city renovated a floor of this medieval palace next to the Textile Museum.

With its dark, overly theatrical lighting, a cliché of 'tribal art' presentation, the museum treats us to many extraordinary pieces from Mexico, Central America, the Andes and the lower Amazon. Some of the exhibits date back to the second millennium BC. Gold and silver objects from Peru and Bolivia complete this good introduction to pre-Columbian art. For early 2001 the display will be entirely altered to accommodate an exhibition on Central America which run throughout the museum. The Barbier-Mueller co-ordinates projects with other museums with connections to the Americas, such as the Museu Marítim and the Museu de la Xocolata.

Aztec god of the hearth, Huehueteotl.
Museu Barbier-Mueller d'Art Precolombí.

Museu Egipci de Barcelona

C/Valencia 284, Eixample (93 488 01 88/
www.fundclos.com). Metro Passeig de Gràcia/7, 16,
17, 22, 24, 28 bus. **Open** 10am-8pm Mon-Sat; 10am-
2pm Sun. **Admission** 900ptas; 700ptas concessions;
free under-5s. **Guided tours** (by appointment)
11am, 5pm Sat; 9pm Fri 1,900ptas. **Discounts** BC.
Credit (shop only) MC, V. **Map** p320 D4.

Jordi Clos was yet a teenager when his fascination
for Ancient Egypt was first sparked, beginning a
small collection with the help of his father. Now a
successful hotelier (he owns Derby Hotels, including the five-star Claris nearby), Clos pours his passion and free time into Barcelona's Egyptian
Museum, which moved into this luminous new
space in May 2000. Run by Clos' prestigious archaeological foundation, reputable enough to do official
digs in Egypt and run university programmes, the
museum is the ideal showcase for a well-chosen collection that includes religious statuary, mummies,
jewellery and elements from everyday life spanning
over 3,000 years of Nile-sprinkled culture. The oldest objects include predynastic ceramics (3,500 BC),
while some of the outstanding pieces are the friezes
from the Tomb of Iny (5th or 6th Dynasty), a *stele*
representing Cleopatra VII, and the little mummy
of the Girl of Kemet, whose afterlife began prema-
turely one day in the Ptolemaic period. Dramatic
recreations of burial settings and impressive x-rays
of mummified animals enhance the display. While
Clos has no rights over the incredible material
retrieved from his archaeological efforts, the foundation continues to buy, adding pieces like a large
stone pharaoh sculpture that greets visitors as they
enter the galleries. In spring 2001 there will be a
temporary exhibit on the influence of Egyptology
on modern fashion and jewellery, while the museum wraps up the year with a show of mummies.
The gift shop is a mine of related books, games and
trinkets, with much in English.

Museu Etnològic

Passeig de Santa Madrona, Montjuïc (93 424 68
07). Metro Poble Sec/55 bus. **Open** 10am-7pm Tue,
Thur; 10am-2pm Wed, Fri-Sun; closed Mon.
Admission 400ptas; 250ptas concessions; group
discounts; free under-12s. **Discounts** BC. **No credit
cards. Map** p323 A6.

Extensive holdings from non-European cultures,
totalling over 30,000 pieces, are shown in
Montjuïc's Ethnology Museum, on a rotating basis.
Shows change every few years, and are designed
to give an idea of different cultures rather than just
displaying objects out of context. The museum is
particularly strong in pre-Columbian artefacts, and
religious sculptures from India and Nepal. It has
also acquired a fine collection of *Mingei*, Japanese
popular crafts, and until June 2001 has an exhibition of gastronomy and culture in present-day
Japan, part of a new permanent Japan display. This
interest in contemporary ethnology has prompted
an exhibition on the current cultural mosaic in
Barcelona, lasting into 2002.

Museu d'Història de Catalunya

Plaça Pau Vila 3, Barceloneta (93 225 47 00/
www.cultura.gencat.es/museus/mhc). Metro
Barceloneta/17, 39, 45, 47, 57, 59, 64, 157 bus.
Open 10am-7pm Tue, Thur-Sat; 10am-8pm Wed;
10am-2.30pm Sun; closed Mon. **Admission** 500ptas;
350ptas concessions; group discounts; free under-7s,
disabled. Temporary exhibitions & combined ticket
prices vary. **Guided tours** noon Sun, public
holidays. **Discounts** BC, BT. **Credit** (shop only)
MC, V. **Map** p327 C4.

This museum is a rarity in Barcelona: it deliberately sets out to explain something thoroughly –
Catalan history – from start to finish. Opened in
1996 in the Palau de Mar by the old port, the MHC
is not so much a collection of valuable objects as a
historical overview from prehistory to the present,
organised thematically with visually dynamic displays. A multitude of materials is used to keep us
entertained – texts, photos, real objects, reproductions, videos, animated models and recreations of
domestic scenes. There are also hands-on exhibitions, such as a waterwheel and wearable armour.
The eight sections have titles like 'Roots', 'Birth of
a Nation' (the consolidation of Catalonia in the
Middle Ages) and so on, coming into the contemporary era with 'The Electric Years', including the
Civil War (with a recreated bomb shelter), and
'Undoing and New Beginnings' on life under Franco
and after. Large temporary shows deal with just
about everything imaginable, from the history of
the Liceu opera house to the experience of Catalan
partisans in the Mauthausen concentration camp
(on until March 2001). A major exhibition on the
Jewish presence in Catalonia in the Middle Ages
opens in November 2001. A Generalitat project, it
is sometimes criticised for ignoring certain realities
in Catalonia – such as the massive immigrations
from the rest of Spain since the 1930s – though
newly-appointed director Jaume Sobrequés, a
socialist historian, is preparing changes. The
exhibits are labelled in English, and English tours
are available for groups. A Mediateca on the upper
floor has material in English, and the top-floor
restaurant has an unbeatable view. There is also an
exceptional gift shop.

Museu d'Història de la Ciutat

C/Veguer 2, Barri Gòtic (93 315 11 11). Metro
Jaume I/17, 19, 40, 45 bus. **Open** *1 Oct-31 May*
10am-2pm, 4-8pm Tue-Sat; 10am-2pm Sun; closed
Mon. *1 June-30 Sept* 10am-8pm Tue-Sat; 10am-2pm
Sun; closed Mon. **Guided tours** by appointment.
Admission 500ptas; 300ptas concessions; free
under-12s & 1st Sat of mth. **Discounts** BC. **No
credit cards. Map** p327 B3.

The City History Museum had a chance beginning:
when the medieval Casa Padellàs was being transferred to this site in 1931, remains of the Roman
city of Barcino were uncovered while digging the
new foundations. They now form a giant
labyrinthine cellar beneath the museum, with
Roman streets and villa layouts still visible. A visit

to the remains takes you right underneath the Plaça del Rei and winds as far as the cathedral itself, beneath which there is a 4th-century baptistery. Busts, monuments and other sculpture found in the excavations are also on display.

The admission fee also gives you access to sections of the former royal palace around the plaça such as the Saló del Tinell, a medieval banquet hall with excellent temporary shows (for mid 2001, on wine, olive oil and bread in Mediterranean culture), and the not-to-be-missed 'Rei Martí' tower, accessible through the Gothic Santa Agata chapel. The Casa Padellàs itself, which is not large enough to accommodate a permanent chronological display of the city's history, will offer an exhibition on Spain under Charles V in early 2001. The bookshop and information centre are useful as well. See also p75.

Museu Marítim

Avda de les Drassanes, Raval (93 342 99 29/ www.diba.es/museus/maritim). Metro Drassanes/14, 20, 36, 38, 57, 59, 64, 91, 157 bus. **Open** 10am-7pm daily. **Admission** 800ptas; 400ptas concessions; free under-7s. **Discounts** BC, BT. **Credit** MC, V. **Map** p327 A4.

The oft-stated remark that Barcelona has lived with its back to the sea is belied by the building this museum occupies – the giant Drassanes or medieval shipyards, one of the finest examples of civil Gothic architecture in the world. Since a 1990s facelift, the museum has also become one of the most visited in the city.

The highlight is the full-scale reproduction of the Royal Galley that was the flagship of Don Juan de Austria at the battle of Lepanto against the Turks in 1571. This battle and the subsequent history of Barcelona's port are now presented in 'The Great Adventure of the Sea', a series of unashamedly audience-pleasing historical simulations, with headphone commentaries (also in English). Visitors are caught in a storm on a 19th-century trade ship, take a steamer to Buenos Aires, and go underwater in the Ictineo, the prototype submarine of Catalan inventor Narcís Monturiol. Another display, 'From the Boat to the Company', recreates dockside-life scenes from the late colonial period. There's lots of space for temporary shows under the Gothic arches, which need restoration work, meaning parts of the collection could get shuttled about from mid 2001 onwards. The museum has a prolific collection of paintings and drawings that show how the port of Barcelona has changed, as well as pleasure boats, traditional fishing craft, figureheads, explanations of boat-building techniques and a section on map-making and navigation. A full visit takes a good hour and a half. Attached to the museum there is also an excellent café-restaurant, La Llotja (*see p138*).

Museu Militar

Castell de Montjuïc, Parc de Montjuïc (93 329 86 13). Metro Paral.lel then Funicular and Telefèric de Montjuïc. **Open** *Oct-June* 9.30am-7pm Tue-Fri;

9.30am-8pm Sat, Sun; closed Mon. *June-Sept* 9.30am-8pm Tue-Sun; closed Mon. **Admission** 250ptas; group discounts. **Discounts** BC. **No credit cards. Map** p323 B7.

The Military Museum has been under fire since late 2000 when the gift shop was found to be selling objects with Franco-era and Nazi symbolism. Already controversial for the portrait gallery of repressive generals and Franco's equestrian statue (the only representation of the dictator left in Barcelona), the museum occupies the 18th-century fortress overlooking the city on the top of Montjuïc. Used to bombard rather than protect Barcelona in past conflicts, and as a prison and place of execution after the Civil War – a monument in the moat to Catalan President Lluís Companys recalls his death here in 1940 – the castle has strong repressive associations. However, its selection of historic weapons from around the world is quite special: armour, swords and lances; muskets (beautiful Moroccan *moukhala*), rifles and pistols; and menacing crossbows. Other highlights include 23,000 lead soldiers representing a Spanish division of the 1920s, and, very strangely, a display of Jewish tombstones from the mountain's desecrated medieval cemetery, the only direct reminder of death in the building.

Science & natural history

Museu de la Ciència

C/Teodor Roviralta, Zona Alta (93 212 60 50/ www.fundacio.lacaixa.es). FGC Tibidabo then Tramvia Blau/17, 22, 73, 85, 158 bus. **Open** 10am-8pm Tue-Sun; closed Mon. **Admission** 500ptas; 250-150ptas concessions; group discounts; free under-7s and 1st Sun of mth. Additional exhibitions 250ptas extra; 200ptas concessions. **Discounts** BC. **Credit** (shop only) MC, V.

The ever-active 'la Caixa' cultural foundation runs Barcelona's Science Museum, fitted into a restored factory building near the foot of Tibidabo. Oriented especially towards school groups and young people, the museum is designed to teach basic scientific principles in the most engaging way possible. The quality of the displays assures there's plenty to interest visitors of all ages, although some of the museum's hands-on exhibits, highly innovative when it opened in the 1980s, look a little 'mechanical' and dated now that many state-of-the-art museums are digitalised. The permanent section uses lively interactive apparatus to explain optical phenomena, quirks of perception, mechanical principles, meteorology, the solar system – there's a planetarium – and many other topics. The *Clik dels nens* section is for small children. A temporary exhibition on form in nature, with over 500 real objects and illustrative experiments, lasts until mid 2001.

Museu de Geologia

Passeig Picasso, Parc de la Ciutadella (93 319 68 95). Metro Arc de Triomf/14, 39, 40, 41, 42, 51, 141 bus. **Open** 10am-2pm Tue, Wed, Fri-Sun; 10am-6.30pm Thur; closed Mon. **Guided tours** by

Sightseeing

appointment. **Admission** 400ptas; 250ptas concessions; free under-12s, 1st Sun of mth; group discounts. **Discounts** BC. **No credit cards**. **Map** p325 E6.

Once known as the Museu Martorell, the oldest museum in Barcelona opened in 1882 in this same building to house the private holdings of Francesc Martorell. In one wing there is a rather dry display of minerals, painstakingly classified, alongside explanations of geological phenomena found in Catalonia. More interesting is the other wing, with a selection from the museum's collection of over 300,000 fossils, including imprints of flora and fauna – even dinosaurs – and fossilised bones from all geological periods. Curiously enough, many were found locally on Montjuïc or inside caves on the site of the Parc Güell.

Museu de Zoologia

Passeig Picasso, Parc de la Ciutadella (93 319 69 12). Metro Arc de Triomf/14, 39, 40, 41, 42, 51, 141 bus. **Open** 10am-2pm Tue, Wed, Fri-Sun; 10am-6pm Thur; closed Mon. **Admission** 400ptas; 250ptas concessions; free under-12s, 1st Sun of mth; group discounts. **Discounts** BC. **No credit cards**. **Map** p325 E6.

Another of the city's older museums in the Ciutadella, the Zoology Museum occupies the much-loved 'Castle of the Three Dragons', built by Domènech i Muntaner as the café-restaurant for the 1888 Exhibition. The separation between structure and façade was considered quite unusual at the time. Downstairs there is the Whale Room with, yes, a whale skeleton, where popular temporary shows are organised on endangered species or other environmentally sound themes. The upper floor has a big collection of dissected and preserved animals, displayed systematically according to group and species. There is a very thorough guidebook, available in English.

Specialities & oddities

Museu d'Autòmates del Tibidabo (Tibidabo Automata Museum)

Parc d'Atraccions del Tibidabo, Zona Alta (93 211 79 42). FGC Av Tibidabo/17, 22, 73, 85 bus, then Tramvia Blau and Funicular de Tibidabo. **Open** as funfair *(see p208)*. **Admission** included in funfair ticket. **Credit** MC, V.

The first automata belonged to the mechanical age, operating without the constant intervention of external energy. In contrast, this collection of electrified toys from the early 20th century, inside the Gran Tibidabo funfair, contains some of the finest examples of coin-operated fairground machines in the world. The entertaining scenarios include a 1924 mechanic's workshop and the saucy *La Monyos* (1913), named after a famed eccentric who cruised the Rambla: she claps her hands, shakes her shoulders and winks, her pigtails flying. Best of all is the depiction of hell (*El Infierno*): look through a small glass hole into a fireball and, to the sound of roar-

ing flames, repentant maidens slide slowly into the pit prodded by naked devils. Admission is pricey if you do not take in the amusement park as well.

Museu de Carrosses Fúnebres (Hearse Museum)

C/Sancho de Avila 2, Eixample (93 484 17 20). Metro Marina/6, 10, 40, 42, 141 bus. **Open** 10am-1pm, 4-6pm daily. **Admission** free. **Map** p325 F5.

Mysteriously invisible from the street (ask the guard at the desk to see it), this incredible collection of historic funeral carriages definitely counts as one of Barcelona's most bizarre cultural assets. The unquestionable charm of these 20 horse-drawn carriages and three motorised vehicles is that they were used in Barcelona from the 18th century up to the 1970s. Carriages vary from delicately ornate white hearses for children and 'single people' (presumably virgins), to a windowless black velour mourning carriage that carried the unfortunate 'second wife' (mistress) to the cemetery gates. Dummy horses and funeral officials in costume complete the scene, with images of the carriages as originally used. The Studebaker used to bury Generalitat President Francesc Macià in 1933 and a hefty Buick Special round off the collection.

Museu de l'Eròtica

La Rambla 96 bis (93 318 98 65/ www.eroticamuseum.com). Metro Liceu/14, 38, 59, N6, N9 bus. **Open** 10am-midnight daily. **Admission** 975ptas; 775ptas concessions; free under-16s (only accompanied by an adult). **Discounts** BT. **Credit** MC, V. **Map** p327 A3.

This private museum would be charming if it were not for the obvious disdain it shows for the intelligence of its guests. Some of the holdings, like a genuinely rare collection of erotic art – *Kama Sutra* illustrations and Japanese erotic drawings, 19th-century engravings by German Peter Fendi, and compelling photos of brothels in Barcelona's *Barrio Chino* in the decadent 1930s – could be appreciated if the displays were not entirely lacking in tact. From the shady-looking staircase on up, the décor looks as though it had deliberately been made as tacky and shabby as possible. A shame in a city with true connoisseurship for the bawdy.

Museu FC Barcelona President Núñez

Nou Camp, Avda Arístides Maillol, access 9, Les Corts (93 496 36 00/93 496 36 08). Metro Collblanc/15, 54, 56, 57, 75, 101, 157 bus. **Open** 10am-6.30pm Mon-Sat; 10am-2pm Sun. **Admission** 525ptas; 350ptas concessions; group discounts. **Discounts** BC, BT. **No credit cards**. **Map** p319 A3.

A must-see for soccer fans, Museu de FC Barcelona (the Núñez bit is for the club's recently retired 20-year President) vies with the slightly higher-brow Picasso as Barcelona's most visited museum. Even non-fanatics might find a certain charm in the paraphernalia and photos that have accumulated since

Heaven's scent. **Museu del Perfum.**

Thousands of people walk past the Regia perfumery (*see p191*) every day without realising that the 'Museu del Perfum' sign is not a promotional gimmick. Entering through a narrow corridor at the back, one comes into a room full of hundreds of scent bottles, dating from predynastic Egypt to the present day. The museum began when owner Ramon Planas moved his shop here in 1960, and began gathering what is now one of the world's finest collections. Hundreds of bottles trace the period before perfumes were labelled, including Egyptian, Greek, Roman and baroque examples. The rest are shown by brands: there are examples from the late 18th century onwards of Guerlain, Dior and 4711; there are limited-edition bottles, such as a Dalí creation for Schiaparelli; and a prized art nouveau flask by René Lalique for the Coty Cyclamen brand. The bottled aromas of many other lands – India, Turkey, Iran, even countries in the former Soviet Union – can also be seen, if not sniffed.

Museu Verdaguer

Vil.la Joana, Carretera de les Planes, Vallvidrera (93 204 78 05). By train FGC from Plaça Catalunya to Baixador de Vallvidrera. **Open** 11am-3pm Sat, Sun; visits by appointment Tue-Fri; closed Mon. **Admission** free.

Priest Jacint Verdaguer (1845-1902) was the foremost poet of the 19th-century Catalan *Renaixença*. His neoromantic poetry, often on nature or spiritual themes, was enormously popular; the epic *L'Atlantida* was later adapted to music by Manuel de Falla. Verdaguer spent his last weeks in this bourgeois summer home on Collserola, now homage to his life and work. Original furnishings, the old kitchen and a small chapel give a clear image of life here a hundred years ago. With the Collserola information centre nearby, a visit complements a walk around the mountain. (*see p102*). On your way back to town muse over his 1883 poem *A Barcelona*: 'Among workshops and factories the bell towers and spires/like fingers through smoke gusts point upward to Heaven.'

Museu de la Xocolata (Chocolate Museum)

Antic Convent de Sant Agustí, Plaça Pons i Clerch, La Ribera (93 268 78 78). Metro Jaume I/17, 19, 39, 40, 45, 51 bus. **Open** 10am-7pm Mon, Wed-Sat; 10am-3pm Sun; closed Tue. **Admission** 400ptas; 340ptas concessions; free under-7s. **No credit cards.** **Map** p317 C3.

The pastry cooks' guild could easily have opted to stick a sweet shop alongside their new school, but to its credit has come up with an attractive museum-quality display. The exhibition includes explanations of chocolate's New World origins; its use in medicine and as an aphrodisiac, and its arrival in Europe, as well as many Catalan Easter '*monos*' – elaborate sculptures for Holy Week which put the rudimentary bunnies we all know to shame. There is also a temporary gallery and, needless to say, a very tempting shop.

Swiss immigrant Joan Gamper founded the club in 1899. The shiniest silver in the trophy case belongs to the European Cup Winners' Cups of 1979, 1982, 1989 and 1997, and the club's greatest treasure, the 1992 European Cup, won at Wembley. Appropriately enough, the museum bought Wembley memorabilia at auction – goalposts, the royal box, stuff from the locker room – for a future recreation of the glorious moment. An old photo reveals the origin of Barça fans' nickname, *culés* (from *culs*, or 'bums', as in arses): spectators used to sit on the high perimeter wall surrounding the old field, their overhanging backsides offering a singular view to those outside. The chronologically arranged collection has been magnificently enhanced with the purchase of Pablo Ornaque's first-class collection of world soccer souvenirs, including old sculptures, posters and magazines, uniforms and boots and balls, often shown in historical recreations. The temporary gallery has a fine show of game posters until mid March 2001; an iffy art collection is upstairs. From the museum one steps into the cavernous Nou Camp (capacity 108,000), a partial substitute if you cannot get to a game. For general information about FC Barcelona, *see also chapter* **Sports & Fitness**.

Museu del Perfum

Passeig de Gràcia 39, Eixample (93 215 72 38/ www.perfum-museum.com). Metro Passeig de Gràcia/7, 16, 17, 22, 24, 28 bus. **Open** 10.30am-1.30pm, 4.30-7.30pm Mon-Fri; 11am-1.30pm Sat; closed Sun. **Admission** free. **Map** p320 D4.

Eat, Drink, Shop

Restaurants

From small, affordable neighbourhood joints to world-renowned shrines to the art of dining, Barcelona's restaurant scene is rich and varied.

Barcelona is a foodie's dream town, teeming with restaurants of every price range and style and inhabited by people who take their food and enjoyment of it seriously. Indeed, in a city where it seems you are constantly overhearing people talking about food, of likes, dislikes and recommendations, the only thing difficult about dining out in Barcelona is choosing a place out of its 2,700 eateries.

Most of these restaurants serve up Catalan specialities, be it a traditional, earthy version or modernised one (*see pp130-3* **Cuisine a la Catalana**). Spanish cuisine cannot really be defined as one entity, but rather consists of very different types of regional cuisines, such as seafood-rich Galician cooking, and Castilian cuisine, which excels at the art of roasting meats. Barcelona has a rich selection of restaurants from different parts of Spain, and much like their Catalan counterparts, they come in all prices and styles. Barcelona's tables have become increasingly international lately, with a growing number of restaurants that either serve very good foreign cuisine or whose cooking is greatly influenced by French, and as of late, Asian methods and ingredients. Strict vegetarians have less to choose from, but as Barcelona's restaurant scene grows so does the number of good vegetarian and vegetarian-friendly places.

Restaurants are scattered generously throughout the city, but some zones stand out for certain types of food and ambience. The neighbourhood of La Ribera is by far the city's trendiest area, with new designer spots opening up regularly. Barceloneta by the sea has long been famous for its seafood establishments, while the heaviest concentrations of traditional Catalan eateries can be found in the Barri Gòtic, Raval and Gràcia. The Eixample and Zona Alta, meanwhile, are home to some of the city's most prestigious places.

EATING HABITS

Catalans eat late: lunch starts around 2pm and goes on to about 3.30 or 4pm, and dinner is served from 9 to 9.30pm until about 11.30pm to midnight in most places, although tourist-oriented restaurants may serve as early as 8pm. Reserving a table in mid-to upper-range restaurants is always a good idea (especially for groups of more than four) and the same goes for

all restaurants at weekends. Children are welcome in most restaurants, but special children's menus are not common, and you don't often see kids dining out in upper range establishments (*see also chapter* **Children**).

As to prices, the lunchtime *menú del dia* is one of Barcelona's best bargains and one way to economise is by making this your main meal and just snacking for dinner (for a selection of *menús, see p141*). In general, lunch menus tend to fall into two types – those which offer good portions of hearty traditional food and those which offer smaller portions of creative, modern cuisine. Most menus include a starter, main dish, dessert, bread and a drink. They can also be a good, economical way of sampling the cuisine at more upscale restaurants. Eating out in the evening is more expensive, but some restaurants now offer menus at night as well, and these can be good value too. There is no percentage rule for tipping: it's common in mid- or upper-range restaurants to leave 200-300ptas – rarely over 500ptas – but many locals leave nothing or just a nominal 25ptas. Menu prices usually, but not always, include the 7% IVA tax (VAT), which is always included in the bill.

Most restaurants close on Sunday, and those that do not fill up quickly. Many establishments also close for holidays, including about a week off around Easter (from Good Friday to Easter Monday), a week or more in August, and often the first week of January. Annual closures are listed where possible, but it's always a good idea to call ahead during holiday seasons just to be sure. Air-conditioning is rare in budget to mid-range places, but is a feature of most upper range spots.

AVERAGES

Average prices listed are based on the average cost of a starter, a main course and dessert, without drink. Set menus, though, often include beer, wine or water.

The Rambla

Amaya

La Rambla 20-24 (93 302 61 38/www.amaya.com-actiu.es). Metro Liceu/14, 38, 59, 91, N9, N12 bus. **Open** 1-5pm, 8.30pm-midnight daily. **Average** 4,000ptas. **Set menu** 950ptas Mon-Fri. **Credit** AmEx, DC, MC, V. **Map** p327 A4.

Restaurants

The best

For lazy lunches
La Oficina (see p144) is the spot for a leisurely lunch on the way to the beach. In the Barri Gòtic, soothe your senses at **Mastroqué** (see p130).

For lunch after eyeballing art at the MACBA
Sink into high-backed sofas at **Silenus** (see p141), or keep the museum in view at **Pla del Angels** (see p139).

For perfect lighting
Cast your partner in an ideal light at the exquisite **Jean-Luc Figueras** (see p151), or relax your eyes at **El Pebre Blau** (see p142).

For romantic tête-a-têtes
Dawdle over dinner at cosy **Octubre 18** (see p151) or sigh with pleasure at **Specchio Magico** (see p152).

To get away from it all
Located in a charming little square, **Els Pescadors** (see p154) is far from the city centre, but worth it for the delicious food.

A big, central Basque restaurant, traditionally popular with actors, writers, opera singers and politicians. Specialities include *angulas* (elvers, baby eels), *lubina* (sea bass) and *besugo* (sea bream), cooked several different ways. The extensive wine list includes Txakoli, a light and dry Basque white wine. Livelier for lunch than dinner.

Barri Gòtic

Agut
C/Gignàs 16 (93 315 17 09). Metro Jaume I/17, 40, 45 bus. **Open** 1.30-4pm, 9pm-midnight Tue-Sat; 1.30-4pm Sun; closed Mon. Closed Aug. **Average** 2,800ptas. **Set lunch** 1,350ptas Tue-Fri. **Credit** MC, V. **Map** p327 B4.
This long-established, comfortable family-run restaurant is well known for appetising traditional Catalan food. Despite its location in a narrow old street near the port it has always drawn a very varied clientele, although recent price rises may augur a (perhaps regrettable) move upmarket. Agut is applauded for its cannelloni, steaks and home-made profiteroles.

Agut d'Avignon
C/Trinitat 3/Avinyo 8 (93 302 60 34). Metro Liceu/14, 38, 59, 91, N9, N12 bus. **Open** 1-3.30pm, 9-11.30pm daily. **Average** 5,500ptas. **Credit** AmEx, DC, MC, V. **Map** p327 B3.

In a small alleyway, one of Barcelona's most prestigious restaurants offers comfort and service belying the shabbiness of much of the surrounding area. Menus are based on classic Catalan dishes (excellent *farcellets de col*, stuffed cabbage leaves), with others from various Spanish regions, such as Castilian roasts, and creations of their own like wild boar with strawberry sauce, duck with figs, or oyster soup.

Café de l'Acadèmia
C/Lledó 1 (93 319 82 53/93 315 00 26). Metro Jaume I/17, 19, 40, 45, N8 bus. **Open** 9am-noon, 1.30-4pm, 8.45pm-11.30 Mon-Fri; closed Sat, Sun. Closed 2wks Aug. **Average** 3,500ptas. **Set lunch** 1,100-1,475ptas. **Credit** AmEx, MC, V. **Map** p327 B3.
Perhaps the best of a clutch of quality restaurants near the Catalan government and City Hall, the Acadèmia serves some 50-odd dishes that range from Catalan classics such as *rossejat* (rice cooked in a fish broth) with prawns to a delicious chicken brochette or quail with sesame and soy sauce. On the floor above, there are magnificent rooms for larger group dinners, offering beautiful views of the medieval Plaça Sant Just.

Can Culleretes
C/Quintana 5 (93 317 30 22). Metro Liceu/14, 18, 38, 59 bus. **Open** 1.30-4pm, 9-11pm Tue-Sat; 1.30-4pm Sun; closed Mon. Closed 3wks July. **Average** 2,500-3,000ptas. **Set menus** 1,600ptas Tue-Thur; 2,100ptas Tue-Fri. **Seafood menu** 3,000ptas. **Credit** MC, V. **Map** p327 A3.
Can Culleretes is the oldest restaurant in Barcelona. It was founded in 1786, and has a rambling interior covered in old photos of local celebrities. The lengthy main menu includes rich traditional dishes like *civet de porc senglar* (wild boar stew) and *cuixa d'oca amb pomes* (goose leg with apples); there's also a lighter seafood menu, which is highly recommended. Culleretes undercharges for wine, and there are good Raïmats at 1,100ptas. This is a popular place, so go early to avoid queuing.

Cervantes
C/Cervantes 7 (93 317 33 84). Metro Jaume I/14, 18, 38, 59, N6, N9 bus. **Open** Bar 7am-8pm Mon-Fri; closed Sat, Sun. *Restaurant* 1-4pm Mon-Fri; closed Sat, Sun. Closed Aug. **Set lunch** 1,200ptas. **No credit cards. Map** p327 B3.
This friendly, low-priced lunch restaurant is run by three sisters. The food is Catalan, including traditional classics such as *botifarra*, paella and *escudella*, and is equally popular with tie-wearing city-hall workers and green-haired students from a nearby art school. Full Catalan breakfasts are also served.

▶ For suggestions on **good tapas bars** and such, see chapter **Cafés & Bars**.
▶ If you're looking for places to have a **late-night nibble**, see chapter **Nightlife**.
▶ See chapter **Gay & Lesbian** for places catering to a **mainly gay** crowd.

Eat, Drink, Shop

Govinda

Plaça Vila de Madrid 4-5 (93 318 77 29).
Metro Catalunya/bus all routes to Plaça Catalunya.
Open 1-4pm, 8.30-11.45pm Tue-Sat; 1-4pm Mon, Sun.
Average 2,000ptas. **Set lunch** 1,300ptas Mon-Fri.
Set menu 1,800pts Fri pm-Sun.
Credit AmEx, DC, MC, V. **Map** p326 B2.
This Indian vegetarian restaurant is in a very handy
location, in a square just off the Rambla. An
excellent salad bar, a choice of two hot dishes and
home-made bread and desserts make up a great-
value lunch menu. Drinkers note, though, that
there's no alcohol or coffee available.

Juicy Jones

C/Cardenal Casañas 7 (93 302 43 30).
Metro Liceu/14, 38, 59, 91, N9, N12 bus.
Open 1pm-midnight daily. **Set menu** 1,100ptas.
No credit cards. Map p327 A3.
With its island-hippy paint job, this could be the
original veggie voodoo lounge. At least 17 different
fresh juices are served from the long thin bar. For
something more substantial, the well-prepared all-
vegetarian food is decent, and can be ordered all
through the day until midnight.

Mastroqué

C/Codols 29 (93 301 79 42). Metro Drassanes/14,
36, 57, 59, 64, 157, N6, N12 bus. **Open** 1.30-
3.30pm, 9-11.30pm Tue-Fri; 9-11.30pm Mon, Sat;
closed Sun. Closed most of Aug. **Average** 3,500-
4,500ptas. **Set lunch** 1,350ptas. **Credit** MC, V.
Map p327 B4.
Despite being located on one of the narrowest streets
in the city, this is a surprisingly roomy restaurant.
Mellow-lit and French-run, Mastroqué offers an
interesting selection of regional dishes from France,
together with others from Catalonia and different
parts of Spain, such as a hot goat's cheese starter
with cooked peppers and tomatoes or a candied
aubergine 'caviar'. The good value set lunch is
generous and excellent.

Cuisine a la Catalana

Eat, Drink, Shop

Catalan food is not just a matter of a few
regional dishes but a complete cuisine easily
distinguishable from neighbours in France
and the rest of Spain. There are four basic
elements that form the basis of many Catalan
dishes: *sofregit*, tomato and onion sautéed
together in olive oil until soft; *samfaina*, a
rather ratatouille-like mixture of aubergine,
garlic, onion, red and green peppers and
tomatoes, which usually accompanies grilled
fish and meats; the fabulous *picada*, the
ingredients of which depend upon which dish
it will be used to enrich and thicken, but
usually contains nuts, garlic, parsley, bread,
sometimes small chilli peppers known as
bichos, ham, or even liver for extra thickening
power, all mashed up with mortar and pestle.
Last is *all i oli*, garlic mayonnaise served with
meat and seafood, best made solely with raw,
crushed garlic and olive oil slowly stirred
together, with an egg added only if the
mixture breaks.

Catalans like their country classics – pork,
sausages, lamb and rabbit *a la brasa* (grilled
over an open charcoal fire) with *all i oli*, and
escalivada – onions, red peppers and
aubergine roasted black and then peeled
clean and sliced into strips. Other traditional
fare special to Catalonia are *calçots*, a special
type of large sweet spring onion served whole
with the thick stalk attached. In season from
late January until early May, *calçots* are
roasted over live coals until charred black; the
charred layer is then yanked off and the

creamy exposed onion bulb is dipped into
romesco sauce (crushed tomatoes, almonds
and hazelnuts, garlic and a special little chilli
pepper, the *nyora*). This delicious, rustic
cooking can be found at numerous *a la brasa*
restaurants around the city, such as **La Parra**
p152). *Cassoles* are fantastic stewy dishes
cooked in large earthenware casseroles, and
range from fairly conventional combinations
such as chicken or meat with tomatoes,
parsley and garlic to *mar i muntanya* ('sea and
mountain'), Catalan surf-n-turf combinations
from the Figueres area such as *conill i cargols*,
rabbit and snails deliciously prepared with a
rich tomato sauce. Many shellfish and fish
dishes are prepared in a large flat pan called a
paella, in which, as you may have already
guessed, the world-famous paella rice dish
from Valencia is also made. Catalans have
their own versions of paella (*see p147* **More
than paella**), which may contain more
tomatoes and no saffron, and include dishes
like *fideuà*, made with noodles instead of rice.

Although meat dishes feature prominently in
traditional Catalan cuisine, there are also a
healthy variety of salads and vegetable
dishes, such as *espinacs a la catalana*,
spinach with onion, pine nuts and raisins,
which is also a prime example of the Catalan
affinity for combining savoury with sweet.
Canelons, much like Italian cannelloni, were
absorbed into Catalan cuisine in the last
century, but are covered with white, rather
than tomato sauce, and may be filled with

Mercè Vins

C/Amargós 1 (93 302 60 56). Metro Urquinaona/17, 19, 40, 45, N8 bus. **Open** 8am-5pm Mon-Thur; 8am-5pm, 9pm-midnight Fri; 9am-noon, 8pm-midnight Sat; closed Sun. **Set lunch** 1,200ptas. **Credit** V. **Map** p326 B2.

Mercè Vins offers short set menus (there's no à la carte list) featuring interesting Catalan dishes such as *llom amb ametlles i prunes* (pork with almonds and prunes) or *estofat* (beef stew). It's tiny, and opening times are eccentric, but it's always packed. In the evenings, there's only a lighter *llesqueria* service (*see below*).

Mesón Jesús

C/Cecs de la Boquería 4 (93 317 46 98). Metro Liceu/14, 38, 59, 91, N9, N12 bus. **Open** 1-4pm, 8-11pm Mon-Fri; 1-4.30pm Sat; closed Sun. Closed Aug-early Sept. **Average** 1,400ptas. **Set lunch** 1,100ptas. **Set dinner** 1,400ptas. **Credit** MC, V. **Map** p327 A3.

Small and cheerful, this restaurant off Plaça del Pi feels like it hasn't changed much in the last 50 years. The hard-working team provide good, reliably satisfying traditional Catalan and Spanish dishes, and it's equally popular with lunching locals and foreign travellers.

Oolong

C/Gignás 25 (93 315 12 59). Metro Jaume I/17, 40, 45 bus. **Open** 8pm-1am Mon-Sat; 8pm-midnight Sun. Closed early Sept. **Average** 1,800ptas. **No credit cards. Map** p327 B4.

Cool and cosy, Oolong serves innovative, 'fun' cuisine, including such dishes as *pollo onoto*, a spicy Venezuelan-style chicken and rice combo, or excellent (even if diminutive) Thai spring rolls. While some meat dishes are available, the emphasis is on vegetarian food, and the generous salads are almost a meal in themselves. Hip, mellow music combined with an uncomplicated but tasteful, detail-conscious decor make for a groovy meal.

---

meat, tuna or spinach or dressed up with wild mushrooms or truffles. Happily, the Catalan food scene is not static, and increasingly includes some delightfully light and modern innovations on Catalan classics (try **Silenus**, *p141*, and **Taxidermista**, *p137*) and keeps changing as it draws on influences from many other world cuisines. The one thing that may never change about Catalan cooking is *pa amb tomaquet* – slices of toasted crusty country bread rubbed with a halved tomato, sprinkled with olive oil and salt, a tasty treat upon which ham, cheese and sausages or any other item is balanced and devoured. Certain places, known as *llesquerias*, specialise in this quintessential Catalan staple; **Mercé Vins** (*see above*) is a good example. For information on wines, see chapter **Shopping**; see chapter **Cafés & Bars** for notes on drinks and coffee.

Words and phrases below are given in Catalan, Spanish and English, respectively.

Essential terminology

una cullera	una cuchara	a spoon
una forquilla	un tenedor	a fork
un ganivet	un cuchillo	a knife
un tovalló	una servilleta	a napkin
una ampolla de	una botella de	a bottle of
una altra	otra	another (one)
més	más	more
pa	pan	bread
oli d'oliva	aceite de oliva	olive oil
sal i pebre	sal y pimienta	salt and pepper
amanida	en salada	salad
truita	tortilla	omelette

(note: **truita** can also mean trout)

la nota	la cuenta	the bill
un cendrer	un cenicero	an ashtray
vinagre	vinagre	vinegar
vi negre/rosat/	vino tinto/	red/rosé/
blanc	rosado/blanco	white wine
bon profit	aproveche	Enjoy your meal
sóc	soy	I'm a
vegetarià/ana	vegetariano/a	vegetarian
sóc	soy	I'm a
diabètic/a	diabético/a	diabetic

Cooking terms

a la brasa	a la brasa	charcoal-grilled
a la graella/ planxa	a la plancha	grilled on a hot metalplate
a la romana	a la romana	fried in batter
al forn	al horno	baked
al vapor	al vapor	steamed
fregit	frito	fried

A Catalan classic: *botifarra amb mongetes.* ▶

Peimong

C/Templaris 6-10 (93 318 28 73). Metro Jaume I/17, 19, 40, 45, N8 bus. **Open** 1-4.30pm, 8pm-midnight, Tue-Sun; closed Mon. Closed Aug. **Average** 1,500ptas. **Credit** MC, V. **Map** p327 B3.

If there's another Peruvian restaurant in town, it hasn't had the success of this small place. No-frills décor is made up for by the food, mainly from northern Peru – such things as *ceviche*, grouper marinated in lemon and spices, or *pato en ají*, duck stewed with peas, potatoes and white rice.

La Poste

C/Gignás 23 (93 315 15 04). Metro Jaume I/17, 19, 40, 45, N8 bus. **Open** 1-4.30pm, 8-11.30pm Mon-Fri; 1-4.30pm Sat, Sun. Closed late Aug-early Sept. **Average** 1,500ptas. **Set menus** 900ptas Mon; 1,100ptas Sat; 1,200ptas Sun. **No credit cards.** **Map** p327 B4.

Faithful provider to postal workers from the nearby *Correus*, a cheap, enjoyable restaurant with time-honoured Spanish and Catalan dishes such as *botifarra amb mongetes*, paella, *faves a la catalana* (broad beans and blood sausage in white wine) and *empanadillas* (tuna pies). The three-course menu (for lunch or dinner) is one of the best deals in town.

Les Quinze Nits

Plaça Reial 6 (93 317 30 75). Metro Liceu/14, 38, 59, 91, N9, N12. **Open** 1-3.30pm, 8.30-11.30pm daily. **Average** 2,000ptas. **Set lunch** 995ptas Mon-Sat; 1,100ptas Sun. **Credit** AmEx, DC, MC, V. **Map** A3. **Map** p327 A3.

This small chain has become hugely successful by offering modern Catalan food at low prices, but lately both food and service often get patchy (or just poor) at busy times, and queues are annoyingly long (other branches can be better than the Plaça Reial base). Menus are all similar, with dishes such as *parrillada de peix* (seafood mixed grill) and *arròs negre*.

Branches: La Dolça Herminia C/Magdalenes 27

▶ ## Cuisine a la Catalana (continued)

rostit	asado	roast
ben fet	bien hecho	well-done
a punt	medio hecho	medium
poc fet	poco hecho	rare

Catalan specialities

amanida catalana/*ensalada catalana* mixed salad with a selection of cold meats
arròs negre/*arroz negro* 'black rice', rice cooked in squid ink, with other seafood usually included
bacallà a la llauna/*bacalao 'a la llauna'* salt cod baked in garlic, tomato, paprika and wine
botifarra/*butifarra* Catalan sausage: variants include *botifarra negre*, blood sausage; *blanca*, mixed with egg
botifarra amb mongetes/*butifarra con judías* sausage with haricot beans
calçots a specially sweet variety of large spring onion (scallion), available only from Nov to spring, and eaten char-grilled, with *romesco* sauce
carn d'olla traditional Christmas dish of various meats stewed with *escudella*, then served separately
conill amb cargols/*conejo con caracoles* rabbit with snails
crema catalana cinnamon-flavoured custard dessert with burnt sugar topping, similar to crème brûlée
escalivada/*escalibada* grilled and peeled peppers, onions and aubergine
escudella thick winter stew of meat and vegetables

espinacs a la catalana/*espinacas a la catalana* spinach quick-fried in olive oil with garlic, raisins and pine kernels
esqueixada summer salad of marinated salt cod with onions, olives and tomato
fideuà/*fideuá* paella made with noodles
pa amb tomàquet/*pan con tomate* bread prepared with tomato, oil and salt
peus de porc/*pies de cerdo* pigs' trotters
romesco a spicy sauce from the coast south of Barcelona, made with crushed almonds and hazelnuts, tomatoes, oil and a special type of red pepper (the *nyora*)
sarsuela/*zarzuela* fish and seafood stew
sípia amb mandonguilles/*sepia con albóndigas* cuttlefish with meatballs
suquet de peix/*suquet de pescado* fish and potato soup
torrades/*tostadas* toasted *pa amb tomàquet*

Carn i aviram/Carne y aves/ Meat & poultry

ànec	pato	duck
bou	buey	beef
cabrit	cabrito	kid
conill	conejo	rabbit
faisà	faisán	pheasant
fetge	hígado	liver
embotits	embotidos	cold cuts of sausage
llebre	liebre	hare
llengua	lengua	tongue
llom	lomo	loin of pork
ous	huevos	eggs
perdiu	perdiz	partridge
pernil (serrà)	jamón serrano	dry-cured ham
pernil dolç	jamón york	cooked ham

(93 317 06 76); **La Fonda** C/Escudellers 10 (93 301 75 15); **Hostal de Rita** C/Aragó 279, Eixample (93 487 23 76); **L'Hostalet de la Mamasita** Avda Sarrià, Zona Alta (93 321 92 96).

Restaurante Pakistani

C/Carabassa 3 (93 302 60 25). Metro Drassanes/14, 36, 57, 59, 64, 157, N6 bus. **Open** 1pm-1am daily. **Average** 1,300ptas. **No credit cards. Map** p327 B4.

Central, just off Plaça George Orwell, this clean, green-walled little place serves good cheap dishes such as chicken with couscous or veggies with rice. The branch down the street is bigger, but similar. **Branch: Cuatro Hermanos** C/Carabassa 19 (93 302 60 25).

El Salón

C/Hostal d'en Sol 6-8 (93 315 21 59). Metro Jaume I/17, 19, 40, 45, N8 bus. **Open** 2-5pm, 8.30pm-midnight Mon-Sat; closed Sun. Closed 2 wks Aug. **Average** 3,200ptas. **Credit** AmEx, MC, V. **Map** p327 B4.

With antique couches, mirrors and high-backed chairs, El Salón has the feel of a 19th-century bohemian living room. The cuisine on offer has French overtones, with a fair amount of creamy sauces, but the base is Catalan, and very good. Of the regulars on the menu, try roast guinea-fowl with chestnut confit and creamy clove sauce, or the aubergine tart with goat's cheese and pesto.

Self Naturista

C/Santa Anna 11-17 (93 318 23 88/93 318 26 84). Metro Catalunya/bus all routes to Plaça Catalunya. **Open** 11.30am-10pm Mon-Sat; closed Sun. **Average** 1,400ptas. **Set menu** 965ptas. **No credit cards. Map** p326 B2.

Barcelona's best-known vegetarian restaurant looks like a college self-service canteen, only cleaner. The good-value set menu includes stews and soups, most made without dairy products, and Catalan dishes such as *escalivada*. It's popular, so be prepared for long queues for lunch.

pollastre	pollo	chicken
porc	cerdo	pork
porc senglar	jabalí	wild boar
ronyons	riñones	kidneys
vedella	ternera	veal
xai/be	cordero	lamb

Peix i marisc/Pescado y mariscos/ Fish & seafood

anxoves	anchoas	anchovies
bacallà	bacalao	salt cod
besuc	besugo	sea bream
calamarsos	calamares	squid
cloïsses	almejas	clams
cranc	cangrejo	crab
escamarlans	cigalas	crayfish
escopinyes	berberechos	cockles
gambes	gambas	prawns
llagosta	langosta	spiny lobster
llagostins	langostinos	langoustines
llenguado	lenguado	sole
llobarro	lubina	sea bass
lluç	merluza	hake
musclos	mejillones	mussels
pop	pulpo	octopus
rap	rape	monkfish
salmó	salmón	salmon
sardines	sardinas	sardines
sípia	sepia	cuttlefish
tonyina	atún	tuna
truita	trucha	trout
(note: **truita** can also mean an omelette)		

Verdures/Legumbres/Vegetables

all	ajo	garlic
alvocat	aguacate	avocado
bolets	setas	wild mushrooms
ceba	cebolla	onion
cigrons	garbanzos	chick peas
col	col	cabbage
enciam	lechuga	lettuce
endivies	endivias	chicory
espinacs	espinacas	spinach
faves	habas	broad beans
mongetes blanques	judías blancas	haricot beans
mongetes verdes	judías verdes	French beans
pastanagues	zanahorias	carrots
patates	patatas	potatoes
pebrots	pimientos	peppers
pèsols	guisantes	peas
tomàquets	tomates	tomatoes
xampinyons	champiñones	mushrooms

Postres/Postres/Desserts

flam	flan	crème caramel
formatge	queso	cheese
gelat	helado	ice-cream
mel i mató	miel y mató	cottage cheese with honey
pastís	pastel	cake
tarta	tarta	tart

Fruita/Fruta/Fruit

figues	higos	figs
maduixes	fresas	strawberries
pera	pera	pear
plàtan	plátano	banana
poma	manzana	apple
préssec	melocotón	peach
raïm	uvas	grapes
taronja	naranja	orange

EL JAPONES

Japanese food in a minimalist setting with long wooden tables, which encourage socialising with fellow diners.

Pasaje de la Concepción, 2
Tel.: 93 487 25 92
Open from 1.30 pm to 4 pm and from 8.30 to 12.30 am. Thursday, Friday and Saturday until 1 am.

NEGRO

A modern and cosmopolitan atmosphere in Barcelona's business district. Presenting a tasty fusion of Mediterranean and Oriental food.

Avda. Diagonal, 640 (Caja Madrid building)
Tel.: 93 405 94 44
Open from 1.30 to 4pm and from 8.30 pm to 12.30 am
Drinks until 3 am on weekends.

AGUA

Seafood restaurant with beach terrace. Try the rice 'al carbón' - a different and exquisite choice.

Paseo Marítimo de la Barceloneta, 30
Tel.: 93 225 12 72
Open from 1.30 pm to 4 pm and from 8.30 pm to 12.30 am
Thursday, Friday and Saturday until 1 am.

TRAGALUZ

Vanguard design with three floors and a sliding glass ceiling on the top floor. Winner of FAD 1991. Atmosphere and quality guaranteed. **TRAGARRAPID** located on the ground floor, offers non-stop cuisine from 1.30 pm to midnight. Until 1 am on Thursdays, Fridays and Saturdays.

Pasaje de la Concepción, 5
Tel.: 93 487 06 21
Horario, de 13.30 a 16 h y de 20.30 a 24.30
Jueves, viernes y sábados hasta la una.

ACONTRALUZ

Garden restaurant in the heart of the quiet Sarrià neighbourhood.

C/ Milanesado, 19
Tel.: 93 203 06 58
Open from 1.30 pm to 4 pm and from 8.30 pm to 12.30 am
Thursday, Friday and Saturday until 1 am.

PRINCIPAL

Located on the first floor of a noble Ensanche flat.
Ideal for group lunches and dinners.

C/ Provença, 286
Tel.: 93 272 08 45

DJ dinners

In the last couple of years hip, clubby restaurants have invaded the city night scene; places where you can chill out to live DJ music, sample some bites off the usually exotically-influenced menus and get geared up for a night out and about.

Bar Ra

Plaça de la Garduña 3, The Raval (93 423 18 78). Metro Liceu/14, 38, 59, N9, N12 bus. **Open** 1.30-4pm, 9pm-midnight Mon-Sat. **Average** 1,500ptas. **Set lunch** 1,200ptas. **Dinner buffet** 2,200ptas. **Credit** AmEx, DC, MC, V. **Map** p326 A2.

In the big car park/square behind the Boqueria market is this lively place with tables outdoors and food from tapas to Mexican, West Indian and Thai dishes. Music covers the bases, from jazz to ethnic beat, with ambient and light drum 'n' bass the sounds of choice. On the back wall a tantric mural depicts a moon goddess smiling down on an orgy of sexy abundance – healthy inspiration, perhaps, for the clientele.

Future

C/Fusina 5, The Born (93 319 92 99). Metro Jaume I/17, 19, 40, 45, N8 bus. **Open** 1.30-3.30pm; 9-11.30pm Mon-Thur; 9pm-midnight Fri, Sat; closed Sun. Closed 2wks Aug. **Average** 2,500ptas. **Set menu** 1,900ptas. **Credit** AmEx, DC, MC, V. **Map** p327 C3.

Located in the trendy Born area, Future serves up classic fare such as hot or cold foie gras and grilled or roasted fish, while the sleek setting is appropriately futuristic. Fridays and Saturdays DJ m.u.g. spins great drum'n'bass and trance.

Mama Café

C/Doctor Dou 10, Raval (93 301 29 40). Metro Catalunya/all routes to Plaça Catalunya. **Open** 1-5pm Mon; 1pm-1am Tue-Sat; closed Sun. Closed 3wks Aug. **Average**

1,500ptas. **Set menu** 1,100ptas. **Credit** DC, MC, V. **Map** p326 A2.

Just a short walk from Bar Ra is Mama Café with pillow benches in its big, colourful space. The innovative food has fine offerings such as a chilled melon soup, or good stir-fried veggies. Music is digestive too, tending to acid jazz and ethnic beat.

Salsitas/Club 22

C/Nou de la Rambla 22, The Raval (93 318 08 40). Metro Liceu/14, 38, 59, N9, N12 bus. **Open** *Bar* 11am-5pm, 8pm-3pm Tue-Sun; closed Mon. *Restaurant* 1-4pm, 8-11pm Tue-Sun; closed Mon. **Average** 3,500ptas. **Set lunch** Tue-Fri, 1,200ptas. **Credit** DC, MC, V. **Map** p327 A3.

An extravagant palace of whiteness, Salsitas combines a spacious dining area – complete with white–cushioned chairs and pillars of sculpted white palm trees – with a bar and club area. Food is a decent if limited selection of salads, pizzas and some white meat dishes. After midnight from Wednesday to Saturday, the entire place is transformed into the ultra-trendy Club 22 – run by the former Octopussy crowd – and fills up with pretty young things who mingle to the sounds of dance and house music.

Suborn

C/de la Ribera 18 The Born (93 310 11 10). Metro Barceloneta/14, 39, 51 bus. **Open** 8pm-3am Tue-Sun; closed Mon. **Average** 2,500ptas. **Credit** MC, V. **Map** p327 C4.

This bustling place over by the Born plays rock'n'roll, sliding into happy house as the night progresses. Facing the Ciutadella, it has an outdoor terrace and sometimes hosts live music. Food is straightforward – paellas, own-made tapas – and it's a popular leap-off point for more fun in the Born or nearby **Woman Caballero** (*see chapter* **Nightlife**).

Help yourself at the **Biocenter**.

Slokai

C/Palau 5 (93 317 90 94). Metro Jaume I/17, 19, 40, 45 bus. **Open** 1.30-4pm, 9pm-midnight Mon-Fri; 9pm-midnight Sat; closed Sun. **Average** 3,000ptas. **Set lunch** 1,200ptas. **Credit** MC, V. **Map** p327 B3.

White-walled and spacious, with only a few tables, this trendy spot is run by a young crowd who serve unabashedly modern dishes such as a terrine of salmon and prawns, or truffle-stuffed duck flan. Portions are nouvelle cuisine-small, but the food is well realised, and prices are within sampling range. For dessert, try tiramisú with strawberry sauce.

Sushi-ya

C/Quintana 4 (93 412 72 49). Metro Liceu/14, 38, 59, 91, N9, N12 bus. **Open** 1-4pm, 8.30-11.30pm daily. **Average** 1,700ptas. **Set menus** 795-1,195ptas. **No credit cards**. **Map** p327 A3.

A small, friendly sushi bar with bargain menus, which can include salad, miso soup, *gryndon* (beef and rice) or a choice of sushi, and exotic ice creams for dessert, such as one of sweet red beans.

Taxidermista

Plaça Reial 8 (93 412 45 36). Metro Liceu/14, 38, 59, 91, N9, N12 bus. **Open** 1.30pm-1am Tue-Sun; closed Mon. *Meals served* 1.30-4pm, 8.30-11.30pm. **Average** 2,600ptas. **Set lunch** 990ptas. **Credit** AmEx, DC, MC, V. **Map** p327 A3.

As its name implies, this airy, elegant spot was once a shop for stuffed animals, patronised by the likes of Dalí and Miró. The newly designed interior, by star architect Beth Galí achieves a calm, precise balance of old and new (minus the animals), while the well-staffed kitchen serves high quality Catalan and international cuisine, with some vegetarian dishes, and all day tapas. Easier to get into than its less satisfying Plaça Reial neighbour, **Les Quinze Nits**.

The Raval

L'Antic Gotan

C/Riereta 8 (93 442 81 79). Metro Sant Antoni/20, 24, 64, 91, N6 bus. **Open** 1-4pm Mon; 1-4pm, 8.30pm-midnight Tue-Sat; closed Sun. **Average** 1,550ptas. **Set lunch** 1,200ptas Mon-Fri. **Set dinner** 1,500ptas Tue-Thur; 2,000ptas Fri, Sat. **Credit** DC, MC, V. **Map** p324 C6.

A small, comfortable restaurant in the old *Barrio Chino*, run by a Catalan-Argentinian couple who serve up grilled meats *al estilo argentino*. Other specialities include varied *torrades* (*see p132*).

Biocenter

C/Pintor Fortuny 25 (93 301 45 83). Metro Liceu/14, 38, 59, N9, N12 bus. **Open** 9am-5pm Mon-Sat; closed Sun. **Average** 1,500ptas. **Set menu** 1,150ptas Mon-Fri; 1,500ptas Sat. **No credit cards**. **Map** p326 A2.

This large, bustling vegetarian restaurant sits across the street from a health-food shop of the same name, and serves a broad range of salads, a filling set menu, and organic beer. Vegan dishes feature on the menu.

El Cafetí

C/Hospital 99, end of passage (93 329 24 19/ www.elcafeti.com). Metro Liceu/14, 38, 59, N9, N12 bus. **Open** 1.30-3.30pm, 8.30-11.30pm Tue-Sat; 1.30-3.30pm Sun; closed Mon. Closed 3wks in Aug. **Average** 3,500ptas. **Set menu** 1,200ptas Tue-Sat. **Credit** AmEx, DC, MC, V. **Map** p324 C6.

This small restaurant has perfected a series of Catalan-French dishes in the last 15 or so years, and built up a clientele that includes London mayor Ken Livingstone, when he's in town. Specialities include paté, salt-cod dishes and home-made desserts. Staff speak English, French and German, and there's a function room for up to 30 people.

Ca l'Isidre

C/es Flors 12 (93 441 11 39/93 442 57 20). Metro Paral.lel/20, 64, 91, N-0, N6 bus. **Open** 1.30-4pm, 8.30-11.30pm Mon-Sat; closed Sun. Closed 2wks Aug. **Average** 8,000ptas. **Credit** AmEx, DC, MC, V. **Map** p324 C6.

A small family-run restaurant near the Paral.lel that receives regular visits from King Juan Carlos. Chef César Pastor's regular dishes include artichoke hearts stuffed with wild mushrooms and duck liver, and loin of lamb broiled English-style. Desserts are made by the daughter of the family, master *pastissera* Núria Gironès. English and French are spoken.

Casa Leopoldo

C/Sant Rafael, 24 (93 441 30 14). Metro Liceu/14, 38, 59, 91, N9, N12 bus. **Open** 1.30-4pm, 9.30-11pm Tue-Sat; 1.30-4pm Sun; closed Mon. **Average** 7,500ptas. **Set dinner** 5,500ptas. **Credit** AmEx, DC, MC, V. **Map** p324 C6.

An old-school Catalan eatery, complete with beautiful tiling around the walls and excellent if somewhat pricey food. The delicious dinner menu features a bounty of seafood, fried and steamed as starters and classic main dishes such as sea bass roasted with garlic and prawns or calamari with meatballs.

El Convent

C/Jerusalem 3 (93 317 10 52). Metro Liceu/14, 38, 59, N9, N12 bus. **Open** 1-4pm, 8pm-midnight daily. **Average** 3,500ptas. **Set lunch** 990ptas Mon-Sat. **Credit** AmEx, DC, MC,V. **Map** p326 A2.

Until 1998 this rambling old four-storey building housed the Egipte, many people's favourite

Eat, Drink, Shop

Crustacea at **Casa Leopoldo**. *See p137.*

Barcelona restaurant. When its owners retired they sold it to their former staff, who have kept it much as it was, although the menu of traditional Catalan dishes has been reduced in variety and length, but not in quality. With its antique fittings, bustling atmosphere and enjoyable food it remains a convivial standby. As always, it's very crowded at peak times, when things can seem a bit chaotic.

Elisabets
C/Elisabets 2-4 (93 317 58 26). Metro Catalunya/bus all routes to Plaça Catalunya. **Open** 1-4pm Mon-Thur, Sat; 1-4pm, 9-11.30pm Fri; closed Sun. Closed 3wks Aug. **Set lunch** 1,050ptas. **Set dinner** 1,500-2,000ptas. **No credit cards. Map** p326 A2.
Classic little lunchtime eating-house with a long history of serving good, cheap Catalan food to the neighbourhood and anyone else who wanders in. The menu gives a wider than average choice, often with good lamb with *all i oli*.

Estevet
C/Valldonzella 46 (93 302 41 86). Metro Universitat/bus all routes to Plaça Universitat. **Open** 1.30-4pm, 9pm-11pm Mon-Sat; closed Sun. Closed 2wks Aug. **Average** 1,700ptas. **Set lunch** 3,500-4,000ptas. **Credit** AmEx, DC, MC, V. **Map** p326 A1.
Estevet is one of the oldest restaurants in town, run for many years by Jordi Suñé. The food is enjoyable and carefully prepared – the langoustines, grilled asparagus and *filet Café de París* are especially good – but it's worth coming here almost as much for the uniquely warm atmosphere, with striking paintings, photos of celebrity diners such as Maradona and Gary Lineker and regulars who treat it a bit like a family dining room.

Fil Manila
C/Ramelleres 3 (93 318 64 87).
Metro Catalunya/all routes to Plaça Catalunya. **Open** noon-4pm, 8-11.30pm Tue-Sun; closed Mon. **Average** 1,500ptas. **Set menu** 1,200ptas. **No credit cards. Map** p326 A2.
The city's only Filipino eatery, this small, friendly place offers a large selection of good coconut milk curries, meats and fish cooked on sizzling stone platters. While there is a lunchtime *menú*, ordering an à la carte plate and rice winds up being more satisfying and just as affordable, as many dishes are in the 600-700ptas range. The banana wrapped in very thin pastry and fried is a great sweet finish.

La Garduña
C/Jerusalem 18 (93 302 43 23). Metro Liceu/14, 38, 59, 91, N9, N12 bus. **Open** 1-4pm, 8pm-1am Mon-Sat; closed Sun. **Average** 2,600ptas. **Set lunch** (incl 1 drink) 1,275ptas. **Set dinner** (no drink incl) 1,575ptas. **Credit** AmEx, DC, MC, V. **Map** p326 A2.
Once located inside the Boqueria market in a charming historic inn, this still popular establishment has been transformed by its relocation to a gleaming, all-new glass and steel building, funkily decorated inside with a mosaic of stone and sand set into the floor. With the market right next door, the Catalan food is still good and fresh, if more pricey than before.

L'Hortet
C/Pintor Fortuny 32 (93 317 61 89). Metro Liceu/14, 38, 59, N9, N12 bus. **Open** 1.15-4pm Mon-Thur, Sun; 9-11pm Fri, Sat. **Set lunch** 1,100ptas Mon-Fri; 1,400ptas Sat, Sun. **Set dinner** 1,400ptas. **Credit** MC, V. **Map** p326 A2.
This homey little place is one of Barcelona's more imaginative vegetarian restaurants. L'Hortet offers a different set menu every day and is cheap, too. It doesn't serve alcohol, but there are good juices.

La Llotja
Museo Marítim, Avda. Drassanes (93 302 64 02). Metro Drassanes/14, 38, 59, N9, N12 bus. **Open** 2-3.45pm Mon-Thur, Sun; 2-3.45, 9-11.30pm Fri, Sat. **Average** 3,000ptas. **Set lunch** 1,250ptas. **Credit** MC, V. **Map** p327 A4.
The setting alone is wonderful: La Llotja, the creation of gourmet and food critic Josep Maria Blasi, sits beneath the lofty arches of the magnificent 14th-century Drassanes, home of the Museu Marítim. The excellent selection of Catalan food includes a medieval dish or two, such as roast chicken with saffron, in homage to the ancient stone edifice. At midday, there's an interesting two-course set menu. The restaurant and the equally attractive café are entered from the garden beside the museum entrance, and are not very visible from the street.

Mesón David
C/Carretas 63 (93 441 59 34). Metro Paral.lel/20, 36, 57, 64, 91, 157, N-0, N6 bus. **Open** 1-4pm, 8-midnight Mon, Tue,Thur-Sun; closed Wed. Closed Aug. **Average** 1,800ptas. **Set lunch** 900ptas Mon-Fri. **Credit** AmEx, MC, V. **Map** p324 C6.

This bustling Galician joint offers delicious deals such as *trucha navarra* (a whole trout stuffed with Serrano ham and cheese, lightly breaded and fried) for just 425ptas, or hearty meats such as the *lechazo* (a huge, sticky, tender roasted pork knuckle). For the full experience, make sure to tip your waiter when you pay at the cash register – he/she will toss the money with a clang into a large metal shoe behind the counter and ring the large cowbell above the register at which point everyone in the restaurant stops eating and cheers.

Els Ocellets

Ronda Sant Pau 55 (93 441 10 46). Metro Sant Antoni or Paral.lel/20, 24, 64, 91, N6 bus. **Open** 1.30-4pm, 8.30-11.30pm Tue-Sat; 1.30-4pm Sun; closed Mon. **Average** 2,300ptas. **Set lunch** 950ptas Tue-Fri. **Credit** AmEx, DC, MC,V. **Map** p324 C6.
This comfortable restaurant, on the Ronda on the edge of the Raval, and its more picturesque parent **Can Lluís**, a little way up a narrow street opposite,

share the same menu and popularity. Try the spicy *romescada*, the *esqueixada* or the *filet de vedella al cabrales* (veal fillet with a powerful goat's cheese sauce). Bookings are only taken for groups, and both restaurants have been popular favourites in the area for years, so get there early to avoid having to wait. Menu prices do not include tax.
Branch: Can Lluís C/de la Cera 49 (93 441 11 87).

Pla del Angels

C/Ferlandina 23 (93 329 40 47). Metro Universitat/bus all routes to Plaça Universitat. **Open** 1.30-4pm Mon; 1.30-4pm, 9pm-midnight Tue-Sat; closed Sun. **Average** 1,500ptas. **Set menus** 2,600ptas. **Credit** DC, MC, V. **Map** p324 C5.
On the square right in front of the MACBA, this modern café-restaurant serves fresh, simple dishes, including pastas, salads, meat and fish. The tables outdoors give you a chance to take in great views of the museum, as well as the cultural melting pot bubbling away in the square.

Two trips out

If unforgettable dining experiences are what you're after, here are two of Catalonia's most famous top-notch restaurants. For transport information, *see p262*.

El Bulli

Cala Montjoi (7km/4.5 miles from Roses) (972 15 04 57/www.elbulli.com). By car A7 or N11/by train RENFE from Sants or Passeig de Gràcia to Figueres, then bus to Roses, then taxi. **Open** *July-early Oct* 8-10pm daily. *Mid Mar-June* 1-3pm, 8-10pm Wed-Sun. Closed mid Oct-early Mar. **Average** 14,500ptas. **Credit** AmEx, DC, MC, V.
A privileged hideaway overlooking a small cove outside Roses on the Costa Brava, El Bulli (pictured) has become known as one of the finest restaurants in Europe through the skill and imagination of chef Ferran Adrià. The long, set gourmet menu includes a parade of nine aperitifs, seven starters, three main dishes and two desserts, with such striking culinary events as candied trout eggs and duck tongues with pears and oysters; a real experience. For more on Roses, *see pp271-2*.

El Racó de Can Fabes

C/Sant Joan 6, Sant Celoni (93 867 28 51/www.racocanfabes.com). By car A7 or C-251 (60 km/37 miles)/by train RENFE to Sant Celoni. **Open** 1.30-3.30pm, 8.30-10.30pm Tue-Sat; 1.30-3.30pm Sun; closed Mon. Closed first 2wks Feb, end June/1st wk July. **Average** 15,000ptas. **Set menu** 13,950ptas. **Credit** AmEx, DC, MC, V.

In a small town at the foot of the Montseny mountains, the Racó has all of three Michelin stars, and presiding figure Santi Santamaria is acclaimed as one of the greatest Catalan chefs. Specialities include scallop salad, cold truffle stews and a superlative grill of Mediterranean seafood. Desserts and cheeses are as fine. A gourmet pilgrimage, and for all its prestige service El Racó is unpretentiously welcoming; those who make the trip don't regret it.

Just off the Rambla, and nearly always full, the Romesco is enshrined as a favourite with young foreigners, and many locals too. House speciality is *fríjoles*, a Spanish-Caribbean dish of black beans, mince, rice and fried banana, a hearty and satisfying bargain at just over 500ptas. Noisy and convivial, this is one of the city's best cheap eating houses. To find it, just head down C/Sant Pau and look to the right.

Restaurante Xironda Orense

C/Roig 19 (93 442 30 91). Metro Liceu/14, 38, 59, 91, N9, N12 bus. **Open** 1-4pm, 8.30pm-2am Mon-Sat; closed Sun. Closed Aug. **Average** 1,100ptas. **No credit cards. Map** p324 C6.
Walk past the narrow, crowded bar to the narrow, crowded dining room, where you can choose from a decent variety of salads and mainly meat-based Galician dishes, in generous quantities at low prices.

Shalimar

C/Carme 71 (93 329 34 96). Metro Liceu/14, 38, 59, 91, N9, N12 bus. **Open** 1-4pm, 8-11.30pm Mon, Wed-Sun; 8-11.30pm Tue. **Average** 1,800ptas. **Credit** DC, MC, V. **Map** p324 C6.
One of the best mid-price Pakistani restaurants in town, the Shalimar serves a selection of South Asian standards, with good tandoori dishes, in pleasant and relaxed surroundings.

Silenus

C/del Angels 8 (93 302 26 80). Metro Liceu/14, 38, 59, 91, N9, N12 bus. **Open** 1-4pm Mon; 9-11.45pm Tue-Sat; closed Sun. **Average** 2,800ptas. **Lunch specials** 1,500-1,800ptas Mon-Fri. **Credit** DC, MC, V. **Map** p326 A2.
A short walk from the MACBA, and a meeting place for local artists, Silenus is laid-back and fresh, with comfy sofas lining the walls and minimalist décor that highlights the open, high-ceilinged space. The food is a creative mix of contemporary Catalan and Spanish dishes including such delights as a *crocantí de bacallà amb caviar d'albergínia i reducció de fórum* (salt cod in almond batter with aubergine caviar simmered in a sweet/sour vinegar). Service is friendly, and there are regular art exhibits on the walls.

Sant Pere, La Ribera & the Born

Bar Mundial

Plaça Sant Agustí Vell 1 (93 319 90 56). Metro Arc de Triomf/39, 40, 41, 42, 51, 141 bus. **Open** *Bar* 9am-11pm Mon, Wed, Thur; 9am-11.30pm Fri, Sat; 9am-5pm Sun; closed Tue. Closed last 2wks Aug. *Restaurant* 1.30pm till close (as bar). **Average** 2,000ptas. **No credit cards. Map** p326 C2.
Mundial is a small, unpretentious bar-restaurant specialising in freshly cooked seafood, mainly plain-grilled. A single *parrilladas* (mixed seafood grill) is ample for two, and costs just 2,200ptas. The standard dishes can have their ups and downs, but on a good day it's a great bargain.

The best **Menús**

Barri Gòtic

Cervantes *(see p129)*; **Mastroqué** *(see p130)*; **Mesón Jesús** *(see p131)*; **La Poste** *(see p132)*.

The Raval

L'Antic Gotan *(see p137)*; **El Cafetí** *(see p137)*; **Restaurant Riera** *(see p141)*.

Sant Pere, La Ribera & the Born

Café de la Ribera *(see p142)*; **Al Passatore** *(see p142)*; **Pla de la Garsa** *(see p143)*; **Restaurante Económico-Borrás** *(see p143)*.

Port Olímpic

Taverna del Cel Ros *(see p145)*.

The Eixample

Marcelino 2000 *(see p148)*; **La Bodegueta** *(see chapter* **Cafés & Bars***)*

Gràcia

SoNaMu *(see p151)*.

Punjab Restaurante

C/Joaquín Costa 1b (93 443 38 99). Metro Liceu/14, 38, 59, 91, N9, N12 bus. **Open** 11am-midnight daily. **Average** 1,900ptas. **Set lunch** 500ptas. **Set dinner** 750ptas. **No credit cards. Map** p324 C5.
When this small Pakistani restaurant first opened it put up a sign daringly offering 25,000ptas to anyone who found a cheaper place to eat. A couple of years later most of the sign remains, but the figure of 25,000ptas has been blanked out. Has someone actually come up with somewhere cheaper than the Punjab? Not that we know of. The menu features basics like chicken tikka or samosas, and the food is good for the price.

Restaurant Riera

C/Joaquín Costa 30 (93 443 32 93). Metro Universitat/bus all routes to Plaça Universitat. **Open** 1-4pm, 8-11pm daily. **Average** 1,000ptas. **Set menu** 825-875ptas. **No credit cards. Map** p324 C5.
In perennial half-light despite the overhead fluorescent tubes, this is a budget traveller's classic, with menus day and night at ultra-low prices. For 750ptas you get three courses of ordinary local grub: soups, salads, paellas, meat or fish. Drinks are extra, unless you go for the 800ptas menu. The cook is from Bangladesh, and sometimes prepares curries and similar things. Vegetarian dishes always available.

Restaurante Romesco

C/Sant Pau 28 (93 318 93 81). Metro Liceu/14, 38, 59, 91, N9, N12 bus. **Open** 1pm-12,30am Mon-Sat; closed Sun. Closed Aug. **Average** 1,000ptas. **Map** p327 A3.

Bunga Raya

C/Assaonadors 7 (93 319 31 69). Metro Jaume I/17, 19, 39, 40, 45, 51, N8 bus. **Open** 8pm-midnight Tue-Sun; closed Mon. **Average** 2,000ptas. **Set menu** 1,795ptas. **No credit cards**. **Map** p327 C3.

This small, charming Malaysian-Indonesian restaurant is home to what many consider to be the best curries in Barcelona. The *rijstafel*, an eight-item combination plate, is delicious and good value. Service can be a bit slow on busy nights, but is kind and friendly enough.

Café de la Ribera

Plaça de les Olles 6 (93 319 50 72). Metro Barceloneta/14, 17, 40, 45, 51 bus. Meals served 1-4pm, 8pm-midnight Mon-Sat; closed Sun. **Average** 1,600ptas. **Set lunch** 1,375ptas Mon-Fri. **Set dinner** 1,500ptas. **Credit** DC, MC, V. **Map** p327 C4.

Dishes at this very popular, ever-crowded place include *revueltos de espinaca* (scrambled eggs with spinach), veal with goat's cheese, and fish soups. The set lunch menu changes daily, with salads, pizzas and fresh juices available all day. From April to October the café stays open one hour later in the evening, and you can eat alfresco at the outside tables.

Cal Pep

Plaça de les Olles 8 (93 310 79 61). Metro Barceloneta/14, 17, 40, 45, 51 bus. **Open** 8pm-midnight Mon; 1.15-4.15pm, 8pm-midnight Tue-Sat; closed Sun. Closed Aug. **Average** 4,000ptas bar; 6,000ptas (groups only) restaurant. **Credit** AmEx, DC, MC, V. **Map** p327 C4.

Most people choose to eat at the bar, although there's also a restaurant – a brick-lined room decorated with a boar's head and antique cash registers. At the bar, Pep himself grills most of the exceptional fish and seafood, while keeping customers amused with a constant stream of chat. He also runs the costlier **Passadís del Pep** *(see below)*.

Comme Bio

Via Laietana 28 (93 319 89 68). Metro Jaume I/17, 19, 40, 45, N8 bus. **Open** 1-4pm, 8.30-11pm Mon-Fri, Sun; 1-4pm, 8.30-midnight Sat. **Average** 1,100ptas. **Set meals** 1,125ptas Mon-Fri; 1,725ptas Sat, Sun. **Credit** AmEx, DC, MC, V. **Map** p327 B3.

An ambitiously large, stylish place that combines a health-food shop and boutique of artisanal products with a vegetarian restaurant. Maybe it's a vision of the future; at any rate the food is good and reasonably priced, with a varied mix of 40-odd dishes.

Branch: Gran Via de les Corts Catalanes 603, Eixample (93 301 03 76).

Havana Vieja

C/Banys Vells 2 (93 93 268 25 04). Metro Jaume I/17, 19, 40, 45, N8 bus. **Open** 10am-4pm, 8pm-midnight Mon-Thur, Sun; 8pm-1am Fri, Sat. **Average** 3,000ptas. **Credit** AmEx, DC, MC, V. **Map** p327 C3.

Dinner at this Cuban restaurant feels like a house party, with its crowds of diners clinking their *mojito* glasses, friendly service and delicious food. Try a saucy meat dish, such as *picado habanero* or *ropa vieja* (ground meat and shredded beef, respectively, cooked in a *sofrito* - a sauce of tomatoes and onions) with *arroz congri* (rice with black beans), and fried sweet bananas. Simple, satisfying desserts include the *pudin de coco* (soft slices of cornmeal-based cake topped with syrup-sweetened coconut).

Passadís del Pep

Pla del Palau 2 (93 310 10 21). Metro Barceloneta/14, 36, 57, 59, 157 bus. **Open** 1.30-3.30pm, 9-11.30pm Mon-Sat; closed Sun. Closed 3wks Aug. **Average** 10,000ptas (incl drink). **Credit** AmEx, DC, MC, V. **Map** p327 C4.

An eccentric restaurant that's impossible to find unless you know where to look (go down a long, unmarked corridor next door to a Caixa office). There is no menu, just some of the best seafood in Barcelona, with a superb first-course buffet and cava included in the price. *Fideus amb llamàntol* (noodles with lobster) are particularly recommended. If this place is too pricey, a cheaper alternative is **Cal Pep** *(see left)*, run by the same family.

Al Passatore

Pla del Palau 8 (93 319 78 51). Metro Barceloneta/14, 36, 57, 59, 157 bus. **Open** 1pm-1am daily. **Average** 1,500-2,000. **Set lunch** 975ptas Mon-Fri. **Credit** MC, V. **Map** p327 C4.

An Italian restaurant very popular for its excellent, wood-fired oven pizzas, Al Passatore also offers a big choice of pasta dishes – *linguini al cartoccio* (linguini with a rich mix of seafood) is recommended – salads, meat and fish dishes. There are outdoor tables as well as a decent lunch menu.

Branches: Al Passatore Moll de Gregal 25, Vila Olímpica (93 225 00 47). **Montello** Via Laietana 42 (93 310 35 26).

El Pebre Blau

C/Banys Vells 21 (93 319 13 08). Metro Jaume I/17, 19, 40, 45, N8 bus. **Open** 8pm-midnight daily. **Average** 3,500ptas. **Credit** MC, V. **Map** p327 C3.

This cosy, inviting place has subtle, lovely lighting and a menu inspired from all over. However, salads

Hip and eclectic, **Salero**. *See p143.*

Contemporary Catalan cuisine and space to unwind at **Senyor Parellada**.

and starters, such as the spinach salad with roquefort ice cream and pine nuts are what shine here, and it is a great place for a light and casual dinner.
Branches: **L'Ou Com Balla** C/Banys Vells 20 (93 310 53 78)

Pla de la Garsa
C/Assaonadors 13 (93 315 24 13). Metro Jaume I/ 17, 19, 40, 45, N8 bus. **Open** 1.15-3.45pm, 8pm-1am Mon-Fri; 1.30-3.45pm, 8pm-1am Sat; 8pm-1am Sun. **Average** 2,500ptas. **Set lunch** 1,050-1,200ptas. **Set dinner** 1,100ptas (summer only); 1,750ptas. **Credit** AmEx, MC,V. **Map** p327 C3.
Antique-dealer Ignasi Soler transformed a 16th-century stables and dairy near C/Montcada into this beautiful restaurant, serving high-quality cheeses, patés and cold meats. At midday there's an excellent, good-value set menu, with larger dishes as well as *torrades*.

Restaurante Económico – Borrás
Plaça Sant Agusti Vell 13 (93 319 64 94). Metro Arc de Triomf/39, 40, 41, 42, 51, 141 bus. **Open** 12.30-4.30pm Mon-Fri; closed Sat, Sun. Closed Aug. **Average** 1,500ptas. **Set lunch** 1,075ptas. **No credit cards. Map** p326 C2.
A pretty restaurant looking onto a centuries-old square. The set lunch gives a choice of around nine first courses and ten seconds, regularly including *fideuà*, baked potatoes, macaroni and *arroz a la Cubana*, rice with tomato sauce, a fried egg, and a fried banana, if you ask for one.

Rodrigo
C/Argenteria 67 (93 310 30 20). Metro Jaume I/17, 19, 40, 45, N8 bus. **Open** 8am-5pm, 8.30pm-1am Mon, Tue, Fri-Sun; 8am-5pm Wed; closed Thur. Closed Aug. **Average** 2,000ptas. **Set lunch** 1,150ptas; 1,475ptas Sun. **Set dinner** 1,475ptas. **Credit** MC, V. **Map** p327 C3.
Home cooking and bargain prices attract huge crowds to Rodrigo's jumble of tables, especially on Sundays. Full meals are not served in the evening,

but there is a wide choice of hot and cold sandwiches. Note the unusual choice of closing day.

Salero
C/Rec 60 (93 319 80 22). Metro Barceloneta/14, 39, 51 bus. **Open** 1.30-4pm, 9pm-midnight Tue, Wed, Sun; 9pm-1am Thur-Sat; closed Mon. Closed 2nd wk Aug. **Average** 1,800ptas. **Set menu** 1,100ptas bar; 1,250ptas restaurant. Tue-Fri. **Credit** AmEx, MC, V. **Map** p327 C3.
Fashionably relaxed, with a white interior and candlelit tables, Salero serves up a delicious and eclectic range of dishes at decent prices. Among the 20-odd offerings are Mediterranean-Japanese mixes such as *kakiage* (sautéed squid, onion, courgettes and carrot). Other treats include an excellent magret of duck with mango, or a beef fillet with foie gras.

Senyor Parellada
C/Argenteria 37 (93 310 50 94). Metro Jaume I/17, 19, 40, 45, N8 bus. **Open** 1-3.30pm, 9-11.30pm Mon-Sat; closed Sun. **Average** 3,000ptas. **Credit** AmEx, MC, CD, V. **Map** p327 B3.
The atmosphere is relaxed, and the décor stylishly combines modern touches with the centuries-old stone walls of this old La Ribera building. As well as the pillared main room there are attractive spaces upstairs. Specialities among the innovative fare include thyme soup, cod with honey, variations on Catalan standards such as *escalivada* and, to finish, great cinnamon *semifreddo* and *crema catalana*. Service is courteous, but the quality of the cooking can be variable at busy times.

Port Vell & Barceloneta

Can Majó
C/Almirall Aixada, 23 (93 358 25 54). Metro Barceloneta/17, 39, 45, 57,59, 64, 157, N8 bus. **Open** 1-4pm, 8-11.30pm Tue-Sat; 1-4pm Sun; closed Mon. **Average** 2,000ptas. **Credit** AmEx, MC, CD, V. **Map** p324 D7.

Around the world

Barcelona doesn't have its own Chinatown or little Italy, but the ranks of good international restaurants has swelled of late to include inventive, no-MSG Asian.

Brazilian
Conducta Ejemplar – El Rodizio, *see p147.*

Cuban
Havana Vieja, *see p142.*

Filipino
Fil Manila, *see p138.*

Indian/Pakistani
Restaurante Pakistani, *see p133;*
Punjab Restaurante, *see p141;* **Shalimar**, *see p141.*

Italian:
Al Passatore, *see p142;* **Specchio Magico**, *see p152 .*

Japanese
Sushi-ya, *see p137;* **SoNaMu** *see p152.*

Mexican:
Cantina Mexicana I & II *see p150.*

Oriental
dZi, *see p144.*

Peruvian
Peimong *see p132.*

Eat, Drink, Shop

Very well regarded within the Barcelona culinary community and a favourite of many of the city's top chefs and restaurant managers, Can Majó has as its speciality excellently prepared seafood. Grilled razor clams and *pescadito frito* (tiny fried fish, eaten whole) are a delicious way to start, and the opulent *zarzuela* (with a touch of anisette liqueur) and *suquet* are superb. There are tables outdoors, although it's generally more comfortable to sit inside, unless you really want to be hassled by rose sellers, whiny singing guitarists and the like.

Can Ramonet
C/Maquinista 17 (93 319 30 64). Metro Barceloneta/17, 39, 45, 57, 59, 64, 157, N8 bus. **Open** 10.30-4pm, 8pm-midnight Mon-Sat; 10.30-4pm Sun. Closed 2wks Jan, 2wks Aug. **Average** 3,500ptas. **Credit** AmEx, MC, CD, V. **Map** p325 E7.
Reportedly the oldest building in Barceloneta, first opened as a harbour tavern in 1763 and run since 1956 by the Ballarín family. A spectacular display of all kinds of fresh seafood greets you at the entrance, and if you're not sure what anything is called, you can just point to it. Eat tapas at the bar,

or larger *raciôns* at a table, perhaps lobster with clams, cod with *romesco*, Serrano ham or some of the very best anchovies in town.

dZI
Passeig de Joan de Borbó, 76 (93 221 21 82). Metro Barceloneta/17, 39, 64 bus. **Open** 1-4pm, 8pm-midnight daily. **Average** 3,000ptas. **Set lunch** 1,200ptas. **Credit** AmEx, MC, V. **Map** p327 C4.
No tacky red lacquer, added MSG or greasy food here – dZI offers a host of creatively updated Asian classics, in the setting of a pleasant, modern interior. The chicken and sticky rice steamed in a banana leaf is an excellent low-fat starter, before going on to specialities such as the potato-wrapped duck or the Thai beef sautéed with mangoes. Service is friendly, and the outside terrace tables offer a fine view of the port.

La Oficina
Passeig de Joan de Borbó 30 (93 221 40 05). Metro Barceloneta/17, 39, 45, 57,59, 64, 157, N8 bus. **Open** 1-4.30pm, 8.30-11.30pm Mon, Wed-Sun; closed Tue. Closed some wks Sept. **Average** 1,500ptas. **Set menus** 1,150ptas Mon-Sat; 1,300ptas Sun. **Credit** AmEx, DC, MC, V. **Map** p324 D7.
With tables outside all year round, and views of Port Vell, La Oficina provides one of the best deals on this harbourside strip. Set menus give a wide choice of dishes, usually including paella.

Ruccola
World Trade Centre, Moll de Barcelona (93 508 82 68). Metro Drassanes/20, 36, 57, 64, 157, N-0, N6 bus. **Open** 1-4pm, 8-11.45pm daily. **Average** 4,500ptas. **Set lunch** 2,200ptas. **Credit** AmEx, MC, V. **Map** p324 C7.
The new darling of the Barcelona restaurant scene, Ruccola steadily attracts flocks of the rich, beautiful and famous, along with a bevy of top Catalan chefs. With views of the water and a couldn't-be-more-modern location in the new (and somewhat sterile) World Trade Centre, glamorous diners chow down on a stylishly eclectic mix of Italian and Asian-influenced Catalan classics. The chef can be a bit heavy-handed, but overall the fare is good, and prices surprisingly reasonable.

Set Portes
Paseo de Isabell II, 14 (93 319 30 33/93 319 29 50/www.7puertas.com). Metro Barceloneta/36, 57, 59, 64, 157, N-0, N6 bus. **Open** 1pm-1am daily. **Average** 4,000ptas. **Credit** AmEx, DC, MC, V. **Map** p327 C4.
Founded in 1836 and a historic institution in itself, the huge 'Seven Doors' is on every tourist list. It's regularly packed with foreigners, but also manages to maintain standards, and despite the frilly fittings and the piano player, prices are generally acceptable. The speciality is *paella de peix*: for maximum flavour ask for the shells to be left on the seafood. Bookings are taken only for meals at 1.30-2.30pm and 8-9.30pm; you can expect long queues at most times, and especially on Sunday evenings.

Xiringuito Escribà

Vila Olímpica - Port Olímpic

Agua
*Passeig Marítim de la Barceloneta 30 (93 225 12
72). Metro Barceloneta/45, 57, 59, 157, N8 bus.*
Open 1.30-4pm, 8.30-midnight Mon-Thur; 1.30-4pm,
8.30pm-1am Fri; 1.30-4pm, 8.30-1am Sat; 1.30-4pm,
8.30pm-midnight Sun. **Average** 4,000ptas. **Credit**
AmEx, DC, MC, V. **Map** p325 F7.
Bona fide beachfront tables and a warm, modern
interior make Agua a reliable bet for an enjoyable
meal. Dishes range from quirky starters such as
Montadito de bacallà amb tomaquet sec (layered cod
cake with sun-dried tomatoes) to pasta or rice dishes such as *arròs salvatgte amb verdures i gingebre*
(wild rice with greens and ginger) and very good
meat and fish. Plus, you can watch the soothing
Mediterranean waves while you eat.

La Taverna del Cel Ros
*Moll del Mestral 26 (93 221 00 33). Metro
Ciutadella-Vila Olímpica/36, 100, N6, N8 bus.* **Open**
1-5pm, 8pm-midnight Mon-Wed, Fri-Sun; closed
Thur. Closed Dec. **Average** 2,000ptas. **Set lunch**
1,250ptas. **Credit** AmEx, DC, MC, V. **Map** p325 F7.
Near the main entrance of the Port Olímpic, this is
one of just a few inexpensive, 'normal' places among
the Port's mass of quayside eateries, and so is
favoured by port workers, sailors and other regulars. The lunch menu is short, but good.

Xiringuitó Escribà
*Litoral Mar, 42 (Platja Bogatell) (93 221 07 29).
Metro Ciutadella-Vila Olímpica/36, N6, N8 bus.*
Open 11am-5pm Tue-Thur; 11am-11pm Fri-Sun;
closed Mon. *Tapas served* 11am-5pm Tue-Sun.
Meals served 1-4.30pm Tue-Thur; 1-4.30pm, 9-11pm
Fri-Sun. **Average** 5,000ptas. **Credit** MC, V.
Map p325 F7.
The main attraction of this beachside restaurant is
the great selection of paellas, seafood or lobster, but
the salads are large and beautiful and the fish dish-
es are very good as well. As one would expect of an
establishment owned by the great pastry-making
Escribà dynasty (*see p187*), desserts (up to three
kinds of deep chocolate cakes) are matchless.

Poble Sec

Elche
*C/Vila i Vila 71 (93 441 30 89). Metro Paral.lel/20,
36, 57, 64, 91, 157, N-0, N6 bus.* **Open** 12.45pm-
12.30am daily. **Average** 2,500ptas. **Set menus**
3,500-5,250ptas. **Credit** AmEx, MC, V. **Map** p324 C6.
This well-regarded, charming establishment has
been specialising in fine paellas and other traditional
rice dishes since 1959. Portions are healthy, and service is friendly. A must for comfort-food lovers.

La Tomaquera
*C/Margarit 58 (no phone). Metro Paral.lel/20, 36,
57, 64, N6, N9 bus.* **Open** 1.30-4.30pm, 8.30-11.30pm
Tue-Sat; closed Mon. Closed Aug. **Average**
2,000ptas. **No credit cards. Map** p323 B6.

Eat, Drink, Shop

More than paella

Love of rice is certainly as strong in Catalonia as it is elsewhere on the Iberian peninsula, and extends far beyond a pan of typical Valencian paella. Unique Catalan rice variations include such dishes as **Gaig**'s (see p154) famous *arròs amb ceps i colomí* (rice with porcini mushrooms and young pigeon) offered in autumn, or prepared with *bacallà* (salt cod) throughout the year; *arròs negre* (a delicious variation on paella prepared with black squid ink) and the very Catalan *arròs de conill i satsitxes* (a saucy rice dish which includes rabbit and chunks of country sausage).

However, if traditional Valencian paella is what you must have, keep in mind that yellowness is no sign of quality, or saffron content for that matter, nor should you be surprised if your paella isn't yellow at all but a lovely stewy brown, as it typically is in Catalonia. **Xiringuito Escribà** (see p145) offers lovely beachside paellas. **Set Portes** (see p144) is home to the legendary paella Parellada (named after the member of the also legendary Parellada restaurant family who created it there years ago) which is also served at the Ramon Parellada's eponymously named **Senyor Parellada**. Famed **Elche** (see p145), meanwhile, over in Poble Sec, specialises in skilfully prepared rice dishes, serving at least ten different variations on paella.

Despite the owner's refusal to have a phone or put an entry into local listings guides, people from all over town visit this enjoyable Poble Sec restaurant, above all for its specialities: *caracoles* (snails) and *a la brasa* meat, with fabulous, utterly fresh *all i oli*. In quality, quantity and preparation the meat is the best in town, and there are also excellent salads and desserts.

The Eixample

El Asador de Burgos

C/Bruc 118 (93 207 31 60). Metro Verdaguer/20, 39, 43, 44, 45, 47, N6, N7 bus. **Open** 1-4pm, 9-11pm Mon-Sat; closed Sun. Closed some wks Aug. **Average** 5,000ptas. **Credit** AmEx, DC, MC, V. **Map** p321 D4.

Castilian food is for confirmed carnivores, with only very little vegetable relief. First courses at this *asador* ('roasting-house') include morcilla blood sausage, roast chorizo, sliced marinated pork, and baby peppers. Main courses are typically roast lamb, roast piglet, grilled ribs of lamb, and a veal steak that looks like it could kick sand in the face of any standard entrecôte. Booking is essential, as roasts are prepared three hours in advance, in a traditional tiled oven.

L'Atzavara

C/Muntaner 109 (93 454 59 25). Metro Diagonal, Hospital Clínic/20, 43, 44, 54, 58, 64, 66, N3, N7 bus. **Open** 1-4pm Mon-Sat; closed Sun. **Average** 2,500ptas. **Set lunch** 1,100-1,250ptas. **Credit** MC, V. **Map** p320 C4.

As the queues of expectant *eixampleros* indicate, this all-veggie restaurant is very popular, and for good reason. The three-course lunch menu offers generous salads and home-made soups, including gazpacho, while the second main dish might be a delicious vegetarian paella. A great bargain.

Café del Centre

C/Girona 69 (93 488 11 01). Metro Girona/7, 50, 54, 56, 62, N1, N2, N3 bus. **Open** 8am-2am Mon-Fri; 7.30-2am Sat; closed Sun. Closed Aug. **Average** 1,500ptas. **Credit** MC, V. **Map** p325 E5.

This early-1900s marble and wood *llesqueria* bar offers fine cheeses (try the Maó), patés, cold meats, smoked fish and ten different salads into the small hours, with live (and untacky) piano music on Thursday, Friday and Saturday nights. A genuine local joint that's well worth a visit.

Casa Calvet

C/Casp 48 (93 412 40 12). Metro Urquinaona/41, 47, 55, 62, 141, N4, N8 bus. **Open** 1-3.30pm, 8.30-11pm Mon-Sat; closed Sun. **Average** 7,000ptas. **Gourmet menu** 6,800ptas. **Credit** AmEx, DC, MC, V. **Map** p326 B-C1.

On the first floor of one of Gaudí's outwardly less spectacular buildings (but with some exquisite details within), this modern restaurant offers updated Catalan cuisine such as smoked foie gras with mango sauce, and roast *canetón* (baby duckling) with a curry dressing. Desserts, such as ginger and cinnamon ice-cream with bananas and mango, are excellent too. Parties of six or more can take one of the spacious private rooms, with velvet chairs, antiques, crystal glasses and service so gracious it feels genuinely Victorian.

Conducta Ejemplar – El Rodizio

C/Consell de Cent 403 (93 265 51 12). Metro Girona/6, 19, 47, 50, 51, 55, N1, N4 bus. **Open** 1-4pm, 8.30-midnight Mon-Thur; 1-4pm, 8.30-1am Fri, Sat; 1-4pm Sun. **Lunch buffet** 1,190ptas Mon-Fri; 1,590ptas Sat. **Evening buffet** 1,590ptas. **Credit** MC, V. **Map** p321 E5.

One of few places in town offering a *rodizio*, a Brazilian meat buffet. Eat as much as you like from a hot and cold buffet, followed by 12 different types of meat – Castilian sausage, steak, turkey, lamb, Brazilian-cut beef, veal, marinated pork. Vegetarians beware.

Eat, Drink, Shop

Le Relais de Venise

C/Pau Claris 142 (93 467 21 62). **Open** 1-3.30pm,
8.30pm-12.30am Mon-Sat; 1.30-4pm, 8.30pm-
midnight Sun. **Average** 2,250-3,200ptas.
Credit MC, V. **Map** p326 B1.
This very French restaurant (complete with waitresses in black dresses and white pinafores) offers
only one main course – succulent entrecôte with Café
de Paris sauce and fries, but makes up for it with an
array of classic French desserts such as profiteroles
with hot chocolate sauce, crêpes and ice-creams.

Tragaluz

*Passatge de la Concepció 5 (93 487 01 96). Metro
Diagonal/7, 16, 17, 22, 24, 28, N4 bus.* **Open** 1.30-
4pm, 8.30pm-midnight Mon-Wed, Sun; 1.30-4pm,
8.30pm-1am Thur-Sat. **Average** 4,500ptas. **Set
lunch** 2,800ptas Mon-Fri. **Credit** AmEx, MC, V.
Map p320 D4.
Tragaluz's light, refreshing and hip interior – by '80s
design star Javier Mariscal – includes a top floor and
roof that have been made into a wonderfully airy,
glass-covered dining room. To go with the stylish
and very mellow surroundings there's a fashionably
eclectic menu of Catalan/Mediterranean themes,
with such things as *lluç al vapor amb esparrecs verds
i salsa de poma àcida* (steamed hake with fresh
asparagus and apple sauce) or *filet de porc amb
figues i formatge de cabra* (pork fillet with figs and
goat's cheese). Below there's a comfortable cocktail
lounge, and across the street there's a spacious and
good if slightly overpriced Japanese restaurant, **El
Japonés**, run by the same crowd.
Branches: **Acontraluz** C/Milanesat 19, Zona Alta
(93 203 06 58); **Casi Negro** Avda. Diagonal 640 (93
405 94 44); **El Japonés** Passatge de la Concepció 2
(93 487 25 92).

Windsor

*C/Còrsega 286 (93 415 84 83). Metro Diagonal/54,
66, 67, 68, N8 bus.* **Open** 1-4pm, 8.30-11pm Mon-
Sat; closed Sun. **Average** 5,000ptas. **Gourmet
menu** 6,500ptas. **Credit** AmEx, DC, MC, V.
Map p320 D4.
Named after a movie theatre that once stood nearby, Windsor serves exquisitely prepared modern,
French-influenced Catalan cuisine in a classy setting
complete with enormous chandeliers and satin wall-
paper. The menu changes seasonally, service is
gracious, and the wine list is impressive. In
particular, the wild mushroom *canelons* and desserts
are very good. Ask to sit by the window for a view
of the lovely fountain in the restaurant's courtyard.

Gràcia

Botafumeiro

*C/Gran de Gràcia 81 (93 218 42 30). Metro
Fontana/22, 24, 28, N4 bus.* **Open** 1pm-1am daily.
Closed 3wks Aug. **Average** 6,000ptas. **Credit**
AmEx, MC, V. **Map** p320 D3.
This spacious restaurant specialises in the best of
Galician food, which means, above all, quality

Gaudí details at **Casa Calvet**. *See p147.*

seafood. The lobster, langoustines, scallops, oysters
and other shellfish selected by chef-proprietor
Moncho Neiras are unbeatable. Botafumeiro stays
open late, and entertains its clientele with two
singers, one with guitar. They only play if you want
them to, or so they claim.

La Buena Tierra

*C/de l'Encarnació 56 (93 219 82 13).
Metro Joanic/39, 55, N6 bus.* **Open** 1-4pm, 8pm-
midnight Mon-Sat; closed Sun. Closed end Jul/Aug.
Average 2,000ptas. **Set lunch** 950ptas. Mon-Fri.
Credit MC, V. **Map** p321 E3.
A pleasant restaurant in a little old house in Gràcia,
with a pretty garden at the back, which has some of
the best vegetarian food in town. Specialities include
canelons de bosc (cannelloni and wild mushrooms),
vol-au-vent with cream of asparagus and refreshing
gazpacho and melon soups in summer.
Branch: **La Llar de Foc** C/Ramón y Cajal 13 (93
284 10 25).

Ca l'Abuelo

*C/Providencia 44 (93 284 44 94). Metro Fontana,
Joanic/39, N6 bus.* **Open** 1pm-4pm Tue-Thur; 1.30-
4pm, 9-11.30pm Fri, Sat; closed Mon. Closed Sept
(phone to check). **Set lunch** 1,100ptas Tue-Fri;
1,395ptas Sat. **Set dinner** 1,395ptas Fri, Sat. **Credit**
AmEx, DC, MC, V. **Map** p321 E3.
This well-run place offers a great deal: an open buffet of over 40 different dishes for just over 1,000ptas.
Gorge yourself silly on prawns, chicken, veal, pork,
fish, stews or salads, and a good choice of desserts.

Caliu II

*C/Francisco Giner 21 (93 217 06 05). Metro
Diagonal/22, 24, 28, 39, N4 bus.* **Open** 1-4pm, 8.30-
11pm Mon-Fri; 8.30-midnight Sat; closed Sun.
Average 2,200ptas. **Set lunch** 995ptas Mon-Fri.
Credit MC, V. **Map** p320 D3.
A taste of the islands: an interesting assortment of
Mallorcan dishes such as *sobrassada*, a spicy
sausage meat, sometimes served with honey, or *tum-
bet*, aubergine, potato, and red pepper baked in
tomato sauce and served with lamb (or without, for
vegetarians). There are also excellent cheeses from
Menorca and island goods for sale. For summer,
there's a pleasant outdoor dining area.

Eat, Drink, Shop

Jaume de Provença

C/Provença 88 (93 430 00 29).
Metro Entença/41, 43, 44, N7 bus.
Open 1-4pm, 9-11.30pm Tue-Sat; 1-4pm Sun;
closed Mon. Closed Aug. **Average** 9,000ptas.
Gourmet menu 8,500ptas. **Credit** AmEx, DC,
MC, V. **Map** p327 B4.

This small restaurant tucked away in the Eixample
has its place consistently as one of the most prestigious in Barcelona for many years. This excellent
reputation is due entirely to the quality and
originality of the cuisine of chef Jaume Barguès:
menus are a mixture of traditional Catalan recipes
and ideas of his own, such as crab lasagne, or a salad
of wild mushrooms with prawns and clams. The
wine list is truly superlative.

Marcelino 2000

C/Consell de Cent 236 (93 453 10 72).
Metro Universitat/all routes to Plaça de la
Universitat. **Open** 1-5pm, 8pm-midnight Mon-Sat;
closed Sun. Closed 2wks Aug. **Average** 2,000ptas.
Set menu 1,000ptas Mon-Fri; 1,200ptas Sat.
Credit AmEx, MC, V. **Map** p324 C5.

The Bodegas Marcelino are a chain of straightforward bar-restaurants found right across the
Eixample (usually on street corners), offering a
decent Galician-oriented menu consisting of stews,
soups and salads for first courses, followed by mainly meat and seafood grills for the main event. The
best way to find out about the other branches is to
visit one and pick up one of the napkins, which give
a complete list.

Seaside dining

Back before EU regulations and the '92
Olympics, Barceloneta used to have quite a
few beach-shack style restaurants located
literally on the beach. A decade later,
Barcelona's shoreline once again has its
allotment of temporary cabana-like
establishments where you can enjoy platters
of steamed seafood or fried fish, great
seafood stews, and yes, paella, beach- or
dock-side. These places are spread between
three main areas, the Port Vell, Barceloneta
and its beaches (Metro Barceloneta/17, 39,
45, 57, 59, 64, 157, N8 bus) and the Port
Olímpic, with more beaches (Metro Ciutadella-
Vila Olímpic/36, N6, N8 bus.)

Within the Port Vell, by the new marina at
the eastern end of the port, there is the well-
restored former warehouse now called the
Palau de Mar, lined with restaurants with
outside tables such as **Emperador**, (Plaça de
Pau Vila, Palau de Mar 93 221 02 20,
average 5,500ptas) and the **Merendero de la
Mari** (Plaça de Pau Vila, Palau de Mar, 93
221 31 41, average 5,500ptas). On a warm
evening you get a superb view of the city back
across the harbour. Behind the Palau,
Barceloneta may have lost its beachfront
paella bars, but it still has the city's largest
concentration of good seafood restaurants.
It's possible to find a table outdoors all year
long at the many places along Passeig Joan
de Borbó, such as the low-priced **La Oficina**
(see p144) or **El Rey de la Gamba** (Passeig
Joan de Borbó 48-53, 93 221 75 98, average
3,500ptas).

When you reach the sea at the end of the
Passeig Joan de Borbo, from April to
November you'll find a handful of *chiringuitos*,
temporary food stands, on the beach. They
serve an assortment of tapas and paellas,
some more elaborate than others, such as
those offered by **Chiringuito Silvestre
Salamanca**, run by the nearby **Salamanca**
restaurant (C/Almirall Cervera 34, 93 221 50
33, average 4,500ptas).

Follow the sea northwards and you come to
the Port Olímpic, most attractive of the 1992
Olympic areas. It's big, modern, and
surrounded by the parasoled terraces of
some 200 bars and restaurants. Some are
overpriced, but it's also by the sea, busy,
smells of fresh-cooked fish, democratic – with
fast-food chains vying for space with luxury
restaurants – and open late, with plenty of
places serving until 2am.

There's a whole range of food on offer, from
fast to Mexican. Nearby, **Agua** (see p145)
offers a more elegant setting and eclectic
food, (almost) on the beach. It's fish
restaurants that predominate, though, and a
wander around the Port leaves you spoilt for
choice. For cheap seafood, try the branch of
El Rey de la Gamba (93 221 00 12) or **La
Taverna del Cel Ros** (see p145). **Tinglado
Moncho's** (Moll de Gregal 5-6, 93 221 83
83, average 4,500ptas) and **El Cangrejo
Loco** (Moll del Gregal 29-30, 93 221 05 33,
average 5,500ptas) are pricier but serve
superb fresh seafood, and for summer the
Cangrejo has an upper terrace with a sea
view. More upmarket is **El Celler del Rocxi**
(Moll de Gregal 26, 93 225 19 65, average
5,500ptas). A further stroll down the beach
away from the port will lead you to the great
Xiringuito Escribà (see p145), which offers
very good paellas, grilled fish, fresh salads
and, a special extra, deliciously morish and
self-indulgent desserts.

Eat, Drink, Shop

Relive the spirit of swinging Barcelona at the **Flash Flash**.

Cantina Mexicana I & II

C/de l'Encarnació 51 (93 210 68 05) &
C/Torrent de les Flors 53 (93 213 10 18).
Metro Joanic/39, 55, N6 bus. **Open** 1-3.30pm, 8pm-
1am Mon-Sat; 8pm-12.30am Sun. **Average**
2,500ptas. **Credit** DC, MC, V. **Map** p321 E3.
Both Cantinas, very close to each other on a street corner, offer the same food – enchiladas, *machaca*, guacamole, *fríjoles* – but Cantina Mexicana II, in
C/Torrent de les Flors, has a larger, more comfortable
space. Ingredients are imported from Mexico, and
dishes much more authentic than standard Tex-Mex.
If one closes for a holiday, the other one will be open.

Casi Casi

C/Laforja 8 (93 415 81 94). FCG Gràcia/22, 24, 25,
28, N4 bus. **Open** 1-4pm, 8pm-midnight Mon-Sat;
closed Sun. **Average** 2,000ptas. **Set lunch**
1,000ptas. **Set dinner** 1,200ptas.
Credit AmEx, DC, MC, V. **Map** p320 D3.
With nearly 70 dishes on its main menu, Casi Casi
mixes purely Andalusian food – fish or chickpeas *a*
la andaluza, or, in summer, cold soups like gazpacho and *ajoblanco* (white garlic soup) – with more
Catalan-orientated cannelloni, pigs' trotters or *pa*
amb tomàquet with cheese or ham.

Flash Flash

C/La Granada del Penedès 25 (93 237 09 90).
FGC Gràcia/16, 17, 22, 24, 27, 28, 31, 32 N4 bus.
Open 1pm-1.30am daily. **Average** 2,500ptas.
Credit AmEx, DC, MC, V. **Map** p320 D3.
This *'sandwicheria'*, opened in 1970, was Barcelona's
first-ever design bar. It's '60s-cool through and
through, all white with photos of Twiggy-esque

models around the walls. House speciality is tortilla,
in many varieties, and there are good burgers and
sandwiches, with lots of vegetarian options. Just
control those bad Austin Powers impersonations.

El Glop

C/Montmany 46 (93 213 70 58). Metro Joanic/39,
55, N6 bus. **Open** 1-4pm, 8pm-1am Tue-Sun; closed
Mon. **Average** 2,500ptas. **Set lunch** 1,100ptas. Tue-
Fri. **Credit** MC, V. **Map** p321 E3.
El Glop ('The Sip') is a long-running success, serving traditional char-grilled meat and seasonal vegetables at good prices. Specialities include snails
cooked *a la llauna* and *xoriço al vi* (chorizo in wine),
washed down with powerful red *vi de Gandesa*, from
the Ebro. In summer the ceiling opens up to create
a kind of indoor patio. The original Glop is often
crowded, but the more spacious **El Nou Glop** is
only a few streets away.
Branches: El Nou Glop C/Montmany 49, torre (93
219 70 59); **El Glop de la Rambla**, Rambla
Catalunya 65, Eixample (93 487 00 97); **Taverna El**
Glop del Teatre C/Casp 21, Eixample (93 318 75 75).

L´Illa de Grácia

C/Sant Doménec 19 (93 238 02 29).
Metro Diagonal/22, 24, 28, N4, N6 bus. **Open** 1-
4pm, 9pm-midnight Tue-Fri; 2-4pm, 9pm-midnight
Sat, Sun; closed Mon. Closed late Aug. **Average**
1,700ptas. **Set lunch** 875ptas Mon-Fri. **Credit** DC,
MC, V. **Map** p320 D3.
An unusual place – while it serves solely vegetarian food, L'Illa allows smoking at its tables, and
serves beer, wine and coffee. The regular specialities include *crep illa de Gràcia* (pancake with mush-

rooms, cream and pepper), and home-made cakes. Prices are very reasonable, with the most expensive dish on the menu at just 675ptas, and the set lunch is excellent value.

Jean-Luc Figueras

C/Santa Teresa 10 (93 415 28 77). Metro Diagonal/6, 15, 22, 24, 28, 33, 34 N4 bus. **Open** 1.30-3.30pm, 8.30-11.30pm Mon-Fri; 8.30-11.30pm Sat; closed Sun. Closed 2wks Aug. **Average** 9,000ptas. **Gourmet menu** 9,500ptas. **Credit** AmEx, DC, MC, V. **Map** p320 D4.

A 19th-century neo-classical palace houses this award-winning restaurant, one of the city's finer culinary jewels. The interior is spacious and understatedly refined, and perfect lighting gives one and all the best of appearances. A Frenchman of Catalan descent, Figueras is an exceptionally skilful and inventive chef, who boasts the traditional French ability with sauces. The special delicacies of the house include his prawn salad with cream of summer squash, ginger, a dab of orange mousse, and soy sauce; or leg of Les Landes duck prepared with pears and liquorice. To finish in style, desserts – such as cold rhubarb soup with cream of pistachio and lemon sorbet – are just as outstanding.

Laurak

C/La Granada del Penedès 14-16 (93 218 71 65). FCG Gràcia/16, 17, 22, 24, 27, 28, 31, 32 N4 bus. **Open** 1-4pm, 9-11.30pm Mon-Sat; closed Sun. Closed Aug. **Average** 2,500ptas. **Set lunch** 2,200ptas. **Set dinner** 5,600ptas. **Credit** AmEx, DC, MC, V. **Map** p320 D3.

The dinner menu at this supreme Basque restaurant offers perhaps the best value to be found in any of Barcelona's upper-range establishments. The six course gourmet menu might include perfectly portioned treats such as creamy lobster gazpacho, crab-filled crêpes, and sweet, *bacalao*-stuffed *piquinillo* peppers. The dessert menu is extensive, creative and frankly fantastic: skilfully combined offerings such as seared foie gras with a toffee-glazed *platano* and tiny cubes of mango are luscious and not at all heavy. Service is suitably attentive.

Octubre 18

C/Julián Romea (93 218 25 18). FCG Gràcia/16, 17, 27, 31, 32 bus. **Open** 1.30-3.30pm, 9-11pm Mon-Fri; 9-11pm Sat; closed Sun. Closed end Aug. **Average** 3,700ptas. **Credit** AmEx, DC, MC, V. **Map** p320 D3.

This intimate and highly romantic little place offers a frequently-changing, seasonally-based menu of modern Catalan dishes, such as warm artichoke hearts stuffed with foie gras, and duck confit with gratinéed potatoes. Desserts include a bittersweet chocolate soufflé cake, plus a lemon bavaroise with raspberry sauce.

SoNaMu

Passatge Josep Llovera 11 (93 209 65 83). FCG Gràcia/27, 32, 58, 64, N8 bus. **Open** 1.30-4pm, 8.30-11.30pm Mon-Sat; closed Sun. **Average** 2,500ptas. **Set menu** 1,200ptas. **Credit** MC, V. **Map** p320 C3.

This outstanding Japanese-Korean restaurant in one of the quieter parts of Gràcia is home to Barcelona's best combination plate – the Bento box. Consisting of compartmentalised trays, the box contains four or five different goodies such as *bulgogui* (Korean-style barbecued beef), *gyoza* (steamed, handmade Japanese dumplings), vegetable and prawn tempura, sushi or sashimi, or a salad of seaweed and rice noodles. If you're not just out for a fast, quality lunch, larger meals are equally impressive: the beatifully presented fish is of the highest quality, and everything is prepared with great pride and care.

Top ten Cheap eats

Eating cheaply in Barcelona doesn't ever have to mean eating poorly, for the city has a fine range of budget eating-places.

Ca l'Abuelo
Gràcia (see p149)

Elisabets
The Raval (see p138)

Fil Manila
The Raval (see p138)

Marcelino 2000
The Eixample (see p148)

Mesón David
The Raval (pictured, see p138)

La Poste
Barri Gòtic (see p132)

Restaurante Económico-Borrás
Sant Pere, La Ribera & the Born (see p143)

Restaurante Pakistani
Barri Gòtic (see p133)

Restaurante Romesco
The Raval (see p141)

Rodrigo
Sant Pere, La Ribera & the Born (see p143)

Eat, Drink, Shop

Barcelona's best-value Bento box, at **SoNaMu**. *See p151.*

See p151.

Specchio Magico

C/Luis Antúnez 3 (93 415 33 71). Metro
Diagonal/22, 24, 28, N4 bus. **Open** 2-4pm, 8.30-
11pm Mon-Sat; closed Sun. **Average** 4,500ptas.
Credit AmEx, DC, MC, V. **Map** p320 D3.
Popular, romantic and pocket-sized, this excellent
Italian restaurant offers a big variety of superior
pastas and sauces (including excellent wild mushroom ravioli or fettucine in autumn) as well as delicious vegetable and chicken terrines, great large
salads, and superb desserts such as panna cotta
(cream custard) with blackberries in syrup. Warm
and friendly service adds to the appeal.

Sants

La Parra

Joan Martorell 3 (93 332 51 34).
Metro Hostafrancs/30, 56, 57, 157, 53N, N2, N14
bus. **Open** 8.30pm-12.30am Tue-Fri; 2-4.30pm,
8.30pm-midnight Sat; 2-4.30pm Sun; closed Mon.
Closed Aug (phone to check). **Average** 3,500ptas.
Credit MC, V. **Map** p323 A4.
A great outlet for stout Catalan country cooking *a
la brasa* within the city asphalt. As you enter this
180-year-old ex-coaching inn you pass a giant, fierce-
ly-flaming wood-fired grill, from which comes forth
one of the best *escalivades* in town and hefty portions
of lamb, rabbit, pork, beef and spare ribs, served on
wooden slabs with fresh *all i oli*. There's no messing
about here: flavours are unreservedly powerful.
Other specialities include roast duck, and an unbeatable *orada a la sal* (gilt-head bream baked in salt),
and from November to March there are *calçots*, specially cultivated spring onions from the Valls area
(*see p130*), eaten on their own, charcoal-grilled, with
romesco sauce. Well-priced wines are served, and
rare *orujos* (fierce Galician spirits), but happily, they
have always refused to stock Coca-Cola.

El Peixerot

C/Tarragona 177 (93 424 69 69).
Metro Sants Estació/27, 30, 109, 215, N-0, N7.
Open 1-4pm, 8-11pm Mon-Sat; 1-4pm Sun. Closed
Sat eve & Sun Aug. **Average** 5,500ptas. **Credit** DC,
MC, V. **Map** p323 A-B4.
A branch of the excellent seafood restaurant of the
same name in Vilanova i la Geltrú (*see p264*), El
Peixerot serves a great *arrós a la marinera* (rice in a
fish broth with seafood), paella, *arròs negre*, fresh fish
and other classic dishes of the Catalan coast. There is
also a very good list of local wines – try Hermita
d'Espiells, a semi-dry white from the Penedès.

Tibidabo & Zona Alta

La Balsa

C/Infanta Isabell 4 (93 211 50 48). FCG Av. del
Tibidabo/22, 58, 73, 75, 85 bus. **Open** 9-11.30pm
Mon; 2-3.30pm, 9-11.30pm Tue-Sat; closed Sun.
Average 6,500ptas. **Credit** AmEx, MC, V.
Surrounded by lush gardens and with an equally
airy interior in an award-winning wooden building
designed by Oscar Tusquets and Lluís Clotets, La
Balsa is one of Barcelona's top-notch restaurants
and a regular haunt of the city's elite. The food is an
impressive array of sophisticated Mediterranean
dishes, with regulars such as superb prawn and salt
cod croquettes with tarragon sauce, and in August
there's an open buffet at the bargain price of
3,500ptas. It is, though, above all the garden setting
that makes eating here a delicious experience.

Neichel

C/Beltrán i Rózpide 16 bis (93 203 84 08/
www.relaischateaux.fr/neichel). Metro Maria
Cristina/7, 33, 63, 67, 68, 78, N12 bus. **Open**
1-3.30pm, 8.30-11pm Tue-Sat; closed Mon, Sun.
Closed Aug. **Average** 9,500ptas. **Gourmet menu**
8,000ptas. **Credit** AmEx, DC, MC, V.

Vegetarian relief

Vegetarians still have it hard in Barcelona, but thankfully times are changing. Along with the city's handful of strictly vegetarian places are an increasing number of decent, popular restaurants that make a point of serving veggie food along with fish or white meat dishes. Strict vegetarians should be on their guard however, particularly at more traditional places, for dishes that may seem vegetarian but in fact include, or have been made with, meat or meat stock. When ordering, especially with stews and soups (lentils or chick peas are prime candidates) ask if your meal contains *carn/carne*, meat, or has been prepared with fat or stock (ask *¿lleva tocino?* to see if it's made with pork fat).

Barri Gòtic
Govinda (see p130); **Juicy Jones** (see p130); **Oolong** (see p131); **Self Naturista** (see p133).

The Raval
Biocenter (see p137); **L'Hortet** (see p138).

Sant Pere, La Ribera & the Born
Comme Bio (see p142).

The Eixample
L'Atzavara (see p147).

Gràcia
La Buena Tierra (see p149); **L'Illa de Gracia** (see p150).

In a modern block in the very best part of town, the Neichel restaurant offers an exquisite array of Mediterranean-inspired dishes, meticulously prepared and presented in high style. Owner-chef Jean-Louis Neichel, originally from Alsace, is the foremost representative of the classic French culinary tradition in Barcelona, and his Michelin-starred restaurant is one of the city's very best. As well as the six-course gourmet menu there is a separate menu, also of six courses, that is devoted entirely to dishes made with black truffles. The wine list, a comprehensive survey of Spanish and French labels, cheeses and desserts are all equally remarkable. A very opulent treat.

La Venta
Plaça Doctor Andreu/FCG Av. del Tibidabo/17, 22, 58, 73, 75, 85, 101 bus, then Tramvia Blau. **Open** 1.30-3.15pm, 9-11.15pm Mon-Sat; closed Sun **Average** 5,000ptas. **Credit** AmEx, DC, MC, V.
In the square at the foot of the funicular on Tibidabo, La Venta has an outside terrace that's a really lovely place to enjoy a meal in the fresh mountain air. The restaurant is also attractive indoors, and in winter a glass conservatory maintains the open-air atmosphere. Regulars on the imaginative menu include sea urchins au gratin and cod tail with vegetables, and there are also moreish desserts. Service is friendly and efficient.

Get intimate at **Octubre 18**. *See p151.*

Eat, Drink, Shop

Supreme modern Basque cuisine awaits at **Laurak**. *See p151.*

Eat, Drink, Shop

Poble Nou

Els Pescadors

Plaça Prim 1 (93 225 20 18). Metro Poble Nou/41 bus. **Open** 1-3.45pm, 8pm-midnight daily. **Average** 5,500ptas. **Credit** AmEx, MC, V.

A very attractive and enjoyable restaurant in a small square in the old village of Poble Nou, back from the beach area, with a beautiful outside terrace. Inside, there are two dining rooms in contrasting styles: the first room is in traditional Barcelona café style, with tiled floor and marble tables; further in, the decor is more plush and more intimate. Its specialities are , above all, refined Catalan fish and seafood dishes, and the oven-cooked fish specials, using the pick of the same day's catch from ports on the coast, are superb. There are also frequently interesting vegetarian options on the menu.

Horta

Can Travi Nou

C/Jorge Manrique (93 428 03 01). Metro Horta/10, 45, 102 bus. **Open** 1.30-4pm, 8.30pm-midnight Mon-Sat; 1.30-4pm Sun. **Average** 5000ptas. **Credit** AmEx, DC, MC, V.

Occupying a huge, beautiful old *masia* or traditional Catalan farmhouse, standing in its own large garden, on a hill above the former village of Horta, this feels more like a country restaurant than somewhere within a city. Even if you don't take a table in the garden, the timbered rooms inside the venerable house are delightfully pretty. The food is traditional Catalan, with speciality *mar i muntanya* dishes such as *sípia amb mandonguilles* and *cueta de rap amb all torrat* (monkfish tail with toasted garlic). Can Travi is difficult to reach by public transport, so take a cab, but very worth finding.

Gaig

Passeig Maragall 402 (93 429 10 17). Metro Horta/19, 45, N4 bus. **Open** 1.30-4pm, 9-11pm Tue-Sat; 1.30-4pm Sun; closed Mon. Closed 3wks Aug. **Average** 6,000ptas. **Credit** AmEx, DC, MC, V.

Founded in 1869 as a café for cart drivers, this renowned restaurant has been in the Gaig family for four generations. Specialities include *arròs de colomí amb ceps* (young pigeon in rice with wild mushrooms) and stuffed pigs' trotters. A favourite dessert is the *pecat de xocolata* ('chocolate sin', a thick mousse). The wine cellar is a sight in itself.

The best Top tables

These restaurants offer luxurious surroundings, supremely smooth service and the finest Catalan or, in the case of **Laurak**, Basque cooking, as well as drawing on a range of Mediterranean cuisines. This all naturally comes at a price, but most offer a *menú degustacion* to showcase the chef's talents, which are good value. Some of these restaurants may be a little formal, but none has any rigid dress code.

Agut d'Avignon *Barri Gòtic.*
Ca l'Isidre *The Raval.*
Passadís del Pep
Sant Pere, La Ribera & the Born.
Casa Calvet, Jaume de Provença, Windsor
all in the Eixample.
Botafumeiro; Jean-Luc Figueras; Laurak
all in Gràcia.
La Balsa; Neichel *Tibidabo & Zona Alta.*
Gaig *Horta.*

Cafés & Bars

The best spots in town to sip, think, chat, meet friends or just plain soak up the world around you.

The sheer number of establishments in Barcelona where you can meet up with others and share a drink is proof positive of the city's famed openness. Some are meeting points around which neighbourhood life turns, others old *bodegas* with an ageing clientele sampling wine from the barrel; there are outdoor cafés on sunny squares, designer spots with imported beer, and small *granges* where you can sample afternoon coffee and cakes. Without paying a few of them a visit, you won't really get to know what Barcelona is about.

Tapas in Barcelona are generally not as varied as in some parts of Spain, but great examples can be found, and most bars offer food of some kind, from sandwiches to a full lunch menu. The listing that follows can only be one selection from all the (uncategorisable) cafés and drinking-holes around the city. Be advised that some of the bars listed do serve a set lunch menu and that if you try to occupy one of their tables during the lunch hours, you will probably be asked to leave. For bars more clearly oriented to night-time socialising, *see chapter* **Nightlife**, for post-club breakfast venues, *see p250,* and for more bar-restaurants *see chapter* **Restaurants**.

OPENING TIMES
Especially in traditional cafés, opening hours will vary (many close earlier or later at night, according to trade), and those listed should be taken as guidelines rather than fixed hours.

The Rambla

There is one main drawback to taking a table on the most famous café pavement in town: the cost. There are exceptions: the new **Zurich** and **Cava Universal** still maintain reasonable prices. The **Opera** has an unchallenged claim to the most class.

Boadas
C/Tallers 1 (93 318 95 92). Metro Catalunya/ bus all routes to Plaça Catalunya. **Open** noon-2am Mon-Thur; noon-3am Fri, Sat; closed Sun. **No credit cards. Map** p326 A2.
This Barcelona institution is a 1933 art deco cocktail bar opened by Miquel Boadas after he learned his trade in the famed Floridita Bar in Havana. The expert barmen can mix a huge variety of cocktails, and the

Reflect on life at the **Café Zurich**.

wood-lined walls are strung with mementoes of famous patrons – including a sketch or two by Miró.

Café de l'Opera
La Rambla 74 (93 317 75 85/93 302 41 80). Metro Liceu/14, 38, 59, N9, N12 bus. **Open** 8am-2.15am Mon-Thur, Sun; 8am-3am Fri, Sat. **No credit cards. Map** p327 A3.
And another institution, the last real 19th-century grand café in the city, and by far the best of the cafés on the Rambla. With genuine *Modernista*-era decor, L'Opera remains enormously popular, with a contentedly mixed clientele – elderly locals, foreigners, a big gay contingent and anyone else. Unbeatable for people-watching on the Rambla.

Café Zurich
Plaça Catalunya 1 (93 317 91 53). Metro Catalunya/bus all routes to Plaça Catalunya. **Open** *June-end Oct* 8am-1am Mon-Sat; 8am-11pm Sun. *End Oct-May* 8am-11pm Mon-Thur, Sun; 8am-midnight Fri, Sat. **No credit cards. Map** p326 B1.

Eat, Drink, Shop

No cava, but great views at **Cava Universal**.

Not so much on the Rambla as staring down it from the corner of Plaça Catalunya, and with one of Barcelona's largest café terraces, the 1920s Zurich was for decades one of the city's universally recognised meeting-points. Hence it was a controversial step when it was swept away in 1997, in another redevelopment scheme. To make amends, the shiny new mall built on the site, El Triangle, has included a new version of the café, opened in 1999. The new-model Zurich has generically old-style decor instead of the quirkiness of the original, with rather over-shiny woodwork, but nonetheless quickly regained its status as meet-up spot par excellence for locals, backpackers and other urban wanderers, and the tables outside are great for watching the parade of humanity flowing in and out of the Rambla.

Cava Universal

Plaça Portal de la Pau 4 (93 302 61 84). Metro Drassanes/14, 20, 36, 38, 57, 59, 64, 91, 157, N6, N9 bus. **Open** 9am-10pm daily. **No credit cards.** **Map** p327 A4.

A landmark bar, oblivious to fashions and more than usually resistant to rising prices. Have a coffee, beer or *bocadillo* (it's not actually a cava bar) at outdoor tables at the foot of the Rambla. Admire the statue of Columbus pointing the way to the New World, and enjoy the optimum view of the crowds heading for the new new world of Maremàgnum.

Barri Gòtic

Bar Celta

C/Mercè 16 (93 315 00 06). Metro Drassanes/14, 36, 57, 59, 64, 157, N6 bus. **Open** noon-midnight Mon-Sat; closed Sun. **No credit cards.** **Map** p327 B4.

Among the survivors of old Barcelona is the line of *tascas* along C/Mercè, near the port – small

---

Café behaviour

BASIC ETIQUETTE

The civilised system of pay-as-you-leave is the norm in Barcelona bars, except in busy night bars and some outdoor terraces, such as those in the Plaça Reial, where you are often asked to pay as soon as drinks are served. If you have trouble getting a waiter's attention, a loud but polite 'Oiga' (literally, 'hear me'), or, in Catalan, 'Escolti' should do the trick. Tipping is entirely discretionary, but it's common to leave something if you've had table service, and food as well as a drink. Most people just round up a bill to the nearest 100ptas, or leave some of the change. Some people also leave a few coins (rarely over 25ptas) when served at the bar, intended more as an old-fashioned courtesy than a real tip.

One other point: Spaniards are the biggest consumers of low-alcohol drinks in the world. Catalans, in particular, do not drink to get drunk, and it's not unusual for people to sit on a drink for an hour or more.

COFFEE AND TEA

A large, milky coffee is a *cafè amb llet* (Catalan) or *café con leche* (Spanish), which locals usually only have with breakfast, although you can order it at any time of day. After mid-morning people are more likely to have a small coffee with a dash of milk, a *tallat* (Catalan)/*cortado* (Spanish), or a black espresso (*cafè sol/café solo*). A *café americano* is a *solo* diluted with twice the normal amount of water, and a *carajillo* is a *solo* with a shot of spirits. It will normally be made with brandy (*carajillo de coñac*), but you can also order a *carajillo de ron* (rum), whisky or whatever else may take your fancy. Decaffeinated coffee (*descafeinado*) is widely available, but if you don't want just instant decaf with hot milk, you need to ask for it *de máquina* (espresso).

Tea, except from places that specialise in it, is frankly a bit of a dead loss in Barcelona, but various herbal teas (*infusiones*) such as *menta* (mint) or *manzanilla* (camomile) are pretty much always available.

BEER

Damm beer reigns supreme in Catalonia. The most popular is Estrella, a good, standard lager; Voll-Damm is stronger and heavier, and Bock-Damm is an interesting, but not widely distributed, dark beer. Bottled beers can be ordered in standard *mitjanes/medianas* (third of a litre; just over half a pint) or smaller *quintos* (a quarter-litre). Draught beer is served in *cañas* (about the same as a *mediana*) or *jarras* (about half a litre). Imported beers are increasingly available, but are pricier than local brands.

traditional bars that are ever popular for a drinks-and-tapas crawl. At Bar Celta, huge trays laden predominantly with seafood line the bar: particularly recommended are the *patatas bravas* and *rabas* (deep-fried chunks of squid), best washed down with Galician white wine served, as is traditional, in white ceramic cups.

Café La Cereria

C/Baixada Sant Miquel 3-5 (no phone). Metro Liceu/14, 38, 59, 91, N9, N12 bus. **Open** 9.30am-10pm Mon-Sat; closed Sun. **No credit cards.** **Map** p327 B3.
This quiet, friendly café is welcome relief from the invasion of overly commercial spots nearby. In a *Modernista* former wax shop, run as a co-op, La Cereria offers home-made cakes, tarts and a big range of teas, herbal and traditional. Its wooden tables are home-made too, as are, of course, the varied *bocadillos* you can order when sitting at them.

Leticia

C/Codols 21 (93 302 00 74). Metro Drassanes/14, 36, 57, 59, 64, 157, N6 bus. **Open** 5pm-3am Mon, Wed-Sun; closed Tue. **Credit** MC, V. **Map** p327 A4.

Located on one of the medieval city's narrowest streets, Leticia is cool and relaxed, with comfy chairs and a sofa on which to chat, play chess, and chill out to the eclectic vibes of drum 'n' bass, rare soul, jazz and flamenco. Should hunger strike, there's an excellent range of salads, home-made *bocadillos*, cakes, and vegetarian dishes. Cocktails and quality teas are also available.

Margarita Blue

C/Josep Anselm Clavé 6 (93 317 71 76). Metro Drassanes/14, 18, 38, 59, N6, N9 bus. **Open** 11am-2am Mon-Wed; 11am-3am Thur, Fri; 7pm-3am Sat; 7pm-2am Sun. **Credit** MC, V. **Map** p327 A4.
This is a roomy, colourful bar/restaurant that serves very good Mexican food at all hours at moderate prices. As you sip your blue drink, observe the weird, winged lightbulbs that serve as lamps, and the tiled artwork depicting nude, flying women. If you find you're in need of a pick-me-up, then try the Ibizan energy cocktail, the *turbital*. The latest branch of the Blue empire, Rita Blue (*see below* **Branches**), serves up a more varied menu,

Eat, Drink, Shop

WINES, SPIRITS AND OTHER DRINKS

All bars stock a basic red (*negro* or *tinto*), white (*blanco*) or rosé (*rosado*). If a red wine is a bit acidic, try asking for it with lemonade (*gaseosa*). Except in bars that are wine specialists, good wines tend to be expensive, and the range limited: for a wider choice, go to a *bodega*. Most bars stock popular brands of cava, but 'champagne bars' have a wider variety Spirit mixes such as *gin-tonic*, *vodka-tónica* or a *Cuba-libre* (rum and coke) are very popular for night-time drinking. Both Catalonia and Andalusia produce high-quality brandies, more full-bodied than French brandies but still subtle; of Catalan labels, Torres 5 and 10 are two of the best.

NON-ALCOHOLIC DRINKS

Very popular alternatives to alcohol are the Campari-like but booze-free Bitter Kas, and tonic water (*una tónica*), drunk with just ice and lemon. Mineral water is *aigua/agua mineral*: ask for it *amb gas/con gas* (fizzy), or *sense gas/sin gas* (still).

FOOD

Most bars have some kind of *bocadillo*, hefty, crusty bread rolls filled with *llom/lomo* (pork), *jamón serrano*, potato tortilla, tuna, cheese and other fillings; some bars use long, thin rolls called *flautes*. When you order a *bocadillo* the waiter will usually check that you want it '*amb tomàquet?*' or '*con tomate?*', spread with tomato Catalan-style. A *sandwich* is made with white sliced bread, and a *bikini* is a toasted ham and cheese sandwich.

Most Barcelona tapas bars offer a fairly standard choice, although there are several Basque bars that have a wider range. Some Catalan bars have a different, *llesqueria* selection (*see chapter* **Restaurants**). Below we list some of the most common tapas (in Spanish only).

Albóndigas meatballs; **anchoas** salted anchovies; **berberechos** cockles; **boquerones** pickled fresh anchovies; **chipirones en su tinta** small squid cooked in their ink; **croquetas (de pollo, de bacalao, etc)** croquettes (with chicken, salt-cod, etc); **empanadas** large flat pie, usually with tuna filling; **empanadillas (de atún)** small fried pastries, usually with tuna filling; **ensaladilla Rusa** mixed 'Russian' salad; **gambas al ajillo** prawns fried with garlic; **habas a la Catalana** broad beans, onions and *botifarra* blood sausage cooked in white wine; **mejillones** mussels; **olivas** olives; **patatas bravas** deep-fried potatoes with hot pepper sauce; **pincho moruno** peppered pork brochette; **pulpo a la gallega** octopus with paprika and olive oil.

A table with a view

When the time comes to just simply stop and admire the world around you, Barcelona's outdoor café terrazas are the place to be. They also make perfect spots in which to write a postcard, read a book, or just join in the great Mediterranean sport of people-watching.

Barri Gòtic & La Ribera

The city's two oldest *barris* offer delightful spots to sit and sip a drink in ancient medieval squares or beside breathtaking gothic churches. Also try the **Tèxtil Café**, **La Vinya del Senyor** (for both, *see p166*) and **Bar Zurich** (*see p155*).

L´Antiquari de la Plaça del Rei

C/Veguer 13 (93 310 04 35). Metro Jaume I/17, 19, 40, 45, N8 bus. **Open** *Mid Sept-May* 5pm-2am daily. *May mid-Sept* 10am-2.30am daily. **No credit cards. Map** p327 B3.
L'Antiquari's outdoor tables are great for enjoying both the charm of the history-dense Plaça del Rei and the frequent public concerts held there. Inside, occasional concerts are staged in the ancient cellar.

Bar del Pi

Plaça Sant Josep Oriol 1 (93 302 21 23). Metro Liceu/14, 38, 59, N9, N12 bus. **Open** 9.30am-11pm Mon-Sat; 10am-3pm, 5-10pm Sun. **Credit** MC, V. **Map** p327 A3.
This much-loved, bustling bar offers a front-row seat for the weekend art market and the

buskers which frequently perform there, as well as side views of the majestic Santa Maria del Pi. Inside, space is cramped, but a friendly atmosphere prevails.

Cafè d´Estiu

Museo Frederic Marés, Plaça Sant Iu 5 (93 310 30 14). Metro Jaume I/17, 19, 40, 45, N8 bus. **Open** *Easter-Sept* 10am-10pm Tue-Sun. Closed Mon. *Oct-May* closed. **No credit cards. Map** p327 B3.
The Gothic courtyard of the Museu Federic Marés, with its stone fish pond and six old citrus trees, is one of the most peaceful spots in the Barri Gòtic to enjoy a quiet drink – but only in the summer, mind, as the literal translation of its name, the Summer Café, indicates.

Glaciar

Plaça Reial 3 (93 302 11 63). Metro Liceu/14, 38, 59, N9, N12 bus. **Open** 4pm-2.15am Mon-Sat; 8am-2.15am Sun. **No credit cards. Map** p327 A3.
Originally intended to be the residences of bankers and wealthy Catalan merchants, the Plaça Reial is now a seething melting-pot of street-life and you won't find a better vantage point than this perennially hip spot.

Vascelum

Plaça Santa Maria del Mar (93 319 01 67). Metro Jaume I/17, 19, 40, 45, N8 bus. **Open** 9.30am-1am Tue-Fri; 10am-2am Sat, Sun; closed Mon. **Credit** MC, V. **Map** p327 C4.
This modern bar in the Ribera is not to be visited for its

similarly hip decor, a terrace in a pleasant square and a subterranean party area.
Branches: El Taco de Margarita Plaça Duc de Medinaceli 1 (93 318 63 21); **Rita Blue** Plaça Sant Agusti 3, Raval (93 412 34 38).

Mesón del Café

C/Libreria 16 (93 315 07 54). Metro Jaume I/17, 19, 40, 45, N8 bus. **Open** 7am-11pm Mon-Sat; closed Sun. **No credit cards. Map** p327 B3.
A charming hole-in-the-wall café that's regularly packed. It's reckoned by many in the know to have the best coffee in town, served by some of the city's fastest moving waiters.

Nostromo

C/Ripoll 16 (93 412 24 55). Metro Urquinaona/17, 19, 40, 45, N8 bus. **Open** 1.30pm-2.30am Mon-Thur; 1.30pm-3am Fri; 8pm-3am Sat; closed Sun. **Credit** V. **Map** p326 B2.
Named after the Conrad novel and run by a retired sailor, this is a relaxed haven for landlubbers and mariners alike. The literary nature of the place is not just a matter of a name: shelfloads of books about the sea, exotic parts and similar topics are distributed about the bar, ready for browsing and/or sale. There's an excellent lunch menu, and dinners are cooked to order (by advance reservation only).

The aptly named **Café del Sol**.

somewhat sterile interior, but shouldn't be missed for its comfortable outdoor tables from which to contemplate the majestic counterposition of verticals and plain space in the façade of Santa Maria del Mar.

Gràcia

Quieter and less-touristed than the Ciutat Vella, this unique area of town has its fair share of pleasant, leafy squares lined with welcoming watering holes.

Cafè del Sol

Plaça del Sol 16 (93 415 56 63). Metro Fontana/22, 24, 28, N4 bus. **Open** 1pm-2am Mon-Thur, Sun; 1pm-2.30am Fri, Sat. **No credit cards. Map** p320 D3.
A more appropriate name – 'Bar of the Sun' – could not have been chosen for this popular bar which, fortunately, also enjoys considerable shade. Inside, ask before playing the piano – and only if you know how to play. Your request may or may not be granted.

Virreina Bar

Plaça de la Virreina 1 (93 237 98 80). Metro Fontana/21, 39, N4 bus. **Open** 10am-2.30am Mon-Sat; 10am-midnight Sun. **No credit cards. Map** p321 E3.

In another human-sized Gràcia square is this friendly meeting place, which serves imported beers, as well as good *bocadillos* and sandwiches. The odd dash of colour on the façade of the church next door is a recent addition.

Montjuïc & Tibidabo

For a breath of fresh air and breathtaking views, the city's two mountains are the place to go. Fortunately, Barcelona's café proprietors know this.

Mirablau

Plaça Doctor Andreu, Tibidabo (93 418 58 79). FGC Tibidabo/17, 22, 58, 73, 75, 85, 101 bus, then Tramvia Blau. **Open** 11am-4.30am Mon-Thur, Sun; 11am-5am Fri, Sat. **Credit**: MC, V.
The most breathtaking panorama of the city is to be had here, at the end of the tramline on Tibidabo. It has both an outside garden terrace and, inside the bar, floor-to-ceiling windows seemingly suspended in space, from where you can admire Barcelona laid out below you by day and by night.

Miramar

Avda Miramar, Montjuïc (93 442 31 00). Metro Paral.lel, then Funicular de Montjuïc/61 bus. **Open** Dec-May 10am-midnight Mon, Tue, Thur-Sun; June-Nov 10am-2am Mon, Tue, Thur-Sun; closed Wed. Closed some wks in Nov. **No credit cards. Map** p323 B6.
This little-known bar on Montjuïc, at the end of the road from the Fundació Miró, offers a sweeping vista of the port and Mediterranean. The views however, are the best thing about it, as the bar itself is nothing special.

La Palma

C/Palma de Sant Just 7 (93 315 06 56). Metro Jaume I/17, 19, 40, 45, N8 bus. **Open** 8am-3.30pm, 7-10pm Mon-Thur; 8am-3.30pm, 7-11pm Fri, Sat; closed Sun. **No credit cards. Map** p327 B3.
A cluster of sausages hanging from the ceiling attests to the speciality of this family-run bar in a beautiful old building. The assorted paintings on the walls are the originals by a group of artists – called the *Internos* – who frequented the place in the 1950s. Don't expect to tap dance on the tables here – the regulars come for a quiet glass of wine, poured from one of the many barrels lining the walls, and the easy familiarity.

Pilé 43

C/N'Agla 4 (93 317 39 02) Metro Liceu/14, 38, 59, N9, N12 bus. **Open** 1.30-4.30pm, 7pm-2am Mon-Thur; 1.30-4.30pm, 7pm-3am Fri, Sat; closed Sun. **Credit** MC, V. **Map** p327 A3.
A mod little spot behind the Plaça Reial filled with furniture collectibles from the 1960s and '70s – lamps, chairs, glasses – all of which are for sale at this combination bar/furniture shop. Hopefully nobody will buy the seat out from under you while you're waiting for your cocktail to arrive. For once, you can get decent vegetarian dishes, and other light foodstuffs are also available.

Eat, Drink, Shop

El Portalón

*C/Banys Nous 20 (93 302 11 87). Metro Liceu/
14, 38, 59, N9, N12 bus.* **Open** 9am-midnight
Mon-Sat; closed Sun. Closed Aug. **No credit cards**.
Map p327 B3.

A charming *bodega* that was created in the 1860s
out of the stables of a centuries-old palace, and
which has been putting out bargain food and wine
ever since. Regulars chat and play dominoes at
marble tables or sit ensconced in wooden booths surrounded by the original stone walls. A substantial
offering of tapas is always available and full meals
at lunch and dinner are served.

Els Quatre Gats

*C/Montsió 3-bis (93 302 41 40). Metro Catalunya/
bus all routes to Plaça Catalunya.* **Open** 9am-2am
Mon-Sat; 5pm-2am Sun. Closed 3wks Aug.
Credit AmEx, DC, MC, V. **Map** p326 B2.

Not so much an institution as a monument. In 1897
a figure-about-town called Pere Romeu opened this
café in a *Modernista* building by Puig i Cadafalch,
and for a few years it was the great meeting-point
of bohemian Barcelona. Major artists of the day
such as Rusiñol and Casas painted pictures especially for it, and the menu cover was Picasso's first
paid commission. It closed in 1903, and was used
for decades as a textile warehouse, until in the 1980s
it was finally restored and reopened, with reproductions by contemporary artists of the original
paintings. Under its current management the present-day Els Quatre Gats is much more smart than
bohemian, but is an attractive place for a coffee, and
to sample some good although pricey tapas. In the
room at the back, where Pere Romeu once presented avant-garde performances, there is a restaurant,
with a good set lunch menu.

Schilling

*C/Ferran 23 (93 317 67 87). Metro Liceu/14, 38,
59, N9, N12 bus.* **Open** 10am-2.30am Mon-Sat;
noon- 2.30am Sun. **Credit** V. **Map** p327 A3.

Proof that Barcelona is a ranking member of
European café society, Schilling could almost be a
sleek modern heir to the sort of grand café that used
to thrive in the days when the Habsburg empire was
still intact (even though the place only opened up in
1997). Spacious and popular – with a particularly

Sweet treats

Originally direct outlets for fresh dairy
produce in the city, *granjas* (literally 'farms')
developed into a genre of café/shop all
their own. They specialise in coffee, cakes,
pastries, dairy products and such things
as *suizos* (thick hot chocolate topped by a
mountain of whipped cream) and *batidos*
(milkshakes), although many will also serve
you a beer if you must. Built to satisfy
Catalans' traditionally sweet tooth, they're
especially popular for call-ins breaking up
an afternoon's shopping.

La Granja

*C/Banys Nous 4, Raval (93 302 69 75).
Metro Liceu/14, 38, 59, 91, N9, N12
bus.* **Open** 9am-2pm, 5-9.30pm Mon-Fri;
9.30am-2pm, 5-9.30pm Sat; 10am-2pm,
6-9.30pm Sun. Closed 2wks end Aug/Sept.
No credit cards. **Map** p327 B3.

Run for years by two gentle old ladies, this
place on one of the oldest streets of the Barri
Gòtic has since passed to a younger crew
who have expanded it a bit, but otherwise
kept the same *granja* mentality. Plus, in the
extra room at the back, there's a section of
Roman wall, clearly visible.

Granja Dulcinea

*C/Petritxol 2, Barri Gótic (93 302 68 24).
Metro Liceu/14, 38, 59, 91, N9, N12 bus.*
Open 9am-1pm, 4.30-9pm daily.
No credit cards. **Map** p326 A2.

Located on a very pretty street, Granja
Dulcinea looks a bit like a mountain cottage,
with a small arched window facing the
street and traditional wooden fittings.
Piping hot *suizos* are swiftly served by
white-jacketed, bow-tied waiters.

Granja M Viader

*C/Xuclà 4-6, Raval (93 318 34 86).
Metro Liceu/14, 38, 59, 91, N9, N12 bus.*
Open 5-8.45pm Mon; 9am-1.45pm, 5-
8.45pm Tue-Sat; closed Sun. Closed 1wk
Aug. **Credit** MC, V. **Map** p326 A2.

The 130 years of service have gradually
filled the walls here with mementoes,
photographs and awards. Enjoy your *mel i
mató* (a cottage cheese-like substance with
honey drizzled on top) at one of the marble-
top tables, or take away a sampling of local
honey, cheese, meat or chocolate.

Cool relief: *orxata/horchata*

Orxateries/horchaterías serve *orxata* (in
Spanish, *horchata*), a delicious milky drink
made by crushing a nut called a *chufa*. Many
don't appreciate it on first tasting, but once
you're used to it it's actually wonderfully
refreshing on a hot day. *Orxata* curdles once

large gay clientele – Schilling serves a variety of *bocadillos*, desserts and teas, as well as a range of other refreshments and alcohol.

Les Tapes

Plaça Regomir 4 (93 302 48 40). Metro Jaume I/ 17, 19, 40, 45, N8 bus. **Open** 9am-11pm Mon-Sat; closed Sun. Closed Aug. **No credit cards.** **Map** p327 B3.
The sign 'We rip off drunks and tourists' above the bar shouldn't worry you, for this place is especially welcoming to English speakers. Run by Santi, who worked in Birmingham as a chef, and his English wife, it has UK football on the TV, shelves of English books to browse through and a noticeboard for foreigners looking for contacts, rooms, jobs and so on.

Taverna Basca Iratí

C/Cardenal Casañas 17 (93 302 30 84). Metro Liceu/14, 38, 59, N9, N12 bus. **Open** noon-midnight Tue-Sat; noon-4.30pm Sun. Closed 3wks Aug, 2wks Christmas. **Credit** AmEx, MC, V. **Map** p327 A3.
A very busy place serving excellent Basque-style tapas, with a long bar displaying the wealth of

Basque imagination when it comes to designing delicious bite-size combinations. Note: the selection dwindles dramatically the later it gets, so don't miss out. There's also a good, full-service restaurant at the back of the bar.

Thiossan

C/Vidre 5 (93 317 10 31). Metro Liceu/14, 38, 59, N9, N12 bus. **Open** 1.30-4pm, 7pm-2am Tue-Sat; 7pm-2am Sun. **No credit cards.** **Map** p327 A3.
A comfortable, laid-back African bar-cum-cultural-centre off Plaça Reial. It features exhibitions, light West African edibles, and regular music sessions.

Venus Delicatessen

C/Avinyó 25 (93 301 15 85). Metro Liceu/14, 38, 59, N9, N12 bus. **Open** noon-midnight Mon-Sat; closed Sun. Closed 2wks Nov. **No credit cards.** **Map** p327 B3.
Two sisters run this innovative place, serving decent deli-style food with a wide choice of pâtés and cheeses, nine different salads, numerous types of *bocadillos*, and dishes such as vegetable lasagne and chilli. The atmosphere is relaxed and international.

made, and so has to be bought fresh on the spot from a specialised *orxateria*.
Orxaterias also sell home-made ice-creams and *granissats/granizados* (fruit or coffee drinks sipped through crushed ice).
Closing times for all the *horchaterias* listed vary as the summer season progresses.

Horchatería Sirvent

C/Parlament 56, Eixample (93 441 27 20). Metro Poble Sec/20, 24, 38, 64, N6 bus. **Open** *Easter-mid Nov* 9am-1.30am daily. *Mid Nov-Jan* 9am-9pm daily. Closed Feb, Mar. **No credit cards. Map** p324 C6.
What this lacks in ambience, it makes up for in an ample offering of treats (which they can ship for you). On summer nights, crowds of people drink standing around the door. Though both this place and the one listed below share the same name and are close to one another, they deny any connection.

Orxateria-Gelateria Sirvent

Ronda Sant Pau 3, Eixample (93 441 76 16). Metro Paral.lel/20, 36, 57, 64, 91, 157, N6 bus. **Open** *Easter-early Nov* 9am-10pm daily. *Mid Nov-Jan* 9am-1am daily. **No credit cards. Map** p324 C6.
Aside from the requisite *orxata* and home-made ice-cream, Orxateria-Gelateria Sirvent

has a wonderful assortment of hand-made chocolates. Its outside tables are a great place to sit out late at night.

El Tío Che

Rambla del Poble Nou 44-46, Poble Nou (93 309 18 72). Metro Poble Nou/36, 71, 141, N6 bus. **Open** *Oct-May* 9am-2pm, 5-9pm Mon, Tue, Thur-Sun; closed Wed in winter. *May-mid Sept* 9am-1am Mon-Thur; 9am-3am Fri, Sat. **No credit cards.**
Open since 1912, this well-known establishment is the only place in town that still does a malt-flavoured *granizado*.

La Valenciana

C/Aribau 1 (93 453 11 38). Metro Universitat/bus all routes to Plaça Universitat. **Open** *Sept-June* 8.30am-10.30pm Mon-Thur; 8.30am-2am Fri; 9am-2am Sat; 9am-10.30 Sun. *July, Aug* 8.30am-2am daily. **Credit** V. **Map** p324 C5.
A big, well-run and long-established *orxateria* and *torroneria* (nougat shop) that serves excellent home-made ice creams and sorbets, as well as other sweet things and savoury café standards. Upstairs there's a good-sized area where you can sit and read, chill out, chat or have lunch, served daily with a drink and dessert for 850ptas.

Robots and beer at the friendly **Bar Fortuny**. Guys lIke it.

The Raval

Bar Almirall

*C/Joaquim Costa 33 (no phone). Metro
Universitat/bus all routes to Plaça Universitat.*
Open 7pm-2.30am Mon-Thur; 7pm-3am Fri, Sat;
closed Sun. **No credit cards. Map** p324 C5.
Opened in 1860, the Almirall has the distinction of
being the oldest continuously functioning bar in the
city, and still has its elegant early *Modernista* woodwork, although for some years it's been charming-
ly unkempt. Iron beams supporting the original
wood crossbeams are the recent result of city-
enforced renovations, but the big, soft sofas lining
the walls have been allowed to stay.

Bar Fortuny

*C/Pintor Fortuny 31 (93 317 98 92). Metro
Catalunya/bus all routes to Plaça Catalunya.* **Open**
10am-midnight Tue-Sun; closed Mon. Closed 2wks
Aug. **No credit cards. Map** p326 A2.
A subtle stroke of genius transformed this one-time
neighbourhood hangout for chess-playing elderly
men into a science-fiction-tinged arena where generations of the culturally hip now sit and smoke
together. The former *bodega*'s wine barrels are still
in place, as are a few of the chess players, now over-
seen by a collection of toy robots. It's also popular
with gay women. Good, wholesome home cooking
is available throughout the day and evening.

Bar Kasparo

*Plaça Vicenç Martorell 4 (93 302 20 72). Metro
Catalunya/bus all routes to Plaça Catalunya.*

Open *Winter* 9am-10pm. *Summer* 9am-midnight
daily. Closed Jan. **No credit cards. Map** p326 A2.
A small bar in the arcades of one of the city's more
peaceful squares, taken over (and renovated) by
three Australian sisters, and offering more varied
fare than basic tapas. The terrace at the front is a
great spot for sitting out on a sunny day.

Bar Pastís

*C/Santa Mònica 4 (93 318 79 80). Metro
Drassanes/14, 38, 59, 91, N12 bus.* **Open** 7.30pm-
2.30am Mon-Thur, Sun; 7.30pm-3.30am Fri, Sat.
Credit AmEx, MC, V. **Map** p327 A4.
Down a tiny alley off the bottom end of La Rambla,
this small, dark, quirky place is another of
Barcelona's 'bar-institutions'. It was opened in the
1940s by Quimet and Carme, a Catalan couple who'd
lived in Marseilles, and the pictures around the walls
were painted by Quimet himself, apparently always
when drunk. They began the tradition of playing
exclusively French music and serving only pastis,
and the bar became a favourite of boxers, French
sailors, *Barrio Chino*-types and the Franco-era intel-
ligentsia. Under its current management the drinks
list has expanded, and there's now live music, 11pm-
1.30am Sun, but the essence remains unchanged.

Iposa Bar

*C/Floristas de la Rambla 14 (93 318 60
86/www.barip05a.com) Metro Liceu/14, 38, 59,
N9, N12 bus.* **Open** 1pm-3am Mon-Sat; closed
Sun. **Credit** MC V. **Map** p326 A2.
Run by a friendly French trio – who speak very
good English – Iposa is a fresh and cool new addition to the Raval. Art photos are projected on to a

Wetting whistles at **The Clansman**.

huge burlap screen covering a back wall and the house DJ spins anything from Cuban rhythms to ambient and house. Excellent meals are served for both lunch and dinner, along with yummy home-made tapas. There are also tables outdoors on a pleasant, leafy square.

(El bar que pone) Muebles Navarro

C/Riera Alta 4-6 (607 18 80 96 mobile). Metro San Antoni/20, 24, 38, 64, N6 bus. **Open** *Mid Sept-June* 5pm-midnight Tue-Thur; 5pm-2am Fri-Sun. *June-mid Sept* 6pm-2am Tue-Thur; 6pm-3am Fri, Sat. **No credit cards. Map** p324 C5.
Once a furniture showroom, now a big, elegantly informal café with excellent, if pricey sandwiches, including New York lox with onion spread. An amal-gam of armchairs, sofas and other furniture allows you to sit in comfort and style while at the same time being on display in the large front windows.

Sant Pere, La Ribera & the Born

Bar Hivernacle

Parc de la Ciutadella (93 295 40 17). Metro Arc de Triomf/39, 40, 41, 42, 51, 141 bus. **Open** 10am-1am daily. **Credit** AmEx, DC, MC, V. **Map** p325 E6.
A bar inside the beautiful iron-and-glass *hivernacle*, or greenhouse, of the Ciutadella park, built by Josep Amargós in 1884. With three parts (one shaded room, one unshaded and a terrace), Bar Hivernacle hosts exhibitions and occasional jazz and classical concerts, and as well as the plants around the bar there's a fine display of tropical plants in one of the rooms alongside.

Café del Born Nou

Plaça Comercial 10 (93 268 32 72). Metro Jaume I/14, 39, 51 bus. **Open** 9am-10pm Mon; 9am-3am Tue-Sat. **No credit cards. Map** p327 C3.
A big, airy café opposite the old Born market. With a soothing interior and music, an interesting food selection, papers to read and the odd exhibition from a local artist, this café makes one of the most relax-ing places in the area to enjoy a coffee or two. Tables outdoors here are also a treat.

The Clansman

C/Vigatans 13 (93 319 71 69). Metro Jaume I/17, 19, 40, 45, N8 bus. **Open** *Sept-May* 6pm-2.30am Mon-Thur; 6pm-3am Fri; 3pm-3am Sat; 3pm-2.30am Sun. *June-Aug* 6pm-2.30am Mon-Thur, Sun; 6pm-3am Fri, Sat. **Credit** MC, V. **Map** p327 C3.
An ever-lively Scottish pub located on a narrow street near the Picasso Museum, the Clansman keeps 'em pleased with Gillespie's Stout, satellite TV and occasional live music.

La Estrella de Plata

Pla del Palau 9 (93 319 60 07). Metro Barceloneta/14, 36, 57, 59, 64, 157, N-0, N6 bus. **Open** 1-4pm, 7pm-2am Mon-Sat; closed Sun. **No credit cards. Map** p327 C4.
Once a hangout for workers from the port, this long, thin bar has been tastefully rehauled and is now known for its 'designer' tapas, among the city's very best. Along with an excellent selection of seafood, such as Cantabrian anchovies served on *requesón* (curd cheese) and superb fresh prawns, there are such offerings as an astounding foie gras simmered in port wine, or spicy lamb meatballs with a may-onnaise and pickle sauce. Though unpretentious in style, the place isn't cheap, as the BMWs often double-parked outside may indicate.

Euskal Etxea

Placeta Montcada 1-3 (93 310 21 85). Metro Jaume I/17, 19, 40, 45, N8 bus. **Open** *Restaurant* 1-3.30pm,

La Estrella de Plata's top-notch tapas.

9-11.30pm Tue-Sat. *Bar* 9am-11.30pm Tue-Sat; 12.45-3.30pm Sun. Closed Aug. **Credit** MC, V. **Map** p327 C3.
Catalonia may not be famous for tapas, but the Basque Country certainly is, and this bar has the best Basque tapas in Barcelona, a mouth-watering array of small *pinchos* (from chunks of tuna and pickles to deep-fried crab claws and complicated mixed tapas) that make a grand entrance at midday and at 7pm. Get there early for the best selection, and be prepared to stand. At the back there's a full restaurant with a Basque menu, and the nearby branch, Txakolín, has a larger dining room and bar.
Branch: **Txakolín** C/Marquès de l'Argentera 19, Barceloneta (93 268 17 81).

Palau Dalmases

C/Montcada 20 (93 310 06 73). Metro Jaume I/17, 19, 40, 45, N8 bus. **Open** 8pm-2am Tue-Sat; 6-10pm Sun. **Credit** MC, V. **Map** p327 C3.
Not a bar, they say, but a 'baroque space' on the ground floor of one of the most beautiful courtyard palaces of C/Montcada, the 17th-century Palau Dalmases. Its promoters aim to provide an 'aesthetic experience' to 'satisfy all five senses': walls are adorned with period paintings, the ornate furniture and semi-religious accoutrements are to match; spectacular displays of flowers, fruit and aromatic herbs give it the look of an Italian still life, and suitably baroque music plays in the background. Fresh fruit drinks are provided as well as the usual alcoholic options, and there are occasional music recitals. Deeply eccentric, decadent, a tad pretentious, but soothing to ear, nose and eye, and worth the elevated prices.

La Tinaja

C/Esparteria 9 (93 310 22 50). Metro Barceloneta/14, 17, 39, 40, 45, 51, 100 bus. **Open** 6pm-2am Mon-Sat; closed Sun. **Credit** AmEx, DC, MC, V. **Map** p327 C4.
Once the ground floor – probably the stables – of a 17th-century palace, this arched-ceiling locale serves

The art of connecting

Over the last year, the door to cyberspace has burst open in Barcelona, as web centres have begun appearing everywhere. Most of these places are straightforward, utilitarian connection centres (*see p295*) with little or no charm. A number of other spots however, are more amenable and happily combine Barcelona's famed café culture with the parallel universe of the WWW. A selection of the city's better netcafés are listed below.

Bcnet-Internet Gallery Café

C/Barra de Ferro 3, La Ribera (93 268 15 07/www.bcnetcafe.com). Metro Jaume I/17, 19, 40, 45, N8 bus. **Open** 10am-1am daily. **Rates** from 400ptas per half-hour. **No credit cards**. **Map** p327 C3.
This small but comfortable space near the Picasso Museum has dark hardwood floors, soft lighting, and cool but unobtrusive music. Regular exhibitions along with good wine and coffee make it a far cry from the cold computer dens of old.

El Café del Internet

Gran Via de les Corts Catalanes 656, Eixample (93 412 19 15/cafe@infonegoci. com). Metro Passeig de Gràcia/7, 50, 54, 56, 62, N1, N2, N9 bus. **Open** 10am-10pm Mon-Sat; closed Sun. **Rates** from 250ptas per half hour. **No credit cards**. **Map** p324 D5.
The colourful if gaudy downstairs restaurant shows no signs of the net, but does offer a straightforward, reasonably-priced lunch

menu. All the technology, meanwhile, is located upstairs in a more visually pleasing space and each computer has its own table with plenty of elbow room.

La Idea

Plaça Comercial 2, Born (93 268 87 87/www.ideaborn.com). Metro Jaume I/ 14, 39, 51 bus. **Open** 9am-midnight Mon-Fri; 10.30am-2am Sat; 10.30am-midnight Sun. **Rates** 300ptas per half-hour. **No credit cards**. **Map** p327 C3.
Spacious and with a comfortable sitting-room feel, La Idea has a small, eclectic selection of books for sale and/or loan, more than a dozen international newspapers and plenty of computers located in a quiet, downstairs space. Regular exhibitions – usually on civil rights issues – are held and light snacks and drinks are available. There's even a small pavement terrace.

a wide variety of Spanish wine, cheese and ham. No two tables are the same, and the ornately carved bar was made from panelled artwork found on the original site in the palace's chapel. With its soft candle-light and subtle guitar music – sometimes live – this is the perfect place for a quiet night out for two.

Tèxtil Cafè

C/Montcada 12-14 (93 268 25 98). Metro Jaume I/17, 19, 40, 45, N8 bus. **Open** 10am-midnight Tue-Thur; 10pm-3am Fri, Sat; 6-10pm Sun. **Credit** MC, V **Map** p327 C3.

Another special bar on Calle Montcada, with tables in the tranquil courtyard of the 14th-century Palau dels Marquesos de Llió, now home to the Museu Tèxtil and Museu Barbier-Mueller (*see chapter* **Museums**). Good for lunch or a drink in special surroundings, the 'Textile Café' is popular with tourists, locals, a sizeable gay clientele and many others round about, and a great place to stop while sightseeing.

La Vinya del Senyor

Plaça Santa Maria 5 (93 310 33 79). Metro Jaume I/17, 19, 40, 45, N8 bus. **Open** noon-1.30am Tue-Sat; noon-4pm Sun. **Credit** DC, MC, V. **Map** p327 C4.

A wine taster's café with a front-row view of the glorious façade of Santa Maria del Mar. Wooden chairs and tables distinguish La Vinya del Senyor from nearby competition, as does a superb list of over 300 wines. There's also a listing of selected cavas, wines, sherries, and *moscatells*, changed every 15 days. Fine Iberian ham and other delicacies can accompany your sips.

El Xampanyet

C/Montcada 22 (93 319 70 03). Metro Jaume I/17, 19, 40, 45, N8 bus. **Open** noon-4pm, 6.30-11.30pm Tue-Sat; noon-4pm Sun. Closed Aug. **Credit** MC, V. **Map** p327 C3.

Forget art and museums for a while, this 'little champagne bar' is one of the eternal attractions of C/Montcada. It's lined with coloured tiles, barrels and antique curios, has a few marble tables, and there are three specialities: anchovies, cider and 'champagne' (a pretty plain cava, if truth be told, but very refreshing), served by the glass or bottle. Other good tapas – particularly good tortilla – are available, too. Owner Sr Esteve – born above the shop in 1930, one year after his father opened the bar – and his family are unfailingly welcoming, and it's one of the best places on the entire planet to while away an afternoon, or a day, or a week. Opening times can vary unpredictably.

Port Vell & Barceloneta

Can Paixano

C/Reina Cristina 7 (93 310 08 39). Metro Barceloneta/14, 36, 69, 51, 57, 59, 64, 157 bus. **Open** 9am-10.30pm Mon-Sat; closed Sun. **No credit cards. Map** p327 C4.

An old-time, standing-room only *bodega* which so many travellers claim to have discovered first, this

An expectant bottle at **La Vinya del Senyor**.

ever-popular, grungy place serves very drinkable no-label cava and a huge range of dead cheap toasted *bocadillos*. It is located smack bang in the middle of the *bazares*, the streets of cheap electrical retailers down by the port.

Jai-ca

C/Ginebra13 (93 319 50 02). Metro Barceloneta/17, 39, 45, 57, 59, 67, 157, N8 bus. **Open** 10am-midnight daily. **No credit cards. Map** p325 E7.

High-quality, no-nonsense Basque tapas bar in the heart of the Barceloneta, specialising in seafood.

Tapas Bar Maremàgnum

Moll d´Espanya (93 225 81 80). Metro Drassanes/14, 36, 57, 56, 64, 157, N6 bus. **Open** 11am-1am Mon-Thur, Sun; 11am-2am Fri-Sat. **Credit** AmEx, MC, V. **Map** p324 D7.

Here you'll get the best views of port and city that Maremàgnum can offer, along with good if pricey tapas of every class: in exchange you get to watch the spectacle of a thousand bobbing heads passing over the Rambla de Mar, or boats slipping through its swing bridge.

El Vaso de Oro

C/Balboa 6 (93 319 30 98). Metro Barceloneta/17, 39, 45, 57, 59, 64, 157, N8 bus. **Open** 9am-midnight daily. Closed Sept. **No credit cards. Map** p325 E7.

A very narrow *cervecería* (beer bar), one of few in Barcelona that makes their own (excellent) brew. Don't go expecting a table (there aren't any); there is, though, a long, often crowded bar that will test your dexterity as you try not to elbow your neighbour's *patatas bravas*. Tapas-lovers' heaven.

Vila Olímpica – Port Olímpic

Port Olímpic has bars one after the other (*see p244* **Party ports**), but worth singling out is:

Café & Café

Moll del Mestral 30 (93 221 00 19). Metro Ciutadella-Vila Olímpica/36, 41, 71, 91, 100, N6, N8 bus. **Open** 4pm-3am Mon-Thur, Sun; 4pm-5am Fri, Sat. **Credit** MC, V. **Map** p325 F7.
Relaxed coffee house/cocktail bar in the Port Olímpic with a mind-boggling range of coffees. Particularly good is the 'Royal', sweetened with cane sugar.

Poble Sec

Bar Primavera

C/Nou de la Rambla 192 (93 329 30 62). Metro Paral.lel/20, 36, 57, 64, 157, N6 bus. **Open** 10am-7pm Mon-Sun; *Nov-Apr* until 5pm only. **No credit cards. Map** p323 B6.
At the very end of C/Nou de la Rambla, halfway up Montjuïc, this peaceful outdoor bar/café feels well away from the urban activity bubbling down below. In the summer, grapevines provide shade, there's always a dog lying around, and it's a great place to stop on the way up or down the hill. Rudimentary *bocadillos* are served as well as drinks.

Cervecería Jazz

C/Margarit 43 (no phone). Metro Paral.lel/20, 57, 64, 157, N-0, N16 bus. **Open** 6pm-2am Mon-Sat. **No credit cards. Map** p323 B6.
German and Belgian beers, a long wooden bar and a rustic-meets-baroque interior make this one of the more original bars in the area. The sandwiches are great – from a standard 'club' to *frankfurt a la cerveza* (Frankfurter in beer) – and the music (mixed jazz) is never so loud as to inhibit conversation.

Quimet & Quimet

C/Poeta Cabañas 25 (93 442 31 42). Metro Paral.lel/20, 36, 57, 64, 157, N6 bus. **Open** noon-4pm, 7-10.30pm Tue-Sat; noon-4pm Sun; closed Mon. Closed Aug. **Credit** MC, V. **Map** p323 B6.
A small, top-quality *bodega* with wines stacked behind the bar and a very healthy selection of tapas. Overwhelmingly crowded around mealtimes.

The Eixample

La Bodegueta

Rambla de Catalunya 100 (93 215 48 94). Metro Diagonal/FGC Provença/7, 16, 17, 20, 31, 43, 44, 67, 68, N7 bus. **Open** 8am-2am Mon-Sat; 6.30pm-1am Sun. **No credit cards. Map** p320 D4.
This faded little cellar bar has, for several decades now, borne witness to the Eixample's upward march but has stubbornly refused to change with

it. Incongruously placed amid high-priced bridal and fashion boutiques, La Bodegueta remains one of the most popular tapas bars in town, with professional, personable service. There is also a very good, well-priced lunch menu.

Bracafé

C/Casp 2 (93 302 30 82). Metro Plaça Catalunya/bus all routes to Plaça Catalunya. **Open** 7am-10.30pm daily. **No credit cards. Map** p326 B1.
A bustling, popular café just off the Plaça Catalunya, patronised by Passeig de Gràcia shoppers and known for its Brazilian coffee, which has made it onto the 'best in Barcelona' list.

Café Torino

Passeig de Gràcia 59 (93 487 75 71). Metro Passeig de Gràcia/22, 24, 28, N4, N8 bus. **Open** 8am-11pm Mon-Thur, Sun; 9am-1.30am Fri, Sat. **No credit cards. Map** p320 D4.
The striking, curved wooden doors are not, as one might suspect, Gaudí's original work, as the wonderfully ornate original Café Torino was demolished in a mindless 1960s reconstruction. The new Torino has its charms, however, including excellent panini and gourmet coffee.

Les Gens Que L'Aime Pub

C/Valencia 286 bajos (93 215 68 79). Metro Passeig de Gràcia/22, 24, 28, N4, N6 bus. **Open** 6pm-2.30am Mon-Thur; 7pm-3am Fri, Sat, 7pm-2.30am Sun. **Map** p320 D4.
A comfy, dimly-lit cellar bar with ageing, red velvet sofas and an incurably romantic air. Ideal for an evening schmooze or a potentially life-altering consultation with the mysterious woman tarot card reader ever-present by the bar.

La Gran Bodega

C/Valencia 193 (93 453 10 53). Metro Universitat, Passeig de Gràcia/20, 43, 44, 54, 58, 63, 64, 66, 67, 68, N3, N7, N8 bus. **Open** 11am-1am Tue-Sun; closed Mon. **Credit** MC, V. **Map** p320 C4.
Bustling tapas bar, a first stop for students and office workers before a night out. Adventurous tourists acquaint themselves here with the *porró* (the drinking jug that has you pour wine down your throat from a long glass spout). It takes several goes to master the art – but it's fun trying.

Laie Libreria Café

C/Pau Claris 85 (93 302 73 10). Metro Urquinaona/22, 28, 39, 41, 45, 55, 141, N1, N2, N4, N8 bus. **Open** *Café* 9am-1am Mon-Fri; 10am-1am Sat. *Bookshop* 10.30am-9pm Mon-Sat; closed Sun. **Credit** AmEx, DC, MC, V. **Map** p326 B1.
Barcelona's original bookshop-café, a hugely successful concept. The upstairs café has its own entrance, but is popular with a literary set and anyone looking for a comfortable bar in which to sit and read. It has great cakes and coffees, magazines for browsing and a good lunch menu for 1,975ptas; there are also outside tables on a covered patio, and live jazz some evenings. *See also p171.*

Eat, Drink, Shop

Gràcia

Bodega Manolo

C/Torrent de les Flors 101 (93 284 43 77). Metro Joanic/39, 55, N6 bus. **Open** *Bar* 9am-9pm Tue, Wed; 9am-10pm Thur-Sat; 10.30am-3.30pm Sun. *Dinner served* 9-11.30pm Thur-Sat. Closed Aug. **No credit cards. Map** p321 E3.

Don't be fooled by the peeling paint of this weathered family-run Gràcia *bodega*. Those old barrels lining the walls really are filled with wine – not great, but good and cheap – and the unassuming kitchen at the back produces dishes such as foie gras with port and apple, or fresh pasta salad with avocado and prawns. Hours can be erratic, so it's worth a phone call before going.

El Roble

C/Lluis Antúnez 7 (93 218 73 87). Metro Diagonal/16, 17, 22, 24, 28, N4 bus. **Open** 7am-1am Mon-Sat; closed Sun. Closed Aug. **Credit** MC, V. **Map** p320 D3.

Large, bright, old-style tapas bar, with a great fresh seafood tapas, well-filled Galician *empanadas* and a wide range of tortillas. One of the better places to eat tapas in Barcelona, and often bustling.

Salambó

C/Torrijos 51 (93 218 69 66). Metro Joanic/39 bus. **Open** noon-2.30am daily. **Credit** V. **Map** p321 E3.

An elegant two-storey café, opened in 1992 but which deliberately echoes the large literary cafés of the 1930s, with plenty of tables, billiard tables and an unusual selection of fragrant teas, sandwiches and salads. Extremely popular, especially with the crowds from the Verdi cinemas.

Sol Solet

Plaça del Sol 21 (93 217 44 40). Metro Fontana/22, 24, 28, N4 bus. **Open** 7pm-2am Mon, Tue; 3pm-2am Wed, Thur; noon-3am Fri-Sat; noon-2am Sun. **No credit cards. Map** p320 D3.

One of the few bars in town that offers wholefood tapas, tabouleh, guacamole, feta and tomato salads, along with a selection of tortillas – and therefore a godsend for vegetarians. Marble tables, wood-lined walls and intimate lighting also add to its appeal. Plus the fact that it's cheap.

Zona Alta

Bar Aula 'O'

Passeig de Santa Eulalia 25 (93 204 13 45). FCG Reina Elisenda/60, 66, N8 bus. **Open** 8.30am-6pm Mon-Fri; 11am-4pm Sat, Sun. **No credit cards.**

In the romantic gardens of the former palace of the Marqués de Sentmenat, high up on Tibidabo above Sarrià, this slickly contemporary bar is shaped like a shipping container, with one side opening onto a garden terrace. Popular with students from the nearby Eina design school, it has a fresh, original feel and great views down onto the city. Its *bocadillos* and *platos combinados* are also well priced.

Mas I Mas

C/Marià Cubí 199 (93 209 45 02). FCG Muntaner/14, 58, 64, N8 bus. Open 7.30pm-2.30am Mon-Thur, Sun; 7.30pm-3am Fri, Sat. **No credit cards. Map** p320 C3.

The Mas family have made a splash throughout the '90s with their music/club venues (La Boîte, Jamboree, Moog: *see chapter* **Nightlife**). They began with this tapas bar-café on the Santaló route, an evergreen favourite with the young uptown set. Defying the upmarket image, the tapas are very good, and reasonably priced. In the Eixample, on C/Còrsega near the junction of Passeig de Gràcia and Diagonal, the Mases have a similarly stylish café-restaurant, with fine tapas and a good, reasonably priced lunch menu.

Branch: C/Còrsega 300, Eixample (93 237 57 31).

Mos

Via Augusta 112 (93 237 13 13). FCG Plaça Molina/16, 17, 27, 31, 32 bus. **Open** 7am-10pm Mon-Sat; 7.30am-10pm Sun. **Credit** MC, V. **Map** p320 D3.

Neither café, nor bar, nor restaurant, this elegantly designed space is more like the headquarters of a caterer's where you can sample their scrumptious offerings in situ or take away goodies for a picnic.

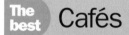

The best Cafés

For breakfast

Start the day with a full-on ham and egg special at **Les Tapes** (*see p161*) or enjoy homemade cakes outdoors at the **Tèxtil Café** (*see p166*). For a stronger sugar fix, try **Sweet Treats** (*see pp160-1*). For morning munchies after an all night dance-a-thon, head for the **Cafeteria Estació de França** (*see p250*).

For laid-back grooves

Check out **Leticia** (*see p157*) to get yourself into a relaxed frame of mind, or sit without worries in the friendly **Café La Cereria** (*see p157*).

For drinking cava on the cheap

Fight your way to the bar for a glass of bubbly at **Can Paixano** or celebrate finding a seat at **El Xampanyet** (for both, *see p166*).

For tapas

Bar Celta (*see p156*) has huge quantities, while **La Estrella de Plata** (*see p164*) serves up exquisite quality. For delicious Basque tapas, don't miss **Euskal Etxea** (*see p164*) or the **Taverna Basca Irati** (*see p161*).

(sidebar) **Eat, Drink, Shop**

Shops & Services

Mammoth malls to quiet corner shops, innovative fashion stores to unique designer goods: shopping in Barcelona will spoil you for choice.

The contrast between old-world and ultra-modern, characteristic of so much in Barcelona, also applies to the city's shopping scene. Big, everything-under-one-roof mixed spaces were slow to arrive, but since the 1980s Barcelona has taken to them with typical verve. Meanwhile, the individual, downright quirky little shops that are one of the glories of Barcelona have been struggling on for years – capacity for survival is one of their common characteristics. The biggest concentration of them is in the old city (*see p172* **Think small**). Larger fashion stores are mainly on or around Passeig de Gràcia, Rambla Catalunya and Plaça Francesc Macià, while many street-fashion outlets are in the old city, especially around C/Portaferrissa and, increasingly, in the Raval (*see p178* **The Riera Baixa**).

OPENING HOURS

Sunday and holiday opening hours have traditionally been closely regulated, though this is due to change by early 2001 when new, liberalised legislation on opening times is scheduled to come into effect: small shops (under 300 square metres/3,200 square feet in size) will now be able to open throughout the day, seven days a week. 'Large spaces' – big stores and malls – are currently allowed to stay open through the day in the week, and on eight Sundays each year, including all four Sundays prior to Christmas (special conditions also apply to **Maremàgnum**, which is open every day). Most smaller shops close for lunch on weekdays, and a diminishing number only open until midday on Saturdays. For standby shops always open outside normal hours, *see p171*, **Open most hours**.

SALES AND TAX REFUNDS

Sales run roughly from the second week in January to the end of February, and during July and August. Value Added Tax (IVA) depends on the classification of the product – seven per cent on food, 16 per cent on most items. In many shops non-EU residents can request a Tax-Free Cheque on purchases of more than 15,000ptas, which can be cashed at customs when leaving Spain to reclaim VAT. Shops in the scheme have a 'Tax-Free Shopping' sticker on their doors.

One-stop

El Corte Inglés

Plaça Catalunya 14, Rambla (93 306 38 00/ www.elcorteingles.es). Metro Plaça Catalunya/bus all routes to Plaça Catalunya. **Open** 10am-10pm Mon-Sat; closed Sun. **Credit** AmEx, DC, MC, V. **Map** p326 B1.
The bulldozer of retailing in Spain, El Corte Inglés provides everything you would expect from a department store, and more: key cutting, shoe repairs, hair and beauty treatments… plus a rooftop café with a fine view. The Portal de l'Angel branch is a leisure megastore specialising in music, books and sporting goods. Should there be anything that you can't find in the main stores (and you have a car) the company also has two giant Hipercor hypermarkets, one in Sagrera, on Avda Meridiana on the north side of the city, and another in Cornellà in the southern suburbs.
Branches: **El Corte Ingles** Avda Diagonal 471-473, Eixample, (93 419 20 20); Avda Diagonal 617-619, Eixample, (93 419 28 28); Portal de l'Angel 19, Barri Gòtic, (93 306 38 00); **Hipercor** Avda Meridiana 350-356, Sant Andreu, (93 346 38 11); C/Salvador Dali 15-19, Cornella de Llobregat, Outer Limits, (93 475 90 00).

Marks & Spencer

Plaça Catalunya 23, Rambla (central number for both branches 93 363 80 90/www.marksandspencer.com). Metro Plaça Catalunya/bus all routes to Plaça Catalunya. **Open** 10am-9.30pm Mon-Sat; closed Sun. **Credit** MC, V. **Map** p326 B1
Despite its more-central-impossible location on the corner of the Plaça and the Rambla, M&S doesn't seem to have won the hearts of the locals, who seemingly find it dull. Still, this six-floor megastore outshines the chain's other Barcelona store at L'Illa mall (*see p170*), and is a good deal fancier than your average M&S in the UK.
Branch: L´Illa, Avda Diagonal 545, Eixample (93 363 80 90).

Malls

Barcelona Glòries

Avda Diagonal 208, Eixample (93 486 04 04). Metro Glòries/7, 56, 60, 92 bus. **Open** *Shops* 10am-10pm Mon-Sat; closed most Sun.
This huge, drive-in mall with over 200 shops is located by the Plaça de les Glòries, near Els Encants. It's built around an open-air *plaça* with bars, restaurants and a multiplex cinema. The northern European

chain Hennes & Mauritz (H&M) has moved in recently and now competes with Zara (*see p181*) for young fashion addicts.

L'Illa

Avda Diagonal 545-557, Eixample (93 444 00 00/ www.lilla.com). Metro Maria Cristina/6, 7, 30, 33, 34, 66, 67, 68, 78 bus. **Open** 10am-9.30pm Mon-Sat. *Supermarkets* 9.30am-9.30pm Mon-Sat; closed most Sun. **Map** p327 B3.

Thanks to its prime location in the fashionable business area on the upper Diagonal, L'Illa attracts a more upmarket clientele than its counterparts on the city's fringes. It has trendier fashion shops (check out the groovy Prestige, 93 444 01 41), and a well-stocked Caprabo supermarket, as well as a Marks & Spencer, the Decathlon sports shop and a Fnac.

Maremàgnum

Moll d'Espanya, Port Vell (93 225 81 00/ www.maremagnum.es). Metro Drassanes/14, 19, 36, 38, 40, 57, 59, 64, 157, N6, N9, N12 bus. **Discounts** BT. **Open** 11am-11pm daily. **Map** p324 D7.

A mall, or what? Maremàgnum is intended as an all-round leisure complex, with restaurants, games, cinemas and nightclubs, and has pretty much succeeded. It's unique because of its Port setting, because it was designed by two of the leading architects of the new Barcelona, Viaplana and Piñón, and because you get to it via a bridge linking it with the Rambla. For those who find normal malls claustrophobic, it's a delight, and the giant mirror-wall above the main entrance creates spectacular visual effects. Its shops, though, are mostly better for fun and souvenir shopping than clothes-or-other-things-you-really-want buying. For other facilities, *see chapters* **Restaurants**, **Cafés & Bars** and **Nightlife**.

El Triangle

C/Pelai 39, Rambla (93 318 01 08/www.triangle.es). Metro Catalunya/bus all routes to Plaça Catalunya. **Open** 10am-10pm Mon-Sat; closed Sun. **Credit** MC, V. **Map** p326 A1.

Dominating one side of Plaça Catalunya, the bunker-like Triangle, which opened in 1999, houses a Fnac, Habitat, and many small, trendy fashion shops including Camper for shoes, but its most spectacular store is the Sephora perfume mega-space. For the nostalgic, the Triangle has a version of the emblematic Cafè Zurich in one corner (*see p155*).

Antiques

The streets around C/de la Palla, in the Barri Gòtic, are crowded with small, idiosyncratic antique shops. Antiques are also found around C/Consell de Cent in the Eixample, and there are some less expensive shops around C/Dos de Maig near Els Encants flea market (*see p192*).

L'Arca de l'Àvia

C/Banys Nous 20, Raval (93 302 15 98). Metro Liceu/14, 38, 59, 91 bus. **Open** 10.30am-2pm, 5-8pm

Ageing gracefully at **L'Arca de l'Àvia**.

Mon-Fri; 10.30am-2pm Sat; closed Sun. **Credit** MC, V. **Map** p327 B3.

The beautifully displayed antique cottons, linens and silks here are not cheap, but the patchwork eiderdowns, dresses and antique beaded bags are lovely to behold. Popular with brides looking for something special.

Bulevard dels Antiquaris

Passeig de Gràcia 55, Eixample (93 215 44 99). Metro Passeig de Gràcia/7, 16, 17, 22, 24, 28 bus. **Open** *Sept-May* 9.30am-1.30pm, 4.30-8.30pm Mon-Sat; *June-Sept* Mon-Fri; closed Sun. **No credit cards**. **Map** p320 D4.

Beside the main Bulevard Rosa fashion mall (*see p180*), this arcade houses 73 shops selling antiques, from fine paintings to religious artefacts and dolls. In Turn of the Century, you'll find miniature musical instruments from the 1930s, and dolls' furniture; Trik-Trak are specialists in old tin toys.

Gothsland Galeria d'Art

C/Consell de Cent 331, Eixample (93 488 19 22). Metro Passeig de Gràcia/7, 16, 17, 22, 24, 28, 63, 67, 68 bus. **Open** 10am-1.30pm, 4.30-8.30pm Mon-Sat; closed Sun. **No credit cards**. **Map** p324 D4-5.

A near-unique specialist in original Catalan *Modernista* art, furniture and decoration. Delights include a spectacular selection of fine furniture (some pieces by Gaspar Homar), polychrome terracotta sculptures by Casanovas, Pau Gargallo or Lambert Escaler, alabaster by Cipriani, *Modernista* vases and mirrors, paintings, and even a marble sculpture by Frederic Marés. It also hosts exhibitions of painting and other work from the era.

La Llar del Col.leccionisme

C/Llibreteria 13, Barri Gòtic (93 268 32 59). Metro Jaume I/17, 19, 40, 45 bus. **Open** 10am-1.30pm, 4.30-8pm Mon-Fri; 10am-1.30pm Sat; closed Sun. **No credit cards**. **Map** p327 B3.

More bric-a-brac than antiques, the 'Home of Collecting' has lots of small items such as old postcards, posters, medals and watches. Owner Jesús Torriente seems to enjoy the company of visitors as much as doing business.

Bookshops

A wide selection of books on Barcelona can be found at the city information centre in the **Palau de la Virreina** on the Rambla, as well as at the city's main tourist office on Plaça Catalunya. The Generalitat's **Palau Robert** on Passeig de Gràcia has a selection of books on both Barcelona and Catalunya. For all, *see p304.*

Documenta

C/Cardenal Casañas 4, Barri Gòtic (93 317 25 27). Metro Liceu/4, 38, 59, 91 bus. **Open** 9.30am-8.30pm Mon-Fri; 10.30am-8.30pm Sat; 11am-2.30pm, 5-8.30pm Sun. **Credit** AmEx, DC, MC, V. **Map** p327 A3.

Just off the Rambla on the way to Plaça del Pi, this well-stocked shop specialises in art and humanities, with a good selection of books in English.

Fnac

El Triangle, Plaça Catalunya 4, Rambla (93 344 18 00/www.fnac.es). Metro Plaça Catalunya/all routes to Plaça Catalunya. **Open** 10am-10pm Mon-Sat; closed Sun. **Credit** AmEx, MC, V. **Map** p326 A1.

This French-owned megastore chain has spread ripples throughout the bookselling world in Spain with its huge stocks of titles (with French and English sections) in modern displays at discount prices. As well as books it has CDs, videos, cameras and games and other software, a very international newsstand and a concert ticket desk (*see p196*).
Branch: L'Illa, Avda Diagonal 549 (93 444 59 00).

Laie Libreria Café

C/Pau Claris 85, Eixample (93 318 17 39/ www.laie.es). Metro Urquinaona/22, 28, 39, 41, 45, 55, 141, N1, N2, N4, N8 bus. **Open** *Bookshop* 10.30am-9pm Mon-Sat. *Café* 9am-1am Mon-Fri; 10am-1am Sat; closed Sun. **Credit** AmEx, DC, MC, V. **Map** p326 B1.

An internationally-oriented, arts-based 'bookshop-café' with extremely helpful staff and a very imaginative selection of stock. The splendid and relaxing café is on the floor above (*see p167*).

Llibreria Francesa

Passeig de Gràcia 91, Eixample (93 215 14 17). Metro Diagonal/7, 16, 17, 22, 24, 28 bus. **Open** 9.30am-2.30pm, 4-8.30pm Mon-Fri; 9.30am-2pm, 5-8.30pm Sat; closed Sat pm June-mid Sept. **Credit** AmEx, MC, V. **Map** p320 D4.

A long-established bookshop with Catalan, Spanish, French and English books, as well as a very good selection of foreign press.

El Lokal

C/de la Cera 1 bis, Raval (93 329 06 43/ www.angea.org/ellokal). Metro Sant Antoni/20, 24, 64, 91 bus. **Open** 5-9pm Mon, Sat; 10am-2pm, 5-9pm Tue-Fri; closed Sun. **No credit cards.** **Map** p324 C6.

More than a bookshop, this anarchists' hideout has over 1,000 titles on anarchism, anti-militarism, history, ecology, feminism and so on. General books are available in the ground-floor 'Amanecer' shop, while in the 'Distri' section you can find comics, fanzines, magazines, CDs, videos, pins and T-shirts. Cool.

Ras

C/Doctor Dou 10, Raval (93 412 71 99/ www.actar.es). Metro Catalunya/bus all routes to Plaça Catalunya. **Open** 11am-2pm, 4-8pm Tue-Sat; closed Sun. Closed 2wks Aug. **Credit** AmEx, DC, MC, V. **Map** p326 A2.

Ras combines a gallery, exhibiting young designers' creations, with a highly stylish bookshop, specialising in recent publications on architecture, photography and design.

Comics

Norma Comics

Passeig de Sant Joan 9, Eixample (93 245 45 26/ www.norma-ed.es). Metro Arc de Triomf/19, 39, 40, 41, 42, 51, 55, 141 bus. **Open** 10.30am-2pm, 5-8.30pm Mon-Sat; closed Sun. **Credit** AmEx, MC, V. **Map** p325 E5.

Open most hours

The only fully 24-hour shops in Barcelona are the convenience stores found at many petrol stations.

Depaso

C/Muntaner 14, Eixample (93 454 58 46). Metro Universitat/bus all routes to Plaça Universitat. **Open** 6am-2.30am Mon-Thur; 6-4am Fri-Sun. **Credit** MC, V. **Map** p324 C5.
General store for non-sleepers or those in dire straits.Takeaway pizzas and bakery plus a bit of everything. Smaller branches are found at many petrol stations.

Drugstore David

C/Tuset 19-21, Gràcia (93 200 47 30). FCG Gràcia/6, 7, 15, 27, 32, 33, 34 bus. **Open** 7.30am-5am Mon-Sat; 9am-10pm Sun. **Credit** MC, V. **Map** p320 C3.
This pioneer in out-of-hours stores has seen better days. It now incorporates a tobacco shop, bookshop, newsstand, and photocopying service

Vip's

Rambla Catalunya 7-9, Eixample (93 317 48 05). Metro Catalunya/bus all routes to Plaça Catalunya. **Open** 8am-3am Mon-Fri; 9am-3am Sat-Sun. **Credit** AmEx, DC, MC, V. **Map** p326 B1.
Vip's houses a restaurant, a supermarket, a fairly good bookshop, a newsstand and a toy and gift section.

Eat, Drink, Shop

Think small

Traditionally, shops in Barcelona kept to a specific trade, and sought to know it well. As a result, the city has an eccentric range of specialists that really is hard to top.

Almacenes del Pilar

C/Boqueria 43, Rambla (93 317 79 84). Metro Liceu/14, 38, 59, 91 bus. **Open** 10am-2pm, 4.30-8pm Mon-Sat; closed Sun. Closed 2wks Aug. **Credit** AmEx, MC, V. **Map** p327 A3. This quaint shop stocks *mantones de Manila* (fringed and embroidered silk shawls), mantillas, and materials used for traditional costumes in all regions of Spain. Pilar also has a good selection of fans.

Aureliano Monge

C/Boters 2, Barri Gòtic (93 317 94 35). Metro Liceu/14, 38, 59, 91 bus. **Open** 9am-1.30pm, 4-8pm Mon-Sat; closed Sun. **Credit** AmEx, DC, MC, V. **Map** p326 B2. Even if old stamps and coins are not your thing, this *Modernista* shop is worth a look through the window. Designed in 1904 by Calonge, a disciple of Gaudí, it has dark mahogany walls and four seats that beat classification.

Casa Morelli

C/Banys Nous 13, Barri Gòtic (no phone). Metro Liceu/14, 18, 38, 59 bus. **Open** 5.30-8pm Mon-Fri; closed Sat, Sun. Closed Aug. **No credit cards. Map** p327 B3. A shop devoted to feathers, wrapped in tissue paper and stored in boxes stacked up high around the room. In the window, there are rather dusty but beautifully made feather masks.

Cereria Subirà

Baixada de Llibreteria 7, Barri Gòtic (93 315 26 06). Metro Jaume I/17, 19, 40, 45 bus. **Open** 9am-1.30pm, 4-7.30pm Mon-Fri; 9am-1.30pm Sat; closed Sun. **Credit** AmEx, MC, V. **Map** p327 B3. Having opened in 1761 as a ladies' fashion store, this has been a candle shop for many decades. It's worth a visit for the original decor alone, with steps swirling down from the gallery, and two black maidens holding up torch-like lights at the foot of the stairs.

Drap

C/del Pi 14, Barri Gòtic (93 318 14 87/ www.ample24.com/drap). Metro Liceu/14, 38, 59, 91 bus. **Open** 9.30am-1.30pm, 4.30-8.30pm Mon-Fri; 10am-1.30pm, 5-8.30pm Sat; closed Sun. **Credit** AmEx, DC, MC, V. **Map** p326 B2. The name means rag (as in dolls), and Drap is the place to find everything related to dolls' houses, much of it handmade. You can buy a chair for 2,000ptas or an empty house (made to your own specifications) for around 50,000ptas.

Flora Albaicín

C/Canuda 3, Barri Gòtic (93 302 10 35). Metro Catalunya/bus all buses to Plaça Catalunya. **Open** 10.30am-1pm, 5-8pm Mon-Sat; closed Sun. **Credit** AmEx, MC, V. **Map** p326 A-B2. This tiny shop piles high flamenco skirts, dresses, *sevillana* dresses, shoes, combs, shawls and everything you need to dance except talent. They also make outfits to measure and stock men's riding boots.

Herboristeria del Rei

C/del Vidre 1, Barri Gòtic (93 318 05 12). Metro Liceu/14, 38, 59, 91 bus. **Open** 10am-2pm, 5-8pm Mon-Sat; closed Sun. **Credit** MC, V. **Map** p327 A3 This unique shop was founded in 1818 by Josep Vilà, as La Lineana, after the great botanist Linnaeus. It was decorated by the theatre designer Francesc Soler i Rovirosa and the interior is ornate: a grand balcony winds around the shop at second-floor level, while the walls below are lined with hundreds of tiny specimen drawers all individually worked in marquetry or decorated with miniature watercolours. In 1858 the shop became official herbalist to Queen Isabel II, and changed its name to Herboristeria del Rei; it went back to La Lineana in the two republican periods. These name changes are still visible in the gold lettering on the door.

El Ingenio

C/Rauric 6, Barri Gòtic (93 317 71 38). Metro Liceu/14, 38, 59, 91 bus. **Open** 10am-1.30pm, 4.15-8pm Mon-Fri; 10am-2pm, 5-8.30pm Sat; closed Sun. **Credit** MC, V. **Map** p327 A3. Ingenio (pictured top right) lives up to its name with an ingenious collection of cardboard, feather and papier mâché masks and party accessories. There are fancy-dress outfits, carnival clothes, decorations, puppets and tricks to choose from. Stick-on Dalí moustaches are 200ptas each, and can be twisted into shape. The shop, naturally, does booming business at Carnival time.

Perfumeria Prat

*La Rambla 68, Rambla (93 317 71 39).
Metro Liceu/14, 38, 59, 91 bus.* **Open** 10am-
2pm, 4-8.30pm, Mon-Sat; closed Sun.
Credit AmEx, DC, MC, V. **Map** p327 A3.
This beautiful perfumery, which until 1997
occupied part of the Liceu building, has been
transported pillar by pillar to a new site across
the Rambla. This undertaking was justified
by its history: it was the first *perfumeria*
established in Spain, by Renaud Germain in
1847. Today it continues to thrive, with a fine
selection of perfumes and cosmetics.

El Rei de la Màgia

*C/Princesa 11, La Ribera (93 319 39 20/
www.arrakis.es/~reimagia). Metro Liceu/14,
38, 59, 91 bus.* **Open** 10am-2pm, 5-8pm
Mon-Fri; 10am-2pm Sat; closed Sun.
Credit AmEx, MC, V. **Map** p327 B-C3.
Founded in 1881, this shop (pictured right) is
many a magician's training ground. Walls are
covered with autographed photos of magicians.
There are no set prices and one doesn't go
there to buy a specific item, but rather to
develop an idea or concept that might require
the use of a special chair, box or mechanism,
made for the purpose. Ritual is perhaps the
key to describing the way things happens here.

San-Do

*C/Cardenal Casañas 5, Barri Gòtic (93 302
64 33). Metro Liceu/14, 38, 59, 91 bus.*
Open 4.30-8.30pm Mon; 10.30am-1.30pm,
4.30-8.30pm Tue-Sat; closed Sun.
Credit AmEx, DC, MC, V. **Map** p327 A3.
Perhaps the smallest shop in Barcelona with
the broadest range in different styles of
jewellery, from the most traditional pieces in
gold to original designs in silver, some by the

owner himself or his son Albert. Small silver
boxes for collectors are also available.

Solingen Paris-Barcelona

*Plaça del Pi 3, Barri Gòtic (93 302 12 41).
Metro Liceu/14, 38, 59, 91 bus.* **Open**
9.45am-1.30pm, 4.15-8pm Mon-Fri; 10am-
2pm, 5-8pm Sat; closed Sun. **Credit** AmEx,
DC, MC, V. **Map** p327A3.
Every cutting instrument under the sun is
available here. Knives and scissors for all
thinkable purposes, and of all shapes and
sizes, are wrapped in green felt and brought
forth for inspection by sombre salesmen.
Seriously weird.

Sombrereria Obach

*C/Call 2, Barri Gòtic (93 318 40 94). Metro
Liceu/14, 38, 59, 91 bus.* **Open** 9.30am-
1.30pm, 4-8pm Mon-Fri; 9.30am-1.45pm,
4.30-8pm Sat; closed Sun, Sat pm Aug.
Credit MC, V. **Map** p327 B3.
Hats of all varieties, from nylon pom-poms
through top-quality felt berets to formal
headgear for men and women.

C

A point of interest

Walking down La Rambla, on the right, quite near the Columbus monument, lies the Cultural Information Point of the Autonomous Government of Catalonia. There you will find addresses, data and information on cultural activities, literary awards, art prizes, museums, the Filmotheque, theatre, exhibitions... and the opportunity to connect to the Internet.

**Rambla de Santa Mònica, 7
08001 Barcelona
publinfo@correu.gencat.es
http://cultura.gencat.es
Fax: 93 316 28 11
Telephone for cultural information:
93 316 27 27**

Generalitat de Catalunya
Departament de Cultura

The largest comic shop in Barcelona: one floor is dedicated to European and US comics, another is dedicated to Japanese Manga, and there are special sections for Star Wars, model kits and the like. Next door, Norma has Tintin Barcelona, which is geared exclusively to Hergé's wonderboy. Norma also has a comics gallery.

English-language bookshops

BCN Books

C/Roger de Lluria 118, Eixample (93 476 33 43). Metro Passeig de Gràcia/7, 16, 17, 22, 24, 28 bus. **Open** 9am-2pm, 4-8pm Mon-Fri; 10am-2pm Sat; closed Sun. **Credit** AmEx, MC, V. **Map** p324 D4.

Everything is here, from computer manuals and teaching materials to the latest bestsellers. There is also a large selection of dictionaries and other reference books.

Come In

C/Provença 203, Eixample (93 453 12 04). Metro Hospital Clínic, FCG Provença/7, 16, 17, 31, 38, 63, 67, 68 bus. **Open** 10am-2pm, 4.30-8pm Mon-Sat; closed Sun. Closed Aug. **Credit** V. **Map** p320 C4.

Barcelona's largest English bookshop has teaching books and general material, from Milton to Shirley Maclaine. Check the notice-board if you're looking for Spanish, Catalan or private English classes.

Second-hand & rare books

Angel Batle

C/Palla 23, Barri Gòtic (93 301 58 84). Metro Liceu/14, 38, 59, 91 bus. **Open** 9am-1.30pm, 4-7.30pm Mon-Fri; 9am-1.30pm Sat; closed Sun. **No credit cards. Map** p326 B2.

Despite the old paperbacks displayed in the window, this is a venerable antiquarian bookshop. Inside, there's also an enormous collection of prints, priced from 2,000ptas.

Travel specialists

Altaïr

C/Balmes 69-71, Eixample (93 454 29 66/ www.altair.es). Metro Passeig de Gràcia/FCG

Altaïr offers you the world.

Provença/7, 16, 17, 63, 67, 68 bus. **Open** 10am-2pm, 4.30-8pm Mon-Sat; closed Sun. **Credit** AmEx, MC, V. **Map** p320 D4.

This travel bookstore also publishes an excellent magazine of the same name. It has a fine stock on Catalonia and Spain, plus anthropology, photography, world music, guidebooks and maps. Many titles are in English.

Llibreria Quera

C/Petritxol 2, Barri Gòtic (93 318 07 43). Metro Liceu/14, 38, 59, 91 bus. **Open** 9.30am-1.30pm, 4.30-8pm Mon-Fri; 10am-1.30pm 5-8pm Sat; closed Sun. **Credit** MC, V. **Map** p326 A2.

If you're planning trips to the Catalan countryside and the Pyrenees, this is the ideal place to find good walking maps for every part of the country. Staff also have information on mountaineering and all kinds of outward-bound adventures.

Women

Pròleg

C/Dagueria 13, Barri Gòtic (93 319 24 25/ www.mallorcaweb.net/proleg). Metro Jaume I/17, 19, 40, 45 bus. **Open** *Sept-July* 5-8pm Mon; 10am-2pm, 5-8pm Tue-Fri; 11am-2pm, 5-8pm Sat; closed Sun. *Aug* 5-8.30pm Mon-Fri; closed Sat, Sun. **Credit** MC, V. **Map** p327 B3.

Barcelona's only feminist bookshop, Pròleg also organises writing workshops, poetry readings and discussions on literature and cinema.

Children

Clothes

Generally, children's clothes are relatively expensive in Spain. Some adult chains, such as **Zara** (*see p181*), also have imaginative and quite reasonably priced children's lines.

Cache Cache

C/Valencia 282, Eixample (93 215 40 07). Metro Passeig de Gràcia/7, 16, 17, 22, 24, 28 bus. **Open** 10am-8pm Mon-Sat; closed Sun. **Credit** V. **Map** p320 D4.

Original everyday, casual clothing in natural fibres – mostly cotton – for children aged 0-12. They have 20 shops throughout Barcelona.

Prénatal

Gran Via de les Cortes Catalanes 611, Eixample, (93 302 05 25/www.prenatal.es). Metro Passeig de Gràcia/7, 16, 17, 22, 24, 28, 50, 54, 56, 67, 68 bus. **Open** 10am-8pm Mon-Sat; closed Sun. **Credit** AmEx, DC, MC, V. **Map** p324 D5.

This French-owned chain has everything: good quality prams and pushchairs, cots, feeding bottles, toys, plus clothes for the pregnant mum and for kids up to eight years old. There are several branches around Barcelona, including a large, central one in Galeries Maldà in the Barri Gòtic.

Eat, Drink, Shop

Young and full of designs

Known since the 1980s for its cutting edge design, Barcelona attracts young designers from all over, many of whom have set up small studios in a scramble for a foothold in the market. The creative design studios mentioned here are all visitable upon request; be prepared to fit into the designer's work schedule, as none of them has permanent showrooms with assistants to attend you.

Coming from Madrid, María Ruíz has applied her art school training to elaborating a unique line of accessories called 'Pequeñopoder'. Her collections feature small, flattened handbags using tweed or denim, like folded dolls' dresses, as well as delicate one-off hairpieces. The Gràcia studio is at C/Progrès 46, baixos, 1ª (667 013 990 mobile).

Josep Abril is Barcelona's sharpest young designer of men's clothing. Abril combines subdued tonalities with a studied asymmetrical tailoring. His small staff works out of an unlikely Eixample studio: C/Consell de Cent 159, down the passageway and up the stairs (93 453 68 92).

Self-taught Nina Pawlowsky is now one of Barcelona's most innovative hat-makers. She has worked with Stephen Jones in London, and regularly does hats for film and theatre. There is a small window display at the entrance to her Barri Gòtic studio at C/Nou de Sant Francesc, 17 (93 412 52 67).

SIG is the brand name of furniture-maker Jonathan Singleton. Manchester-born, he founded Zeta design shop in 1994, but has since gone back to producing his polished stainless steel pieces, as well as doing many interiors. The ramshackle charm of his Poble Nou space is in the industrial compound at Marquès de Santa Isabel, 40 (ask for 16 bis).

As graphic design has gone electronic, the best place to see it is online. The young designers of Vasava Artworks are leading the way, combining their culture sector clientele with purely creative projects, such as the magazine Evolutive and participation in the international website encounter of My City, all accessible via www.vasava.es.

Eat, Drink, Shop

Toys

Joguines Foyé

C/Banys Nous 13, Raval (93 302 03 89). Metro Liceu/14, 38, 59, 91 bus. **Open** 10am-2pm, 4.30-8pm Mon-Fri; 5-8.30pm Sat; closed Sun. **Credit** AmEx, MC, V. **Map** p327 B3.
As well as all the usual novelties, Joguines Foyé also stocks a wonderful collection of tin toys made from original moulds, English and German music boxes, porcelain dolls, furniture for dolls' houses and more oddities. Unusual PVC dolls from eastern Europe are also available.

Joguines Monforte

Plaça Sant Josep Oriol 3, Barri Gòtic (93 318 22 85). Metro Liceu/14, 38, 59, 91 bus. **Open** 9.30am-1.30pm, 4-8pm Mon-Sat; closed Sun. **Credit** AmEx, MC, V. **Map** p327 A3.
A traditional toy shop that's one of the oldest in Barcelona. The owner tells how she once got rid of 'all those old toys in the back room', only to see them later being sold as valuable antiques.

Cleaning & repair

There is also a good range of services, including shoe repair, dry-cleaning, custom tailoring and alterations, available at **El Corte Inglés** (see p169).

5 a Sec

L'Illa, Avda Diagonal 545-557, Eixample (93 444 00 34). Metro Maria Cristina/6, 7, 33, 34, 63, 66, 67, 68, 78 bus. **Open** 9.30am-9.30pm Mon-Sat; closed Sun. **Credit** MC, V. **Map** p327 B3.
This efficient dry cleaners has several branches throughout the city.

Jaimar

C/Numància 91-93, Sants (93 322 78 04). Metro Sants Estació/30, 43, 78 bus. **Open** 9.30am-1.30pm, 5-8pm Mon-Fri; 11am-1.30pm Sat; closed Sun. **No credit cards**. **Map** p327 B3.
This place near the Sants Estació will repair or alter virtually any piece of clothing.

Mr Minit

Centre Barcelona Glòries, Avda Diagonal 208, Eixample (93 486 03 52). Metro Glòries/7, 56, 60, 92 bus. **Open** 10am-10pm Mon-Sat; closed Sun. **Credit** V.
On-the-spot shoe repairs (heels, 700ptas) and key cutting (from 150ptas) at many points around town.

Qualitat Servei

C/Amargós 10, Barri Gòtic (93 318 31 47/93 301 36 87). Metro Urquinaona/17, 19, 40, 45 bus. **Open** 9am-10pm Mon-Sat; closed Sun. **No credit cards**. **Map** p326 B2.
This shop will clean and iron clothes and deliver them to you within 24 hours, though it won't pick them up. Also does minor repairs.

Crafts & gifts

See also *p188* **Art Escudellers** for food.

Cerámica Villegas

C/Comtal 31, Barri Gòtic (93 317 53 30) Metro Urquinaona/17, 19, 40, 45 bus. **Open** 10am-2pm, 4-8.30pm Mon-Sat; closed Sat pm. Closed July, Aug. **Credit** AmEx, DC, MC, V. **Map** p326 B2.
This worldwide distributor of ceramics has everything from one-off art pieces to popular rustic styles, plus antique water jugs and ceramic jewellery.

2 Bis

C/Bisbe 2 bis, Barri Gòtic (93 315 09 54). Metro Jaume I/17, 19, 40, 45 bus. **Open** 10am-8.30pm Mon-Sat; closed Sun. **Credit** AmEx, DC, MC, V. **Map** p327 B3.
Quirky objects for everyone – toys for kids and adults, tin planes, life-sized Tintin characters, and lots of other items in wood, paper and papier mâché.

Germanes García

C/Banys Nous 15, Barri Gòtic (93 318 66 46). Metro Liceu/14, 38, 59, 91 bus. 4.30-7.30pm Mon; 9.30am-1.30pm, 4.30-7.30 Tue-Sat; closed Sun. **Credit** MC, V. **Map** p327 B3.
There's no name on the shopfront, but it's impossible to miss this wickerwork outlet from the baskets in the entrance. Inside, there are fruit baskets at 800ptas, laundry baskets for 3,500ptas, and screens or chests of drawers made in the workshop.

Taller de Marionetas Travi.

Kitsch

Placeta de Montcada 10, Born (93 319 57 68). Metro Jaume I/17, 19, 40, 45 bus. **Open** 11am-3pm, 5-8pm Mon-Sat; noon-3pm Sun. **Credit** AmEx, MC, V. **Map** p327 C3.
Guadalupe Bayona is a lawyer with a passion for papier mâché. Most of her creations are inspired by Klimt, Botero, Dalí or Picasso, but she also recreates living personalities. La Rocío, a life-sized lady in a flamenco dress who stands at the entrance, is the symbol of the shop. Prices start from 3,000ptas and go up to around 100,000ptas.

Taller de Marionetas Travi

C/Amargós 4, Barri Gòtic (93 412 66 92/ www.teleline.terra.es/personal/moya.monllor). Metro Urquinaona/17, 19, 40, 45 bus. **Open** noon-9pm Mon-Sat; closed Sun. **No credit cards.** **Map** p326 B2.
Entering the puppet workshop of Teresa Travieso (whose surname means 'naughty') is like going back into a world of fantasy and childhood. The former pupil of an English puppeteer, Teresa creates pieces for theatre and television. Prices for handmade puppets go from 35,000ptas up to 200,000ptas for the most intricate. Opening hours can be very unpredictable.

Design/household

Aspectos

C/Rec 28, La Ribera (93 319 52 85). Metro Jaume I/14, 39, 51 bus. **Open** 4.30-8pm Mon-Fri; 10.30am-2pm Sat; closed Sun. Closed Aug. **Credit** MC, V. **Map** p327 C3.
A prestigious shop which houses work by international furniture and product designers such as Mendini, Kima, Garouste-Bonetti, Lowenstein or Josep Cerdà. It also showcases work by younger, as yet unknown, designers.

BD Ediciones de Diseño

Casa Thomas, C/Mallorca 291, Eixample (93 458 69 09/www.bdbarcelona.com). Metro Passeig de Gràcia/20, 39, 43, 44, 45, 47 bus. **Open** 10am-2pm, 4-8pm Mon-Fri; 10am-2pm, 4.30-8pm Sat; closed Sun. Closed 3wks Aug. **Credit** AmEx, DC, MC, V. **Map** p320 D4.
One of the institutions of Barcelona's design world, BD stocks a sleekly impressive array of (reproduction) furniture by design gurus such as Macintosh and Gaudí, as well as more contemporary designers – Ricard Bofill, Mariscal, Oscar Tusquets – and objects by the Memphis group, Owo and others. The magnificent *Modernista* house, by Domènech i Montaner, is well worth wandering round, even if you can't afford so much as a chair leg.

Dos i Una

C/Roselló 275, Eixample (93 217 70 32). Metro Diagonal/7, 16, 17, 22, 24, 28 bus. **Open** 10.30am-2pm, 4.30-8.30pm Mon-Sat; closed Sun. **Credit** AmEx, DC, MC, V. **Map** p320 D4.

The Riera Baixa

Tucked away in the Raval, C/Riera Baixa (Metro Liceu or 14, 38, 59, 91 bus, map p324 C6) has become home to a clutch of interesting small fashion, music and unclassifiable shops. This is where you'll find the hottest trends and the best second-hand bargains, together with antiques, records, tattoos and piercings, dance accessories and other urban styles.

In addition, a *mercat alternatiu* or 'alternative street market' of fashion, second-hand clothes and other things is also held in the street, every Saturday from May to September and in December, and on the first Saturday of every other month from October to April.

@WC

C/Riera Baixa 4-6, Raval (93 443 90 11). **Open** 10.30am-2pm, 5-8.30pm Mon-Sat; closed Sun. **Credit** MC, V.
@WC offers a truly continental selection of slick new ultra-trendy clubwear for men and women from Spain, France, the UK, Italy and even further afield.

Cyborg

C/Riera Baixa 4, Raval (93 442 66 79/ www.cyborg.com). **Open** 11am-2pm, 5-9pm Mon-Sat; closed Sun. **Credit** MC, V.
Going up from the C/Hospital end, Cyborg has its own techno-inspired, futuristic collection.

Lailo

C/Riera Baixa 20, Raval (93 441 37 49). **Open** 10.30am-2pm, 5-8.30pm Mon-Sat; closed Sun. **Credit** AmEx, MC.
A delightfully quirky second-hand store with everything from leather coats to bridalwear, including recent designer labels (in perfect condition). Worth a look, are the opera-costumes of the Liceu theatre.

Recicla Recicla

C/Riera Baixa 13, Raval (616 110 118/699 443 800). **Open** 11am-2pm, 5-9pm Mon-Sat; closed Sun. **No credit cards.**
This place has a great selection of second-hand clothing, with around 150 new pieces each week, including vintage party dresses, shoes, jewellery and even furniture.

The first ever design shop in Barcelona (established in 1977), and an early patron of Mariscal, Dos i Una has grown up into a high-class gift shop, selling designer crockery, wacky lamps, postcards, earrings and T-shirts.

Gema Povo

C/Banys Nous 5-7, Raval (93 301 34 76/ www.gemapovo.com). Metro Liceu/14, 39, 59, 91 bus. **Open** 10am-1.30pm, 4.30-8pm Mon-Sat; closed Sun. Closed 2wks Aug. **Credit** AmEx, DC, MC, V. **Map** p327 B3.
A family-run, artisan shop specialising in beautiful wrought-iron lamps and bedsteads, all designed by the owner. She also sells Mallorcan glass vases, and rustic tables. Well worth a browse.

Gotham

C/Cervantes 7, Barri Gòtic (93 412 46 47). Metro Jaume I/17, 40, 45 bus. **Open** 10.30-2pm, 5-8.30pm Mon-Sat; closed Sun. **Credit** AmEx, DC, MC, V. **Map** p327 B3.
On a corner of Plaça Sant Miquel, behind the Ajuntament, this hip, off-the-wall shop has a highly original exterior. A second glance reveals that most of its great range of furniture is from the 1930s and '40s, while accessories – lamps, vases, glassware – hail from the '50s or '60s, and there are also many completely new, up-to-the-minute items. The owners are interior designers, and will undertake restorations.

Ici et Là

Plaça Santa Maria del Mar 2, La Ribera (93 268 11 67/www.icietla.com). Metro Jaume I/17, 19, 40, 45 bus. **Open** 4.30-8.30pm Mon; 10.30am-8.30pm Tue-Sat; closed Sun. **Credit** AmEx, MC, V. **Map** p327 C3-4.
The brainchild of three women – two French and one Spanish – who believe that original furniture and accessories shouldn't be limited to the well-heeled. Wacky ethnic objects and striking contemporary creations are sourced from Barcelona, Europe and the world, and sold at deliberately reasonable prices.

Insòlit

Avda Diagonal 353, Eixample (93 207 49 19). Metro Verdaguer/6, 15, 33, 34 bus. **Open** 10am-1.30pm, 4.30-8pm Mon-Fri; 11am-2pm, 5-8pm Sat; closed Sun. Closed Aug. **Credit** AmEx, DC, MC, V. **Map** p320 D4.
One of few shops to stock entirely original work, since most of the owners' own witty designs are sold only through this outlet. Pick up a star-shaped table in wood and iron for 20,000ptas, or tableware, bizarre lamps and colourful kitsch furniture.

Matarile

Passeig del Born 24, La Ribera (93 315 02 20). Metro Jaume I/14, 39, 51 bus. **Open** 5-9pm Mon, Sat; 10am-2pm, 5-9pm Tue-Fri; closed Sun. **Credit** MC, V. **Map** p327 C3.

Owner Mauricio sells his own lamps and other types of lighting. He uses unusual materials, recycled and otherwise, and has some restored lamps from the 1970s.

Vinçon
Passeig de Gràcia 93, Eixample (93 215 60 50/ www.vincon.com). Metro Diagonal/7, 16, 17, 22, 24, 28 bus. **Open** 10am-2pm, 4.30-8.30pm Mon-Sat; closed Sun. **Credit** AmEx, MC, V. **Map** p320 D4.
Barcelona's most renowned design palace, with everything for the home down to the smallest accessory. You may find the superbly extravagant furniture a tad expensive, but the lighting, kitchen, bathroom and fabric departments offer affordable alternatives. Each December Vinçon hosts Hipermerc'art, an 'art supermarket' where astute buyers can pick up originals by young artists for as little as 9,000ptas. There is a feeling that as it has expanded and become steadily more 'corporate' Vinçon has also become steadily less innovative, but it's still an attractive place to browse, and for art and architecture buffs there's the consolation that the upper floor is the former apartment of Santiago Rusiñol, one of the greatest *Modernista* artists.

Fashion

Designers

Adolfo Domínguez
Passeig de Gràcia 32, Eixample (93 487 41 70/ www.adolfodominguez.es). Metro Passeig de Gràcia /7, 16, 17, 22, 24, 28 bus. **Open** 10am-8.30pm Mon-Sat; closed Sun. **Credit** AmEx, DC, MC, V. **Map** p324 D5.
One of the foremost names in Spanish fashion, Galician Adolfo Domínguez deserves his reputation as a designer of well-made, timeless clothes for men and women, usually in stylishly austere colours. **Branches:** Avda Diagonal 490, Gràcia (93 416 17 16); Avda Pau Casals 5, Pau Casals (93 414 11 77); Passeig de Gràcia 89, Eixample (93 215 13 39).

Armand Basi
Passeig de Gràcia 49, Eixample (93 215 14 21/ www.armandbasi.com). Metro Passeig de Gràcia/7, 16, 17, 22, 24, 28 bus. **Open** 10am-8.30pm Mon-Sat. **Credit** AmEx, DC, MC, V. **Map** p320 D4.
The pleasant flagship shop of this ultra-hip Spanish designer is suitably in the centre of things, and is the only place in town where you can find everything in his men's and women's collections, from soft leather jackets to more timeless suits, classic knitwear, evening dresses and a wide variety of accessories.

David Valls
C/València 235, Eixample (93 487 12 85). Metro Passeig de Gràcia/7, 16, 17, 20, 43, 44, 63, 67, 68 bus. **Open** 10am-2pm, 5-8.30pm Mon-Fri; 10.30am-2pm, 5-8.30pm Sat; closed Sun. Closed 2wks Aug. **Credit** AmEx, DC, MC, V. **Map** p320 D4.

David Valls produces original upmarket knitwear for new bohemians, using the latest technology to create unique textures and fabrics. His shop has an extensive collection of body-hugging jumpers for women and stylish yet classic sweaters for men.

Giménez y Zuazo
C/Elisabets 20, Raval (93 412 33 81). Metro Catalunya/bus all routes to Plaça Catalunya. **Open** 10.30am-2pm, 5-8.30pm Mon-Sat; closed Sun. **Credit** MC, V. **Map** p326 A2.
This duo won a national competition for young Spanish designers back in 1984. Fabric is the essential starting point of their garments: designs mix and play with different textures, using clean cuts and surprising, original details. In spring/summer 2001 unisex pieces will appear as a first step towards a collection for men.

Groc
Rambla Catalunya 100, Eixample (93 215 01 80). Metro Diagonal/FGC Provença/7, 16, 17, 20, 22, 24, 28, 43, 44 bus. **Open** 10am-2pm, 4.30pm-8.30pm Mon-Sat; closed Sun. **Credit** AmEx, DC, MC, V. **Map** p320 D4.
Groc is the place to find men's and women's clothing by one of the most admired of current Catalan designers, Toni Miró. His clothes are designed with a very distinctive flair, in irresistible materials. Shoes by Miró and jewellery by Chelo Sastre also feature in the range.
Branch: C/Muntaner 385, Zona Alta (93 202 30 77, 93 202 00 01).

Jean-Pierre Bua
Avda Diagonal 469, Eixample (93 439 71 00). Bus 6, 7, 15, 33, 34. **Open** 10am-2pm, 4.30-8.30pm Mon-Sat; closed Sun. **Credit** AmEx, DC, MC, V. **Map** p320 C3.
The first, and for many years, the only Barcelona shop to sell avant-garde international designer fashion. Enjoy exclusive selections from Dries van Noten, Sybilla and personal friend Jean-Paul Gaultier: this is also the place to go for if you are looking for stylish and modern bridalwear. Luis and Adolfo make everyone welcome, and it's worth checking for special sales.

Josep Font
Passeig de Gràcia 106, Eixample (93 415 65 50). Metro Diagonal/22, 24, 28, 100, 101 bus. **Open** 10am-8.30pm Mon-Sat; closed Sun. **Credit** AmEx, MC, V. **Map** p320 D4.
The Mediterranean influence in Josep Font's designs is evident as soon as you walk through the door of this attractive shop. Elaborated styles and an imaginative way of dealing with colours and textures create beautiful, extraordinary clothes.

Noténom
C/Pau Claris 159, Eixample (93 487 60 84). Metro Passeig de Gràcia/22, 24, 28, 39, 43, 44, 45 bus. **Open** 4.30-8.30pm Mon; 10.30am-2pm, 4.30-8.30pm Tue-Sat; closed Sun. **Credit** AmEx, DC, MC, V. **Map** p320 D4.

Eat, Drink, Shop

Noténom ('It has no name') is a focal point for all the newest trends and lines, selected from around the world (labels such as Exté, Comme des Garçons, Maurizio Pecoraso and D2). The two-level store sells wear for both sexes and especially men can find daring pieces difficult to find anywhere else in town. There is also a selection of fashion jewellery and accessories.

Designer bargains

Contribuciones

C/Riera de Sant Miquel 30, Gràcia (93 218 71 40). Metro Diagonal/6, 7, 15, 16, 17, 22, 24, 28, 33, 34 bus. **Open** 11am-2pm, 5-9pm Mon-Sat; closed Sun. **Credit** AmEx, DC, MC, V. **Map** p320 D3.

Labels – usually Spanish and Italian ones such as Dolce & Gabanna – vary according to what's available. The great bonus point of this spacious fashion store is that everything is sold at half-price.

Stockland

C/Comtal 22, Barri Gòtic (93 318 03 31). Metro Urquinaona/17, 19, 40, 45 bus. **Open** 10am-8.30pm Mon-Sat; closed Sun. **Credit** AmEx, DC, MC, V. **Map** p326 B2.

Originally known as Preu Bo ('good price') this outlet for designer clothes still lives up to its former name, with up to 65% off end-of-lines by Roberto Verinno, Jordi Cuesta, Purificación Garcia, Joaquin Verdú, María Encarnación and C'est Comme Ça. The staff are very friendly, too.
Branches: C/Balmes 308, Zona Alta (93 414 44 57); C/Craywinckel 5, Zona Alta (93 418 81 74).

Fashion malls

Galeries of individual small shops sprouted apace during the 1980s, some occupying the interiors of whole Eixample blocks, and have stayed among the most popular places for fashion browsing.

Bulevard Rosa

Passeig de Gràcia 55, Eixample (93 309 06 50/www.bulevardrosa.com). Metro Passeig de Gràcia/7, 16, 17, 22, 24, 28 bus. **Open** 10.30am-8.30pm Mon-Sat; closed Sun. **Credit** AmEx, DC, MC, V. **Map** p320 D4.

A major 1980s success story, this arcade began the *galeria* boom and has attracted some of the most interesting designers of clothes, shoes and jewellery. It has about 120 shops, including both luxury and more casual outlets for men and women.

Gralla Hall

C/Portaferrissa 25, Barri Gòtic (93 412 32 72). Metro Liceu/14, 38, 59, 91 bus. **Open** *Mall* 9.30am-8.30pm Mon-Sat; closed Sun. *Shops* 10.30am-8.30pm (some close 2-4.30pm) Mon-Sat; closed Sun. **Map** p326 B2.

In the middle of the Portaferrissa shopping area, the Gralla is one of Barcelona's favourite places for club-wear and street fashion. For (relatively) expensive club fashion, Fantasy and Loft Avignon are two of the best in town; Club is home to two local talents – you won't find the same design twice. Young clubbers get ready for Saturday night in Mayday.

El Mercadillo

C/Portaferrissa 17, Barri Gòtic (93 301 89 13). Metro Liceu/14, 38, 59, 91 bus. **Open** 11am-9pm Mon-Sat; closed Sun. **Credit** MC, V. **Map** p326 B2.

Neon lights and a life-sized fibre-glass camel mean it's hard to miss the entrance to Barcelona's grungier fashion mall. Patience is necessary for discovering the trousers, heavy boots or garish tops you like in the crammed shelves. You can find colourful shirts by Replay and discounts on classics such as Levi 501s. The wonderful bar at the back opens to an old patio.

Unstoppable chains

Mango

Passeig de Gràcia 65, Eixample (93 215 75 30/ www.mango.es; www.mangoshop.com). Metro Passeig de Gràcia/7, 16, 17, 22, 24, 28 bus. **Open** 10.15am-8.30pm Mon-Fri; 10.15am-9pm Sat; closed Sun. **Credit** AmEx, DC, MC, V. **Map** p320 D4.

Since its first opening in Barcelona in 1984, Mango has extended into around 500 branches worldwide, and has become a point of reference for young modern urban women. Well-designed clothes in good-

Clubwear at **Gralla Hall**.

For lifestyles hard to kick, **Bad Habits**.

quality fabrics reflect innovative trends at reasonable prices, with ranges for work, free time and party wear. Several branches around Barcelona.

Zara

C/Pelai 58, Eixample (93 301 09 78). Metro Catalunya/bus all routes to Plaça Catalunya. **Open** 10am-9pm Mon-Sat; closed Sun. **Credit** AmEx, DC, MC, V. **Map** p326 A1.
Lately, fashion-watchers and shoppers alike in other countries have become aware of the qualities of Zara, now a real international empire with 200 shops in 17 countries. The secret of its success is a simple, functional formula of reasonable prices, intelligent copies of top designs and an unbelievable capacity to react to changes in consumer taste, enabling them to draw in a clientele running from the very hip to those just looking for good, wearable clothes. There are several branches dotted around Barcelona.

Street style & second-hand

Most street-fashion shops are around C/Portaferrissa and other streets near the Rambla. Malls like **El Mercadillo** and **Gralla Hall** offer a good choice, and C/Avinyó is worth a look to find work by young local designers. In the last couple of years, also, C/Riera Baixa in the Raval has become the new centre for small, innovative style shops in Barcelona (*see p178*, **The Riera Baixa**). It's also worth checking out **Els Encants** market (*see p192*), for old and new objects, and some vintage clothes stalls.

Bad Habits

C/Valencia 261, Eixample (93 487 22 59). Metro Passeig de Gràcia/20, 22, 24, 28, 43, 44 bus. **Open** 10.30am-2.30pm, 4.30-8.30pm Mon-Sat; closed Sun. **Credit** AmEx, DC, MC, V. **Map** p320 D4.
You might almost miss the low entrance to Bad Habits (which is the name of the label, too), where Mireya Ruiz sells her line created with an intelligent philosophy: individual, tasteful, comfortable – a chic and classy look with a sexy twist. The shop also stocks shoes by Dorotea for Toni Miró.

Four Elements

C/Duc de la Victòria 5, Barri Gòtic (93 412 61 66). Metro Liceu/14, 38, 59, 91 bus. **Open** 10.30am-8.30pm Mon-Sat; closed Sun. **Credit** MC, V. **Map** p326 B2.
A tasteful selection of pieces by the likes of Sabotage, Acupuncture, and E-pure. makes this shop the perfect place to get your club- and urbanwear. Cool Japanese-style outfits and jewellery in the popular Locking Shocking guarantee success in Barcelona's in-scene.

Pisamorena

C/Consolat de Mar 41, La Ribera (93 268 09 04). Metro Jaume I, Barceloneta/14, 17, 19, 36, 40, 45, 57, 59, 64, 157 bus. **Open** 10am-8pm Mon-Sat; Aug 10am-3pm, 4-8pm Mon-Sat; closed Sun. **Credit** AmEx, DC, MC, V **Map** p327 B4.
Feminine, coquettish and discreet fashion for everyday wear, with a slightly retro touch. Only one or two pieces are available of each design. Handbags and other glittering accessories are available.
Branch: La Tienda de los Milagros, C/Rera Palau 7, La Ribera (93 319 67 30).

So_da

C/Avinyó 24, Barri Gòtic (93 412 27 76/93 342 45 29). Metro Liceu/14, 38, 59, 91 bus. **Open** 11am-2.30pm, 4.30pm-9pm Mon-Sat. *Bar* 9pm-2am daily. **Credit**: MC, V **Map** p327 B3.
This very minimalist-designed shop offers a small but choice selection of men's and women's clothes by The Point, Miss Sixty, Levi's Red, etc. The pieces combine classic colours with modern styles (and vice versa), others show interesting material mixes and surprising details. At night in the back there's a groovy bar which attracts a hip and pretty crowd.

Tactic

C/Enric Granados 11, Eixample (93 451 03 87). Metro Plaça Universitat/bus all routes to Plaça Universitat. **Open** 10.45am-2.30pm, 5-8.15pm Tue-Sat; closed Mon, Sun. **Credit** AmEx, MC, V. **Map** p320 C4.
This laid-back shop just behind the central university provides fashion for surfers and skaters, including Quiksilver, Ripcurl, Volcom and many others. Of course they also sell all kinds of boards and accessories, even for children.

Eat, Drink, Shop

LaRoca COMPANY STORES

Come and enjoy outlet shopping in the cool, shaded style of a 19th century Catalan town, eat at the terraced restaurants or simply sit at a café and count your savings.

- Discover your favourite brand names at **discounts of up to 60%** only 30 minutes north of Barcelona
- Men's and women's fashions, accessories, childrenswear and sportswear from end-of-lines and previous seasons
- Terraced restaurants
- Children's play area and supervised crèche
- Free parking

Exit 12 (Cardedeu)
Barcelona   A-7 Motorway   Girona

So_da. *See p181.*

Tribu

*C/Avinyó 12, Barri Gòtic (93 318 65 10). Metro
Jaume I/17, 19, 40, 45 bus.* **Open** 11am-2.30pm,
4.30-8.30pm Mon-Sat; closed Sun. **Credit** AmEx, MC,
V. **Map** p327 B3.

More than just a fashion store, Tribu is one of the
hippest places for modern urban trendies to hang
out and finger radical unisex designs by Diesel, e-
play, Silvia Rielle, and so on. The selection of shoes
has been widened recently and on the first floor there
are monthly changing exhibitions by young, mainly unknown artists.

Join the trendy tribe at **Tribu**.

Fashion accessories

Dress & costume hire

Casa Peris

*C/Junta de Comerç 20, Raval (93 301 27 48). Metro
Liceu/14, 38, 59, 91 bus.* **Open** 9am-2pm, 3.30pm-
6.30pm, Mon-Fri; closed Sat, Sun. **No credit cards.**
Map p327 A3

A old family firm which has supplied the Liceu and
Madrid operas and stocks close to a million theatrical costumes. A walk through the warehouse reveals
a Don Giovanni outfit from the opera and many film
costumes as well as military uniforms. More mun-
danely, men's formal wear can be hired for 8,000ptas.

Jewellery

Forvm Ferlandina

*C/Ferlandina 31, Raval (93 441 80 18/
www.forvmjoies.com). Metro Universitat/24, 41, 55,
64, 91, 141 bus.* **Open** 10.30am-2pm, 5-8.30pm Tue-
Sat; **Map** p324 C5.
Near the MACBA, this space features all styles of
contemporary jewellery. It has exclusively designed
pieces in materials from precious stones to plastic;
there are also exhibits by leading jewellery artists.
For further information, check the frequently
updated webpage.

Hunting for mushrooms & other treasures

Eat, Drink, Shop

Catalonia has as much of a passion for wild mushrooms as any part of the Mediterranean. There's a great deal of culture attached to funghi (*bolets* in Catalan, in Spanish *setas*). Prime season for them is the autumn, when families take to the hills on *bolet* hunts, but there are varieties available at other times of year. Few Catalan *bolets* have English names (or sometimes Spanish ones). Many fruit and vegetable shops sell woodland mushrooms each autumn – especially the highly valued, sweet *rovellons*. Lesser known but equally tasty are *llenegues*, the nutty *girgoles* and *reig bord*. Another funghi to keep an eye out for is the *moixernon*, a sweet, earthy, small wild mushroom found only in Catalonia.

If you don't trust your ability to collect them yourself – many kinds are poisonous, after all – the best bet is to visit *bolet* specialist Llorenç Petras at stalls 869 and 870 in the Boqueria, who stocks nothing but them – up to 30 varieties at any time. While the best season is still autumn, he can provide *bolets* all year round: when a variety is not available locally, he gets them from other parts of Spain, Portugal, Turkey, or even Pakistan or Afghanistan if necessary.

From the baskets displayed at the stall you can choose bitter-tasting Japanese *matsutakes* for about 2,000ptas per kilo, or a mixed kilo of eight to ten varieties of local *bolets* for 1,100ptas. Petras also freezes, dries and tins mushrooms; dried varieties include *ceps* and *moixarnons*, and a mixed assortment, *barretxa*, is available in tins. He will even grind mushrooms to make seasonings for soups and stews. Some tips from the master: break *bolets* up by hand, not with a knife; contact with water should be kept to a minimum, as they get spongy; use olive oil in cooking, and avoid overcooking – if grilling, keep heat low. Crushed garlic, *jamón serrano* and chopped parsley can be added to them, but not much else, so as not to drown their natural flavour.

HAMS, *EMBOTITS* & CHEESES

A more widespread favourite, almost a totem of the Spanish diet, is dry-cured ham, *jamón serrano* (*pernil serrà* in Catalan). The very best comes from southwest Spain, but it's found everywhere, and is one thing that

unites Catalans with the rest of the country. The quality of *jamón* varies a great deal, and you can expect to pay up to 14,000ptas a kilo for the best, entirely traditionally cured ham. The biggest distinction is that between *jamón del país* (or just generic *serrano*), from conventional pigs, and *jamón ibérico* or *pata negra* ('black foot'), from the native Iberian breed of black pig, raised in an entirely free-range manner, and fed on acorns. Traditionally, the best *pata negra* ham comes from Jabugo in Andalusia, which accordingly tends to be the most expensive. For expert advice, stop off at La Pineda (*see p189*).

As well as *jamón,* ham shops offer many other cold meats such as chorizo, *salchichón*, Catalan *botifarra* and spicy Mallorcan *sobrassada*. All cheese shops in Spain have many kinds of classic *manchego* – fans of strong, dry cheeses should try *seco* (or even *seco añejo*); *semi* or *tierno* is milder.

Hipótesis

Rambla Catalunya 105, Eixample (93 215 02 98).
FGC Provença/7, 16, 17, 20, 22, 24, 28, 43, 44 bus.
Open 10am-8.30pm Tue-Fri; 10am-1.30pm, 5-8.30pm
Mon, Sat. **Credit** AmEx, DC, MC, V. **Map** p320 D4.
A wonderful place to see fine original gold and silver jewellery, and striking costume pieces by
Spanish and foreign designers.

Joaquín Berao

C/Rosselló 277, Eixample (93 218 61 87/
www.joaquinberao.com). Metro Diagonal/7, 16, 17,
22, 24, 28 bus. **Open** 10.15am-2pm, 5-8.30pm Mon-
Sat; closed Sun. Closed Sat pm Aug. **Credit** AmEx,
DC, MC, V. **Map** p320 D4.
Though one of the most avant-garde jewellery
designers in Barcelona, Berao at present works
classically with gold, diamonds and silver. Not
cheap, but very beautiful.

Magari

C/Horaci 20, Zona Alta (93 418 88 10). Bus 14, 22,
58, 64, 70, 72, 75. **Open** 5-9pm Mon-Thur; closed
Fri-Sun. **Credit** V.
Less a shop than a jewellery gallery, Magari, in a
distinctly upmarket location near Plaça Bonanova,
has a permanent collection of original and exclusive
pieces and hosts exhibitions of international jewellery. It's recommended to call before a visit or to
arrange an appointment outside opening hours.

Leather & luxury

Calpa

C/Ferran 53/Call 22, Barri Gòtic (93 318 40 30).
Metro Liceu/14, 38, 59, 91 bus. **Open** 9.30am-2pm,
4.30-8pm Mon-Fri; 10am-2pm, 5-8.30pm Sat; closed
Sun. **Credit** AmEx, DC, MC, V. **Map** p327 B3.
Bags for every taste, from 3,000ptas carry-alls to
beautifully finished leather cases for 30,000ptas.
Branch: C/del Pi 5, Barri Gòtic (93 412 58 22).

Casa Antich SCP

C/Consolat del Mar 27-31, La Ribera (93 310 43
91/www.casaantich.com). Metro Jaume I/17, 19, 40,
45 bus. **Open** 9am-8pm Mon-Fri; 9.30am-8.30pm Sat;
closed Sun. **Credit** AmEx, MC, V. **Map** p327 B4.
This part of the Ribera has dealt in luggage for centuries, and family-owned Antich is one of a clutch
of shops that keeps up the tradition, with a vast
range of bags, briefcases, suitcases and enormous
metal trunks at reasonable prices. If they haven't got
what you want, they'll make it for you.

Loewe

Passeig de Gràcia 35, Eixample (93 216 04 00).
Metro Passeig de Gràcia/7, 16, 17, 22, 24, 28 bus.
Open 9.30am-8pm Mon-Sat; closed Sun.
Credit AmEx, DC, MC, V. **Map** p324 D5.
The celebrated leather company Loewe has its main
Barcelona store in the Casa Morera in the Mansana
de la Discòrdia (*see p96*). Inside there are high-priced
bags, suitcases, scarves and other accessories of
superb quality.

Branches: Avda Diagonal 570, Eixample (93 200 09
20); Avda Diagonal 606, Eixample (93 240 51 04).

Lingerie & underwear

Casa Ciudat

Avda Portal de l'Àngel 14, Barri Gòtic (93 317
04 33). Metro Catalunya/bus all routes to Plaça
Catalunya. **Open** 10am-8.30pm Mon-Fri; 10.30am-
9pm Sat; closed Sun. **Credit** AmEx, DC, MC, V.
Map p326 B2.
This charming shop opened in 1892, and sells some
of the prettiest women's underwear you can find.
The sign at the door says 'manufacturers of combs
and articles for the dressing-table'; its collection of
combs is something to behold. Opening times
might vary in August.

Janina

Rambla Catalunya 94, Eixample (93 215 04 21).
Metro Diagonal or FGC Provença/22, 24, 28 bus.
Open 10am-8.30pm Mon-Sat; closed Sun.
Credit AmEx, DC, MC, V. **Map** p320 D4.
A well-established shop that sells its own exclusive
silk and satin underwear, nightwear and robes, as
well as stockings by Risk and La Perla. A large selection of swimsuits and bikinis is also available.

Scarves & textiles

Though there are textile shops and workshops
all over the old city, the largest concentration is
in La Ribera, especially around C/Banys Vells,
which runs parallel to C/Montcada – making
workshop-browsing one more way to explore
the charms of the area. The **Museu Tèxtil** (*see
chapter* **Museums**) has a free leaflet with a
map and workshop addresses (note, though,
that workshops may not keep consistent hours).

Almazul

C/Amargós 15, Barri Gòtic (93 412 20 45/93 430
01 21). Metro Urquinaona/17, 19, 40, 45 bus. **Open**
10am-2pm, 4.30-8.30pm Mon-Fri, 10am-2pm, 5pm-
8.30pm Sat; closed Sun. **Credit** MC, V. **Map** p326 B2.
Violeta and Ana, the friendly owners of this shop
near Portal de l'Àngel, sell anything from scarves to
tablecloths and rugs, all handmade from beautiful
natural fibres and dyes, perfectly worked and
exquisitely elegant.

Botiga Tèxtil

C/Montcada 12, La Ribera (93 310 74 03). Metro
Jaume I/17, 19, 40, 45 bus. **Open** 10am-8.30pm Tue
Sat; 10am-3pm Sun; closed Mon. **Credit** AmEx, DC,
MC, V. **Map** p327 C3.
Located in the Museu Tèxtil, this is one of the best
museum shops in the city, with items related to the
world of fashion and textiles: designer sweaters
(around 16,000ptas), collectors' sewing thimbles
(1,500ptas), miniature period shoes in ceramics
(2,000ptas) and great throws and original textiles by
local designers (at good prices).

Eat, Drink, Shop

Botiga Tèxtil. *See p185.*

Entretelas

Plaça Vicenç Martorell 1, Raval (93 317 76 14/
www.looknbuy.com; www.cidem.com/artesania).
Metro Catalunya/bus all routes to Plaça Catalunya.
Open 10am-2pm, 5-8pm Mon-Sat; closed Sun.
(also closed Sat in summer.) **Credit** MC, V.
Map p326 A1-2.
Entretelas is both small workshop and shop, and
specialises in beautiful and imaginative printed
fabrics for the home, accessories with a markedly
individual stamp, and an irresistible collection of
hand-painted baby clothes.

Otman

C/Banys Vells 21 bis, La Ribera (93 319 29 34).
Metro Jaume I/17, 19, 40, 45 bus. **Open** 11am-
2pm, 5-9pm Mon-Sat; closed Sun. **No credit cards**.
Map p327 C3.
Otman is a Moroccan-run shop with unusual, light
cotton clothing that's just perfect for a hot
Mediterranean summer.

Rafael Teja

C/Santa Maria 18, La Ribera (93 310 27 85).
Metro Jaume I/17, 19, 40, 45 bus. **Open** 10am-
2pm, 4.30-8.30pm daily. **Credit** AmEx, MC, V.
Map p327 C3.
In his shop by Santa Maria del Mar, Rafael Teja
offers beautiful hand-printed silk foulards and other
scarves, from 3,000-15,000ptas.

Tela Marinera

C/Banys Vells 5, La Ribera (93 310 21 34). Metro
Jaume I/17, 19, 40, 45 bus. **Open** 4-8pm Mon-Sat;
closed Sun. **Credit** MC, V. **Map** p327 C3.
Olga López produces very attractively original cush-
ions, tablecloths and other items in hand-printed and
painted cotton.

Shoes

The most traditional Catalan shoe
(*espardenyes/alpargatas*) is a type of espadrille
with ribbons attached. It's now used as
leisurewear, and by performers of the *sardana*
(*see p205*, **A load of *coblas***).

Camper

El Triangle, C/Pelai 13-37, Eixample (93 302 41
24/www.camper.es). Metro Plaça Catalunya/bus
all routes to Plaça Catalunya. **Open** 10am-10pm
Mon-Sat; closed Sun. **Credit** AmEx, DC, MC, V.
Map p326 A1.
Camper is to shoes what Zara is to clothes – with
the same very clever and customer-friendly mix of
style, wearability, quality and price. Camper shoes
are increasingly becoming known as style items
throughout the world, but buying them in Spain
can still save you a significant amount of money.
There are seven branches in Barcelona – this one
is the most central.

Muxart

C/Rosselló 230, Eixample (93 488 10 64). Metro
Diagonal/7, 16, 17, 22, 24, 28 bus. **Open** 10am-
2pm, 4.30-8.30pm Mon-Fri; 10am-2pm, 5-8.30pm Sat;
closed Sun. **Credit** AmEx, MC, V. **Map** p320 D4.
Started in the Balearics in the 1980s and now one of
Spain's most fashionable shoe brands, Muxart combines design and traditional handmade manufac-
turing. Irresistible sandals, bags and accessories,
including a small, tasteful range for men.
Branch: Rambla Catalunya 47, Eixample
(93 467 74 23).

Noel Barcelona

C/Pelai 46, Eixample (93 317 86 38). Metro Plaça
Catalunya/bus all routes to Plaça Catalunya.
Open 10am-9pm Mon-Sat; closed Sun.
Credit MC, V. **Map** p326 A1
All kinds of shoes, from practically unwearable
30cm platform boots in garish colours to the trendi-
est sneakers. Noel Barcelona's footwear is undoubt-
edly not for the shy.

Flowers

Florists and plant shops can be found all
over Barcelona; many of them offering the
Interflora delivery service. As well as the
flower stalls on the Rambla, there are stalls at
the Mercat de la Concepció, on the corner of
C/València and C/Bruc (map p321 E4), which
are open all night.

Food

Chocolate, cakes & bread

Escribá Pastisseries

Gran Via de les Cortes Catalanes 546, Eixample (93 454 75 35). Metro Urgell/9, 14, 20, 38, 50, 56, 59 bus. **Open** 8am-9pm daily. **Credit** MC, V. **Map** p324 C5.

Antoni Escribà, many times champion *pastisser* of Barcelona, is a local celebrity. He is particularly known for his elaborate chocolate reproductions of famous buildings which have won him victories in Barcelona's Easter cake competition. At other times, his most delectable cake is the *rambla*, made from biscuit, truffle and chocolate (250ptas).

The Rambla branch is in the Antigua Casa Figueras, with a beautiful mosaic façade (*see p189*), while down by the Port Olimpic, the family runs a popular restaurant, Xiringuito Escribá (*see p145*), which specialises in seafood and paella, and has tables outdoors.

Branch: La Rambla 83 (93 301 60 27).

Forn de Pa Sant Jordi

C/Libreteria 8, Barri Gòtic (93 310 40 16). Metro Jaume I/17, 19, 40, 45 bus. **Open** 7am-9pm Mon-Sat; 8am-2pm Sun. **No credit cards. Map** p326 B3.

There's nearly always a queue outside the Sant Jordi bread shop – testimony to the delicious cakes on sale inside. The bread is good, and the *xuxos/chuchos* (cream doughnuts) are extremely tasty.

La Mallorquina

C/Vidreria 15, La Ribera (93 319 38 83). Metro Barceloneta/14, 17, 40, 45, 51, 100 bus. **Open** 8am-2pm, 4.30-8.30pm Mon-Sat; closed Sun. Closed Aug. **No credit cards. Map** p327 C4.

The irresistible smell of baking *carquinyolis* (a Catalan biscuit made with almonds) hits you whenever you walk past La Mallorquina. The chocolate croissants and cream cakes are also well worth tucking into.

Pastisseria Maurí

Rambla Catalunya 102, Eixample (93 215 10 20). Metro Diagonal/FGC Provença/7, 16, 17, 22, 24,

Red, white & rosé

The prime Catalan wine area, the Penedès, produces good reds, whites and rosés: the Torres and René Barbier labels are reliable, and Bach whites have a great dry tang. The most famous of Spanish wines, Rioja, can be found everywhere, but quality can be pretty variable; in recent years the Ribera del Duero and Navarra regions have been as highly regarded as Rioja for red wines.

Catalan cava, sparkling wine, is also from the Penedès. *Caves* are labelled, according to quality and sweetness, *brut nature*, *brut*, *seco* and *semi-seco* – the latter may be not *seco* at all but very sweet, and is the cheapest.

El Celler de Gèlida

C/Vallespir 65, Sants (93 339 26 41/ www.mestres-celler.com). Metro Plaça del Centre or Sants Estació/bus all routes to Estació de Sants. **Open** 9am-2pm, 5-8pm Mon-Fri; 9.30am-2.30pm, 5-8.30pm (*July-Sept* closed pm) Sat; closed Sun. Closed Aug. **Credit** MC, V. **Map** p323 A4.

A little way off the beaten track in Sants, this modern cellar has over 3,000 labels and an unbeatable selection of Catalan wines. Knowledgeable staff advise many restaurants on their wine lists.

Lafuente

C/Johann Sebastian Bach 20, Zona Alta (93 339 26 41). FGC Bonanova/14 bus. **Open**

9am-2pm, 4.30-8.30pm Mon-Fri; 9am-2pm Sat; closed Sun. **Credit** MC, V. **Map** p320 C2.

Smart wine store with another huge stock of wines, *caves* and spirits. A good selection of non-Spanish wines.

Vila Viniteca

C/Agullers 7-9, La Ribera (93 310 19 56/ www.vilaviniteca.es). Metro Jaume I/17, 19, 45 bus. **Open** 8.30am-2.30pm Mon-Sat; closed Sun. **Credit** AmEx, DC, MC, V. **Map** p327 B4.

Joaquim Vila took over the shop (pictured) from his grandfather, who opened it in 1932. From outside, it looks like a grocery store, but inside there's a huge range of wine and cava.

Vins i Caves La Catedral

Plaça Ramon Berenguer el Gran 1, Barri Gòtic (93 319 07 27). Metro Jaume I/17, 19, 40, 45 bus. **Open** 4.30-8.30pm Mon; 10.30am-2.15pm, 4.30-8.30pm Tue-Sat; Closed Sun. **Credit** AmEx, DC, MC, V. **Map** p327 B3.

A good supply of wines from all over Spain, including fine *caves* and Catalan wines.

28 bus. **Open** 8am-9pm Mon-Sat; 9am-3pm, 5-9pm Sun; (July-Aug closed Sun pm). **Credit** MC, V. **Map** p320 D4.

Granja Maurí opened in 1885 as a grocery specialising in cakes, and the elaborate painted ceiling is a relic from that time. Enjoy delicate sandwiches or cakes in the tea room, or take away a ready-to-eat meal from what remains of the grocery store. **Branch**: Rambla Catalunya 103, Eixample (93 215 81 46).

Colmados/general food stores

Colmado Quilez

Rambla Catalunya 63, Eixample (93 215 23 56/ www.lafuente.es). Metro Passeig de Gràcia/7, 16, 17, 22, 24, 28 bus. **Open** 9am-2pm, 4.30-8.30pm Mon-Sat (Jan-Sept closed Sat pm); closed Sun. **Credit** MC, V. **Map** p320 D4.

One of the monuments of the Eixample. The walls of this fabulous emporium are lined with cans and bottles from all over the world; there are huge quantities of hams and cheeses, and every type of alcohol: saké, six types of schnapps, a wall of whiskies, and cava from over 55 *bodegas* – one, Cava La Fuente, is sold exclusively in this shop. The excellent own-brand coffee, Cafe Quilez, is imported from Colombia, and ground for you on the spot.

Queviures Murrià

C/Roger de Llúria 85, Eixample (93 215 57 89). Metro Passeig de Gràcia/20, 39, 43, 44, 45, 47 bus. **Open** 10am-2pm, 5-9pm Mon-Sat; closed Sun. **Credit** DC, MC, V. **Map** p320 D4.

This magnificent *Modernista* shop, photographed time and again for its original 1900s tiled decoration by Ramon Casas and still run by the Murrià family, is not only an architectural attraction: it also stocks wonderful food, including a superb range of individually-sourced farmhouse cheeses, and over 300 wines, including their own-label Cava Murrià. *See also p77.*

Food specialities

Art Escudellers

C/Escudellers 23-25, Barri Gòtic (93 412 68 01/www.escudellers-art.com). Metro Drassanes/14, 38, 59, 91 bus. **Open** 11am-11pm Mon-Sun. **Credit** AmEx, DC, MC, V. **Map** p327 A-B3.

A shop that defies all attempts at classification. From street level it looks likes an exceptionally large ceramics shop, but descend to the cellar and you'll find a fantastic selection of wines, olive oil and the best *jamón serrano* and other meats. There's a small bar where you can try out some of these delights, and manager Iván is helpful and knowledgeable.

Cafés Magnífico

C/Argenteria 64, La Ribera (93 319 60 81). Metro Jaume I/17, 19, 40, 45 bus. **Open** 8.30am-1.30pm, 4-8pm Mon-Fri; 9.30am-2pm Sat; closed Sun. Closed 3wks Aug. **Credit** AmEx, MC, V. **Map** p327 C3.

Since 1919 the Sans family has imported, prepared and blended coffees from around the world. Prices vary from 1,400ptas per kilo for a simple blend to 13,000ptas per kilo for the especially smooth Jamaican coffee. They also stock over 300 cases of tea, including blends from Taiwan, Nepal, India, Sri Lanka, China, Japan and Sikkim. They exhibit a great collection of antique tea and coffee cups .

Casa del Bacalao

C/Comtal 8, Barri Gòtic (93 301 65 39). Metro Urquinaona/17, 19, 40, 45 bus. **Open** 9am-2.30pm, 5-8.30pm Mon-Sat; closed Sun. **Credit** AmEx, MC, V. **Map** p326 B2.

The 'house of cod', and the shop sells nothing else – salted and dried, with no chemical additives. Salt-cod features in many Catalán and Spanish dishes, which require different parts of the fish: the cheek (*mejilla*) for *bacalao* with *salsa verde*; broken-up pieces (2500ptas/kilo) for *esqueixada* and small *cocotxes* for Basque *bacalao al pil-pil*. Travellers note – staff can now vacuum-pack your choice piece to take home; don't, though, forget to de-salt it overnight before cooking.

Casa Gispert

C/Sombreres 23, La Ribera (93 319 75 35). Metro Jaume I/17, 19, 40, 45 bus. **Open** 9am-1.30pm, 4-7.30pm Mon-Fri; 10am-2pm, 5-8pm Sat; closed Sun. *Aug* 10am-2pm, 5-8pm Mon-Fri; closed Sat, Sun. **Credit** DC, MC, V. **Map** p327 C3.

Founded in the 1850s, Casa Gispert is a wholesale outlet famous for top-quality nuts, dried fruit and coffee. All are roasted on-site in the magnificent original wood-burning stove. The minimum order is 100g. Delve into enormous baskets of almonds and hazelnuts, still warm from the oven. Monica will help you choose one of their 'packs' with recipes and ingredients for making a *romesco* sauce, *crema catalana*, the *coca de Sant Joan*, and many other local specialities.

Formatgeria Cirera

C/Cera 45, Raval (93 441 07 59). Metro Sant Antoni/20, 24, 64, 91 bus. **Open** 9am-2pm, 5.30-8.30pm Mon-Fri; 9am-2pm Sat; closed Sun. **Credit** MC, V. **Map** p324 C6.

As well as home-made cheesecakes (including some suitable for diabetics) this shop has a great selection of cheeses, pâtés, hams, *caves* and fine *sobresada* from Mallorca.

Mel Viadiu

C/Comtal 20, Barri Gòtic (93 317 04 23/ www.viadiu.com). Metro Catalunya/bus all routes to Plaça Catalunya. **Open** 10am-2pm, 5-8.30 Mon-Sat; closed Sun. **Credit** AmEx, DC, MC, V. **Map** p326 B2.

Founded in 1898 and supplier to Fortnum & Mason, this is the only shop in Barcelona to specialise in honey – 14 types from different parts of Spain. Choose honey with ginseng or royal jelly, try honey throat sweets, or buy some of the good local cava. They also stock *turrón* (a Christmas delicacy) all year round.

La Pineda

C/del Pi 16, Barri Gòtic (93 302 43 93). Metro Liceu/14, 38, 59, 91 bus. **Open** 9am-3pm, 5-10pm Mon-Sat; 11am-3pm, 7-10pm Sun. **Credit** AmEx, DC, MC, V. **Map** p326 B2.

La Pineda has specialised in *jamón serrano* since 1930, together with other fine cold meats, and a wide range of cheeses and wines. The shop – a charming Barri Gòtic survivor – also functions as a local *bodega*, with a few humble tables and stools where you can snack on these delicacies, washed down with a good Rioja.

Tot Formatge 2

Passeig del Born 13, La Ribera (93 319 53 75). Metro Liceu/14, 38, 59, 91 bus. **Open** 7.30am-1.15pm, 4.30-7.30pm Mon-Fri; 9am-1.15pm Sat; closed Sun. **No credit cards. Map** p327 C3.

Probably the most comprehensive cheese specialist in Barcelona, with cheeses from all over Catalonia and Spain, France, Italy and many other parts of Europe. The goats' cheeses from Extremadura are excellent; if you prefer something milder, try the Catalan *mató* (cream cheese).

Health & herbs

See also p172 **Herboristeria del Rei.**

Herbolari Ferran

Plaça Reial 18, Barri Gòtic (93 304 20 05). Metro Liceu/14, 38, 59, 91 bus. **Open** 9.30am-2pm, 4.30-8pm Mon-Sat; closed Sun. **Credit** MC, V. **Map** p327 A3.

Herbolari Ferran has been serving a faithful public since the 1940s. Its large new basement area is a combination of an old-fashioned herb shop, a modern self-service store, a coffee/teashop, a bookshop and an exhibition area, providing a very all-round health store service. The branch nearby has special gift-wrapped products.

Branch: El Regal de l'Herbolari Passatge Bacardi 1, Plaça Reial, Barri Gòtic (93 301 78 39)

Macrobiòtic Zen

C/Muntaner 12, Eixample (93 454 60 23). Metro Universitat/bus all routes to Plaça Universitat. **Open** 9am-2pm, 5-8pm Mon-Fri; closed Sat, Sun. Closed 2wks Aug. **No credit cards. Map** p324 C5.

All kinds of cheeses suitable for macrobiotic, diabetic and vegetarian diets, with a self-service canteen at the back of the shop.

Supermarkets

Caprabo and **Dia** are local chains of small supermarkets with at least one branch in every district; another, **Champion**, has a branch on the Rambla (No.113, Map p326 A2). Large hypermarkets such as **Hipercor** (*see p169*, **El Corte Ingles**) or **Carrefour** (near the north and south exits to Barcelona on the *Rondes*) are designed to be visited by car, but the **Glòries** mall also has a **Carrefour** hypermarket that is accessible by Metro, and has a wide range of Spanish and international foodstuffs.

Eat, Drink, Shop

The delicious exterior of **Escribá Pastisseries**. *See p187.*

Hair & Beauty

Beauty treatments

Instituto Francis

Ronda de Sant Pere 18, La Ribera (93 317 78 08).
Metro Càtalunya/bus all routes to Plaça Catalunya.
Open 9.30am-8pm Mon-Fri; 9.30am-4pm Sat; closed
Sun. **Credit** DC, MC, V. **Map** p326 B1.
Eight floors dedicated to making you look and feel
great; from make-up and make-overs on the first
floor, up through hairdressing, waxing, facials, slim-
ming and massages. Not cheap, but a real treat.

Masajes a 1000

C/Mallorca 233, Eixample (93 215 85 85). Metro
Diagonal/FGC Provença/7, 16, 17, 22, 24, 28
bus. **Open** 7am-1am daily. **Credit** AmEx, V.
Map p320 D4.
Inexpensive, professional massages (from ten minutes for 1000ptas to an hour at 5,500ptas), perfect
for unwinding after (or during) a day of shopping
or sightseeing.

Cosmetics & perfumes

For **Perfumería Prat**, *see p173* **Think
small**.

Regia

Passeig de Gràcia 39, Eixample (93 216 01
21/www.perfum-museum.com). Metro Passeig de
Gràcia/7, 16, 17, 22, 24, 28 bus. **Open** 10am-
8.30pm Mon-Fri; 10.30am-2pm, 5-8.30pm Sat; closed
Sun. **Credit** AmEx, DC, MC, V. **Map** p320 D4.
Regia has been serving a very select Barcelona clientele in its main shop and beauty salon on Passeig de
Gràcia since 1928. It stocks over 60 types of scent,
plus all the best beauty potions. For those interested in nasal nostalgia, it also contains the remarkable
Museu del Perfum, tucked away at the back of the
shop (*see chapter* **Museums***)*.

Talk about your cut with **Antoni Llobet**.

Sephora

El Triangle, C/Pelai 13-39, Rambla (93 306 39
00/www.sepora.com). Metro Catalunya/bus all
routes to Plaça Catalunya. **Open** 10am-10pm
Mon-Sat; closed Sun. **Credit** AmEx, DC, MC, V.
Map p326 A1.
Truly the most sophisticated of perfumeries, this
French mega-shop in the Triangle shopping centre (*see p170*) has taken Barcelona by storm. The
'perfume street', with a striking red, black and
white colour scheme, occupies almost 2,500 square
metres/26,800 square feet of space in what was
once a dingy underground arcade; all of the huge
stock is on display, and you are invited to try out
each and every one, if your sense of smell can
stand it. Shoppers can consult the 'perfume stock
market' wall panel for fluctuating prices of perfumes in capitals around the world, browse
through a perfume and fashion library, or log on
to the free Internet service.

Hairdressers

Antoni Llobet

C/Sant Joaquim 28, Gràcia (93 415 42 10/639 931
555 mobile). Metro Fontana/22, 24, 28 bus. **Open**
11.30am-8pm Mon-Fri; closed Sat, Sun. Closed Aug.
Credit MC, V.
If you don't trust your Spanish , this is the place for
you. Antoni and his team all speak English and are
very competent hairdressers. Located in the fun barrio of Gràcia, their prices are reasonable.

Clear

C/del Pi 11, pral 10, Barri Gòtic (93 317 08 22/
www.clear-bcn.com). Metro Liceu/14, 38, 59, 91 bus.
Open 10am-8pm Mon-Sat; closed Sun. **Credit** MC,
V. **Map** p326 B2.
Welcome to the place where the stylish go for minimalist cuts or the craziest extensions. Even if you're
not after a make-over, the all-white futuristic décor
is worth a visit.

Llongueras

C/Balmes 162, Eixample (93 218 61 50/
www.llongueras.com). Metro Diagonal/FGC
Provença/7, 16, 17, 31, 67, 68 bus. **Open** *Sept-June*
9.30am-6.30pm Mon-Sat; closed Sun. *July, Aug*
9.30am-6.30pm Mon-Fri; 9.30am-2pm Sat; closed Sun.
Credit AmEx, DC, MC, V. **Map** p320 D4.
This is the best known hairdressing chain in Spain,
with over a dozen branches in the city. It's also
expensive, but the Balmes salon's hairdressing
school offers cheaper cuts.

Peluquería Vicente

C/Tallers 11, Raval (no phone). Metro Catalunya/bus
all routes to Plaça Catalunya. **Open** 9am-1pm, 4-8pm
Mon-Fri; 9am-1pm Sat; closed Sun. **No credit
cards. Map** p326 A1.
Gentlemen: for a no-nonsense haircut and one of the
closest shaves in the world, try out this small traditional barber's shop.

Eat, Drink, Shop

Markets: flea, art & antique

Antique Market
Avda de la Catedral 6, Barri Gòtic (93 291 61 00/93 291 61 89). Metro Jaume I/17, 19, 40, 45 bus. **Open** *Jan-Nov* 10am-10pm Thur. **No credit cards.** **Map** p326 B2.

Art Market
Plaça Sant Josep Oriol (93 291 61 00). Metro Liceu/14, 38, 59 bus. **Open** (first weekend each month) 11am-10pm Sat; 10am-3pm Sun. **No credit cards.** **Map** p327 A3.

Various bric-a-brac and antique stalls are spread in front of the cathedral every week. There aren't many bargains to be had, but it's always enjoyable to rummage through the religious artefacts, pipes, watches, lace handkerchiefs and old telephones. Before Christmas, the market transfers to the Portal de l'Àngel.

An art market of variable quality is held in Plaça del Pi and Plaça Sant Josep Oriol on the first weekend of each month throughout the year.

Book & Coin Market
Mercat de Sant Antoni, C/Comte d´Urgell 1, Eixample (93 423 42 87). Metro Sant Antoni/20, 24, 38, 64, 91 bus. **Open** 9am-2pm (approx) Sun. **No credit cards.** **Map** p324 C5.

This Sunday second-hand book and coin market is something of an institution in Barcelona. Struggle through the crowds to rummage through boxes of dusty tomes, old magazines and video games, and whole collections of old coins. If it gets too much, sit at one of the nearby bars to watch the bargain-hunters pass by.

Brocanters del Port Vell
Moll de les Drassanes, Port Vell. Metro Drassanes/14, 36, 38, 57, 59, 64, 100, 157 bus. **Open** 11am -9pm Sat, Sun. **No credit cards.** **Map** p327 A4.

Now in its fourth year, this relatively new bric-a-brac and antique market,is held in a prime position on the seafront between the monument to Columbus and the Maremàgnum bridge. The only antiques market on Sundays, it's popular with locals on the look-out for china, coins, collectors' records, costume jewellery, mantillas and old lace, toys, pocket watches, old fountain pens, or even military gear. Prices are more reasonable than at the Barri Gótic market.

Els Encants (flea market)
C/Dos de Maig, corner Plaça de la Glories, C/Cartagena, Eixample (93 246 30 30). Metro Glories/62, 92 bus. **Open** 8.30am-6pm (auctions 9am-5pm) Mon, Wed, Fri, Sat; closed Sun, Tue, Thur. **No credit cards.** **Map** p325 F5.

Els Encants (also known as the Mercat de Bellcaire) remains the most authentic of flea markets – from its fringes, where old men lay out battered shoes and toys on cloths spread on the ground, to the centre, where a persistent shopper can snaffle up enough bargains to furnish a whole flat: earthenware jugs and country furniture from La Mancha, second-hand clothes, new textiles, and loads of fascinating junk. If possible avoid Saturdays, when it's very crowded, and watch out for short-changing and pickpockets. The market is officially open in the afternoons, but many stalls pack up at midday; for the best stuff and real bargains, get there early in the morning.

Stamp & Coin Market
Plaça Reial 1, Barri Gòtic (93 318 93 12/ www.bcn.es). Metro Liceu/14, 38, 59 bus. **Open** 9am-2.30pm (approx) Sun. **No credit cards.** **Map** p327 A3.

This somewhat incongruous gathering for enthusiasts blends surprisingly well with the goings-on in the Plaça Reial. Having inspected the coins, stamps and rocks, take an aperitif in the sun and watch the experts poring over each other's collections.

Stock up on **La Pineda**'s endless bounty. *See p189.*

Eat, Drink, Shop

Markets of plenty

There are over 40 food markets in Barcelona – every *barri* has its own. La Boqueria is deservedly the most famous, but there are others worth visiting. Sant Antoni, near the Paral.lel, has a clothes market around the edge and food stands in the middle; Mercat de la Llibertat in Gràcia has a village atmosphere. Mercat del Ninot at C/Mallorca–C/Casanova has everything you could think of, and Mercat de la Concepció at València/Bruc is famous for flowers.

Markets open early (from 8am or earlier) and most close up by around 2-3pm. Monday is not a good day to go, as stocks are low. Don't expect stalls to take credit cards, and for a note on queueing, *see p305.*

La Boqueria (Mercat de Sant Josep)

La Rambla 91 (93 318 25 84). Metro Liceu/ bus 14, 38, 59, 91. **Open** 8am-8.30pm Mon-Sat. **Map** p326 A2.

One of the greatest markets in the world, and certainly the most attractive and comprehensive in Barcelona, the Boqueria is always full of tourists, locals and gourmands. Even amid all the bustle, it's possible to appreciate the orderliness of its structure: fruit and vegetables around the edge, meat and chicken kept apart, and fish and seafood

stalls in the centre, arranged in a circle. Enter through the main gates, set back from the Rambla, amid great colourful heaps of red peppers, cucumbers and fruit. Don't buy here, though: the stalls by the entrance are more expensive than those further inside. They do, however, offer delights such as *palmitos* (palm roots), *higos chumbos* (Indian figs) or *caña dulce* (sugar cane sticks). J Colomines (stall 477), to the right of the entrance, specialises in fresh herbs, tropical fruit and African food. It's one of the few places selling fresh coriander, tarragon, ginger and okra throughout the year. At the back of the market, there's a stall that's a monument in itself, Llorenç Petras (stall 869-870) (*see p184* **Hunting for mushrooms**). On the way, admire the glistening meat and fish stalls, kept firmly in order by perfectly made-up ladies in spotless white overalls. Or stop at one of the cheese stalls offering selections of the 81 types of Spanish cheeses with a *denominación de origen*: try pungent *cabrales*, dry *mahón* from Menorca, or the delicious *garrotxa*, a Catalan cheese made from goat's milk, not to mention the many delicious lamb's milk *manchegos*. Specialised stalls selling over 40 varieties of olives are dotted all over the market.

Music

Comprehensive mainstream music stores can also be found in the huge Portal de l'Angel branch of **El Corte Inglés** (*see p169*) and the **Fnac** (*see p171*).

La Casa

Plaça Vicenç Martorell 4, Raval (93 412 33 05). Metro Catalunya/bus all routes to Plaça Catalunya. **Open** 11am-2pm, 5-9pm Mon-Sat; closed Sun. **Credit** MC, V. **Map** p326 A1-2.

Probably the most respected record shop for the dance music scene. Its owners are mines of information on dance music across the board, and the vinyl selection never disappoints.
Branch: C/Portaferrisa 17, Barri Gòtic (93 317 11 80).

New Phono

C/Ample 37, Barri Gòtic (93 315 13 61). Metro Jaume I/14, 17, 19, 36, 40, 45, 57, 59, 64, 157 bus. **Open** 9.30am-2pm, 4.30-8pm Mon-Wed, Fri; 9.30am-8pm Thur; 9.30am-2pm Sat; closed Sun. **Credit** AmEx, DC, MC, V. **Map** p327 B4.

Founded in 1834, this is one of the oldest shops in Spain, which specialises in the manufacture, sale

and repair of musical instruments. Included within the very wide selection of guitars are some fine ones by Ramirez.

Discos Castelló

C/Tallers 3, Raval (93 318 20 41/ www.discoscastello.es). Metro Catalunya/bus all routes to Plaça Catalunya. **Open** 10am-2pm, 4.30-8.30pm Mon-Sat; closed Sun. **Credit** AmEx, DC, MC, V. **Map** p326 A2.

A chain of small shops, each with a different emphasis. This one specialises in classical; the branch in Nou de la Rambla is good for ethnic music and flamenco.
Branches: (all Raval) C/Nou de la Rambla 15 (93 302 42 36); C/Sant Pau 2 (93 302 23 95); C/Tallers 7 (93 302 59 46); C/Tallers 9 (93 412 72 85); C/Tallers 79 (93 301 35 75).

Edison's

C/Riera Baixa 9-10, Raval (93 441 96 74/ www.discos-edisons.com). Metro Liceu/20, 64, 91 bus. **Open** 10am-2pm, 4.30-8.30pm Mon-Sat; closed Sun. **Credit** AmEx, DC, MC, V. **Map** p324 C6.

C/Riera Baixa now has music specialists to cater for all tastes. Edison's buy and sell unlisted vinyl LPs and singles, and CDs of every persuasion.

Etnomusic

C/Bonsuccés 6, Raval (93 301 18 84/ www.etnomusic.com). Metro Catalunya/bus all routes to Plaça Catalunya. **Open** 5-8pm Mon; 11am-2pm, 5-8pm Tue-Sat; closed Sun. **Credit** MC, V. **Map** p326 A2.

This ethnic music shop in the Raval has music from all over the planet, although most foreign visitors seem to be hunting for rare flamenco. Staff know their business and are extremely helpful.

Musical instrument rental

La Lonja del Instrumento

C/Gran de Gràcia 206, Gràcia (93 415 77 77/ www.lonjadelinstrumento.com). Metro Fontana/22, 24, 25, 28 bus. **Open** 10am-2pm, 4-8.30pm Mon-Sat; closed Sun. **Credit** AmEx, MC, V. **Map** p320 D3.

One of very few places in Barcelona for selling, exchanging or repairing musical instruments, particularly second-hand ones. Instruments can also be rented out; hiring an electric guitar for a weekend costs from 2,000ptas plus a deposit (10 per cent of the guitar's value). A saxophone costs around 20,000ptas.

Opticians

Grand Optical

El Triangle, Plaça Catalunya 4, Rambla (93 304 16 40). Metro Catalunya/bus all routes to Plaça Catalunya. **Open** 10am-10pm Mon-Sat; closed Sun. **Credit** AmEx, MC, V. **Map** p326 A1.

English-speaking staff at Grand Optical offer eye-tests and can provide new glasses within two hours, or one hour if you have your prescription. Lens prices begin at about 4,500ptas.
Branch: Centre Barcelona Glòries, Avda Diagonal 208, Eixample (93 486 02 77).

Photocopying

A great many local *papereries* (stationers) have photocopiers, and also fax machines.

Shopping by area

Old City

Barri Gòtic

2 Bis (Crafts, p177); **Angel Batle** (Books, p175); **Almazul** (Textiles, p185); **Antique Market** (Market, p192); **Art Escudellers** (Food, p188); **Art Market** (Market, p192); **Aureliano Monge** (Stamps and coins, p172); **Calpa** (Leather, p185); **Casa Ciutat** (Lingerie, p185); **Casa del Bacalao** (Food, p188); **Casa Morelli** (Feathers, p172); **Cerámica Villegas** (Crafts, p177); **Cereria Subirà** (Candles, p172); **Clear** (Hair, p191); **Copisteria Miracle** (Photocopying, p194); **Decathlon** (Sports, p196); **Drap** (Dolls, p172); **Documenta** (Books, p171); **Flora Albaicín** (Flamenco, p172); **Forn de Pa Sant Jordi** (Food, p187); **Four Elements** (Fashion, p181); **Germanes García** (Crafts, p177); **Gotham** (Design, p178); **Gralla Hall** (Fashion, p180); **Herboristeria del Rei** (Herbalist, p172); **Herbolari Ferran** (Health, p189); **El Ingenio** (Party, p172); **Joguines Monforte** (Toys, p176); **La Llar del Col.leccionisme** (Antiques, p170); **Llibreria Quera** (Travel, p175); **Mel Viadiu** (Food, p188); **El Mercadillo** (Fashion, p180); **New Phono** (Music, p193); **La Pineda** (Food, p189); **Pròleg** (Books, p175); **Qualitat Servei** (Cleaning, p176); **San-Do** (Jewellery, p173); **So_Da** (Fashion, p181); **Solingen Paris-Barcelona** (Knives and scissors, p173); **Sombreria Obach** (Hats, p173); **Stamp and Coin Market** (Market, p192); **Stockland** (Fashion, p180); **Tribu** (Fashion, p183); **Taller de Marionetas Travi** (Crafts, p177); **Vins Caves La Catedral** (Wines, p187).

The Raval

Almacenes del Pilar (Silks and wools, p172); **L'Arca de l'Àvia** (Antiques, p170); **Arpi Foto Video** (Camera, p195); **@WC** (Fashion, p178); **La Boqueria (Mercat de Sant Josep)** (Markets, p193); **La Casa** (Music, p193); **Casa Peris** (Costume hire, p183); **El Corte Inglés** (Department store, p169); **Cyborg** (Fashion, p178); **Discos Castelló** (Music, p193); **Edison's** (Music, p193); **Entretelas** (Fashion, p186); **Etnomusic** (Music, p194); **Fnac** (Books, p171); **Fnac** (Ticket agent, p196); **Formatgeria Cirera** (Food, p188); **Forvm Ferlandina** (Jewellery, p183); **Fotoprix** (Photography, p195); **Gema Povo** (Design, p178); **Giménez y Zuazo** (Fashion, p179); **Grand Optical** (Opticians, p194); **Joguines Foyé** (Toys, p176); **Lailo** (Fashion, p178); **El Lokal** (Books, p171); **Marks and Spencer** (Department store, p169); **Peluquería Vicente** (Hair, p191); **Perfumeria Prat** (Perfume, p173); **Ras** (Books, p171); **Recicia Recicia** (Fashion, p178); **Sephora** (Perfume, p191); **Tel-entrada - Caixa Catalunya** (Ticket agent, p196); **El Triangle** (Mall, p170).

Copisteria Miracle

C/Dr Joaquim Pou 2, Barri Gòtic (93 317 12 26/93 412 18 12). Metro Jaume I/17, 19, 40, 45 bus. **Open** 9am-1.30pm (July-Sept 8am-1.30pm), 4-7.30pm Mon-Fri; closed Sat, Sun. **Credit** MC, V. **Map** p326 B2.

This store is the best in the city for high-quality copying of all kinds, at reasonable prices. Again, be prepared to wait around, as queues are long. The other branches do not close at midday.

Branches: C/Rector Ubach 6, Zona Alta (93 200 85 44/fax 93 209 17 82); Passeig Sant Joan 57, Eixample (93 265 53 54/fax 93 265 30 70).

Photographic

Arpi Foto Video

La Rambla 38-40, Rambla (93 301 74 04/fax 93 317 95 73). Metro Drassanes or Liceu/14, 38, 59, 91 bus. **Open** 9am-2pm, 4-8pm Mon-Sat; closed Sun. **Credit** AmEx, DC, MC, V. **Map** p327 A3.

This giant specialist camera store has a wide range of professional-standard cameras and accessories

and a good basic repair department. Although service has improved, it can still be snail-like at times, but the staff do know what they are doing. Stock ranges from happy-snappers to studio Hasselblads.

Fotoprix

C/Pelai 6, Raval (93 318 20 36/information 902 500 600). Metro Universitat/bus all routes to Plaça Universitat. **Open** 9.30am-2pm, 4.30-8.30pm Mon-Sat; closed Sun. **Credit** V. **Map** p326 A1.

Over 100 branches in the city, offering one-hour film developing, photocopying and fax services.

Sports

La Botiga del Barça

Maremàgnum, Moll d'Espanya, Port Vell (93 225 80 45). Metro Drassanes/14, 19, 36, 38, 40, 57, 59, 64, 157 bus. **Open** 11am-11pm daily. **Credit** AmEx, DC, MC, V. **Map** D7.

If you feel a visit to Barcelona would be incomplete without acquiring some FC Barcelona paraphernalia,

La Ribera & Born

Aspectos (Design, p177); **Botiga Tèxtil** (Gifts, p185); **Cafés Magnifico** (Food, p188); **Casa Antich SCP** (Luggage, p185); **Casa Gispert** (Food, p188); **L'Estanc de Laietana** (Tobacco, p196); **Ici et Là** (Design, p178); **Instituto Francis** (Beauty, p191); **Kitsch** (Crafts, p177); **La Mallorquina** (Food, p187); **Matarile** (Design, p178); **Otman** (Fashion, p186); **Pisamorena** (Fashion, p181); **Rafael Teja** (Fashion, p186); **El Rei de la Màgia** (Magic, p173); **Tela Marinera** (Fashion, p186); **Tot Formatge 2** (Food, p189); **Vila Viniteca** (Wines, p187).

The Eixample

5 a Sec (Cleaning, p176); **Adolfo Domìnguez** (Fashion, p179); **Altaïr** (Books, p175); **Armand Basi** (Fashion, p179); **Barcelona Glòries** (Mall, p169); **Bad Habits** (Fashion, p181); **BCN Books** (Books, p175); **BD Ediciones de Diseño** (Design, p177); **Book and Coin Market** (Market, p192); **Bulevard dels Antiquaris** (Antiques, p170); **Bulevard Rosa** (Fashion, p180); **Cache Cache** (Children, p175); **Camper** (Shoes, p186); **Colmado Quilez** (Food, p188); **Come In** (Books, p175); **David Valls** (Fashion, p179); **Depaso** (24 hour, p171); **Dos i Una** (Design, p177); **Els Encants** (Market, p192); **Escribá Pastisseries** (Food, p187); **Gimeno** (Tobacco, p196); **Gothsland Galeria d'Art** (Antiques,

p170); **Groc** (Fashion, p179); **Halcón Viajes** (Travel services, p196); **Hipótesis** (Jewellery, p185); **L'Illa** (Mall, p170); **Insòlit** (Design, p178); **Janina** (Lingerie, p185); **Jean-Pierre Bua** (Fashion, p179); **Joaquín Berao** (Jewellery, p185); **Josep Font** (Fashion, p179); **Laie Libreria Café** (Books, p171); **Libreria Francesa** (Books, p171); **Llongueras** (Hair, p191); **Loewe** (Leather, p185); **Macrobiòtic Zen** (Food, p189); **Mango** (Fashion, p180); **Masajes a 1000** (Beauty, p191); **Mr Minit** (Cleaning, p176); **Muxart** (Shoes, p186); **Noel Barcelona** (Shoes, p186); **Norma Comics** (Books, p171); **Noténom** (Fashion, p179); **Nouvelles Frontières** (Travel services, p196); **Pastisseria Maurí** (Food, p187); **Prénatal** (Children, p175); **Queviures Murrià** (Food, p188); **Regia** (Perfume, p191); **Tactic** (Fashion, p181); **Vinçon** (Design, p179); **Vip's** (24 hour, p171); **Zara** (Fashion, p181).

Gracia

Antoni Llobet (Hair, p191); **Contribuciones** (Fashion, p180); **Drugstore David** (24 hour, p171); **La Lonja del Instrumento** (Music, p194).

Port Vell

Brocanters del Port Vell (Market, p193); **La Botiga del Barça** (Sports, p195); **Maremàgnum** (Mall, p169).

look no further. The Botiga del Barça has every permutation of Barça merchandise imaginable, from scarves, towels and hats through (of course) shirts to an appalling range of claret-and-blue clocks. Barça being a club that fancies itself, there are also 'classy' items like champagne glasses, or silver spoons. Why go to any other souvenir shop?
Branches: Gran Vía de les Corts Catalanes 418, Eixample (93 423 59 41); Museu del FC Barcelona, Nou Camp (93 496 36 00).

Decathlon

C/Canuda 25, Barri Gòtic (93 342 61 61/ www.decathlon.es). Metro Catalunya/bus all routes to Plaça Catalunya. **Open** 10am-9pm Mon-Fri; 10am-9.30pm Sat; closed Sun. **Credit** MC, V. **Map** p326 B2.
After functioning successfully in L'Illa shopping centre (*see p170*) for the past few years, this international sports goods chain has recently opened up this centrally located, very well stocked sports shop just off La Rambla.
Branch: L'Illa, Avda. Diagonal 549, Eixample (93 444 01 54).

Ticket agents

Tickets for many concerts and events are sold through savings banks. The best places to get advance tickets are often the venues themselves; concert tickets for smaller venues may be sold in record shops (see above); look out for details on posters. The bullring has its own ticket office (*see p98*) and football tickets can only be bought from the clubs (*see chapter* **Sport & Fitness**).

Fnac

El Triangle, Plaça Catalunya 4, Rambla (93 344 18 00). Metro Catalunya/bus all routes to Plaça Catalunya. **Open** 10am-10pm Mon-Sat; closed Sun. **Credit** AmEx, DC, MC, V. **Map** p326 A1.
The Fnac has an efficient ticket desk to compete with the *caixes*. Mainly good for rock/pop concerts.

Servi-Caixa – la Caixa

902 33 22 11/www.serv" serviticket.com. **Credit** MC, V.
Next to the cash machines in branches of the biggest of them all, the Caixa de Pensions, better known just as la Caixa, you find a machine called a Servi-Caixa, through which you can with a Caixa account or a credit card obtain T2 and T50/30 travel cards, local information and tickets to a great many attractions and events, including Port Aventura, the Teatre Nacional and the Liceu, 24 hours a day. You can also order tickets by phone (many of the staff speak reasonable English) or by going through their website.

Tel-entrada – Caixa Catalunya

Phoneline 902 10 12 12/http://cec.caixacat.es. Central desk Plaça Catalunya, La Rambla (no phone). Metro Catalunya/bus all routes to Plaça Catalunya. **Open** 9am-9pm Mon-Sat; closed Sun. **Credit** MC, V. **Map** p326 B1.

Tel-entrada sells tickets for many theatres over the counter at all its branches. You can also reserve tickets over the phone with a credit card (many of the staff speak reasonable English); you will be given a reference number, and then must collect the tickets at the venue itself. You can phone from outside Spain (on 34 93 479 99 20), or buy tickets on the Internet. Also, you can get tickets for half-price by buying them (cash only) within three hours of a performance at the Tel-entrada desk at Plaça Catalunya.

Tobacco & cigars

L'Estanc de Laietana

Via Laietana 4, La Ribera (93 310 10 34/www.geocities.com/estanc). Metro Jaume I/17, 19, 40, 45 bus. **Open** 9am-2pm, 4-8pm Mon-Fri; 10am-2pm Sat; closed Sun. **Credit** (for gifts, not cigarettes) MC, V. **Map** p327 B4.
The busiest and most famous of the tobacco shops in Barcelona, run with zest and enthusiasm by Sr Porta. Over 100 brands of cigarettes and 100 types of rolling tobacco are on sale; he also has a humidor at sea level in his underground cellar to store his exceptional range of fine cigars.

Gimeno

Passeig de Gràcia 101, Eixample (93 237 20 78/www.gimeno101.com). Metro Diagonal/7, 16, 17, 22, 24, 28 bus. **Open** 10am-2pm, 4-8.30pm Mon-Sat; closed Sun. **Credit** AmEx, DC, MC, V. **Map** p320 D4.
Gimeno has anything and everything to do with smoking, with hundreds of pipes and lighters. Plus, an interesting collection of ornate walking sticks.

Travel services

Travel agents have become more competitive here, and it pays to shop around to find good deals.

Halcón Viajes

C/Aribau 34, Eixample(93 454 59 95/902 30 06 00/www.alcon-viajes.es). Metro Universitat/bus all routes to Plaça Universitat. **Open** 9.30am-1.30pm, 4.30-8pm Mon-Fri; 10am-1.30pm Sat; closed Sun. **Credit** AmEx, DC, MC, V. **Map** p324 C5.
This chain travel agency is part of a group that also owns the airline Air Europa, and so often has exclusive bargain deals on its Spanish domestic and European flights. Also a hotel booking service, and good deals on car rental.

Nouvelles Frontières

C/Balmes 8, Eixample (93 304 32 33/reservations 902 21 21 20/www.nouvelles-frontieres.es). Metro Universitat, Plaça Catalunya/bus all routes to Plaça Catalunya. **Open** 9.30am-8pm Mon-Fri; 10am-6pm Sat; closed Sun. **Credit** AmEx, DC, MC, V. **Map** p324 D5.
A no-nonsense agency with very competitive prices, sometimes offering savings of over 10,000ptas on European flights compared to larger agencies.

Eat, Drink, Shop

Arts & Entertainment

By Season

Dates for your diary from the Catalan calendar.

Something is always happening in Barcelona. The official public holidays are evenly spread throughout the year, and in between them there is always a music, art, theatre or cinema festival of some kind going on. With its Gothic squares and narrow streets, the colourful hubbub of the Rambla, and the calming vistas of the harbourfront and the beach, Barcelona lends itself to outdoor, communal life.

Each area of the city has its own local celebration, the Festa Major. The main one in Barcelona is the **Mercè** in September, though there are smaller, but very popular, versions in Gràcia, Sants, Barceloneta and most local districts. This is the best place to witness Catalan folk traditions, including human castles, giants, fatheads and the pyromaniac pandemonium of the *correfoc*, as well as concerts and street parties.

And in addition there is a lively calendar of other activities, including events like the **Fiesta de la Diversidad** that celebrates the city's cultural diversity, the summer **Grec** festival of theatre, music and dance, myriad trade fairs encompassing widgets to wedding dresses, and mass participation sports events, including the **Day of the Bicycle**.

INFORMATION

The best places for finding out what's going on are tourist offices or the city's cultural information office in the Palau de la Virreina, (*see pp304-5*). Another good source is the city's information phone line on **010** as well as their website at **www.bcn.es** – go to the cultural agenda section. The daily press also carry details, especially in their Friday or Saturday supplements. In the listings below events that include public holidays are marked *.

Spring

Festes de Sant Medir de Gràcia

Gràcia to Sant Cugat and back, usually via Plaça Lesseps, Avda República Argentina & Carretera de l'Arrabassada. Metro Fontana/bus 22, 24, 28. **Information** tourist offices & 010. **Date** 3 Mar. **Map** p320 D2-3.

Without a horse or a lot of stamina, it's difficult to follow the Sant Medir procession as it leaves Plaça Rius i Taulet in Gràcia on horseback and heads up along the winding Arrabassada road to the Hermitage of Sant Medir in the Collserola hills above Barcelona.

In a tradition that has been celebrated since 1830, the procession is joined by 'pilgrims' who come on foot or horseback from nearby Sant Cugat to celebrate mass, dance *sardanas* and enjoy a traditional Catalan lunch. As the riders leave Barcelona, they shower the cheering crowds with sweets, as do others on carts and trucks that drive around different parts of the city all morning, particularly in Gràcia, Sarrià and Sants, trailing scrabbling children (and adults) in their wake.

Setmana Santa* (Holy Week)

Information *tourist offices, Centre d'Informació de la Virreina & 010.* **Dates** Easter (8-15 Apr 2001).

In general, Easter celebrations in Barcelona are not as extravagant as those in the south of the country. Holy Week starts on Palm Sunday with the blessing of the palms – these are often full-sized bleached palm leaves woven and plaited into extravagant shapes and designs. They are traditionally given to a child by his or her godmother, and kept until the following year. On Good Friday, there is a series of small processions and blessings which takes place in front of the cathedral, starting with the Via Crucis in the morning, the blessing of The Christ of Lepanto in the afternoon, and a procession that sets out from the church of Sant Agustí in C/Hospital at around 5pm and arrives at the cathedral a couple of hours later.

Sant Jordi: the book of love.

Barcelona day by day

Many of the things worth seeing and doing in Barcelona take place once or twice a week on specific days. The following are some examples. For more information on markets, *see chapter* **Shopping**.

Monday: Cheap night at most cinemas. Museums and galleries closed.

Tuesday: Cheap night at most theatres.

Wednesday: Reduced price entrance for most museums. Cheap night for some cinemas (when not Monday).

Thursday: Antique market in front of the cathedral. Savings banks open in the afternoon. Paella is on the *menú del dia* of many restaurants.

Friday: Market selling handmade chocolates, cheeses, honey and other produce, Plaça del Pi (alternate weeks – continues on Saturday). Folk dancing, Plaça del Rei, 9-11pm.

Saturday: Art market, Plaça Sant Josep Oriol. Antique and flea market, Plaça George Orwell. Handicrafts market, Rambla Santa Monica. *Sardanas*, Plaça de la Catedral 6.30-8.30pm.

Sunday morning: Art market, Plaça Sant Josep Oriol. Coin and stamp market, Plaça Reial. Second-hand book market (including computer games, role playing cards, postcards, etc), Mercat Sant Antoni. Badges and pins market, Arc de Triomf. *Sardanas*, Avinguda de la Catedral, noon-2pm.

Sunday afternoon: Most museums close early (around 2-3pm). Theatre performances start earlier (usually 5 or 7pm). *Sardanas*, Plaça Sant Jaume, 6-8pm.

Sant Jordi

La Rambla, and all over Barcelona. **Date** 23 Apr.

As the patron saint of Catalunya, Saint Jordi (England's Saint George) can be seen all over the city slaying his dragon. This is the day when you demonstrate your feelings to your beloved – men traditionally give their beloved a red rose. In return women are supposed to give men a book, as this has also been National Book Day since 1923, when a local bookseller drew attention to the fact that both Cervantes and Shakespeare had died on this day in 1616. Now that it is generally accepted that women can read as well as men, and that men like flowers, it is perfectly fine to give either gift to either sex, generally in person, with none of the shifty anonymity that surrounds Saint Valentine's day. Bookshops have stands out on the streets and offer healthy discounts, writers are wheeled out for marathon book signing sessions, and rose sellers, from entrepreneurial students to hardened pros, sell roses at every street corner across the city; though the Rambla de Catalunya, Passeig de Gràcia and La Rambla are the main focus of activity, and get very crowded as the day goes on. This is also, traditionally, the day of the year when the public go to visit the **Palau de la Generalitat** to see the palace's own dazzling displays of red roses (queues are huge, *see p76*).

Feria de Abril

Diagonal-Mar, Sant Adrià del Besòs. Metro Besòs-Mar, then special buses. **Information** Federación de Entidades Culturales Andaluces en Cataluña (93 488 02 95). **Dates** 28 Apr-6 May.

For ten days each spring this satellite of the world-famous April Feria in Seville brings a breath of fiery Andalusia to cool Catalonia, with song, dance, food, wine and a real taste of southern culture – a great chance to catch good flamenco and *sevillanas*. It began as a migrant get-together in the '70s, and it now draws some two million people. It looks set to be held for the time being in the newly-developed Diagonal-Mar are near the Besòs river; there are special buses for those who don't have a traditional horse and flower-cart.

Festival de Música Antiga

Information Centre Cultural de la Fundació la Caixa, Passeig de Sant Joan 108 (93 476 86 00). Metro Verdaguer/6, 15, 33, 34, 55 bus. **Dates** Apr-May. **Tickets** 500-1,500ptas; some concerts free.

The festival of early music in May is the highpoint in Fundació La Caixa's admirable series of cultural events. Ensembles are brought from all over Europe to perform in several of the most beautiful spaces of the old town, indoors and out. Recent performers have included Thomas Zehetmair, Christophe Coin, Rinaldo Alessandrini, Andreas Staier and Musica Antiqua Köln. At the same time, the fringe offers young performers the chance to practise and perform alongside more established musicians.

Dia del Treball* (May Day)

Date 1 May.

The larger trades unions organise a march from Passeig de Gràcia to Plaça Sant Jaume, which receives a modest following, though for most workers the day is a good chance to celebrate the imminent arrival of summer.

Saló International del Còmic

Estació de França (93 301 23 69). Metro Barceloneta/14, 39, 40, 51 bus. **Information** Ficòmic, C/Palau 4 entrl 1ª (93 301 23 69/ www.ficomic.com). **Dates** 3-6 May. **Map** p327 C4.

Barcelona's comics fair, which is considered one of the best in the world, draws crowds from across Europe, America and Japan.

Arts & Entertainment

Medieval mayhem

There is something satisfyingly historical about Catalan traditions, most of which are at least four centuries old, maintaining links with the past as solid as the stones of the old city walls. All three of the events below can be seen in the Mercè festival.

Castellers

Catalans are a very civic people, with a strong sense of community, and this is reflected in several of their traditions. A good example are the *castells*, or human towers (*pictured far right*), a group of people all working together towards a common goal. A thick knot of people (the *pinya* or pine cone) clings together to form the base of the tower, with sometimes a second support layer (*folre*) standing on their shoulders, and occasionally a third (*manilles*) on theirs. The tower is then erected stage by stage, with anything up to five people per level (although nine is occasionally attempted), until the penultimate level, when a single, small kid (the *aixecador*) squats across the shoulders of the level below to provide a solid base for an even smaller kid (the *anxaneta*) whose job it is to get to the top and raise one hand – and then climb down again. Collapses are frequent, though, which is one reason why the base is so large. *Castells* are enjoying a resurgence of interest at the moment, and towers are being completed that have not been seen for a century, mostly different combinations of nine levels (a *tres de nou amb folre*, for example, is a nine-floor tower with three people per storey, and a support ring). Local and national press has details of forthcoming '*trobadas*' (meetings), as does 010.

Correfoc

Medieval overtones of a darker, more pagan kind abound with the *correfoc* (literally 'fire-running'). A parade of dragons (*dracs*) carves its way through crowded streets, spitting fire, while attendant devils (*dimonis*) dance around (*pictured top right*), chasing onlookers and showering them with sparks from powerful fireworks spinning at the end of trident-like poles. Groups of marching drummers make sure adrenaline levels and pulse rates do not fall. Well-protected youths from the crowd stand or even kneel in the dragon's path, shouting "No pasaran" ('You will not pass'), getting covered with sparks in the process. This is organised pandemonium at its most exciting, and certainly not for the agoraphobic. It's safe, but not that safe, and you are advised to wear some form of head covering, a scarf over your mouth and old, cotton clothes. If it all sounds too dangerous, the dragons usually do a dry run the night before.

Gegants and Capsgrossos

The gegants, or giants – lofty figures of wood and papier-mâché, each supported by a person peeping out through a mesh in the

Arts & Entertainment

Sant Ponç

C/Hospital. Metro Liceu/14, 38, 59, 91 bus. **Date** 11 May. **Map** p326-7 A2-3.
This charming market fills C/ Hospital for one day a year, commemorating the patron saint of bee-keepers and herbalists. Stalls sell all kind of natural products from the surrounding countryside, including honey straight from the barrel, bunches of fresh and dried herbs, candied fruit, sweet wine, perfumes and candles.

Festa de la Diversitat

Moll de la Fusta. Metro Drassanes/14, 36, 38, 57, 59, 64, 157, N4, N6, N9 bus. **Information** SOS Racisme, Passatge de la Pau 10 bis (93 301 05 97/fax 93 301 01 47/www.sosracisme.org). **Dates** 11-13 May. **Map** p327 A-B4.
SOS Racisme monitors and works against racism of all kinds both within the city and throughout Spain. Their main public event is a three-day jamboree on the harbour-front that celebrates the city's cultural and ethnic diversity. The event draws over 50,000 visitors, taking over the harbour-front for a packed programme of concerts, conferences, children's activities and workshops, as well as stalls run by the various immigrant organisations and associations, providing information, food, jewellery and clothes.

Festa de la Bicicleta

C/Aragó to Plaça de les Glories. **Information** Servei d'Informació Esportiva (93 402 30 00). **Date** one Sun in May.
The bicycle is slowly gaining acceptance in Barcelona as an alternative means of transport, though it has some way to go before it challenges the dominance of either cars or motorbikes. First established in 1936, The Festa de la Bicicleta was revived by 'Olympics Mayor' Joan Maragall, a keen cyclist who could regularly be seen pedalling from one mayoral meeting to another. It's a relaxed, family affair, drawing around 40,000 participants for a 16-km (10-mile) ride round the city centre, starting in C/ Aragon and ending at the Plaça de les Glories. Special bike hire is available.

Arts & Entertainment

skirts – were originally part of the Corpus Christi festival, instituted by the Church in 1264 partly in order to incorporate pre-Christian figures into conventional ritual. There are many theories on their origin – one that they are based on David and Goliath – but they represent many folkloric characters. In Barcelona two of the most historic are the Gegants del Pi, kept in the church of Santa Maria del Pi; more recent are the city's 'official' giants, who represent King Jaume I

and his queen, Violant of Hungary. Equally popular are the capgrossos , 'fatheads' (pictured bottom left) who accompany the giants, wearing huge papier-mâché and wood heads, usually with bizarre fixed smiles. Mischievous, leprechaun-like figures, they once represented the biblical tribes of Shem, Ham and Japheth, but the heads can now resemble celebrities or all sorts of popular figures. One of the most skilled makers of them is El Ingenio (*see p172*).

Barcelona Poesia

All over Barcelona. **Date** 15 May.

The *Jocs Florals* (Flowery Games) were poetry contests started by King Joan I in 1393. Having died out in the middle of the 15th century, they were resuscitated in 1859 and have been held ever since, with prizes awarded for the three best poems. The Jocs were recently combined with the annual International Poetry Festival and expanded to a week of poetry, including thematic readings as well as a poetic walk through Barcelona. While mostly in Catalan and Spanish, the International Festival, held on the final day, features poets who write in half a dozen other languages.

Summer

Marató de l'Espectacle

Mercat de Les Flors, C/Lleida 59. **Information** Associació Marató de l'Espectacle, C/Trafalgar 78, 1er 1ª (93 268 18 68). Metro Espanya/bus all routes to Plaça Espanya. **Dates** 8-9 June. **Map** p323 B6.

Two nights of performance mayhem in a condensed burst of non-stop action and colour that goes some way to filling the Grec Festival's lack of alternative performance. Pieces last from 30 seconds to ten minutes, with continuous action each evening and a continuous flow of people, as members of the audience drift between spaces, go up and perform their bits before returning to their seats or head for the bar for a rest and some networking.

There are over 80 performances, mostly from Spain, but there are always several groups from the rest of Europe and a handful from further afield. Dance, theatre, music and puppets are among the delights on offer, as well as installations and film-screenings. This is an excellent showcase for new talent, with inevitable peaks and troughs.

L'Ou com Balla

Venues *Ateneu Barcelonès, C/Canuda 6; Casa de l'Ardiaca, C/Santa Llúcia 1; Cathedral Cloister; Museu Frederic Marès. Metro Jaume I/17, 19, 40, 45 bus.* **Date** Corpus Christi (14-17 June). **Map** p327 B3.

Before the 19th century, Corpus Christi was one of the most important celebrations in the year, though it has lost a lot of its earlier significance. The tradition of L'Ou com Balla ('the egg that dances') continues: a hollowed-out egg is placed on the spout of a small fountain, where it spins and bobs. Fountains are garlanded with spectacular flower displays, and a funnel-like structure guides the egg back onto the water spout whenever it falls off. L'Ou com Balla can also be seen in the cathedral during Easter week.

Festa de la Música

All over Barcelona. **Information** Centre d'Informació de la Virreina. **Date** 21 June.
International Music Day, initiated by the then French minister of culture Jack Lang in 1982 and since exported all over the world, has been officially celebrated in Barcelona since 1996. Hundreds of performances take place in squares, parks, museums and cultural centres all over the city, and all of it is free, though not always of very high quality.

Sound echoes

It's three days of electronica and excess. It's a three-day rave. It's a stop-press snapshot of the latest in multimedia music and art. Most of all it's a fantastic, fabulous, fathomless festival of fun. Sónar, Barcelona's massively successful electronic music and media festival, almost defies description, metamorphosing from day to night and back to day again, changing as it does so. It started life in 1995 as a modest event for hard-core web-heads and techno-types. Since then it has just grown and grown, drawing 53,000 people from across Europe for its weekend of intense, feverish activity.

The key is its multi-disciplined, many-faceted nature. Not just three delirious nights of pumping dance music, not just three days of communal chill-out, it incorporates concerts, DJ-sets, exhibitions, demos, a record fair, a meeting place for professionals and, if all else fails, good old-fashioned bumper-cars.

For most people, Sónarnight is the main draw, with concerts and DJ-sets on four different stages, from mainstream techno and house to more experimental electronica to down-tempo rhythms to practically anything you can think of that requires binary code and an amplifier. Even for the techno-phobe, it's an irresistible affair, if only for its sheer, unstoppable exuberance and energy.

Sónarday is more relaxed, shot through with that febrile morning-after feeling, as concert-goers from the night before drift like ghostly pilgrims to the main base at the CCCB, to lie recovering in the sunshine on artificial grass (and other artificial substances), gathering energy for the night to come, and turning the area into a futuristic refugee camp/airport lounge. There's more music, more DJs but also exhibitions of electronic and net art, a record fair, hardware demos, people talking shop, people not talking shop, before drifting back to Sónarnight for another night of mayhem.

Alas, not all is rosy in Sónarland. A victim of its size and success, in 2001 Sónar is forsaking its traditional night-time venue for an as yet undisclosed new home big enough for the growing hordes. The Pabellón de la Mar Bella, the converted sports centre with its privileged location yards from the beach, will be sorely missed, as will the unforgettable sight of the blood-red sun coming up over the Mediterranean as the party pounded on. Without it, Sónar might never be the same again.

Sónar 2001 – Barcelona International Festival of Advanced Music and Multimedia Art. June 14-16 2001 **Information** 93 442 29 72/www.sonar.es/advance@sonar.es

Sant Joan*

All over Barcelona. **Date** night of 23 & 24* June.
One could argue that Catalans are a nation of pyromaniacs (witness the *correfoc*): there's no better evidence for this than the night of 23 June, the eve or *verbena* of Sant Joan (24 June), strictly speaking the feast of Saint John the Baptist. This is La Nit del Foc, the 'night of fire', throughout Catalonia and the Balearics; marking the summer solstice (to which Saint John's is the nearest saint's day). It's clearly pagan in origin, and the wildest night of the year. Nowadays the huge bonfires that used to burn at every road junction in the city have been banned, but they still fill the *ramblas* of towns up and down the coast, and even in the city there are still one or two 'private initiatives'.

For a week before Sant Joan, the June air is ripped apart by explosions, as every schoolkid in town spends his or her pocket-money on terrifying bangers. Come the night itself, the city sounds like a virtual war zone, with impromptu firework displays exploding from balconies and squares. There are big displays on Tibidabo, Montjuïc and, especially, by the beach, with live bands to dance to – good places to head for. There are also smaller events in squares across the city, and countless house and terrace parties.

Marking the 'official' start of summer, this is the night of the year when Catalans really let their hair down, and the atmosphere is thick with excitement and gunpowder as midsummer madness takes a grip. De rigueur things to consume are *coca de Sant Joan*, a shallow, bread-like cake decorated with very sweet candied fruit, and as much cava as you can manage (sold from improvised stalls along the Rambla). The best thing to do is keep going all night, and a 'traditional' way to end Sant Joan is to head for the beach at dawn, to watch the sunrise. Afterwards, 24 June is a public holiday, and nothing moves before mid-afternoon.

Classics als Parcs

Information Parcs i Jardins, C/Tarragona 173, Sants, (93 413 24 00/www.bcn.es/parcsijardins). Metro Tarragona/27, 30, 109, 215, N-0, N7 bus. **Open** 8am-3pm Mon-Fri. **Dates** June-July. **Tickets** approx 800ptas. **No credit cards.**
A season of classical concerts is held alfresco in early summer in some of the city's more attractive parks. The programme varies, and there are usually two or three different concerts to choose from every Friday and Saturday evening in venues such as Gaudí's Parc Güell, and the Ciutadella and Laberint parks. *See section* **Sightseeing**.

Festival del Grec

Teatre Grec, Mercat de les Flors and other venues.
Information Centre d'Informació de la Virreina. Tickets available from Centre d'Informació de la Virreina (*see p304*) & Tel-entrada (*see p196*). **Dates** 1 June-31 July. **Map** (Grec theatre) p323 B6.
Barcelona's main performing arts festival, the Grec takes its name from the mock-Greek open-air theatre on Montjuïc where several of the performances are staged. Unlike its counterparts in Edinburgh and Avignon, it has remained consistently mainstream, and even the non-official elements are semi-official. Most of the theatre is in Catalan or Spanish, with a smattering of work in other, mainly European, languages – the official festival booklet makes clear which. Dance is mostly contemporary and is similarly weighted to home-grown talents, though again there is still plenty of work from abroad. Music is particularly strong on flamenco and jazz, and this is also, inevitably, the most international, and eclectic, section, providing something to suit most tastes. Tickets generally cost between 2,000 and 3,000ptas and can be bought from the special booth in Plaça Catalunya, from El Palau de la Virreina (La Rambla, 99) or with a credit card from Tel-entrada (902 10 12 12 or www.telentrada.com).

Festa Major de Gràcia

All over Gràcia. Metro Fontana/22, 24, 28, N4 bus. **Information** Centre d'Informació de la Virreina (*see p304*), 010 & 93 291 66 00. **Dates** 15-21 Aug. **Map** pp320-21 D-E2-3.
Held since the 1820s, Gràcia's *festa major* has now almost outgrown the *barri* itself, attracting thousands from all over the city, to an extent that can annoy true locals. A unique feature is the competition between streets for the best decoration: they are decked out to represent elaborate fantasy scenarios, from desert islands to satires on current events. Each street also has its own programme of entertainment, plus an open-air meal for all the neighbours. District-wide events are centred on Plaça Rius i Taulet, and there's music nightly in Plaça de la Revolució, Plaça del Sol and Plaça de la Virreina. The festa opens with *gegants* and *castells* in Plaça Rius i Taulet, and climaxes on the last night with a *correfoc* and more fireworks.

Festa Major de Sants

All over Sants. Metro Plaça de Sants, Sants Estació/bus all routes to Estació de Sants. **Information** Centre d'Informació de la Virreina & 010. **Dates** 24 Aug-2 Sept. **Map** p323 A4.
Following right after Gràcia, the smaller *festa major* in Sants has not had the benefit of the same historical continuity, and had to be revived after the dictatorship. Major events, such as the *correfoc*, are held in the Parc de L'Espanya Industrial; others are centred on Plaça del Centre, C/Sant Antoni, Plaça de la Farga and Plaça Joan Peiro, behind Sants station.

Autumn

Diada National de Catalunya*

(Catalan National Day) All over Barcelona.
Date 11 Sept.
On 11 September 1714, after a 13-month siege, Barcelona fell to the Castilian/French army in the War of the Spanish Succession, a national disaster that led to the loss of all Catalan institutions for 200 years (*see p13*). This heroic defeat is commemorat-

Arts & Entertainment

ed as Catalan National Day. In 1977, the first time it could be celebrated openly after the dictatorship, over a million people took to the streets. It's now lost some of its vigour, but is still a day for national reaffirmation. Flags are displayed on balconies, and separatist groups hold demonstrations.

Dies de Dansa
Parc Güell, MACBA, CCCB, Pati Manning, Piscines Picornell, Fundació Miró, SGAE and Mercat de Los Flors. **Dates** 14 -16 Sept.
Three days of dance performance in various venues, day and night, featuring both local and international dance companies. Some of the performances are free, particularly those taking place outdoors. The most spectacular of the venues are Parc Güell and the terrace of the Miró Foundation.

Festa Major de la Barceloneta
All over Barceloneta. Metro Barceloneta/17, 36, 39, 40, 45, 57, 59, 64, 157, N6, N8 bus. **Dates** 22-30 Sept. **Map** p327 C4.
One of the liveliest of the smaller district *festes*, the Festa Major de la Barceloneta coincides, in 2001, with the Mercè. Activities centre around Plaça de la Barceloneta and Plaça de la Font. A grotesque – supposedly French – general, General Bum Bum (Boom Boom, possibly named after Prosper Verboom, the French army engineer who designed the *barri*), leads a procession of children around the district, firing off cannons. The tradition is said to date from 1881. There's dancing on the beach at night, and some people take to boats to eat, drink and watch the firework display from the sea.

Festes de La Mercè*
All over Barcelona. **Information** Centre d'Informació de la Virreina (see *p304*), 010 & tourist offices. **Dates** 24-30 Sept.
If Sant Joan celebrates the beginning of summer, La Mercè marks its end, rounding off with a resounding bang the Indian summer that is (usually) September in Barcelona. Nostra Senyora de la Mercè (Our Lady of Mercy) joined Santa Eulàlia as one of the patron saints of Barcelona in 1637 after stamping out a plague of locusts, and has had the city's annual celebrations dedicated to her since 1871.

The celebration lasts for a week and combines all the ingredients of a traditional Catalan *festa major*. It starts with an early-morning clarion call, as drummers and musicians march around the Barri Gòtic to wake everyone up, and mass is held in the Basilica de la Mare de Déu de la Mercè; unmistakable, especially from the port, with its towering statue of the virgin on the roof. The week includes processions of giants, two major displays of human towers, and a spectacular *correfoc*, preceded the night before by a dry run for the faint-heated as the dragons lumber through town without their attendant devils (*see pp200-1* **Medieval mayhem**).

There are also *sardanas*, folk dances, a run round town, a swim across the port, kites, air displays and parachuting on the beach, and a firework display up

on Montjuïc. Added to which, there are dozens of concerts in Plaça de Catalunya, Avinguda del Catedral and Moll de la Fusta, among other venues, with flamenco, folk, rock, *rai*, dance, classical and jazz in the main programme, or associated events such as the BAM music festival.

Mostra de Vins i Caves de Catalunya
Maremàgnum. **Information** INCAVI (93 487 67 38). **Dates** 4 days coinciding with La Mercè.
The Penedès region, Catalonia's most important wine- and cava-producing area and home to cava labels like Freixenet and Codorniu, is less than an hour from Barcelona. For four days (coinciding with the dates of La Mercè) the Catalan Institute of Wine and Cava brings together around 50 of the province's wine producers, along with makers of other Catalan specialities including cheese, *embotits* (charcuterie) and anchovies.

Festival International de Jazz de Barcelona
Palau de la Música, Luz de Gas. **Information** 010. **Dates** Oct-Dec.
Barcelona has a strong jazz tradition, and this is the key event in the annual jazz-lovers' calendar, attracting a handful of major and less major international names. Around a dozen concerts are held either in the Palau de la Música or Luz de Gas.

Festival de Jazz de Ciutat Vella
All over the old city. **Dates** 1-31 Oct.
Inevitably more low-key than the international festival with which it overlaps, the Festival de Jazz de Ciutat Vella features dozens of concerts in bars and other small venues around the old city. All kinds of jazz feature, ranging from trad jazz to bossa nova, and both local and some international groups.

Tots Sants* (All Saints' Day)
All over Barcelona. **Date** 1 Nov.
This is the day to remember the dead, and it is traditional to visit the cemetery where your loved ones are buried. Most people take the opportunity to clean up the grave, bringing with them cloths and window-cleaner, replacing the flowers and generally making the grave look tidy for another year. Known colloquially as the *Castanyada*, it is customary to eat *castanyas* (roast chestnuts), *moniatos* (sweet potatoes) and *panellets*, small sweet cakes made from almonds and pine-nuts, washed down with sweet wines like *moscatell* or *malvasia*.

Fira del Disc de Col.leccionista
Fira de Barcelona, Avda Reina Maria Cristina 1 (93 233 20 00/firadisc@catradio.com). Metro Espanya/bus all routes to Plaça d'Espanya. **Date** 2-4 Nov 2001. **Map** p323 A4.
Curiously, Barcelona hosts the largest second-hand record fair in Europe: a vast array of vinyl LPs, 45s, tapes and CDs, ending in an auction of rock memorabilia that draws buyers from around the world.

A load of *coblas*

Catalonia's traditional folk dance, the *sardana*, is not an exciting dance to watch. No hey-ho, hey nonny-no, no swiping at each other with wooden staves, and certainly no waving pigs' bladders. You stand in a circle, holding hands, and bob lightly up and down on the balls of your feet in time to the music, taking the occasional step to the left, followed almost immediately by another one back.

Though it might look extremely simple, it is in fact fiendishly difficult and, apparently, a joy to dance. The music is played by a traditional band called a *cobla*, consisting of 11 musicians playing traditional tubas, trombones and reedy, squeaky wind instruments similar to clarinets and oboes. Anyone can join in – provided you don't break up a couple, so you should break in to the man's left. And of course it is frowned upon to join a circle above your level. Instead look

for the groups of muddlers. There are always a couple.

The origins of the dance are somewhat obscure. Some have traced it back to Ancient Greece, though more, perhaps, on romantic than historical grounds. Others see its origins in the *ballo sardo* of Sardinia – the island was once a Catalan colony. In fact the first written reference of the *sardana* comes in 1552, though early sources all relate to the dance being banned in front of, and sometimes inside, various Catalan churches, on account of the noise.

Sardanas are danced at all traditional festivals, including the *festa major* of every neighbourhood and village, as well as every weekend in front of the cathedral (6.30-8.30pm Sat; noon-2pm Sun) and in Plaça Sant Jaume (6pm-8pm Sun). For details of classes, contact the Federació Sardanista 93 319 76 37.

Winter

Fira de Santa Llúcia

Pla de la Seu & Avda de la Catedral. Metro Jaume I/17, 19, 40, 45 bus. **Dates** 1-22 Dec. **Map** p319 B2-3.

The annual Fira de Santa Llúcia huddles round the cathedral for all the world like a medieval market on the front of a Christmas card. Heralding in the arrival of the Christmas season, the market sells all the necessary paraphernalia, from trees and decorations to Christmas logs (for the significance of which, see under Nadal, below) and handmade gifts. The stalls in front of the cathedral's main entrance specialise in small figures for the nativity scenes that Spanish familes build up year by year: donkeys, shepherds and other stable staples, plus the wonderful Catalan character of the *caganer*, or 'shitter' – a small figure literally caught with his trousers down. No one seems to know quite where this came from, but there is even a *caganer* collectors' club, and an endless variety of *caganers*, including film stars, politicians and Barça football players. There is also a huge, life-size nativity scene erected each year in Plaça Sant Jaume, though without a *caganer*, alas.

Nadal* & Sant Esteve* (Christmas Day & Boxing Day)

All over Barcelona. **Dates** 25* & 26* Dec.

Pity poor Catalan kids. Traditionally, Christmas comes and goes with no presents, and they have to wait for the three kings to arrive, twelve long days later, before finally getting their sacks filled. And then it's usually back to school the next day, before they've barely had a chance to break their new toys. In these impious times, families increasingly split the present-giving between Reis (see below) and Christmas Day, or at least offer a small advance to keep the kid going on Christmas Eve. These come courtesy of the Christmas log, the *Caga Tió* (or 'shitting log'). The kid beats the log with a stick, singing a short, sweet song that ends with the words "¡Caga, Tió! ¡Caga!" ("Shit, Log! Shit!"), whereupon, the log does so, in the form of a small gift!

Cap d'Any (New Year's Eve)

All over Barcelona. **Date** 31 Dec & 1 Jan*.

As on Sant Joan (*see p203*), discos and bars charge outrageous admission for New Year parties: the mass public celebrations around the city are cheaper. Wherever you are at midnight – well announced on TV – you'll be expected to start stuffing 12 grapes

It's **Carnival** time!

into your mouth, one for every chime of the bell, without stopping until the New Year has been fully rung in. Otherwise, it's bad luck. Many taxi drivers take the night off, so it can be hard to get around.

Cavalcada dels Reis (Three Kings' Parade)

Route *Kings normally arrive at Moll de la Fusta, then parade up the Rambla to Plaça Sant Jaume, and continue to Passeig de Gràcia; detailed route changes each year.* **Information** Centre d'Informació de la Virreina & 010. **Date** 5 Jan. **Map** p326-327 A-B1-4.
The kings arrive in the harbour at around dusk, and are ceremoniously driven around town in an open carriage, throwing sweets to the cheering crowds. (Don't tell the kids this, but there are usually three teams of kings working different beats; it's a big city for three travel-weary kings.) The route is published in the morning papers, and lined with crowds of parents with their overexcited offspring. There is also a toy market in Gran Via for some last-minute gift shopping. The next day, El Dia dels Reis, children awake to their presents, unless they have been particularly naughty over the past twelve months, in which case they get a lump of (edible) coal.

Festa dels Tres Tombs

District of Sant Antoni. Metro Sant Antoni/20, 24, 38, 64, N6 bus. **Date** 17 Jan. **Map** p323-4 B-C5.
Sant Antoni Abat (Saint Anthony the Abbot) is patron saint of domestic animals and muleteers. There may no longer be any members of this trade left, but a small procession of horsemen, dressed in tailcoats and top hats, still commemorates his day by riding three times (*Tres Tombs*, three turns)

around a route from Ronda Sant Antoni, through Plaça Universitat, Pelai and Plaça Catalunya, down the Rambla and back along Nou de la Rambla. This coincides with the *festa major* of the *barri* of Sant Antoni, which continues for a week.

Carnestoltes (Carnival)

All over Barcelona. **Date** usually late Feb.
The opening event is a procession of figures in outrageous outfits, from Brazilian dancers to the usual Catalan monsters, led by *el Rei Carnestoltes* and *Don Carnal*, amid a confusion of confetti, blunderbuss salvos and fireworks. The origins of Carnival are in a once-traditional outburst of eating, drinking and fornicating prior to the limitations of Lent; King Carnestoltes – the masked personification of the carnival spirit – also used to criticise the authorities and reveal scandals, a tradition that unfortunately has died out. Other events in the city's ten-day modern carnival include dancing in Plaça Catalunya, concerts in different venues and a *Gran Botifarrada Popular* on the Rambla, when sausage is handed out. There are children's fancy-dress carnivals, so it's common to see kids in the street dressed up as bees or Marie Antoinettes, and Carnival is also a big show in the city's markets, where even the traders get dressed up. The end of Carnival on Ash Wednesday is marked by the *Enterrament de la Sardina*, the burial of the sardine, on Montjuïc or in Barceloneta, when a humble fish – symbol perhaps of the penis – is buried to emphasise that even frugal fare will not be consumed for 40 days. More concentrated than Barcelona's Carnival are those in Vilanova i la Geltrú and Sitges (*see pp263-4*).

Children

Big fun with the little ones.

Barcelona has a wealth of activities to capture the imagination of both children and adults. From Gaudí's fairy tale-like buildings to street mimes on the Rambla, the city abounds with ageless pleasures that make sightseeing enjoyable with children in tow. Though it's difficult to manoeuvre a pushchair through the old city's cobblestone streets, Barcelona's compact layout means you don't have to travel far to reach child-oriented attractions.

Due to the declining birth rate, Catalan families are decreasing in size, but family bonds remain strong. Children are very much a part of daily life and are often treated like little adults. It's not unusual to see toddlers out for dinner with their parents at 11pm or to see teenagers playing impromptu football matches in city squares. Your children will be made welcome wherever you go, and even the most boisterous behaviour or worst temper tantrum will be met with patient smiles.

PRACTICALITIES

Unfortunately, the relaxed attitude towards children also means a lack of child-specific concessions and facilities. Public transport is free only for children under four and a half, and few places have baby-changing facilities. Barcelona restaurants rarely offer children's menus, but will provide small portions or simple dishes on request. To avoid frustration during your stay, be sure to adapt to the local timetable: most restaurants don't serve lunch before 2pm or dinner before 8pm.

While few hotels offer special services, some of the more upmarket establishments do have family suites and a childminding service. Some (but not enough) even have child-friendly pools (*see chapter* **Accommodation**). If you need baby equipment and supplies or want to buy a special toy, *see p176*.

Attractions

Children's attractions are clustered around Montjuïc, Tibidabo and the Port Vell and there's a host of fun ways to get around them: funiculars, trams, cable cars and *golondrines* (swallow boats), as well as the open-top Bus Turístic. The latest special attraction, located behind the **Zoo** in the Vila Olímpica, is a spectacular **balloon ride** (for all of the above *see section* **Sightseeing**). **Poble Espanyol** is

Who's watching who at the **Aquàrium**?

a bit of a tourist trap, but popular with kids, who enjoy the daily arts and crafts demonstrations, such as the resident glass-blower and the puppet and circus shows that take place most Sunday mornings (*see p91*). On a rainy day, a good (expensive) standby can be the IMAX 3-D cinema (*see p215*). For advance ticket outlets, *see p196*.

L'Aquàrium de Barcelona

Moll d'Espanya, Port Vell (93 221 74 74/ www.aquariumbcn.com). Metro Barceloneta/ 14, 19, 36, 40, 57, 59, 64, 157, N6 bus. **Open** *Sept-June* 9.30am-9pm Mon-Fri; 9.30am-9.30pm Sat, Sun. *July, Aug* 9.30am-11pm daily. **Admission** 1,550ptas; 950ptas concessions; free under-4s. **Advance sales** Tel-entrada. **Discounts** BC, BT. **Credit** MC, V. **Map** p324 D7.

Barcelona's aquarium is considered to be Europe's best display of Mediterranean marine life, with more than 360 species contained in 21 tanks. A highlight is the 80-metre (260-foot) glass tunnel through a shark tank where you might find yourself face to face with a sand tiger shark. For young children, the Explora exhibit offers 50 touch-and-feel activities. The aquarium's newest addition, Planeta Aqua, features penguins, piranhas and alligators.

Nits hípiques a Barcelona (horse shows)

Pista Hípica de la Foixarda, Avda Montanyans 1, Parc de Montjuïc. Metro Espanya/9, 13, 38, 61, 65, 91 bus. **Performances** *Late June-Sept* 9pm Fri. **Tickets** tourist offices & Tel-entrada. **Admission** 700ptas; 500ptas under-10s. **Credit** MC, V. **Map** p323 A5.

On Friday evenings during summer, the city police display team dons fancy uniforms and hops aboard Andalusian horses to present a dainty show in which the horses time their fancy footwork to music.

Arts & Entertainment

Tibidabo funfair

Parc d'Atraccions del Tibidabo, Plaça del Tibidabo (93 211 79 42). FGC Av Tibidabo/17, 22, 58, 73, 85 bus, then Tramvia Blau and Funicular to park. **Open** *Late Mar-April* noon-7pm Fri-Sun; closed Mon-Thur. *May* noon-7pm Thur-Sun; closed Mon-Wed. *June* noon-7pm Wed-Sun; closed Mon, Tue. *July, Aug* noon-10pm Mon-Thur, Sun; noon-1am Fri, Sat. *Early Sept* noon-8pm Mon-Thur; noon-10pm Fri-Sun. *Late Sept-early Oct* noon-8pm Sat, Sun. **Admission** entrance & 6 rides 1,200ptas; free children under 1m 10cm tall. Pass & unlimited number of rides 2,500ptas; 700ptas under 1m 10cm. **Discounts** BC, BT. **Credit** MC, V.

Make a day of it by catching the Tramvia Blau up the hill to the Funicular, which takes you through the woods to the top of the mountain and the funfair. Few amusement parks can compete with this spectacular mountaintop view. The park has lots of good old-fashioned attractions (bumper cars, Ferris wheel, and so on), as well as the infamous house of horrors, Hotel Krueger. Also worth a visit is the Museu d'Automates, a wonderful collection of old fairground machines.

Zoo de Barcelona

Parc de la Ciutadella, La Ribera/Port Olímpic (93 225 67 80/fax 93 221 38 53). Metro Barceloneta, Ciutadella/14, 39, 40, 41, 42, 51, 141 bus. **Open** *Nov-Feb* 10am-5pm daily. *Mar, Oct* 10am-6pm daily. *Apr, Sept* 10am-7pm daily. *May-Aug* 9.30am-7.30pm daily. **Admission** 1,550ptas; 975-900ptas concessions; free under-3s. **Discounts** BC, BT. **Credit** MC, V. **Map** p325 E6.

The cramped, concrete enclosures are not ideal for the animals, but children enjoy the regular shows at the Dolphinarium, picnics on the grass, the cuddly creatures in the farm area and the new penguin aquarium. Be sure to meet *Copito de Nieve* (Snowflake), the only albino gorilla in captivity.

Museums

Barcelona has a wide variety of museums that you can share with your children. In July and August, many museums take part in the **Estiu als Museus** ('summer in the museums') programme, with fun educational activities for kids. Details can be found at tourist offices and **La Virreina** centre (*see p304*). The children's exhibitions at the **Museu de Zoología** in the Ciutadella Park will delight budding zoologists, while the Museu Marítim offers life-sized models of boats and cabins, an oared galley and an audio-visual exhibit on life at sea. Also enjoyable is the hands-on **Museu de l'Historia de Catalunya** where kids can participate in activities including mounting a medieval horse and exploring air raid shelters. The biggest hit with kids, though, is often the Barça football museum, **Museu del FC Barcelona**. For all, *see chapter* **Museums**.

Museu de Cera (Wax Museum)

Passatge de la Banca 7, Rambla (93 317 26 49). Metro Drassanes/14, 38, 59, 91 bus. **Open** *Mid Sept-mid July* 10am-1.30pm, 4-7.30pm Mon-Fri; 11am-2pm, 4.30-8.30pm Sat, Sun. *Mid July-mid Sept* 10am-10pm daily. **Admission** 1,100ptas; 625ptas concessions; free under-4s. **No credit cards. Map** p327 A4.

Not a patch on Madame Tussauds, but worth a trip on a rainy day, the museum is home to over 300 wax figures, with good costumes. In the square outside is a bar, El Bosc de les Fades, with fairy-grotto décor.

Museu de la Ciència

C/Teodor Roviralta 55, Tibidabo (93 212 60 50/www.fundacio.lacaixa.es). FGC Tibidabo, then Tramvia Blau/17, 22, 73, 85, 158 bus. **Open** 10am-8pm Tue-Sun; closed Mon. **Admission** 500ptas; 250-150ptas concessions; free under-7s; additional exhibitions 250ptas extra. **Discounts** BC. **Credit** MC, V.

The science museum uses hands-on fun and gadgetry to teach children about everything from mechanics to the layout of the human body. For children between three and seven, the museum offers a special touchy-feely exhibit called *Clik del nens*. Children over ten enjoy the Planetarium's enlightening films on space.

Beaches

Barcelona's coastline is blessed with a stretch of beaches, all offering reasonably easy access, passably clean sands, lifeguards, showers, play areas and plenty of ice-cream kiosks. Unfortunately, there are few toilets and baby-changing facilities. While the city beaches are considered safe for swimming, some parents nonetheless prefer to make a short trip out of town to the more shallow waters of Casteldefells or Sitges (*see pp263-4*).

You talkin' to me? **Zoo de Barcelona**.

Parks & playgrounds

Many of the city's most beautiful parks are outside the centre, and those in the old town are often disappointing paved squares. The exception is lush, green and fun **Ciutadella** (*see pp82-3*), which also contains the city zoo, where you can hire bikes or a boat to paddle in the lake. The bright ceramic sculptures in **Parc Güell** (*see p100*) appeal to kids, and, further away, **Parc del Laberint** (*see p106*) has a fun maze and picnic areas. For a real day out, head for the huge **Parc de Collserola** (*see p102*) behind Tibidabo, which is dotted with pine forests and picnic spots.

Parc del Castell de l'Oreneta

Camí de Can Caralleu & passage Blada, Zona Alta (93 424 38 09/ www.bcn.es/parcsijardins/). By car Ronda de Dalt Exit 9; by bus 60, 66. **Open** *Nov-Feb* 10am-6pm daily. *Mar, Oct* 10am-7pm daily. *Apr, Sept* 10am-8pm daily. *May-Aug* 10am-9pm daily.

One of Barcelona's largest parks, not far from the Monestir de Pedralbes (*see p103*). Attractions here include a pony club, several play areas, a sports circuit and a snack bar. On Sundays from 11am-2pm, you can hop aboard the miniature steam train (200ptas per person).

Entertainment

Every three months, the Ajuntament local government presents an official programme of entertainment for children ages three and up called **Espectacles Infantils + a prop** (roughly, 'Children's performances closer to you'). Events include concerts and marionette and magic shows that usually take place in neighbourhood civic centres. Information is available at **La Virreina** (*see p304*).

Film

The Verdi has one screen that shows children's films undubbed, and the Filmoteca has a children's session on Sundays at 5.30pm. S*ee pp214-5.*

Music

The auditorium of the **Fundació la Caixa** (*see chapter* **Museums**) presents top-notch family concerts complete with entertainers, usually on Saturday mornings or Sunday afternoons from September to May. In March and April, the **Liceu** will put on a special production of Mozart's *The Little Magic Flute* for children and their families (*see p237*). On June and July evenings, orchestras play in the city's parks for the **Classics als Parcs** cycle (*see chapter* **By Season**).

Theatre

Barcelona hosts some excellent children's theatre, but basic understanding of Catalan or Spanish is essential. In late June and July, **Petit Grec**, part of the Grec cultural festival, will present special performances for children. Information is available at La Virreina.

Throughout the rest of the year, plays and puppet shows can be seen at the **Jove Teatre Regina** (C/Sèneca 22, 93 218 15 12, shows 5.30pm Sat, Sun, admission 900-1,100ptas); **Teatre Goya**, **Teatre Malic** and **Artenbrut** (*see chapter* **Theatre**). On Sundays there are children's shows at Turó Parc, Poble Espanyol, Fundació Miró and the CCCB. For English-language theatre check ads in English bookshops (*see p175*) and *Metropolitan* magazine.

Festivals & seasons

See also chapter **By Season**.

February: Carnaval

Miniature Batmen, fairies and bumble bees fill the streets of Barcelona during Carnival week. Colourful parades are held along the Rambla, with King Carnestoltes as the star of the show.

March, April: Easter

Treat them to a *mona*, which is an elaborate chocolate treat that is traditionally bought by godparents for their godchildren.

May: La Tamborinada

For a whole Saturday the Ciutadella is taken over by performers, puppets, magicians and circus acts.

June: Sant Joan

Sant Joan enters with a bang on 23 June, Midsummer's Eve, when bonfires are lit and firecrackers are set off all over the city. Hectic for small children, but very much a teen favourite.

August: Festa Major de Gràcia

Street parties are held in each area of Barcelona for a week during the summer. The best by far is in Gràcia. Besides enjoying the decorated streets, kids can join in the games, rides and competitions.

September: La Mercè

A huge street party: for a whole week, squares fill with clowns, puppets, concerts and theatre.

December: Christmas

In the run-up to 25 December, Barcelonans flock to Santa Llúcia market in the Cathedral square to buy Christmas trees and crib figures. Children traditionally receive presents from the Three Wise Men on 6 January, **El Dia dels Reis**.

Out of town

For a day at the seaside, **Sitges** is easygoing and pretty, with pleasant, safe beaches; for a more hectic experience you can't beat a visit to **Port Aventura**, one of Europe's best theme parks. *See pp264-5.*

Arts & Entertainment

Catalunya en Miniatura

Can Balasch de Baix, Torrelles de Llobregat,
Outer Limits (93 689 09 60/www.catalunyaen
miniatura.com). By bus Oliveras from Plaça
d'Espanya/by car N-II to Sant Vicens dels Horts,
then left (10km/6 miles). **Open** *Nov-Mar* 10am-6pm
daily. *Apr-Oct* 10am-7pm daily. **Admission**
1,200ptas; 800ptas over-65s; 700ptas under-14s; free
under-3s. **No credit cards.**

Apparently this is the largest model village in
Europe, comprising over 170 miniatures of Catalan
monuments and buildings, and a mini train to take
you all around. Clowns put on an act on Sundays
and holidays at 12.30pm.

Parc de les Aus

Carretera de Vilassar de Mar a Cabrils,
Vilassar de Mar, Outer Limits (93 750 17 65/
www.elparcdelesaus.com). By car A19 or N-II north
to Vilassar, then left (24km/15 miles)/by train
RENFE from Sants or Plaça Catalunya to Vilassar,
then taxi. **Open** *Sept-Feb* 10am-5pm Tue-Sun.
Mar-June 10am-8pm Tue-Sun. *July, Aug* 10am-9pm
Tue-Sun. Closed Mon all year round. **Admission**
750-1,300ptas; 950ptas 3-12s; free under-3s.
Credit AmEx, DC, MC, V.

Enjoy over 300 local and exotic bird species, extensive gardens, picnic spots and play areas.

Vintage trains

Information & reservations (93 205 15 15/
www.fgc.catalunya.net). **Dates** Sept-June. **Tickets**
1,800ptas return; 1,000ptas return concessions; free
under-3s. **No credit cards.**

An FGC steam train departs from Abrera (near
Martorell) to Monistrol de Montserrat every Sunday
at 11.30am, returning at 13.30pm. To reach Abrera,
catch the 10.17am FGC train from Plaça d'Espanya.
If you prefer a 1920s electric train, vintage rolling
stock is in action, with live jazz on board, from Plaça
Catalunya to Reina Elisenda on the first Sunday of
each month. For both, booking well in advance is
essential. Railway buffs also enjoy the Museu del
Ferrocarril (railway museum) in Vilanova i la Geltrú
(Plaça Eduard Maristany, 93 815 84 91).

Waterparks

For fun cooling off, Catalonia has seven
waterparks. Options further afield include
Aqua Brava (Roses), **Aquadiver** (Platja
d'Aro) and **Water World** (Lloret de Mar)
along the Costa Brava, **Marineland** in
Palafolls and **Aqua Park** near Port Aventura.

Aqualeón Safari

Finca les Basses, Albinyana, Outer Limits
(977 68 76 56/www.aspro-hocio.es). By car A2,
then A7 via Vilafranca, or N340 to El Vendrell,
then right to Albinyana (65km/40 miles). **Open** (9
June-16 Sept) *Safari park* 10am-6pm daily. *Water*
park 11am-7pm Mon-Fri; 11am-8pm Sat, Sun.
Admission 2,300ptas; 1,300ptas concessions;
free under-3s. **Credit** AmEx, DC, MC, V.

An all-in-one water and safari park between
Barcelona and Tarragona, with tigers, birds of prey
and parrots as well as giant water slides, fun pools
and wave machines. Captive dolphins too.

Isla de Fantasia

Finca Mas Brassó, Vilassar de Dalt, Outer Limits (93
751 45 53/www.islafantasia34w.com). By car A19 or
N11 north, left at Premià de Mar (24km/15 miles).
Open *Water park* (June-mid Sept) 10am-7pm Mon-
Fri, Sun; 10am-7pm, 9pm-4am Sat. *Disco* (all year)
10pm-6am Sat. **Admission** (water park) 1,500ptas;
1,000ptas 2-10s; free under-2s. **Credit** MC, V.

In the evenings this park becomes a water disco.

Babysitting & childcare

The agencies below employ qualified
childminders, and can supply an English-
speaker if necessary. Supervised daycare
centres offer parents the chance of a few
child-free hours.

Cangur Serveis

C/Aragó 227 pral, Eixample (93 487 80 08/24-hour
mobile 639 66 16 06). Metro Passeig de Gràcia/7, 16,
17, 22, 24, 28 bus. **Open** *Sept-June* 9am-6pm Mon-
Fri; closed Sat, Sun. *July, Aug* 9am-2pm Mon-Fri;
closed Sat, Sun. **No credit cards. Map** p320 D4.

This specialist agency provides babysitters at two
hours' notice on any day of the year. Charges begin
at 1,000ptas per hour, moving to 8,000ptas for an
all-night service, with discounts for longer-term
arrangements.

Cinc Serveis

C/Pelai 50, Eixample (93 412 56 76/24-hr mobile
639 36 11 11/609 80 30 80). Metro Catalunya/bus
all routes to Plaça Catalunya. **Open** *Office* 9.30am-
1.30pm, 4.30-8.30pm Mon-Fri; closed Sat, Sun.
No credit cards. Map p326 A1.

The basic babysitting rate at Cinc Serveis, after 9pm,
is 1,200ptas per hour plus the sitter's taxi home; day
and longer-term rates are less, phone for details.

Happy Parc

C/Comtes de Bell.lloc 74-78, Sants (93 490 08 35).
Metro Sants Estació/bus all routes to Estacio de
Sants. **Open** 5-9pm Mon-Fri; 11am-9pm Sat, Sun.
Rates 550ptas hr daily; 125ptas each subsequent
15mins. **No credit cards. Map** p327 A3.

An indoor fun park and drop-in daycare centre
for kids aged from two-12.
Branch: C/Pau Claris 97, Eixample
(93 317 86 60).

Xiqui Park

C/Manuel de Falla 31, Zona Alta (93 205 46 76).
FGC Les Tres Torres/bus 34, 66. **Open** 4.30-9pm
Mon-Fri; 11am-2.30pm, 4 -9pm Sat, Sun. **Rates**
600ptas per hr. **No credit cards. Map** p319 B2.

Xiqui Park entertains children aged one to 12 with
a range of fun activities, and also organises birth-
day parties. Phone for further details.
Branch: C/Marina 228, Eixample (93 231 40 59).

Dance

Despite a lack of resources, Barcelona is a hotbed for contemporary dance.

While Madrid is home to Spain´s two national dance companies, Barcelona is acknowledged as the most vibrant centre for contemporary dance. Though no one big, public institution presides over the scene, the city has cultivated a wide range of small and medium-sized professional groups that consistently produce exciting and original work.

Contemporary dance blossomed in Barcelona during the late 1970s, as new freedoms gave way to experimentation and young dancers found themselves free to try any and everything. In 1981, Toni Gelabert and Norma Axenfeldt founded a private, avant-garde dance school called La Fàbrica, which attracted dancers and teachers from around the world. The school trained such artists as Cesc Gelabert of **Gelabert-Azzopardi**, Ramón Oller of **Metros**, María Muñoz of **Mal Pelo** and Juan Carlos García of **Lanònima Imperial**, whose cutting-edge productions have earned international acclaim.

The creative spirit still reigns today, and a solid core of young dancers and companies have appeared who are recognised for their innovative choreography, which often mixes theatre and dance. In recent years, however, economic cutbacks have taken their toll, most notably with the break-up in 2000 of one of Catalonia's most emblematic troupes, Danat Dansa. This event sparked controversy in the community, causing choreographers and dancers alike to band together to ask politicians for more backing. Traditionally, most of the Generalitat´s funding has paid for performances rather than the development of new talents, and Catalan troupes find themselves competing with European groups that receive up to ten times the level of public support.

While some private schools nurture serious dancers, Barcelona´s only subsidised dance academy is the Escola de Dansa i Coreografia (School of Dance and Choreography) at the **Institut del Teatre**. To ease the transition from student to professional, the institute created IT Dansa in 1997, a contemporary company of young graduates that performs around Catalonia and at the **Grec** festival each summer.

NON-CONTEMPORARY DANCE

While contemporary dance has become an integral part of the local arts scene, opportunities to see other kinds of dance in Barcelona (except folk dancing, for which see p205), are relatively few. Dance is not at the top of the agenda at the new Liceu, but it will host several prestigious classical ballet companies in 2001, including the Zurich Ballet, Ballet Víctor Ullate, Ballet Maurice Béjart and Spain's Compañía Nacional de Danza, from Madrid (see chapter **Music: Classical & Opera**).

As for Spanish dance and flamenco, the best of the genre is not permanently in residence here, but high-quality flamenco companies such as those of Joaquín Cortés or Sara Baras do pass through Barcelona regularly, and major groups from Madrid are likely to visit the Liceu. The Barcelona groups Color and Increpación Danza perform flamenco with a contemporary twist. At the city's flamenco *tablaos*, performers are rarely first-rate, although even middling flamenco can provide a memorable evening. For venues, see chapter **Music: Rock, Roots & Jazz**.

INFORMATION

For programme information, check the *Guía del Ocio* and the free *Barcelona en Música*, available in record shops and at venues. These and other venue leaflets are also available at the **Centre de la Virreina** (see p304).

Associació dels Professionals de Dansa de Catalunya

Via Laietana 52, entresol 7 (93 268 24 73/ www.dancespain.com). Metro Urquinaona/bus 17, 19, 40, 45. **Open** 10am-2pm Mon-Fri; closed Sat, Sun. **Map** p326 B2.

Acts as a clearing-house for the dance companies, with information on who is doing what at any time.

Venues

L'Espai is the only venue with a permanent slot for dance, but the **Teatre Nacional de Catalunya** has provided a new main stage for Catalan dance companies, usually in its Sala Tallers (Workshop Space). The **Teatre Lliure** and **Mercat de les Flors** present dance with reasonable frequency, and **Sala Beckett** hosts small-scale, fringe events (for all, see chapter **Theatre**). There are experimental dance shows at the **CCCB** (see chapter **Museums**).

An officially promoted dance programme, **Dansa + a prop** ('Dance closer to you') features performances by well- and lesser known companies in a wide range of venues with a new schedule presented every three months. Another event, the annual **Dies de dansa**, offers a three-day dance programme of performances by Catalan, Spanish and international dance companies, mostly free-of-charge, in various architecturally significant locations, including Parc Güell and the MACBA. The 2001 dates are 14, 15 and 16 September. Information for both of the above is available at La Virreina.

L'Espai
Travessera de Gràcia 63 (93 414 31 33/www.cultura.gencat.es/ espai). FGC Gràcia/16, 17, 27, 31, 32, N4 bus. **Open** *Box office* 6.30-9.30pm Tue-Sat; 5-7pm Sun; closed Mon. Advance sales also from Servi-Caixa. *Performances* Sept-June usually 10pm Mon-Sat; 7pm Sun. **Tickets** 1,000-2,000ptas (subject to change). **Credit** AmEx, DC, MC, V. **Map** p320 C3.
This Catalan government show-case for the performing arts combines dance programmes (nearly always contemporary) with contemporary, experimental and (sometimes) other music.

From the **Dies de dansa**.

France and Cunningham in America. Since 1986 he has used his extensive training to develop a rich and very physical language, with philosophical content. For more information, see www.lanonima.com

Mal Pelo
The name means 'bad hair' implying a rebellious spirit, and its choreography combines abstract dance with a strong storyline. Formed in 1989 by two well-respected dancers, Pep Ramis and María Muñoz, this group has performed across Europe and the US. Mal Pelo published a book and organised an exhibit in 2000 called *L'Animal a L'Esquena* (Animal on the Shoulders) in celebration of its 12th anniversary. In May and June 2001, Mal Pelo will perform a duet of the same name at the Teatre Nacional.

Metros
Ramón Oller, an award-winning Catalan choreographer with a substantial theatrical background, created Metros in 1984. In 2001, the company will present *Pecado Pescado* (Sin Fish) and *Suite Rodrigo* (Rodrigo Suite) at Barcelona festivals and will also be touring Spain performing its latest work, *Frontera, el jardin de los gritos* (Frontier: The Garden of Cries).

Mudances
Director Angels Margarit has been gaining in stature as a choreographer throughout the last decade, producing highly structured, complex work. Mudances features two male dancers and four women, and has had many international successes, beginning in 1991 with *Atzavara*. Mudances will premiere *El Somriure del Laberint* (The Labyrinth's Smile) at the Grec festival in July 2001.

La Porta
This collective performs more or less monthly at the Sala Beckett or the Metrònom gallery (*see chapter* **Galleries**), and represents a team drawn from Barcelona's top young dancers and choreographers, as well as visiting foreign companies. In February 2001, La Porta will present *Tempo*, a series of one-minute performances, at the CCCB.

Contemporary dance groups

Other groups to look out for include **Búbulus**, **Companyia Andrés Corchero/Rosa Muñoz**, **Las Malqueridas**, **Nats Nus**, **Sol Picó** and **Transit**.

Gelabert-Azzopardi
Companyia de Dansa
Cesc Gelabert studied at the Cunningham School in New York and on his return became an influential figure in Catalan contemporary dance, helping develop a particular style concentrating more on form than emotion, and forming a crop of new dancers at La Fàbrica school. Lydia Azzopardi, previously at The Place in London, has contributed a sophisticated level of traditional dance knowledge. The group will perform its successful, *Useless Information Meets Boy*, 'dedicated to Buster Keaton', at the Teatre Nacional in early April 2001.

Lanònima Imperial
Companyia de Dansa
Juan Carlos García, who founded and choreographs Lanònima Imperial Companyia de Dansa, benefited from time with Galotta in

Film

Cine-literate Barcelona offers many spots to see English-language movies.

Movie-going is very much a part of life in Barcelona and the city has no shortage of cinemas, from charming, single-screen venues to monumental, old-fashioned pleasure palaces and spanking new multi-screens that serve up popcorn and pap in equal, industrial quantities. Film programming is similarly heterogeneous, catering for all ages and tastes. There is a flourishing Spanish film industry, plus an intuitive link with Latin American cinema and plenty of interest in other European work, as well as, of course, a huge market for the ubiquitous and inescapable McMovies that Hollywood shoves this way.

Most big foreign films are dubbed into Spanish, but subtitled films have enjoyed huge expansion over the last few years, so that over 30 screens now offer subtitled versions around town. This means that almost everything released can bee seen in at least one venue in its original language, including even the most shamelessly commercial blockbusters, for when you just have to hear Bruce, Arnold, Pierce or Russell in their mother tongue.

The biggest crowds still turn out for Hollywood movies, and films like *The Sixth Sense* and *Gladiator* top the league. However, Spanish and Catalan films are in no way shunned by Barcelona audiences, and one consequence of the current boom in cinema-going in Spain has been to give a significant new boost to domestic production. In 1999, almost 14 per cent of film tickets bought in Spain were for Spanish productions, up from a lowly 9.3 per cent in 1996.

Spain's best-known director is still Pedro Almodóvar, who made a dramatic return to form with *Todo Sobre Mi Madre* (*All About My Mother*), winning Best Director at the 1999 Cannes Festival, and Best Foreign Film at the 2000 Oscars. One of his strongest films, it was also shot in Barcelona, the first ever of his 17 features not to be filmed in Madrid. This could, maybe, signal a new chic for Barcelona as backdrop. Indeed, 2001 will see the release of *Gaudí Afternoon*, a social comedy based on a novel by Barbara Hershey, directed by Susan Seidelman (*Desperately Seeking Susan*) and starring Judy Davies, Marcia Gay Harden, Lili Taylor and Juliette Lewis.

Almodóvar apart, a lot of current Spanish cinema tends to consist either of period drama –

mostly shot in Portugal, which is both cheaper and more 'authentic' – or gritty contemporary urban drama, with a side-helping of unsophisticated comedy. Two young directors who have carved out a name for themselves with interesting and idiosyncratic film-making are Alex de la Iglesia and Julio Medem. De la Iglesia (*El Día de la Bestía, La Comunidad*) specialises in a violent, comic-book aesthetic mixed with semi-surreal humour. Medem (*Vacas, Tierra, Los Amantes del Círculo Polar*) is far more poetic, producing enchanting, almost dream-like films shot in his native Basque Country. His latest work, *Lucía y el Sexo*, is due to start shooting in 2001.

CATALAN CINEMA

In the first part of the 20th century, Barcelona itself was a major film centre. By the 1960s, though, Madrid exerted its influence more and more, and became the unquestioned centre of Spain's film industry. Today, the Catalan government offers its own subsidies to local productions, on condition that the film be shown in Catalan inside Catalonia. Two Catalan-language films shot in 2000 were *Pau i el seu germà*, the second feature by well-regarded young director Marc Recha and *Anita Amorosa*, by Ventura Pons, who churns out an annual diet of light social drama. Meanwhile a newly established offshoot of Filmax, Fantasy Factory, has chosen Barcelona as a base for producing American-style horror films in English. Its first bloody offering, *Faust*, by Brian Yuzma, was premiered at the 2000 Sitges film festival.

After years without any organisation to promote it as a place to make films, Barcelona has finally acquired a film office, Barcelona Plató (www.bcn.es/icub/filmoffice), whose task is to offer help for productions being filmed here. But be warned; it has a reputation for Soviet-style service and efficiency. In 1998 Catalan President Jordi Pujol threatened to impose quotas on the screening of Hollywood films if studios did not pay for a percentage of their work to be dubbed into Catalan. Distributors in Spain set up a howl, while Hollywood just shrugged its shoulders and made it clear that it had no intention of complying. The Generalitat was forced to back down, and it is still rare to find any films shown dubbed into Catalan.

GOING TO THE MOVIES

Films shown with subtitles are labelled *versió original*, and identified by the letters VO. A list of the main VO cinemas follows below.

Current programme details will be found in the *Guía del Ocio* and daily papers (*see p300*). Like most things in Barcelona, film-going tends to happen later than in northern countries, and the most popular sessions are those that start at around either 7.45-8.30pm or 10.30pm, when there are big queues at weekends. On Sundays, it's a good idea to arrive at the cinema in very good time, especially for the 8.30pm show. Real 'late' shows take place after midnight on Fridays and Saturdays.

All cinemas have a cheap day (*dia del espectador*), usually Monday or Wednesday. A few take phone bookings, and most sell advance tickets via Servi-Caixa (*see p196*) or by Internet (www.serviticket.com). However, getting a ticket at the door is rarely a problem except on weekend evenings. Generally, box offices are open 15 minutes before the first performance. All the cinemas listed here have air-conditioning. For information on film screenings for kids, *see chapter* **Children**.

VO cinemas

Casablanca

Passeig de Gràcia 115, Eixample (93 218 43 45). Metro Diagonal/22, 24, 28, N4 bus. **Tickets** 600ptas Mon; 800ptas Tue-Fri; 825ptas Sat, Sun, public holidays. **No credit cards. Map** p320 D4.
Two-screen art cinema mostly showing US and European non-mainstream films, currently unchallenged as the most uncomfortable cinema in the city.

Icària Yelmo Cineplex

C/Salvador Espriu 61, Vila Olímpica (93 221 75 85). Metro Ciutadella-Vila Olímpica/41, 71, 92, 36, N6, N8 bus. **Open** *Box office* 11am-11pm Mon-Thur, Sun; 11am-1am Fri, Sat. **Late shows** 12.50am Fri, Sat. **Tickets** 600ptas Mon, before 2.30 pm Tue-Sun; 800ptas after 2.30 pm Tue-Sun, late shows. **No credit cards. Map** p325 F7.
Part of an American-style mall just behind the Port Olímpic, this 15-screen cinema mostly shows American-style movies. Almost all of its films are also shown in English, with a propensity towards commercial, Hollywood productions, plus a few independent pictures. Weekend late shows (in all 15 screens) show recent-run blockbusters.

Maldà

C/del Pi 5, Barri Gòtic (93 317 85 29). Metro Liceu/14, 38, 59, N9, N12 bus. **Tickets** 550ptas Mon; 750ptas Tue-Fri; 800ptas Sat, Sun, public holidays. **No credit cards. Map** p326 B2.
A pokey old dive of a cinema housed in an 18th-century palace now fallen on hard times, the Maldà is nevertheless a much-loved city institution. Its

Verdi, the independents' favourite.

weekly double bill changes every Friday, and usually features recent releases or slightly older favourites. The entrance is up a staircase just inside the Galerías Maldà, up from the Plaça del Pi.

Méliès Cinemes

C/Villaroel 102, Eixample (93 451 00 51). Metro Urgell/14, 20, 38, 59, N12 bus. **Tickets** 400ptas Mon; 600ptas Tue-Sat, public holidays. **No credit cards. Map** p324 C5.
This two-screen Eixample cinema opened in 1997, filling a gap for popular classics not covered by the more arid, purist fare at the **Filmoteca**. The frequently changing programme often features up to eight films at any one time. In the summer there are weekly cycles of films, linked by director, actors or subject matter.

Renoir-Les Corts

C/Eugeni d´Ors 12 , Les Corts (93 490 55 10). Metro Les Corts/15, 43, 59, 70, 72, N3 bus. **Open** *Box office* 3.45-11pm Mon-Thur, Sun; 3.45-11pm, midnight-1am, Fri, Sat. **Tickets** 600ptas Mon; 800ptas Tue-Sun. **Late shows** from 12.30am Fri, Sat, public holidays. **No credit cards. Map** p319 A3.
Located a short walk from Les Corts Metro, this six-screen complex shows both Spanish and non-Spanish films exclusively in their original language. There are usually at least two films in English. Sound quality and comfort are of a high standard, and there are also unusually good facilities for disabled people, but it's a bit of slog to get back from, especially midweek, when the Metro shuts at 11pm.

Verdi

C/Verdi 32, Gràcia (93 237 05 16). Metro Fontana/22, 24, 28, N4 bus. **Late shows** 12.45am Fri, Sat. **Tickets** 600ptas Mon, Tue-Fri 1st 2 shows; 800ptas Tue-Fri; 825ptas Sat, Sun, public holidays. **Late shows** from 12.30am Fri, Sat. **Map** p320 D3.
A cinematic institution, the Verdi started out in 1992 with just three screens. In 1993 it added two more, and in 1995 the four-screen Verdi Park opened at the back of the same block. Drawing large numbers of cinema-goers, C/Verdi and the area around it is a lively place at night. The Verdi mostly shows contemporary international releases, particularly independent films at the art-house end of the mainstream. It also has a good reputation for

championing less familiar work, such as the new wave of Chinese and Japanese cinema. Wheelchair toilet access is available at Verdi Park only.
Branch: Verdi Park C/Torrijos 49, Gràcia (93 238 79 90).

The Filmoteca

Filmoteca de la Generalitat de Catalunya

Cinema Aquitania, Avda Sarrià 31-33, Eixample (93 410 75 90). Metro Hospital Clínic/27, 32, 63, 66, 68 bus. Closed Aug. **Tickets** 400ptas; 300ptas concessions; 5,000ptas block ticket for 20 films; 10,000ptas for 100 films. **Credit** *for block tickets only* MC, V. **Map** p320 C3.

Offering a virtual master class in the history of cinema, the Catalan government-funded Filmoteca shows overlapping, short cycles of films from the distant and recent past, grouped by theme, country, style or director. The programme changes daily, with most films appearing two or three times in the space of a couple of weeks. Sessions start at 5pm, 7.30pm and 10pm, and latecomers are not admitted. A fortnightly information leaflet is published, and a children's programme is shown at 5pm on Sundays.

Mega-screen movies

IMAX Port Vell

Moll d'Espanya, Port Vell (902 33 22 11). Metro Barceloneta/14, 36, 57, 59, 64, 157 bus. **Tickets** 1,000 ptas; 2 tickets 1,500 ptas. **Discount** BT. **Credit** MC, V. **Map** p324 D7.

Barcelona's IMAX is the white monolith squatting at one end of the port's Maremagnum complex. Opened in 1995, it offers a choice of mega-formats, including 3-D and towering OMNIMAX. The problem is that there are very few decent films made for these screens, so programmes rarely stray from a repetitive round of nature films and uninspiring documentaries. You're probably better off spending your time and money at the excellent Aquarium next door.

Events & festivals

Cine Ambigú

Sala Apolo, C/Nou de la Rambla 113, Paral.lel (93 441 40 01/www.retinas.org). Metro Paral.lel/20, 36, 57, 64, 91, 157, N-0, N6 bus. **Shows** 8.30pm, 10.30pm Tue. **Tickets** 500 or 800ptas (incl 1 drink). **No credit cards.** **Map** p324 C6.

This hip, happening dance venue screens independent films not given a general release in Spain; films are subtitled in Spanish, and often in English as well.

Mostra Internacional de Films de Dones de Barcelona (Women's Film Festival)

Venue: *Filmoteca de la Generalitat de Catalunya.* **Dates** first half of June. **Details:** Dracmàgic (93 216 00 04).

An exhibition (not a competition) of women's cinema, past and present. Directors also speak about their work in lively debates.

Festival Internacional de Cinema de Catalunya, Sitges

Information *Avda Josep Tarradellas 135, esc A, 3er 2a, 08029 Barcelona (93 419 36 35/fax 93 439 73 80).* **Dates** first half of Oct.

While not one of the big-league film festivals, the Sitges festival nevertheless has its charm. The 'Fantastic' element was dropped from the title a few years ago, as the festival tried to make itself more respectable and less nerdy, although fantasy is still where its heart is, with about half the programme made up of 'fantasy' films – sci-fi, horror, gore, or preferably a mixture of all three. The other half is defiantly mainstream. In 2000 the main prize in the fantasy section went to Chuck Parello's true story portrait of serial killer Ed Gein, while the general section, voted on by audiences, was won by Tim Robbins' *The Cradle Will Rock*. Tickets are usually snapped up quickly, so start queuing early or book ahead via Tel-entrada. A special train service runs back to Barcelona after the final session, at 1.30am.

Arts & Entertainment

Barcelona as backdrop: shooting winter on the cathedral steps.

Galleries

You never know what could pop up next in Barcelona's diffuse art scene.

The oddest thing about Barcelona's art scene is that it doesn't exist, at least not in the way you would expect in a city with such a captivating visual culture and vibrant streetlife. Unlike their counterparts in Williamsburg or Mitte, Barcelona artists are loath to hang out *ensemble*, tending to labour in standoffish solitude until opening night (preferably theirs) requires them to emerge from the cave. Visiting critics often remark that there are many strong artists in this city, but a lack of collective energy and engaged dialogue, which explains why those yearning for more (whether scene or sales) make a beeline for New York or Berlin. Successful artists internationally – including granddaddy Antoni Tàpies, the slightly senior generation of Antoni Muntadas, Francesc Torres, and Susana Solano, or the younger crop led by Eulàlia Valldosera, Antoni Abad, and Montserrat Soto – mostly make it on their own, with little help from local dealers or curators.

Although Barcelona was a minor hot spot of the early 20th-century avant-garde, with Picasso, Miró and Dalí the most luminous figures, the city's creative spirit was all but paralysed by the Franco regime. Following the city's triumphant reawakening in the 1980s and '90s, the Barcelona art world was convinced that simply by invoking the mood of the pre-Civil War years, and adding in a hefty dose of self-promotion, the city would be able to offer another generation of top-flight artists to the world. Dealers anxiously waited to cash in on the results. In the end the ploy seems to have worked, though only in part. While a new generation of artists have come to share in the benefits of globalised culture, participating in biennials and museum shows worldwide, the verve of Barcelona art-making has had little effect on the local art market. Amid the city's overall economic buoyancy the flaccidity of the market has cut in on many dealers' room for manoeuvre; even the most prestigious private galleries are losing their reputation as trendsetters, descending into caprice, conservatism, and at times plain bad taste.

The slack has been picked up by public institutions and private foundations (*see chapter* **Museums**), which together make up a formidable phalanx on the contemporary art front. In 2001, many of these institutions will join in on a citywide project for an art Triennial.

Galeria Joan Prats.
See p218.

The Triennial has come under fire by Barcelona artists for its aloof treatment of the local community and its eminently political-promotional motives, leading to the resignation of the first appointed director, although the promise of a generous programme of installations in the city's historic quarters is bound to make Barcelona an art destination in the summer of 2001.

There is no definitive guide to galleries and artistic activities. Listings appear in the *Guía de Ocio* and some papers, but are rarely comprehensive (*see chapter* **Directory**). It can be just as easy to go to a gallery district and do the rounds. All galleries are closed on Sundays and Mondays and for the whole of August. Show openings typically take place around 8pm midweek, and are open to anyone.

Commercial galleries

The Barri Gòtic and C/Consell de Cent are Barcelona's longest-established gallery areas, but in recent years new clusters of contemporary spaces have developed in La Ribera, near the Born market, and around MACBA in the Raval.

Barri Gòtic

Also of interest are **Galeria Segovia Isaacs**, C/Palla 8 (93 302 29 80), and **Met.Room**, C/Nou de Sant Francesc 4, a new space oriented towards architecture and urban themes.

Antonio de Barnola

C/Palau 4 (93 412 22 14). Metro Liceu, Jaume I/ 14, 38, 59, 91 bus. **Open** 5-9pm Tue-Fri; noon-2pm, 5-9pm Sat; closed Sun, Mon. Closed Aug. **No credit cards. Map** p326 B3.

This handsome space presents impeccable shows of Spanish contemporary artists. Regulars include Manuel Saiz (preparing an installation for early 2001), national photography prize-winner Humberto Rivas, and José Manuel Ballester, who applies his disturbing realism to modern architecture, one of Barnola's favoured themes.

Sala d'Art Artur Ramon

C/Palla 23 (93 302 59 70). Metro Liceu/14, 38, 59, 91 bus. **Open** 5-8pm Mon; 10am-1.30pm, 5-8pm Tue-Sat; closed Sun. Closed Sat July, Sept. Closed Aug. **No credit cards. Map** p326-7 B2-3.

The best of the local dealers in historic art, Artur Ramon puts together intelligent exhibits of Spanish and European painters and artisans, along with thematic shows (from Piranesi engravings to Catalan *Modernista* drawings), spending years digging through private collections.

Sala Parés

C/Petritxol 5 (93 318 70 08/www.salapares.com). Metro Liceu/14, 38, 59 bus. **Open** 10.30am-2pm, 4.30-8.30pm Mon-Sat; 11.30am-2pm Sun. Closed Sun June-Sept. Closed 3wks Aug. **Credit** MC, V. **Map** p326 A2.

The Sala Parés opened in 1840 and is owned by relatives of Catalan socialist leader Pasqual Maragall. It promoted *Modernista* painters (Rusiñol, Mir, Nonell) and it was here that Picasso had his first one-man painting show. The spacious renovated gallery specialises in figurative and historical painting. Across the street, the associated Galeria Trama offers work that is more contemporary.
Branch: Galeria Trama C/Petritxol 8, Barri Gòtic (93 317 48 77).

The Raval

Other venues worth a look are **Galeria Ferran Cano**, Plaça dels Àngels 4 (93 310 15 48), **Cotthem Gallery**, C/Dr Dou 15 (93 270 16 69), with an interest in American post-pop, and nearby **Alter Ego**, C/Dr Dou 11 (93 302 36 98).

Galeria dels Àngels

C/Àngels 16 (93 412 54 54). Metro Catalunya/bus all routes to Plaça Catalunya. **Open** noon-2pm, 5-6.30pm Mon; noon-2pm, 5-8.30pm Tue-Sat; closed Sun. Closed Aug. **No credit cards. Map** p326 A2.

This somewhat awkward space is used by collector Emilio Álvarez, who has begun to deal in the work of his preferred artists, including abstract painters Miquel Mont and Santi Moix, and the conceptual photography-based work of Juan Urrios.

Galeria Claramunt

C/Ferlandina 27 (93 441 88 17/ galeriaclaramunt@teleline.es). Metro Catalunya/bus all routes to Plaça Catalunya. **Open** 10.30am-2pm, 5-8.30pm Mon, Wed-Sat; closed Tue, Sun. **No credit cards. Map** p324 C5.

From her new gallery space directly facing the MACBA, Carmen Claramunt is doing a good job for the city in presenting new contemporary work in all media, including Barcelona-based Japanese artist Akané, and Catalans Joana Cera and Ester Partagás, who recently have been finding significant success in New York.

La Ribera & the Born

Also worth a look are **Tristan Barberà**, C/Fusina 11 (93 319 46 69), for limited-edition prints, and **Galeria 44**, C/Flassaders 44 (93 310 01 82), a space that works with many Barcelona cutting-edge artists.

Galeria Berini

Plaça Comercial 3 (93 310 54 43/www.berini.com). Metro Jaume I/14, 39, 51 bus. **Open** Sept-July 10.30am-2pm, 5-8.30pm Tue-Sat; closed Mon, Sun. Closed Sat July. Closed Aug. **Credit** MC, V. **Map** p327 C3.

This is one of few prestige Born galleries to have resisted the MACBA fanfare. Toni Berini has turned her back on her once-beloved painting to specialise in photography and new media. The fashion photography of Sarah Moon and the witty collages of Sara Huete will be shown in 2001.

Galeria Maeght

C/Montcada 25 (93 310 42 45/www.artbarcelona.es). Metro Jaume I/17, 19, 40, 45 bus. **Open** 10am-2pm, 4-8pm Tue-Sat; closed Sun, Mon. **Credit** AmEx, DC, MC, V. **Map** p327 C3.

The Paris-based Maeght gallery opened this handsome space in the 1970s. Occupying a Renaissance palace near the Picasso museum, with a lovely courtyard and staircase, it shows established Spanish and European painters and sculptors. In spite of its prestigious name, the Maeght struggles for relevance in the Barcelona scene.

Metrònom

C/Fusina 9 (93 268 42 98/metronomon@retemail.es). Metro Jaume I/39, 51 bus. **Open** 10am-2pm, 4.30-8.30pm Tue-Sat; closed Sun, Mon. Closed Aug. **Map** p320 C3.

Run by collector Rafael Tous, this was Barcelona's most lively art space in the 1980s. After a brief hiatus, it has now won back some of its original impetus, focusing on photography and multimedia installations. In 2001 there will be an exhibition by Basque artist Txomin Badiola, while Catalan conceptualist Francesc Torres has mysteriously announced a final career installation for late May-June. Metrònom organises annual festivals of experimental music (January) and dance (July) beneath its gorgeous belle époque glass ceiling; there is a video space upstairs.

The Eixample

Galeria Carles Taché

C/Consell de Cent 290 (93 487 88 36/ www.artbarcelona.es). Metro Passeig de Gràcia/ 7, 16, 17, 63, 67, 68 bus. **Open** *Oct-May* 10am-2pm, 4-8.30pm Tue-Sat; closed Sun, Mon. *June-July* 10am-2pm, 4-8.30pm Tue-Fri; closed Mon. Closed Aug. **No credit cards**. **Map** p324 D5.

Carles Taché has the good fortune to represent some of the most established senior Spanish painters, like Eduardo Arroyo and Miguel Angel Campano. He also shows Sean Scully, Jannis Kounellis, and Barcelona sculptor Jordi Colomer, set to exhibit in 2001.

Galeria Estrany-de la Mota.

Passatge Mercader 18 (93 215 70 51). FGC Provença/7, 16, 17, 20, 31, 43, 44, 67, 68 bus. **Open** *Sept-June* 10.30am-1.30pm, 4.30-8.30pm Tue-Sat; closed Mon, Sun. *July* 10.30am-1.30pm, 4.30-8.30pm Mon-Fri; closed Sat, Sun. Closed Aug. **No credit cards**. **Map** p320 D4.

This iron-columned basement gallery works well for Antoni Estrany's selection of Spanish neo-conceptualists, including Jorge Ribalta and the often-impervious Pep Agut. Other artists include Montserrat Soto, whose intelligent photographic montages are gaining her an international reputation. The gallery has extensive holdings in 20th-century art.

Galeria Joan Prats

Rambla Catalunya 54 (93 216 02 84/ www.galeriajoanprats.com). Metro Passeig de Gràcia/7, 16, 17, 22, 24, 28, 63, 67, 68 bus. **Open** 10.30am-1.30pm, 5-8.30pm Tue-Sat; closed Mon, Sun. Closed Sat in July. Closed Aug. **Credit** AmEx, V. **Map** p324 D4-5.

This gallery was born out of the 1920s friendship between Joan Prats, son of a fashionable hat maker, and Joan Miró. The only remnant of the original business is the name and the headgear motifs on the storefront – Prats' collection of his friend is now in the Fundació Miró. The interior was designed by Miró architect Sert. 'La Prats' represents senior Catalan painters like Hernández Pijuan, the quirky Perejaume (showing in April 2001), British photographer Hannah Collins, as well as Spain's highest profile emerging artist, Eulàlia Valldosera. Limited edition prints are sold at the nearby Joan Prats-Artgràfic space at C/Balmes 54 (93 488 13 98).

Kowasa Gallery

C/Mallorca 235 (93 487 35 88/www.kowasa.com). FGC Provença/7, 16, 17, 20, 31, 43, 44, 67, 68 bus. **Open** 11am-2pm, 5-8.30pm Tue-Sat; closed Mon, Sun. **Credit** AmEx, MC, V. **Map** p320 D4.

Kowasa is Barcelona's only gallery dedicated exclusively to photography. Located above the excellent specialised bookstore of the same name, Kowasa rep-

resents the work of Spaniards Martí Llorens, Ramon David and the estate of famed Civil War chronicler Agustí Centelles. The gallery has holdings of many international photographers, including Cartier-Bresson, Josef Sudek, Brett Weston and Ralph Gibson.

Gràcia & the Zona Alta

Galeria Alejandro Sales

C/Julián Romea 16 (93 415 20 54/ www.alejandrosales.com). FGC Gràcia/16, 17, 22, 24, 27, 28, 31, 32 bus. **Open** 11am-2pm, 5-8.30pm Tue-Sat; closed Mon, Sun. Closed Sat July, Sept. Closed Aug. **No credit cards**. **Map** p320 D3.

Alejandro Sales is one of the city's most successful young dealers. As well as hosting impeccable shows by international blue-chip artists, he represents Barcelona photographer Mabel Palacín and sculptor Alberto Peral (showing in 2001). In the 'Blackspace', young creators do smaller exhibitions with less commercial pressure.

Galeria H₂0

C/Verdi 152 (93 415 18 01). Metro Lesseps/22, 24, 25, 28, 31, 32, 39, 74 bus. **Open** 11am-1pm, 5.30-8pm Tue-Fri; 11am-1pm Sat; closed Mon, Sun. Closed Aug. **No credit cards**. **Map** p321 E2.

Industrial designers run this space on one floor of a small Gràcia house, showing international design, photography, architectural projects and contemporary art. Performance art and literary readings are often presented in the charming back garden.

The fringe scene

Present-day art activism in Barcelona is typified by a distinctly iconoclastic Catalan style. Some initiatives imitate 1970s models (art parties, performance art, open studios), while others are aligned with the city's squatter movement, now thrown headlong into anti-globalisation cyber-activism. Many independent galleries are run by collectives and work as mini cultural centres, offering concerts, film screenings and lecture series.

Other initiatives worth checking out are **Fundació La Lavanderia**, C/Ramallers 15 (93 412 06 99), a new space with shop included in a converted launderette near MACBA, and the window installations at **Schilling**, C/Ferran 23 (*see chapter* **Cafés & Bars**).

Established centres complementing the fringe are **Metrònom**, the **Mediateca** at Fundació La Caixa, and the **CCCB** (*see chapter* **Museums**) which hosts the Mostra de Video Independent and the Sonar music festival in June (*see p202*). The alternative scene – naturally enough – blends into frontier nightlife, where many of Barcelona's loose ends eventually meet. For more on all this, and more venues, *see chapter* **Nightlife**.

Net art BCN

Is Internet art from anywhere? The gurus of cyberspace cry ubiquity, leaving us to wonder whether the World Wide Web leaves any room for local identities in artistic expressions able to resist the globalisation of form – generalised copying, ignorance of tradition, technological naïvety – that has pervaded the art world. In Barcelona things are no different, although artists in the city have opted for a particularly sardonic approach to art available online. Rather than using the web as just another catalogue for art made in other media, in Barcelona Net art is a new genre with its own set of challenges and perils.

Net art receives considerable support from art centres and educational institutions. Permanent displays are offered by the Media Centre for Art and Design, based in nearby Sabadell (www.mecad.org), and Hangar, which also funds the production of Internet art (www.hangar.org).

www.evru.org

Projects can also be viewed through the websites of the Audiovisual Institute of the Pompeu Fabra University (www.iua.upf.es) and through the private channel of Connect-Arte (www.connect-arte.com). A good Spanish platform is at www.aleph-arts.org.

With his brother Narcís, Roc Parés runs the Galeria Virtual, specialising in producing art using virtual reality. Both independently and through the Pompeu Fabra University, where he teaches, he has created a variety of challenging online works, such as a reflection on the supposed internal geometry of the web. They can be found at www.aleph-arts.org/art/rpares/webometria.

Antoni Abad is an established sculptor who brings a sense of physical tension to his Net projects. The first was a metaphorical tug-of-war between Barcelona and Wellington, its antipode (Sisyphus, at www.iua.upf.es/abad/sisif). He has recently opted for humour to reflect on our dependency on the mouse (in *Z*, www.mecad.org/net_condition/z/) and on the Internet as a locus of sensual stimuli (read porn), which he dishes up liberally (*1,000,000*, www.aleph-arts.org/1.000.000/indexv.htm).

Jodi are Joan Heemskerk and Dirk Paesmans. This Dutch-Catalan project has created a paradigmatic style in Net art, based on the simulation of computer errors and breakdowns in information systems. In pieces like www.404.jodi.org, www.asdfg.jodi.org, www.sod.jodi.org, and plain old www.jodi.org, Jodi play with the potential hysteria and crisis lurking in the backwaters of the World Wide Web.

Zush has been chipping away at an awry vision of reality since the Sixties, developing what he has come to call the Evrugo Mental State. His art is heavily influenced by surrealism, and a kind of radical animistic humanism. His discovery of CD-Rom and now the Internet has allowed him to bring this freaky world alive. At www.evru.org.

Hangar

Passatge del Marquès de Santa Isabel 40, Poble Nou (tel/fax 93 308 40 41). Metro Poble Nou/40, 42 bus. **Open** *Information* 9am-2pm Mon-Fri; closed Sat, Sun. Closed Aug. **No credit cards.**
Besides being a multi-disciplinary production centre with studios and facilities for the production of video and Internet art, Hangar organises a regular "Showroom" of residents' work. Run by the Catalan Association of Visual Artists, Hangar also spearheads an open studio project for Poble Nou artists in June. Those interested in visiting the space should call ahead first.

Espai 22A

C/Margarit 70, Poble Sec (93 319 51 31).
Metro Paral.lel/20, 57, 64, 157 bus. **Open** 5-8pm Thur-Fri, 11am-2pm Sat; closed Sun-Wed. Closed Aug. **No credit cards. Map** p323 B6.

This small space in the unlikely upper reaches of Poble Sec offers some of the most experimental programming in Barcelona. Run by a group of artists and critics, in 2001 the gallery will organise a series on recent Mexican video, an exhibit of nomadic design, and concerts of improvised music.

Box 23

C/Ample 23 entresol Barri Gòtic (93 302 38 82).
Metro Drassanes/14, 36, 57, 59, 64, 157 bus. **Open** 5-8.30pm Wed-Sat; closed Mon,Tue, Sun. Closed Aug. **No credit cards. Map** p317 B4.
Brazilian Edgar Dávila started this Barri Gòtic gallery with the idea of challenging the conventional gallery space, as the curtain-lined walls attest. Shows include conceptual reflections on ephemeral architecture, such as the 2001 'Box Hotel', where a group of Canadian artists will turn the space into a live-in installation.

Gay & Lesbian

Barcelona's gay scene is bursting with bars, clubs and more, and then of course there's Sitges...

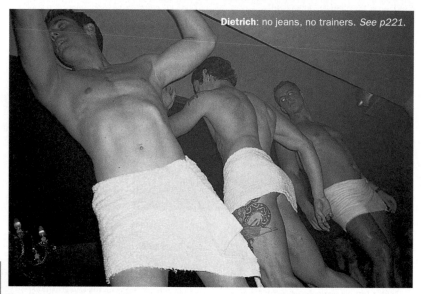

Dietrich: no jeans, no trainers. *See p221.*

Barcelona's gay scene, as well as the gay tourist count, keeps growing at a phenomenal rate. There are now more than 200 establishments catering specifically to the gay and lesbian market. These include gay bars, dance clubs, gymnasiums, restaurants, services and a variety of interesting shops. Moreover, this architecturally majestic port city also offers the visitor the beautiful beach town and gay mecca of **Sitges** a few kilometres away.

The city hosts a lively gay community that flexes its economic muscle even on the political scene. One area of the Eixample, roughly in the blocks around the junction of C/Muntaner and C/Consell de Cent (map p324 C5), has acquired such a concentration of gay venues that it has become known as the *Gaixample*, and is well on the way to becoming the Soho or West Hollywood of Barcelona. It comes as no surprise to learn that Barcelona is one of the few Spanish cities to recognise significant rights of gay domestic partners. At the same time, however, while it's true that attitudes are changing rapidly, it is still not uncommon to meet young *guapos* (good-looking men) who cannot invite

you back to their place because they live with their parents. So, be prepared.

The visitor should also keep in mind that some of the best places to have 'a gay old time' are not strictly gay. Nightlife here brings many different types of people together to *pasarlo bien* (have a good time). The gay scene, sometimes called *el ambiente* – which can equally be translated just as 'atmosphere' – is quite gender- and persuasion-mixed. Don't worry about dress codes – you can wear just about anything or almost nothing. Like most things in Spain, gay nightlife goes on long and late, so make the most of it; you can always rest on your return from your trip. If you like to stroll and/or you're an eye-candy addict, then this is your town: cruising and sightseeing combine fluidly.

A *Gay Barcelona* map and answers to questions are available in Sestienda and Zeus (*see p225*). In addition, there are several free city gay rags that you can pick up for more information about current events and updated listings. The sleek local magazine *Nois* is comprehensive, accurate, has a great map, and offers information on gay-owned and/or -friendly places throughout Catalonia. *Nois* also has a related website (www.revistanois.com). For information on gay organisations, *see p297*.

The biggest concentration of gay venues may be in the Eixample – making it easy to wander from one to the next – but even venues located in other areas are never too far from the centre of town. Naturally, spring and summer are the best times to visit the city, but don't underestimate the fun to be had at Carnaval in mid February (*see p206*).

Cafés & bars

It's worth mentioning here that, although **Cafè de L'Opera**, **Schilling**, the **Tèxtil Cafè** (*see chapter* **Cafés & Bars**) and the **Marsella** (*see p239*) are not gay per se, they are regularly frequented by gays and lesbians.

Acido Oxido

C/Joaquín Costa 61, Raval (93 412 09 39). Metro Universitat/24, 41, 55, 64, 91, 141, N6 bus. **Open** 10pm-2.30am daily, plus 5-10.30am Thur-Sun. **No credit cards. Map** p324 C5.

A trendy oblong industrial-style venue with a panoramic view of the main floor from the men's urinal. Tattoos and piercings are accessories for much of the clientele. They can be a little hard on women visitors. A different sort of place to have a drink before Metro.

Café de la Calle

C/Vic 11, Eixample (93 218 38 63). Metro Diagonal/16, 17, 22, 24, 28, N6, N9 bus. **Open** 6pm-2.30am Tue-Sun; closed Mon. **No credit cards. Map** p320 D3.

Where does one go for light-hearted, intimate conversation with someone special or in a small group? Café de la Calle is a well-lit, cosy and orderly environment where there's pleasant music and good sandwiches. Women like it just as much as men.

Café Dietrich

C/Consell de Cent 255, Eixample (93 451 77 07). Metro Universitat/bus all routes to Plaça Universitat. **Open** 10.30pm-2.30am Mon-Thur; 10.30pm-3am Fri, Sat; 6pm-2.30am Sun. **No credit cards. Map** p324 C5.

For a while now one of the most popular gay places in BCN. The elegant deco entrance leads to a small dancefloor and good music. Well-done short drag performances are put on at regular intervals each night for the good-looking crowd.

Caligula

C/Consell de Cent 257, Eixample (no phone). Metro Universitat/14, 54, 58, 64, 66, N3 bus. **Open** 8pm-3am Tue-Sun; closed Mon. **No credit cards. Map** p324 C5.

New café-bar theatre that acts as an escape valve when the pressure gets too much in the ever popular Café Dietrich located practically next door.

The Eagle

Passeig de Sant Joan 152, Eixample (93 207 58 56/ www.eaglespain.com). Metro Verdaguer/15, 55 bus. **Open** 10pm-2.30am Mon-Thur, Sun; 10pm-3am Fri, Sat. **No credit cards. Map** p325 E4.

On the rough side: the Eagle has a moustached and bearded clientele, and appropriately subdued lighting which enhances that rustic darkroom effect. The dress code stipulates jeans and leather, and some nights only underwear.

Medusa

C/Casanova 75, Eixample (93 454 53 63/ www.medusacafe.com). Metro Urgell/9, 50, 54, 56, 58, 64, 66, N1, N2, N3 bus. **Open** 11pm-3am Sun-Thur; 11pm-3.30am Fri, Sat. **No credit cards. Map** p324 C5.

One of the most popular of the recently opened nightspots for a youthful, trendy crowd, Medusa's minimalist decor leaves space for browsing and/or dancing (to some good grooves). It also has furnished corners and wall sofas for chatting or checking out the crowd. Boys have preference for entry on busy nights.

New Chaps

Avda Diagonal 365, Eixample (93 215 53 65). Metro Diagonal or Verdaguer/6, 15, 33, 34, N4, N6 bus. **Open** 9pm-3am daily. **No credit cards. Map** p320 D4.

The cowboy bar atmosphere still lingers, but times have changed. New Chaps mostly attracts the mature and manly, and regular theme nights as well as the downstairs darkroom draw an ample crowd.

Ouí Café

C/Consell de Cent 247, Eixample (93 531 03 38). Metro Universitat/14, 54, 58, 59, 64, 66, N3 bus. **Open** 5pm-2am Mon-Thur, Sun; 2.30pm-3am Fri, Sat. **No credit cards. Map** p324 C5.

Situated near several other popular bars, Ouí Café is a pleasant, stylish place in which to down the first cocktail of the night.

Punto BCN

C/Muntaner 63-65, Eixample (93 453 61 23/93 451 91 52). Metro Universitat/14, 54, 58, 59, 64, 66, N3 bus. **Open** 6pm-2am Mon-Thur, Sun; 6pm-2.30am Fri, Sat. **No credit cards. Map** p324 C5.

Punto BCN is one of few places to open in the early evening. Plenty of seating upstairs offers a full view of the entrance and the main bar, and the friendly air and pleasant decor lend themselves to the mingling of people of all sizes, shapes, ages and types.

Zeltas Club

C/Casanova 75, Eixample (93 454 19 02). Metro Urgell/9, 50, 54, 56, 58, 64, 66, N1, N2, N3 bus. **Open** 11pm-3am Wed-Sat; closed Mon, Tue, Sun. **No credit cards. Map** p324 C5.

The up-and-coming place in the *Gaixample* is very large and has a very friendly crowd. It is next door to, and has surpassed the popularity of, Medusa. Absolutely everybody is welcomed with a smile, even on the busiest nights.

Arts & Entertainment

The Sitges scene

Gay men from around the world agree that it's hard to beat the offerings of this little gay home from home. The Mediterranean climate and beautiful beaches seduce even the most city-hardened. A good deal of its enchanting old fishing village charm remains, but the night comes alive with song, dance and rowdy camaraderie. Sitges attracts many other people as well as the gay crowd, but tolerance makes it an easy place to relax and be yourself. Even if you don't stay overnight, Sitges is a must for the gay traveller to Barcelona.

The gay scene in Sitges is at its height from June to September, when gay males from just about every country converge here. However, perhaps the most emblematic event is Carnaval in the middle of February. If you've ever wanted to dress up in drag, this extravagant celebration is your chance to join in the parade of thousands on the climax night. Although most gay venues in the town close up at the end of summer, they reopen for this very special week. For more on Sitges, including how to get there, *see p263*.

ACCOMMODATION

If you really want to take advantage of the nightlife in Sitges you should stay overnight in one of its abundant hotels and *hostals*, most of which welcome gay clients. Just remember to book ahead. The **Hotel Romàntic** (C/Sant Isidre 33, 93 894 83 75/fax 93 894 81 67, rates 11,000-14,000ptas) and **La Renaixença** (C/Illa de Cuba 7, 93 894 83 75/fax 93 894 81 67, rates 11,000-14,000ptas) are two of Sitges' most popular places – the Romàntic is in a beautifully restored 19th-century house with palm-filled patio – managed by the same people and very gay-friendly. The Renaixença is not quite as architecturally or historically distinctive, but they both offer well-kept, attractive gardens and reasonable prices.

The **Hotel Liberty** (C/Illa de Cuba 35, 93 811 08 72/fax 93 894 16 62, rates 10,000-14,000ptas) is another option that's less attractive yet still popular, and has recently undergone a complete renovation. In the hills ten kilometres (six miles) inland from Sitges, **La Masia Casanova** (Passatge Casanova 8, 93 818 80 58, rates 15,000ptas) offers luxury suites with all the trimmings, a pool, a bar and lots of tranquillity. Book well in advance for the minimum three-day stay. If

you're at a loss, RAS (607 14 94 51/fax 93 894 42 72/ www.raservice.com), formed by Peter and Rico, is a very professional agency that can alleviate all your worries about finding your choice of accommodation in Sitges or Barcelona.

BARS

There is no lack of bars in Sitges, whatever your style. **Trailer** is still about the only one that charges admission, and you can forget about using your credit cards in any of them. Crowds move around, and venues change hands and names from season to season, so it's best to refer to the free *Gay Maps* of Barcelona and Sitges (available from **Sestienda** or **Zeus**, *see p225*) for orientation. The year-round pub **Bar 7** (C/Nou 7, no phone) makes an interesting stop early in the evening. **Bourbons** (C/Sant Bonaventura 9, 93 894 33 47) and **El Horno** (C/Juan Tarrida 6, 93 894 09 09) are mature men's hangouts that could be included as stopping-off points, especially in high season, and the two-floored **Mediterraneo** (C/Sant Bonaventura 6, no phone) is still an international happening spot; an appearance here is obligatory before going on to Trailer. Go to **Parrot's Pub** (Plaça de l'Industria, no phone) for a cool drink on the streetside terrace after a hard day at the beach. **Organic** (C/Bonaire 15, no phone) is a very popular all-gay disco that almost outdoes the long-running **Trailer** (C/Angel Vidal 36, no phone). However, absolutely everybody generally ends up here. The international DJs and scene are hot and heavy until its closing time of 5am.

RESTAURANTS

Sitges is loaded with places to have a good meal. Moreover, the number of gay-owned and/or gay-friendly restaurants has more than tripled recently. The garden environment at **Flamboyant** C/Pau Barrabeitg 16 (93 894 58 11, set menu 2,500ptas) still appeals to the gay clientele. It would be difficult to be displeased, equally, with a meal at **El Trull** (Passeig Mossèn Fèlix Clarà 3, 93 894 47 05, closed Wed, average 3,500ptas), the more apparently traditional **Can Pagés** (C/Sant Pere 24-26, 93 894 11 95, closed Mon, average 3,500ptas) or **Sucre Salé** (C/Sant Pau 39, 93 894 23 02, average 3,000ptas).

Clubs

As with bars in general, there are several locales that are not strictly gay but which have a big and established gay following, especially among the young and hip, especially **La Terrrazza**, **Discothèque**, **Bar Six** and **Woman Caballero** (*for all, see chapter* **Nightlife**).

Arena Madre

C/Balmes 32, Eixample (no phone). Metro Passeig de Gracia or Universitat/7, 16, 17, N1, N2 bus. **Open** midnight-5am Tue-Sun. **Admission** 700ptas Sun-Fri (incl beer or soft drink); 1,300ptas Sat (any drink incl). **No credit cards. Map** p324 D5.

In the tradition of Martins and Metro, this large spacious dancefloor with good lighting and special effects, and pounding house and garage sounds, attracts a younger crowd with energy to burn.

Arena VIP

Gran Via de les Corts Catalanes 593, Eixample (93 487 83 42). Metro Universitat/bus all routes to Plaça Universitat. **Open** midnight-5am Fri, Sat. **Admission** 700ptas Fri (incl beer or soft drink); 1,300ptas Sat (any drink). **No credit cards. Map** p324 D5.

Even the latest hotspots haven't diminished this club's drawing power. A cross-section of gays, lesbians and straights make it an interesting place to move the feet. Great new and not-so-new dance music on tap.

Martins

Passeig de Gracia 130, Gràcia (93 218 71 67) Metro Diagonal/22, 24, 28, N4, N6 bus. **Open** midnight-5am daily. **Admission** 1,200ptas (incl one drink). **Credit** MC, V. **Map** p320 D3-4.

Martins is now experiencing a comeback after many years in waiting. Three floors give plenty of room to roam about, and the music gets you dancing. New Chaps and Eagle empty into here as they close, especially on co-operative theme nights.

Metro

C/Sepúlveda 185, Eixample (93 323 52 27). Metro Universitat/24, 41, 55, 64, 91, 141, N6

Bar Six.

bus. **Open** midnight-5am Mon-Thur, Sun; midnight-6am Fri, Sat. **Admission** 1,500ptas (incl one drink). **Credit** MC, V. **Map** p324 C5.

Surprisingly, this club is yet to lose its hold on BCN gay nightlife. It's unbearably packed at the weekend, but the punters keep coming back for more. Women are welcome, but they almost always have to pay. There are regular mid-week party nights. The backroom can be an entertaining labyrinth, but take care with valuables.

Salvation

Ronda Sant Pere 19-21, Eixample (93 318 06 86/www.matineegroup.com). Metro Urquinaona/16, 17, 18, 19, 40, 45 bus. **Open** midnight-5am daily. **Admission** 1,500ptas. **No credit cards. Map** p324 D5.

Two large dancefloors, decent music and handsome, muscular, barebacked personnel have made this a very popular night stop on the gay circuit. If the door men don't select you for immediate entry, don't push it. They can get pushy, too.

Restaurants

Castro

C/Casanova 85, Eixample (93 323 67 84). Metro Universitat/bus all routes to Plaça Catalunya. **Open** 1-4pm, 9pm-midnight Mon-Fri; 9pm-midnight Sat; closed Sun. **Average** 3,500ptas. **Set menu** 1,200ptas. **Credit** DC, MC, V. **Map** p320 C4.

A new, modern mix of industrial and elegant decor keeps the eye entertained while you enjoy one of the best Mediterranean-style menus available in gay Barcelona, with truly excellent food. The place is very popular, so book ahead.

Ovlas

C/Portaferrissa 25, Barri Gòtic (93 412 38 36). Metro Plaça Catalunya/14, 16, 17, 38, 41, 59, N6, N9 bus. **Open** 9.30am-8.30pm Mon-Sat; closed Sun. **Set menu** 1,200-1,500ptas. **Credit** AmEx, MC, V. **Map** p326 B2.

A new if rather antique-style accompaniment to the Ovlas men's store next door, serving varied Italian dishes, pastas and salads.

Roma

C/Alfons XII 39-41, Gràcia (93 201 35 13). Metro Fontana/14, 16, 17, 24, 25, 30, 31, 58, 64 bus. **Open** 8.30-1am Mon-Fri; 7pm-1am Sat; closed Sun. **Average** 3,500-4,000ptas. **Set lunch** 1,250ptas. **Set dinner** 3,300ptas. **Credit** AmEx, MC, V. **Map** p320 D3.

This long-time uptown favourite continues to serve a more-than-decent Mediterranean-style meal at a reasonable price. You can't help but be pleased with the congenial staff, warm setting and the after-dinner cocktails at its well-populated bar.

Cabaret-restaurants

In all three of these gilded, lushly decorated venues dining is really secondary to the highly professional (each in its own way) and very entertaining drag shows on offer. Opinions vary, but word is out that one eats better in Miranda and Diva. Try them all and judge for yourself.

Café Miranda

C/Casanova 30, Eïxample (93 453 52 49). Metro Universitat/bus all routes to Plaça Catalunya. **Open** 9pm-1am daily. **Average** 4,000ptas. **Credit** MC, V. **Map** p324 C5.

La Diva

C/Diputació 172, Eixample (93 454 63 98/ www.ladivagay.com). Metro Universitat/bus all routes to Plaça Catalunya. **Open** 1-3.30pm, 9pm-midnight Tue-Fri; 9pm-midnight Sat, Sun; closed Mon. **Average** 4,500ptas. **Set lunch** 1,275ptas. **Credit** MC, V. **Map** p324 C5.

Eterna

C/Casanova 42, Eixample (93 453 17 86). Metro Universitat/bus all routes to Plaça Catalunya. **Open** 1-3.30pm, 9.30pm-midnight Mon-Fri; 9.30pm-midnight Sat, Sun. **Average** 4,900ptas. **Set lunch** 975ptas. **Credit** DC, MC, V. **Map** p324 C5. **Branch**: Eterna, C/Consell de Cent 127-129, Eixample (93 424 25 26).

Gay services

Accommodation

Hostal Qué Tal

C/Mallorca 290, Eixample (93 459 23 66). Metro Passeig de Gracia, Verdaguer/6, 15, 33, 34, 45, N4, N6 bus. **Rates** 4,800ptas single; 7,200-9,500ptas double. **No credit cards. Map** p320 D4.
What a nice place to spend the night. The 'Hostal How Are You' is exceptionally clean, with very attractive simple decor and fantastically helpful staff. This combination will make your stay comfortable and memorable, and it's close to everything, so you won't get lost on the way home. Book well in advance as it is an extremely popular place. **Hotel services** *Lift. Multilingual staff. Telephone. TV.*

Hotel California

C/Rauric 14, Barri Gòtic (93 317 77 66/fax 93 317 54 74). Metro Liceu/14, 18, 38, 59, N6, N9 bus. **Rates** 6,000ptas single; 9,500ptas double. **Credit** AmEx, MC, V. **Map** p327 A3.
California is very comfortable and centrally located, in the heart of the old city. All 31 rooms have individual bathrooms; there's no bar, but breakfast and drinks can be had.
Hotel services *Air-conditioning. Laundry. Multilingual staff. Safe.* **Room services** *Bathroom. Air-conditioning. Heater. Room service (24hrs). Telephone. TV.*

Bookshops

Antinous

C/Josep Anselm Clavé 6, Barri Gòtic (93 301 90 70/ www.antinouslibros.com). Metro Drassanes/14, 18, 36, 38, 57, 59, 64 bus. **Open** 11am-2pm; 5-9pm Mon-Fri; noon-2pm, 5-9pm Sat; closed Sun. **Credit** AmEx, DC, MC, V. **Map** p327 A4.
Bright natural lighting and ample space make this a great place to browse and cruise or to have some refreshment in the cute little café at the back. It stocks a wide range of gay literature (books, magazines and the press) and announcements of cultural events of interest to the gay community abound.

Complices

C/Cervantes 2, Barri Gòtic (93 412 72 83/ www.personal1.ideo.is/complices). Metro Jaume 1/17, 19, 40, 45 bus. **Open** 10.30am-8.30pm Mon-Fri; noon-8.30pm Sat; closed Sun. **Credit** MC, V. **Map** p327 B3.
Complices was Barcelona's first gay bookshop, run by a largely female group. Although its stock in English is limited, it does have a very wide selection of materials in Catalan and Spanish.

Saunas

There are at least eight gay saunas in the city; here you have the most popular. All have showers, open bar, porno lounge and cubicles.

Complices: tomes for homes.

Girls' night out at the **Café Bar Aire.**

You get a locker, towel and shower sandals, and everything is charged to your locker/key number. **Casanova, Thermas** (lots of rent boys) and **Condal** are the most visited, especially after hours and on their 'Client's (Discount) Day'.

Sauna Casanova

C/Casanova 57, Eixample (93 323 78 60). Metro Urgell/9, 45, 56, 58, 64, 66, N1, N2, N3 bus. **Open** 24hrs daily. **Admission** 1,700ptas Mon, Wed, Fri-Sun; 1,300ptas Tue, Thur. **Credit** MC, V. **Map** p324 C5.

Sauna Condal

C/Espolsa Sacs 1, Barri Gòtic (93 301 96 80). Metro Urquinaona/16, 17, 18, 19, 40, 45 bus, and all nightbuses to Plaça Catalunya. **Open** 11am-5am Mon-Thur, 11am Fri-5am Sun. **Admission** 1,300ptas Mon, Wed; 1,700ptas Tue, Thur-Sun. **Credit** MC, V. **Map** p326 B2.

Galilea

C/Calabria 59, Eixample (93 426 79 05). Metro Rocafort/9, 27, 50, 56, 109, 127, N1, N2 bus. **Open** noon-midnight daily. **Admission** 1,400ptas Mon, Tue, Fri-Sun; 1,000ptas Wed, Thur; 800ptas from noon-2pm Mon-Fri; 900ptas concessions. **Credit** MC, V. **Map** p323 B5.

Thermas

C/Diputació 46, Eixample (93 325 93 46). Metro Rocafort/9, 27, 50, 56, 109, 127, N1, N2 bus. **Open** noon-2am Mon-Thur; noon Fri-2am Mon. **Admission** (incl lunch) 1,700ptas. **Credit** AmEx, DC, MC, V. **Map** p323 B5.

Sex shops

Two exclusively gay sex shops with friendly and helpful staff. Both produce free gay maps of Barcelona and Sitges, updated annually.

Sestienda

C/Rauric 11, Barri Gòtic (93 318 86 76/ www.sestienda.com). Metro Liceu/14, 16, 38, 59, N6, N9 bus. **Open** 10am-8.30pm Mon-Sat; closed Sun. **Credit** MC, V. **Map** p327 A3.

Zeus

C/Riera Alta 20, Raval (93 442 97 95). Metro San Antoni/24, 64 bus. **Open** 10am-9pm Mon-Sat; closed Sun. **Credit** V. **Map** p324 C5.

Lesbian Barcelona

The lesbian lifestyle doesn't stand out as much in Barcelona as the gay male's, but don't be fooled by appearances. Women may always have been more discreet, but they aren't hiding in the closet. Gay women's idea of social life is less tied to the bar scene: instead, there are weekly and monthly events and women-only dances, organised by a whole variety of collectives and groups: **Complices** – as much a gay women's as a men's bookshop – and **Ca La Dona** (*see p297*) are good places to get information. Of other gay venues, **Café de la Calle** is almost as popular with lesbians as with gay men (see *p221*). Films on lesbian themes are enthusiastically received at the Women's Film Festival in June (*see p215*).

Cafés, bars, restaurants, clubs

Bahia

C/Sèneca 12, Gràcia (no phone). Metro Diagonal/6, 7, 15, 22, 24, 27, 28, 33, 34, N4, N6 bus. **Open** 10pm-3am daily; plus 6-9am Fri, Sat. **No credit cards**. **Map** p320 D3.
Pleasant laid-back Gothic bar with a friendly ambience and good music. It is especially popular as a place to go with a group of friends.

Café Bar Aire

C/Valencia 236, Eixample (93 451 58 12). Metro Passeig de Gracia/7, 16, 17, 54, 58, 64, 66, N3 bus. **Open** 10pm-3am Tue-Sun; closed Mon. **No credit cards**. **Map** p320 C4.
The colourful decor and light environment put you at your ease, and there are lots of intimate tables for chatting up. Gay men are not turned away at the door.

Free Girls

C/Marià Cubí 8, Zona Alta (93 217 22 96). FGC Muntaner/58, 64, N8 bus. **Open** 10pm-5am Fri, Sat. **No credit cards**. **Map** p320 D3.
Once known as Imagine, this is an interesting little '70s-style dance bar that attracts a younger set.

La Rosa

C/Brusi 39, Zona Alta (93 414 61 66). FGC Sant Gervasi/16, 17, 27, 58, 64, 127, N8 bus. **Open** 10pm-3am Fri, Sat. **No credit cards**. **Map** p320 C2.
A little on the tacky side, but this veteran bar still draws a crowd of mature women at weekends.

La Singular

C/Francisco Giner 50, Gràcia (93 237 50 98). Metro Diagonal/22, 24, 28, N4, N6 bus. **Open** 1-4pm, 8pm-midnight Mon, Fri; 1-4pm, 8pm-1am Sat; closed Sun. Closed end Aug-end Sept. **Average** 2,000ptas. **Set lunch** 1,100ptas. **Credit** MC, V. **Map** p320 D3.
This place offers very good tapas and home-cooked meals for your pleasure, and the women who run it are very friendly and attentive.

Music: Classical & Opera

Barcelona is ablast with music as it celebrates a refurbished opera house and an all new, state-of-the-art concert hall.

Through a combination of coincidence and urban planning, the year 2000 marked something of a renaissance in the city's musical fortunes. Following the fire that destroyed the **Liceu** opera house in 1994, the newly rebuilt Liceu was officially opened in October 1999, and enjoyed a sell-out first season. The hi-tech municipal concert hall, **L'Auditori**, also celebrated its first full year, with a dizzying number of concerts in a dazzling range of genres. And not to be outdone, the beautiful **Palau de la Música**, which up until the arrival of the Auditori in 1999 was Barcelona's only sizeable concert hall, began major renovations to add a 600-seat subterranean chamber hall and display its modernist charms to better effect.

Whether it's symphonies, string quartets, synthesisers or *sardanas* you're after, there is always something on offer. The main musical calendar mimics the school calendar, stretching from September to June. During this period, the city orchestra, the **OBC**, offers weekly concerts at the Auditori, mostly playing a repertoire of orchestral classics. As well as the OBC, the Auditori also plays host to cycles of concerts by independent promoters, as does the Palau. Of these, Ibercamera at the luxury end of the market provides a regular supply of international big-name orchestras, ensembles and soloists, while Promoconcert is more modest in its talent and its ticketing. Between the two is Euroconcert, which follows its own musical score and manages to be both accessible and eclectic.

In general Catalan audiences know what they like, like what they know, and like to let the orchestra know when they like it. Not so much undiscerning as easy to please, they prefer their composers to be mostly male, preferably Germanic and entirely dead, and this is generally what they get. There is, however, also support for Spanish and Catalan composers and it is not unusual for a contemporary work to be slipped in beside a couple of classics. Xavier Montsalvatge and Frederic Mompou are two of the more highly considered representatives of the old guard, while of the current generation,

Albert Guinovart, Joan Guinjoan and Salvador Brotons enjoy healthy reputations. Independent of the mainstream, Carles Santos composes, stages and performs in his own idiosyncratic creations of manic, surreal works that blur the lines between opera, performance and theatre.

While the majority of concerts stick to more traditional repertoire, there are also various cycles of contemporary music, both 'conventional' and experimental, which attract a small but enthusiastic following.

Over the summer the focus of activity moves. Various public art galleries and museums hold small, outdoor evening concerts in their courtyards or on their roofs, including the Maritime Museum, the Barbier-Mueller Museum and La Pedrera. There are also weekly concerts in several of the city's parks (*see chapter* **By Season**). The more serious musical activity, though, follows its audience and heads up the coast, to major international festivals in the towns of Perelada, Cadaques and Toroella De Montgrí.

INFORMATION

Apart from the venues themselves, the most thorough source of information is the monthly leaflet *Informatiu Musical*, detailing concerts across all genres. You can pick a copy up at tourist offices, record shops or at the cultural information centre in the **Palau de la Virreina** (*see p304*), or at the Generalitat's bookshop almost opposite. The weekly entertainment guide *La Guía del Ocio*, available from news kiosks, has a music section. Both *El País* and *La Vanguardia* carry information for forthcoming concerts in their classified ads sections, and on most days also publish details for that day's more important concerts. The Ajuntament's web page (www.bcn.es) also provides full listings of events.

BUYING TICKETS

Tickets for most major venues can be bought by phone, over the Internet (www.serviticket.com, or check venue listing), or in person via **Tel-Entrada**, or at La Caixa's **Servi-Caixa** machines (*see p196*).

Venues

L'Auditori

C/Lepant 150, Eixample (93 247 93 00/
www.auditori.com). Metro Marina/6, 7, 10, 56, 62,
N2, N3 bus. **Open** *Information* 8am-3pm, 4-6pm
Mon-Fri. *Box office* 10am-9pm daily. *Performance*
from 8pm daily, plus 11am-1pm Sun. **Tickets** prices
vary. **Discounts** (OBC concerts) BC. **Credit** MC, V.
Map p325 F5.

One of the raisons d'être of the new auditorium was
to give the city a modern, world-class music venue,
and at the same time provide a permanent home for
the city's symphony orchestra, the OBC. Rafael
Moneo's 1999 concert hall is worlds away from the
modernist exuberance of the Palau de la Música.
Unprepossessing to the point of soulless on the
outside, the main, 2,300-seat auditorium, the Sala
Simfónica, manages to be both minimalist and
warmly welcoming, with excellent, hi-tech acoustics,
though the public foyer areas are less friendly. It is
also more populist – if you don't mind or don't notice
acoustic imbalance and like to see the conductor's
face, there are cheaper seats in the wings above the
orchestra's heads, although inevitably these can be
irritatingly distracting for the rest of the audience.
A smaller hall, the Sala Polivalent, literally the All
Purpose Room, with 400 seats, is used for less popular concerts, although it does not match the main
hall for either comfort or acoustics. As well as classical music, the Auditori also plays host to jazz and
world music concerts, as well as the occasional
awards ceremony, including the 1999 Goyas (the
Spanish equivalent to the Oscars).The Metro is only
a few minutes walk away, and a special bus service
runs to Plaça Catalunya after concerts.

Auditori Winterthur

Auditori de l'Illa, Avda. Diagonal 547, Les Corts-
Sants (93 290 10 90/www.winterthur.es). Metro
Maria Cristina/6, 7, 33, 34, 63, 66, 67, 68, N12
bus. **Open** *Information* 8.30am-4.30pm Mon-Fri;
closed Sat, Sun. **Tickets** & **credit** vary according
to production. **Map** p319 B3.

An intimate, modern venue in the unlikely surrounds of the Illa shopping centre that hosts a dozen
or so chamber concerts, including an annual
Schubert cycle and a series of song recitals.

Gran Teatre del Liceu

La Rambla 51-59, Rambla (93 485 99 00/
www.liceubarcelona.com). Metro Liceu/14, 38, 51,
91, N9, N12 bus. **Open** *Information* 9am-2pm,
4-7pm Mon-Fri; (summer) 8am-3pm Mon-Fri; closed
Sat, Sun. **Tickets** *Box office* 10am-1pm, 3-7pm Mon-
Fri. **Discount** 30% 2hrs before performance
concessions. **Credit** MC, V. **Map** p327 A3.

Though it might be heretical to say so, the welder's
spark that burnt the original Liceu down in 1994
was a blessing in disguise. Plans for expansion had
already been afoot for some time before that fateful
morning, and the fire provided a useful excuse to
enlarge the new building. In place of a creaking,

The revamped **Gran Teatre del Liceu**.

dusty, wooden wreck, the theatre is now a spanking new building of three times the size, equipped
with all the latest technology. Lovers of the original will be pleased to know that the auditorium has
been recreated in all its red velvet and gold-leaf
glory, for that authentic, luxuriant 19th-century
opera feel. A large subterranean foyer has been
added, which is used for talks, late-night recitals,
children's puppet shows and other musical activity
linked to the main programme.

One advantage of the new 2,340 seat opera house
is that it can now join up with its counterparts
elsewhere in Europe to bring exciting and innovative co-productions to a city that was long used
to somewhat duller, more complacent work.
Consequently, season ticket sales have soared from
around 7,000 before the fire to around 18,000, making it sometimes difficult to get hold of tickets.
Several of the productions feature a couple of
reduced-priced nights sung by understudies.

Palau de la Música Catalana

C/Sant Francesc de Paula 2, Eixample (93 295 72
00/www.palaumusica.org). Metro Urquinaona/17,
19, 40, 45, N8 bus. **Open** *Box office* 10am-9pm
Mon-Sat; 1hr before concert Sun (concert days only);
Advance sales box office, phone & Servi-Caixa
or Caixa de Catalunya. **Tickets** prices vary.
Credit MC, V. **Map** p326 B-C2.

The Palau de la Música has never been an ideal concert hall musically, but visually it is unbeatable,
arousing loyalty and affection from regular performers and concert-goers alike. Commissioned and
paid for by the Orfeó Català (*see p228*) in 1908,
Domènech i Montaner's *Modernista* masterpiece has
long been seen as the spiritual home of Catalan
music. The busts of Beethoven and local composer
Anselm Clavé look out over the audience, with the
Valkyries' chariots soaring above them, while performers are encircled by a ring of musical muses.
The effusive detail and florid decoration both complement and are complemented by music in performance, and while it is possible to visit on a guided
tour (*see p82*), the experience is just not the same.
Although it was conceived with very populist intentions, the narrow shape of the auditorium means
the majority of seats are rather distant from the
stage. Try and avoid the rear half of the upper

Arts & Entertainment

circle (here called the 2nd floor) if you possibly can. Acoustically, the hall is somewhat flawed, although since the renovation of 1989 extraneous street sounds are at least muffled, if not always entirely absent. A further renovation is currently under way to add a 600-seat hall for chamber music.

Sala Cultural de la Caja de Madrid
Plaça Catalunya 9, Rambla (93 301 44 94). Metro Plaça Catalunya/bus all routes to Plaça Catalunya. **Open** *Information* 6-9pm Mon; 11am-1pm, 6-9pm Tue-Sat; closed Sun. **Tickets** prices vary. **No credit cards. Map** p326 B1.
This small, idiosyncratic space hosts a regular programme of recitals and chamber pieces by predominantly local musicians, with the occasional visiting soloist. Concerts take place almost every night of the week, and many of them are free. Seats are either uncomfortable, Franco-era cinema style or folding chairs at 45° to the stage, often behind pillars.

CHURCHES
Churches around Barcelona, particularly in the old town, hold concerts from time to time. The most beautiful is probably Santa Maria del Mar (*see p83*), whose tall, ghostly interior exemplifies the gothic intertwining of music, light and spirituality. Concerts include everything from Renaissance music to gospel singers. Other venues include the main cathedral, Santa Maria del Pi, Sant Felip Neri, Santa Anna and the Monastery in Pedralbes. Also, in May, keep an eye out for the Festival de Música Antiga (*see p199*) in which concerts of early music are held in different locations of the old city.

Orchestras & ensembles

La Capella Reial de Catalunya, Le Concert des Nations, Hespèrion XX
Widely respected early music specialist Jordi Savall is the driving force behind all three of these ensembles, each of which has a strong international reputation and an envious discography of prize-winning recordings. La Capella Reial specialises in Catalan and Spanish Renaissance and baroque music, vocal or instrumental, Le Concert des Nations is a period-instrument ensemble playing orchestral and symphonic work from 1600 to 1850, while Hespèrion XX limits itself to pre-1800 (*see also* **Festival de Música Antiga,** *p199*).

Orfeó Català
Information *see* **Palau de la Música,** *p227.*
The Orfeó Català is a choral society that had its origins in the patriotic and social movements at the end of the 19th century, and was just one of over 150 choral groups that sprang up in Catalonia at this time. It was sufficiently successful to be able to commission the Palau de la Música, with which it is inseparably identified. Although no longer as pre-

The stunning **Palau de la Música Catalana.**

eminent as they once were, the Orfeó still offers around 25 performances a year, giving *a cappella* concerts as well as providing a choir for the OBC and other Catalan orchestras when necessary. The Orfeó Català is largely non-professional, though it includes a small professional nucleus, the Cor de Cambra del Palau de la Música, which gives around 50 performances a year.

Orquestra Simfònica de Barcelona i Nacional de Catalunya (OBC)
C/Lepant 150, Eixample (93 247 93 00/www.obc.es). Metro Marina/6, 10, 62 bus. **Open** 9am-3pm, 4-6pm Mon-Fri; closed Sat, Sun. **Map** p325 F5.
Under the baton of American conductor Lawrence Foster, and principal guest conductor Franz-Paul Decker, the orchestra performs weekly concerts on Friday and Saturday evenings and Sunday mornings from October to May. The OBC also hosts an annual Mozart festival in September, under the direction of Christopher Hogwood. Despite regular appearances by guest conductors and soloists, the orchestra is yet to develop a strong reputation beyond Catalonia. It is more of a steady workhorse, delivering the classics with confidence, if without great flair. At the same time it provides an occasional outlet for young Catalan composers, with first performances during the 2000/2001 season of works by Salvador Brotons, Francesc Taverna-Bech, Joan Amargós and Pere Puértolas.

Orquestra Simfònica i Cor del Gran Teatre del Liceu
Information *see* **Gran Teatre del Liceu,** *p227.*
The Liceu season runs from October to July, offering around a dozen opera, mostly taken from the classics, but also including a couple of slightly risqué productions. In 2000 a staging of Wagner's

Lohengrin set in a school room managed to shock the stalwarts. To add to the excitement, the 2000/2001 season opened with the worldwide premiere of *D.Q., Don Quijote* in Barcelona by José Luis Turina, but staged by hi-tech performance troupe La Fura del Baus.

This current season is devoted to old favourites like Wagner, Mozart, Strauss, Rossini et al, with productions of Verdi's *Aïda*, Saint-Saëns' charming *Samson et Dalila* and Handel's rarely heard *Giulio Cesare* planned for spring/summer 2001, as well as Benjamin Britten's *Billy Budd* in April to commemorate the 25th anniversary of the composer's death.

In addition to opera, there are also a handful of concert performances by the resident orchestra and several recitals by major international soloists, with Catalan diva Montserrat Caballé usually making an annual appearance. There are also a couple of ballets by both national and international companies every year, with the Zurich Ballet and the Ballet Victor Ullate both appearing in February 2001, and Ballet Maurice Béjart in July.

Orquestra Simfònica del Vallès

Information *C/Narcis Giralt 40, Sabadell, Outer Limits, (93 727 03 00/www.osv.sumi.es).* FCG Sabadell Rambla/RENFE Sabadell Centre. **Open** 9am-2pm, 3-5pm Mon-Fri; closed Sat, Sun. **Tickets** prices vary. **No credit cards.**
One of the main beneficiaries of the OBC's departure from the Palau de la Música, this orchestra, founded in 1987, continues to enjoy a healthy reputation, thanks largely to its dynamic young conductor/composer Salvador Brotons. Based in the nearby town of Sabadell, where it performs regularly at the Teatre Municipal La Faràndula, it also gives a series of concerts between October and June at the Palau de la Música, as well as appearing occasionally at the Auditori.

Contemporary music

Barcelona's contemporary music scene offers a varied programme of events, from 'classical' contemporary music to more avant-garde work, including experimental and electronic music and improvisation. Along with the venues and events listed below, the Metrònom (*see p217*) hosts an annual experimental music festival in late January.

Avuimusics

Associacio Catalana de Compositors, Passeig Colom 6, space 4, Barri Gòtic (93 268 37 19/ www.accompositors.com). Metro Jaume I/14, 36, 57, 59, 64, 157, N6 bus. **Open** *Information* 9.30am-1.30pm Mon-Fri; *Box office* 30 min before concert. **Concerts** *Oct-May* 9pm Thur. **Tickets** 900ptas; 500ptas students; season tickets also available. **Credit** Auditori only, MC,V. **Map** p326 B4.
This increasingly successful series offers 17 concerts from October to May. Run by the Association of Catalan Composers, the repertoire is approximately

half by living Catalans, and half by international 20th-century heavyweights. Concerts are held at the Auditori, the Sociedad General de Autors (Passeig Colom 6; 93 268 9000) and the Church of Santa Ana.

Festival de Músiques Contemporànies

Information *see* **L'Auditori,** *p227.*
Recently re-located to the Auditori, this festival aims to provide a wide, international showcase of current thinking in contemporary music of all kinds. Several works are specially commissioned and premiered here, including, in 2000, compositions by Lawrence D Butch Morris, John Butcher and Joan Saura.

Fundació Joan Miró

Parc de Montjuïc, Montjuïc (93 329 19 08/ www.bcn.fjmiro.es). Metro Paral.lel, then Funicular de Montjuïc/50 bus. **Open** *Box office* 7.30pm Thur. **Sales** box office & Tel-Entrada.**Tickets** 800ptas; 2,000ptas for 3 concerts, 4,500ptas for 7 concerts. **Credit** MC, V. **Map** p323 B6.
It may not be the world's best auditorium, but the brief series of concerts at the Fundació Miró that run from end June to September features an eclectic and interesting selection of improvised music by an array of international musicians. Several of the more light-hearted concerts are held on the roof terrace overlooking the city.

Gràcia Territori Sonor

C/Mozart 24, Gràcia (93 237 37 37/www.graciaterritori.com). Metro Diagonal, Fontana/22, 24, 28, N4 bus. **Dates** 30 Sept-18 Nov. **Tickets** free. **No credit cards. Map** p320 D3.
An anarchic, irreverent but highly organised umbrella organisation that runs a dazzling range of musical activities of all types and genres throughout the year. Their LEM festival (LEM stands – bafflingly and meaninglessly – for Logarithm Elastic Metabolic), consists of over 30 concerts of experimental music held in various bars and other venues in the Gràcia district in October and November.

Nick Havanna

C/Rosello 208, Eixample (93 215 65 91/ www.nickhavanna.com). Metro Diagonal, FCG Provença/7, 16, 17, 31, 67, 68 bus. **Open** 11pm-4.30am Mon-Wed; 11pm-5.30am Fri, Sat; *Apr-June* 9pm Mon, admission free. **Admission** free Mon-Wed; 1,500ptas (incl 1 drink) after midnight Fri, Sat. **Credit** AmEx, MC, V. **Map** p320 D4.
The owner of this slick, Old-Baghdad-meets-*Bladerunner*-style cocktail bar Albert Sardà has been a long-time supporter of contemporary classical music. A short season of eight concerts takes place in May and June, with concerts held on Monday or Tuesday nights. The emphasis is on 'written' music, with a wide selection from Cage to Xenakis, and including local composers like Brotons, Santos and Guinovart.

Arts & Entertainment

Music: Rock, Roots & Jazz

DJs may rule the roost in Barcelona, but the buzz of live jazz, rock, salsa and flamenco is never far away.

Barcelona's live music scene makes up for in both liveliness and diversity what it lacks in size. Several local events, such as the alternative music festival, BAM, and above all, the internationally renowned electronic music festival, Sonar (*see p202*), have become key dates in the city's music calendar. Other important festivals include the summer festival, Grec, and the Festival de Flamenco. And, although the DJ-based dance scene is currently the rave, there is still a wide variety of live rock, jazz, Latin music, and flamenco to choose from.

The ever-changing rock scene boasts a number of noteworthy bands. Granada's **Los Planetas** are considered the uncrowned kings of Spanish indie rock, while local bands such as **Dusminguet** (*mestizo* rock) or **7 Notas 7 Colores** (hip hop) are currently enjoying their moment of fame. *Rock català* is another important part of the local mix, defined by (and receiving institutional support for) its Catalan lyrics. Musically, it tends towards the rock mainstream, and groups like **Sopa de Cabra**, **Lax 'n' Busto** or **Els Pets** have huge followings in Catalonia.

The folkish Catalan music known as *nova cançó* was often politically inspired when it appeared in the '60s and '70s during the dictatorship. Now, however, it has lost its radical edge even though some of its original exponents – such as **Lluís Llach**, **Maria del Mar Bonet**, **Raimon**, and **Joan Manuel Serrat** remain popular. A younger generation of Catalan singers include the duo **Sílvia Comas** and **Lídia Pujol**, and Catalan-American, **Paul Fuster**, who sings in English.

Two other genres with firm roots in Barcelona are related to gypsy culture: *rumba catalana* and flamenco. **Peret**, a gypsy from the Raval, is the king of *rumba*, an infectious dance music with a Latin/flamenco sound, and groups such as **Sabor de Gràcia** have followed in his footsteps. Catalan flamenco is sustained by the children of Andalusian migrants, and local artists **Mayte Martín**, **Miguel Poveda** and **Duquende** are considered among the most accomplished voices in Spain.

The jazz scene in Barcelona, bolstered by two schools, the **Taller de Músics** and the **Aula de la Música**, is very vibrant. It has a traditionally strong base, with competent musicians and established festivals such as the **Festival Internacional de Jazz** (*see p204*). Locally-based jazz artists include singer/pianist/showman, **Lucky Guri**; pianist, **Lluís Vidal**; double bass player, **Horacio Fumero**; and singer, **Laura Simó**.

Latin rhythms and various African music styles also have a strong following. Cuban singer **Lucrecia** is based in Barcelona, as is **Cheb Samir**, the urban-style *rai* group. Big-name concerts by the likes of **Los Van Van**, **Marisa Monte**, **Khaled** or **Cesária Évora** take place regularly, especially during the summer. Tango is yet another feature in the city's musical mélange; the local **Trío Argentino de Tango** and jazz/tango artist **Emilio Solla** are frequent performers.

VENUES AND GIG INFORMATION

Big-name international acts often perform in one of the sports venues at Montjuïc, either at the **Palau d'Esports** (despite its poor acoustics) or the preferable **Palau Sant Jordi** (*see chapter* **Sports & Fitness**). An era came to an end when Barcelona's best and most long-running venue for less overblown concerts, **Zeleste**, closed down in 2000. The venue has since been reopened under the not altogether serious sounding name **Razzmatazz**, but it's still too early to say how successfully the space will stage concerts. Meanwhile, medium-sized bands keep Bikini heavily booked. Smaller clubs like **Magic**, **Garatge** and **Sidecar** play host to lesser known bands on the other end of the stardom spectrum.

Many smaller venues shut down for August. Summer outdoor spaces are important in this festival-oriented town: get to a concert in the magical Plaça del Rei if you can, and the CCCB and its Pati de les Dones provide great atmosphere for all kinds of music. There's no completely foolproof listings guide; you can get the weekly *Guía del Ocio*

Working nights at the **Sidecar Factory Club**.

(www.guiadelociobcn.es) at any newsstand, while in bars and shops you can pick up the monthly giveaways *Barcelona Metropolitan* (in English), *AB* and *Go BCN* (dance/style/bands), and *Mondo Sonoro* (the complete rock chronicle). Several of the record shops along C/Tallers near Plaça Catalunya display concert information on noticeboards by the door, and local papers publish entertainment supplements on Fridays; *Tentaciones*, in *El País*, is the best one for music (www.elpais.es/tentaciones).

See also **London Bar**, **KGB** and the **Sidecar Factory Club**, *all in chapter* **Nightlife**.

Abaixadors Deu

C/Abaixadors 10 pral, La Ribera (no phone). Metro Jaume I/17, 19, 40, 45 bus. **Open** 11pm-3am Wed, Thur, Sun; 11pm-4am Fri, Sat; closed Mon, Tue. **Admission** 1,000ptas Fri, Sat (incl 1 drink); free entrance Wed, Thur, Sun. **No credit cards**. Map p319 B3.

Abaixadors Deu (the name is the address) is a new, multi-room, multifaceted venue in the heart of the trendy Born district, with an exquisite programme of events that includes live music, poetry readings, cinema, and supper parties. Concerts usually start at around 9pm, with music styles ranging from jazz and flamenco to experimental and pop music. The Lounge Social Club, from Wednesday to Saturday starting at 11pm, provides a laid-back atmosphere in which to chill out and socialise while sipping a tropical cocktail.

Astin

C/Abaixadors 9, La Ribera (93 442 96 69/ www.nitsa.com/astin). Metro Jaume I/17, 19, 40, 45 bus. **Open** 11pm-3am Wed, Thur, Sun; 11pm-4am Fri, Sat; closed Mon, Tue. **Admission** 500ptas Fri,

Sat (1 drink incl); free entrance Wed, Thur, Sun. **No credit cards**. Map p319 B3.

This hip new little bar, across from Abaixadors Deu and just down the street from Santa Maria del Mar, features pop, rock, and electronic music concerts by both local and foreign bands in a modern, industrial-like setting. Sit and chat in a cloud of smoke upstairs, check out the scene from the bar, or mingle with the crowd while taking in the latest in hip hop or lounge. Live music usually starts at 9pm.

Bikini

C/Déu i Mata 105, Les Corts (93 322 08 00/ www.bikinibcn.com). Metro Les Corts/15, 30, 43, 59 bus. **Open** midnight-4.30am Tue-Thur; midnight-5.30am Fri, Sat; closed Sun, Mon. **Admission** (incl one drink) 1,500ptas. **Credit** AmEx, V. Map p319 B3.

The original (and legendary) Bikini was torn down in 1990 to make way for L'Illa shopping mall. Reopened by the same management within the new building, it now looks a bit like a cinema multiplex, but its eclectic musical policy survives; from Venezuelan dance fiends Los Amigos Invisibles to dour post-rockers Labradford, the variety is incredible and quality is consistently high. With good acoustics and the flexibility of one large space or two smaller ones, Bikini reigns supreme in city music venues. *See p249.*

La Boîte

Avda Diagonal 477, Eixample (93 419 59 50/ www.masimas.com). Bus 6, 7, 15, 27, 32, 33, 34, 63, 67, 68, N12. **Open** 11pm-5.30am daily; *live music* midnight-1.30am daily. **Admission** (incl one drink) *disco* 1,800ptas; *gigs* 1,800-3,000ptas. **No credit cards**. Map p320 C3.

Barcelona's live music scene owes a lot to the dynamic Mas siblings, who have restored and reinvented venues such as Jamboree and Los Tarantos, and proved to the sceptics that you can maintain musical credibility while also attracting the bigger-spending dance crowd. La Boîte, an uptown basement club, was their first music venue, and has featured everything from blues, kitschy cabaret and South American *cantautores*, to a month-long residency by The Supremes. *See p247.*

Apolo/Nitsaclub

C/Nou de la Rambla 113, Paral.lel (93 441 40 01/ www.nitsa.com/astin). Metro Paral.lel/36, 57, 64, 91, N6, N9 bus. **Open** *disco* midnight-6am Fri, Sat; *gigs* times vary. **Admission** *disco* (incl 1 drink) 1,500ptas; *gigs* 1,800ptas. **No credit cards.** **Map** p324 C6.

As well as being one of the best clubs in town, this ex-music hall hosts top live acts of the world music/reggae, pop/rock and salsa varieties, and more avant-garde events like the weekly Cine Ambigú, an alternative film night. A balcony ensures a good view even for big-name acts. After the gig, the Nitsaclub takes over and the crowds pour in to dance the night away. *See p245.*

Garatge Club

C/Pallars 195, Poble Nou (93 309 14 38). Metro Llacuna/40, 42, 92, N11 bus. **Open** midnight-5.30am Fri, Sat; closed Sun-Thur. Closed 2wks Aug. **Admission** depends on band. **No credit cards.**

If rock 'n' roll is the devil's music, then his satanic majesty would be right at home in the Garatge Club, with a Stratocaster hanging off his shoulder and belting out one hell of a noise. The Poble Nou 'garage' is one of Barcelona's hotbeds of harder-edged guitar and home-made pop, taking in a range of styles from ska to speed metal to psychodelia. Performers at the club include some of the better Spanish indie groups and foreign visitors.

Jamboree

Plaça Reial 17, Barri Gòtic (93 301 75 64/ www.masimas.com). Metro Liceu/14, 38, 59, N9, N12 bus. **Open** 10.30pm-5.30am daily; *gigs* 11pm-12.30am daily; *advance tickets* 93 319 17 89 & ServiCaixa. **Admission** 1,800ptas (incl 1 drink). **No credit cards.** **Map** p327 A3.

Inaugurated in 1959, this cellar was the first jazz 'cave' in Spain, and was reopened by the Mas brothers (*see above*, La Boîte) in 1993. Barcelona-based and visiting names in jazz, blues, funk, and hip hop all play at this enormously popular venue. The Sunday night blues sessions are an institution, and a club is held after the gigs. *See p237.*

Jazz Sí Club/Cafè

C/Requesens 2, Raval (93 329 00 20/ www.tallerdemusics.com). Metro Sant Antoni/20, 24, 38, 41, 55, 64, N6 bus. **Open** 9am-11pm Mon-Fri; 6-11pm Sat, Sun. **Admission** 600ptas (incl 1 drink) Sat. **No credit cards.** **Map** p324 C5.

This quirky club/café in a tiny street in the Raval is run by the proactive Barcelona contemporary music school, Taller de Músics (across the street at Requesens, 5), and is a meeting place for musicians. There's live music every night of the week, catering, like the school, for diverse interests, with music from

the experimental vanguard on Mondays; pop/rock on Tuesdays; jazz jams on Wednesdays; Cuban music on Thursdays; flamenco on Fridays, and rock/blues/pop on Saturdays and Sundays. Good, reasonably-priced lunchtime *menús*, sandwiches and snack food are also available during the day.

Luz de Gas

C/Muntaner 246, Eixample (93 209 77 11/93 209 73 85). Bus 6, 7, 15, 27, 32, 33, 34, 58, 64, N8. **Open** *gigs* 11pm-4.30/5.30am daily; closed Sun in Aug. **Admission** (incl 1 drink) 2,500ptas. **Credit** AmEx, DC, MC, V. **Map** p324 C3.

This beautiful belle époque music hall usually maintains a regular weekly live programme: soul/funk artist Monica Green has a Thursday spot, and there's jazz, salsa, pop and stand-up comedy on other nights. The club sometimes suffers from uptown snootiness, but its atmosphere changes when an international guest passes through: recent guests include Pink Martini, jazz guitarist Ronny Jordan, and salsa violinist Alfredo de la Fe.

Magic

Passeig Picasso 40, La Ribera (93 310 72 67). Metro Barceloneta/14, 39, 51 bus. **Open** 11pm-6am Thur; 11pm-7am Fri, Sat. **Admission** *gigs* 500-2,000ptas; *disco* (incl 1 drink) 1,000ptas. **No credit cards.** **Map** p325 E6.

Despite an odd and claustrophobic layout, over the last few years Magic has become an important venue for independent music in the city. Acts vary from young, green and noisy local bands, to somewhat unlikely (but often wonderful) tourists, such as US surf band Man or Astroman, ex-Minuteman Mike Watt, and a steady stream of northern European guitar groups.

Razzmatazz

C/Almogàvers 122-C/Pamplona 88, Poble Nou (93 272 09 10). Metro Marina/6, 40, 42, 141, N6 bus. **Open** *gigs* 9pm-midnight; *disco* 1-5am Fri, Sat; closed Mon. **Admission** *gigs* depends on band; *disco* 1,200ptas (incl 1 drink). **No credit cards.** **Map** p325 F6.

Before the now vanished Zeleste went bankrupt in 2000, it was the city's best mid-sized rock venue (with memorable shows by PJ Harvey, Lou Reed and others). The new Razzmatazz opened up on the old premises in late 2000 with a strong injection of cash and a facelift; only time will tell whether it lives up to its predecessor. Two large disco spaces (Spanish rock and techno/house) provide fun for the masses on weekend nights.

Toguná

C/Tiradors s/n, La Ribera (93 268 20 27/ www.inicia.es/de/toguna). Metro Jaume I/17, 19, 39, 40, 45, 51, N8 bus. **Open** 8.30pm-2am Thur-Sun; closed Sun-Wed. Closed July-Sept. **No credit cards.** Toguná, which bills itself as 'a place for culture wanderers and travelling hearts', is located off Plaça Sant Agustí Vell in La Ribera, and is the home of Mamá-Latido, an active cultural association. Events

Hitting all the right notes at the **Jazz Sí Club**. *See p232.*

in this funky, unpretentious venue include anything from African cinema to live world music and flamenco concerts. Snack food is also available.

Flamenco

See also **Abaixadors Deu** (*see p231*) and Jazz Sí Club/Cafè (*see p232*).

La Macarena

C/Nou de Sant Francesc 5, Barri Gòtic (93 317 54 36). Metro Liceu/14, 38, 59, N9, N12 bus. **Open** 11pm-4am Mon-Sat; closed Sun. **Map** p327 A4.
With an interior like an Almodóvar film set and an owner who could be one of the extras, La Macarena is a once-in-a-lifetime experience. It's completely unpredictable: you could be treated to anything from a thrilling, spontaneous session from visiting flamenco artists to a cursory ten-minute spot from the regulars who hang around the bar. Be warned that either way, you'll be expected to pay. There's no cover charge, but be warned: if they ask you after the show if you would like to buy a drink for the artists', it could well empty your wallet. An acceptable way out is to leave a tip as you go; the amount should depend on the length and quality of the 'show'. Go late (2am onwards) and, if possible, with somebody who lives in the city.

El Tablao de Carmen

C/Arcs 9, Poble Espanyol, Montjuïc (93 325 68 95/ www.tablaodecarmen.com). Metro Plaça d'Espanya/13, 50, 61 bus. **Open** approx 8pm-2am Tue-Sun; flamenco shows 9.30pm, 11.30pm, Tue-Thur, Sun; 9.30pm, midnight Fri, Sat; closed Mon. **Admission** *Poble Espanyol* 950ptas; 525ptas concessions. *El Tablao de Carmen* show incl 1 drink

4,450ptas; show incl dinner 8,400ptas. **Credit** AmEx, DC, MC, V. **Map** p323 A5.
A high-quality supper/flamenco show venue in the Poble Espanyol (*see p91*), with a full *tablao* of guitarists, singers and dancers, frequented by locals and tourists alike. It's great fun, and if you book in advance you don't have to pay the Poble entry fee.

Los Tarantos

Plaça Reial 17, Barri Gòtic (93 319 17 89/tablao 93 389 16 61). Metro Liceu/14, 38, 59, 91, N9, N12 bus. **Open** 9.30pm-5am daily; *flamenco show (tablao)* 10-10.30pm Mon-Sat. **Admission** *disco* (incl 1 drink) 1,800ptas; *tablao* (incl 2 drinks) 4,000ptas; *other performances* depends on the artist. **Credit** MC, V. **Map** p327 A3.
When Mas i Mas (*see p247* La Boîte) took over Los Tarantos on Plaça Reial, they retained the long-established flamenco *tablao* for tourists, but also began booking straight concerts, too. The concerts often feature the best Catalan flamenco artists, as well as tangos, Latin, salsa, and *cantautores*, complementing the music on offer at the Jamboree next door. When the live gigs finish, the door between the two clubs opens, to give a choice of two dancefloors.

Folk

L'Espai acts as a showcase for mostly Catalan musicians. There are no specific criteria; performances can be anything from flamenco to folk or experimental, but the aim is to give unknown performers a space to display their talent. Folk, Celtic music and other mainly acoustic sounds are also on offer in many of the city's British or Irish-style pubs, although the standard can vary considerably.

Arts & Entertainment

CAT (Centre Artesà Tradicionàrius)

*Travía de Sant Antoni 6-8, Gràcia (93 218 44 85/
www.personal4.iddeo.es/tramcat). Metro Fontana/22,
24, 28, 39, N4 bus.* **Open** *bar* 5pm-midnight Mon-
Fri; *gigs* about 10pm Fri; closed Sat, Sun. Closed mid
July-end Aug. **Admission** 1,000-1,500ptas. **No
credit cards. Map** p320 D3.

This centre is dedicated to the teaching of indigenous music from Catalonia, Spain and occasionally
the rest of Europe. Performances usually take place
on Friday nights in the centre's hall, with classes and
workshops during the week. From January to March
the annual Tradicionàrius folk festival offers at least
three concerts and dances a week, featuring visiting
musicians from countries all over the world.

Jazz-based

See also **Jamboree**, (*see p232*), and **Jazz Sí
Club**, (*see p232*). Although live gigs no longer
take place in the Pipa Club in the Plaça Reial (*see
p236*), the club currently uses the atmospheric
lounge area of the Hotel Oriente on the Rambla
(*see p50*) as a temporary venue for concerts
featuring both local and foreign jazz talent, as
well as *boleros* or tangos on some nights. Consult
their website (www.bpipaclub.com) for the latest
information.

La Cova del Drac

*C/Vallmajor 33, Zona Alta (93 200 70 32). FGC
Muntaner/14, 58, 64, N8 bus.* **Open** *gigs* 6.30pm-
1.30am Tue; 10.30pm-1.30am Wed; 11pm-1.30am
Thur-Sun; *disco* 1.30-5am Thur-Sat; closed Mon.
Admission *disco* 1,000ptas (incl 1 drink); *gigs* extra
800ptas on minimum consumption. **No credit
cards. Map** p320 C2.

Few echoes remain of the days when this swish
uptown jazz club was a bohemian/intellectual hangout in the final years of Francoism. The current club
has live acts (with bigger names at weekends) at
11.30pm Thursday to Saturday, preceded by 'new
talent' gigs at 9.30pm – usually folk, pop or jazz
fusion; and followed by the 'Classic Plastics Disco'
from 1.30am. On Tuesday nights there are poetry
readings at 6.30pm, followed by a jam session.
Drinks are on the pricey side, but La Cova has a
reputation for excellence.

Harlem Jazz Club

*C/Comtessa de Sobradiel 8, Barri Gòtic (93 310 07
55). Metro Jaume I/17, 19, 40, 45, N8 bus.* **Open**
8pm-4am Tue-Thur, Sun; 9pm-5am Fri, Sat. *Gigs*
10.30pm, midnight, Tue-Thur, Sun; 11.30pm, 1am,
Fri, Sat; closed Mon. Closed some wks Aug.
Admission free (but you must have a drink).
No credit cards. Map p327 B3.

This intimate Barri Gòtic club has a wonderful
atmosphere and is a real favourite with Barcelona
jazz aficionados. Creative programming mixes jazz
and blues with sounds that hail from Cuba, Senegal,
or other points of the compass. The club also hosts
popular story-telling sessions (for adults).

Teatreneu

*C/Terol 26-28, Gràcia (93 285 79 00). Metro
Fontana, Joanic/22, 24, 28, 39, N4, N6 bus.* **Open**
gigs from 8.30-10.30pm Tue, Wed; 8.30pm-midnight
or 3am Thur, Fri, Sat; 6pm-midnight Sun; closed
Mon. **Admission** 2,000-2,800ptas. **Credit** MC, V.
Map p320 D3.

Part of the Teatreneu complex, which also includes
a theatre and a restaurant, this intimate club in the
heart of Gràcia features events that include world
dance performances and world music concerts, followed by late-night jazz.

Latin

Other venues for Latin music are **Apolo/
Nitsaclub** (*see p232*), **Jazz Sí Club/Cafè** (see
p232), **Luz de Gas** (*see p232*), **Los Tarantos**
(*see p233*), **Toguná** (*see p232*), and **Harlem
Jazz Club**.

Antilla Barcelona

*C/Aragó 141, Eixample (93 451 21 51). Metro
Hospital Clínic/43, 44, N7 bus.* **Open** 11pm-4am
Mon-Thur, Sun; 11pm-5am Fri, Sat. **Admission** (incl
1 drink) 1,500ptas; *salsa classes* free. **Map** p320 C4.

Great live bands get the crowd moving and grooving from Sunday to Thursday in this popular
salsa/Latin venue. There are free dance classes of
the 'follow the leader' variety on Thursdays and
Fridays starting at 11.30pm, right up until the
band starts. On Fridays and Saturdays there's a
'salsateca'. *See p247*.

Àtic

*C/Tarragona 141-147, Eixample (93 426 84 44).
Metro Tarragona/10, 30, 44, 109, N7 bus.* **Open**
midnight-4.30am Thur, Sun; midnight-5.30am Fri,
Sat; closed Mon-Wed. **Admission** (incl 1 drink)
1,500ptas. **No credit cards. Map** p323 A-B4.

Formerly known as Quinta Avenida, this big club
for mostly Latin rhythms has a large dancefloor,
three bars and lots of chrome. Sala Àtic manages to
book big names in merengue, son and other music
styles from the Caribbean – among them, Cuba's
Eliades Ochoa and his Cuarteto Patria – to entertain
the well-dressed, cosmopolitan crowd.

La Paloma

*C/Tigre 27, Raval (93 317 79 94). Metro
Universitat/bus all routes to Plaça Universitat.* **Open**
11.30pm-5am Thur; 3-5am Fri. **Admission** 800-
1,000ptas. **No credit cards. Map** p314 C5.

This fabulous 1902 dance hall is a Barcelona classic
patronized by an eclectic crowd of old-timers, young-
timers and out-of-towners. La Paloma currently
schedules concerts by well-known artists, both Latin
and others, including part-time Barcelona resident,
Manu Chao, Cuba's NG La Banda, or Arto Lindsay.
On Thursday nights from 11.30pm to 5am and on
Friday nights from 3am to 5am, Bongo Club's 'Afro-
Latin style' takes over: Latin rhythms, electronic
music and rare grooves spun by resident DJs Angel
Dust and Lippo. *See p238*.

Nightlife

Welcome to the biggest party on the Mediterranean.

Fonfone's green house effect. *See p236.*

For a city of its size, Barcelona offers an overwhelming variety of venues within easy reach on foot or a short taxi ride away. Bar owners and punters from cities as different as New York, Rio de Janeiro, La Habana or Kingston, Jamaica, make a wicked cocktail to suit all tastes. Nightlife is concentrated around certain zones. Apart from the two packed port areas, **Maremagnum** and **Port Olímpic**, there are hundreds of places in the old city, mostly in and around the **Plaça Reial**, the traditional starting point for most night-owls. Here, all-time favourites like the **Jamboree** with its funk and soul sounds or the pop rock hangout **Karma** mingle with newer spots such as the electro/dance **Fonfone**. The area also has the greatest concentration of cheap bars and the **Plaça George Orwell**, particularly, has become one big, student/grunge hangout.

Across the Via Laietana in the unstoppable **Born** area, the influx of new residents with spending power is reflected in the designer 'wine bar' style, and likewise attracts a more upmarket clientele. Back on the other side of the Rambla in the **Raval**, established bars (**Marsella**, **London Bar**) are great meeting

places for long-time residents. For serious clubbers who want non-stop all-nighters with techno, underground, progressive or just plain happy house, clubs up on **Montjuïc** such as **Discothèque** and **La Terrrazza**, or the ultra-trendy **Row** in the Eixample are the places to be. These spots host international DJs and the resident DJs are often Ibiza nightlife veterans. If you still want more you'll find Latin places with hot dance floors and free lessons in salsa, merengue, samba and tango in the **Eixample** and **Gràcia**. If you feel the need to observe the city's affluent at play, go up to the **Zona Alta** on the Tibidabo Avenue to the serious posing places and you might just get to rub shoulders with Barça footballers, fashion designers or the latest gossip column star. Don't forget the Burberry and Louis Vuitton accessories!

As dawn breaks, many restless souls still search for a place to continue the party but in central Barcelona at least, the number of **after-hours clubs** has diminished drastically due to a city clamp-down in 2000. Hope is still at hand for die-hard ravers in the outskirts of Barcelona, however – take flyers from PRs outside nightclubs for further information.

Arts & Entertainment

A non-stop weekend in BCN

Barcelona is a trendsetter when it comes to club culture. Top artists wouldn't miss the city off their tour lists and Barcelona's proximity to Ibiza and the city's various music festivals throughout the year (**Sonar**, **BAM**) encourage the world's top DJs to play at the city's clubs. Think of any internationally famous DJs and they will have played here: Jeff Mills, Carl Cox, Eric Morillo, Laurent Garnier, Fatboy Slim, Cesar del Melero... the list is endless.

Homespun talent is also very thick on the ground. Barcelona has, over the years, nurtured a healthy base of resident DJs and the city's size means that once a DJ becomes well known you're likely to see him at various venues in the city. Don't be surprised to see Professor Angel Dust, Angel Molina, Sergio Patricio or Tony Verdi at different clubs throughout the week.

The scene is constantly evolving. The 'specialised club nights' phenomenon has caught on here at last and new specific music nights are being organised all the time. Drum 'n' bass, funk, rare groove, Latino, hard house, techno, reggae and Afro-Brazilian music is all on offer. Bars and clubs open, close and change management often, so it's important to pick up all the flyers when you arrive and check out what's in. Free city magazines publish a listings section and have ads for clubs and bars. Check out the *Barcelona Metropolitan*, *Punto H* or *Mes & Mes* for the latest.

If you're in Barcelona for a mad rave here's a challenging suggestion:

Thursday

11.30pm Start the night off at **Malpaso** listening to acid jazz. Marvel at how many people really fit into such a small place. Have a beer, pace yourself.

12am Decide you've had enough and cross the Rambla to the Raval. Next stop **Benidorm**. Another jammed bar but quick service. Try not to spill your beer as you sway to the groove.

1am You're getting closer to your destination as you enter the too cool **Bar Six**. Order a long drink or try some lethal knock-backs. Practise your dance moves to DJ Leo's Balearic beats.

2.30am Make new friends in the line outside **La Paloma**. Don't worry if you forget their names, it won't matter once you're getting down to the funky music inside.

5am Suitably sweaty and starving make your way to the **Bar Estudiantil** for a hot chocolate and sandwich.

6am Figure out if it's going to be quicker to walk back or find a cab.

Friday

10pm Attack the Born in style at the **Barroc**. See how long you can last in a bar that plays great dance music but doesn't have any dance space.

11.30pm A rumbling stomach takes you in the direction of **Suborn**. Have a snack or even a heavier dish to prepare yourself for a heavy night.

1.30am By now you're sick of trying to find dance space. Pile out of Suborn for some

Barri Gòtic

Barcelona Pipa Club

Plaça Reial 3, pral (93 302 47 32/ www.bpipaclub.com). Metro Liceu/14, 38, 59, N9, N12 bus. **Open** 10pm-6am daily. **Admission** (incl 1 drink) 1,000ptas. **No credit cards. Map** p327 A3.
One of Barcelona's best all-night bars – push the buzzer next to the sign of the pipe in a corner of the Plaça Reial. It's a genuine pipe-smoker's club but its late-night incarnation attracts a mix of night-owls who ensure that the meerschaums rattle in their stands until early morning. *See also p234.*

Dot

C/Nou de Sant Francesc 7 (93 302 70 26/ www.dotlightclub.com). Metro Drassanes/14, 38, 91, N9, N12 bus. **Open** 10pm-2.30am Mon-Thur, Sun; 10pm-3am Fri, Sat. **No credit cards. Map** p327 A4.

A smallish dance bar in the dark and alley-like back streets around the Plaça Reial, this groovy, popular place calls itself a 'light club', and consists of two spaces: a red-lit bar area for chat, and an intimate dancefloor, where cult movies are projected onto one wall. The sound system is top, as is the music – drum 'n' bass, lounge, space funk and club/dance.

Fonfone

C/Escudellers 24 (93 317 14 24). Metro Drassanes/14, 38, 59, 91, N9, N12 bus. **Open** 10pm-2.30am Mon-Thur, Sun; 10pm-3am Fri, Sat. **Credit** MC, V. **Map** p327 A3.
A colourful new bar whose cool tonal geometric designs, upfront music policy and fresh feel stand out on the traditionally seedy Escudellers. With resident and international guest DJs selecting breakbeat, drum 'n' bass, nu jazz and house, guests in to play with the visuals and no entrance fee, it's starting to draw its own streetwise, up-for-it crowd.

fresh air. Walk down to the Paseo Colon having a quick *carajillo* – espresso with a shot of alcohol – in any café on the way before hailing a cab up to Poble Espanyol.
2am Congratulate yourself on having beaten the queues and saved yourself the rigorous door selection as you make your way into Poble Espanyol. Take in a cheap bar and even some sights before going to **Discothèque/La Terrrazza** (*pictured*).
4am By now you're getting bleary-eyed, don't be afraid to get up onto a podium and join the crazies in sunglasses.
6.30am Leave Poble Espanyol having danced to your heart's content. Prepare yourself for the long downhill walk to Plaça Espanya before you see even one cab.

Saturday

It's time for a multicultural experience and Gràcia's the place.
10.30pm Take your pick of bars in the Plaça del Sol after having wolfed down a shawarma (or two). Check out the cool lounge feel of **Mond Bar**, or fuel up on *carajillos* in Café del Sol. If you're lucky it should be warm enough to hang out on a terrace and take in the buskers in the square.
12.15am Having planned your route it's time to see how many different kinds of music you can hear in Gràcia. First stop **Terrasamba** – for samba and *caipirinhas*!

12.45am Sway across to **Sabor Cubano**. Salsa and *mojitos*: a lethal cocktail heightened by the stuffy heat in the bar. See if you can persuade a new person to join the group on its quest.
1.30am Check out the tiny **Zimbabwe** (C/Mozart 13, open 7pm-3am daily) for a bit of spontaneous reggae dancing before peering into **Sal de Gràcia**. Ogle a live band playing something between country and western and grunge.
2.45am Get out before things get too blurred and grab a cab to meet up with the rest of your friends downtown.
3.15am Enter **Nitsa** satisfied after having tried something different. Get in, get down and before you know it, it's time to leave.
7am If you still have energy delve into your pocket for the after-hours club flyer given to you yesterday. After a unanimous decision of 'can't be bothered', stumble on back to your resting place.

Hook

C/Ample 35 (93 442 09 84). Metro Jaume I/14, 17, 19, 36, 40, 45, 57, 59, 64, 157, N6, N8 bus. **Open** 7pm-2am Tue-Thur, Sun; 7pm-3am Fri, Sat; closed Mon. **No credit cards. Map** p327 B4.
The eccentric collection of clocks and other antique bits and pieces that clutter this warm, cosy place are just this side of authenticity, and for an instant here, it's possible to believe Peter Pan might actually enjoy beer. The clientele consists of young foreigners and Catalans getting to know each other, as well as the occasional serious drinker mumbling to one of the clocks in the corner.

Jamboree

Plaça Reial 17 (93 301 75 64/www.masimas.com). Metro Liceu/14, 38, 59, N9, N12 bus. **Open** 10.30pm-5.30am daily. *Gigs* 11pm-12.30am daily. **Admission** (incl 1 drink) 1,800ptas. **No credit cards. Map** p327 A3.

Live acts end around 1am, and the club, which is famed for soul, R&B and low-grade swinger sounds, begins. This subterranean brick vault is hugely popular, and gets very cramped. Total gridlock is averted by a steady stream of people going upstairs (for free) to Tarantos, to chill to Latin and Spanish music. *See also p232.*

Karma

Plaça Reial 10 (93 302 56 80). Metro Liceu/14, 38, 59, N9, N12 bus. **Open** midnight-5am Tue-Sun; closed Mon. **Admission** (incl 1 drink) 1,000ptas Fri, Sat. **No credit cards. Map** p327 A3.
Right on Plaça Reial and with bouncers at the door, Karma is impossible to miss. It has long served tourists and a cross section of locals, but the young student crowd normally dominates. Intense competition from the nearby clubs has lowered attendances, but this bomb-shelter of a club still remains crammed at weekends. The doormen let you walk

Arts & Entertainment

The Dope Brothers

Paco (*pictured right*) and Diego (*pictured left*), alias Professor Angel Dust and DJ Lippo, are the Dope Brothers, two total music addicts as well as rising stars of the Barcelona night. Brothers for real and Mexican by birth, they've seen a fair bit of the world, having cut their teeth on the Toronto scene in Canada, where they once played in punk bands, got into breakdancing in a big way and threw some of their first parties.

In Barcelona, the Brothers have made names for themselves, playing at important clubs – Dot, La Terrrazza and Moog. Then, at the end of 1999 they were offered their own club nights (the '**Bongo Lounge**', Thursdays and Fridays) in **La Paloma** (*see* p241), and

haven't looked back since. Instead of creating yet another copycat 'cool' techno/dance club, the Brothers have stuck to what they know best: freestyle with a generous mix of Latino, rare groove, soul and funk. Finding the breakdancing Quassit B-Boy Crew in 2000 put the icing on the cake for a scene that has gained something of a cult status among hard-to-please funk lovers. Mainstream recognition has followed. Paco's funked-up version of 'Oye Como Va' from the album *Guapacheando* (Professor Angel Dust and PH Force) got airplay and then rose up into the top 40. Brother Diego, in the meantime, has recently released an LP of juicy breakbeat and funk, *It's Easy*.

in if they like the look of you; if not, you pay. Music is mainstream rock with lapses into electronica.

Malpaso

C/Rauric 20 (93 412 60 05/www.atiza.com). Metro Liceu/14, 38, 59, N9, N12 bus. **Open** 8pm-2.30am Mon-Thur, Sun; 8pm-3am Fri, Sat. **No credit cards. Map** p327 A3.

Tucked down a back alley from the Plaça Reial is this busy little bar, complete with decks and a buzzy young crowd. It's a good warm-up for Moog (*see p240*) – the music flits unpredictably from indie to jungle to French touch disco all in one evening, but is consistently lively.

New York

C/Escudellers 5 (93 302 70 26). Metro Drassanes/14, 38, 59, 91, N9, N12 bus. **Open** 10.30pm-5.30am Thur-Sat; closed Mon-Wed, Sun. **Admission** (incl 1 drink) 1,400ptas. **No credit cards. Map** p327 A3.

Students and teenagers thrash it out to Britpop in this former sex club, which metamorphosed overnight in the late '90s into a hang-out for Barcelona's own version of Generation Z. It's a big place, and has a mezzanine above the dancefloor and couches dating from the club's licentious origins in the 1970s. Unfortunately, it has no air-conditioning, which means the air becomes a sweaty soup. Panams, close by at La Rambla 27, is a similar former sex club venue (which still has a live show) also hosting club nights.

Branches: **Panams**, Rambla 27, Rambla (93 318 10 40); **Starlets**, Av. Sarrià 44, Zona Alta (93 430 91 56); **Mr. Dollar**, Plaça Macià, Zona Alta (93 439 18 15).

Ovisos

C/Arai 5 (no phone). Metro Liceu/14, 38, 59, N9, N12 bus. **Open** 10pm-2.30am Mon-Thur, Sun; 10pm-3am Fri, Sat. **No credit cards. Map** p317 B3.

This is a deep recess of a friendly grunge bar in Plaça George Orwell on C/Escudellers that attracts a young, hip, relaxed crowd. The music is excellent and ranges from ambient and garage to sip-hop, and surprisingly sophisticated (and surprisingly pricey) food is also available. Nearby on the narrow C/Aglà, Ovisos has a sister bar, Shanghai, which is smaller and more refined, but is still packed at weekends.

Paradís Reggae

C/Paradís 4 (no phone). Metro Jaume I/17, 19, 40, 45, N8 bus. **Open** 6-9pm; midnight-5am Thur, Sun; 11.30pm-6am Fri, Sat; closed Mon-Wed. **Admission** (incl 1 drink) 800-1,000ptas. **No credit cards. Map** p327 B3.

A reggae, Afro-Latin music club, Paradís occupies a vaulted basement, next door to the local government palaces. The place doesn't really get going until after 2 or 3am, when other places have closed. Occasionally, live gigs are held, and there are also dub reggae and rap sessions.

Sidecar Factory Club

C/Heures 4-6 (93 302 15 86). Metro Liceu/14, 38, 59, N9, N12 bus. **Open** 10pm-3am Tue-Sat. **Gigs** normally 10/11pm Tue-Sat; closed Mon. Closed Aug. **Admission** *Gigs* depends on band. *Club* 400ptas (1 beer incl). **No credit cards**. **Map** p327 A3.

A basement club tucked into a corner of the Plaça Reial, Sidecar is place to chill, play pool or listen to concerts by local and touring indie-pop bands. On Tuesdays, the G's Club takes over, offering 'alternative' performances by a local arts collective – everything from theatre and poetry readings to video art and experimental music. The 'underground' crowd is friendly.

The Raval

Aurora

C/Aurora 7 (93 442 30 44). Metro Paral.lel/14, 20, 24, 38, 59, 64, 91, N6, N9, N12 bus. **Open** 8pm-3am daily; plus 6am-noon Fri, Sat. **No credit cards**. **Map** p324 C6.

A small, red-walled bar in the *Barrio Chino* with an eclectic selection of music that attracts the perkier, more artistic elements of the neighbourhood. On Fridays and Saturdays it's not clear if the bar ever shuts. On Sunday at any rate, it's open at dawn, and steadily fills up with those restless types still out and about, until almost noon.

Benidorm

C/Joaquim Costa 39 (93 317 80 52). Metro Universitat/bus all routes to Plaça Universitat. **Open** 7pm-2am Mon-Thur, Sun; 7pm-2.30am Fri, Sat. **No credit cards**. **Map** p324 C5.

Here is the eye-catching proof of just what can be achieved with a little money and a lot of imagination. This Catalan/Finnish creation in the heart of the Raval is a charming, dimly-lit venue for sipping mint tea or knocking back vodkas. It's small, but the owners have made the most of the space to fit in plenty of seating and a pair of gleaming Technics. Local and international DJs play every day of the week – the music ranges from smooth East Coast rap and sounds from the Bristol massive to obscure Spanish electronica. Whatever the mood or the music playing, the atmosphere is always welcoming and warm.

Benidorm, and not a Union Jack in sight.

La Confiteria

C/Sant Pau 128 (93 443 04 58). Metro Paral.lel/14, 20, 24, 38, 59, 64, 91, N6, N9, N12 bus. **Open** 10am-2am Tue-Thur; 10am-3am Fri; 6pm-3am Sat; noon-midnight Sun; closed Mon. **No credit cards**. **Map** p324 C6.

A friendly hangout with murals of rural scenes dating from the 1920s, and a mirrored booth offering a curved view of infinity. The clientele is lively, without a defined tendency, encompassing local characters, foreigners and normal-looking Catalans. The non-polarizing music is mostly Spanish and Catalan rock and pop, but ethnic sounds also feature. Very good if slightly pricey *bocatas* and other light goodies are served.

Kentucky

C/Arc del Teatre 11 (93 318 28 78). Metro Drassanes/14, 38, 59, N9, N12 bus. **Open** 9pm-3am Tue-Sat; closed Mon, Sun. Closed Aug. **No credit cards**. **Map** p327 A4.

An old red-light bar left over from the 1960s, when Barcelona was a port of call for US Navy ships. The bar looks essentially unchanged since then: a long, narrow space with an old juke-box, which holds a surprisingly large selection of music. The Kentucky is popular among an assortment of foreigners, Raval locals and slumming uptowners.

London Bar

C/Nou de la Rambla 34 (93 318 52 61/ tonoyeli@eresmas.com). Metro Liceu/14, 38, 59, N9, N12 bus. **Open** 7pm-4am Tue-Thur, Sun; 7pm-5am Fri, Sat; closed Mon. Closed 2wks end Aug. **No credit cards**. **Map** p327 A3.

With its 1910 bar and wall mirrors, the London does not look much like an English pub, but is reminiscent of England in that people tend to arrive and settle in for the rest of the evening. It has been open since 1910, and for a while it became a popular hangout for Catalan hippies. It was then taken over, a few years back, by a livelier management who have kept it popular among young resident expats and a mixed bunch of partying Barcelonans. There are regular live gigs, for which there's no entrance fee, but drink prices go up accordingly.

Marsella

C/Sant Pau 65 (93 442 72 63). Metro Liceu/14, 38, 59, N9, N12 bus. **Open** 10pm-2am Mon-Thur; 10pm-3am Fri, Sat; closed Sun. **No credit cards**. **Map** p327 A3.

The Marsella is another survivor of the *Barrio Chino*'s colourful past. This is a well-loved bar that's been in the same family for five generations. Dusty, untapped 100-year-old bottles sit in tall glass cabinets (they still have locally made absinthe, *absenta*), old mirrors line the walls, and assorted chandeliers loom over the cheerful clientele. It's another one that's very popular with the expat crowd, and attracts many gays too. The bar can get very crowded late night on weekends, so come a bit earlier if you want to secure a comfortable spot at one of the old wooden tables.

Arts & Entertainment

Staying alive at **La Paloma**.

Moog

C/Arc del Teatre 3 (93 301 72 82/
www.masimas.com). Metro Drassanes/14, 38, 59,
N9, N12 bus. **Open** 11.30pm-5am daily. **No credit**
cards. Map p327 A4.

Moog expands the Mas family's empire (*see p237*
Jamboree, *p247* La Boîte) to encompass techno and
electronic dance. An excellent programme of name
DJs keeps this place perennially popular with a
happy, young, lively crowd. The dancefloor is smallish and can get tight, but the upstairs '70s dance
lounge offers some relief. International DJs usually
guest on Wednesday nights.

La Paloma

C/Tigre 27 (93 301 68 97). Metro Universitat/
bus all routes to Plaça Universitat. **Open** 6-9.30pm,
11.30pm-5am Thur-Sat; 6-9.30pm Sun; closed
Mon-Wed. **Admission** 800-1,000ptas.
No credit cards. Map p324 C5.

Loved by many, old and young, La Paloma is a
Barcelona institution. Until 1am on Thursdays,
(until 2.30am on Fridays and until closing time on
Saturdays and Sundays) this ornate old ballroom
offers live music (*paso doble*, cha cha cha or buga-
loo, and the occasional visiting group) for a mixed,
mostly middle-aged, but always happy crowd. After
the live band on Thursday and Friday nights, things
change drastically. The place becomes the Bongo
Lounge and fills up with a steady stream of sexy
young things all ready to groove to the Dope
Brothers' (*see p238*) mix of breakbeat, funk and
Latino grooves. Don't miss the super-cool break-
dance show by Quassit B-Boy Crew around 3am on
Fridays. If you need to catch your breath or
exchange numbers with a new 'friend', check out the
hidey-holes with plush red sofas. *See also p234.*

Sant Pere, La Ribera & the Born

Abaixadors Deu

C/Abaixadors 10 pral (93 268 10 19). Metro Jaume
I/17, 19, 40, 45 bus. **Open** 11pm-3am Wed, Thur,
Sun; 11pm-4am Fri, Sat; closed Mon, Tue. **Admission**
(incl 1 drink) 1,000ptas Fri, Sat; free entrance Wed,
Thur, Sun. **No credit cards. Map** p327 B3.

Abaixadors Deu is stylish and original without
being cliquey and elitist. It's approached through an
internal courtyard and up the stone stairway. To
your left there is a high-ceilinged red bar which
serves expensive but exquisite food until 2am; to
your right there is a dimly lit ex-theatre that hosts
concerts, performances and the Lounge Social Club,
an offbeat mix of lo-fi electronica, and easy listening
for a crowd of genuine and aspiring beatniks and
artists. *See also p231.*

Astin Bar Club

C/Abaixadors 9 (93 442 96 69/www.nitsa.com/
astin). Metro Jaume I/17, 19, 40, 45 bus. **Open**
11pm-3am Wed, Thur, Sun; 11pm-4am Fri, Sat;
closed Mon, Tue. **Admission** (incl 1 drink)
500ptas Fri, Sat; free Wed, Thur, Sun.
No credit cards. Map p327 B3.

Right opposite Abaixadors Deu, this tight little bar
and club is the nose cone of the cutting edge but
mass-market music missile which is **Nitsa** (*see*
p245) – just reverse the letters. On a quiet night its
curious shape, steel fittings and bare walls can feel
cold and unconducive to fun, but the self-styled
'Adidactic pedagogy' of its super-select music policy (it means you need to be in the know already)
attracts the black-clad music cognoscenti for small
but intense concerts and DJ sessions across the spectrum. *See also p231.*

Barroc

C/Antic de St. Joan 10, C/Rec 67 (93 268 46 23).
Bus 14, 17, 36, 39, 45, 51, 57, 59, 64. **Open** 6pm-
3am Mon-Fri; 7pm-3am Sat, Sun. **No credit cards.**
Map p327 C3.

Passeig del Born and the maze of surrounding
streets are packed with great places for a drink, all
competing for style, ambience and spectacle. There's
no excuse for not exploring, but this could be a good
place to start, with its high ceiling, cheeky cherubs
and chunky sound system.

Bass Bar

C/Assanadors 25 (no phone). Metro Jaume I/17, 19,
40, 45, N8 bus. **Open** 7pm-3am daily. **No credit**
cards. Map p327 C3.

A quietly alternative scene clusters in this small,
artsy bar. Regular exhibits of local artists and collectives adorn the walls, and the music is anything
goes, from Spanish ska or world drumming to Latin.

Bass Bar: mine's a treble.

Groovin' on the underground

Art bars & spaces

A night at a 'Cultural Association' may not initially sound promising, but this is how some of the coolest and most original places in town are organised. You start with a *local*, which could be a gutted shop or warehouse space, or an old bar; then you need a network of talented mates that includes enough artists and general bon viveurs to give the place the decor and feel you're after. Organise live events and exhibitions and finish it off with a buzzer and a note on the door, lay on the bar, and you're away. In these spots, tucked away around the Raval, Poble Sec and Gràcia, you'll find congenial private bars, cool sounds, and the occasional full-on party. Look out, too, for posters and flyers for one-off events, which you can find in bars like Bar Fortuny (*see p163*), Aurora, Ovisos and Malpaso.

L'Atelier – Art de Vivre Total

C/Cadena 49, Raval (93 441 07 16/ atelier@retemail.es). Metro Liceu/14, 38, 59, N9, N12 bus. **Open** sporadically. **No credit cards. Map** p324 C6.
A huge 'life-art' space that in another era was a laundry and bathhouse. It still maintains three stone wash basins ten metres (30 foot) long, which now serve as performance spaces and chill-out rooms whenever it hosts experimental drum 'n' bass electro-music parties or DJ sessions. This is also a good place to call to find out about **free parties** (*see p243*).

Ateneu del Xino

C/d'en Robador 25, Raval (sau89@hotmail.com). Metro Liceu/14, 38, 59, N9, N12 bus. **Open** 9pm-3am Fri-Sat; 9-11.30pm Sun; closed Mon-Thur. Closed Aug. **No credit cards. Map** p324 C6.
A relaxed, alternative venue with a weekend programme of live, mostly acoustic concerts.

Conservas

C/Sant Pau, 58 baixos, Raval (93 302 06 30). Metro Liceu or Paral.lel/14, 20, 38, 59, 64, 91 bus. **Performance** days and times vary. **Admission** according to performances. **No credit cards. Map** p324 C6.
This medium-sized, well-kept space is run by the gifted performance artist Simona Levi. It has excellent, sporadic programmes featuring contemporary theatre performances, poetry readings and up-and-coming comedy acts, and is extremely popular with those in the know. In early July 2000 Conservas is holding 'In Motion', a combination theatre/ performance/dance/film event on the patio of the CCCB in the Raval (*see p114*), with professional artists and performers from around Europe. Entry price also includes supper. Call for more information.

Mau-Mau

C/d'en Fontrodona 33, Poble Sec (606 860 617). Metro Paral.lel/20, 57, 64, 157, N6 bus. **Open** 11.30pm-4.30am Fri, Sat; closed Mon-Thur, Sun. **No credit cards. Map** p323 B6.
Local brothers Frank and Alex run this laid-back warehouse chill-out up a back street from Paral.lel. Keep following C/d'en Fontdrona up after it zig-zags across C/Blesa – if you're lucky, you'll find a bit of paper on the anonymous white door. You pay to 'join' the club and get 'a membership card'.

Colombo

Passeig de Picasso 26 (93 310 75 50). Metro Jaume I/40, 41, 42, 141 bus. **Open** *7am-2.30am Mon-Sat, 5am-noon Sun.* **No credit cards. Map** *p327 E6.*
A cool oasis in the Born that's resisted conversion into one more designed-up, pretty place. With a good view of the park, the terrace in summer is a relaxed and funky hangout, with local DJs playing whatever they like, from Jungle Book music to rare soultracks and self-created ambient sounds. Most of this happens at the weekend; other nights it's a quiet, local bar that serves decent lunches and light dinners.

Suborn

C/de la Ribera 18 (93 310 11 10). Metro Barceloneta/14, 39, 51 bus. **Open** *8pm-3am Tue-Sun; closed Mon.* **Credit** MC, V. **Map** *p327 C4.*
Just about as popular as it can get without exploding, Suborn starts the evening as a relatively relaxed café, with tables under the arches outside, and ends

Passing through an airlock you enter a huge space where gorgeous projections cover every surface. The music is deep house at conversation-friendly volume, lovingly dovetailed onstage; the crowd chill with beers on the sofas and chairs that fill the floor. People turn up after midnight and it's so relaxed many find it hard to move before the early morning.

The Merry Ant

C/Peu de la Creu 23, Raval (626 787 126). Metro Sant Antoni/20, 24, 38, 64, N6 bus. **Open** 7pm-12.30am Tue, Wed, Sun; 9pm-2.30am Thur-Sat; closed Mon. **No credit cards. Map** p324 C5.

Behind the heavy chalk-scrawled door (ring the bell) and through an up-lit floor-to-ceiling arch of reclaimed jetsam, you enter a space which is all installation, a 3-D collage assembled by an obsessive skip-trawler with a nailgun and lots of red paint. Right down to the details, the salvaged domestic water pipe mobiles, the kitchen wall of aluminium utensils caught in netting, the inconspicuously stapled little red toy ants, it's a street scavenger's *Wunderkammer*, usually busy with an alternative, arty, but presentable crowd, from stoner teens up to more mature residents in the know.

Heliogabal

C/Ramón y Cajal 80, Gràcia (679 894 866/ 609 762 622). Metro Joanic/39, 55, N6 bus. **Open** 10pm-2am Mon-Wed, Sun; 11pm-5am Thur-Sat. **No credit cards. Map** p321 E3.

Heliogabal has an eclectic programme of live happenings, starting after 11pm. It's a classic Gràcia after-hours hangout, comfortably heaving on Saturday nights with a relaxed and open alternative crowd until well into Sunday morning. There's an extremely cute courtyard at the back, the walls are exhibition space and you can keep drinking long after most places in Gràcia have closed

down. You'll recognise the red and black painted shutter which is usually down: to get in, ring the bell on the left of the entrance.

Trsdimensiones

C/Mila y Fontanals 42, Gràcia (654 585 221). Metro Joanic/39, 55, N6 bus. **Open** 6pm-midnight Sun; closed Mon-Sat. **No credit cards. Map** p321 E3.

On Sunday nights, a back room chill-out is staged in this collective art workshop. It's a scruffy, homey space that looks and feels like what it is, a studio kitchen, but with a bar, toytown tables and chairs, home-made cakes and tea, and decks in the corner. Intelligent drum 'n' bass and comedown house and the mellow vibe make it an excellent spot to untwist at the end of the weekend.

Free parties

Barcelona's real underground is thriving with techno and trance parties all year long in warehouses, abandoned properties and some truly stunning one-off locations in the city's mountain hinterland. It's happening, but you'll need to get informed, go prepared and probably find your own transport. Bars on **Plaça George Orwell** are good for contacts, or **L'Atelier** (*see p242*), but **Tazmaniac Records**, techno and trance specialists, is the best place to ask and pick up flyers: you want the cheap-looking photocopied ones with directions, or at least the all-important info line number. Just remember, though: for many people this is a lifestyle, not a night out, and look after yourselves out there.

Tazmaniac Records

Plaça Vicenc Martorell 2, Raval (93 301 25 66/www.tazmaniac.org). Metro Catalunya/all buses to Plaça Catalunya. **Open** 11.30am-2.30pm, 5-9pm Mon-Fri; 11.30am-9pm Sat; closed Sun. **Credit** AmEx, DC, MC, V. **Map** p326 A1.

up as a heaving, jostling party, and woe betide you if you happen to have picked a table on the dancefloor and haven't finished your salad. Squeeze your way in and get intimate with a fashionable crowd inured to elbows in the ribs and up for a boogie. (*See also p136*.)

Port Vell & Port Olímpic

See also p244, **Party Ports.**

Baja Beach Club

Paseo Maritimo, s/n (93 225 91 00/10, 36, 45, 57, 59, 71, 92, 157, N8 bus. **Open** *Oct-May* noon-5am Thur-Sun; closed Mon-Wed. *June-Sept* noon-1am Mon-Wed; noon-5am Thur-Sun. **Admission** (incl 1 drink) 1,800ptas. **No credit cards. Map** p325 F7.

With decor that has the feel of a cruise ship disco and non-stop top 40 music to match, the Baja Beach Club is the place to go if you feel like experiencing

Party ports

PORT OLIMPIC

All year round, this zone gets massively pumped up after midnight on Fridays and Saturdays (daily in summer), as bar after bar along the lower strip offers a mass-pleasing mix of blaring top 40 dance music and gorgeous, scantily clad go-go dancers. What's on offer tends not to vary a great deal from place to place, but a select bunch are listed below.

Transport for all venues: *Metro Ciutadella-Vila Olímpica/10, 36, 45, 57, 59, 71, 92, 157, N8 bus.* **Map** for all venues: p325 F7.

Pachito

Moll Mestral 43 (93 221 32 89).
Open 5pm-5am daily. **Credit** MC, V.
A branch of the famous Ibizan disco, Pachito's plays only techno/house and has a bevy of huge drag queen performers.

Joker

Moll Mestral 10-11 (93 221 40 40).
Open 6pm-5am daily. **Credit** MC, V.
A bit more spacious than other discos along the strip, Joker also has some of the hottest girl go-go dancers.

Kennedy Irish Sailing Club

Moll Mestral 27 (no phone). **Open** 4.30pm-3.30am daily. **Credit** MC, V.
More relaxed than other spots nearby, this 'authentic' pub has live Irish and country-western music from Thursday through Saturday evenings.

Gran Casino

Marina Village, Marina 19-21 (93 225 78 78).
Open 1pm-5am daily. **Credit** MC, V.
At the base of the Hotel Arts, this large casino opened in 2000 and offers an array of gambling tables, slot machines and a 'Mystery bar' with live lounge music.

MAREMAGNUM

Maremagnum gleams temptingly in the middle of the Port Vell and draws in huge crowds both night and day via the wooden footbridge. The list below is again only a small selection of what is on offer.

Transport: *Metro Drassanes/14, 36, 57, 56, 64, 157, N6 bus.* **Map** p325 D7.

Mojito Bar

Moll d'Espanya 59 (93 225 80 14).
Open 5pm-4.30am daily. **Credit** MC, V.
A hot salsateca on the ground floor, Mojito's is always jammed with dancers.

Irish Winds

Moll d'Espanya, top floor (93 225 81 87).
Open 1pm-2.30am Mon-Thur, Sun; 1pm-5am Fri, Sat. **Credit** V.
An interestingly named disco-pub with an outdoor terrace and live Irish music on Saturday nights.

Nayandei

Moll d'Espanya, top floor (no phone).
Open 10.30am-5am daily. **Credit** MC, V.
A mega-disco with crowds of happy revellers and music that never strays from the top 40.

---

a giant hen/stag night – complete with the obligatory topless barmen and bikini-clad waitresses, and a mock strip show thrown in for good measure. This one is definitely for single people looking for a good time.

Base Nàutica de la Mar Bella

Espigó de la Mar Bella, Platja de la Mar Bella, Av. Litoral s/n (93 221 04 32/www.basenautica.net). Bus 36, N6, N8. Open *Mar-Oct* 9am-11pm daily. Closed Nov-Apr. **Credit** V. **Map** p325 F7.
This seaside bar in the windsurfing club on the Mar Bella beach has DJs playing from about 9am through to the evening. It's right on the beach and has a sandwich bar, which makes it the perfect place to spend the whole day eating, drinking, sunbathing and chilling out to happy house and Balearic beats. Top city DJs such as Sergio Patricio (La Terrrazza) and DJ Lippo (Dope Brothers) play regularly at Barcelona's answer to Ibiza beach bars. Worth

checking out are the special one-off all-nighters organised here over the summer and during the Mercé. Also, on Friday nights, there are organised outings in sea kayaks.

Woman Caballero

Estació de França, Av. Marqués de l'Argentera 6 (93 300 50 50). Metro Barceloneta/14, 36, 39, 51, 57, 59, 64, N0, N6 bus. **Open** 1.30-6am Thur-Sat; closed Mon-Wed, Sun. **Admission** (incl 1 drink) 1,500ptas. **No credit cards. Map** p327 C4.
In the basement of Estació de França, this subterranean darkland consists of three spaces: a very large cement dancefloor, a medium-sized cement dancefloor (both of which cater for the house and techno crowds), and a small, slightly less cementy lounge where drum 'n' bass often degenerates into R&B and disco. When you eventually leave, don't forget to stop in at the station's café/bar (*see p250* **Breakfast Clubs**).

Montjuïc & Poble Sec

La Bella Bestia

C/Mexic 7-9 (no phone). Metro Espanya/bus all routes to Plaça d'Espanya. **Open** 11pm-5am Thur-Sun; closed Mon-Wed. **No credit cards. Map** p323 A5.
The 'Beautiful Beast' isn't beautiful at all. It's a stark, warehouse space set off by two zebra-striped columns and a stone lion in the corner. You start to understand the theme once you hear the music – calypso, soca, African music or roots reggae – and the mood is relaxed as members of Barcelona's African community get down. Check out the photo exhibition and the tribal masks in and around the bar area as you have a cocktail and soon you'll be joining in the gentle swaying to 'Reggae Nights'.

Club Apolo/Nitsaclub

C/Nou de la Rambla 113 (93 441 40 01/ www.nitsa.com/astin). Metro Paral.lel/36, 57, 64, 91, N6, N9 bus. **Open** midnight-6am Fri, Sat. **Admission** (incl 1 drink) 1,500ptas. **No credit cards. Map** p324 C6.
This elegant old ballroom has changed hands many times over the years, but has always drawn a crowd. The most recent management has put it to good use with techno-oriented dance parties and concerts. On Fridays, Saturdays and the eves of public holidays, it becomes the Nitsaclub, a hugely popular, very young Detroit techno/hard house/electro dance-a-thon. However, two smaller, separate rooms on the balcony level act as chill-out rooms with popular downbeat sets from residents Coco, djd!, and Fra, among others. At 4am queues to get in still snake as far as the Paral.lel. On other nights Apolo hosts live concerts (*see p232*).

Discothèque

Behind Poble Espanyol, Avda. Marqués de Comillas (93 423 12 85/www.nightsungroup.com). Metro Espanya/13, 50, 61E bus. **Open** 19 Oct-11 May midnight-6am Thur-Sat; closed Mon-Wed, Sun. Closed 12 May-18 Oct. **Admission** (incl 1 drink) 2,000ptas. **No credit cards. Map** p323 A4.
La Terrrazza's (*see below*) other half is an indoor club which opens for the winter. A heavier beat to please the demanding, more specialised crowd keeps it at number one for the ravers. Even though many international DJs pass through, it's the excellent Sergio Patricio, Xavi VII, DJ Cad and Hector Herrera who keep Discothèque packed. House and dance music features all night long on the main floor and there's a chill-out zone upstairs to replenish energy and get you back on the central podium. Don't be surprised by the half-naked go-go dancers at the top of the towers, they're there to make the more outrageous clientele blend in!

Rouge

C/Poeta Cabanyes 21 (93 442 49 85). Metro Paral.lel/20, 57, 64, 157, N16 bus. **Open** 11pm-4am Tue-Sat; closed Mon, Sun. **No credit cards. Map** p323 B6.

In contrast to the ambience, which is chilled, and the clientele, who are cool, the decor here is a raging, blazing, thermometer-busting… well, what did you expect with a name like that? It's highly appreciated by a hip, young crowd who like their cocktails as well-mixed as their tunes: try the West Indian punch with fresh lime juice, kick back and relax to a backdrop of top quality grooves, from future jazz to select electronica.

La Terrrazza

Behind Poble Espanyol, Avda. Marqués de Comillas (93 423 12 85/www.nightsungroup.com). Metro Espanya/13, 50, 61E bus. **Open** 18 May-12 Oct midnight-6am Thur- Sun; closed Mon-Wed. Closed 13 Oct-19 May. **Admission** (incl 1 drink) 2,000ptas Fri; 2,300ptas Sat. **No credit cards. Map** p323 A4.
Only functioning in the summer months, this outdoors venue is a literal breath of fresh air. Don't let the 300-plus queue with a door policy to match put you off. Get dressed to sweat and get down to some of the best dance music on offer. It's definitely worth the wait. Luke Slater, Angel Molina and Frankie Knuckles played here in 2000 and top names are the norm. Heavy dance tunes and plenty of podium space make La Terrrazza the perfect place for wild-eyed pouting posers.

Tinta Roja

C/Creu dels Molers 17 (93 443 32 43). Metro Poble Sec/57, 157, 61E bus. **Open** 5pm-1.30am Tue-Thur, Sun; 5pm-3am Fri, Sat; closed Mon. **No credit cards. Map** p323 B6.
Buenos Aires, anyone? You could well have stepped through a time warp into this small, smoky bar painted a rusty red and green and decorated with items recycled, rescued or bought at fleamarkets. The walls are packed with yellowing photos of tango shows and old Argentina set off by dozens of '60s and '70s style dressing table mirrors and fairy lights. Deeper into the bar and you're pleasantly surprised by an avant-garde art exhibition which opens up to a theatre. If you're lucky the owners Hugo and Carmen might be doing a tango show (Fridays and Saturdays) or giving tango lessons to new disciples of this sensual art (Tuesdays).

Torres de Avila

Entrance to Poble Espanyol, Avda. Marqués de Comillas (93 424 93 09/www.welcome.to/ torresdeavila). Metro Espanya/13, 50, 61E bus. **Open** 12.30pm-7am Fri, Sat; closed Mon-Thur, Sun. **Admission** (incl 1 drink) 1,500ptas. **Credit** MC, V. **Map** p323 A5.
The Torres de Avila is the ultimate product of the '80s/'90s Barcelona design-bar phenomenon, and Javier Mariscal's most spectacular creation. There are actually seven bars within this building, inside the main entrance to the Poble Espanyol (*see p91*). The entrance is a copy of one of the gates to the medieval city of Ávila – hence the name. The main theme of the design, by Javier Mariscal and architect Alfredo Arribas, was day and night, and the whole edifice is full of (tongue-in-cheek) symbols.

Only the best materials were used in the construction and fittings, and the whole thing cost millions, in any currency. Whatever you think of that, the result is beautiful, at times magical. For years it was more a monument than a bar, but in the last few years the stiff drink prices have been lowered to more moderate levels, and it now functions as a trance-techno disco. When the rooftop terrace bar opens in summer, it's a stunning vantage point for views of the city. In July and August, it may also be open on Tuesdays and Wednesdays.

The Eixample

Antilla Barcelona

C/Aragò 141-143 (93 451 21 51). Metro Hospital Clínic/43, 44, N7 bus. **Open** 10.30pm-4am Mon-Tue, Sun; 10.30pm-5am Wed; 11pm-6am Fri, Sat. **Admission** (incl 1 drink)1,500ptas. **No credit cards. Map** p320 C4.
Don't go to Antilla expecting to hear Ricky Martin or Gloria Estefan. Expect real salsa, hot merengue and crowds of Barcelona's Cuban residents. It looks like something from a film set, but once you get over the Miami tackiness accentuated by plastic palm trees and plenty of neon, a good time is assured. The house band Los Angelitos Negros gets the party going and the dance teachers (free classes 11.30pm-12.30am Mon-Thur) will soon have you swaying away like professionals.

Bar Six

C/Muntaner 6 (93 453 00 75). Metro Universitat/ bus all routes to Plaça Universitat. **Open** 8pm-3am Tue-Sat; 9pm-3am Sun; closed Mon. Closed 2wks end Aug. **Credit** AmEx, DC, MC, V. **Map** p324 C5.
Designer bar par excellence, Bar Six is the ideal place to get warmed up before some serious raving. Heavenly kitsch (check out the toilets) and smooth style blend together along with cool party tunes. The very low lighting and plush red velvet sofas are perfect for getting intimate and if you're lucky, owner Ronaldo might invite you to join him in one of his lethal knock-backs.

La Boîte

Avda. Diagonal 477 (93 419 59 50/ www.masimas.com/boite@masimas.com). Bus 6, 7, 15, 27, 32, 33, 34, 63, 67, N12. **Open** 11pm-5.30am daily. **Admission** (incl 1 drink) 1,800ptas. *Gigs* 1,800-3,000ptas (incl 1 drink). **No credit cards. Map** p320 C3.
One of a handful of clubs uptown that pulls in people from across the city, La Boîte is another place owned by the Mas brothers (of Jamboree and Moog), and is also a good music venue (*see pp231-2*). The long bar hugs the curved walls, and mirrored columns make the space surprisingly intimate. The resident DJ usually plays mainly soul, funk and old Motown favourites, but recently some decent progressive house fixtures have started to attract a younger crowd. The rather small dancefloor can get crowded at weekends.

Costa Breve

C/Aribau 230 (93 414 27 78). Bus 31, 58, 64, N8. **Open** midnight-5am Thur; midnight-6am Fri, Sat; closed Mon-Wed, Sun. **Admission** (incl 1 drink) 1,500ptas. **No credit cards. Map** p320 C3.
Costa Breve has long attracted a varied (largely uptown) clientele. The low ceilings, dim lights and curved bar help create an atmosphere for unwinding, while more energetic visitors really get into it on the dancefloor, grooving mainly to funk and popular dance tunes.

La Fira

C/Provença 171 (no phone). Metro Hospital Clínic/31, 38, 63, N3, N8 bus. **Open** 10pm-3am Mon-Thur; 10.30pm-4.30am Fri, Sat; closed Sun. **No credit cards. Map** 320 C4.
Large, airy space that calls itself a 'bar museum' – possibly the wackiest museum in town. It's furnished entirely with old fairground equipment: dodgems, waltzers, or swings provide the seating, and the several bars and food stands are designed like stalls. One of the liveliest of Barcelona's more extravagant bars.

La Pedrera de Nit

C/Provença 261-265 (93 484 59 95). Metro Diagonal/7, 16, 17, 22, 24, 28 bus. **Open** *July-Sept* 9pm-midnight Fri, Sat; closed Mon-Thur, Sun. Closed Oct-June. **Admission** (incl 1 drink) 1,500ptas. **Credit** MC, V. **Map** p320 D4.
The Eixample now has a unique new space that shouldn't be missed off any visitor's itinerary: in summer the swerving, rolling roof terrace of Gaudí's visionary La Pedrera is opened on Friday and Saturday evenings for drinks, live music, and fine views of the city. *See also p96.*

Perfumes Con Atxe

C/Provença 43 (93 321 10 75). Metro Entença/ 43, 44, N7 bus. **Open** midnight-6am Thur-Sat; 7pm-midnight Sun; closed Mon-Wed. **Admission** (incl 1 drink) 1,000ptas. **No credit cards. Map** p319 R4.
Without a doubt one of the most popular salsa clubs in the city, this place is big, with two floors of dancing space and surrounding lounge areas in which to take a breather. It is also seriously fun, even though it has the air of a club not to be messed with (take care with the bouncers at the door). The serious action begins late, after 1am, and keeps on getting hotter and hotter into the night. The rhythm-frenzied crowd represents a broad cross section of refugees from the electronic dance scene, along with a main core of real-life Latinos and eager neighbourhood locals.

Row Club (at Nick Havanna)

C/Rosselló 208 (93 215 65 91/ www.rowclub.com). Metro Diagonal, FCG Provença/7, 16, 17, 31, 67, 68 bus. **Open** *Row Club* 11.30pm-5.30 am Thur; closed Mon-Wed, Fri-Sun. *Nick Havanna* 11pm-4.30am Mon-Wed; 11pm-5.30am Fri, Sat; closed Thur. **Admission** *Row Club* (incl 1 drink) 1,500ptas. **Credit** AmEx, MC, V. **Map** p320 D4.

Keeping reality at bay in **Illusion**.

Located in the sleek 1980s design bar Nick Havanna, Row is a Thursday nightclub run by the same folks who put on the Sónar festival *(see p202)*. If you missed that, here's a second chance to hear the most coveted international DJs; Sven Vath, Francesco Farfa, John Acquaviva are just some of the regulars. It isn't comfortable and cosy but if you want dance music with a high ceilinged, breathable space then row, row, row yourself this way.

Zsa Zsa

C/Rosselló 156 (93 453 85 66) FGC Provença/14, 54, 58, 59, 63, 64, 66, N3, N8. **Open** 10pm-3am Mon-Sat; closed Sun. **Credit** V. **Map** p320 C4.
A chic bar patronised by designers, media people and older types, who go to talk and sample a sophisticated range of cocktails. An innovation of designers Dani Freixes and Vicente Miranda was the lighting, which changes continuously and subtly, so the mirrored wall may appear completely black, and at other times be ablaze with colour.

Gràcia

Buda

C/Torrent de l'Olla 134 (93 415 77 14). Metro Fontana/22, 24, 25, 28, 39, N4 bus. **Open** 9pm-2.30am Mon-Thur, Sun; 9pm-3am Fri, Sat. **No credit cards**. **Map** p320 D3.
If you're looking for a relaxed evening playing pool, chatting and drinking at reasonable prices, this is the place. There's low, comfortable lighting, the music's not overloud and the wait to get on the one pool table is not too long. It can get packed on Saturdays but otherwise it's all about relaxation.

Illusion (Cathedral Sunday T-Dance Session)

C/Lepant 408 (93 347 36 00/ www.matinegroup.com). Metro Alfons X/10, 15, 20, 25, 45, 47, N4 bus. **Open** midnight-6am Fri, Sat; 7pm-midnight Sun; closed Mon-Thur. **Admission** (incl 1 drink) 1,000ptas Fri; 1,300ptas Sat; 1,200ptas Sun. **No credit cards**. **Map** p321 F3.
Sunday nights haven't been the same since this special early session was started at Illusion, a warehouse-style club with a spacious dancefloor that always gets packed with a funky crowd. House music blares out on the main floor and there are the most outrageous floor shows, with drag queens, g-stringed go-go boys and girls, and painted fire-eaters: if you got too drunk you'd be forgiven for thinking you'd imagined the whole thing. The Sunday sessions are a must but if scooter boys and teenie boppers are not your scene don't go there on a Friday or Saturday.

KGB

C/Alegre de Dalt 55 (93 210 59 06). Metro Joanic/39, 55, N6 bus. **Open** 9pm-5am Thur-Sat. *Gigs* 9pm-12.30am. **Admission** *Gigs* depends on the band. *Disco* 1,000ptas (incl 1 drink) or 1,500ptas (incl 2 drinks). **No credit cards**. **Map** p321 E3.
The best time to go to this stark, industrial-style warehouse is 2am or later. The crowd are a lively alternative bunch. Despite its residential Gràcia location, KGB stays open late enough to attract hardcore insomniacs: by 5am, the place is thick and thumping. The drill-hammer house beat gets harder and faster the later it gets. Frenetic live concerts are held here sometimes, and international DJs do occasionally pass through.

Mond Bar

C/Plaça del Sol (607 310 015). Metro Diagonal/22, 24, 28, 39 bus. **Open** 8.30pm-2.30am Mon-Thur, Sun; 8.30pm-3am Fri, Sat. **No credit cards**. **Map** p320 D3.
The quintessential Gràcia meeting point for fashion conscious/music press-reading twenty-somethings.

A harmonious mix of pop/lounge, downbeat and trip hop emanates from this tiny split-level bar, where calming pastels and happy punters create a brilliant atmosphere. DJs are mostly home-grown talent, many of whom have resident slots elsewhere in town – at Moog, Nitsaclub or Malpaso.

Mond Club

Sala Cibeles, C/Còrsega 363 (93 317 79 94). Metro Diagonal/22, 24, 28, 39 bus. **Open** 1-5.30am Fri; closed Mon-Thur, Sat, Sun. **Admission** (incl 1 drink) 1,500ptas. **No credit cards.** Map p320 D4.
Friday nights, the big sister of Mond bar converts a stylish dance hall of the old school into a temple of pop, with candy-jar projections bathing the upper galleries and the stage, three sparkling bars and plush seats for louche posturing on the balconies. A steady stream of celeb DJs (Jarvis Cocker, Marc Almond and et al) at the decks are given free rein to take whatever trip down the primrose path of pop tickles their fancy. Fresh-faced Catalan kids and immaculate indie stylists hardly make for a hi-octane dancefloor, but if you have no demons to exorcise and can party on three centilitres of apple schnapps and a juicy slice of hand-picked pop, make a date on Friday night.

Otto Zutz Club

C/Lincoln 15 (93 238 07 22). FGC Gràcia/16, 17, 25, 27, 31, 32, N4 bus. **Open** 11pm-6am Tue-Sat; closed Mon. **Admission** 1,500ptas. **Credit** AmEx, DC, MC, V. **Map** p320 D3.
A landmark among the city's nocturnal offerings, the Otto Zutz Club offers three levels of hard-edged but elegant decor, with galleries overlooking the dancefloor. In times past it was the hottest club in town, but with the years it's moved inexorably towards the mainstream. On an average weekend night the place fills up with wannabes and expensive clothing labels, handsome himbos and their destined mates; the door policy can be a bit snooty. Even so, when a good DJ is visiting, it's a great place to dance. The Hot Club is a separate space with a softer, funkier tone. There's also live music, usually jazz, on some nights.

Sabor Cubano

C/Francisco Giner 32 (93 217 35 41). Metro Diagonal/22, 24, 28, 39, N4 bus. **Open** 9pm-3am Mon-Sat; closed Sun. **No credit cards.** Map p320 D3.
One of Barcelona's first salsa clubs, it doesn't try too hard on the decor but relies on its reputation and no-nonsense atmosphere to keep you coming back. Traditional Cuban music is mixed in with salsa and son – La Banda, Celia Cruz, and Manolito el Medico de la Salsa all feature – and it's frequented by Cuban band members resident in Barcelona.

Sal de Gràcia

C/Tordera 42 (607 230 952). Metro Joanic/15, 20, 39, 45, 47, 55, N4, N6 bus. **Open** 9pm-3am Mon-Thur, Sun; 6pm-3.30am Fri, Sat. **No credit cards.** Map p321 D3.

An ex-pat hangout for those who don't want to go home when the last bar has shut. Sal de Gràcia has a grunge look, so come here if you can't be bothered to dress up and are tired of the trendy music scene. It helps if you've already drunk yourself into oblivion before you arrive.

Terrasamba

C/La Perla 34 (no phone). Metro Fontana, Joanic/22, 24, 28, 39, N4, N6 bus. **Open** 9pm-3am Tue-Sun; closed Mon. **No credit cards.** Map p321 E3.
Named after the famous Brazilian band, this place is unmissable for all aspiring samba dancers. Shake your thing to the instructions of Toninho on Wednesdays, when you can get a free *brasileiro* dance lesson for the price of a *caipirinha*. An hour and a couple of *caipirinhas* later everyone is dancing samba and/or falling over. Terrasamba's compact size means it can get kind of stuffy so be sure to dress to sweat.

Tibidabo & Zona Alta

Atlantic Bar

C/Lluís Muntadas 2 (93 418 71 61). FGC Avinguda del Tibidabo/60 bus. **Open** 10.30-3am Thur-Sat; closed Mon-Wed, Sun. **Credit** V.
Directly opposite the Partycular, this bar is easy to check out on the same night. Murals of mermaids and roman statues decorate the place and you'll hear the same top 40 dance music as everywhere else. On the plus side, there is an outdoor bar serving cocktails, seating for a quiet chat and a swimming pool combined with being high up on the hill, making it a true 'alfresco' experience.

Bikini

C/Déu i Mata 105 (93 322 08 00/ www.bikinibcn.com). Metro Les Corts/15, 30, 43, 59 bus. **Open** midnight-4.30am Tue-Thur; midnight-5.30am Fri, Sat; closed Sun, Mon. **Admission** (incl 1 drink) 1,500ptas. **Credit** AmEx, V. **Map** p319 B3.
If there were such a thing as a state disco, it would probably be something like Bikini. Its institutional feel can be explained from its past: dating from the 1950s, the original Bikini called itself a 'multi-space' and had rooms for concerts and activities. A hub of late 1980s revels, it was closed when a huge mall, L'Illa, was built on the site. In 1996 the new, stately Bikini opened within the mall. It still offers three distinct spaces: a club, a Latin room and a cocktail lounge. *See also p231.*

Partycular

Avda Tibidabo 61 (93 211 62 61/ www.partycular.com). FGC Avinguda del Tibidabo/17, 22, 58, 73, 75, 85 bus. **Open** 6.30pm-2.30am Wed, Thur; midnight-3.30am Fri, Sat; closed Mon,Tue, Sun. **Credit** AmEx, MC, V.
Pleasant all year, this enormous bar located in a mansion on the hill up to Tibidabo really comes into its own in summer. It has rambling gardens sprinkled with bars, from where you can look across to

Arts & Entertainment

Breakfast clubs

For when hunger strikes at dawn...

Bar Estudiantil

*Plaça Universitat 12, Eixample (93 302 31
25). Metro Universitat/bus all routes to
Plaça Universitat.* **Open** 6am-2am Mon-Fri;
5am-3am Sat, Sun. **Credit** AmEx, MC, V.
Map p326 A1.

From 6am, wired punters arrive at this big
café in Plaça Universitat – at other times a
normal bar – to grab a *bocadillo* or a tapa
before committing to the next move. The
atmosphere at weekends is buoyant, owing
greatly to the staff's clever idea to tune into
a local techno station.

Bar-Kiosko Pinocho

*Mercat de la Boqueria, stall 66-67, Rambla
(93 317 17 31). Metro Liceu/14, 38, 59,
N9, N12 bus.* **Open** 6am-5pm Mon-Sat;
closed Sun. Closed 3wks Aug. **No credit
cards. Map** p326 A2.

A bar-stall tucked inside the Boqueria market
(take a right turn, if you're coming in from the
Rambla) that's a popular breakfast spot for
night-birds on their way home. During the day,
it's also good for lunch, although it's not as
cheap as it looks.

Cafeteria Estació de França

*Estació de França, Avda Marquès de
l'Argentera, Barceloneta, (93 310 16 33).
Metro Barceloneta/14, 36, 39, 51, 57, 59,
64, N0, N6 bus.* **Open** 6.45am-9pm Mon-Fri;
5am-9pm Sat, Sun. **Map** p327C4.

The grand, spacious and early-opening
station bar beneath the lofty ceilings of the
Estació de França is a breakfast favourite
for revellers (especially those turning out of
Woman Caballero downstairs). The perfect
place for winding down and filling up at the
end of the night.

El Horno

*C/Lancaster 6 (no phone). Metro Liceu,
Drassanes/14, 38, 59, N9, N12 bus.*
Open 11pm-8am daily. **Map** p327 A4.

Right around the corner from Moog, this
bakery is open through the night till 8am:
just lean in the door/window and shout
out your order to get *croissants de xocolata*
(chocolate croissants), *xuxos* (cream
doughnuts) or just plain croissants, hot
and fresh straight from the oven.

---

the lights of the funfair: there's plenty of space, beautiful people to look at, dance areas, tables for chatting and dark corners to be romantic in. If the
weather's cold, the grandeur of the rooms still makes
Partycular a good place for an after-dinner drink. All
in all, it's a class act. However, we repeat, it's up the
hill, so don't bother trying to get there by public
transport; take a cab.

Universal

*C/Marià Cubi 182 bis-184 (93 201 35 96). Bus 6, 7,
14, 15, 27, 32, 33, 34, 63, 67, 68.* **Open** 11pm-
4.30am Thur-Sat; closed Mon-Wed, Sun. **Credit** MC,
V. **Map** p320 C3.

Divided over two floors, Universal has two distinct
atmospheres. Downstairs, the music is loud, the
decor dark, and away from the bar there's plenty of
space for dancing. Upstairs is a light, high-ceilinged
bar-room, big enough to seat many but still quiet
enough for conversation. The trendy crowd is no
longer the wide cross section of characters it once
was: today, it tends towards a happy homogenous
band of surburbanites, and as such, the place gets
packed at the weekends.

The outer limits

Walden Eight

*Avda. Industria 12, Sant Just Desvern (93 499 03
42/www.elmirador.org). Bus 63.* **Open** midnight-
5.30am Fri, Sat; closed Aug. **Admission** 1,000ptas. **Credit** MC, V (only
for restaurant).

In the suburb/town of Sant Just Desvern on the western edge of metropolitan Barcelona, Walden Eight
is a post-industrial, sci-fi fantasy housed in a defunct
cement factory, with a crystal-ceilinged, flying-
saucer-like restaurant 30 metres (100 feet) up the factory's chimney. It was designed by Alfredo Arribas,
architect of the Torres de Avila, and sits next door
to Ricard Bofill's famous Walden building. In terms
of music style it's a techno/house club, with a wide
range of programming, including concerts by international groups, performances by bizarre circus people and a bevy of very skilled go-go dancers. At the
very top of the chimney, 100 metres (330 feet) up,
there's a viewing area from where you can gaze
down on the city's twinkling lights. Wow.

Sport & Fitness

Barcelona's enjoyment of sports – and not only football – grows year by year.

Though football may often seem like the only game in town, the 1992 Olympic Games were the starting point for an upswing in sports interest and an improvement in facilities that continues today. Currently, more than 500,000 people make use of the city's sports services, and the numbers are growing.

Spectator sports

Tickets can often be purchased in advance by credit card through Servi-Caixa or Tel-entrada (*see p196*).

Major sports venues

Montjuïc venues
Estadi Olímpic de Montjuïc *Avda de l'Estadi.*
Palau Sant Jordi *Passeig Olímpic 5-7 (both 93 426 20 89). Metro Espanya, then escalators, or Paral.lel then Funicular de Montjuïc/61 bus.* **Map** p323 A6.
Palau dels Esports *C/Lleida (93 423 15 41). Metro Espanya, Poble Sec/55 bus.* **Map** p323 B5-6.
The Olympic Games left Barcelona these three large-scale, multi-purpose sports venues, which have been fairly underused. However, the Estadi Olímpic has taken on new life since it became home to the Espanyol football club and the Barcelona Dragons (*see below*). In addition to sport, the venues are also used for concerts and other events (*see chapter* **Music: Rock, Roots & Jazz**). The Palau dels Esports, at the foot of Montjuïc, was constructed before 1992, but was rebuilt for the Olympic year.

Velòdrom d'Horta
Passeig Vall d'Hebron 185, Vall d'Hebron, (93 427 91 42). Metro Montbau/27, 73 bus. **Open** 4-8pm daily. Closed Aug. **Admission** free.
Least used of the Olympic installations, the Velòdrom incorporates centres for tennis and archery as well as cycling.

American football

Barcelona Dragons
Estadi Olímpic de Montjuïc, Avda de l'Estadi 17-19, Montjuïc (93 425 49 49/www.dragons.es). Metro Espanya, then escalators, or Paral.lel then Funicular de Montjuïc/61 bus. **Ticket office** match days from 2hrs before kick-off. **Tickets** 1,100-3,500ptas; VIP ticket (incl refreshments) 8,000ptas. **Advance tickets** Caixa de Catalunya, Servi-Caixa. **Games** 5pm Sat, from April to June. **Credit** MC, V. **Map** p323 A6.

Runners-up in the 1999 NFL European final, the Dragons have been surprisingly successful in gaining support in a city with very little experience of the game (average attendance is around 10-12,000). They play in the Estadi Olímpic, usually on Saturdays and Sundays at 7pm from April to June. The promoters liven up the games with all the razzle-dazzle Americana, including cheerleaders. Most players are American, but there are a few locals in the squad.

Basketball

The second most popular sport after football. The season runs from September to May; most league games are played on Saturday and Sunday evenings.

FC Barcelona
Palau Blaugrana, Avda Arístides Maillol s/n, Les Corts (93 496 36 75/www.fcbarcelona.com). Metro Maria Cristina, Collblanc/15, 52, 53, 54, 56, 57, 75 bus. **Ticket office** from 2 days before match, 9.30am-1.30pm, 4.30-7.30pm, or Servi-Caixa.
Tickets 500-3,700ptas. **No credit cards**.
Barça's basketball team is fanatically well supported, and it's advisable to book in advance. League games are mainly on Saturdays at 7.15/9pm and Sundays at noon/7pm; Cup and European games 8/8.30pm during the week. Though Barça has played in the European final five times, it has yet to win.

Club Joventut Badalona
C/Ponent 143-161, Badalona, Outer Limits (93 460 20 40/www.penya.com). Metro Gorg/44 bus. **Ticket office** from 1hr before match times. **Tickets** 2,400-3,300ptas. **No credit cards.**
Badalona's standard-bearers stand head-to-head with their wealthier neighbours, and unlike them, have actually won the European Basketball Cup. Most Sunday games are at 6pm; fans can be even more passionate than in Barcelona.

Football

The city's two first-division clubs are **FC Barcelona** and **RCD Espanyol**. Such is Barça's all-absorbing power that lower-division teams tend to be reduced to semi-pro status through lack of support, but fans of Brentford or Raith Rovers might want to commune with Hospitalet, or Jupiter, from Poble Nou. The season runs from late August to May, and league games have traditionally been played at 5pm or 7pm on Sundays. Due to pressure from TV, at least one game a week is played at 8.30-

Big *Bad* Barça

Former club president Josep Lluis Nuñez was probably only half-joking when he suggested that Futbol Club Barcelona had lent its name to the Mediterranean city where it was founded 100 years ago. Certainly the club's near-religious significance to the city cannot be overstated: *Barça, més que un club* (more than a club) is, for many, the very embodiment of Catalan identity itself.

However, one of many ironies at the core of '*Barcelonisme*' is that the club was actually founded by non-Catalans. The Swiss Joan Gamper is widely acknowledged as founder and mentor, but there were also Englishmen within the original group of football enthusiasts who shaped Barça's early years. The club's links with foreigners continues to be strong. Despite all the Catalan rhetoric, many Barça fans are only too aware of the fact that their most recent footballing campaigns have been fought by highly-paid foreign mercenaries.

Recent Barça history has been dominated by two men: former club president of 20 years, Josep Lluis Nuñez, and football legend, Johan Cruyff. Under Cruyff's charismatic leadership during the early 1990s, Barça enjoyed the most successful spell in its history, winning the European Cup in 1992, a 'must' for a club with such huge aspirations. But, in 1996 Johan went the way of all coaches. Nuñez in turn resigned bitterly in the summer of 2000, having failed to erase the Dutchman from Barça memory. No subsequent coach has managed to equal Cruyff's successes. The most recent sacking was of another Dutchman, Louis Van Gaal, who had arrived in Barcelona with impressive credentials but couldn't satisfy the exacting demands of *Barcelonisme*, and further alienated fans by filling the team with his own protegés from Holland. In June 2000, following their most dismal season in a decade (they failed to win a single trophy), the doors opened for the third new manager in four years.

Meanwhile, Barcelona's second club, RCD Espanyol, have also recently celebrated their centenary, but by contrast, the poor relations of city football have just enjoyed their most successful season ever, winning the Spanish Cup, the first major trophy in their history. Enmity between the clubs has been intensely political. Due to its name, Espanyol is viewed by many as Spanish rather than Catalan;

however, yet another contradiction is that the 'Spanish' club, who currently play their matches in the Olympic Stadium, actually have more Catalan players on their books than Barça, Catalonia's self-appointed national team.

WHAT NEXT?

Barça is rare among major European clubs in that the fans, its 100,000-plus members, elect the board. As the club enters a new millenium, another round of drastic change is under way. The new President, former Vice-President Joan Gaspart – elected after Nuñez' resignation – has promised renewal and continuity: a return to trophy-winning ways, and naturally, ever-increasing financial returns. The loss of the club's identity through over-reliance on foreigners brought a response in the hiring of its first Spanish coach in over a decade, the Mallorcan Llorenç Serra Ferrer. A few new players have been brought in to put a smile back on fans' faces, in the wake of the heartbreaking defection to Madrid of Portuguese star and long-serving Barça idol, Luis Figo.

The Gaspart era began falteringly, however. Following one of their worst League starts for several years, and still reeling in shock from the traumatic loss of Figo, Barça had to endure further humiliation: an early exit from Europe's premier competition, the Champions' League, while other Spanish sides – Real Madrid among them – qualified with ease.

The new coach may be discovering that unlike money, time, a precious commodity for creating great football teams, is scarce at the Camp Nou. Meanwhile, Barça remains as impatient as ever for footballing triumphs to match its name and sacred reputation.

Arts & Entertainment

9pm on Saturday; midweek cup games are usually at 8.30pm, but European matches can be as late as 10pm. *See also p252.*

FC Barcelona

Camp Nou, Avda Arístides Maillol, Les Corts (93 496 36 00/www.fcbarcelona.com). Metro María Cristina, Collblanc/15, 52, 53, 54, 56, 57, 75 bus. **Ticket office** 9.30am-1.30pm, 4.30-7.30pm Mon-Fri; tickets available a week before each match. **Tickets** 3,000-15,000ptas. **Advance tickets** (league only) Servi-Caixa. **No credit cards. Map** p319 A3.

Barça now has more season-ticket holders than its giant stadium, the Camp Nou (or Nou Camp), has seats, and it has become very difficult to get tickets for even the most ordinary game. However, there are various options. A week before each match, Barça puts around 4,000 tickets up for sale. Phone the club in advance to find out exactly when the tickets will go on sale and queue at the ticket office on Travessera de les Corts an hour beforehand. Another option is to try your luck with the ticket touts who usually stand in front of the ticket office before each match. Finally, you can always try asking at the entrance gates if anyone has an extra ticket – '*si us plau, li sobra un carnet?*' – it does work. There's a range of ticket prices, but since the *entrades generals* areas (for non-members) are very high up, it's worth spending more for a decent view. Barcelona also has teams in the Spanish second (the old third) division and at amateur level. The second-division Barça-B plays in the Mini-estadi, a 16,000-seat arena connected to the main stadium. Tickets cost about 1,000-2,000ptas, and games are usually at 5pm on Saturdays. If A and B teams are both at home, a joint ticket allows you to see both games. There is also the option of watching a training session (usually at 10am) or visiting the ultra-popular club museum (*see chapter* **Museums**).

RCD Espanyol

Estadi Olímpic, Passeig Olímpic 17-19, Montjuïc (93 292 77 00/www.rcdespanyol.com). Metro Espanya or Paral.lel, then Funicular de Montjuïc/61 bus (special buses on match days). **Ticket office** 10am-1.30pm, 5-8pm Fri; 10am-2pm Sat; match days 10am-match time. **Tickets** 3,000-7,000ptas. **No credit cards. Map** p323 A6.

Getting a ticket to see an Espanyol game is a lot easier than getting into the Camp Nou, but the Olympic athletics stadium lacks the atmosphere of a genuine football ground. On match days, free buses transport ticket holders up Montjuïc from a special stop at Plaça Espanya two hours before kick-off. To buy a ticket, head to the ticket booth at the right-hand side of the stadium entrance.

Ice hockey

FC Barcelona

FC Barcelona Pista de Gel, Avda Arístides Maillol, Les Corts (93 496 36 00/www.fcbarcelona.com). Metro María Cristina, Collblanc/15, 52, 53, 54, 56, 57, 75 bus. **Admission** free.

Once again, it's Barça that sponsors the only professional ice hockey team in town. The rink, open to the public on non-match days, is part of the club's vast sports complex. The season runs from October to March and a match schedule is available by phone or from the arena.

Roller hockey

FC Barcelona

Palau Blaugrana, Avda Arístides Maillol, Les Corts (93 496 36 00). Metro María Cristina, Collblanc/15, 52, 53, 54, 56, 57, 75 bus. **Ticket office** 2hrs before match times. **Tickets** prices vary. **No credit cards.**

Roller hockey is extremely popular in Catalonia. The game follows ice hockey regulations, with one notable exception – body-checking and most other forms of contact are prohibited. Matches are played at the Palau Blaugrana indoor arena; for match times, see the local press or phone the number above.

Other events

Barcelona Marathon (Marató de Catalunya-Barcelona)

Information & entry forms *C/Jonqueres 16, 15°, La Ribera (93 268 01 14/fax 93 268 43 34/ www.redestb.es/marathon_cat). Metro Urquinqona/ 17, 19, 40, 45 bus.* **Office** 5.30-8.30pm Mon-Fri; closed weekends. **Date** March 18. **Price** 6,000ptas. **No credit cards. Map** p326 B1.

Barcelona's Marathon celebrates its 24th anniversary in 2001. The race begins along the coast in Mataró, and ends in Plaça d'Espanya. Prospective participants should apply between October and the end of February. The city also holds two half-marathons, and the Cursa de la Mercè, during the Mercè (*see p204*). The sports information centre (*see p254* **Servei d'Informació Esportiva**) has details.

Motor sports

Circuit de Catalunya, Carretera de Parets del Vallès a Granollers, Montmeló, Outer Limits (93 571 97 00/fax 93 572 27 72/www.circuitcat.com). By car A7 or N152 to Parets del Vallès exit (20km/13 miles). **Times & tickets** vary according to competition; available from Servi-Caixa. **Credit** MC, V.

This motor racing circuit at Montmeló, north of Barcelona, was inaugurated in 1991. Motor sports have become very popular here in the last few years, mainly due to the success of Catalans Alex Crivillé and Carles Checa in 500cc motorbike competitions. The Spanish Formula-1 Grand Prix will be held in 2001 from April 27 to 29, and a motorcycle Grand Prix in mid-June.

Tennis

Reial Club de Tennis Barcelona-1899, C/Bosch i Gimpera 5-13, Les Corts (93 203 78 52/fax 93 204 50 10/ www.rctb1899.es). Bus 63, 78. **Open** club (members only except during competitions) 8am-10pm daily. **Ticket office** 9am-6pm daily during competitions.

As part of the men's ATP tour, Barcelona's most prestigious tennis club hosts a prestigious ten-day international tournament, the Trofeig Comte de Godó, during the last week of April. Tickets, available through Servi-Caixa or the club, cost 3,000-9,800ptas; *bono* tickets give you admission to all ten days (23,500-45,000ptas).

Participation sports

The Ajuntament runs an extensive network of *poliesportius* or sports centres: some have basic gyms and indoor halls suitable for basketball and five-a-side; others a lavish range of facilities including pools and running tracks. Charges are low, and you don't have to be a resident to use them. For cycle hire, *see p292*.

All of Barcelona's beaches have ramps for wheelchair access and most of the city's pools are fully equipped for disabled people (one exception, however, is the ageing Piscina Municipal Folch i Torres). For a list of facilities with disabled access, check with the Servei d'Informació Esportiva (*see below*).

Servei d'Informació Esportiva

Avda de l'Estadi 30-40, Montjuïc (information phoneline 93 402 30 00). Metro Espanya, then escalators, or Paral.lel then Funicular de Montjuïc/61 bus. **Open** *24 June-24 Sept* 8am-3pm Mon-Thur; closed Fri-Sun. *25 June-23 Sept* 8am-2.30pm, 4-6.15pm Mon-Thur; 8am-2.30pm Fri; closed Sat, Sun. **Map** p323 A6.
The Ajuntament's sports information service is located alongside the Piscina Bernat Picornell (*see p256*). It distributes leaflets listing district sports centres, or you can phone to ask which is the one nearest to you. Staff are helpful, but only some speak English.

Billiards, snooker, pool

Many Barcelona bars have tables for Spanish billiards (*carambolas*, blue, and without pockets) or American pool, and a few can offer full-size snooker tables.

Club Billars Monforte

La Rambla Santa Mònica 27, Rambla (93 318 10 19). Metro Drassanes/14, 18, 38, 59, 64, 91 bus. **Open** 10am-10pm daily. **Rates** membership 4,500ptas per trimester; members 200ptas per hour; non-members 800ptas per hour.
No credit cards. Map p327 A4.
Men of a certain age play cards, dominoes and billiards in a room of faded glory in this old-fashioned club. Officially, Club Billars Monforte is members only, but non-members are welcome to play American pool. It doesn't hurt to phone ahead and you should knock after 10pm. Make a point of going to the toilet to see the amazing domed roof of the ballroom on the way.

Bowling

Bowling Pedralbes

Avda Dr Marañón 11, Les Corts (93 333 03 52). Metro Collblanc/7, 54, 67, 68, 74, 75 bus. **Open** 10am-1am daily (Aug open from 5pm only). **Rates** per game 345ptas per person until 5pm Mon-Fri; 525ptas from 5pm Mon-Thur; 675ptas from 5pm Fri, all day Sat, Sun. Shoe hire included. **Credit** MC, V.
At this well-equipped facility, you can bowl or play snooker, pool or darts. Best time is early afternoon, but if it's full (which it often is), leave your name at reception and they will page you at the bar or restaurant when a lane becomes free.

Football

Barcelona International Football League

Information *(93 218 67 31/ nicksimonsbcn@yahoo.co.uk)*.
Wandering expats in Barcelona are able to bond on the football field thanks to the BIFL, created in 1991. The league is now made up of 17 teams, with many local and international members as well as British and Irish players, who play from September to June. If you're new in town, contact league president Nick Simons, who will help you find a team. Games can also be set up for visiting teams.

Golf

Club de Golf Sant Cugat

C/Villa s/n, Sant Cugat del Vallès, Outer Limits (93 674 39 58). By car Túnel de Vallvidrera (E9) to Valldoreix/by train FGC from Plaça Catalunya to Sant Cugat. **Open** 7.30am-9pm Tue-Sun; closed Mon. **Rates** (non-members) 7,000ptas Mon; 9,000ptas Tue-Fri; 20,000ptas Sat, Sun. **Credit** MC, V.
A young Seve Ballestros made his professional debut at this attractive and well-equipped 18-hole course, which was first designed and laid out in 1919, making it one of the oldest in Spain. Visitors can hire clubs and trolleys, and green fees allow access to several other facilities such as the bar, restaurant and pool.

Horse riding

Hípica Severino de Sant Cugat

Passeig Calado 12, Sant Cugat del Vallès, Outer Limits (93 674 11 40). By car Carretera de l'Arrabassada Km 10-11 Sant Cugat. **Open** 8am-8pm daily. **Rates** *Lessons* 1,700ptas per hr; 12 classes 25,000ptas. *Rides* by arrangement.
No credit cards.
This school takes groups riding with experienced guides through the pretty countryside around Sant Cugat and the Serra de Collserola. All-day rides include lunch. It is recommendable to book weekend rides at least two days in advance.

By the Port Olímpic you can jog...

Hípica Sant Jordi

Carretera de Sant Llorenç Savall, km. 42, Cànoves i Samalús (93 843 40 17). By car A18 or N150 to Sabadell, then B124 to Sant Llorenç Savall. **Rates** from 3,000ptas per 1½ hrs. **No credit cards.**
A child-friendly riding establishment in the hills near the Montseny (*see pp 279-82*), which offers varied programmes and excursions both for beginners and for experienced riders. One of the owners is English, so there are no language problems. Call ahead to book and get directions to the centre.

Ice skating

The skating rink in the Barça complex (*see p253*) is open to the public whenever it is not needed for ice hockey games. The rink is quite functional, and prices are low (1,000ptas per session on weekdays, which includes skate hire; rates are slightly higher at weekends).

Skating Roger de Flor

C/Roger de Flor 168, Eixample (93 245 28 00/ www.skatingbcn.com). Metro Tetuan/6, 19, 50, 51, 54,55, N1, N3, N4, N5 bus. **Open** 10.30am-1.30pm Tue-Sun; 5-10pm Wed, Thur; 5pm-midnight Fri, Sat; 5-9pm Sun; closed Mon. **Rates** (incl skates) 1,450ptas. **No credit cards. Map** p325 E5.
This modern rink, with good bar and restaurant facilities, offers discounts to groups of ten or more if you arrange your visit at least one day in advance.

...or take to sail.

Jogging & running

An enjoyable place to jog is the seafront, from Barceloneta past the Vila Olímpica. Away from the water, head to Montjuïc: run up from Plaça d'Espanya, or start at the top. For a flat, dirt road and a great view of the city, jog along the Carretera de les Aigües at the top of Avenida Tibidabo in the Collserola.

Sailing

The city's sailing facilities are concentrated in the Port Olímpic. For sailing outside Barcelona, *see pp266-7.*

Base Nàutica de la Mar Bella

Avda Litoral s/n, between Patja Bogatell & Platja de Mar Bella, Port Olímpic (93 221 04 32/ www.basenautica.net). Bus 36, 41. **Open** *Winter* 9.30am-5.30pm daily. *Summer* 9.30am-9pm daily. **Rates** *Membership* 22,000ptas per year. *Boat hire & courses* rates vary. **Discounts** BC. **Credit** MC, V.
Base Nàutica de la Mar Bella, on the third beach north after the Port Olímpic, hires out windsurfing and snorkelling equipment. Experienced sailors can choose from among many types of boats. The well-trained staff run courses for beginners.

Centre Municipal de Vela

Moll del Gregal, Port Olímpic (93 225 79 40/ www.vela-barcelona.com). Metro Ciutadella-Vila Olímpica/10, 36, 45, 59 bus. **Open** 9am-9pm Mon-Fri; 9am-8pm Sat, Sun. *Office* 10am-8pm daily. **Rates** individual sessions from 3,600ptas per hr; 17½ hr course 26,600ptas; 14,000ptas children. **Credit** MC, V. **Map** p325 F7.
A relaxed city sailing club offering courses at reasonable prices. The five-day programme is the same price for all classes of boat. For the complete novice, Centre Municipal de Vela offers a sea-christening session.

Squash

Squash 2000

C/Sant Antoni Maria Claret 84-86, Gràcia (93 458 22 02). Metro Joanic/15, 20, 45, 47 bus. **Open** 7.30am-11.30pm Mon-Fri; 8am-10pm Sat; 8am-3pm Sun. **Rates** non-members from 1,375ptas per hour. **Credit** AmEx, MC, V. **Map** p321 E3.
Squash 2000 has ten courts (book in advance), plus a sauna, bar and restaurant.

Swimming pools

There are 27 municipal pools in Barcelona; for a full list contact the **Servei d'Informació Esportiva** (*see p254*). The most spectacular of the Olympic pools, the **Piscina Municipal de Montjuïc** (93 443 00 46), used for the diving events, is only open from June to September.

At the **Club Natació Barceloneta**.

Club de Natació Atlètic Barceloneta

Plaça del Mar, Port Vell (93 221 00 10). Bus 17, 45, 57, 59, 64. **Open** *June-mid Sept* 7am-11pm Mon-Sat; 8am-8pm Sun. *Mid Sept-June* 7am-11pm Mon-Sat; 8am-5pm Sun. **Admission** (non-members) 1,025ptas per day. **No credit cards. Map** p324 D7.
The club's indoor and outdoor pools are located at Banys de Sant Sebastià (Passeig Joan de Borbó 93), where the Passeig meets the beach. Other facilities include a bar and restaurant, a massage/sauna area and a gym.

Piscina Bernat Picornell

Avda de l'Estadi 30-40, Montjuïc (93 423 40 41). Metro Espanya, then escalators, or Paral.lel then Funicular de Montjuïc/61 bus. **Open** 7am-midnight Mon-Fri; 7am-9pm Sat; 7.30am-4pm (June-Sept 7.30am-8pm) Sun. **Admission** *Open-air pool* 700ptas; 475ptas under-15s; free under-6s. *All facilities*, 1,300ptas; 700ptas under-15s; free under-6s. **Discounts** BT. **Credit** MC, V. **Map** p323 A6.
Built in 1969, this pool was lavishly renovated for the 1992 games. There are two Olympic-size pools, one indoor and the other outdoor (heated in early spring). You can also tone up in a gym/weights room. During the Grec festival (*see p203*), the pool hosts a joint swimming/film session from around 10.30pm, and on Saturdays, from 9 to 11pm, there is a session for naturists.

Piscina Municipal Folch i Torres

C/Reina Amalia 31, Raval (93 441 01 22). Metro Paral.lel/20, 36, 57, 64, 91 bus. **Open** *Sept-July* 7am-9.30pm Mon-Fri; 8am-7.30pm Sat; 8.30am-1.30pm Sun. *Aug* 7am-3pm daily. **Admission** (non-members) 900ptas; 250-500ptas children.
No credit cards. Map p324 C6.
This city complex on the edge of the Raval has three covered pools and a sauna and weights room.

Tennis

Barcelona Tenís Olímpic

Passeig de la Vall d'Hebron 178-196, Vall d'Hebron (93 427 65 00/ bto@fctennis.org). Metro Montbau/10, 27, 60, 73, 76, 85, 173 bus. **Open** 8am-11pm Mon-Fri; 8am-9pm Sat; 8am-7pm Sun. **Rates** courts for non-members 2,260ptas per hour; 650ptas for floodlights. **No credit cards.**
The city tennis centre, built for the Olympics, is some way from the centre of town. It has 17 clay courts, seven asphalt courts and four paddle courts. Racquets can be hired and balls are for sale.

Club Vall Parc

Carretera de l'Arrabassada 97, Tibidabo (93 212 67 89). Bus A6. **Open** 8am-midnight daily. **Rates** 2,200ptas per hour (courts); 600ptas for floodlights. **No credit cards.**
On Tibidabo, near Vall d'Hebron, this club offers 14 outdoor asphalt courts and two open-air pools. Tennis balls can be hired, but you must bring your own racquet.

Fitness

If you want to stay fit on a visit here, a good bet are the sport centres run by the city – they are cheaper and generally more user-friendly than private clubs. Check with the **Servei d'Informació Esportiva** (*see p254*) for centres with the right facilities.

Centres de Fitness DIR

C/Casp 34, Eixample (901 30 40 30/93 450 48 18). Metro Catalunya/bus all routes to Plaça Catalunya. **Open** 7am-11pm Mon-Fri; 9am-3pm Sat, Sun. **Rates** from 1,800ptas a day; 4,060ptas seven days. **No credit cards. Map** p326 B1.
Centres de Fitness DIR is a chain of seven centres in Barcelona, all with excellent facilities (weights machines, pools, saunas, and more) and flexible rates for non-members. Call the 901 number above for information about the one nearest to you.

Europolis

Jardín de les Infantes, between C/Vallespir and C/Marquès de Sentmenat, Zona Alta (93 363 29 92). Metro Les Corts/15, 43, 59, 30, 78, 54 bus. **Open** 7am-11pm Mon-Fri; 8am-8pm Sat; 9am-3pm Sun. **Rates** (non-members) 1,200ptas per day; membership 5,800ptas per month plus 10,000ptas joining fee. **Credit** MC, V.
Inaugurated in May 2000, this modern sports complex is located in Les Corts, a block from Diagonal. Fitness rooms are equipped with new machinery and there are 38 classes a day (spinning, aerobics, yoga, etc). The 'thermal zone' includes saunas, vapour baths and two indoor pools. A one-day pass permits access to all sports facilities, but appointments at the health and beauty centre are extra.
Branch: **Europolis** C/Sardenya 549-553, Gràcia (93 210 07 66)

Theatre

Barcelona's thriving, crowd-pleasing theatre scene has them lining up.

Catalan theatre has its own distinct style, less dependent on literary dialogues than on an ingenious blend of music, choreography, multimedia showmanship and spectacular production. This crowd-pleasing approach easily crosses language barriers, drawing ecstatic reactions from critics and audiences around the world for groups like **La Fura dels Baus** and **La Cubana**. On a local level, the influence of puppetry, circus and vaudeville is widely visible in a great variety of companies and festivals.

The vibrancy of this kind of theatre, added to Barcelonans' love for musicals and light comedy, has sparked a spectacular growth in attendances. As a result, private promoters and producers now surpass public ones in prestige and power; more and more venues are dedicated to unabashedly commercial shows, with actors from Catalan TV often serving as box office draws. The Generalitat-sponsored **Teatre Nacional de Catalunya** (TNC) opened in 1997, and the 2001 advent of the city-inspired **Ciutat del Teatre** ('City of Theatre'), a modern complex combining office, educational and performance space, can do little to alter the balance.

SEASONS AND FESTIVALS
The main theatre season runs from September to June, but the success of the **Festival del Grec** (*see p203*) has led some promoters to present programmes in July and August. The Grec is the best time to catch visiting theatre and dance companies, both international and from other parts of Spain. There's no fringe festival per se in Barcelona (Catalonia's best experimental showcase is in Tàrrega, in Lleida, in September), but worth watching out for are the **Marató del Espectacle** weekend in June (*see p201*), the autumn puppetry and masked theatre festival and the world-class clown festival in nearby Cornellà.

TICKETS AND TIMES
Main shows at most theatres start late, around 9-10.30pm. Many theatres also have earlier (and cheaper) performances at 6-7pm, often on Wednesday and Saturday or Sunday; on weekend nights there are also late shows. Most theatres are closed on Mondays. Advance bookings are best made through the ticket sales operations of savings banks, Servi-Caixa or Tel-entrada (www.telentrada.com, or *see p196*). Theatre box offices often take cash sales only. The best places to find current programmes are

Teatre Nacional de Catalunya. *See p258.*

the *Guia del Ocio*, newspapers (*see p300*) and, for Tel-entrada theatres, the *Guia del Teatre*, free at Caixa Catalunya branches.

Major companies

Els Comediants
The Comedians have been around for nearly 30 years, 17 of them spent living together as a community up the coast from Barcelona. Built around director/guiding light Joan Font, Els Comediants have a unique style of performance based in street theatre, mime, circus, music and Mediterranean traditions of folklore and the village holiday. While often accused of a naïve optimism, Comediants claim to defend the child within us all, making no distinction between creating a street ambience for a town celebration and elaborating a complex piece of staged theatre based on Cervantes' short dramas (*Maravillas de Cervantes*, seen in Barcelona in 2000).

La Cubana
Perhaps the Catalan company with the widest appeal, La Cubana has thrived on a dazzling mix of satire, gaudy showbiz effects, camp music and audience participation. Its productions *¡Cómeme el Coco, Negro!* and *Cegada de Amor* (Blinded by Love) were huge successes; the latter, exploiting and inter-mixing film and theatre conventions, blew audiences away at the 1997 Edinburgh Festival. Since then they have inexplicably lowered their profile. In 2000 they did an ironic combination of theatre and museum exhibit at the CCCB called *Equipaje para el 2000: más deprisa, más deprisa* (Luggage for 2000: Faster, Faster).

Dagoll Dagom
Under the direction of Joan Lluís Bozzo this company has honed a Catalan musical genre almost of its own, with striking use of colour and comedy.

Its productions *Mar i Cel* and *Flor de Nit* – inspired by the anarchist 1920s – were box-office hits; their latest show, *Cacao*, exposes the rough side of Caribbean immigration to Barcelona while ironising on the local love for salsa.

La Fura dels Baus

With their primitivist rituals, industrial music and latent threat of danger, La Fura burst onto the international scene in the 1980s with productions like *Suz-O-Suz* ('85) and *Tier Mon* ('88), where liquids, fire, and raw meat formed part of the messy recipe, and audience members were treated like refugees in a sea of noise, nudity, incessant banging and sundry mayhem. After their impressive Olympic opening ceremony came productions with more narrative, as La Fura went upscale, designing a version of Berlioz's *Damnation of Faust* for the prestigious Salzburg Festival in 1999 and producing a brand new opera, *Don Quijote en Barcelona,* in 2000 for the Liceu. A new piece, *OBS* (for 'obsession'), recalls earlier post-punk Fura chaos (and will travel to New York in February, and London at the end of 2001).

Els Joglars

A company that revolves around Albert Boadella, its founder, ideologist and leader, a veteran theatrical provocateur who was imprisoned under the Franco regime for his political stances. Using sardonic humour and text as well as the customary Catalan mime and dance skills, Boadella has kept to a line of caustic satire, with creations such as *Ubu President*, a biting caricature of Catalan president Jordi Pujol. A bit reiterative in their spoofs of Church, state and nationalist clichés, Joglars have now done *Daaalí*, a sympathetic portrait of the eccentric painter (scheduled for London's Barbican in September 2001).

Teatre Lliure

Probably Barcelona's most reputable theatre company, since 1976 the Lliure has presented classic and contemporary drama by Catalan and international authors. The Ciutat del Teatre project has been designed as their future base, although the enormous new ambitions – and budgets – attached to the project have lead to infighting and haggling with politicians. The Lliure also has a fine chamber orchestra (*see chapter* **Music: Classical & Opera**).

Mainstream theatres

Mainstream theatres

The boom in commercial theatre in Barcelona since the mid 1990s has meant that some theatres have lost their identification with any one genre or company. Large central theatres like the **Borràs** (Plaça Urquinaona 9, 93 412 15 82) or **Tivoli** (C/Casp 10-12, 93 412 20 63) are used for big-draw productions. The **Goya** (C/Joaquín Costa 68, 93 318 19 84), where García Lorca premièred many of his plays, often hosts flamenco music and Spanish-language theatre.

Mercat de le Flors

Plaça Margarida Xirgu, C/Lleida 59, Montjuïc (93 426 18 75/www.bcn.es/icub/mflorsteatre). Metro Espanya, Poble Sec/55 bus. **Box office** 1hr before performance. **Advance sales** also from Tel-entrada & Centre de la Virreina. **Tickets** prices variable. **No credit cards. Map** p323 B6.

A huge converted flower market with another adjacent space, the Mercat is due to become part of the Ciutat del Teatre project, to be opened in 2001. It has become the usual venue for flexible staging and multidisciplinary performances like those by La Fura dels Baus, and major visiting productions such as those of Peter Brook, La La La Human Steps and Cheek by Jowl. Also a major venue for the Grec festival (*see p203*).

Teatre Lliure

C/Montseny 47, Gràcia (93 218 92 51/ www.teatrelliure.com). Metro Fontana/22, 24, 28, 39, N4 bus. **Box office** from 5pm Tue-Sat; 4pm Sun. **Advance sales** also from Tel-entrada. **Tickets** 2,000ptas Tue-Thur; 2,500ptas Fri-Sun. **No credit cards. Map** p320 D3.

Long the most prestigious venue in Catalan theatre, a breeding ground for fine actors and directors such as Anna Lizarán and Lluís Pascual. The Gràcia space is charming and intimate; the scheduled move to the mega-Ciutat del Teatre has aroused tensions, leading to Pascual's resignation from the Lliure board.

Teatre Nacional de Catalunya (TNC)

Plaça de les Arts 1, Eixample (93 306 57 00/ www.tnc.es). Metro Glòries/7, 18, 56, 62, N3, N9 bus. **Box office** noon-3pm, 4-9pm Mon; noon-9pm Tue-Sat; noon-6pm Sun. **Advance sales** also from Servi-Caixa. **Tickets** 2,500-3,000ptas; discounts concessions and standby tickets from 50min before performance. **Credit** MC, V. **Map** p325 F5.

Architect Ricard Bofill's Parthenon-like TNC is by far the most imposing theatre building in the city, standing alone on a grand lot near the Plaça de les Glòries. After a controversial opening in 1997 (the prestigious actor/director Josep Maria Flotats was unceremoniously sacked as the institution's director for political reasons), the TNC has since been at peace with self and fellow man, although some programming is at times hard to distinguish from overtly commercial proposals. Productions to note in its two auditoria for 2001 include the Compagnie DCA production of *Shazam!,* in line with the Catalan non-textual genre, and *Useless (Information meets boy)*, a dance work by choreographer Cesc Gelabert.

Teatre Poliorama

La Rambla 115, Eixample (93 317 75 99/ www.teatrepoliorama.com). Metro Catalunya/bus all routes to Plaça Catalunya. **Box office** 5-8pm to performance Tue-Sat. **Advance sales** also from Servi-Caixa. **Tickets** prices variable; some discounts concessions. **Credit** MC, V. **Map** p326 A2.

This theatre was acquired by the Catalan government in 1984 to house the Flotats company, but since the opening of the TNC has been used by commercial producers tresX3, run by groups like Dagoll Dagom.

Multi-man Marcel.lí Antúnez

Actor, artist, musician and multimedia showman Marcel.li Antúnez has forged a unique theatrical persona since leaving the famed Fura dels Baus in 1989. As one of the Fura's founders, he was a key in honing their radical style; his break with the group just as mainstream success beckoned has won him the respect of a loyal following, drawn to his more personal, less anonymous approach to theatre. The son of a small town butcher, Antúnez is at home with blood and entrails in a way that makes urbanites cringe. He has shown his sewn pigskin sculptures in contemporary galleries, in 1992-93 coming up with *Joan l'Home de Carn* (Joan, the Flesh-Man), where a robotised caricature of Dr. Frankenstein's poor suturing was activated by viewers via sound and motion sensors.

His return to total art was with *Epizoo* (1994), where he attached clamps and pincers to his body and allowed audience members sadistically to manipulate his parts via a joystick connected to a computer.

Ulysses' trauma-ridden voyage home is the theme of *Afasia*, his newest production. Alone on stage with controls attached to his body, Antúnez manipulates a series of home-made instruments against a projected backdrop of mystical vignettes – including filmed scenes of actors – drawn from some imaginary Aegean. *Afasia* adds narrative and a strong dose of humour – his own wife and daughter embrace him onscreen at journey's end – to Marcel.li Antúnez' apparently sinister facade.

Teatre Principal

La Rambla 27, Rambla (93 301 47 50). Metro Drassanes/ 14, 38, 59, 91, N9, N12 bus. **Box office** from 4.30-8pm Tue-Sun; closed Mon. **Advance sales** also from Servi-Caixa. **Tickets** *Plays* 3,000-4,000ptas. *Opera* 2,000-4,500ptas. *Recitals* 2,000ptas. Some concessions. **No credit cards. Map** p327 A3.
The Principal stands on the site of Barcelona's first theatre, the Teatre de la Santa Creu, opened in 1597 and rebuilt in the 1850s. Recently refurbished, it offers everything from music to opera and serious drama.

Alternative & fringe

Barcelona's alternative theatre scene is holding its own, even growing, amid the enthusiasm for anything staged. Quality productions can be seen in intimate spaces like **Artenbrut** (C/Perill 9-1, 93 457 97 05), **Nou Tantarantana** (C/Flors 22, 93 441 70 22), **Espai Escènic Joan Brossa** (C/Allada Vermell 13, 93 310 13 64), **Abaixadors Deu** (C/Abaixadors, 10, 93 268 10 19) and **Conservas** (C/Sant Pau 58, 92 302 06 30).

Institut del Teatre

Plaça Margarida Xirgú (93 227 39 00/ www.diba.es/iteatre). Metro Espanya/55 bus. **Box office** 2hrs before performance Mon-Sat; 1hr before performance Sun. **Advance sales** also from Tel-entrada. **Tickets** 1,700-1,900ptas; 25% discount concessions; free Mar, May-June (student shows). **No credit cards. Map** p323 B6.

Three stages in the spacious new premises of Barcelona's Theatre School, part of the spanking new Ciutat del Teatre next to the Mercat de les Flors, offer interesting (and inexpensive) shows. Student productions and workshop projects with prestigious visiting directors are often staged. The expanded dance school also means more new choreography.

Sala Beckett

C/Alegre de Dalt 55 bis (93 284 53 12/ www.teatral.net/beckett). Metro Joanic/24, 25, 31, 32, 39, 55, 74, N6 bus. **Open** *Information office* 10am-2pm, 4-8pm Mon-Fri. **Box office** from 8pm Sat; from 5pm Sun. **Advance sales** also from Tel-entrada. **Tickets** 2,200ptas; discounts concessions. **No credit cards. Map** p321 E3.
Founded by the Samuel Beckett-inspired Teatro Fronterizo group, whose guiding light José Sanchis Sinisterra is one of Spain's best contemporary playwrights, this small Gràcia space offers varied new theatre, and also contemporary dance.

Teatre Malic

C/Fusina 3, La Ribera (93 310 70 35). Metro Jaume I/ 39, 51 bus. **Open** performances at 9pm. **Box office** from 7pm. **Advance sales** also from Tel-entrada. **Tickets** 1,800ptas. **Credit** MC, V. **Map** p327 C3.
A tiny (60-seat) theatre in a Born basement, the Malic does everything from mini-musicals to one-person diatribes. It has hosted English-language productions from local company Escapade, while a new English theatre group based in Barcelona will appear during the 2001 Festival del Grec.

Trips Out of Town

Getting Started

All partied out? Get out of town for a while – here's how.

Barcelona residents are fond of saying that their schoolkids are the luckiest in Europe, because they have the whole of Catalonia as their playground. Certainly, few other countries allow you to go from snow-capped mountain tops to crystal-clear Mediterranean bays after just a few hours' ride through woodland and green plains. In addition to the sheer beauty of the scenery, Catalonia's towns and villages also offer an astonishing variety of architecture and many of them are worth more than just a passing visit.

The information centre in the **Palau Robert** (*see p304*) and local offices have brochures (many multilingual) on the districts (*comarques*) into which Catalonia is divided, as well as parks, topics (*Modernisme* or Roman sites) and activities. Staying in the countryside is now easier with the number of *masies* taking guests (*see p274*) – a guide to them (*Residències – Casa de Pagès*) is available at the Palau Robert, local offices and bookshops. Other Generalitat guides include *Hotels Catalunya* and *Catalunya Campings*, and a good website (*www.gencat.es/probert*). For travel agents, *see p196*.

By bus

Coach services around Catalonia are operated by about half a dozen private companies, concentrated mostly (but not entirely) at the **Estació d'Autobusos Barcelona-Nord**, C/Ali Bei 80 (Metro Arc de Triomf/map E5). General information is on **93 265 65 08**, but each company has its own phone lines. Two areas better served by buses than trains are the high Pyrenees (with the Alsina-Graëlls company) and the central Costa Brava (with Sarfa).

By road

One great addition brought by the 1992 Olympics was the ring road, built to ease traffic into, around and out of the city. **The Ronda**

de Dalt** runs along the edge of Tibidabo, and the **Ronda Litoral** along the coast, meeting north and south of the city. They intersect with several motorways (*autopistes*): from north to south, the **A19** (from Mataró), the **A17/A7** (Girona, France) and **A18** (Sabadell, Manresa, Puigcerdà), which both run into Avda Meridiana; **A2** (Lleida, Madrid), a continuation of Avda Diagonal, which connects with the **A7** south (Tarragona, Valencia); and the **A16** (Sitges), reached from the Gran Via; all toll roads. Where possible, toll-free alternatives are given in the pages that follow. The **Túnel de Vallvidrera**, the continuation of Via Augusta that leads out of Barcelona under Collserola to Sant Cugat and Terrassa, also has a high toll. Further north, the **C25** (*Eix Transversal*) highway between Girona and Lleida is a means by which long-distance traffic can avoid the Barcelona hub. For more on driving and car hire, *see pp290-2*.

By train

Spanish Railways (**RENFE**) within Catalonia are particularly useful for the coast, Girona, the Montseny and the Penedès. All trains stop at **Barcelona-Sants** station. Tickets for local and suburban (*Rodalies/Cercanías*) services are sold at separate windows. In the city centre, some routes (the coast north, the Montseny, the Penedès) stop at the **Plaça Catalunya**; others (the coast south, Girona), **Passeig de Gràcia**.

Regional trains are *Regulars*, stopping at every station, *Deltas*, at nearly all of them, or *Catalunya Exprés*, stopping less often and costing a bit more. Long-distance (*Largo Recorrido*) services also stop at main stations, but supplements are paid for high-speed services. RENFE fare structures are complicated, but special deals are available and there are also *dias azules*, blue days (usually midweek) when long-distance services are cheaper. For **RENFE information**, call **902 24 02 02** (English spoken); or see the RENFE website (partly in English) at www.renfe.es.

Catalan Government Railways (**FGC**) serves some destinations from its two stations: **Plaça d'Espanya**, for Montserrat and Manresa, and **Plaça Catalunya** for the line within Barcelona and trains to Sant Cugat, Sabadell and Terrassa. **FGC information** is on **93 205 15 15**.

Beaches

Sun, sea, sand, scuba diving… you might even find the occasional relatively uncrowded beach.

Soaking up the **Sitges** sun.

Now that Barcelona has beaches of its own, the temptation to escape up or down the coast is not as strong as it was. Having said which, there are still plenty of coastal towns well worth a visit, and not just for their beaches.

In addition to the places to stay listed here, check out the Generalitat's *Residències – Casa de Pagès* guide (*see p274*) for low-price farmhouse accommodation, particularly in remoter areas.

South

To Sitges & Vilanova

Used in summer by generations of Barcelona residents, **Castelldefels** has now become a year-round suburban residence. Just 20km (12 miles) south of Barcelona, the town has kilometres of windswept beaches and fine seafood restaurants. A few minutes' ride further is **Garraf**, a tiny village with a small, recommended beach served by a couple of beach bars, and the **Celler de Garraf**, a *Modernista* gem designed by Gaudí for the Güell family in 1895.

Just on the other side of the Garraf mountains – a nature reserve – **Sitges** is one of Catalonia's most famous resorts. First 'discovered' in the 1890s by writer/artist Santiago Rusiñol (whose circle included Manuel de Falla, Ramon Casas and the teenage Picasso) it has a character all of

its own. Since the 1960s, Sitges has also become a favourite international gay destination (*see chapter* **Gay & Lesbian**). There are nine beaches along the seafront, and quieter, if snobbier, beaches at the (artificial) port of **Aiguadolç** – to get there, turn left out of the station. For nudist beaches, get to the seafront, turn right, and keep going (it's quite a walk).

Even when crowded, Sitges is charming, with a long promenade, the Passeig de la Ribera, curving along the beaches. Beautiful buildings cluster around the town's most visible monument, the 17th-century church of **Sant Bartomeu i Santa Tecla**. Almost adjacent are the old market, the Ajuntament and the **Museu Cau Ferrat** (C/Fonollar s/n, 93 894 03 64, admission 500ptas). Nearby is Santiago Rusiñol's old home, bequeathed to the town as a ready-made museum, chock-full of paintings – including some early Picassos – archaeological finds, *Modernista* ironwork and other fascinating objects.

Opposite is the **Palau Mar i Cel**, a delightful old residence with a finely crafted door, unusual interior and eclectic collection of medieval and baroque artwork. The **Museu Romàntic** in Casa Llopis, (C/Sant Gaudenci 1, 93 894 29 69, admission 500ptas), has a valuable collection of antique dolls. Sitges hosts a string of events through the year, including the spectacular *carnaval* in February, a theatre festival in June, and the **Film Festival** in October (*see p215*).

Vilanova i la Geltrú is the largest port between Barcelona and Tarragona, and has some good beaches. It also has several museums, including the important **Biblioteca-Museu Balaguer** (Avda Víctor Balaguer s/n, 93 815 42 02, admission 300ptas), with some El Grecos and many other artefacts, and a distinguished main square, the Plaça de la Vila. The town is known for its *carnaval*, and its ultrafresh seafood, especially served with *xató* – a spicy variant of *romesco* sauce.

Where to stay & eat

In Castelldefels, there are several cheap seafront paella restaurants, or the more upmarket **Nàutic** (Passeig Marítim 374, 93 665 01 74, average 6,000ptas).

Trips Out of Town

In Sitges, the **Sitges** C/Parellades 61, (93 894 34 93, closed Mon, average 2,000ptas) and **La Salseta** (C/Sant Pau 35, 93 811 04 19, closed Mon, set menu 1,400ptas) are both good value. For really good seafood at a price, go to **La Nansa** (C/Carreta, 24 93 894 19 27, closed Wed, average 4,500ptas).

If you want to stay over in Sitges, the **Celimar** (Passeig de la Ribera 18, 93 811 01 70, rates 12-16,000ptas) is a comfortable seafront hotel, while the **Hotel Romàntic** (C/Sant Isidre 33, 93 894 83 75, rates 10-14,000ptas) is a Sitges classic, an almost over-the-top hotel in a delicately restored set of 19th-century villas. **Hostal Maricel** (C/d'en Tacó 11, 93 894 36 27, rates 6,000ptas) is a good budget option, while the **Parellades** (C/Parellades 11, 93 894 08 01, rates 4,000ptas) is both good and cheap. *See also chapter* **Gay & Lesbian** for more accommodation options.

In Vilanova i la Geltrú **Avi Pep** (C/Llibertat 128, 93 815 17 36, closed Mon, average 2,000ptas) is cheap and cheerful; **Peixerot** (Passeig Marítim 56, 93 815 06 25, closed Mon, average 5,000ptas) gets the pick of the day's fish; and excellent grilled meat can be had at **Can Pagès** (C/Sant Pere 24-6, 93 894 11 95, closed Mon, average 4,000ptas).

At Cubelles (4km/2½ miles west of Vilanova) there is the **Llicorella** (93 895 00 44, rates 20,000ptas), a comfortable upscale hotel with a pool and sculptures in the garden, and a very highly regarded restaurant.

Getting there

By car
A16 to Castelldefels, Garraf, Sitges (41km/25 miles) and Vilanova (extra tunnel toll of 620ptas between Garraf and Sitges); or C246 via a slow, winding drive around the Garraf mountains.

By train
RENFE approx every 20min from Sants or Passeig de Gràcia to Platja de Castelldefels, Sitges (30min) and Vilanova (40min); not all stop at Castelldefels and Garraf.

Tourist information

Oficina de Turisme de Castelldefels
Plaça de l'Igliesa 1 (93 664 23 61). **Open** 8am-3pm Mon-Fri; closed Sat, Sun.

Oficina de Turisme de Sitges
Passeig de Vilafranca (93 894 42 51). **Open** 9am-2pm, 4-6.30pm Mon-Fri; 9am-2pm Sat; closed Sun.

Turisme de Vilanova i la Geltrú
C/Torre de Ribarroges/Platja (93 815 45 17). **Open** 10 am-2pm, 4-7pm Tue-Fri; 10am-2pm Sat, Sun; closed Mon.

Altafulla: sand, sea and sights to see.

Tarragona & Costa Daurada

If you're looking for castles and sand, **Altafulla**, between Vilanova and Tarragona, has both, plus one of the best-preserved medieval centres on the coast. The modern section is close to the seafront, where there are fine white sand beaches between rocky outcrops, and a picturesque seaside castle at nearby **Tamarit**. The old walled town – which is crowned by the imposing **Castell d'Altafulla** and floodlit at night – is ten minutes' stroll inland.

Tarragona, a busy city of over 100,000 people, is overlooked by most foreign visitors, despite the fact that as Roman Tarraco it was the capital of half the Iberian peninsula, and so contains the largest ensemble of Roman buildings and ruins in Spain, an extraordinary architectural legacy: the original town walls, an amphitheatre, circus, aqueduct and forum. Much later, Catalan colonisers spent 61 years constructing the majestic **Catedral de Santa Maria**, which dominates the beautiful *ciutat antiga* (old city). A walkway around the Roman walls, the **Passeig Arqueològic**, provides a breathtaking view of the sea and the flat hinterland, the Camp de Tarragona. Below are a busy modern boulevard, the Rambla Nova, and an attractive fishermen's district with good seafood restaurants. The Platja del Miracle ('Beach of the Miracle') lies just beyond the amphitheatre.

Further south-west is **Salou**, resort hub of the Costa Daurada, with sand, sea, hotels, discos, bars, calamares'n'chips and suncream all on tap. It also has some *Modernista* buildings, and, on another note, the popular **Port Aventura** theme park is just nearby.

Universal Studios Port Aventura
(977 77 90 00). **Open** *Mar-late June, mid Sept-early Nov* 10am-8pm daily. *Late June-mid Sept* 10am-12am daily. *Nov-Jan* call to confirm times. **Admission** *One day* 4,800ptas; 3,600ptas concessions; free under-5s. *Two consecutive days* 7,200ptas; 5,500ptas concessions; free under-5s. *Three consecutive or*

alternate days 9,600ptas; 7,400ptas concessions; free under-5s. *Night ticket* (7pm-midnight, mid June-mid Sept only) 3,500ptas; 2,400ptas concessions. **Credit** AmEx, DC, JCB, MC, V. **Getting there**: By car A2, then A7 to exit 35, or N340 (108km/67 miles). By train from Sants or Passeig de Gràcia (1hr 15min). The park has its own station, on the Barcelona-Tarragona-Tortosa line; in season 7 southbound and 10 northbound trains stop there daily.

Port Aventura continues to draw in the crowds. Top attraction is the stomach-crunching Dragon Khan, largest roller-coaster in Europe, with eight 360° loops; there are also special rides for little kids, and all sorts of floor shows. There is also an excellent virtual underwater journey called Sea Odyssey. Theme park fans rate Port Aventura very highly; non-addicts might note that it's more authentic than most, in terms of the design of the buildings and the goods on sale. Admission gives you unlimited rides. Facilities include video and buggy hire, and wheelchairs and other disabled services. Food and drink cannot be taken into the park, but there are food outlets (serving alcohol) on every corner.

Where to stay & eat

In Altafulla there is the **Faristol** (C/Sant Martí 5, 977 65 00 77, closed Mon, average 3,000ptas), a well-priced bar-restaurant in an 18th-century house run by an Anglo-Catalan couple, with a pleasant outdoor terrace. A decent bed can be found at **Yola** (Via Augusta 50, 977 65 02 83, rates 13,000ptas), a modern place with a brand-new swimming pool. To rent rooms in the old town, ask at **El Corral** bar (977 65 04 86) or the above-mentioned Faristol.

Tarragona offers cheap and enjoyable meals at the **Bufet el Tiberi** (C/Martí d'Ardenya 5, 977 23 54 03, average 2,000ptas). **Sol-Ric** (Via Augusta 227, 977 23 20 32, closed Mon, average 5,000ptas) is famous for seafood *romesco* and its fine wine list. A bed fit for a king can be found at the **Imperial Tarraco** (Rambla Vella 2, 977 23 30 40, rates 11,000 -18,000ptas); cheaper digs are at the **Forum** (Plaça de

l'Ajuntament, 977 23 17 18, rates 6,000ptas). A highly recommended in-between hotel is the three-star **Lauria** (Rambla Nova 20, 977 236 712, rates 10,000ptas).

Eating in Salou is pricey. The **Goleta** (C/Gavina-Platja Capellans, 977 38 35 66, closed Mon, Sun pm, average 5,000ptas) has good salt-baked fish. **El Racó** (Platja del Racó, 977 37 02 16, rates 6,500ptas) has good, clean rooms.

Getting there

By car
A2, then A7 via Vilafranca (Tarragona 98km/60 miles); or toll-free N340 (Molins de Rei exit from A2).

By train
RENFE from Sants or Passeig de Gràcia to Altafulla (55min), Tarragona (1hr 6min) and Salou (1hr 18min). Trains hourly approx 6am-9.30pm.

Tourist information

Oficina de Turisme de Altafulla
Plaça dels Vents (977 65 07 52). **Open** *May-Oct* 10am-2pm Mon-Sat; closed Sun. Closed Nov-April.

Oficina de Turisme de Tarragona
C/Fortuny 4 (977 23 34 15). **Open** 10am-2pm, 4pm-6.30pm Mon-Fri; 10am-2pm Sat; closed Sun.

Oficina de Turisme de Salou
Passeig Jaume I 4 (977 35 01 02). **Open** 9.30am-1.30pm, 4-7pm Mon-Sat; 9.30am-1.30pm Sun.

The Ebre Delta

About an hour down the coast from Tarragona is the **Delta de l'Ebre** nature reserve, an ecologically remarkable 320 square km (125 square mile) protected area that's home to almost 300 species of birds (60 per cent of all the species found in Europe) including flamingoes, great crested grebes, herons, marsh harriers and a huge variety of ducks.

The Ebre Delta.

Having a splash

Scuba diving

Scuba diving is hugely popular in Catalonia. The coastal waters are relatively deep, and the effects of mass tourism are often easy to see, but there is some very decent diving to be had, especially among the rocky coves and caves of the Costa Brava. Wetsuits, tanks, regulators and guides can be hired at diving clubs in towns along the coast (masks, fins, and snorkels are also available, but it's more common to bring your own). Prices generally run from about 5,000 to 8,000ptas per dive, including equipment and guide. A valid diver's certificate is required. Scuba clubs in Barcelona also arrange trips up the coast, but inevitably charge a bit more.

The **Illes Medes,** near Estartit, are an official underwater reserve, with some of the last beds in the western Mediterranean of the sea's native red coral. Unfortunately, this means that diving areas at the Medes are often uncomfortably crowded, with bunches of 50 divers being dumped into the sea every half-hour or so.

If you've never dived before it's also possible to try a simple baptismal dive with a guide, or sign up for a course. Courses usually last from a few days to a week, and cost around 50,000ptas.

Diving clubs, north to south

Cadaqués
Sotamar *Avda Caritat Serinyana 17 (972 25 88 76).* Open all year. Ten dive routes.

Roses
Poseidon *C/Bernd i Barbara Mörker (972 25 57 72/25 44 07/929 58 15 06).* Open all year.

L'Estartit (for Illes Medes)
Diving Center La Sirena *C/Camping La Sirena (972 75 09 54).* Open all year.

Unisub *Ctra Torroella de Montgrí 15 (972 75 17 68).* Open Mar-Nov.

Quim's Diving Center *Ctra Torroella de Montgrí, km 4.5 (972 75 01 63).* Open all year.

Begur
Aqualògik *Cala d'Aiguafreda (972 62 42 47).* Open all year. Ten dive routes.

Barcelona
Aquamarina *C/Castillejos 270 (93 455 29 62).* Open all year. Map p321 F4. Equipment for sale and rent.

The towns of the delta are nothing special, but the natural beauty of the place – the immense, flat, green expanse of wetlands, channels, dunes and still productive rice fields – makes it fascinating all year round.

The town of **Deltebre** is the base for most park services. From there it's easy to make day trips to the bird sanctuaries, especially the remote headland of **Punta de la Banya.** The delta's flatness makes it ideal for walking or cycling (for bicycle hire, check at the information office in Deltebre). Small boats offer trips along the river from the north bank about 8km (5 miles) east of Deltebre.

Where to stay & eat

In Deltebre there is **El Buitre** (Ctra de Riumar, 977 48 05 28, rates 5,000ptas), a box-style hotel with low-budget James Bond undertones; the restaurant serves very good Delta rice dishes (average 2,500ptas). Another excellent restaurant is **Galatxo** (Desembocadura Riu Ebre, 977 26 75 03, average 2,500ptas) at the mouth of the Ebro.

There are two official campsites between Deltebre and the river mouth, **L'Aube** (Urbanització Riumar, 977 44 57 06, rates 1,500ptas per car), and **Riomar**, which has a pool (Urbanització Riumar, 977 26 76 80, rates 1,800ptas per car).

Getting there

By car
A2, then A7 via Vilafranca, or N340 (Molins de Rei exit from A2). Barcelona-Amposta 172km/107 miles.

By train & bus
RENFE from Sants or Passeig de Gràcia to L'Aldea-Amposta (2 hrs), then bus (HIFE 977 44 03 00) to Deltebre.

Tourist information

Centre d'Informació – Parc de Deltebre
C/Doctor Martí Buera 22 (977 48 96 79). **Open** 10am-2pm, 3-6pm Mon-Fri; 10am-1pm, 3.30-6pm Sat; 10am-1pm Sun.

Sailing/windsurfing/kayaking

Nearly every coastal town has a Club Nàutic (boat club) that rents small sailboats or windsurf-boards by the hour. Yachts (with or without a captain) for day trips or longer adventures are also available, as are sea kayaks. Other rental places specialise in different types of boat, catamarans being the most common. Coastal campsites may also have boats or windsurfing equipment for rent. Prices range between 2,500ptas and 4,500ptas an hour for smaller class craft, and from 25,000ptas up per day for yachts. For boat hire within Barcelona, see p255.

Barcelona & further south

Barcelona

Jack London Charters C/Riera Alta 10 (tel/fax 93 442 08 69/639 35 89 92/ jalondon@teleline.es). Open all year. Two 42ft/13m yachts can be hired with English-speaking captain for trips along the coast, to the Balearics, or the Caribbean, if need be.

Castelldefels

Catamaran Center Port Ginesta, Local 324 (93 665 22 11). Open all year. All classes of catamarans for rent, including a 16m/53ft cat-yacht. Sea kayaks also available.

Sitges

Club Nàutic Sitges Espigon s/n (93 894 09 05). Open all year. Catamarans for rent.

Calafell (south of Vilanova i la Geltrú)

Windcat House Passeig Marítim 51 (Mas Mel) (977 69 30 72). Open all year. Catamarans, kayaks and courses.

North of Barcelona

Calella de la Costa

Club Nàutic Calella Passeig Platja s/n (93 766 18 52). Open all year. Cats, estells, kayaks and windsurf equipment for rent.

L'Escala

Kayaking Costa Brava Passeig Lluís Albert 11 (972 77 38 06). Open all year. Kayak hire, courses and guided group trips from Tamariu to Aiguablava. Half-day trips, 6,000ptas.

Sant Pere Pescador

La Ballena Alegre C/Despoblat Sector Sud (972 52 03 02). A campsite on the Costa Brava that rents windsurf equipment.

North

The Costa del Maresme

The Maresme coast, immediately north-east of Barcelona, is close enough to visit in a day. Of the string of small towns along the shoreline, **Caldes d'Estrac**, also known as **Caldetes**, and **Sant Pol de Mar** both have good beaches (some nudist), and plenty of tourists, local and foreign. Caldetes has some interesting *Modernista* houses, a spa, and a recently restored park with fine views; and Sant Pol is a tranquil, mostly unspoilt, if yuppified, fishing village. In contrast to many places along this coast, where railway tracks run close to the beach, some of Sant Pol's beaches are separated from roads and rail by rocky cliffs.

Between these two villages is the larger town of Canet, the former home of *Modernista* architect Domènech i Muntaner, and containing some of his best work. It was also home in the '70s and '80s to theatre group Els Comediants.

Getting there

By car

N-II from Barcelona to Caldes d'Estrac (36km/22 miles), Sant Pol (48km/30 miles), Canet (42km/26 miles).

By train

RENFE from Sants or Plaça Catalunya. Trains every 30min, journey time approx 45min-1hr.

Where to stay & eat

In Caldetes, **Emma** (Baixada de l'Estació 5, 93 791 13 05, open Apr-Oct, average 2,500ptas) is one of the town's best mid-priced restaurants. If you want to stay over, **Pinzón** (C/El Callao 4, 93 791 00 51, rates 5,500ptas) is a good bet. In Sant Pol, the **Hostalet I** (C/Manzanillo 9, 93 760 06 05, rates 5,000ptas) and **Hostalet II** (C/Antonio Soleda 1, 93 760 02 51, rates 5,000ptas), are pleasant hotels. Canet has the **Mitus** (Riera de la Torre, 937 942 903, rates 4,000ptas) a charming family-run hostal. There are plenty of places to eat on the tree-lined Passeig del Maresme.

Dalí-rama

Figueres had an on-off relationship with its most famous son while he was still alive – not least due to his ambiguous relationship with the Franco regime – but since Salvador Dalí's death the town has become an obligatory visit for anyone curious about the great masturbator's special universe. The **Teatre-Museu Dalí** (pictured bottom right), in Figueres' former theatre, was designed by Dalí complete with music, optical illusions and bizarre installations, and contains his tomb. From July to September, the museum stays open later, with Dalí's own choice of lighting and music and a free glass of cava. The **Torre Galatea**, Dalí's egg-topped Figueres residence (pictured top right), is next door.

Since 1998 the two other Empordà properties associated with the great man have been opened to the public, forming a new 'Dalí Triangle' (*triangle dalinià*) for aspiring surrealists to disappear into. Dominating the cove of **Port Lligat** just outside Cadaqués is his own favourite house, a Dalí image in itself with two giant cracked heads on the top wall seen against the rocky hillside and azure sea. The house, designed for Dalí with many strange features, was all but abandoned for years and is in very poor condition. Only eight people are allowed in at one time, so bookings are essential. In Púbol, about 35 kilometres (22 miles) south of Roses in the Baix Empordà, is the 12th-century castle that Dalí bought for his wife and 'muse' Gala. Here she entertained a string of young men, while Dalí himself was not allowed to visit without an appointment. Today, reservations are only obligatory for very large groups.

Casa-Museu de Port Lligat

(972 25 10 15). **Open** *14 Mar-14 June, 16 Sept-6 Jan* 10.30am-6pm Tue-Sun. *15 Jun-15 Sept* 10.30am-9pm Tue-Sun. Closed Mon. Closed 7 Jan-13 Mar. **Admission** 1,300ptas; 800ptas concessions. **No credit cards**.

Castell de Púbol

(Enquiries:Teatre-Museu Dalí, 972 67 75 00). **Open** *15 Mar-14 June, 16 Sept-1 Nov* 10.30am-6pm Tue-Sun. *15 Jun-15 Sept* 10.30-8pm Tue-Sun. Closed Mon. Closed 2 Nov-14 Mar. **Admission** 700ptas; 500 ptas concessions. **No credit cards**. Púbol is best reached via Girona, not Figueres: by train to Girona or Flaçà, and then by Sarfa bus to La Bisbal, which stops at Púbol village. In a car, take the N-II north from Girona, and then the C255 towards La Bisbal.

Teatre-Museu Dalí

Plaça Gala-Salvador Dalí 5, Figueres (972 67 75 00). **Open** *Oct-June* 10.30am-5.45pm Tue-Sun. *July-Sept* 9am-7.45pm Tue-Sun. Closed Mon. **Admission** 1000ptas; 800ptas concessions. **Credit** AmEx, MC, V.

The Costa Brava

The area which most visitors usually think of as the Costa Brava consists of a clutch of towns around the local hub of **Blanes**, which have been given over to big-scale package tourism since the 1960s. For the sake of simplicity, over the years different towns along the stretch have come to specialise in different nationalities: **Calella de la Costa** is known as the coast's German *burg* – with its very own summer *bierfest*; in **Lloret de Mar** there are more British and Dutch, and so pubs and places selling chips with mayonnaise. If you're looking for the full disco-blow-out-fall-asleep-on-the-beach experience, head for Lloret.

Oddly enough, this is not really the Costa Brava proper at all, which actually lies 50km (30 miles) further north in the Baix Empordà. This rocky peninsula was the original 'rugged coast' for which journalist Ferran Agulló dreamt up the name 'Costa Brava' in the early 1900s. It is still the Costa's most unspoilt section: there are no big sandy beaches, and public transport is limited, so the area has largely escaped mass tourism. Accommodation facilities are also relatively small-scale (it's essential to book in high season), as are nightlife and organised activities for children and families. This does not mean the area is undiscovered, though: it's a favourite holiday and second-home location for prosperous Catalans, and in summer it's best to visit midweek to avoid the crowds.

The first town of interest in the *comarca* is **Sant Feliu de Guíxols**, for centuries the principal port for Girona (*see p283-4*) and the cork industry. Sant Feliu has some stunning *Modernista* buildings, a charming Passeig Marítim, and a treasure trove of ancient ceramics in the town museum. The curved sandy beach gets crowded, but offers respite from an otherwise rocky coast. A less-visited beach lies 3km (2 miles) north at **Sant Pol**. Nearby is **S'Agaró**, a private village of luxury beach houses built when tourist facilities were scarce on this coast. It's worth visiting for its spectacularly ritzy architecture – the cliffside balconies are favourites for perfume ads.

Heading north about 20km (12 miles) and avoiding the more crassly touristy areas of **Platja d'Aro** and **Palamós**, you arrive at the main inlets on the peninsula. The northern ones (**Sa Riera**, **Sa Tuna**, **Aiguablava**) are most accessible from Begur; those further south (**Tamariu**, **Llafranc** and **Calella**) are best reached from Palafrugell.

Begur is an attractive old town dominated by the remains of a 14th-century castle. It's set just inland on a rocky hillside commanding magnificent views. From there it's a steep 3km (2

mile) walk down to the coast (no public transport). A little further inland is the very carefully preserved medieval village of **Pals**, now seemingly converted almost entirely into second homes. It is nonetheless a remarkable survivor, with a core of fine 12th- to 15th-century buildings, and beautiful views over the surrounding countryside.

Sa Riera, at the end of the road from Pals to the coast, is the northernmost cove of the peninsula, with one of its largest sandy beaches and good views of the Medes islands to the north. There's a popular nudist beach, the **Illa Roja**, between Sa Riera and La Platja del Racó. From Sa Riera a road leads south to **Sa Tuna**, a picturesque fishing village with a stony beach. Its one hostal-restaurant has a great position on the seafront. From there a 40-minute walk along a coastal path takes you northwards through **Aiguafreda**, a small wooded cove, to a spectacular building cut into the promontory beyond. Steps lead down to swimming pools cut into the precipitous cliff-face.

Heading south via Begur, you'll reach **Fornells** and **Aiguablava**, both in a larger bay. Aiguablava has a beach with beautiful white sand, a small yacht harbour, and an old, luxurious hotel. **Tamariu**, in an intimate bay, is slightly larger, with hotels and bars known for excellent seafood. You can swim from the rocks, and hire boats for exploring, water skiing or fishing (call Paco Heredia on 972 30 13 10 or 607 29 25 78). Tamariu and nearby **Llafranc** are the only places on this stretch easily accessible by public transport, with regular buses from **Palafrugell**, the peninsula's transport hub, which also hosts a lively Sunday market.

Leaving the Costa Brava outcrop, further up the coast is the small town of **Estartit**, a water-sports centre situated opposite the islands known as the **Illes Medes** (Catalonia's only underwater nature reserve). Glass-bottomed boats leave Estartit every hour (June to September; in April, May, October, according to demand) to tour the now rare coral deposits for which the rocky islets are renowned. The more adventurous can go scuba diving (*see p266*). A little inland is the **Castell de Montgrí**, an unfinished but imposing 12th-century castle with fine views.

Where to stay

In Sant Feliu de Guíxols, the **Hotel Les Noies** (Rambla del Portalet 10, 972 32 04 00, rates 5,000ptas) has reasonably-priced rooms in town. More intimate is the **Florida** (Plaça del Monestir 7, 972 32 03 79, rates 6,000ptas). The **Casa Rovira** (C/Sant Amanç 106, 972 32 12 02, rates 6,000ptas) is a rambling old bohemian-style *hostal* run by the heirs of English journalist John Langdon-Davies, who wrote some of the finest reports ever about Catalonia in the Civil War. **Camping Sant Pol** is at Ctra de Palamós km 0.8 (972 32 10 19, rates 2,300-5,400ptas).

In S'Agaró, meanwhile, the luxury choice is **Hostal de la Gavina** (Plaça de la Rosaleda, 972 32 11 00, rates 35,000-50,000ptas) a true-blue five-star with real antiques, but don't go expecting a funky atmosphere.

Begur has the **Hotel Begur** (C/De Coma i Ros 8, 972 62 22 07, rates 10,700ptas) is centrally placed and open all year; **Hotel Rosa** (C/Forgas i Puig 6 (972 62 30 13, rates 5,200ptas) is less expensive but pleasant. Pals has the **Barris** (C/Enginyer Algarra 51, 972 63 67 02, rates 4,800ptas). There are two campsites near Begur: at Sa Riera (El Maset Platja de Sa Riera, 972 62 30 23, rates 2,400-4,500ptas); and on the Palafrugell road, Begur (Ctra de Begur a Palafrugell, 972 62 32 01, rates 2,000-4,300ptas).

Nearby Sa Tuna has the **Hostal Sa Tuna** (Platja Sa Tuna, 972 62 21 98, rates 12,500ptas), with five rooms in a perfect spot by the sea. In Aiguablava there's the four-star, family-run **Hotel Aiguablava** (Platja de Fornells, 972 62 20 58, rates 13,700ptas), one of the coast's grand hotels. Choose from standard rooms or almost self-contained villas.

Tamariu is home to **Hotel Hostalillo** (C/Bellavista 28, 972 30 01 58, open June-Sept only, rates 14,200ptas, the largest hotel in town. Open all year round is the **Sol d'Or** (C/Riera 18, 972 30 04 24, rates 6,000ptas). Llafranc has the **Hotel Llafranc** (Passeig de Cipsela 16, 972 30 02 08, rates 11,000ptas), or try the two-star Hotel Casamar (C/de Nero 3-11, 972 30 01 04, rates 9,000ptas). The campsites near Calella are: **La Siesta** (C/Chipitea 110-20, 972 61 51 16); and **Moby Dick** (C/Costa Verda 16-28, 972 61 43 07).

In L'Estartit is the **Santa Clara** (Passeig Marítim 18, 972 75 17 67, rates 6,500ptas).

Where to eat

For superb seafood in Sant Feliu de Guíxol, try the **Nàutic** (Passeig Marítim, 972 32 06 63, set menu from 1,500ptas), in the **Club Nàutic** sailing club with great port views. In Begur, good Catalan home cooking can be had at **Can Torrades** (C/Pi Itato 7, 972 62 28 81, closed Mon, average 2,500ptas). The **Fonda Platja** (C/Ramon Lluc 3, 972 62 21 97, average 3,000ptas) is expensive, but excellent. On the road toward Palafrugell is **Mas Comangau** (972 62 32 10, average 2,500ptas), a popular traditional restaurant. In Pals, **Alfred** (C/La Font 7, 972 63 62 74, average 3,000ptas) has fine home cooking.

In Tamariu, there's not much to choose between the restaurants on the seafront, but family-run **Snack Bar Es Dofí** (972 61 02 92, average 1,500ptas) is open all year.

Getting there

By bus
Sarfa (93 265 11 58), 15 buses daily to Sant Feliu de Guíxols from Estació del Nord (1hr 20min); nine daily to Palafrugell (2hrs), some continue to Begur. Change in Palafrugell or Torroella for Estartit.

By car
A7 north to exits 9 or 7 onto C253 or C250 for Sant Feliu de Guíxols, then C255 for Palafrugell (123km/76 miles); or A7 exit 6 for Palafrugell and Begur via La Bisbal. A slower option is the coastal N-II, then C250, C253, C255.

Tourist information

Oficina de Turisme de Sant Feliu de Guíxols
Plaça Monestir s/n (972 82 00 51). **Open** 10am-1pm, 4-7pm Mon-Sat; 10am-2pm Sun.

Oficina de Turisme de Begur
Plaça de l'Església 8 (972 62 40 20). **Open** 10am-1pm, 4-7pm Tue-Sat ; closed Mon, Sun.

Oficina de Turisme de Pals
C/Aniceta Figueras 6 (972 68 78 57). **Open** 10am-1pm, 4-7pm Mon-Fri; 10am-2pm Sat; closed Sun.

Oficina de Turisme de Palafrugell
C/Carrilet 2 (972 30 02 28). **Open** 10am-1.30pm, 4-7pm Mon-Fri; 10am-2pm Sat; closed Sun.

Oficina de Turisme de L'Estartit
Passeig Marítim (972 75 89 10). **Open** 10am-1pm, 4-7pm Mon-Sat; 10am-2pm Sun.

Figueres to France

The centre of the northern Costa Brava and the comarca of Alt Empordà is **Figueres**. From here it's possible to travel to every other place of interest in the area. The *tramontana* wind regularly sweeps this area, allegedly leaving the locals slightly touched (read, crazy), a fact apparently borne out by two of Figueres' most famous sons: Narcís Monturiol, the utopian socialist and inventor (some say) of the first submarine, and Salvador Dalí.

Figueres has an attractive centre (despite exceptionally hideous outskirts), with a lively Rambla, and boasts one of Catalonia's most visited attractions, the **Teatre-Museu Dalí** (*see p268*). Also worth visiting is the **Museu de l'Empordà** (972 50 23 05) on the Rambla, for a good overview of the area's art and history.

Island hopping

Due to their status as Europe's number-one holiday patch, it's nearly always cheaper and easier to reach **Mallorca, Menorca, Eivissa** (aka **Ibiza**, in Spanish) or **Formentera** by direct flight from northern Europe than via Barcelona. Even so, the islands are only a short hop away, and fast shuttle ferries have made getting to them much easier.

Life on the islands is conditioned, obviously enough, by their 6.5 million annual foreign visitors – including an estimated 1.5 million clubbers to Ibiza alone – few of whom are aware that a vibrant local cultural life is going on behind their backs, especially in the visual arts and literature. As in Barcelona, the islands' main language is Catalan (used monolingually on many roadsigns, for example). Spanish, English and German are also widely spoken.

Getting there

By air

There are over ten flights daily, Barcelona-Mallorca, and two daily to Ibiza and Menorca. Companies compete on prices: return flights to Mallorca cost about 22,000ptas for a weekend or 16,000ptas if you stay a bit longer, but this may vary.

By sea

Trasmediterránea (*Estació Marítima de Balears, Moll de Barcelona 902 45 46 45*) is the main ferry operator to the islands. Ferries leave from the Estació Marítima at the foot of the Rambla. Standard ferries leave regularly for Mallorca, Ibiza and Menorca. Since the collapse of Trasmediterránea's main fast-ferry rival, the company has been revising its timetables which now vary from month to month. The best thing is to call or check out the website: www.trasmediterranea.es.

Tourist information

Oficina de Turisme – Ibiza & Formentera
Paseo Vara del Rey 13, Ibiza (971 30 19 00). **Open** 10am-1.30pm Mon-Sat; closed Sun.

Oficina de Turisme de Mallorca
Avda Jaime III, Palma (971 71 22 16). **Open** 10am-1.30pm, 4.30-7pm Mon-Sat; 10am-2pm Sun.

Oficina de Turisme de Menorca
Plaça de la Esplanada 40, Mahón (971 36 37 90). **Open** 10am-1.30pm, 4.30-7pm Mon-Sat; 10am-2pm Sun.

East of Figueres, **Roses** was once a major port and is now the area's largest tourist town. It has a glut of hotels, discos, and (often overpriced) restaurants, but also some good beaches and a 16th-century citadel, the **Ciutadella**. To the south are the **Aiguamolls de l'Empordà**, a nature reserve in the wetlands at the mouth of the Fluvià river that's a bird-watcher's paradise. Some 300 species of birds winter or rest here, and fish and amphibians (and mosquitoes, so take insect repellent) are also plentiful.

From Roses the road climbs through spectacular switchbacks with fabulous views to take you to **Cadaqués**, in splendid isolation at the end of the Cap de Creus peninsula. This once remote fishing village was first brought to outside attention by Dalí and friends in the 1920s, and later became the favourite summer resort of Barcelona's cultural elite. In the tourist-boom years high-rise hotel-building was barred from Cadaqués, so it has kept its narrow streets and whitewashed houses. The village's cultural season includes a summer classical music festival. Due to its chic rating Cadaqués

is relatively expensive, but still strikingly beautiful. The peninsula around it is an extraordinary mass of rock, lined by tiny coves (many reachable only by boat) offering the chance for complete relaxation. Cadaqués natives, whose ancestors lived for centuries in total isolation from anywhere inland, are well known for their lack of interest in outsiders.

A short walk and you're in **Port Lligat**, the tiny bay where Dalí built his main home (*see p268*). Beyond it a road continues to **Cap de Creus** ('Cape of Crosses'), with its lighthouse, nature reserve and unique, pock-marked rock formations used as a location in many science-fiction movies.

Port de la Selva, on the cape's north side, has never received the accolades showered on Cadaqués, yet is similarly unspoilt, quieter, and closer to the magnificent Romanesque monastery of **Sant Pere de Rodes**, often lost in clouds on the mountain above the town. Sant Pere was founded in 1022, and large sections of it are still intact.

Alternatively, south of Figueres are the well-preserved remains of the ancient city of

Trips Out of Town

Cadaqués, loved by Dalí. *See p271.*

Empúries, founded in 600 BC by the Phoenicians, recolonised by the Greeks and finally by the Romans in the year AD 2. Ruins from all three periods, as well as the layout of the original Greek harbour, are clearly visible. It's a picturesque and atmospheric ancient site, and right next to a beach. The nearest town, **L'Escala,** has an attractive beach and port. It is noted for its fine anchovies, and as the birthplace of Caterina Albert, author – under the pseudonym Victor Català – of the savage Catalan proto-feminist novel *Solitud* (1911) now available in English.

Sant Pere de Rodes
No phone. **Open** *Oct-May* 10am-1.30pm, 3-5pm Tue-Sun; closed Mon. *June-Sept* 10am-7pm Tue-Sun; closed Mon. **Admission** 300ptas; 150ptas students. **No credit cards.**

Getting there

By bus
Barcelona Bus (93 232 04 59), several buses daily to Figueres from Estació del Nord (2hrs 30min); Sarfa (93 265 11 98) has two buses daily direct to Roses and Cadaqués (2hrs 15min). The easiest way to get anywhere on the coast is by train to Figueres, then Sarfa bus from the depot next door. Sarfa has services to Llança, Roses, Port de la Selva, Cadaqués and L'Escala.

By car
A7 or N-II to Figueres (120km/74 miles). From Figueres, C260 to Roses.

By train
RENFE from Sants or Passeig de Gràcia to Figueres (1hr 45min) or Llançà.

Tourist information

Oficina de Turisme de Figueres
Plaça del Sol (972 50 31 55). **Open** 10am-1pm, 4-7pm Mon-Sat; 10am-2pm Sun.

Oficina de Turisme de Roses
Plaça de les Botxes (972 25 73 31). **Open** 10am-1pm, 4-7pm Tue-Fri; 10am-2pm Sat; closed Mon, Sun.

Oficina de Turisme de Cadaqués
C/Cotxe 2A (972 25 83 15). **Open** 10am-1pm, 4-7pm Mon-Sat; 10am-2pm Sun.

Oficina de Turisme de L'Escala
Plaça de les Escoles 1 (972 77 06 03). **Open** 10am-1.30pm, 4-7pm Tue-Fri; 10am-2pm Sat; closed Mon, Sun.

Where to stay & eat

In Figueres, the **Hotel Duran** (C/Lasauca 5, 972 50 12 50, rates 9,500ptas) is a comfortable place, while the **Hostal Bon Repòs** (C/Villalonga 43, 972 50 92 02, rates 4,000ptas) is a good budget option. Most restaurants in Figueres are in the old town. The ones in C/de la Jonquera are cheapish, with tables outside in summer. **Presidente** (Ronda Firal 33, 972 50 17 00, closed Mon, average 3,000ptas) offers good, solid Catalan fare.

Roses has any number of hotels. Among them are: **Nautilus** (Platja Salatar, 972 25 62 62, rates 5,700ptas) which faces the beach; **Hostal Can Salvador** (C/Puig Rom 43, 972 25 78 11, rates 5,500ptas) is one of the cheaper *hostals*. **El Bullí** (*see chapter* **Restaurants**), which is an international mecca for gourmets, and rightly so, is a must.

Further north in Cadaqués, there are not many hotels for the summer demand, and smaller *hostals* may be closed out of season, so always book. The tourist office has lists of hotels and of families who rent rooms. Try **Hostal Marina** (C/Frederic Rahola 2, 972 25 81 99, rates 7,000ptas), and the **Pension Vehí** (C/de l'Església 6, 972 25 84 70, rates 3,900ptas). The best-known restaurant is **La Galiota** (C/Narcís Monturiol 9, 972 25 81 87, closed Mon, average 5,000ptas). **Casa Anita** (C/Miguel Roset, 972 25 84 71, average 3,000ptas) is a long-running, very popular family-owned place with excellent seafood; cheaper but also good is **Pizzeria Plaza** (Passeig Marítim 10, no phone, average 1,200ptas).

In Port de la Selva, the **Germán** (C/Poeta Sagarra 11, 972 38 70 92, rates 6,400ptas) is a reasonably-priced small hotel; **Porto Cristo** (C/Major 48, 972 38 70 62, rates 17,000ptas) is the luxury option.

Near Empúries, if you have a car, the best place to stay is the village of **Sant Martí d'Empúries,** which has the comfortable, beautifully situated **Riomar** (Platja del Riuet, 972 77 03 62, rates 8,000ptas), or the cheaper **Can Roura** (Plaça de l'Església 12, 972 77 03 05, rates 4,800ptas).

Inland

Escape the coast and you will find stunning scenery, pristine mountain forests, cava cellars and wild village parties.

Catalonia's climate and coastline attract millions to its shores, but comparatively few explore the country's insides. Those who do discover striking beauty: Mediterranean colours and rugged hills mix with lush verdure, merging into alpine landscapes in the Pyrenees. The Pyrenean valleys are also one of the birthplaces of Romanesque architecture, with exquisite early medieval buildings in every second town and village.

The Vallès

To begin with, however, you don't have to go very far: just half an hour on a train will take you into an area of virtually unspoilt countryside dotted with fine examples of *Modernista* architecture.

Just behind the mountain of **Tibidabo**, there stretches the plain of the **Vallès**. A little way further along from the road and rail tunnels, Les Planes is a picnic area on the edge of Collserola park, with cheap restaurants and a *merendero*, an area with tables and charcoal grills where Sunday visitors bring their own food for long, leisurely barbecues. There's an attractive walk or cycle ride from **Les Planes** towards **El Papiol**, a town with a medieval castle, unusual rock formations – signposted as **Les Escletxes** – and the remains of an Iberian settlement.

A little further north is **La Floresta**, a garden suburb located on a quiet, pine-covered hillside. It was once called 'La Floresta Pearson', after the Canadian engineer who brought mains electricity to Barcelona in 1911, and planned the village. In the 1970s it was Barcelona's hippy haven – legendary 'Fat Freddy's Cat' cartoonist Gilbert Shelton even lived here a while. La Floresta is a great place for an easy, short walk, with beautiful views. For **Collserola** walks within Barcelona, *see p102*.

Below Collserola stands **Sant Cugat**, a fast-growing town with a Romanesque monastery and, on the Arrabassada road back towards Barcelona, the **Casa Lluch**, a striking 1906 *Modernista* creation with superb tiling. The Vallès also contains two large towns that were at the centre of Catalonia's industrial revolution. **Terrassa** – also known as the

'Catalan Manchester' – is rarely seen as a tourist attraction (it once won a Japanese award as the world's ugliest city) but has at its centre three unique Visigothic-Romanesque churches, **Santa Maria**, **Sant Miquel** and **Sant Pere**, parts of which date from the sixth century. The town also has a host of *Modernista* buildings connected with the textile industry, such as the outlandish **Masia Freixa**, and the **Aymerich i Amat** factory, which is home to the **Museu de la Ciència i de la Tècnica**, a largely historical museum dedicated to science and technology – not to be confused with the more modern Museu de la Ciència in Barcelona.

Terrassa's eternal rival, **Sabadell**, also has its *Modernista* buildings: an unmissable covered market (*el mercat*), the **Torre de les Aigües** (water-tower) and the original Caixa d'Estalvis de Sabadell savings bank.

Museu de la Ciència i de la Tècnica
Rambla d'Egara 270, Terrassa (93 736 89 66). **Open** 10am-7pm Tue-Fri; 10am-2.30pm Sat, Sun; closed Mon. **Admission** 400ptas; 275ptas concessions; free under-7s and first Sun of the month.

Getting there

By car
To Les Planes, La Floresta, Sant Cugat: A7 via Túnel de Vallvidrera (exit 8 off Ronda de Dalt, toll), or the winding but scenic Ctra de l'Arrabassada (exit 5 off Ronda de Dalt) for free. To El Papiol: A7, then B30 from Molins de Rei. To Terrassa, Sabadell: A18 or N150 (exit 1 off Ronda de Dalt).

By train
FGC from Plaça Catalunya, Terrassa or Sabadell trains. Journey time 15-25min.

Where to eat

Sant Cugat has a very good grilled-meat restaurant, **Braseria La Bolera** (C/Baixada de l'Alba 20, 93 674 16 75, closed Mon, average 3,500ptas). In Terrassa, **Casa Toni** (Ctra de Castellar 124, 93 786 47 08, closed Sun pm, average 4,000ptas) has a fine range of wines. In Sabadell, **Forrellat** (C/Horta Novella 27, 93 725 71 51, average 5,500ptas) is quite pricey but the food is top quality.

Rural relaxation

Until recently, opportunities for spending time in certain areas of the Catalan countryside and mountains were limited by a shortage of suitable places to stay. Previously you either had to camp rough, or stay in the odd – and usually equally rough – boarding house. The rapid expansion of *turisme rural*, however, has opened up a whole range of new possibilities.

The characteristic house found in the Catalan countryside is the *masia*, a manor-farmhouse with massive stone walls and sloping roof. Many *masies* are working farms; others are now second homes. Between these two extremes there are a few hundred *masies* that are now open to visitors. Some can be rented complete as self-catering accommodation, while others have introduced the B&B principle into the local countryside.

The Catalan Generalitat produces an annual guide, *Residències – Casa de Pagès* (500ptas), available from bookshops or the Palau Robert information centre (*see p304*), which lists over 500 houses around Catalonia. Facilities vary enormously: some are very simple farm B&Bs, others offer real hotel service and luxuries such as pools; some give a choice of rooms or self-catering annexes around the farm; some are on remote mountainsides, some are near a beach. There is no central booking service, nor does the guide indicate whether other languages are spoken (although several houses are actually foreign-owned). The thing to do is get on the phone, find out as much as you can from the owner and take the plunge. There are idyllic spots to be found.

Three especially attractive *masies* are described here. Exploring villages is, predictably, easier with a car, but many can be reached by public transport with a little effort.

Masia Can Cardús

08775 Torrelavit, Alt Penedès (93 899 50 18). **Getting there**: By car A2, A7 to Sant Sadurní d'Anoia, then north-west to Torrelavit village. By bus/train the nearest are at Sant Sadurní (4km/2½ miles). **Rates** (incl breakfast) 5,500ptas.

This giant earth and stone *masia*, in the Penedès wine country north of Sant Sadurní, is a former Benedictine monastery and dates from the 11th century. Six rooms sleep two, three or four people. A working farm and vineyard, Can Cardús has information on eight more *masies* nearby.

Mas la Garganta

17814 La Pinya (La Vall d'en Bas), La Garrotxa (972 27 12 89). **Getting there**: By car A7 or N-II to Girona, then C150 to Olot: then C153 Vic road, and before reaching Les Presses turn right to La Pinya. Nearest buses Olot, Les Presses (3km/2 miles). **Rates** 7,000ptas Mon-Thur; 9000ptas Fri, Sat, Sun; Self-catering 8,000ptas per cabin (available weekdays only). Children 50% discount. **Set dinner** (incl wine) 1,800ptas.

A *masia* (pictured) offering B&B or self-catering in the hills of La Garrotxa, with magnificent views. The 18th-century building, with seven double rooms, is extremely well preserved. Local cheeses, liqueurs, meats, and patisserie – some of them made by the same family that runs the *masia* – can be bought from the house. There are farm animals around for the kids to play with, and the *masia* also organises walking tours with two *masies* nearby, so you can stay a night or two in one place and spend a day walking (without bags) to the next.

El Molí

17569 Siurana d'Empordà, Alt Empordà (972 52 51 39). **Getting there**: By car A7 to Figueres (exit 4), then C252 toward L'Escala and right turn to Siurana. By bus local service from Figueres. Nearest stop 2km/1.2 miles. **Rates** (incl breakfast) 7,000ptas.

Amid a large delicious garden full of medicinal herbs, this is a beautifully restored large *masia* with six rooms about 7km (4.4 miles) from Figueres, and slightly further from the Costa Brava. Meals are available at this working farm, and homemade produce can be sampled and bought. The owners speak English and French, and can provide ready-prepared cycle and walking routes in the area.

Trips Out of Town

Montserrat

Geologically distinct from the terrain that surrounds it, Montserrat (the literal translation, 'saw-tooth mountain', describes it to a T) emerges on the horizon with striking visual force. Perched halfway up this dramatic ridge are the monastery and hermitages that form the traditional spiritual centre of Catalonia. The fortress-like atmosphere is emphasised by difficult access – the road meanders hair-raisingly, and the only other way up, more spectacular still, is by cable car.

Hermits were attracted to this isolated place as early as the fifth century, a Benedictine monastery was founded here in 1025 and the so-called '**Black Virgin**', a small wooden figure of the Madonna and child, was installed here in the 12th century. All kinds of legends and traditions have grown up around the statue over the centuries. It is the patron virgin of Catalonia, and Montserrat is still the most common name for Catalan women. In the Middle Ages, the monastery became an important place of pilgrimage. It grew rich and powerful, its remote position helping to ensure its independence. During the Franco era, the monastery became a bastion of pacific Catalan nationalism.

The shrine of the Black Virgin, inside the 16th-century basilica, can be visited and even touched by queuing to the right of the main door and up behind the altar. The museum houses liturgical gold and silverware, archaeological finds and gifts presented to the virgin, including some Old Master paintings and three Picassos. The monastery itself is not particularly interesting, and the cafeterias and souvenir shops tend to take the edge off the place's spirituality, although these are currently undergoing a slow process of reformation and modernisation – they were badly damaged in floods in 2000. A new audiovisual attraction called Espai Temàtic now offers an interesting overview of the day-to-day life of the Montserrat monks.

It's the walks and views around the site that are truly spectacular. The whole mountain, 10km (6 miles) long, is a nature reserve, and the monastery occupies a very small part of it. As well as the cave where the virgin was discovered (20 minutes' walk from the monastery) there are 13 hermitages, the most accessible of them **Sant Joan**, reached by funicular from beside the monastery or a 20-minute walk with superb views. There are also longer walking routes (*see p276*), including a circuit of all the hermitages and the (relatively easy) trek to the peak of **Sant Jeroni**, at 1,235m (4,053ft). Rock climbing is popular amid the unique geology, and enthusiasts can find several thrilling climbs on well-marked routes (inquire at the tourist office).

Where to stay & eat

Restaurants on Montserrat are expensive and unimpressive. The café at the top of the Funicular de Sant Joan is better, but only open in summer. Best bet is to take a picnic lunch.

Montserrat.

Visiting a vineyard

Catalonia's most famous wines and almost all of its cava or sparkling wine come from the Alt Penedès district, west of Barcelona, one of the most respected wine-producing areas in Spain. **Vilafranca del Penedès**, capital of this area, has a **Museu del Vi** (wine museum) in the middle of town, with a fascinating display of equipment from across the centuries (93 890 05 82, closed Mon). The region's largest winemaker, **Bodegues Torres**, offers guided tours daily (93 817 74 87, booking essential) at its Vilafranca headquarters.

Sixty per cent of the Alt Penedès is given over to vineyards. Vilafranca is the main centre for table wine and brandies, but neighbouring **Sant Sadurní d'Anoia** is the capital of cava. Codorniu was the first company to begin production. Manuel Raventós, heir to the estate, worked in the Champagne region in the 1870s, and, after extensive note-taking as he trundled wagons of grapes hither and thither for his French bosses, then went home and reproduced the *méthode champenoise* in his native land. The **Can Codorniu** building with its vast cellars (*pictured right*) is a beautiful *Modernista* work by Josep Puig i Cadafalch, from 1896-1906. **Caves Freixenet** was established in the 1920s. Several other companies in Sant Sadurní offer tours, tastings and sometimes food; the tourist office has a full list.

Catalonia has several other *denominació d'origen* wine regions. The small **Alella**, just east of Barcelona, is best known for whites. More important are **Priorat** and **Terra Alta**, either side of the Ebre river west of Tarragona

and renowned for powerful, heavy reds – **Falset** and **Gandesa**, respectively, are their capitals. The better Priorat reds, in particular, are now internationally sought after (try Scala Dei or Rocafort de Queralt). Local tourist offices have information on visits and tastings; look out too for the **Bodega Cooperativa** in Falset, by Gaudí's disciple César Martinell, and the splendidly weird **Cooperativa Agrícola** in Gandesa, two more great *Modernista* contributions to the wine trade.

Cava cellars

Canals i Domingo
Ctra de Sant Sadurní a Vilafranca (C243) km 1, Sant Sadurní d'Anoia (93 891 03 91).
Open 10am-5pm Sat, Sun.
A small cava producer that gives tastings and tours at weekends (English spoken), followed by a meal in the cellars: Catalan country

---

There are two hotels run by the monks – the recently renovated **Hotel Abat Cisneros** (93 877 77 01, 11,650ptas, 16,900ptas or 20,600ptas double per night, depending on whether you want breakfast, half-board or full-board respectively; reductions mid Nov-mid Mar). The lower-category **Hotel-Residéncia Monestir** is currently closed for repairs and renovation and will remain so until an undetermined date in 2001. There is a campsite (93 835 02 51) beyond Sant Joan funicular; look for the sign.

Getting there

By bus
Julià-Via, 9am from Sants bus station (journey time approx 80min). Julià-Via also run guided tours to Montserrat.

By car
Take the N-II to exit km 59; or the A2 to the Martorell exit, then through Abrera and Monistrol (60km/37 miles). The road to the monastery is steep with sharp bends; for this reason it's often crowded and very slow, especially at weekends, public holidays and on holy days.

By train
FGC from Plaça d'Espanya runs every 2hrs from 7.10am daily, to the Aeri de Montserrat (journey time approx 1hr); then take a cable car (leaving every 15min) to the monastery. Return fare (including cable car) is 1,905ptas.

Tourist information

Oficina de Turisme de Montserrat
Montserrat (93 877 77 77). **Open** 10am-5pm daily.

classics (chargrilled lamb, rabbit or *botifarra* sausages, salads, huge *torrades*, masses of *all i oli*), accompanied by cava and/or the vineyard's own Cabernet red.

Can Soniol del Castell
Masia Grabuac, Ctra de Vilafranca a Font Rubí (BV2127) km 6, Font Rubí (93 897 84 26). **Open** by appointment.
A limited quantity of very fine cava is produced at this vineyard, centred on a historic *masia*. Tours (English spoken) are followed by a tasting.

Caves Codorníu
Avda Codorníu, Sant Sadurní d'Anoia (93 818 32 32). **Open** 9am-5pm, Mon-Fri; 9am-1pm Sat, Sun. **Admission** free Mon-Fri, 200ptas Sat, Sun (incl free champagne glass to take away).
Visits include a short film, a mini-train ride through the cellars and a tasting.

Caves Freixenet
C/Joan Sala 2, Sant Sadurní d'Anoia (93 891 70 00). **Tours** 9am, 10am, 11.30am, 3.30pm, 5pm Mon-Thur; 9am, 10am, 11.30am Fri. **Admission** free. Groups of more than ten should book in advance.

Wine festivals

Most of the main wine-towns have festivals in autumn to celebrate the grape harvest (*verema*). In Alella it takes place very early, around the first weekend in September. Much larger are events in Vilafranca on the first Sunday in October, and Sant Sadurní, which is usually a week later, featuring concerts, dances, exhibitions, tastings and more. The **Reina del Cava**, the Cava Queen, is crowned in Sant Sadurní, and the crowd are treated to several free glasses of the product as well. Smaller towns have their own events; ask at the Palau Robert (*see p304*) and local tourist offices for details.

Getting there
Alella By bus Autocars Casas (93 798 11 00) from corner of Gran Via and C/Roger de Flor. By car N-II north to Montgat, left turn to Alella (15km/9 miles).
Alt Penedès By car A2 then A7 to Sant Sadurní (44km/27 miles) and Vilafranca (55km/34 miles), or A2 then N340 from Molins de Rei, which is much slower. By train RENFE from Sants or Plaça Catalunya, trains hourly 6am-10pm (45min).
Falset & Gandesa By car A2, then A7 to Reus, and right onto N420 for Falset (143km/89 miles) and Gandesa (181km/112 miles). By train RENFE from Sants or Passeig de Gràcia to Marçà-Falset. Six trains daily (approx 2hrs). For Gandesa continue to Mora d'Ebre (another 20min) and catch local bus.

Tourist information
Sant Sadurní d'Anoia *Plaça de l'Ajuntament 1, baixos (93 891 12 12)*; **Vilafranca del Penedès** *C/Cort 14 (93 892 03 58)*; **Gandesa** *Avda Catalunya (977 42 06 14)*.

The Royal Monasteries

Montblanc, 112 kilometres (70 miles) due west of Barcelona and inland from Tarragona and the Costa Daurada, is one of the most beautiful towns in western Catalonia. For some reason it is still all but unknown to foreign visitors. Around it, roughly forming a triangle, are three exceptional Cistercian monasteries: **Poblet**, **Santes Creus** and **Vallbona de les Monges**.

In the Middle Ages Montblanc was a prosperous town with an important Jewish community, a past that is reflected in its **Carrer dels Jueus** ('Jews' Street'), the magnificent 13th-century town walls (two-thirds of which are still intact), the churches of **Santa Maria la Major**, **Sant Miquel** and **Sant Francesc**, the **Palau Reial** (Royal Palace) and the **Palau del Castlà** or chamberlain's palace.

The great monasteries of the region enjoyed a uniquely close relationship with the Catalan-Aragonese monarchs, and were all built partly to house royal tombs. **Poblet**, a few kilometres west of Montblanc, was founded as a royal residence as well as a monastery in 1151 by Ramon Berenguer IV, who created the joint Catalan-Aragonese monarchy and gave generous grants of land to the Cistercian order. The remarkable complex includes a **14th-century Gothic royal palace**, the **15th-century chapel of Sant Jordi** and the main church, housing the tombs of most of the Count-Kings of Barcelona. The monastery can be seen by guided tour only, conducted by a monk.

Trips Out of Town

Monserrat monastery. *See p275.*

Santes Creus, founded in 1158 and perhaps still more beautiful than Poblet, grew into a small village when families moved into abandoned monks' residences in 1843. Fortified walls shelter the **Palau de l'Abat** (abbot's palace), a monumental fountain, a 12th-century church, and a superb Gothic cloister and chapterhouse. Visits to Santes Creus now include an audio-visual presentation.

Vallbona de les Monges, the third of these Cistercian houses, was, unlike the others, a convent of nuns. It was particularly favoured by Catalan-Aragonese queens, especially Violant of Hungary (wife of Jaume I), who was buried here. It has a fine part-Romanesque cloister, but is less grand than the other two. All three of these monasteries still house religious communities.

Monestir de Poblet

(977 87 02 54). **Open** *Mar-Sept* 10am-12.30pm, 3-6pm Mon-Fri; 10am-12.30pm, 3-5.30pm Sat, Sun. *Oct-Feb* 10am-12.30pm, 3-5.30pm daily. **Admission** 500ptas; 300ptas concessions.

Monestir de Santes Creus

(977 63 83 29). **Open** *Mid Sept-mid Jan* 10am-1.30pm, 3-5.30pm Tue-Sun; closed Mon. *Mid Jan-mid Mar* 10am-1.30pm, 3-6pmTue-Sun; closed Mon. *Mid Mar-mid Sept* 10am-1.30pm, 3-7pm Tue-Sun; closed Mon. Turn up at least 20 mins before closing time. **Admission** 600ptas; 400ptas concessions; free on Tuesdays.

Monestir de Santa Maria de Vallbona

(973 33 02 66). **Open** 10.30am-1.30pm, 4.30-6.45pmTue-Sat (closing at 5.30pm in the winter); 12-6.30pm Sun. **Admission** 300ptas; 250ptas concessions. Hours can vary according to times of services.

Getting there

By bus

Hispano Igualadina (93 430 43 44) runs daily services to Montblanc from C/Europa (behind the branch of El Corte Inglés on Avda Diagonal; Metro Maria Cristina). There are more buses running from Valls and Tarragona.

By car

Take the A2, then A7, then back again on the A2 to exit 9, or take the N340 to El Vendrell then the C246 for Valls and Montblanc (112km/70 miles). For Poblet, take the N240 west from Montblanc and turn left in L'Espluga de Francolí. Santes Creus is connected by a slip road to the C246. For Vallbona de les Monges, take the C240 north from Montblanc towards Tàrrega and turn left onto a signposted side road.

By train

RENFE from Sants or Passeig de Gràcia to Montblanc, five trains a day (journey time approx 2hrs).

Serra de Montsant, near **Montblanc.**

Where to stay & eat

Montblanc has an inn, **Fonda Colom** (C/Civaderia 3, 977 86 01 53, rates 3,000ptas, average meals 3,000ptas), behind the Plaça Major. Highly recommended in Montblanc is **Els Àngels** (Plaça dels Àngels 1, 977 86 01 73, rates 4,000ptas) where you can also eat. **L'Espluga de Francolí**, on the way to Poblet, has **Hostal del Senglar Plaça** (Montserrat Canals, 977 87 01 21, rates 3,000ptas), a country hotel known for great Catalan food. Poblet's neighbouring village of **Vimbodí** has the **Fonoll** (C/Ramon Berenguer IV 2, 977 87 03 33, rates 2,500ptas). Santes Creus has the equally cheap **Hostal Grau** (C/Pere III 3, 977 63 83 11, rates 2,300ptas).

Montseny to the Pyrenees

Vic, Rupit & Les Guilleries

Vic, an easy day-trip from Barcelona, is surrounded by the wonderful mountain nature reserves and ideal walking territory of **Montseny**, **Les Guilleries** and **Collsacabra**. It began life as the capital of the Ausetian tribe, became a Roman city, and later fell briefly to the Moors, who lost it to Wilfred the Hairy (*see* p8-9) in the ninth century. Since then it has remained a religious, administrative and artistic centre.

Vic has many late medieval houses, and its **Plaça Major** is one of the finest and liveliest in Catalonia, particularly on Saturdays (when the market is held) and during the **Mercat del Ram** (livestock market), which is held the week before Easter. Monuments worth seeing are the **Temple Romà** (Roman temple), which is now an art gallery, and the neo-classical **Catedral de Sant Pere**, which has a perfectly preserved 11th-century bell tower, and a set of sombre 20th-century murals painted by Josep Lluís Sert. In a corner of the Plaça Major is the **Casa de la Ciutat**, which was built in the 14th century. Vic is also famous for its *embotits* (charcuterie), and shops selling *botifarres*, *llonganisses* and various other kinds of sausages can be found in almost every street.

The district of **Osona**, of which Vic is the capital, is full of interesting villages, and can be recommended to anyone with limited time who seeks a taste of the Catalan countryside at its best. The most rewarding route is up the C153 road towards Olot into **Les Guilleries**,

stopping at Rupit, an extraordinarily beautiful and ancient village built against the side of a medieval castle. An 11th-century sanctuary, **Sant Joan de Fàbregues**, and massive farmhouses such as **El Bac de Collsacabra** and **El Corriol** (which has a collection of ceramics and historical artefacts), are all within walking distance.

Getting there

By bus

Empresa Sagalès (93 231 27 56) from the corner of Passeig Sant Joan-C/Diputació (Metro Tetuan) to Vic. There is no direct bus to Tavertet and Rupit from Barcelona, so get a train or bus to Vic and then a Pous company (93 850 60 63) local bus.

By car

N152 from Barcelona, signed for Puigcerdà, to Vic (65km/40 miles). For Tavertet and Rupit, take C153 out of Vic (signposted to Olot).

By train

RENFE from Sants or Plaça Catalunya to Vic, approx two trains per hour (journey time 1hr).

Tourist information

Oficina de Turisme de Vic

Plaça Major 1 (93 886 20 91). **Open** 9am-8pm Mon-Fri 9am-1.30pm, 4-7pm Sat; 10am-1pm Sun.

Where to stay & eat

Vic has good medium-price restaurants. **Basset** (C/Sant Sadurní 4 , 93 889 02 12, closed Mon, average 4,000ptas), has great seafood. **Ca l'U** (Plaça Santa Teresa 4-5, 93 889 03 45, average 3,500ptas) is a more traditional inn with pork specialities. For something special, take the N152 Ripoll road and before Sant Quirze de Besora turn onto a 2km (1¼ mile) signposted road to the **Rectoria d'Oris** (C/Rectoria, 93 859 02 30, average 5,500ptas), one of the best restaurants in the area, which also has a great view.

The luxury option for hotels is the **Parador de Vic** (Paratge Bac de Sau, 93 812 23 23, rates 14,000-19,000ptas) – relatively modern and in a fabulous location overlooking the Ter gorge. Vic's own top-range hotel is the **Ciutat de Vic** (C/Jaume el Conqueridor, 93 889 25 51, rates 13,000ptas). **Can Pamplona** (Crta. de Vic a Puigcerdà, 93 883 31 12, rates 8,000ptas) is cheaper. In Tavérnoles, just off the C153 from Vic, **Mas Banús** (93 812 20 91, rates 7,000ptas) is a giant old *masia* with rooms and self-catering. In Rupit, there's the delightful *hostal*-restaurant **Estrella** (Plaça Bisbe Font 1, 93 852 20 05, rates 6,500ptas).

Trips Out of Town

Head for the hills

Barcelona is surrounded by easily accessible mountain regions with spectacular landscapes, many now national parks, and hiking and hill-walking are hugely popular. The mountains are mostly low- to medium-height, and in many places walking is made easier by GR (*gran recorregut*) long-distance footpaths, indicated with red and white signs.

If you try any walking take local walking maps, suitable clothing and light walking boots, water and food supplies. Best shops for buying maps are **Llibreria Quera** and **Altaïr** (*see chapter* **Shopping**); as usual, **Palau Robert** (*see p304*) is also a good source of information.

Organised walks

Spain Step by Step *C/Casp 55, 3º 1ª (93 245 82 53)* Tailor-made group walking tours all over Spain.

Sant Llorenç del Munt i l'Obac

A wild craggy landscape cut with narrow ravines hosting a huge range of flora. Its highest point is **La Mola**, crowned by the 11th-century monastery of **Sant Llorenç del Munt**.

Circular route from Matadepera via Sant Llorenç del Munt (4hrs)

From Matadepera village, follow the **Les Arenes** stream, before bearing right towards **Can Prat**. Pick up a signposted track that runs left off a sharp bend to connect with the **Camí dels Monjos** (C31). Walk along this marked track and climb, zig-zagging at times, to the peak of **La Mola** (1,104 metres/3,622 feet), with an information centre. Continue north to a rocky outcrop, the **Morral del Drac** (dragon's snout), and drop down into the ravine of **Canal de Santa Agnès**, until you reach a path on the right marked with a cross, the **Camí de la Font Soleia**. Follow this until it meets the Camí dels Monjos, to return to Matadepera by the same route.
Getting there: By car A18 and N150 to Terrassa, then BV1221 to Matadepera. By train and bus RENFE or FGC from Plaça Catalunya to Terrassa, then Thireo bus to Matadepera.

Montserrat

The most emblematic and most visited massif in Catalunya. For the history of the monastery and information on how to get there, *see pp275-6*.

Circular route from the monastery via Sant Jeroni (4hrs 30min)

Walk up the steps from the **Font el Portal** by the monastery to the **Via Crucis**, and cross the stream, the **Torrent de Santa Maria**. Follow this to its source, through several passes. Continue up to the hermitage of Sant Jeroni on the col at **Pou de Calaç**; this is about 15 minutes below the peak of **Sant Jeroni**. Return to the monastery down the steep ravine of Sant Jeroni, turning right on to the GR72 (also called the Camí de l'Arrel), which skirts the north-east face of the main massif, before you reach the road. Continue to the monastery via the **Pla de la Trinitat**.

The 'Hermitage Route' (3hrs)

Leave the main monastery the same way as the previous route and follow the path to the **Plaça de Santa Anna**. Turn right here towards the hermitage of **Sant Benet** (now a refuge) and the cave-hermitage of **Sant Salvador**. Continue on over a less steep stretch and turn left when you reach the **Pla dels Ocells**. Traverse the small peak of Trencabarrals to pick up the **Camí Nou de Sant Jeroni**. From this path you can take in the circuit of panoramic views and hermitages, including **Sant Jaume, Sant Onofre, Sant Joan, Santa Caterina** and **Santa Magdalena**. Return to the monastery via the **Camí de Les Ermites** and **Camí de Sant Miquel**, along the top of the main ridge.

Trips Out of Town

Life's a beech in **Olot**.

Montseny

The Montseny massif north of Barcelona is sacred to Catalan ramblers, and has been a reserve since 1978. Several of its peaks top 1,700 metres (5,577 feet), and woodland covers about 60 per cent of the area.

Getting there

By bus Sagalès from corner of Passeig de Sant Joan-C/Diputació to El Figueró and Aiguafreda. By car N152 (El Figueró 40km/25 miles). Also A7 or C251 to Sant Celoni and BV5301 to Montseny. By train RENFE from Sants or Plaça Catalunya to El Figueró and Sant Martí de Centeller-Aiguafreda, Vic line (approx two trains hourly).

Circular route from El Figueró via Tagamanent (5hrs)

From the station in Figueró walk along the track towards **Vallcárquera**, until you reach the **Font del Molí** and church of **Sant Pere**. Continue, leaving the **Vallcárquera** stream on your right, and pick up another track signposted **Tagamanent** via **Sant Martí** col. Climb up the promontory from here to the hermitage of **Santa Maria de Tagamanent**. From the peak, drop down again to the col and go on to **Can Bellever** and **L'Agustí**. Turn right along a path through woods to **La Roca Centella**, which you leave on your left. Drop down, bearing right, towards the hermitage at **San Cristòfol** and a col at **Creu de Can Plans**. Follow a power line to the Vallcárquera stream to return to Figueró.

Circular route from Aiguafreda via Serra de l'Arca (4hrs)

From Aiguafreda village take the track along a stream called the **Riera de l'Avencó**. After crossing bridges at **Pere Curt** and **La Bisbal** (by a *masia* at **Casa Nova de Sant Miquel**), you come to a third bridge at **Picamena**. Don't cross it, but continue along the track to the left through holm oaks to **Pla de la Creu**, a beautiful mountain pasture above the **Serra de l'Arca**. There is a neolithic dolmen nearby at **Pla del Boix**. Go on south-west to the GR92 path, and follow it left to reach another dolmen. At a fork soon after that, go right past two dolmens to the dolmen at **Cruïlles**. Pass an abandoned *masia* at **Can Serra** and return to Aiguafreda.

Olot & La Garrotxa

There are over 20 old lava flows and 30 volcanic cones around Olot. **El Croscat** was the last to erupt, about 11,500 years ago. The forms, textures and colours of the lava contrast strongly with the leafy, damp forests. For Olot town and information on how to get there, *see p274*.

Circular route from Olot via Fageda d'en Jordà & the volcanoes of Santa Margarida & El Croscat (7hrs)

From the Park Information Centre (**Casal dels Volcans**), follow itinerary three (green) through the beech forest of **Fageda d'en Jordà** (*pictured*), on an old lava flow from El Croscat. When you reach the junction with itinerary two (red), take this path to the right. Pass the Romanesque church of **Sant Miquel de Sacot** and walk up the southern slope of **Santa Margarida**. There is a hermitage in the centre of the crater. Drop down the northern slope until you reach the car park at Santa Margarida, cross the GI524, and continue round El Croscat to the information centre at **Can Serra**. Pick up itinerary three here to return to Olot. Local maps and ideas for many other itineraries are available from the **Casal dels Volcans**.

Ripoll to the Vall de Núria

Ripoll, north of Vic, grew up around the unique church and monastery of **Santa Maria de Ripoll**. Known as the 'cradle of Catalonia', the church has a superb 12th-century Romanesque stone portal. This valley was the original fiefdom of Hairy Wilfred, Guifré el Pilós, before he became Count of Barcelona. He is buried in **Santa Maria**, which he founded in 879.

Wilfred the Hairy also founded the monastery and town of **Sant Joan de les Abadesses**, 10km (6 miles) up the C151 road east, and worth a visit for its Gothic bridge as well as the 12th-century monastery itself. The monastery museum (972 72 00 13) covers a thousand years of local life.

From Sant Joan the road leads to **Camprodon**, on the river Ter, known for a crunchy almond biscuit called a *carquinyoli*. It has a fine Romanesque church. From here a local road veers left up the main Ter valley to the tiny mountain village of **Setcases**, a famous beauty spot now, sadly, taken over by second homes. By now you are well into the Pyrenees; the valley road comes to an end at **Vallter 2000** (972 13 60 75), the easternmost ski station in the mountains. As with all ski resorts in the area, the best way to stay there is to book a package, available at any travel agent in Barcelona.

Ribes de Freser, the next town on the N152 north of Ripoll, is an attractive base from which to travel to the pretty if slightly gentrified villages of **Campelles** and **Queralbs** (where the Catalan president has his summer residence). Ribes is also the starting point for the *cremallera*, the FGC's narrow-gauge 'zipper train', which runs via Queralbs along the Freser river up to the sanctuary of **Núria**. Núria itself nestles by a lake on a plateau at over 2,000 metres (6,500 feet). Home to the second most famous of Catalonia's patron virgins, a wooden statue of the Madonna carved in the 12th century, it was a refuge and place of pilgrimage long before then. The mostly 19th-century monastery that surrounds the shrine is not especially attractive, but its location is spectacular. The zipper-train makes it an accessible place to try relatively high-mountain walking (the tourist office has maps). It's also a winter sports centre (972 73 07 13), suited to novice skiers.

Getting there

By bus

TEISA (972 20 48 68) from the corner of C/Pau Claris-C/Consell de Cent to Ripoll, Sant Joan de les Abadesses and Camprodon.

By car

N152 direct to Ripoll (104km/65 miles). For Sant Joan de les Abadesses and Camprodon, C151 out of Ripoll.

By train

RENFE from Sants or Plaça Catalunya, approx two trains each hour (to Ripoll approx 1hr 30min). For Queralbs and Núria change to the *cremallera* train in Ribes de Freser.

Tourist information

Oficina de Turisme de Ribes de Freser

Crta a Ripoll s/n, (972 72 71 84). **Open** 10am-1pm, 4.30-6.30pm Mon-Fri; 10am-1.30pm Sat; closed Sun.

Where to stay & eat

In Ripoll, decent rooms area available at **Ca la Paula** (C/Berenguer 8, 972 70 00 11, rates 4,820ptas). **La Trobada** (Passeig Honorat Vilamanya 4, 972 70 23 53, rates 7,500ptas), is more comfortable. For meals, **El Racó del Francés** (Plà d'Ordina 11, 972 70 18 94, average 4,500ptas) serves French dishes. In **Sant Joan de les Abadesses**, the best beds are at **Janpere** (C/Mestre Andreu 3, 972 72 00 77, rates 6,000ptas). **Sant Pere** (C/Mestre Andreu 3, 972 72 00 77, average 2,500ptas) offers local food at reasonable prices. In **Ribes de Freser**, very comfortable rooms can be had at **Catalunya Park Hotel** (Passeig Salvador Mauri 9, 972 72 71 98, rates 7,000ptas; closed in winter) **Traces** (C/Nostra Senyora de Gràcia 1, 972 72 71 37, rates 4,000ptas) is cheaper. In Queralbs, **L'Avet** (C/Major, 972 72 73 77, rates 4,600ptas), is tiny; slightly larger is **Sierco** (C/Major 5, 972 72 73 77, rates 4,800ptas). The one good place to eat in Queralbs is **De la Plaça** (Plaça de la Vila 5, 972 72 70 37). In Núria, there's a three-star hotel, the **Vall de Núria** (C/Santuari Mare de Dèu de Núria, 972 73 20 00, rates 10,050ptas double), and a youth hostel, the **Alberg Pic de l'Aliga** (972 73 20 48, rates 2,000ptas).

Berga & Puigcerdà

Some 50km (31 miles) west of Ripoll on the C149 (or on the C154, from Vic) is Berga, capital of the *comarca* of the Berguedà. Just north from there the giant cliffs of the Serra del Cadí, one of the ranges of the 'Pre-Pyrenees' or Pyrenees foothills, loom impressively above the town. Berga also has a medieval castle, **Sant Ferran**, with a suitably storybook air, and a charming old centre, with a Jewish quarter going back to the 13th century. It's famous for a frenzied festival of devils, drink and drums each May called **La Patum** and for its annual mushroom-hunting competition on the first Sunday of October in the **Pla de Puigventós**. Great basketloads of different wild mushrooms (*bolets*) are weighed in before an enthusiastic public. Prospective participants should contact the tourist office, which has information on whereabouts to hunt.

Heading north along the C1411, uphill into the Cadí, you'll come to the small town of **Bagà**, with partially preserved medieval walls and a central square with Romanesque porticoes. It marks the beginning of the **Parc Natural del Cadí-Moixeró**, a gigantic mountain park of 159 square miles/410 square kilometres containing wildlife and forest reserves and some 20 or so ancient villages. All retain some medieval architecture, and many offer stunning views. Picasso stayed and painted in one village, **Gósol**, for several weeks in 1906. Rugged and austerely beautiful, the Cadí is rich in wildlife, and can feel more like the American West than the Mediterranean. Chamois, roe and red deer roam the slopes. There are also golden eagles, capercaillies and black woodpeckers.

Above Bagà the C1411 road enters the Túnel del Cadí to emerge into the wide, fertile plateau of the **Cerdanya**. Described by writer Josep Pla as a 'huge casserole', the Cerdanya has an obvious geographical unity, but since a treaty signed in 1659, the French and Spanish frontier has run right across its middle, with one Spanish village, Llívia, left stranded in French territory.

The snow-capped peaks that ring the valley are laced with ski resorts, including **La Molina** (972 89 20 31), and **Masella** (972 14 40 00). The capital of the area (on the Spanish side), **Puigcerdà**, is a sizeable town heavily touristed by Catalans and French, where discos and après-ski bars mix with remnants of things medieval. Other places of interest in the Cerdanya are the cross-country ski centre of **Lles**, with a Romanesque church, and Bellver de Cerdanya, a hilltop village on the edge of the Cadí-Moixeró that was the unlikely scene of a battle during the Civil War. The village has a park information centre.

Getting there

By bus
ATSA (93 873 80 08), five buses daily to Berga from corner of C/Balmes-C/Pelai (journey time approx 2hrs). Alsina Graëlls (93 265 68 66) daily to Puigcerdà from Estació del Nord (3hrs).

By car
C1411 via Manresa to Berga (118km/73 miles) and Bagà. For Gósol turn off before Bagà onto B400. From Bagà continue on C1411 through Túnel de Cadí

(toll) for Puigcerdà; a scenic alternative is the N152 through Vic and Ripoll. Lles and Bellver are both off the N260 west from Puigcerdà.

By train
RENFE from Sants or Plaça Catalunya to Puigcerdà, about two trains each hour (approx 3hrs).

Tourist information

Oficina de Turisme de Berga
C/Ciutat 12 (93 821 13 84) **Open** 9am-2pm Mon-Sat; 5-7pm Fri, Sat; closed Sun.

Oficina de Turisme de Puigcerdà
C/Querol, Baixos (972 88 05 42). **Open** 9am-1.30pm, 4.30-7pm Mon-Fri; 10am-2pm Sat; closed Sun.

Where to stay & eat

In Berga, a good place to lie down is the **Estel Hotel** (C/Sant Fruitos 39, 93 821 34 63, rates 5,000ptas). In the medieval centre is the **Queralt Hotel** (Plaça de la Creu 4, 93 821 06 11, rates 4,700ptas). The **Casino** is cheap and cheerful (Ronda de Queralt 15, 938 211 795, rates 2,900 ptas), and run by a friendly TV actor. Great local dishes can be sampled at **La Sala** (Passeig de la Pau 27, 93 821 11 85, average 4,000ptas).

Puigcerdà has plenty of hotels in the town centre, including the small and charming **Avet Blau** (Plaça Santa Maria 14, 972 88 25 52, rates 13,000ptas). The **Hotel Alfonso** (C/Espanya 5, 972 88 02 46, rates 6,000ptas) is more moderate. A little further out in Bolvir, the **Torre del Remei** (C/Camí Reial s/n, 972 14 01 82, rates 26,000ptas) is sumptuous and also has one of the best (and most expensive) restaurants in the area (average 11,000ptas). Cheap, very friendly and dead central is the **Cerdanya** (C/Ramon Cosp 7, 972 880 010, 2,400ptas). Good regional food, moderately priced, is served at **El Galet** (Plaça Santa Maria 8, 972 88 22 66, closed Mon, average 2,000ptas). A pizzeria that also offers good regional dishes is **La Tieta** (C/Dels Ferrers 20, 972 88 01 56, average 1,500ptas).

Girona, Besalú & Olot

The most interesting and vibrant Catalan city after Barcelona, Girona was one of the first Paleolithic communities in the region. It was a major trading town under the Romans, and a flourishing centre throughout the Middle Ages. Its spectacular cathedral, built between the 11th and the 15th centuries, has a Romanesque cloister, a soaring Gothic nave and a five-storey tower. From the cathedral's

Trips Out of Town

main façade, 90 steep steps lead down to the main street and the river Onyar, where the buildings packed along the side of the river have been attractively renovated.

Back at the top, Carrer de la Força, just off the cathedral square, leads to the uniquely atmospheric **Call**, the medieval Jewish quarter. The centre for Jewish studies here is run by the last surviving native Jewish community in the peninsula. Add to this the **Banys Àrabs** – a 13th-century Muslim/Jewish bathhouse; the **Passeig Arqueològic**, a walk around the old city wall; seven other impressive churches; an iron bridge (*pont de ferro*) designed by Eiffel; and the Palau **Episcopal**, with a fine art museum, and you have some idea of the beauty of Girona. The city today is also a highly active artistic and literary centre.

Banyoles, 16km (10 miles) north of Girona, is an attractive town divided into the Vila Vella (Old Town) and Vila Nova (New Town), both of which contain medieval buildings. Its main attraction, though, is the **Estany de Banyoles**, a huge, peculiarly placid lake in an ancient volcanic crater, surrounded by smaller lakes and containing rare species of fish. It is a very delicate environment, and only eco-friendly watersports are permitted.

Besalú, another 14km (9 miles) north, is a gem: a small, wonderfully peaceful medieval town founded in the tenth century. The whole town centre has been declared a monument and, with few modern buildings, seems suspended in time. Of special interest are the streets of the old Jewish **Call** and the *mikveh* (Jewish baths), the two main squares and the church of **Santa Júlia**, but most eye-catching of all is the entirely intact 12th-century fortified bridge over the Fluvià.

The N260 road continues west past extraordinary villages, such as **Castellfollit de la Roca**, perched atop a precipitous crag, to **Olot**. The medieval town was destroyed in an earthquake in 1427, but it has imposing 18th-century and *Modernista* buildings. In the last century it was home to a school of landscape painters; the local **Museu de la Garrotxa** (C/ de Hospice 8, 972 27 91 30, admission 300ptas) has works by them and Casas, Rusiñol and other *Modernista* artists. Olot's most unusual feature, though, is its 30-odd extinct volcanoes and numerous lava-slips, sometimes no more than green humps in the ground, that surround it to form the **Parc Natural de la Zona Volcànica de la Garrotxa**. Just south of the town on the Vic road there is a museum and information centre, the **Casal dels Volcans** (Ctra Santa Coloma 43, 972 26 67 62, admission 300ptas). On the pretty back road south-east to Banyoles (GI524) is a delightful beech forest, **La Fageda d'en**

Jordà, made famous by poet Joan Maragall, grandfather of Barcelona's former mayor (for walks, *see p281*).

Getting there

By bus

Barcelona Bus (93 232 04 59) to Girona from Estació del Nord; TEISA (972 20 48 68) runs to Banyoles, Besalú, Olot from the corner of C/Pau Claris-C/Consell de Cent (more frequent services from Girona).

By car

A7 or toll-free N-II to Girona. For Banyoles, Besalú, Olot, take C150 from Girona (direction Besalú).

By train

RENFE from Sants or Passeig de Gràcia to Girona, hourly approx 6am-9.15pm (journey time 1hr 15min, Catalunya Exprés).

Tourist information

Oficina de Turisme de Girona

Rambla Llibertat 1 (972 22 65 75). **Open** 8am-8pm Mon-Sat 9am-2pm Sun.

Oficina de Turisme de Olot

C/Bisbe Lorenzana 15 (972 26 01 41). **Open** 10am-2pm, 4.30-7pm Mon-Fri; 10am-2pm Sat; closed Sun.

Where to stay & eat

In Girona, a reasonably priced, comfortable place is the **Europa** (C/Juli Garreta 21, 972 20 27 50, rates 6,500ptas). **Pensión Bellmirall** (C/Bellmirall 3, 972 20 40 09, rates 6,400ptas) is an unusually charming *hostal*. For quality dining in a historic building, try the **Albareda** (C/Albareda 7, 972 22 60 02, average 4,000ptas). Cheaper and simpler is **Casa Marieta** (Plaça

Olot's lush volcanic terraces.

Alpine splendour at **Sant Maurici.**

Independéncia 5, 972 20 10 16, average 3,000ptas). A good bed in Banyoles can be had at **Can Xabernet** (C/Carme 27, 972 57 02 52, rates 6,000ptas). **L'Ast** (Passeig Dalmau, 972 57 04 14, rates 9,000ptas) has a pool and garden. A famous gourmet restaurant is **La Rectoria** (C/Espinavesa, 972 55 35 31, average 5,000ptas).

In Besalù, there's the **Venència** (C/Major 8, 972 59 12 57, rates 4,250ptas) or try the riverside **Siqués,** which is above the **Fonda Siqués** restaurant (Avda Lluis Companys 6-8, 972 59 01 10, rates 5,300ptas). For good, cheap eats try the **Cúria Reial** (Plaça de la Llibertat 15, 972 59 02 63, average 2,000ptas). Olot has the **Borrell** (C/Nònit Escubós 8, 972 26 92 75, rates 8,000ptas) and at a bargain price there's the **Garrotxa** (Plaça de Móra 3, 972 26 16 12, rates 3,750ptas). Best value for dining is probably the **Ramón** (Plaça Clarà 10, 972 26 10 01, average 1,500ptas).

The High Pyrenees

The *comarques* of the High Pyrenees, to the west of Andorra, reach altitudes of well over 3,000 metres (9,800 feet), and contain some of the most spectacular scenery in the whole mountain range. These high valleys and crags form Catalonia's main districts for real mountain walking, climbing, adventure sports and skiing. Too far from Barcelona to be comfortably visited in a couple of days, they are wonderful places to explore over a week or even a long weekend.

The Pallars Sobirà

The Pallars Sobirà runs up to the French frontier alongside Andorra, a region of steep-sided valleys and flashing rivers, snow-covered in winter and idyllic in summer, with centuries-old villages of stone and slate that seem encrusted into the mountain sides. The capital of the *comarca* is **Sort**, the centre for organised sports in the area. Several companies in Sort organise rafting and kayaking trips, caving and other adventure sports, and hire out equipment (the tourist office has details). The town is also known for its lottery centre, **La Bruixa**, which has sold a phenomenally improbable number of winning tickets over the last few years: not for nothing, apparently, does the word '*sort*' mean 'luck' in Catalan.

For winter, the area has two ski stations: **Super Espot** (973 62 40 15), a large, fully equipped resort near the village of Espot, 24km (14 miles) north of Sort on a turn to the left after Llavorsí, and the smaller **Port Ainé** (973 62 03 25), near the town of **Rialb**, just to the north of Sort. A special attraction of Super Espot is a blue run that allows even the most inexperienced skiers to descend from the highest point on the mountain all the way to the base. As at Vallter (*see p282*), stays at these resorts are best booked direct from Barcelona, at any travel agency.

From spring to autumn there are different attractions. The same road that leads to Espot continues to the nature reserve of Aigüestortes (winding waters), with a network of paths

Trips Out of Town

through alpine wilderness. Its centre is the Estany de Sant Maurici, a fabulously beautiful, crystal-clear mountain lake beneath the peaks of Els Encantats, popular with serious rock climbers. There are several smaller lakes dotted all through the mountains. In the park there are mountain shelters with full-time wardens. Given the remoteness of most areas, you are advised to contact the well-organised park information centre in Espot (973 62 40 36) and equip yourself with good walking maps before embarking on any long hikes.

Getting there

By bus
Alsina Graëlls (93 265 68 66), daily bus to Sort from Estació del Nord, leaves 7.30am and arrives 12.20pm.

By car
For Sort (approx 250km/155 miles), take A18 to Manresa, C1410/C1412 to Tremp, then N260 north-east via Pobla de Segur.

Tourist information

Oficina de Turisme de Sort
Avda. Condes del Pallars 21(973 62 11 30). **Open** 10am-2pm, 4-8pm Mon-Fri; 10am-1pm, 5-8pm Sat; 10am-1pm Sun.

Where to stay & eat

By the river in Sort there's the **Pey** (Avda Montserrat 3, 973 62 02 54, rates 7,000ptas with breakfast and lunch or dinner included). **Hotel Pessets II** (C/Diputació 3, 973 62 00 00, rates 10,700ptas), offers a bar, pool, tennis courts and restaurant. There are plenty of traditional *fondes* in the old town. **Hotel Pessets II** specialises in high-quality local cuisine (average 3,000ptas), with a rich wild boar stew (*civet de porc senglar*).

Espot has the luxury hotel, **Saurat** (C/Sant Martí, 973 62 41 62, rates 14,000ptas), and the cheaper, simpler **La Palmira** (C/Marineta s/n, 973 62 40 72, rates 4,600ptas).

The Val d'Aran

North of Sort the old C142 road begins to wind tightly up to one of the most spectacular mountain passes in Europe, the **Port de la Bonaigua** at 2,072m (6,800ft). The valley you are entering, the **Val d'Aran**, is north of the Pyrenees, and the source of the river Garonne, which meets the sea at Bordeaux. This is a district with its own architectural style, administration and even language (Aranese, a dialect of Provençal), and that it happens to be in Spanish territory is an accident of history.

Vielha e Mijaran (usually just called Vielha), the valley's capital, is a fascinating mountain town with very distinctive medieval houses such as **Çò de Rodés**, and slate churches such as **Sant Pèir d'Escunhau** and **Sant Miquèu**. The Val d'Aran is a great walking area, but is best known for winter sports. It has two big ski stations: **Tuca-Malh Blanc** (973 64 10 50), which is not far south of Vielha, near Betren, and the giant **Vaquèira-Beret** (973 64 44 55), one of the largest and smartest winter sports complexes in the Pyrenees, and one which is occasionally patronised by the Spanish royal family. The Val d'Aran has its own local government, the **Conselh Generau d'Aran,** which runs a frequent internal bus service (timetable available from the Vielha tourist office).

Getting there

By bus
Alsina Graëlls (93 265 68 66), two buses daily from Estació del Nord, at 6.30am and (via Sort) 7.30am (journey time 5hrs 45min, more if via Sort).

By car
From Sort (see above), C147 and C142 continue to Port de la Bonaigua (55km/34 miles, allow over an hour). Most direct route from Barcelona is A18 to Manresa, C1410/C1412 to Tremp and N260 north-east from Pobla de Segur, to enter Val d'Aran by the Vielha tunnel at the western end of the valley.

Tourist information

Oficina de Turisme de Vielha
C/Sarriulera 6 (973 64 01 10). **Open** 10am-1pm, 4.30-7.30pm Mon-Sat; closed Sun.

Where to stay & eat

The town of Viehla is expensive, but **Aran** (Avda Castiero 5, 973 64 00 50, rates 14,700ptas) is a decent place to stay. Cheaper is the small **Busquets** (C/Major 9, 973 64 02 38, rates 4,000ptas), as is the equally charming **Casa Vicenta** (Reiau 7, 973 640 819, rates 4,500ptas). A good, cheap place to eat is **Nicolàs** (C/Castèth 10, 973 64 18 20, average 2,000ptas), while **Era Mola** (C/Marrec 8, 973 64 24 19, average 3,500ptas), is the most typically Aranese restaurant.

In Betren, the only hotel is the **Tuca** (Ctra Salardú s/n, 973 64 07 00, rates 7,100-15,500ptas). **La Borda de Betren** (C/Major, 973 64 00 32, average 2,500ptas), is a rustic-style restaurant. The Vaquèira ski resort has the two-star **Val de Ruda** (Ctra de la Bonaigua, 973 64 58 11, rates 7,800ptas), dwarfed by two very expensive luxury hotels nearby.

Directory

Directory

Getting Around

Barcelona is a compact city and much of it is easy to explore on foot. For longer journeys, a fast, safe Metro (underground) system and buses will get you to most places within half an hour during daytime. Bicycles are great for moving about the old city and port while motorbikes or mopeds can be handy in traffic; a car is usually more of a liability, and only comes into its own for trips out of town. For more details of transport outside Barcelona, *see p262*.

Arriving & leaving

By air

Barcelona's Aeroport del Prat is 12 kilometres (7 miles) south of the city in El Prat de Llobregat. Each airline is allocated to one of the two main terminals – A or B – for all its arrivals and departures. In A and B there are tourist information desks, cash machines, exchange offices (open 7am-11pm daily) and other services. For airport information, call 93 298 38 38, or check the airport website: www.aena.es/ae/bcn/homepage. htm, which includes updated flight information.

Aerobús

This special bus service is usually the most convenient means of getting to central Barcelona. Buses run from stops outside each terminal, via Gran Via, to a stop in Plaça Catalunya near the El Corte Inglés store. Buses to the airport go from Plaça Catalunya via C/Aragó, and also pick up at Sants railway station and Plaça Espanya. Buses leave the airport every 15 minutes from 6am to midnight Monday to Friday (6.30am-midnight Sat, Sun, public holidays); and in the opposite direction from Plaça Catalunya, 5.30am to 11.15pm Monday to Friday (6am-11.20pm Sat, Sun, holidays). The trip takes about 30 minutes; a single ticket costs 500ptas.

Two local buses, the EA and EN, also run between the airport (Terminal B) and Plaça d'Espanya; they are slow and infrequent but the EN runs late (last departure from the airport 2.40am, from Plaça d'Espanya 3.15am; single ticket 150ptas).

Airport trains

Trains to and from the airport stop at four stations in Barcelona: Sants, Plaça Catalunya, Arc de Triomf and Clot-Aragó, all of which are also Metro stops. Trains leave El Prat at 13 and 43 minutes past each hour, 6.13am to 10.43pm Monday to Friday; from the city, trains leave Plaça Catalunya at 8 and 38 minutes past the hour, 5.38am to 10.08pm Monday to Friday (five minutes later from Sants). At weekends and on public holidays, timings vary slightly but there are still trains every half hour. The journey takes about 25 minutes, or 20 minutes to/from Sants. A single ticket costs 335ptas (365ptas on Saturdays, Sundays and public holidays). Be aware that tickets on local trains are only valid for two hours after you purchase them.

Taxis from the airport

The taxi fare to central Barcelona should be about 2,000-2,500ptas (depending very much on traffic), which includes a 300ptas airport supplement. Fares are about 20 per cent higher after 10pm and at weekends (*see p290*). There is a minimum charge for trips to/from the airport of 1,600ptas, and a 125ptas supplement for each large piece of luggage placed in the car boot. It's best to ignore any cab drivers who approach you inside the airport; use the ranks outside the terminal.

Airlines

The appropriate terminal is shown in brackets.
Air Europa (B) 902 401 501 www.air-europa.com
British Airways (B) 902 111 333 www.british-airways.com
Delta Airlines (A) 901 116 946 www.delta.com
Easyjet (A) 902 299 992 www.easyjet.com
Go (A) 901 333 500 www.go-fly.com
Iberia (B) 902 400 500 www.iberia.com
Virgin Express (A) 900 467 612 www.virgin-express.com

By bus

Most long-distance coaches (national and international) stop or terminate at Estació d'Autobusos Barcelona-Nord at C/Ali Bei 80, next to Arc de Triomf rail and Metro station (map p325 E5; general information 93 265 65 08). The Estació d'Autobusos Barcelona-Sants, by Sants rail station and Sants-Estació Metro, is only a secondary stop for many coaches, but some international Eurolines services (information 93 490 40 00) stop only at Sants.

By sea

All Balearic Islands ferries (*see p271*) dock at the Moll de Barcelona quay, at the bottom of Avda Paral.lel (Metro Drassanes, map p324 C7). There is also a ferry three times a week between Barcelona and Genoa in Italy, from the Moll de Ponent, 400 metres (440 yards) further south (Grimaldi Lines; for information phone its agents Condeminas, 93 443 98 98). Cruise ships use several berths around the harbour; when cruisers are in port, a PortBus shuttle service transports passengers on shore leave to the foot of the Rambla.

By train

The giant Barcelona-Sants station (map p323 A4) is the stop or terminus for most long-distance trains run by Spanish state railways, RENFE. It's about three kilometres (two miles) from the centre, but has a Metro stop (Sants-Estació) on line 3 (green, the most direct for the centre) and line 5 (blue).

Some international services from France do not go to Sants but terminate at the 1920s Estació de França, near Ciutadella park and Barceloneta Metro (map p327 C4). Other trains stop at both stations, and many also stop between the two at Passeig de Gràcia (map p320 D4), which can be the handiest for the city centre. *See also p262.*

RENFE information

902 24 02 02/www.renfe.es.
Open 5am-11.50pm daily.
Credit AmEx, DC, JCB, MC, V.
Some English-speaking operators. RENFE tickets can be bought or reserved by phone and delivered to an address or hotel for a small extra fee. For information on non-Spanish European trains, call 93 490 11 22 (open 7am-10pm daily).

Left luggage lockers

Aeroport del Prat

Terminal B. **Open** 24 hours daily. **Rates** 625ptas per day.

Estació d'Autobusos Barcelona-Nord

C/Ali Bei 80. Metro Arc Triomf/19, 39, 40, 41, 42, 55, 141, N4, N11 bus. **Open** 24hrs daily. **Rates** 300, 400, 600ptas per day. **Map** p325 E5.

Estació Marítima (Balearics Ferry Terminal)

Moll de Barcelona. Metro Drassanes/14, 20, 36, 38, 57, 59, 64, 91, 157, N6, N9 bus. **Open** 8am-11.30pm daily. **Rates** 300, 500ptas per day. **Map** p324 C7.

Train stations

There are lockers at Sants and Passeig de Gràcia (both open 5.30am-11pm daily) and França (6am-11pm daily), but not at the smaller stations. **Rates** 400, 600ptas per day.

Maps

Metro and central area street maps are included at the back of this guide. Tourist offices provide a reasonably detailed free street map, and the City tourist offices also have a better map for 200ptas. Metro maps are available free at all Metro stations (ask for '*una guia del Metro*') and city transport

information offices (*see below*), which also have free bus maps. Metro and bus maps also indicate access points for the disabled on to public transport. You can find an interactive Barcelona street map on the web at: www.bcn.es/guia.

Public transport

The Metro is generally the quickest, cheapest and most convenient way of getting around the city, although buses give you a view, operate all night and cover some 'holes' in the underground network – notably around Plaça Francesc Macià. Public transport, although now generally integrated, is still run by different organisations. Local buses and the Metro are run by the city transport authority (TMB). Two more underground lines (from Plaça Catalunya to Reina Elisenda, Les Planes, or Avda Tibidabo; and from Plaça d'Espanya to Cornellà) connect with the Metro but are run by Catalan government railways, the Ferrocarrils de la Generalitat de Catalunya (FGC, often just called '*els Ferrocarrils*'), which also has suburban services.

For transport information call the 010 information line. For details of the Barcelona Card, which gives unlimited travel on public transport, and guided tours, *see p64.*

FGC Information

Vestibule, Catalunya FGC station (93 205 15 15/www.fgc. catalunya.net). **Open** *Sept-June* 7am-9pm Mon-Fri; closed Sat, Sun. *July, Aug* 8am-8pm Mon-Fri; closed Sat, Sun. **Map** p326 B1.
Branches: FGC Provença (open 9am-7pm Mon-Fri); FGC Plaça d'Espanya (open 9am-2pm, 4-7pm Mon-Fri).

TMB Information

Main vestibule, Metro Universitat (93 318 70 74/www.tmb.net). **Open** 8am-8pm Mon-Fri; closed Sat, Sun. **Map** p326 A1.
Branches: Vestibule, Metro Sagrada Família; Vestibule, Metro Sants-Estació. Both open 7am-9pm Mon-Fri; 10am-2pm, 3-6pm Sat, Sun.

Metro & FGC

The five Metro lines are identified by a number and a colour on maps and station signs. At interchanges, lines in a particular direction are indicated by the names of the stations at the end of the line, so you should know which they are when changing between lines. On FGC lines, note that some suburban trains do not stop at all stations.

Metro hours

5am-11pm Mon-Thur; 5am-2am Fri, Sat; 6am-midnight Sun. The FGC has similar hours, but weekday trains on some routes start slightly later, and many services run later at night.

Buses

City bus stops are easy to find: many routes originate in or pass through Plaça Catalunya, Plaça Universitat and/or Plaça Urquinaona. Because of the many one-way streets, buses often do not follow exactly the same route in both directions, but run along parallel streets.

Taking the bus

Most bus routes function between 6am and 10.30pm, Monday to Saturday, although many begin earlier and finish later. Services usually run every 10-15 minutes, but frequency is lower before 8am, after 9pm and on Saturdays. On Sundays buses are less frequent still on most routes, and a few do not run at all. You board buses at the front, and get off through the middle or rear doors. Only single tickets can be bought on board; if you have a *targeta*, insert it into the machine just behind the driver as you board, which will register and return it. With a *targeta* (but not a single ticket) you can change for free to another bus, Metro or train, inside a 75-minute period. Fares increase on a zone system outside the city limits.

Useful routes

Buses that connect Plaça Catalunya with popular parts of town include:
22, via Gràcia to the Tramvia Blau on Tibidabo and the Pedralbes Monastery.
24 goes up Passeig de Gràcia and is the best way to get to Parc Güell.
41 and **66** go to Plaça Francesc Macià, an area not served by the Metro.
41 goes to Ciutadella and the Vila Olímpica.
45 stops in Plaça Urquinaona and goes down to the beach near Port Olímpic.
Three good crosstown routes are:
50 goes from north-east Barcelona past Sagrada Família, along Gran Via and then climbs Montjuïc from Plaça d'Espanya to Miramar.
64 goes from Barceloneta beach, past Colom, Avda Paral.lel, Plaça Universitat to Sarrià and Pedralbes.
7 runs the length of Avda Diagonal, from the Zona Universitària to Diagonal Mar, but deviates in the centre (along Passeig de Gràcia and Gran Via to Glòries).

Night buses

There are 16 Nitbus (night bus) routes, most of which run 10.30pm to 4.30am nightly, with buses every 20-30 minutes. Most pass through Plaça Catalunya, and some also run out of town to Badalona, Castelldefels and the airport. Standard *targetes* are not valid on night buses; instead, you must buy single tickets (165ptas) or the special 10-trip night bus *targeta* (1,050ptas), both available only on board.

TombBus

A special shoppers' bus service (the spooky-sounding name actually means 'round trip') that runs only between Plaça Catalunya and Plaça Pius XII on the Diagonal (7.30am-9.38pm Mon-Fri; 9.30am-9.20pm Sat). Again, normal *targetes* are not valid on the bus, and single tickets cost 180ptas.

Local trains

For trips into the suburbs and surrounding towns there are, as well as buses, regional rail lines run by the FGC and RENFE. From FGC Plaça Catalunya (the same station as for the Sarrià and Tibidabo lines) trains go to Sabadell, Terrassa and other towns beyond Tibidabo, and from FGC Plaça d'Espanya, to Hospitalet and Montserrat. All trains on the RENFE local network (signed Rodalies/Cercanías at mainline stations) stop at Sants, but many lines also converge on Plaça Catalunya (for Vic and the Pyrenees, Manresa, the Penedès and the Maresme coast to the north) or Passeig de Gràcia (for the southern coastal line to Sitges and the Girona-Figueres line north). Fares vary according to zones. For more on rail services, *see p262*; for a map of local RENFE lines, *see p331*.

Taxis

Barcelona's 10,500 black and yellow taxis are among its most distinctive symbols, and are at most times easy to find. Fares are reasonable. Taxis can be hailed on the street when they show a green light on the roof, and a sign saying *Lliure/Libre* (free) behind the windscreen. There are also ranks at railway and bus stations, main squares and other locations throughout the city.

FARES

Current official rates and supplements are shown inside each cab (in English). The current minimum fare is 300ptas, which is what the meter should register when you set off. After the first couple of kilometres (or minutes) the fare begins to increase at a rate per kilometre, or on a time rate at slow speeds. The basic rates apply 6am to 10pm Monday to Friday; at all other times (including midweek public holidays) the rate is about 20 per cent higher. There are also supplements for each item of luggage and for animals (150ptas), and a waiting charge. Note also that taxi drivers are not officially required to carry more than 2,000ptas in change, and that very few will accept credit card payment.

RECEIPTS & COMPLAINTS

To get a receipt, ask for '*un rebut, si us plau/un recibo, por favor*'. It should include the fare, the taxi number, the driver's NIF (tax) number, the licence plate and the date; if you have a complaint of any kind about a cab driver insist on all these, and the more details the better (driver's signature, time, route). Call transport information on 010 to explain your complaint, and follow their instructions.

RADIO CABS

The companies listed below take bookings 24 hours daily. Only some operators speak English, but if you are not at a specific address give the name of a street corner (ie Provença/Muntaner), or a street and a bar or restaurant where you can wait. Note that phone cabs start the meter as soon as a call is answered.
Barnataxi 93 357 77 55.
Fono-Taxi 93 300 11 00.
Ràdio Taxi 93 225 00 00.
Ràdio Taxi Verd 93 303 70 70.
Servi-Taxi 93 330 03 00.
Taxi Groc 93 490 22 22.
Taxi Miramar 93 433 10 20.
Taxi Ràdio Móbil 93 358 11 11.

Driving

Driving in Barcelona can be wearing. There's seldom enough driving space, let alone parking space. Within the city limits a car is rarely a time-efficient form of transport, and it's only out in the country where one becomes an asset. If you do drive here, bear these points in mind:

● You can drive in Spain with a valid licence from most other countries. An international driving licence or EC photo licence can be useful as a translation/credibility aid.

● Keep your driving licence, vehicle documents and insurance Green Card with you at all times.

A ticket to ride

The standard fare for a single ticket on the Metro, FGC and buses is currently 160ptas. The fare is the same, no matter how far you travel, within a zone that includes all of Barcelona city and many outlying suburbs. Unless you plan to make just a few journeys, however, it's much cheaper and more convenient to buy one of the different types of multi-journey tickets or *targetes*. From the start of 2001, the basic all-purpose *targeta* is to be the T-10, which is valid on all three systems and on local RENFE trains. It can be shared by two or more people, so long as one unit is cancelled on the card for each person travelling.

Moreover, with the four 'integrated' *targetes* (T-10, T50/30, T-Mes, and T-Dia) you can now change between the different public transport networks without paying a second fare within a time limit of one hour 15 minutes after the initial validation. In some cases, such as changing from one bus to another, or from the Metro to the FGC, you have to insert your *targeta* into a machine a second time, but an extra unit will not be deducted if you are within the time limit. A single ticket, however, does not let you make free transfers.

T-10 and T-50/30 cards can be purchased at ticket desks and automatic machines in Metro and FGC stations, at transport offices, by credit card from Servi-Caixa machines (*see page 196*) and at many newsstands and lottery shops around town. Outlets for other cards are listed below. You cannot buy *targetes* on buses. Note that there are also more expensive multiple-zone versions of the basic *targetes*, which are used to travel to the outer parts of Barcelona's metropolitan region. The Barcelona Card discount scheme (*see page 64*) also gives unlimited travel for one, two or three days.

INTEGRATED *TARGETES*

T-10 Valid for ten trips on Metro, FGC, buses and local trains. Can be shared by two or more people, and costs 885ptas.

T-50/30 Gives 50 trips within any 30-day period on Metro, FGC, buses and local trains. It can be shared, and currently costs 3,700ptas.

T-Mes One month's unlimited travel on all four transport systems for one person only, costing 5,825ptas. Note, though, that this means a calendar month, not 30 days from date of purchase. With your first month's card you must obtain an identity card (which costs 200ptas and requires a photograph), available only at the TMB and FGC offices. In succeeding months you can renew your card at any Metro/FGC station.

T-Dia Unlimited travel for one person on all four transport systems for one day (670ptas). The T-Dia is sold at transport offices and Metro/FGC stations.

OTHER *TARGETES*

3 Dies Unlimited travel for one person on Metro and buses (not FGC) for three days, for 1,600ptas. Available from the same outlets as the T-Dia, and the Plaça Catalunya and Sants tourist offices.

5 Dies The same, but valid for five days' travel, for 2,400ptas.

Aerobús+Bus+Metro The same as the previous two, but also including a return bus trip from and to the airport. Valid for three (2,200ptas) or five days (2,800ptas) and bought on board the Aerobús.

● It is compulsory to wear seat belts and carry warning triangles, spares (tyre, bulbs, fanbelt) and tools to fit them.
● Legal alcohol limits for drivers are low, similar to those in most EU countries.
● Children under 12 may not travel in the front of a car except in a child car seat.
● Do not leave anything of value, including car radios, in your car, nor bags or coats in view. Foreign numberplates can attract thieves.

● Many drivers ignore speed limits, and it's common to race through lights changing from amber to red (so don't brake suddenly in this situation, or you may be hit from behind).
● When oncoming drivers flash lights at you this means they will not slow down. On main highways, flashing lights is usually a helpful warning of a speed trap ahead.
● Be on your guard against thefts at motorway rest areas, or thieves who may try to make you stop and get out, perhaps by indicating you have a flat tyre. Sometimes they can be violent. Keep your car doors and boot locked when travelling, and be wary of 'helpful' fellow motorists.

Car & motorbike hire

Car hire is relatively expensive here, but it's a competitive market so it's worth shopping around. The key is to carefully check what's included: unlimited mileage, 16 per cent VAT tax, and especially full insurance cover, rather than the third-party minimum (*seguro obligatorio*). You will need a credit card, or a large cash deposit. Most companies also have a minimum age limit and require you to have had a licence for at least a year. Larger companies often advertise special offers on their websites.

Europcar

Pl Paisos Catalans s/n, Sants (93 491 4822/www.europcar.com). Metro Sants Estació/30, 44, 100, 109, N0, N7 bus. **Open** 7.30am-10.30pm Mon-Fri; 8am-1pm Sat; closed Sun. **Map** p323 A4. **Credit** AmEx, DC, MC, V.
Large international agency with several offices in Barcelona. A Renault Clio for 14,500ptas for a three-day weekend; Seat Toledo 63,000ptas a week (both include IVA, full insurance and 500 km/day).
Airport branch: 93 298 3300.

Vanguard

C/Viladomat 297 Eixample (93 439 38 80/93 322 79 51/www.vanguard rent.com). Metro Hospital Clínic/41, 54, N3 bus. **Open** 8am-2pm, 4-8pm Mon-Fri; 9am-1pm Sat, Sun, public holidays. **Credit** AmEx, DC, MC, V. **Map** p323 B4.
Scooter and motorcycle hire. All-inclusive weekend rates from 9,280ptas (50cc Honda) to 29,000ptas (Yamaha 600); you must be 18 to hire a moped and have had a licence a year, 25 and three years for larger bikes.They hire cars too at good rates.

Parking

Parking is never easy in central Barcelona. The Municipal Police readily give out tickets (which many people never pay), or tow cars away. Be careful not to park in front of doorways with the sign *Gual Permanent*, indicating an entry with 24-hour right of access. In some parts of the old city, notably La Ribera and the Barri Gòtic, access is limited to residents for much of the day. Look out for signs.

Pay & display areas

Many streets in the central area and the Eixample are pay-and-display areas (Zones Blaves, Blue Zones), with parking spaces marked in blue on the street. Ticket machines will be nearby. Parking restrictions in the zones apply

from 9am to 2pm and 4 to 8pm, Monday to Saturday, when you can park for a maximum of two hours; in the centre, the rate is 255ptas per hour, less in other districts. If you overstay by no more than an hour you can cancel the fine by paying an additional 500ptas; to do so, press Anul.lar denùncia on the ticket machine, insert 500ptas and take the receipt that comes out. Machines accept credit cards (MC, V) but do not give change.

Car parks

Car parks (*parkings*) are signalled by a white 'P' on a blue sign. The city parking company, charging 240ptas per hour, is SMASSA; another big player is SABA, charging 255ptas. You are especially advised to use a car park if you have foreign plates. Car parks listed below are central and open 24 hours daily.

SABA

Plaça Catalunya, Plaça Urquinaona, Arc de Triomf, Avda Catedral, Passeig de Gràcia, C/Diputació-C/Pau Claris.

SMASSA

Plaça dels Àngels-MACBA, Moll de la Fusta, Avda Francesc Cambó, Av Paral.lel.

Metro-Park

Plaça de les Glòries, Eixample (93 265 10 47). Metro Glòries/7, 56 bus. **Open** 5am-11pm Mon-Thur; 5am-11.30am Fri, Sat; closed Sun. **Credit** AmEx, DC, MC, V. **Map** p325 F5.
A park-and-ride facility recommended for anyone coming in to Barcelona with a car for the day. The 700ptas ticket gives unlimited travel for one person for one day on Metro and city buses (but not the FGC). The car park is at the junction of three traffic arteries (the Diagonal, Meridiana and Gran Via), a short Metro ride from the centre.

Towing away

Municipal Police 93 428 45 95. **Credit** AmEx, DC, MC, V.
If your car has been towed away by the Municipal Police they will leave a triangular sticker on the pavement. Call the number on the sticker or the one above (open 24 hours) to be told which pound it has gone to. Staff do not normally speak English. It will cost 15,775ptas to recover the vehicle during the first four hours after it was towed away, plus 275ptas for each additional hour after that, plus (probably) a parking fine.

Petrol

Most *gasolineres* have unleaded fuel (*sense plom/sin plomo*), regular (*super*) and diesel (*gas-oil*).

Cycling/blading

Recreational bike-riding in Barcelona is on the up, and there is an incomplete but growing network of bike lanes (*carrils bici*) along major avenues and the seafront. Mass bicycle commuting is a long way off, though, for in weekday traffic cyclists still face daunting risks – and tourists are not advised to try it, unless they're experts at home. Rollerblading is also popular. Tourist offices (*see pp304-5*) have route details.

Un Cotxe Menys

C/Esparteria 3, Barri Gòtic (93 268 21 05). Metro Jaume I/14, 17, 39, 40, 45, 51 bus. **Open** 10am-2pm Mon-Fri and by arrangement. **No credit cards.** **Map** p327 C4-3.
The name means 'one car less'; bike hire costs 600ptas per hour; 1,500ptas per half day; or 2,000ptas per full day. Staff also run guided cycle tours (*see p58*).

...al punt de trobada

C/Badajoz 24, Poble Nou (93 225 05 85/bicipuntrobada@hotmail. com). Metro Llacuna/36, 92 bus. **Open** *Apr-Sept* 9am-2pm, 4-9pm Mon-Fri; 9am-2pm, 4-10pm Sat, Sun. *Oct-Mar* 9am-2pm, 4-8pm Mon-Fri; 9am-2pm, 4-7pm Sat, Sun. **Credit** AmEx, MC, V.
Near the beach: mountain bikes and rollerblades cost 500ptas per hour, 1,500ptas a half day, 2,500ptas a whole day. Also tandems, baby seats, bike tours, and other services.

Walking

Barcelona is one of the world's best walking cities; one of the few where the needs of traffic are subordinate to the needs of pedestrians. Its compact centre makes getting around on foot a sensible option, but take care at pedestrian crossings. After the green 'cross' signal lights up, a couple more cars will usually come speeding through to beat the red light. Be careful too of vehicles turning on to the street you are crossing, as they will often speed up or veer to avoid a pedestrian rather than actually give way, green pedestrian light or not.

Resources A-Z

Business

Though Barcelona is Spain's most open city for doing business, anyone wanting to set up shop here needs to be aware of the intricacies of local, Spanish and European Union regulations. It's a waste of time trying to deal with this system single-handed. A visit to the Cambra de Comerç is a must; some consulates can also refer you to English-speaking professionals, and a good *gestoria* will save you time and a lot of frustration.

Institutions & info

Catalan Government: Generalitat de Catalunya

General information 012/ www.gencat.es. Business development 93 476 72 00/new businesses 902 20 15 20.
The Generalitat provides a range of consultancy and other services.

City council: Ajuntament de Barcelona

Plaça Sant Miquel 4-5, Barri Gòtic (93 402 70 00). Metro Jaume I/17, 19, 40, 45 bus. **Open** *Sept-June* 8.30am-5.30pm Mon-Fri; closed Sat, Sun. *July, Aug* 8.15am-2.15pm Mon-Fri; closed Sat, Sun. **Map** p327 B3.
Permits for new businesses are issued by the ten municipal districts.

Borsa de Valors de Barcelona (Stock Exchange)

Passeig de Gràcia 19, Eixample (93 401 35 55/www.borsabcn.es). Metro Passeig de Gràcia/22, 24, 28 bus. **Open** *Visits/ information* 9am-6pm. *Library* 9am-noon, Mon-Fri; closed Sat, Sun. **Map** p324 D5.

British Society of Catalunya

Via Augusta 213, Zona Alta (tel/fax 93 209 06 39). Metro Diagonal/16, 17, 22, 24, 28 bus. **Map** p320 C2.
Keep in touch with fellow expats in monthly get-togethers and other events. Membership 1,500ptas a year.

Cambra de Comerç, Indústria i Navegació de Barcelona (Chamber of Commerce)

Avda Diagonal 452-454, Eixample (93 416 93 00/www.cambrescat.es). Metro Diagonal, FCG Provença/6, 7, 15, 16, 17, 33, 34 bus. **Open** 9am-5pm Mon-Thur; 9am-2pm Fri; closed Sat, Sun. Closed July, Aug. **Map** p320 D4.
The most important institution for business people, the Chamber of Commerce offers databases along with a wealth of other information and advice.

Conference services

Barcelona Convention Bureau

C/Tarragona 149, Eixample (93 423 18 00). Metro Tarragona/27, 30, 109, 215 bus. **Open** *Sept-June* 9am-2.30pm, 4-7pm Mon-Thur; 9am-3pm Fri; closed Sat, Sun. *July, Aug* 8am-3pm Mon-Fri; closed Sat, Sun. **Map** p320 D4.
Specialised arm of the city tourist authority that assists organisations and individuals holding conferences or similar events in the city.

Fira de Barcelona

Avda Reina Maria Cristina, Montjuïc (93 233 20 00/www.firabcn.es). Metro Espanya/bus all routes to Plaça d'Espanya. **Open** *mid Sept-mid June* 9am-2pm, 4-6pm Mon-Fri; closed Sat, Sun. *Mid June-mid Sept* 9am-2pm Mon-Fri; closed Sat, Sun. **Map** p323 A5.
The Barcelona 'trade fair' is one of the largest permanent exhibition complexes in Europe. In addition to the main area at Plaça d'Espanya it includes a huge state-of-the-art new site, Montjuïc-2, in the Zona Franca towards the airport, and administers the Palau de Congressos conference hall in the Plaça d'Espanya site, which can be let separately.

Gestories/admin aid

The *gestoria* is a very Spanish institution, the main function of which is to lighten the weight of local bureaucracy by dealing with it for you. A combination of bookkeeper, lawyer and business adviser, a good *gestor* can be very helpful

in handling paperwork and pointing out shortcuts that foreigners are usually unaware of. Unfortunately, local *gestoria* employees rarely speak English.

LEC

Travessera de Gràcia 96, 2° 2ª Gràcia (93 415 02 50). Bus 27, 31, 32. **Open** 9am-2pm, 4-7pm Mon-Fri; closed Sat, Sun. Closed Aug. **Map** p320 D3.
Lawyers and economists as well as a *gestoría*. Some English speakers on the staff.

Tutzo Assessors

C/Aribau 226, Eixample (93 209 67 88/email: tutzoass@fonocom.es). Bus 31, 58, 64. **Open** 8.30am-2pm, 4-7pm Mon-Fri; closed Sat, Sun. Closed Fri pm Aug. Closed July. **Map** p320 C3.
With years of experience, Tutzo offers legal, fiscal, accounting, social security, contracts and other services. Some English is spoken.

Office space & facilities

Centro de Negocios

C/Pau Claris 97, 4° 1ª (93 301 69 96/www.centro_negocios.com). Metro Passeig de Gràcia/7, 50, 54, 56, bus. **Open** *Sept-July* 8am-9pm Mon-Fri; closed Sat, Sun. *Aug* 9am-3pm Mon-Fri; closed Sat, Sun. **Map** p324 D5.
Office space, desk space in shared offices, mailboxes, meeting rooms, secretarial services and a wide range of administrative services for hire.

Picking Pack Megaservice

C/Consell de Cent 276 (93 487 61 31/www.pickingpack.es). Metro Universitat/bus all routes to Plaça Universitat. **Open** 9am-9pm Mon-Fri; 9am-2pm Sat. **Credit** AmEx, MC, V. **Map** p324 D5.
Computers, Net, fax, design, printing, mail-outs, meeting rooms and more.

Translation agencies

DUUAL

C/Ciutat 7, 2° 4ª (93 302 29 85/fax 93 412 40 66/duual@costacatalana. com). Metro Jaume I/17, 19, 40, 45 bus. **Open** *Oct-May* 9am-2pm, 4-7pm Mon-Thur; 9am-2pm Fri; closed Sat, Sun. *June-Sept* 8.30am-3pm Mon-Fri; closed Sat, Sun. **Map** p327 B3.

Good rates, services in many languages and excellent desktop publishing facilities.

Traductores Jurados (Official translators)

Many official bodies demand that foreign-language documents be translated by legally certified translators. Rates are higher than for conventional translators.

Teodora Gambetta

C/Escorial 29-31, escala C, àtic 2ª (tel/fax 93 219 22 25/teogam @teleline.es). Metro Joanic/39, 55 bus. **Open** by appointment only. **Map** p321 E3.

Communications

Internet & email

Net centres great and small have been popping up (and down) all over Barcelona. For cybercafés, *see p165* **The Art of Connection**; for other computer services *see p295*.

easyEverything

Ronda Universitat 35, Eixample (93 412 1058/www.easyeverything.com). Metro, FCG Catalunya/bus all routes to Plaça Catalunya. **Open** 24 hours. **No credit cards. Map** p324 D5.
The big kid on the Internet block, with 300 terminals at this address and 450 at La Rambla 31. Prices vary according to demand: 200ptas will get you over three hours online if it's empty (early mornings are the best times), but only about 20 minutes when it's at its most busy (lunchtime and early evening).

Inetcorner

C/Sardenya 306, Eixample (93 244 8080/www.inetcorner.net). Metro Sagrada Família/19, 33, 34, 43, 44, 50, 51 bus. **Open** 10am-10pm Mon-Sat; noon-8pm Sun. **No credit cards. Map** p321 F4.
Small online centre next to the Sagrada Família. iMacs available. First 15 minutes 300 ptas, then 10ptas per minute.
Branch: Plaça Ramon Berenguer 2, 1ª (near Via Laietana), Barri Gòtic.

Realnet

C/Perla 28, Gràcia (93 218 98 61/ www.realnet.es). Metro Joanic/39 bus. **Open** 10am-2pm, 4-11pm Mon-Thur; 10am-2pm, 4pm-2am Fri; 11am-2am Sat; 4-11pm Sun. **No credit cards. Map** p320 D3.
One of many pocket-sized Net-and-games centres around Gràcia. Half-hour on the Internet, 300ptas.

MAIL

Normal-rate stamps for cards or letters can most easily be bought in any *estanc* or tobacco shop (*see p196*). Postal information is on 902 197 197 or at www.correos.es.

Correu Central

Plaça Antoni López, Barri Gòtic (93 486 83 02). Metro Jaume I or Barceloneta/14, 17, 19, 36, 40, 45, 57, 59, 64, 157 bus. **Open** 8.30am-9.30pm Mon-Sat; reduced service 9am-2pm Sun. **Map** p323 B4.
In the imposing main post office, there is an information desk in the middle of the hall; most services are available at any of the Admissió Polivalent windows straight ahead of you as you enter. There's a separate window for fax sending and receiving, offered at all post offices (more expensive than at fax shops, but with the option of courier delivery in Spain). Letters sent Poste Restante (General Delivery) to Barcelona should be addressed to Lista de Correos, 08070 Barcelona, Spain; to collect them go to the windows to the left, with your passport. To send something express, you want to send it *urgente*. Note that within the general opening hours not all services are available at all times; also, some post offices close in August.
Branches: Plaça Urquinaona 6, Eixample, open 8.30am-2.30pm Mon-Fri, 9.30am-1pm Sat; C/València 231, Eixample, open 8.30am-2.30pm Mon-Fri, 9.30am-1pm Sat; C/Aragó 282, Eixample, open 8.30am-8.30pm Mon-Fri, 9.30am-1pm Sat.

Postal rates & post boxes

Letters and postcards weighing up to 20 grammes cost 35ptas within Spain; 70ptas to the rest of Europe; 115ptas to North and South America, Africa and much of Asia; and 155ptas to Australasia and East Asia. Mail to other European countries generally arrives in three to four days, and to North America in about a week. Aerogrammes (*aerogramas*) cost 85ptas for all destinations. Normal post boxes are yellow. There are also a few special red post boxes for urgent mail, with collections approximately every two hours.

Postal Exprés

Available at all post offices, an express post system with guaranteed next-day delivery to provincial capitals, and 48-hour delivery elsewhere in Spain. The most convenient and reliable way of sending small packages within Spain.

Telephones

Thanks to competition in the Spanish phone market, prices are coming down and new options are constantly appearing. Former state operator Telefónica still has a monopoly on local calls, and controls most calls from public phones, but this is likely to change. International calls cost less from 8pm to 8am on weekdays and all day at weekends; other timings for lower rates vary. Some phone cards and phone centres (*see below*) give cheaper rates than Telefónica.

PHONE NUMBERS

All normal Spanish phone numbers have nine digits, as the area code (93 in Barcelona and its province) must be dialled with all calls, local or long-distance. If you're ever given a Barcelona number with only seven digits, chances are you simply need to add the 93 in front of it. Spanish mobile phone numbers begin with 6. Numbers beginning 900 are freephone lines; other 90 numbers are special-rate services – the higher the third digit, the higher the rate.

PUBLIC PHONES

The most common model of payphone accepts coins, Telefónica phonecards and credit cards, and has a digital display with instructions in English and other languages. The minimum charge for a local call is currently 20ptas. A call to a mobile phone in daytime will cost around 80ptas for the first minute; to a 902 number, 50ptas. This type of phone also gives you credit to make further calls without having to reinsert money. Most bars and cafés also have phones for public use, but they often cost 50 per cent more than regular booths.

INTERNATIONAL & LONG-DISTANCE CALLS
To make an international call, dial 00 and then the country code: Australia 61; Canada 1; Irish Republic 353; New Zealand 64; United Kingdom 44; USA 1, followed by the area code (omitting the first zero in UK numbers) and number. To call Barcelona from abroad, dial the international code (00 in the UK), then 34 for Spain. To call Barcelona from anywhere else in Spain the number is now the same as the local number, beginning with 93.

PHONE CARDS
Post offices, newsstands and *estancs* sell 1,000 and 2,000ptas Telefónica phone-cards, which save on money and inconvenience if you're making several calls. Also on sale at newsstands and shops are cards from many other companies, which offer cheaper rates than Telefónica on all but local calls. The cards give you a toll-free number to call; an operator or automatic system then connects you with the number you want and can also tell you how much you have left on the card.

PHONE CENTRES
Phone centres (*locutorios*) can also bring down call prices, and avoid the need for change. Most private centres offer international call rates that are cheaper than Telefónica's for all countries. There are many phone centres along C/Sant Pau in the Raval, and C/ Carders-C/Corders in the Casc Antic. Some also offer international money transfer, currency exchange, and other services.

Cambios Sol
La Rambla 88 (93 318 97 53). Metro Catalunya/bus all routes to Plaça Catalunya. **Open** 8.30am-9pm daily. **Map** p327 A3.
Branches: Vestibule, Estació de Sants (93 491 45 37); C/Colón 7 (93 310 6065).

Telefónica Phone Centre
Estació d'Autobusos del Nord C/Alí Bei 8, Eixample. Metro Arc Triomf/19, 39, 40, 41, 42, 55, 141, N4, N11 bus. **Open** 9am-9pm Mon-Fri. *July, Aug* also 10am-1pm Sat, 5-9pm Sun. **Map** p325 E5.

MOBILE PHONES
Many mobile phones from other countries can be used in Spain with a 'Roaming' system, but you probably need to contact your operator to set it up before you leave home. However, this can be expensive and it may well be cheaper to buy a Spanish mobile phone.

Every second Spaniard now has a *móvil*. You pay either with a monthly bill or by using easily rechargeable pre-paid cards. Call costs vary greatly according to contract options; in 2000 a very general average was around 40 ptas/minute.

Rent a Phone
Numància 212, Eixample (93 280 21 31/www.rphone.es). Metro María Cristina/7, 33, 63, 67, 68, 78 bus. **Open** 9.30am-2pm, 4-7pm Mon-Fri. **Credit** AmEx, MC, V.
Mobiles phone and accessories for rent, either for use in Spain or to take to other countries. Daytime Spanish calls charged at 150-200ptas/minute.
Branch: Maremagnum centre, 1ª planta (93 225 81 06) Open 11am-10.30pm daily.

OPERATOR SERVICES
Normally operators will speak Catalan and Spanish only.
National directory 1003.
International directory 025.
National operator 1009.
International operator Europe & North Africa 1008; rest of world 1005.
Telephone breakdowns 1002.
Telegrams 933 222 000.
Time 093.
Weather 906 365 365.
Alarm calls 096. Key in the time at which you wish to be woken, in 24-hour clock, in four figures, for example punch in 0830 if you want to be called at 8.30am.

General information
098.
A local information service provided by Telefónica, with information particularly on duty pharmacies in Barcelona. Otherwise, generally less reliable than the 010 line (*see p305*).

To find a Net terminal, *see p294*.The options for putting your own computer online can be expected to keep changing. At present, basic choice is between using one of the 'free' Internet service providers such as Eresmas (information 900 844 844), Teleline (900 600 800) and others; or paying a provider maybe 12,000ptas a year for better service, extra email addresses and so on.

Cinet
C/Àvila 45, 2ª, Poble Nou (93 502 0339/ www.cinet.es). Metro Bogatell, Llacuna/71 bus. **Open** 9am-2pm, 4-7pm Mon-Fri; closed Sat, Sun. **Credit** MC, V. **Map** p315 F6.
Internet service provider that can connect you directly or via the Retevision data system. Also consultancy services.

GeoMac
No office address (606 30 89 32/cowdery@nexo.es). **Open** by appointment. **No credit cards**.
Experienced US technician George Cowdery offers maintenance and trouble-shooting for Macs.

Microrent
C/Provença 385-387, 3º1ª, Eixample (93 459 26 86/fax 93 459 09 79/ www.microrent.es). Metro Verdaguer or Sagrada Família/19, 33, 34, 43, 44, 50, 51 bus. **Open** 9am-6pm Mon-Fri; closed Sat, Sun. **No credit cards**. **Map** p321 E4.
Computer equipment of all kinds for rent: PCs, Macs, laptops, peripherals, faxes and photocopiers.

A full list of consulates in Barcelona is in the phone book under *Consolats/Consulados*. Outside office hours most have answerphones that give an emergency contact number.

American Consulate
Passeig Reina Elisenda 23, Zona Alta (93 280 22 27/fax 93 205 52 06/

www.embusa.es). FCG Reina
Elisenda/22, 64, 75 bus.
Open 9am-12.30pm, 3-5pm,
Mon-Fri. **Map** p319 A1.

Australian Consulate

*Gran Via Carles III 98, Zona Alta (93
330 94 96/fax 93 411 09
04/www.embaustralia.es). Metro
María Cristina/59, 70, 72 bus.* **Open**
10am-noon Mon-Fri; closed Sat, Sun.
Closed Aug. **Map** p319 A2-3.

British Consulate

*Avda Diagonal 477, Eixample (93
366 62 00/fax 93 366 62 21/email
bcon@cyberbcn.com). Metro Hospital
Clinic/6, 7, 15, 33, 34.* **Open** *end
Sept-mid June* 9.30am-1.30pm, 4-5pm
Mon-Fri; closed Sat, Sun. *Mid June-
mid-Sept* 9am-2pm Mon-Fri; closed
Sat, Sun. **Map** p320 C3.

Canadian Consulate

*C/Elisenda de Pinós 10, Zona
Alta (93 204 27 00/fax 93 204
27 01/www.canada-es.org). FCG
Reina Elisenda/22, 64, 75 bus.*
Open 10am-noon Mon-Fri; closed Sat,
Sun. **Map** p320 D4.

Irish Consulate

*Gran Via Carles III 94, Zona Alta (93
491 50 21/fax 93 411 29 21). Metro
María Cristina or Les Corts/59, 70,
72 bus.* **Open** 10am-1pm Mon-Fri;
closed Sat, Sun. **Map** p319 A3.

New Zealand Consulate

*Travessera de Gràcia 64, Gràcia (93
209 03 99/fax 93 202 08 90). Metro
Passeig de Gràcia/22, 24, 28 bus.*
Open *Sept-June* 9am-2pm, 4-7pm
Mon-Fri; closed Sat, Sun. *July, Aug*
call for reduced hours. **Map** p320 C3.

Courier services

Estació d'Autobusos Barcelona-Nord

*C/Ali Bei 80 (93 232 43 29).
Metro Arc Triomf/19, 39, 40, 41, 42,
55, 141, N4, N11 bus.* **Open** 7am-
7.45pm Mon-Fri; 7am-12.45pm Sat;
closed Sun. **No credit cards.**
Map p315 E5.
Inexpensive service at the bus station
for sending parcels on scheduled
buses to towns within Spain.

Missatgers Trèvol

*C/de la Verneda 18 (93 266 07 70/
www.trevol.com). Metro Clot/33, 43,
44, 92 bus.* **Open** 8am-7pm Mon-Fri.
No credit cards.
Cycle couriers who also have
motorbikes and vans. Price for
delivering a package (up to 6kg) by
bike within the central area is 470ptas,
plus tax unless you have an account.

UPS

*C/Miguel Hernández, corner of
C/Indústria, Polígon Industrial Zona
Franca, L'Hospitalet de Llobregat
(freephone 900 10 24 10/fax 93 263
39 09/www.ups.com). FCG Ildefons
Cerdà/65 bus.* **Open** 7am-8pm
Mon-Fri; closed Sat, Sun.
Credit AmEx, MC, V.
Next-day delivery to many
destinations. Call three hours
before required pick-up time. The
depot is at Avda Diagonal 511
(open 8.30am-8.30pm Mon-Fri,
Metro María Cristina); parcels
dropped there before 7.30pm leave
that evening for EU destinations.

Customs & immigration

EU residents do not have to
declare goods imported into
Spain for their personal use if
tax has been paid on them in
the country of origin. Customs
can still question whether
large amounts of any item
really are for your own use,
and random checks are made
for drugs. Quantities accepted
as being for personal use are
as follows:
● 800 cigarettes, 400 small
cigars, 200 cigars and 1kg of
loose tobacco;
● 10 litres of spirits (over
22% alcohol), 90 litres of wine
(under 22% alcohol) and 110
litres of beer.
Non-EU residents can bring in:
● 200 cigarettes or 100 small
cigars or 50 cigars or 250
grams (8.82 ounces) of tobacco;
● 1 litre of spirits (over 22%
alcohol) or 2 litres of fortified
wine or other alcoholic drinks
with under 22% alcohol;
● 2 litres of wine;
● 50 grammes (1.76 ounces)
of perfume.
There are no restrictions on
cameras, watches or electrical
goods, within reasonable limits
for personal use, and visitors
can carry up to 1,000,000ptas
in cash without having to
declare it. Non-EU residents
can also reclaim VAT (IVA)
paid on some large purchases
when they leave Spain. *For
details, see p169.*

IMMIGRATION & VISAS

Spain is one of the European
Union countries covered by
the Schengen agreement, with
many shared visa regulations
and reduced border controls
(the other countries currently
included are Portugal, France,
Belgium, the Netherlands,
Luxembourg, Germany,
Austria, Italy and, partially,
Greece). To travel to Schengen
countries British and Irish
citizens need full passports;
most EU nationals only need
carry their national identity
card. Passports, but not visas,
are needed by US, Canadian,
Australian and New Zealand
citizens for stays of up to three
months. Citizens of South
Africa and many other
countries also need visas
to enter Spain, obtainable
from Spanish consulates and
embassies in other countries
(or from those of other
Schengen countries that you
are planning to visit).
EU citizens intending to
work, study or live long-term
in Spain are required to obtain
a residency card, which has to
be done after you have arrived
here; non-EU nationals have a
different procedure and should
get a special visa in their home
country before entering Spain
to work (or study for more
than three months). For more
on the formalities of living in
Spain, *see p306.*

Disabled travellers

Transport facilities and access
in general for disabled people
still leave a lot to be desired,
despite steady improvements.
For wheelchair users, buses
and taxis are usually the best
public transport options.
There is a special transport
information phoneline (*see
p297*), and transport maps,
which you can pick up
from transport information
offices (*see p289*), indicate
wheelchair access points and
adapted bus routes.

Access to sights

New museums such as the MACBA have good access, but the process of converting older buildings is slow and difficult – the Picasso Museum, for example, now has a lift, but still has internal stairs as well. Phoning ahead to check is always a good idea even if a place claims to be accessible: access might depend, for example, on getting a lift key in advance. Below are listed wheelchair-friendly venues.

Museums

Fundació Joan Miró
Col.lecció Thyssen-Bornemisza-
Monestir de Pedralbes (wheelchair access to art collection only)
MACBA
MNAC
Museu d'Art Modern
Museu de les Arts Decoratives
Museu d'Arqueologia de Catalunya
Museu d'Historia de Catalunya
Museu de la Ciència
Museu de Zoologia

Exhibition spaces

La Capella
CCCB
Col.legi d'Arquitectes
Fundacio Antoni Tàpies
Palau de la Virreina

Institut Municipal de Persones amb Disminució

Av Diagonal, 233, Eixample (93 413 27 75/fax 93 413 28 00). Metro Glories/7, 56 bus. **Open** *mid Sept-mid June* 9am-2pm, 4-6pm Mon-Thur; 9am-2pm Fri; closed Sat, Sun. *Mid June-mid Sept* 9am-3pm Mon-Fri; closed Sat, Sun.
The city's organisation for the disabled has info on building access (theatres, museums, restaurants, and more) and other facilities.

Transport

Information

93 486 07 52/fax 93 486 07 53. **Open** 9am-9pm Mon-Fri; 9am-3pm Sat. Closed Sun. *Aug* closed Sat, Sun. English speakers sometimes available; if not, call the 010 information line (*see p305*).

Buses

All Aerobús buses from the airport and most on the Bus Turístic route are fully accessible to wheelchair users. Similar fully adapted buses

also alternate with standard buses on all Nitbus services and about half the daytime city routes, which are shown on transport maps and at bus stops.

Metro & FGC

Access is limited. Only line 2 (Paral.lel-La Pau) has lifts and ramps at all stations; some line 1 stations have lifts. The Montjuïc Funicular is also adapted for wheelchairs. FGC stations at Provença, Muntaner and Av Tibidabo are accessible, as are many FGC stops further out of town: Sant Cugat, Sabadell and others.

RENFE trains

Sants, França, Passeig de Gràcia and Plaça Catalunya stations are accessible to wheelchairs, but the trains are not. At Sants, if you go to the Atenció al Client office ahead of time, help on the platform can be arranged for you.

Taxis

All taxi drivers are officially required to transport wheelchairs (and guide dogs) for no extra charge, but their cars can be inconveniently small, and in practice the willingness of drivers to co-operate varies widely. Special minibus taxis adapted for wheelchairs can be ordered from the Taxi Amic service.

Taxi Amic

93 420 80 88. **Open** 7.30am-11pm Mon-Fri; 9am-10pm Sat, Sun. Fares are the same as for standard cabs, but the numbers of such taxis in Barcelona are limited, so you should call hours in advance to get one for a specific time.

Emergencies

See p300 **Emergencies**.

Gay & lesbian

Actua

C/Gomis 38, baixos, Zona Alta (93 418 50 00/fax 93 418 89 74). Bus 22, 73, 85. **Open** 9am-2pm, 4pm-7pm Mon-Fri; closed Sat, Sun.
Similar to Act-Up in the UK and US, it provides counselling and info to people living with HIV.

Ca la Dona

C/Casp 38, pral, Eixample (93 412 71 61). Metro Urquinaona/bus all routes to Plaça Catalunya. **Open** office 10am-2pm, 4-8pm Mon-Thur; closed Fri, Sat. Closed Aug. **Map** p324 D5.
Barcelona's main women's centre. It houses a variety of women's groups. *See also p291.*

Casal Lambda

C/Ample 5, Barri Gòtic (93 412 72 72/fax 93 412 74 76). Metro Drassanes/14, 18, 36, 38, 57, 59, 64 bus. **Open** 5-9pm Mon-Thur; 5pm-midnight Fri; noon-10pm Sat; closed Sun. **Map** p327 A4.
Gay cultural organisation that regularly hosts a wide range of activities and publishes the monthly magazine, LAMBDA. It has a nice interior patio that's used more by men than women, but all are welcome.

Coordinadora Gai-Lesbiana

C/Buenaventura Muñoz 4, Eixample (900 601 601/fax 93 218 11 91). Metro Arc del Triomf/39, 41, 51 bus. **Open** 5pm-9pm Mon-Fri; closed Sat, Sun. **Map** p325 E6.
The gay umbrella organisation in Barcelona works with the Ajuntament on all issues of concern to the gay community.

Front d'Alliberament Gai de Catalunya

(FAG) C/Verdi 88, Gràcia (93 217 26 69). Metro Fontana/22, 24, 28, ND, NG bus. **Open** 5-8pm Mon-Fri; closed Sat, Sun. **Map** p320 D-E3.
Vocal multi-group that produces the Barcelona Gai information bulletin.

Phone Lines

Teléfon Rosa (900 60 16 01). **Open** 6-10pm daily.
The phoneline of the Coordinadora Gai-Lesbiana (*see above*) is at your service if you need help or advice.

Health

All visitors can obtain emergency health care through the local public health service (*Servei Català de la Salut*, often just referred to as the **Seguretat Social/ Seguridad Social**). EU nationals are entitled to free basic medical attention if they have an E111 form (if you can get an E111 sent or faxed within four days, you are still exempt from charges). Many medicines will be charged for. In non-emergency situations short-term visitors will usually find it quicker to use private travel insurance rather than the state system. Similarly, non-EU nationals with private medical insurance can also make use of state health services on a paying basis, but other than in emergencies it will usually be simpler to use a private clinic. If you are a resident registered with the Seguretat Social (see p297) you will be allocated a doctor and a local health clinic. Information on health services is available from the 010 phoneline (see p305).

Emergencies

In a medical emergency the best thing to do is go to the casualty (Urgències) department of any of the main public hospitals. All those listed are open 24 hours daily. In the central area, go to the Clínic or the Perecamps. If necessary, call an ambulance on 061.

HOSPITALS

Centre d'Urgències Perecamps

Avda Drassanes 13-15, Raval (93 441 06 00). Metro Drassanes or Paral.lel/14, 20, 36, 38, 57, 59, 64,91 bus. **Map** *p327 A4.*
Located near the Rambla, this clinic specialises in primary attention for injuries and less serious emergencies.

Hospital Clínic

C/Villarroel 170, Eixample (93 227 54 00). Metro Hospital Clínic/14, 59, 63 bus. **Map** *p320 C4.*
The main city-centre hospital, in the Eixample. The Clínic also has a first-aid centre for less serious emergencies two blocks away at C/València 184 (93 227 93 00; open 9am-9pm Mon-Fri, 9am-1pm Sat).

Hospital de la Creu Roja de Barcelona

C/Dos de Maig 301, Eixample (93 507 27 00). Metro Hospital de Sant Pau/15, 19, 20, 25, 35, 45, 47, 50, 51, 92 bus. **Map** *p321 F4.*

Hospital del Mar

Passeig Marítim 25-29 (93 221 10 10). Metro Ciutadella-Vila Olímpica/45, 57, 59, 157, N8 bus. **Map** *p325 E7.*

Hospital de la Santa Creu i Sant Pau

C/Sant Antoni Maria Claret 167 (93 291 90 00). Metro Hospital de Sant Pau/15, 19, 20, 25, 35, 45, 47, 50, 51, N1, N4 bus. **Map** *p321 F4.*

LOCAL CLINICS

A Centre d'Assistència Primària (CAP) is a lower-level local health centre where you can be seen by a doctor and, if necessary, sent on to a hospital. They are open 8am to 9pm Monday to Friday and 9am to 5pm on Saturday.

CAP Doctor Lluís Sayé

C/Torres i Amat 8 (93 301 25 32/93 301 24 24). Metro Universitat/bus all routes to Plaça Universitat. **Map** *p326 A1.*

CAP Drassanes

Avda Drassanes 17-21 (93 329 44 95). Metro Drassanes or Paral.lel/14, 20, 36, 38, 57, 59, 64, 91 bus. **Map** *p327 A4.*

CAP Casc Antic

C/Rec Comtal 24 (93 310 14 21/310 50 98). Metro Arc de Triomf/39, 40, 41, 42, 51, 141 bus. **Map** *p326 C2.* **CAP Manso** *C/Manso 19 (93 325 28 00). Metro Paral.lel/13, 38, 57, 157 bus.* **Map** *p323 B5.*

CAP Vila Olímpica

C/Joan Miró 17 (93 221 37 85). Metro Ciutadella-Vila Olímpica/14, 41, 71, 92 bus. **Map** *p325 F6.*

Private healthcare

Centre Mèdic Assistencial Catalonia

C/Provença 281, baixos, Eixample (93 215 37 93). Metro Diagonal/6, 15, 22, 24, 28, 33, 34 bus. **Open** 8am-8pm Mon-Fri; closed Sat, Sun. **No credit cards.** **Map** *p320 D4.*
Dr Lynd is a British doctor who has practised in Barcelona for many years. She is at this surgery from 3.30-7pm on Wednesdays; at other times, call for an appointment and she will ring you back.

Dr Mary McCarthy

C/Aribau 215, pral 1ª, Eixample (93 200 29 24/mobile 607 220 040). FCG Gràcia/58, 64 bus. **Open** by appointment. **No credit cards.** **Map** *p320 C3.*
An internal medicine specialist from the US. Also treats general patients.

AIDS/HIV

As in many developed countries, the actual death rate from AIDS is now falling in Spain, but the HIV virus continues to spread in many groups, among them young

heterosexuals. Many local chemists take part in a needle-exchange and condom-distribution programme for intravenous drug users.

AIDS Information Line

900 21 22 22. **Open** *mid Sept-May* 9am-5.30pm Mon-Fri; closed Sat, Sun. *June-mid Sept* 8am-3pm Mon-Fri; closed Sat, Sun.

Alternative medicine

Integral: Centre Mèdic i de Salut

Plaça Urquinaona 2, 3° 2ª, Eixample (93 318 30 50). Metro Urquinaona/bus all routes to Plaça Urquinaona. **Open** information 9am-9pm Mon-Fri (call for appts). Closed Aug. **Map** *p326 B1.*
Acupuncture, homeopathy, and many other forms of complementary medicine are offered by a team of 20 professionals at this well-established clinic. Some speak English.

Contraception

All pharmacies sell condoms (*condons/condones*) and other forms of contraception. Condom vending machines can also be found in the toilets of many night-time bars and clubs, and in petrol stations.

Centre Jove d'Anticoncepció i Sexualitat

C/La Granja 19-21, Gràcia (93 415 10 00/www.centrejove.org). Metro Lesseps/24, 31, 32, 74 bus. **Open** *Oct-May* 10am-7pm Mon; noon-7pm Tue-Thur; 10am-2pm Fri; closed Sat, Sun. *June-Sept* 10am-5pm Mon-Thur; 10am-2pm Fri; closed Sat, Sun. Closed Aug. **Map** *p321 E2.*
A family planning centre aimed at young people (officially, under 23) which has very friendly staff and a tolerant attitude towards social security status and residency papers. The hours given may vary.

Dentists

Not covered by EU reciprocal agreements, so private rates, which can be costly, apply.

Centre Odontològic de Barcelona

C/Calàbria 251, Eixample (93 439 45 00). Metro Entença/41, 54 bus.

Open *Sept-July* 9am-9pm Mon-Fri;
9am-2pm Sat; closed Sun. *Aug* 9am-
1pm, 3pm-8pm Mon-Fri; closed Sat,
Sun. **Credit** DC, MC, V. **Map** p323 B4.
Well-equipped clinics providing a
complete range of dental services.
Several of the staff speak English.
Branch: Institut Odontològic de la
Sagrada Familia, C/Sardenya 319,
baixos (93 457 04 53).

Pharmacies

Pharmacies, *farmàcies*, are
signalled by large green or red
crosses, often in flashing neon,
and are plentiful throughout
the city. They are normally
open from 9am to 1.30pm and
4.30 to 8pm, Monday to Friday,
and 9am to 1.30pm on
Saturdays. At other times a
duty rota is in operation:
every pharmacy has a list of
farmàcies de guàrdia (duty
pharmacies) for that day
posted outside the door. Those
listed as *diürn*, marked in
green, are open all day from
9am to 10pm; those in the
nocturn list (marked red) are
open all night from 10pm to
9am, and often for the full 24
hours. This list is also given in
local newspapers, and on the
010 and 098 phonelines. Note
that at night, duty pharmacies
often appear to be closed, and
it's necessary to knock on the
shutters to be served.

Out of hours

A growing number of
pharmacies are open late or
24 hours, every day of the
year; these also appear on the
night duty list. Among them
are the following:

Farmàcia Alvarez

*Passeig de Gràcia 26, Eixample
(93 302 11 24). Metro Passeig de
Gràcia/7, 16,17, 22, 24, 28 bus.*
Credit MC, V.

Farmàcia Clapés

*La Rambla 98 (93 301 28 43). Metro
Liceu/14, 59, 91 bus.* **Credit** MC, V.

Farmàcia Vilar

*(93 490 92 07). Metro Plaça de Sants/
30, 56, 57, 215, N2, N14 bus.* **Open**
7am-10.30pm Mon-Fri; 8am-10.30pm
Sat, Sun. **Credit** Amex, MC, V.
In the vestibule of Sants train station.

Alcoholics Anonymous

93 317 77 77. **Open** 10am-1pm, 5-
8pm Mon-Fri; 7-9pm Sat, Sun; answerphone at other times.
Among the local AA groups there are
several that have dedicated English-
speaking sections.

Telèfon de l'Esperanca

(93 414 48 48). **Open** 24 hours daily.
A local helpline that offers a listening
ear. Staff here can also consult an
extensive database to put you in
touch with other specialist help
groups, from psychiatric to legal.
English sometimes spoken, but not
guaranteed. A private foundation.

EU nationals are entitled to
make use of the Spanish state
health service, provided they
have an E111 form, which in
Britain is available from post
offices, health centres and
Social Security offices. This
will cover you for emergencies,
but for short-term visitors it's
usually simpler to avoid the
bureaucracy and take out
private travel insurance before
departure, which will also
normally cover you in the case
of theft or other expenses.
Some non-EU countries
have reciprocal healthcare
agreements with Spain, but,
again, for most travellers
it will end up being more
convenient to have private
travel insurance.

Barcelona has over 20
municipal public libraries;
among their many services
some offer novels in English
and free Internet access. Call
010 for the address of the
nearest or click on to this site:
www. bcn.es/icub/biblioteque.

Ateneu Barcelonès

*C/Canuda 6, Barri Gòtic (93
343 61 21). Metro Catalunya/
bus all routes to Plaça Catalunya.*
Open 9am-10.45pm daily.
Map p326 B2.

This venerable cultural and
philosophical society has the best
private library in the city, open nearly
every day of the year, plus a deliciously peaceful interior garden patio and
bar. Initial membership costs
20,000ptas (payable in instalments),
and the subsequent fee is 2,100ptas
per month.

Biblioteca de Catalunya

*C/Hospital 56, Raval (93 317 07
78/www.gencat.es/bc). Metro
Liceu/14, 38, 59 bus.* **Open** 9am-8pm
Mon-Fri; 9am-2pm Sat; closed Sun.
Map p326 A2.
The largest of the city's libraries, the
Catalan national collection is housed
in the medieval Hospital de la Santa
Creu and has a wonderful stock reaching back centuries. Readers' cards are
required, but one-day research visits
are allowed (take your passport).
The library has Net terminals, and
the catalogue is online. On the
ground floor is the city's most central
public library, the Biblioteca de Sant
Pau i Santa Creu.

British Council/ Institut Britànic

*C/Amigó 83, Zona Alta (93 241 97
11). FGC Muntaner/14, 58, 64 bus.*
Open *Oct-June* 9.30am-9pm Mon-Fri;
10.30am-1.30pm Sat; closed Sun. *July,
Sept* 9.30am-2pm, 4-8.30pm Mon-Fri;
closed Sat, Sun. Closed Aug-early
Sept. **Map** p320 C2.
UK press, English books, satellite
TV and a big multimedia section
oriented towards learning English.
Access is free; borrowing costs
8,000ptas a year (16,000ptas with
Net access included).

Mediateca

*Centre Cultural de la Fundació la
Caixa, Passeig de Sant Joan 108,
Eixample (93 458 89 07/
www.lacaixa.es/fundacio/). Metro
Verdaguer/15, 55 bus.* **Open** 11am-
8pm Tue-Fri; 11am-3pm Sat. Closed
Aug. **Map** p321 E4.
A high-tech art, music and media
library in the arts centre of Fundació
la Caixa, housed in a *Modernista* mansion by Puig i Cadafalch (*see chapter*
Museums). Most materials are open-
access; borrowing costs 1,000ptas (for
ever), for which you will need to show
your ID card or passport.

Airport & rail stations

If you lose something land-
side of check-in at Prat
Airport, report the loss
immediately to the Aviación
Civil office in the relevant

Directory

Emergencies

terminal, or call airport information on 93 298 38 38. There is no central lost property depot for the RENFE rail network: if you think you have mislaid anything on a train, look for the Atención al Viajero desk or Jefe de Estación office at the nearest main station to where your property has gone astray, or call ahead to the destination station of the train. To get information by phone on lost property at main railway stations, call their general information numbers and ask for Objetos Perdidos.

Municipal lost property office

Servei de Troballes C/Ciutat 9, Barri Gòtic (lost property enquiries 010). Metro Jaume I/17, 19, 40, 45 bus. **Open** 9am-2pm Mon-Fri; closed Sat, Sun. **Map** p327 B3.
All items found on public transport and taxis in the city, or picked up by the police in the street, should eventually find their way to this office near the Ajuntament. If an item is labelled with the owner's name or a serial number, the 010 phone information service will be able to tell you if it has been handed in. Within 24 hours of the loss you can also try ringing the city transport authority on 93 318 70 74, or, for taxis, the Institut Metropolità del Taxi on 93 223 40 12.

Media

Most of Barcelona's main print and broadcast media are young, like Spain's democracy. But that doesn't mean they're innocent: the worlds of journalism and politics tend to overlap. The linguistic factor is also important, with the Catalan language strong in the broadcast media, and now beginning to gain ground in print, where Spanish still dominates.

Daily newspapers

As in most of Spain, regional rather than national dailies lead the market.

Avui
For many years this was the city's only Catalan-language newspaper; though decent, it's predictably pro-Generalitat.

El País
The third force in the Barcelona press is this rigorous, socialist-leaning paper, Spain's only real national daily. It has good entertainment and arts supplements (Friday and Saturday respectively).

El Periódico
A populist paper with a tabloid look but solid content. In 1997 it introduced a Catalan-language version, which today accounts for 40% of its sales.

La Vanguardia
Traditionally conservative, but now a lively, well-designed paper with a good listings magazine on Fridays.

English language

Foreign newspapers are available at most kiosks on the Rambla and Passeig de Gràcia.

Barcelona Business
A monthly newspaper combining business news with a more general focus on Catalonia.

Barcelona Metropolitan
A monthly city magazine aimed at English-speaking Barcelona residents, distributed free in bars and Anglophone hangouts.

b-guided
Quarterly bilingual style magazine for bars, clubs, shops, restaurants and exhibitions, sold at hip venues.

Listings & classifieds

The main newspapers have daily 'what's on' listings, with in-depth entertainment supplements on Fridays. For monthly listings, see *Metropolitan* and music/scene freebies like *Mondo Sonoro*, *AB*, and *Punto H* (distributed in bars and music shops). Of the dailies, *La Vanguardia* has the best classified section, especially on Sundays.

Guía del Ocio
A weekly listings magazine whose pocket-sized format and availability in any kiosk make it convenient but not always complete.

Anuntis
Largest of the classified-ad magazines, it's published on Mondays, Wednesdays and Fridays (phone 902 508 508 to place a free ad).

TV

Spanish television can take some getting used to: interminable ad breaks, unreliable programme start times, and, perhaps most irritating of all, out-of-sync voices on the mass of dubbed US and British programmes that are shown here. For undubbed films look for VO in listings and a Dual symbol at the top of the screen.

TVE1 (La Primera)
The Spanish state broadcaster with news that can be heavily pro-government.

TVE 2 (La Dos)
Also state run, La 2 offers less commercial fare with some good late-night movies.

TV3
Regional Catalan television – entirely in the Catalan language with mainstream programming.

Canal 33
Also regional and also entirely in Catalan but full of documentaries and extra sports programming.

Antena 3
A private channel with an emphasis on family entertainment and late-night salaciousness.

Tele 5
Also private. Audiences went sky-high in 2000 with a version of the Dutch voyeuristic popularity contest *Big Brother*.

Canal +
A subscriber channel based around movies and sport, although its news and other programmes are shown unscrambled.

BTV
Most innovative of all, but also the hardest to receive in some areas, the Ajuntament's city channel features a lot of student-produced programming.

Radio

The local radio dials – especially the FM band – are packed, and the Catalan language has a greater presence than in any other medium. Catalunya Música (101.5 FM) is mainly classical. Rádio 3 (98.7 FM) has rock/roots. On shortwave, the BBC World Service can be heard on 15485, 12095, 9410 and 6195 KHz, depending on the time of the day.

Money

For the moment, Spain's everyday currency is the peseta, abbreviated as ptas (pesseta, ptes in Catalan). There are coins for 1, 5, 10, 25, 50, 100, 200 and 500 pesetas. A 5ptas coin is called a *duro*. Notes are green 1,000ptas, 2,000 (red), 5,000 (brown) and 10,000ptas (blue).

THE EURO
In Spain, as in 11 other EU countries, local money is technically now only one outward form of the future European currency, the euro. It is already the reserve currency for banking, and euro prices appear next to peseta ones in most shops and on receipts.

Euro notes and coins go into circulation on 1 January 2002, after which banks, bureaux de change and ATMs will dispense only euros. The euro and the peseta will circulate together for a relatively short transition period – a maximum of two months, though the exact duration has yet to be decided – but by 1 March 2002, the peseta will no longer be acceptable for general use, although it will still be possible to convert all the old currencies into euros at national central banks.

One euro (€1) equals 166.386ptas. An easy rule of thumb for conversion is this: 500 ptas is almost exactly €3, 1,000ptas is close to €6, etc.

For euro-information in Spain, call 901 11 20 02.

Banks & foreign exchange

Banks and savings banks readily accept travellers' cheques (you must show your passport), but usually refuse to cash any kind of personal cheque except one issued by that bank. Commission rates vary a good deal, and it's always worth shopping around before changing money. Given the rates charged by Spanish banks, the cheapest way to obtain money may be through an ATM machine with a debit or credit card rather than with travellers' cheques, despite the fees charged for withdrawals.

Bank hours
Banks are normally open from 8.30am to 2pm Monday to Friday, and from 1 October to 30 April most branches also open on Saturday mornings from 8.30am to 1pm. Hours vary a little between banks: some open slightly earlier or later. Savings banks (Caixes d'Estalvis/Cajas de Ahorros), which offer the same exchange facilities as banks, open from 8am to 2pm Monday to Friday, and from October to May they also open on Thursdays from 4.30pm to 7.45pm. Savings banks never open on Saturday. Banks and *caixes* are closed on public holidays.

Out-of-hours services
Outside normal hours there are bank exchange offices open at the airport (Terminals A and B, open 7am-11pm daily) and Barcelona-Sants station (open 8am-9.30pm daily). There's a private bureau de change (*cambio*) at the Estació d'Autobusos Barcelona-Nord (open 8am-9pm Mon-Fri; 9am-4pm Sat, 10am-4pm Sun), and many more in the city centre. Some in the Rambla are open until midnight, or 3am from July to September. *Cambios* do not charge commission, but their exchange rates are usually less favourable than bank rates. At the airport, Sants and outside some banks there are automatic cash exchange machines that accept notes in major currencies, as long as they are in good condition.

American Express
C/Rosselló 261, Eixample (93 217 00 70). Metro Diagonal, FCG Provença/7, 16, 17, 31, 67, 68 bus. **Open** 9.30am-6pm Mon-Fri; 10am-noon Sat; closed Sun. **Map** p320 D4. All the usual AmEx services, and an ATM for AmEx cards. 24-hour money transfers anywhere in the world (charges paid by the sender). **Branch**: La Rambla 74 (93 301 11 66).

Western Union Money Transfer

Loterías Manuel Martín, La Rambla 41 (93 412 70 41). *Metro Liceu or Drassanes/14, 38, 59, 91 bus.* **Open** 9.30am-midnight Mon-Sat; 10am-midnight Sun. **Map** p327 A3.

The quickest, although not the cheapest, way of having money sent from abroad.

Branches: Mail Boxes C/València 214, Eixample (93 454 69 83).

Credit cards

Major credit and charge cards are widely accepted in hotels, shops, restaurants and many other services (including Metro ticket machines, and pay-and-display parking machines in the street). With major cards you can also withdraw cash from most bank cash machines, which provide instructions in different languages at the push of a button. Banks also advance cash against a credit card, but prefer you to use the machine. Don't forget that interest will be charged.

Card emergencies

All lines have English-speaking staff and are open 24 hours daily.

American Express card emergencies 91 572 0303/travellers' cheques freephone 900 99 44 26. **Diners Club** 901 10 10 11. **MasterCard** 900 97 12 31. **Visa** 900 974 445.

Police & street crime

There are two sides to street crime in Barcelona: on the one hand, the general atmosphere on the street is relaxed, and violent crime less common than in many large cities. On the other hand, bag-snatching and pickpocketing are a real problem, reaching epidemic levels in 2000, with tourists the prime target. The constant increase in visitor numbers in the last few years has also been accompanied by an

increase in street crime. Favourite spots for thieves are the Rambla, Barri Gòtic and the old town in general; public transport, particularly the Metro; and, sometimes, quieter areas such as Parc Güell or the beach.

Most street robberies, though, are aimed very much at the unwary, and could be avoided if you take a few simple, common-sense precautions:

● Whenever you put your bag or coat down in a public place, indoors or out, keep it right beside you, clearly visible to you but inaccessible to any passers-by.

● When sitting in a café, especially outdoors, *never* leave a bag on the back of a chair, on the floor or on a chair where you cannot see it clearly. If in doubt, keep it on your lap.

●In crowded spaces be aware, in a relaxed way, of people moving around you. If you're at all suspicious about someone, simply move somewhere else. Don't carry your wallet or any valuables in the back pockets of your trousers or your backpack.

● Keep your shoulder bag closed and pulled to the front (not at your back), and always keep a hand on it.

● Avoid pulling out big-denomination notes or bulging wallets in public places; try not to get stuck with large notes when changing money.

● Be aware that street thieves often work in pairs or groups: one may ask you the time, or attempt to start a conversation, while his friend hovers behind you and then grabs your bag. This is often done very crudely, so it's not hard to recognise: be on your guard.

● Sudden requests to shake your hand, or 'helpful' passers-by who say you've got something spilled on your back and offer to clean it off, should likewise be ignored, as they may be part of the same game.

● A more subtle scam is pulled by people (mostly other foreigners) who approach you with a hard-luck story about how they themselves have been ripped off, and ask for a loan of 6,000ptas or so, which they will send you once they get back to Zurich, Amsterdam or wherever. They won't.

Police forces

Barcelona has several police forces. Most numerous are the local Guàrdia Urbana, who wear navy and pale blue, and are concerned with traffic, local regulations, and general law and order in the city. The Policía Nacional, in darker blue uniforms and white shirts (or blue combat-style gear) also patrol the street, and have primary responsibility for dealing with more serious crime. The Catalan government's police, the Mossos d'Esquadra, in navy and light blue with red trim, are gradually expanding their role, and are now responsible for traffic control in Barcelona province, although not in the city itself. A fourth body is the Guardia Civil, who wear military green uniforms and watch over many Spanish highways and customs posts and some government buildings, but are not often seen within Barcelona.

Reporting a crime

If you are robbed or attacked, report the incident as soon as possible to the Turisme-Atenció station on the Rambla, a special police service to assist foreign visitors in difficulties. Officers on duty can speak French, German, Italian and English. If you report a crime you will be asked to make an official statement (*denuncia*). It is frankly unlikely that anything you have lost will ever be recovered, but you need the *denuncia* to make an insurance claim. In other areas report the incident to the nearest Policía Nacional station (Comisaría), which will be listed in the phone book. For emergency phone numbers, *see p300.*

Turisme-Atenció

La Rambla 43 (93 301 90 60/93 344 13 00). Metro Liceu or Drassanes/14, 38, 59, 91 bus. **Open** 24 hours daily. **Map** p327 A3.

Religious services

Anglican: Saint George's Church

C/Horaci 38, Zona Alta (93 417 88 67). FGC Av Tibidabo/22, 64, 75 bus. **Main service** 11am Sun.
A British church with a multicultural congregation.

Catholic Mass in English: Parròquia Maria Reina

Carretera d'Esplugues 103, Zona Alta (information 93 203 41 15). Metro Zona Universitaria/63, 78 bus. **Mass** 11am Sun. **Map** p319 A1.

Jewish Orthodox: Sinagoga de Barcelona

C/Avenir 2, Zona Alta (93 200 61 48). FCG Gràcia/58, 64 bus. **Prayers** call for times. **Map** p320 C3.
A Sephardic, Orthodox synagogue.

Jewish Reform: Comunitat Jueva Atid de Catalunya

C/Castanyer 27, Zona Alta (93 417 3704/atid@arquired.es). FCG El Putxet, Avinguda del Tibidabo/17 bus. **Prayers** call for times.
Reform synagogue.

Moslem: Mosque Tarik Bin Ziad

C/Hospital 91, Raval (93 4419 149). Metro Liceu/14, 38, 59, 91 bus. **Prayers** Friday 2pm, call for other times.

Removals

Gil Stauffer

C/Pau Claris 176, Eixample (93 215 55 55/www.gil-stauffer.com). Metro Passeig de Gràcia or Diagonal/7, 16, 17, 20, 22, 24, 43, 44 bus. **Open** 9am-7pm Mon-Fri; closed Sat, Sun. **Credit** AmEx, MC, V. **Map** p320 D4.
Reliable national and international movers with worldwide links.

Study

Catalonia is ardently Europhile, and its universities lend enthusiastic support to EU student exchange programmes. The vast majority of foreign students in Spain under the EU's Erasmus scheme are enrolled at Catalan universities. The main teaching language in universities is usually Catalan, although lecturers (and students) are often relaxed about using Castilian in class for the first few months with non-Catalan speakers. Foreign students who stay for over three months, including European Union nationals, are officially required to have a residence permit.

Centre d'Informació i Assessorament per a Joves (CIAJ)

C/Ferran 32 (93 402 78 00/ www.bcn.es/ciaj). Metro Liceu/14, 38, 59, 91 bus. **Open** 10am-2pm, 4pm-8pm Mon-Fri; closed Sat, Sun. Closed afternoons Aug. **Map** p327 A-B3.
City council youth info centre, with advice and information on work, study, travel and more; also small ads, noticeboards and free web terminals.

Secretaria General de Joventut – Punt d'Informació Juvenil

C/Calabria 147-C/Rocafort 116 (93 483 83 83/93 483 83 84/www. bcu.cesca.es). Metro Rocafort/41 bus. **Open** 9am-2pm, 3-5.30pm Mon-Fri; closed Sat, Sun. Closed afternoons June-mid Sept. **Map** p323 B5.
Generalitat-run centre hosting a range of services: a 'youth information point' with information on travel, work and study and Net access. Other services include: **Habitatge Jove** *(93 483 83 92/www.habitatgejove.com).* **Open** 10am-1pm, 3.30-5pm Mon-Thur; 9am-2pm Fri; closed Sat, Sun. Reduced hours Aug.
A youth accommodation service; Erasmus students can use the website to find a place to live before they arrive in Barcelona. **Viatgeteca** *(93 483 83 81).* **Open** 9am-2pm, 3-7pm Mon-Fri; closed Sat, Sun.
Travel information centre, where you can consult guidebooks and the web, buy all kinds of student cards and book youth hostels.

Universities

EU programmes: Socrates, Erasmus, Lingua

The Erasmus student exchange scheme and Lingua project (specifically concerned with language learning) are the most important parts of the European Union's Socrates programme to help students move between member states. Erasmus is open to students from their second year onwards; anyone interested should approach the Erasmus co-ordinator at their home college. General information is available in Britain from the UK Socrates & Erasmus Council, R&D Building, The University, Canterbury, Kent CT2 7PD (01227 762712/fax 01227 762711/www.ukc. ac.uk/ERASMUS/erasmus).

Universitat Autònoma de Barcelona

Campus de Bellaterra, 08193 (93 581 10 00/student information 93 581 11 11/www.uab.es). FCG, RENFE Unversidad Autonoma; by car A18 to Cerdanyola del Valles. **Open** Information Sept-June 10am-1.30pm, 3.30-4.30pm Mon-Thur; 10am-1.30pm Fri; closed Sat, Sun. July, Aug 10am-1.30pm Mon-Fri; closed Sat, Sun.
The Autonomous University occupies a rambling 1960s campus outside the city at Bellaterra, near Sabadell. There are frequent FGC train connections.

Universitat de Barcelona

Gran Via de les Corts Catalanes 585 (93 403 54 17/www.ub.es). Metro Universitat/bus all routes to Plaça Universitat. **Information** Servei d'Atenció a la Comunitat Universitària (Pati de Ciències entrance). **Open** Sept-June 9am-6pm Mon-Fri; closed Sat, Sun. July, Aug 9am-2pm Mon-Fri; closed Sat, Sun. **Map** p324 C-D5.
Barcelona's oldest and biggest university with faculties in the main building on Plaça Universitat, in the Zona Universitària as well as in other parts of town.

Universitat Pompeu Fabra

Plaça de la Mercè 10-12, Barri Gòtic (93 542 22 28/www.upf.es). Metro Drassanes/14, 36, 57, 59, 59, 64, 157 bus. **Open** 8am-9pm Mon-Fri. **Map** p327 B4.
This social sciences-based university has faculties in central Barcelona, many of them in the old city. It was founded as recently as 1991.

Universitat Ramon Llull

C/Claravall 1-3, Zona Alta (93 602 2200/www.url.es). FCG Avinguda del Tibidabo/22, 58, 73, 75, 85 bus. **Open** *Information* 9am-2pm, 4-6.30pm Mon-Fri; closed Sat, Sun. Closed Aug.

Private university bringing together a number of previously separate institutions owned and/or run by the Jesuits, including the prestigious ESADE business school (93 280 2995/www.esade.edu); there is no strong religious presence in teaching. Fees are high.

Language learning

In bilingual Barcelona, many who come to stay for a while will want (or need) to learn some Catalan, but the city is also a hugely popular location for people studying Spanish. For full lists of course options, try youth information centres (*see p303*).

American-British College

C/Guillem Tell 27, Zona Alta (93 415 57 57/www.ambricol.es). FGC Plaça Molina/16, 17, 22, 24, 25, 27, 28, 31, 32 bus. **Open** 9am-9pm Mon-Fri; closed Sat, Sun. Aug closes 8pm. **Map** p320 D2.

An established school offering reasonably priced intensive Spanish courses. Accommodation can be arranged either with families or in student residences.

Bla Bla & Company

C/Muntaner 82, Eixample (93 454 6877/www.blabla.es). Metro Universitat/bus all routes to Plaça Universitat. **Open** 8am-10pm Mon-Fri; 10am-2pm Sat; closed Sun. Aug closed Sat, Sun. **Map** p320 C4.

A multimedia-based language school, offering Spanish courses, drop-in facilities and flexible, personalised tuition schedules.

Consorci per a la Normalització Lingüística

Central office C/Mallorca 272, 8ª, Eixample (93 272 31 00/ www.cpnl.org). Metro Passeig de Gràcia or Diagonal/20, 22, 24, 28, 43, 44 bus. **Open** *Sept-mid June* 9am-2pm, 4-6.30pm Mon-Fri; closed Sat, Sun. *Mid June-Sept* 8am-3pm Mon-Fri; closed Sat, Sun. **Map** p320 D4.

The official Generalitat organisation for the support of the Catalan language has centres around the city offering Catalan courses at low prices from beginners' level upwards, with intensive courses in summer, and self-study centres.

Escola Oficial d'Idiomes

Avda Drassanes (93 324 9330/www.eoibd.es). Metro Drassanes/14, 38, 59, 91 bus. **Open** 9am-2pm Mon, Fri; 9am-2pm, 4-7pm Tue-Thur. Closed afternoons June-Sept. **Map** p323 A4.

The 'official school' has semi-intensive three-month courses at all levels in Catalan, Spanish and other languages. It's cheap, and the Escola has a good reputation, so demand is very high and classes are big. It also has summer courses, a self-study centre and a good library.
Branch: Avda del Jordà 18, Vall d'Hebrón (93 418 74 85).

International House

C/Trafalgar 14, entresol (93 268 45 11/www.ihes.com/bcn). Metro Catalunya/bus all routes to Plaça Catalunya. **Open** 8am-9pm Mon-Fri; 9.30am-1.30pm Sat; closed Sun. **Map** p326 C1.

Intensive Spanish courses all year; IH is also the leading Barcelona centre for TEFL teacher training.

Tourist information

The city council (Ajuntament) and Catalan government (the Generalitat) both run tourist information offices, and the City of Barcelona also has an efficient information service for local citizens that's useful to visitors. Information on what's on in music, theatre, galleries and so on can be found in local papers and listings magazines (*see p301*). For youth and student agencies, *see p303*.

City tourist offices sell multi-journey transport tickets, tourist bus (Bus Turístic) tickets and the Barcelona Card discount card. City and Generalitat also have useful websites (in English).
City of Barcelona
www.bcn.es
City tourist authority
www.barcelonaturisme.com
Generalitat
www.gencat.es
Palau Robert
www.gencat.es/probert

Oficines d'Informació Turística

Main office: Plaça Catalunya (906 30 12 82/from outside Spain 93 368 9730). Metro Catalunya/bus all routes to Plaça Catalunya. **Open** 9am-9pm daily. **Map** p326 B1.

The main office of the city tourist board (Turisme de Barcelona) is underground beneath the Corte Inglés side of the square (look for big red signs with 'i' in white). It has a full information service, money exchange, a souvenir and book shop, a hotel booking service and coin-in-slot Net access.
Branches: Plaça Sant Jaume (in Ajuntament building, side entrance), Barri Gòtic; Barcelona-Sants station; Palau de Congressos (Trade Fair office), Avda Reina Maria Cristina, Montjuïc.

Temporary office & 'Red Jackets'

Information booth located at Sagrada Família. **Open** *late June-late Sept* 10am-8pm daily. Closed late Sept-late June. **Map** p321 F4.

In summer Turisme de Barcelona opens this temporary booth (no hotel booking service). 'Red Jacket' information officers (in red uniforms) also roam the Barri Gòtic and Rambla, ready to field questions in a heroic variety of languages from 10am to 8pm daily.

Palau Robert

Passeig de Gràcia 107, Eixample (93 238 40 00). Metro Diagonal/22, 24, 28 bus. **Open** 10am-7pm Mon-Sat; 10am-2pm Sun. **Map** p320 D4.

The Catalan government's lavishly equipped information centre is in the Palau Robert, a grand mansion at the junction of Passeig de Gràcia and the Diagonal. It doesn't have as much on Barcelona itself as the City offices – although it still has maps and other essentials – but has a huge range of information in different media on other parts of Catalonia, activities and so on. It also hosts interesting exhibitions on different aspects of the country.
Branches: Airport Terminal A (93 478 47 04); Airport Terminal B (93 478 05 65).

Centre d'Informació de la Virreina

Palau de la Virreina, La Rambla 99 (93 301 77 75). Metro Liceu/14, 38, 59, 91 bus. **Open** 10am-2pm, 4-8pm Mon-Fri. Closed Sat, Sun.
Ticket sales 11am-8pm Tue-Sat; 11am-2.30pm Sun; closed Mon. **Map** p326 A2.

Not a tourist office as such, but the information office of the City culture department, with details of exhibitions, concerts, theatres and so on. Also the best place to buy tickets for events in the Grec summer festival (*see p203*), and some other city-sponsored events and venues. In the same building is the Botiga de la Virreina bookshop, which has a wide choice of books on Barcelona, some of them in English editions.

010 phoneline

Open 8am-10pm Mon-Sat.
City-run information line that's again mainly aimed at local citizens, but does an impeccable job of answering all kinds of queries. Calls are taken in French and English as well as Catalan and Spanish, but you may have to wait for an English-speaking operator. From outside Barcelona, call 93 402 70 00.

Useful information

Addresses

Most apartment addresses consist of a street name followed by a number, floor level and flat number. So to go to C/València 246, 2n 3a, find number 246; go up to the *segon pis/segundo piso* – second floor and the *tercera porta/puerta*, the third door.

Ground-floor flats are usually called *baixos* or *bajos* (often abbreviated bxs/bjos); one floor up is usually the *entresol/ entresuelo* (entl), and the next is often the *principal* (pral). Confusingly, numbered floors start here, first, second, up to the *àtic/ ático* at the top.

Electricity

The standard current in Spain is now 220V. A diminishing number of old buildings still have 125V circuits, and it's advisable to check before using electrical equipment in old, cheap hotels. Plugs are all of the two-round-pin type.

The 220V current works fine with British-bought 240V products with a plug adaptor (available at El Corte Inglés). With US 110V equipment you will also need a current transformer.

Estancs/Estancos (tobacco shops)

The tobacco shop, usually known as an *estanc/estanco* and identified by a brown and yellow sign with the words *tabacs* or *tabacos*, is a very important Spanish institution. First and foremost, as the sign suggests, they supply cigarettes and every other kind of tobacco, but they are also the main places to buy postage stamps, as well as many official forms demanded by Spanish state bureaucracy in all kinds of minor procedures. They also sell sweets, postcards, public transport *targetes* and phonecards.

Opening times

Most shops open 9/10am to 1/2pm and 4.30/5 to 8/9pm, Monday to Saturday, but many do not reopen on Saturday afternoons. Markets open earlier, at 7/8am, and most smaller ones are closed by 2/3pm. Major stores, shopping centres and a growing number of shops open all day, 10am to 9pm, Monday to Saturday. Larger shops are also allowed to open some Sundays and holidays, mostly around Christmas time. In summer, staggered holidays have become more common, but many restaurants and shops still close up for all or part of August. Many businesses work a shortened day from June to September, from 8/9am till 3pm. Most (but not all) museums are open at weekends, but close one day each week, usually Monday. They do not close in summer. For restaurant times, *see p128*.

Public toilets

Not common: the main railway stations have clean toilets, and in some places there are pay-on-entry cubicles that cost 25ptas. Generally, when in need, you're best advised to pop into a bar or café; proprietors usually don't mind. Major stores or fast food restaurants are, of course, staple standbys.

Queuing

Catalans, like other Spaniards, have a highly developed queuing culture. In small shops and at market stalls people may not stand in line, but they are generally well aware of when it is their turn. Common practice is to ask when you arrive, to no one in particular, 'Qui es l'últim/la última?' ('Who's last?'); see who nods back at you, and follow after them. Say 'jo' ('me') to the next person who asks the same question.

Smoking

People in Barcelona still smoke – a lot. Non-smoking areas are rare in bars and restaurants, although smoking bans in cinemas, theatres and on trains are generally respected. Smoking is banned throughout the Metro and FGC, but many people take this to mean on trains only, not station platforms. For places to buy tobacco, *see chapter* **Shopping**.

Time

Local time is one hour ahead of GMT, six hours ahead of US Eastern Standard Time and nine ahead of Pacific Standard Time. So, when it's 6pm in Barcelona it's 5pm in London and noon in New York. Summer Time operates in Spain from late March to late October, with the same changeover days as the UK.

Tipping

There are no fixed rules, nor any expectation of a set ten per cent or more, and many locals tip very little. It is common to leave around five per cent for a waiter in a restaurant, up to and rarely over 500ptas, and people may also leave something in a bar, maybe part or all of the small change. It's also usual to tip hotel porters, and toilet attendants. In taxis, the usual tip is around five per cent; more for longer journeys, or if the driver has helped with luggage.

Water

Barcelona tap water is entirely safe and drinkable, but has a minerally taste. By preference most people drink bottled water, and if you ask for water in a restaurant you will automatically be served this unless you specifically request otherwise.

When to go

One of the best times to visit is during one of the many *festes* (*see p198*). Barcelona sees a lot of blue sky all year round, and temperatures are rarely extreme, although there can be surprises (midsummer downpours, or cold snaps in mid-spring).

Spring

Average temperatures 9°C-18°C (48°C-64°F). Spring is often the most unpredictable season, when warm sunny days alternate with cold winds and showers, but generally by Easter locals are casting off winter coats, and May is one of the most enjoyable of all times to be in Barcelona, warm enough to sit out through the night but never oppressive.

Summer

Average temperatures 18°C-27°C (64°C-80°F). In early summer the weather is delicious, and Barcelona's streetlife is at its most vibrant. The real heat hits from late July to mid August; more of a problem than the temperature is humidity. Many locals escape the city altogether, leaving visitors to explore a tranquil, partly closed Barcelona with an atmosphere of its own. As August goes on there's more chance of thunderstorms – intense but refreshing.

Autumn

Average temperatures 13°C-21°C (55°C-70°F). September weather is again beautiful, warm and fresh, although autumn is also the wettest season, with sporadic downpours. In October the weather can visibly

Directory

'break': temperatures drop, and there may be torrential storms. Pavement tables mostly go in by November, although some remain out all year.

Winter

Average temperatures 5°C-14°C (41°C-57°F). Crisp winter sunshine is common, although where it doesn't reach the cold can be damp and penetrating. Snow is rare.

Holidays

On public holidays (*festes/ fiestas*) virtually all shops, banks and offices, and many bars and restaurants, are closed. Public transport runs a Sunday service, or a very limited service on Christmas and New Year's Day. When a holiday falls on a Tuesday or Thursday, some people take the intervening day before or after the weekend off as well, in a long weekend called a *pont/puente* (bridge). Few offices now close the whole of Easter week, but activity diminishes greatly from the Wednesday on. For more information, *see chapter* **By Season**.

Women

The Catalan capital is in many ways a female-friendly city. Sexism can certainly be found – some shocking cases of domestic violence against women in particular have recently drawn attention to this issue. However, from the point of view of the visitor, a woman can have a drink in a bar or go out alone without anyone making much of it, and probably feel safer in general than in many other large cities.

Women's health programmes are run in most CAPs (*see p298*).

Organisations

Ca La Dona

C/Casp 38, pral, Eixample (93 412 71 61/email: caladona@pangea.org). Metro Catalunya, Urquinaona/22, 28, 39, 45 bus. **Open** *Office* 10am-2pm,

4-8pm Mon-Thur; closed Fri-Sun. Closed Aug. **Map** p326 B1.
Women's centre hosting over 30 groups of varying orientations: political, artistic, social and so on. Among them is the Coordinadora Feminista de Catalunya, the most important local feminist organisation: a good place to get general information. It also has a magazine (of the same name, in Catalan) with event listings.

Centre Municipal d'informació i Recursos per a Dones

Av Diagonal 233, 5ª, Eixample (93 413 2722/ 93 413 2723/www.cird. bcn.es). Metro Monumental/7, 56, 62 bus. **Open** noon-2pm Mon-Fri, 4-7pm Tue-Thur; closed Sat, Sun. *July, Sept* noon-2pm Mon-Fri; closed Sat, Sun. Closed Aug.
This is the Ajuntament's women's resource centre. Its publications include a monthly events guide, *Agenda Dona*.

Institut Català de la Dona

Head office/library: C/Viladomat 319, entresol, Eixample (93 495 16 00/icd@correu.gencat.es). Bus 41, 54. **Open** 9am-2pm, 3-5.30pm Mon-Thur; 9am-2pm Fri; closed Sat, Sun. *Information centre: C/Portaferrissa 1-3 (93 317 92 91/icdcentredoc @cor- reu.gencat.es). Metro Liceu/14, 38, 59 bus.* **Open** 9am-2pm, 4-6pm Mon-Fri; closed Sat, Sun. Reduced hours June-Sept. **Map** p326 A2.
The women's affairs department of the Catalan government.

Working in Barcelona

Barcelona's many pleasures attract ever-growing numbers of foreign residents and working visitors. Not many from developed countries, though, are drawn here by filthy lucre – the reverse is often the case, for Barcelona can be a difficult place to find well-paid work, and yet is still a not-too-painful place to live (relatively) cheaply.

Common recourses for English-speakers are tourist-sector jobs (often seasonal and outside the city), translation, and language teaching – probably still the best chance of finding work quickly.

For a contract in a school, a recognised English-teaching qualification such as TEFL is near-essential (*see p304* International House for local TEFL courses). There is also demand for private classes.

If you come here contracted from your country of origin, legal papers should be dealt with by your employer. Otherwise, the quickest way to deal with the Spanish state's love of form-filling is to resort to one of the agencies called *gestories* (*see p293*).

EU CITIZENS

All EU citizens have the right to live, work and study in Spain, but must become legally resident if they stay for more than three months. If you have a job or study course lined up, you are ready to make an appointment to present your residency application. In Barcelona, you do this at the foreigners' office (Oficina de Extranjeros) at the Delegación del Gobierno (*see below*).

NON-EU CITIZENS

While immigration laws have relaxed greatly for EU nationals, they have tightened for people from the rest of the world. First-time applicants officially need a visa, obtained from a Spanish consulate in your home country, although you can start the bureacratic ball rolling in Spain if you don't mind making at least one trip home. This, combined with the length of the process, means that good legal advice from a *gestor* (*see p293*) is especially important.

Delegación del Gobierno – Oficina de Extranjeros

Avda Marqués de l'Argentera 2 (93 482 05 44/appointments 93 482 05 60 8am-3pm Mon-Fri). Metro Barceloneta/14, 39, 51 bus. **Open** 9am-2pm Mon-Fri. **Map** p327 C4.
Arrive early – you'll need the time to wait in line. There are various queues; make sure you're in the right one before you start. You can expect shorter waits on Fridays.

Catalan Vocabulary

Catalan is a Latin language that's readily comprehensible with a little knowledge of French or Spanish grammar. The extent to which Catalans expect visitors to speak it varies, but it is certainly useful to have some recognition of the language if only to be able to read signs and pronounce place names correctly.

Catalan phonetics are significantly different from those of Spanish, with a wider range of vowels and soft consonants. Catalans use the familiar (*tu*) rather than the polite (*vosté*) forms of the second person very freely, but for convenience verbs are given here in the polite form. For food and menu terms, *see p131*.

Pronunciation

In Catalan, as in French but unlike in Spanish, words are run together, so *si us plau* (please) is more like *sees-plow*.

à at the end of a word (as in Francesc Macià) is an open **a** rather like when you say **ah**, but very clipped;
ç, and **c** before an **i** or an **e**, are like a soft **s**, as in **s**it. **c** in all other cases is as in **c**at;
unstressed **e**, in a plural such as cerveses (beers), or Jaume I, is a weak sound like cent**re** or comfort**a**ble;
g, before an **i** or an **e**, and **j** are pronounced like the **s** in pleasure; **tg** and **tj** are similar to the **dg** in ba**dg**e; **g** after an **i** at the end of a word (Puig) is a hard **ch** sound, as in wat**ch**; **g** in all other cases is as in **g**et;
h beginning a word is normally silent;
ll is like the **lli** in mi**lli**on;
l.l the 'split double-l', the most unusual feature of Catalan spelling, refers to a barely audible difference, a slightly stronger stress on a single **l** sound;
o at the end of a word is like the **u** sound in flu; **ó** at the end of a word is similar to the **o** in tomato; **ò** is like the **o** in hot.
A single **r** beginning a word and **rr** are heavily rolled; **r** at the end of a word strengthens the previous vowel but is almost silent, so *carrer* (street) sounds like *carr-ay;*
s at the beginning and end of words and **ss** between vowels are soft, as in s**i**t. A single **s** between two vowels is a **z** sound, as in la**z**y.

x is like the **sh** in **sh**oe, except in the combination **tx**, which is like the **tch** in wa**tch**;
y after an **n** at the end of a word or in **nys** is not a vowel but adds a nasal stress and a y-sound to the n.

Things everyone here knows

please *si us plau;* **very good/great/OK** *molt bé*
hello *hola;* **goodbye** *adéu*
open *obert;* **closed** *tancat*
entrance *entrada;* **exit** *sortida*
nothing at all/zilch *res de res* (said with both s silent)
price *preu;* **free** *gratuit/de franc;*
change, exchange *canvi*
llogar *to rent;* (de) **lloguer** (for) *rent, rental*
up with Barcelona FC *Visca el Barça* (corny, yes, but often good for a cheap laugh)

More expressions

hello (when answering the phone) *hola, digui'm*
good morning, good day *bon dia;*
good afternoon, good evening *bona tarda;* **good night** *bona nit*
thank you (very much) *(moltes) gràcies*
you're welcome *de res*
do you speak English? *parla anglès?*
I'm sorry, I don't speak Catalan *ho sento, no parlo català*
I don't understand *no entenc*
can you say it to me in Spanish, please? *m'ho pot dir en castellà, si us plau?*
how do you say that in Catalan? *com se diu això en Català?*
what's your name? *com se diu?*
Sir/Mr *senyor (sr);* **Madam/Mrs** *senyora (sra);* **Miss** *senyoreta (srta)*
excuse me/sorry *perdoni/disculpi;*
excuse me, please *escolti* (literally 'listen to me'); **OK/fine** *val/d'acord*
how much is it *quant és?*
why? *perquè?;* **when?** *quan?;* **who?** *qui?;* **what?** *què?;* **where?** *on?;* **how?** *com?;* **where is…?** *on és…?;* **who is it?** *qui és?*
is/are there any…? *hi ha…?/n'hi ha de…?*
very *molt;* **and** *i;* **or** *o;* **with** *amb;* **without** *sense;* **enough** *prou*
I would like… *vull…* (literally, 'I want'); **how many would you like?** *quants en vol?;* **I don't want** *no vull*
I like *m'agrada;* **I don't like** *no m'agrada*
good *bo/bona;* **bad** *dolent/a;* **well/ badly** *bé/malament;* **small** *petit/a;*

big *gran;* **expensive** *car/a;* **cheap** *barat/a;* **hot** (food, drink) *calent/a;* **cold** *fred/a*
something *alguna cosa;* **nothing** *res;* **more** *més;* **less** *menys;* **more or less** *més o menys*
toilet *el bany/els serveis/el lavabo*

Getting around

a ticket *un bitllet;* **return** *d'anada i tornada*
card expired (on Metro) *títol esgotat*
left *esquerra;* **right** *dreta;* **here** *aquí;* **there** *allí;* **straight on** *recte;* **at the corner** *a la cantonada;* **as far as** *fins a;* **towards** *cap a;* **near** *a prop;* **far** *lluny;* **is it far?** *és lluny?*

Time

In Catalan quarter- and half-hours can be referred to as quarters of the next hour (so, 1.30 is two quarters of 2)

now *ara;* **later** *més tard;* **yesterday** *ahir;* **today** *avui;* **tomorrow** *demà;* **tomorrow morning** *demà pel matí*
morning *el matí;* **midday** *migdia;* **afternoon** *la tarda;* **evening** *el vespre;* **night** *la nit;* **late night** (roughly 1-6am) *la matinada*
at what time…? *a quina hora…?* **in an hour** *en una hora;* **the bus will take two hours (to get there)** *l'autobús trigarà dues hores (en arribar)*
at 2 *a les dues;* **at 8pm** *a les vuit del vespre;* **at 1.30** *a dos quarts de dues/a la una i mitja;* **at 5.15** *a un quart de sis/a las cinc i quart;* **at 22.30** *a vint-i-dos-trenta*

Numbers

0 *zero;* 1 *u, un,una;* 2 *dos, dues;* 3 *tres,* 4 *quatre;* 5 *cinc;* 6 *sis;* 7 *set;* 8 *vuit;* 9 *nou;* 10 *deu;* 11 *onze;* 12 *dotze;* 13 *tretze;* 14 *catorze;* 15 *quinze;* 16 *setze;* 17 *disset;* 18 *divuit;* 19 *dinou;* 20 *vint;* 21 *vint-i-u;* 22 *vint-i-dos, vint-i-dues;* 30 *trenta;* 40 *quaranta;* 50 *cinquanta;* 60 *seixanta;* 70 *setanta;* 80 *vuitanta;* 90 *noranta;* 100 *cent;* 200 *dos-cents, dues-centes,* 1,000 *mil;* 1,000,000 *un milló*

Date & season

Monday *dilluns;* **Tuesday** *dimarts;* **Wednesday** *dimecres;* **Thursday** *dijous;* **Friday** *divendres;* **Saturday** *dissabte;* **Sunday** *diumenge* **January** *gener;* **February** *febrer;* **March** *març;* **April** *abril;* **May** *maig;* **June** *juny;* **July** *juliol;* **August** *agost;* **September** *setembre;* **October** *octobre;* **November** *novembre;* **December** *desembre*
spring *primavera;* **summer** *estiu;* **autumn/fall** *tardor;* **winter** *hivern*

Directory

Spanish Vocabulary

Note that in Catalonia, still more than in the rest of Spain, this language is generally referred to as *castellano* (Castilian), rather than *español*. Like other Latin languages it has different familiar and polite forms of the second person (you). Many young people now use the familiar *tú* most of the time; for foreigners, though, it's always advisable to use the more polite *usted* with anyone you do not know, especially older people. All verbs here are given in the *usted* form. For help in making your way through menus, *see p131*.

Spanish pronunciation

c, before an i or an e, and **z** are like **th** in **th**in;
c in all other cases is as in **c**at;
g, before an i or an e, and **j** are pronounced with a guttural h-sound that doesn't exist in English – like **ch** in Scottish lo**ch**, but much harder;
g in all other cases is as in **g**et;
h at the beginning of a word is normally silent;
ll is pronounced almost like a **y**;
ñ is like **ny** in ca**ny**on.
A single **r** at the beginning of a word and **rr** elsewhere are heavily rolled.

Useful expressions

hello *hola;* **hello** (when answering the phone) *hola, diga*
good morning, good day *buenos días;* **good afternoon, good evening** *buenas tardes;* **good evening** (after dark), **good night** *buenas noches*
goodbye/see you later *adios/hasta luego*
please *por favor;* **thank you (very much)** *(muchas) gracias;* **you're welcome** *de nada*
do you speak English? *¿habla inglés?*
I don't speak Spanish *no hablo castellano*
I don't understand *no entiendo*
can you say that to me in Catalan, please? *¿me lo puede decir en Catalán, por favor?*

what's your name? *¿cómo se llama?*
speak more slowly, please *hable más despacio, por favor*
wait a moment *espere un momento*
Sir/Mr *señor (sr);* **Madam/Mrs** *señora (sra);* **Miss** *señorita (srta)*
excuse me/sorry *perdón*
excuse me, please *oiga* (the standard way to attract someone's attention, politely; literally 'hear me')
OK/fine/(or to a waiter) **that's enough** *vale*
where is...? *¿dónde está...?*
why? *¿porqué?;* **when?** *¿cuándo?;* **who?** *¿quién?;* **what?** *¿qué?;* **where?** *¿dónde?;* **how?** *¿cómo?*
who is it? *¿quién es?;* **is/are there any...?** *¿hay...?*
very *muy;* **and** *y;* **or** *o;* **with** *con;* **without** *sin*
open *abierto;* **closed** *cerrado;* **what time does it open/close?** *¿a qué hora abre/cierra?*
pull (on signs) *tirar;* **push** *empujar*
I would like... *quiero...*(literally, 'I want')
how many would you like? *¿cuántos quiere?*
how much is it *¿cuánto es?*
I like *me gusta*
I don't like *no me gusta*
good *bueno/a;* **bad** *malo/a;* **well/badly** *bien/mal;* **small** *pequeño/a;* **big** *gran, grande;* **expensive** *caro/a;* **cheap** *barato/a;* **hot** (food, drink) *caliente;* **cold** *frío/a*
something *algo;* **nothing** *nada*
more/less *más/menos;* **more or less** *más o menos*
Do you have any change? *¿tiene cambio?*
price *precio;* **free** *gratis;* **discount** *descuento;* **bank** *banco;* **alquilar** to **rent; (en) alquiler** (for) **rent, rental;** **post office** *correos;* **stamp** *sello;* **postcard** *postal;* **toilet** *los servicios*

Getting around

airport *aeropuerto*
railway station *estación de ferrocarril/estación de RENFE* (Spanish railways)
Metro station *estación de Metro* **entrance** *entrada;* **exit** *salida*
car *coche;* **bus** *autobus;* **train** *tren;* **a ticket** *un billete;* **return** *de ida y vuelta*
bus stop *parada de autobus;* **the next stop** *la próxima parada*
excuse me, do you know the way to...? *¿oiga, señor/señora/etc, sabe cómo llegar a...?*
left *izquierda;* **right** *derecha*
here *aquí;* **there** *allí;* **straight on** *recto;* **to the end of the street** *al final de la calle;* **as far as** *hasta;* **towards** *hacia;* **near** *cerca;* **far** *lejos*

Accommodation

do you have a double/single room for tonight/one week? *¿tiene una habitación doble/para una persona para esta noche/una semana?*
we have a reservation *tenemos reserva;* **an inside/outside room** *una habitación interior/exterior* **with/without bathroom** *con/sin baño;* **shower** *ducha;* **double bed** *cama de matrimonio;* **with twin beds** *con dos camas;* **breakfast included** *desayuno incluído;* **air-conditioning** *aire acondicionado;* **lift** *ascensor;* **swimming pool** *piscina*

Time

now *ahora;* **later** *más tarde;* **yesterday** *ayer;* **today** *hoy;* **tomorrow** *mañana;* **tomorrow morning** *mañana por la mañana* **morning** *la mañana;* **midday** *mediodía;* **afternoon/evening** *la tarde;* **night** *la noche;* **late night** (roughly 1-6am) *la madrugada*
at what time...? *¿a qué hora...?;* **at 2** *a las dos;* **at 8pm** *a las ocho de la tarde;* **at 1.30** *a la una y media;* **at 5.15** *a las cinco y cuarto;* **at 22.30** *a veintidos treinta*
in an hour *en una hora*
the bus will take 2 hours (to get there) *el autobus tardará dos horas (en llegar)*

Numbers

0 *cero;* 1 *un, uno, una;* 2 *dos;* 3 *tres;* 4 *cuatro;* 5 *cinco;* 6 *seis;* 7 *siete;* 8 *ocho;* 9 *nueve;* 10 *diez;* 11 *once;* 12 *doce;* 13 *trece;* 14 *catorce;* 15 *quince;* 16 *dieciséis;* 17 *diecisiete;* 18 *dieciocho;* 19 *diecinueve;* 20 *veinte;* 21 *veintiuno;* 22 *veintidos;* 30 *treinta;* 40 *cuarenta;* 50 *cincuenta;* 60 *sesenta;* 70 *setenta;* 80 *ochenta;* 90 *noventa;* 100 *cien;* 200 *doscientos;* 1,000 *mil;* 1,000,000 *un millón*

Date & season

Monday *lunes;* **Tuesday** *martes;* **Wednesday** *miércoles;* **Thursday** *jueves;* **Friday** *viernes;* **Saturday** *sábado;* **Sunday** *domingo*
January *enero;* **February** *febrero;* **March** *marzo;* **April** *abril;* **May** *mayo;* **June** *junio;* **July** *julio;* **August** *agosto;* **September** *septiembre;* **October** *octubre;* **November** *noviembre;* **December** *diciembre*
spring *primavera;* **summer** *verano;* **autumn/fall** *otoño;* **winter** *invierno*

Further Reference

Reading

Guides & walks

Amelang, J, Gil, X & McDonogh, GW: *Twelve Walks through Barcelona's Past* (Aj de Barcelona)
Well thought-out walks by historical themes. Original, and better-informed than many walking guides.
Güell, Xavier: *Gaudí Guide* (Ed. Gustavo Gili)
Handy, with good background on all the architect's work.
Pomés Leiz, Juliet, & Feriche, Ricardo: *Barcelona Design Guide* (Ed. Gustavo Gili)
An eccentrically wide-ranging but engaging listing of everything ever considered 'designer' in BCN.

History, art, architecture, culture

Burns, Jimmy: *Barça: A People's Passion*
The first full-scale history in English of one of the world's most overblown football clubs.
Elliott, JH: *The Revolt of the Catalans* Fascinating, detailed account of the Guerra dels Segadors and the Catalan revolt of the 1640s.
Fernández Armesto, Felipe: *Barcelona: A Thousand Years of the City's Past*
A solid, straightforward history.
Fraser, Ronald: *Blood of Spain*
A vivid oral history of the Spanish Civil War and the tensions that preceded it. It is especially good on the events of July 1936 in Barcelona.
Hughes, Robert: *Barcelona*
The most comprehensive single book about Barcelona: tendentious at times, erratic, but beautifully written, and covering every aspect of the city up to the 1900s.
Kaplan, Temma: *Red City, Blue Period – Social Movements in Picasso's Barcelona*
An interesting book, tracing the interplay of avant-garde art and avant-garde politics in 1900s Barcelona.
Orwell, George: *Homage to Catalonia*
The classic account of Barcelona in revolution, as written by an often bewildered, but always perceptive observer.
Paz, Abel: *Durruti, The People Armed*
Closer to its theme, a biography of the most legendary of Barcelona's anarchist revolutionaries.

Solà-Morales, Ignasi: *Fin de Siècle Architecture in Barcelona* (Ed. Gustavo Gili)
Large-scale and wide-ranging description and evaluation of the city's *Modernista* heritage.
Tóibín, Colm: *Homage to Barcelona*
Evocative and perceptive journey around the city: good on the booming Barcelona of the 1980s, but also excellent on Catalan Gothic, Gaudi and Miró.
Vázquez Montalbán, Manuel: *Barcelonas*
Idiosyncratic but insightful reflections on the city by one of its most prominent modern writers.
Zerbst, Rainer: *Antoni Gaudí*
Lavishly illustrated and comprehensive survey.

Literature

Calders, Pere: *The Virgin of the Railway and Other Stories*
Ironic, engaging, quirky stories by a Catalan writer who spent many years in exile in Mexico.
Català, Victor: *Solitude*
This masterpiece by woman novelist Caterina Albert shocked readers in 1905 with its open, modern treatment of female sexuality.
Marsé, Juan: *The Fallen*
Classic novel of survival in Barcelona during the long *posguerra* after the Civil War.
Martorell, Joanot, & Joan Martí de Gualba:
Tirant lo Blanc
The first European prose novel, from 1490, a rambling, bawdy shaggy-dog story of travels, romances and chivalric adventures.
Mendoza, Eduardo:
City of Marvels and *Year of the Flood*
A sweeping, very entertaining saga of Barcelona between its great Exhibitions, 1888 and 1929, and a more recent novel of passions in the city of the 1950s.
Oliver, Maria Antònia: *Antipodes and Study in Lilac*
Two adventures of Barcelona's first feminist detective.
Rodoreda, Mercè: *The Time of the Doves* and *My Cristina and Other Stories*
A translation of *La Plaça del Diamant*, most widely read of all Catalan novels. Plus a collection of similarly bittersweet short tales.
Vázquez Montalbán, Manuel: *The Angst-Ridden Executive and An Olympic Death*
Two thrillers starring Vázquez Montalbán's detective and gourmet extraordinaire, Pepe Carvalho.

Food & drink

Andrews, Colman: *Catalan Cuisine*
A mine of information on food and much else besides (but also with usable recipes).
Casas, Penelope: *Food and Wines of Spain*
A useful general handbook.

Music

Lluís Llach An icon of the 1960s and early '70s protest against the fascist regime combines melancholic tone with brilliant musicianship. One of the first to experiment with electronic music.
Maria del Mar Bonet Though from Mallorca, del Mar Bonet always sings in Catalan and specialises in her own compositions, North African music and traditional Mallorcan music.
Raimon Has put some of the greatest Catalan language poets, like Ausiàs March, to music.
Els Pets Kings of the Catalan language pop-rock scene, led by the highly charismatic Lluís Gavaldà.
Sangtraït Heavy metal in Catalan.
Pep Sala Excellent musician and survivor of the extremely successful Catalan group Sau. Sala now produces his own music, much of which has a rockabilly and Country influence.
Quimi Portet The brains behind the now defunct but legendary Spanish language band Último de la Fila. His latest CD 'Cançoner electromagnètic' was a big hit.
Sopa de Cabra (Goat Soup) Led by the highly popular Gerard Quintana: good adolescent pop-rock and powerful live set.

Barcelona online

www.barcelonareview.com
Online literary review.
www.barcelonaturisme.com
Tourist information from the city's official tourist authority.
www.bcn.es The city council's information-packed website.
www.diaridebarcelona.com
Local online newspaper with good English content.
www.barnanetro.com Barcelona entertainment listings (in Spanish).
www.timeout.com/barcelona The online city guide, with links and a monthly agenda.
www.vilaweb.com Catalan web portal and links page. In Catalan.
www.vilaweb.com/webcams/ Barcelona webcams links page.

Directory

Advertisers' Index

Maps

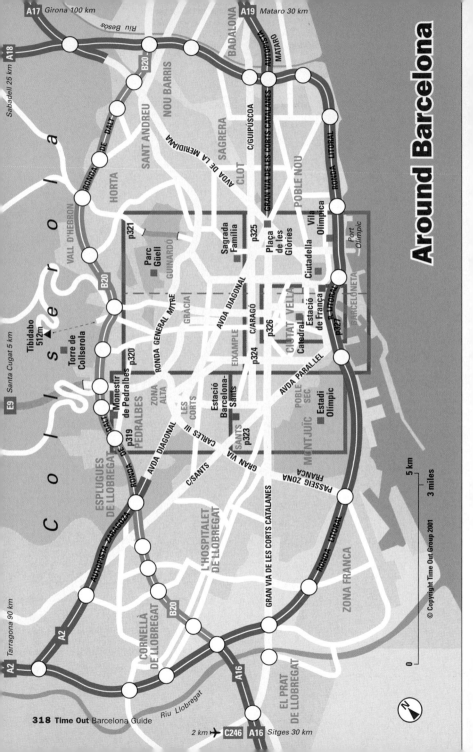

Around Barcelona

A17 *Girona 100 km*
A19 *Mataro 30 km*
A18

Sabadell 25 km **B20**

Santa Cugat 5 km **E9**

Tibidabo
512m ▲
Torre de
Collserola

Tarragona 90 km

A2
A2

AUTOPISTA MATARO

BADALONA

RIU Besòs

Riu Besòs

RONDA DE DALT

NOU BARRIS

SANT ANDREU

SAGRERA

C/GUIPUSCOA

AVDA DE LA MERIDIANA

CLOT

POBLE NOU

RONDA LITORAL

VALL D'HEBRON

HORTA

B20

GRAN VIA DE LES CORTS CATALANES

p321
Parc
Guell
GUINARDÓ

Sagrada
Familia
p325
Plaça
de les
Glòries

Vila
Olímpica

Ciutadella

Port
Olímpic

BARCELONETA

RONDA GENERAL MITRE

GRACIA

AVDA DIAGONAL

C/ARAGÓ

p326

EIXAMPLE

p324

CIUTAT VELLA

Catedral

Estació
de França

p327

Monestir
de Pedralbes
p320

ZONA
ALTA

LES
CORTS

RONDA DE DALT

p319
PEDRALBES

Estació
Barcelona-
Sants

SANTS
p323

CARLES III

GRAN VIA

C/SANTS

AVDA PARALLEL

POBLE
SEC

MONTJUÏC

Estadi
Olímpic

AVDA DIAGONAL

ESPLUGUES
DE LLOBREGAT

AUTOPISTA PEDRALBES

RONDA DE DALT

L'HOSPITALET
DE LLOBREGAT

GRAN VIA DE LES CORTS CATALANES

PASSEIG ZONA FRANCA

RONDA LITORAL

ZONA FRANCA

CORNELLÀ
DE LLOBREGAT

B20

A16

EL PRAT
DE LLOBREGAT

Riu Llobregat

2 km ✈ **C246** **A16** *Sitges 30 km*

318 Time Out Barcelona Guide

0 *5 km*
3 miles

© Copyright Time Out Group 2001

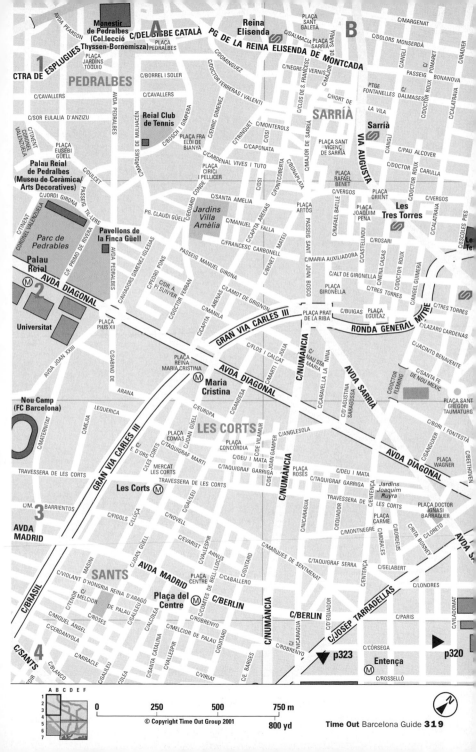

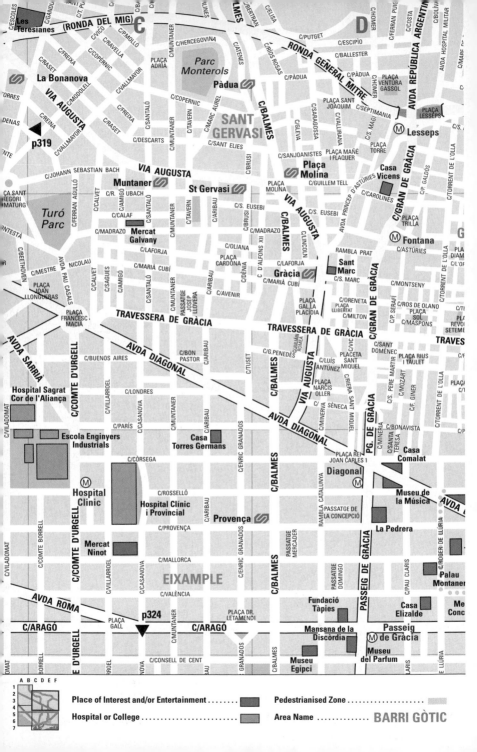

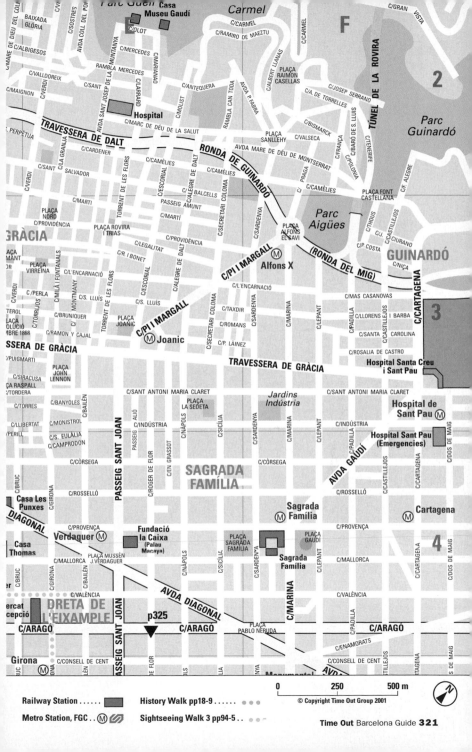

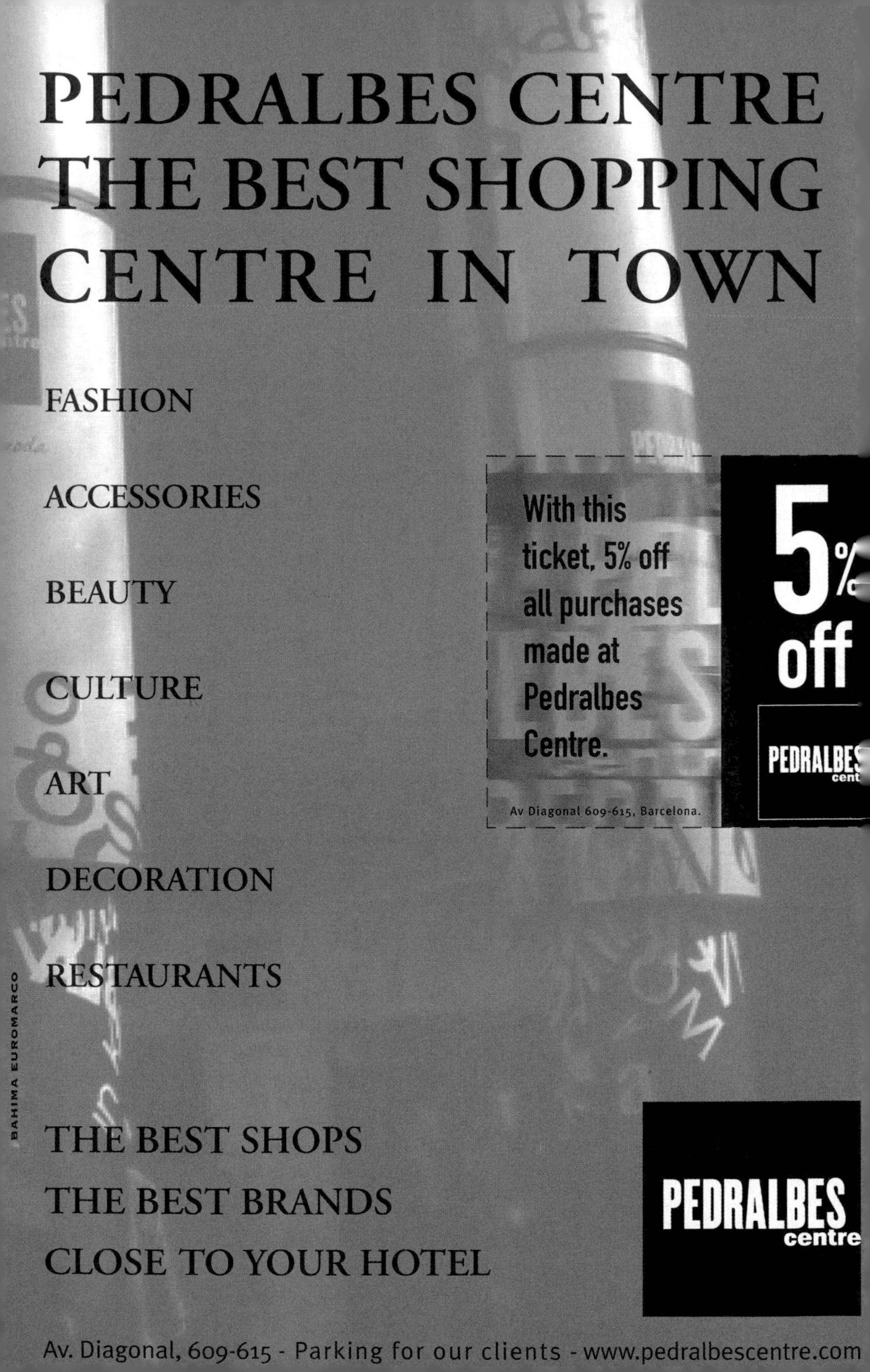
PEDRALBES CENTRE
THE BEST SHOPPING
CENTRE IN TOWN
FASHION
ACCESSORIES
BEAUTY
CULTURE
ART
DECORATION
RESTAURANTS
With this ticket, 5% off all purchases made at Pedralbes Centre.
Av Diagonal 609-615, Barcelona.
5% off
PEDRALBES
THE BEST SHOPS
THE BEST BRANDS
CLOSE TO YOUR HOTEL
PEDRALBES
centre
BAHIMA EUROMARCO
Av. Diagonal, 609-615 - Parking for our clients - www.pedralbescentre.com

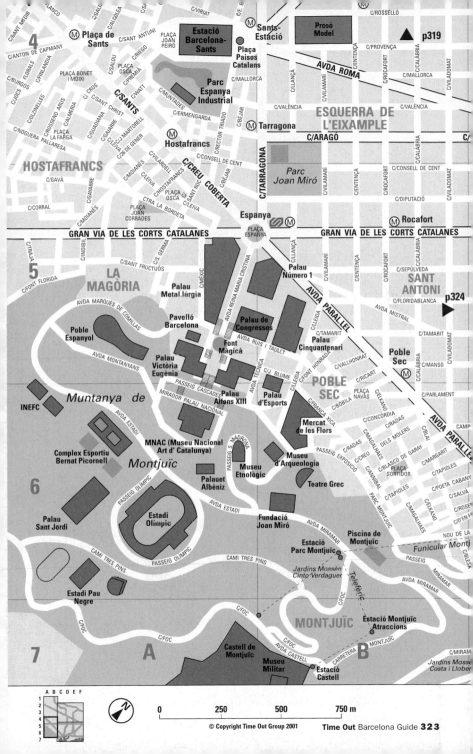

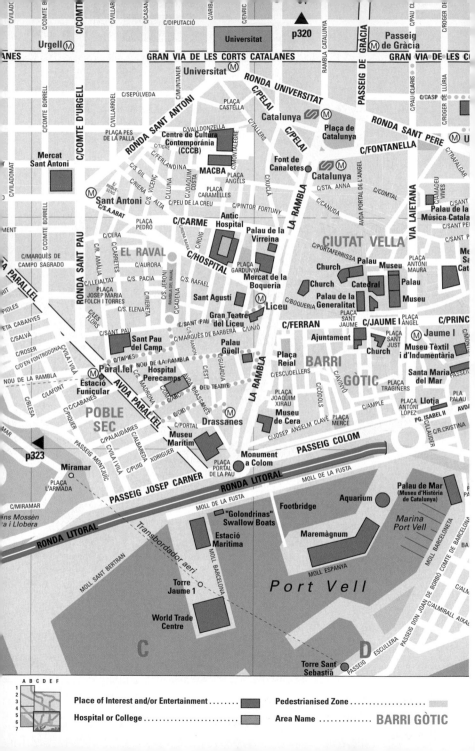

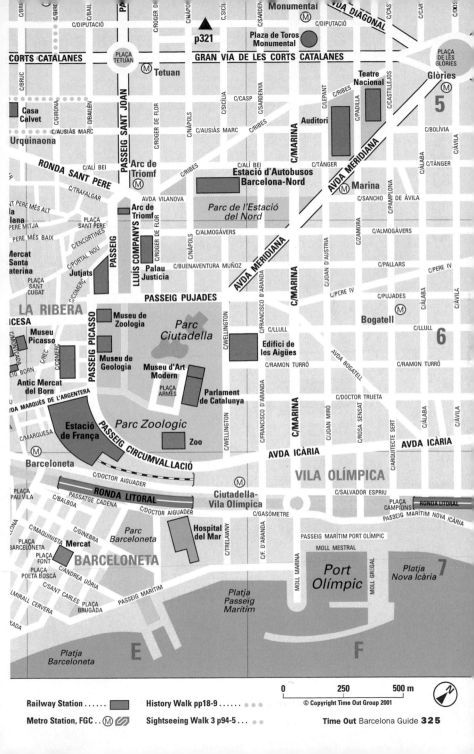

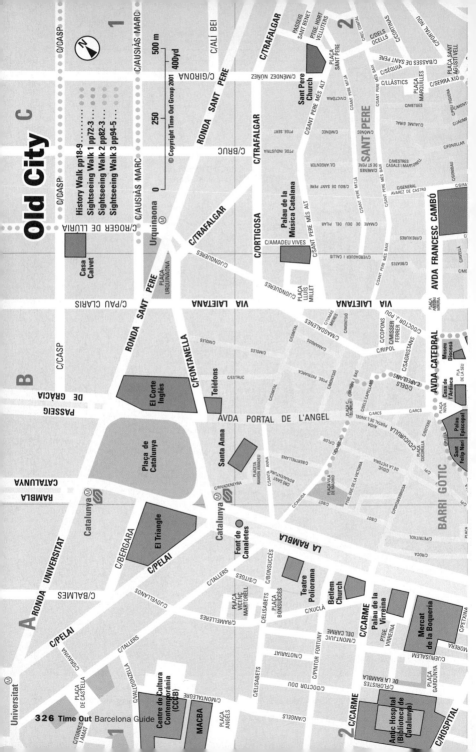

Old City C

History Walk pp18-9 ....
Sightseeing Walk 1 pp72-3 .....
Sightseeing Walk 2 pp82-3 .....
Sightseeing Walk 3 pp94-5 .....

© Copyright Time Out Group 2001

500 m
400yd

0   250   500

Casa Calvet

Palau de la Música Catalana

Sant Pere Church

SANT PERE

AVDA FRANCESC CAMBÓ

PLAÇA URQUINAONA

PLAÇA LLUÍS MILLET

El Corte Inglés

Teléfons

Santa Anna

Plaça de Catalunya

El Triangle

Catalunya

Font de Canaletes

Teatre Poliorama

Betlem Church

Palau de la Virreina

Mercat de la Boqueria

Antic Hospital (Biblioteca de Catalunya)

Centre de Cultura Contemporània (CCCB)

MACBA

Casa de l'Ardiaca

Museu Diocesà

AVDA CATEDRAL

Palau Episcopal

Sant Felip Neri

BARRI GÒTIC

LA RAMBLA

AVDA PORTAL DE L'ANGEL

VIA LAIETANA

RONDA SANT PERE

C/CASP

C/AUSIÀS MARC

C/ROGER DE LLÚRIA

C/BRUC

C/TRAFALGAR

C/ORTIGOSA

C/AMADEU VIVES

PASSEIG DE GRÀCIA

C/FONTANELLA

RONDA UNIVERSITAT

C/PELAI

C/BALMES

C/CARME

C/HOSPITAL

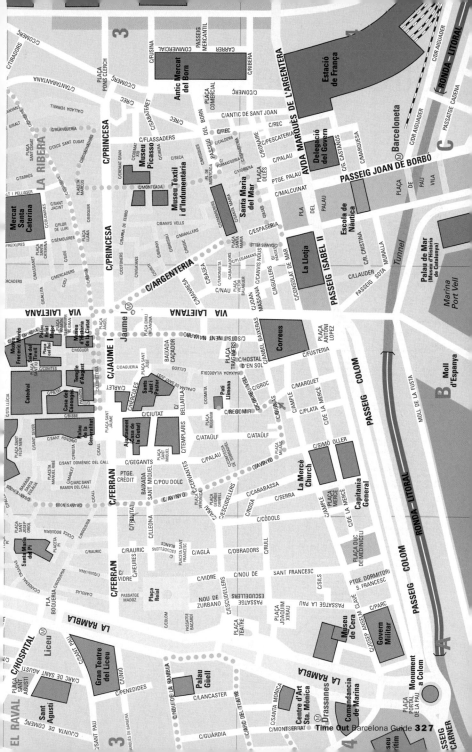

Street Index

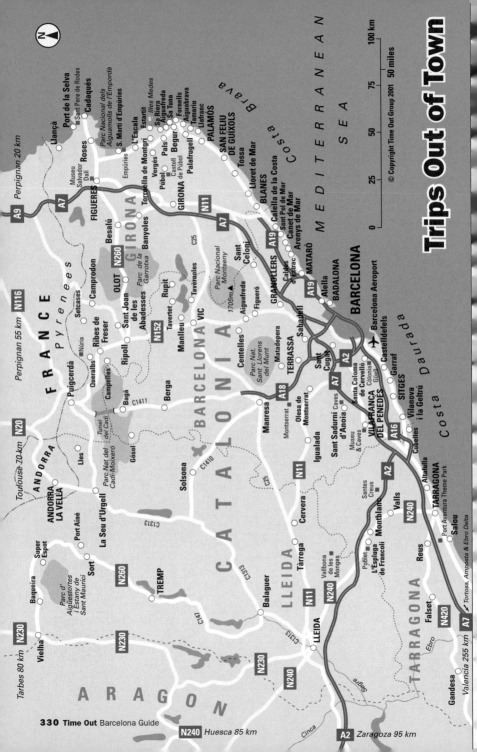

Trips Out of Town

RENFE Local Trains

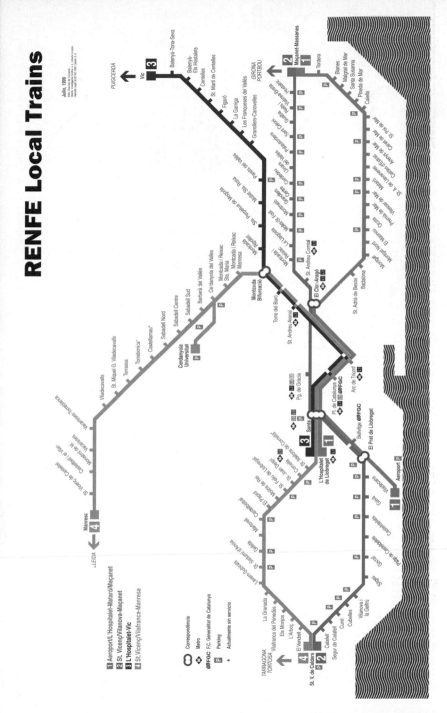

Time Out

Barcelona — Please let us know what you think

About this guide...

1. How useful did you find the following sections?

	Very	Fairly	Not very
In Context	☐	☐	☐
Accommodation	☐	☐	☐
Sightseeing	☐	☐	☐
Eat, Drink, Shop	☐	☐	☐
Arts & Entertainment	☐	☐	☐
Trips Out of Town	☐	☐	☐
Directory	☐	☐	☐
Maps	☐	☐	☐

2. Did you travel to Barcelona...?

Alone ☐   With children ☐
As part of a group ☐   On vacation ☐
On business ☐   To study ☐
With a partner ☐   I live here ☐

3. How long was your trip to Barcelona? (write in)

_____ days

4. Where did you book your trip?

Time Out Classifieds ☐
On the Internet ☐
With a travel agent ☐
Other (write in) ☐

---

5. Where did you first hear about this guide?

Advertising in *Time Out* magazine ☐
On the Internet ☐
From a travel agent ☐
Other (write in) ☐

6. Is there anything you'd like us to cover in greater depth?

_____
_____

7. Are there any places that should/ should not* be included in the guide?
(* delete as necessary)

_____
_____
_____
_____
_____
_____

---

8. How many other people have used this guide?

none ☐ 1 ☐ 2 ☐ 3 ☐ 4 ☐ 5+ ☐

9. What city or country would you like to visit next? (write in)

_____

About other Time Out publications...

10. Have you ever bought/used *Time Out* magazine?

Yes ☐   No ☐

11. Have you ever bought/used any other Time Out City Guides?

Yes ☐   No ☐

If yes, which ones?

_____

12. Have you ever bought/used other Time Out publications?

Yes ☐   No ☐

If yes, which ones?

_____

About you...

13. Title (Mr, Ms etc):

First name: _____
Surname: _____
Address: _____

Postcode: _____
Email: _____
Nationality: _____

14. Date of birth: ☐☐/☐☐/☐☐

15. Sex: male ☐   female ☐

16. Are you...?

Single ☐☐
Married/Living with partner ☐☐

17. What is your occupation? ☐☐☐☐☐☐

18. At the moment do you earn...?

under £15,000 ☐
over £15,000 and up to £19,999 ☐
over £20,000 and up to £24,999 ☐
over £25,000 and up to £39,999 ☐
over £40,000 and up to £49,999 ☐
over £50,000 ☐

☐ Please tick here if you do not want to hear about offers and discounts from Time Out and relevant companies.

Time Out Guides

FREEPOST 20 (WC3187)
LONDON
W1E 0DQ

ISBN	title	retail price	quantity	total
0140289445	Time Out Guide to **Amsterdam**	£10.99		
0140294023	Time Out Guide to **Barcelona**	£11.99		
0140289399	Time Out Guide to **Berlin**	£10.99		
0140293906	Time Out Guide to **Boston**	£11.99		
0140289429	Time Out Guide to **Brussels**	£10.99		
0140286330	Time Out Guide to **Budapest**	£10.99		
0140290788	Time Out Guide to **Chicago**	£10.99		
0141000287	Time Out Guide to **Copenhagen**	£10.99		
0140281738	Time Out Guide to **Dublin**	£10.99		
0140289453	Time Out Guide to **Edinburgh**	£10.99		
0140274537	Time Out Guide to **Florence & Tuscany**	£10.99		
0141000295	Time Out Guide to **Havana**	£11.99		
0140274502	Time Out Guide to **Istanbul**	£10.99		
0140289402	Time Out Guide to **Las Vegas**	£10.99		
0140293868	Time Out Guide to **Lisbon**	£11.99		
0140293884	Time Out Guide to **London**	£10.99		
014029385X	Time Out Guide to **Los Angeles**	£11.99		
0140293876	Time Out Guide to **Madrid**	£10.99		
0140266852	Time Out Guide to **Miami**	£9.99		
014027314X	Time Out Guide to **Moscow**	£9.99		
0140295380	Time Out Guide to **Naples**	£10.99		
0140289461	Time Out Guide to **New Orleans**	£10.99		
0140293922	Time Out Guide to **New York**	£10.99		
0140293892	Time Out Guide to **Paris**	£10.99		
0140289488	Time Out Guide to **Prague**	£10.99		
0140287558	Time Out Guide to **Rome**	£10.99		
0140289364	Time Out Guide to **San Francisco**	£10.99		
014029077X	Time Out Guide to **The South of France**	£10.99		
0140274464	Time Out Guide to **Sydney**	£10.99		
0140293981	Time Out Guide to **Tokyo**	£12.99		
0140293914	Time Out Guide to **Venice**	£11.99		
0140280677	Time Out Guide to **Vienna**	£10.99		
0140284591	Time Out Guide to **Washington, DC**	£10.99		
		+ postage & packing		£1.50
		Total Payment		

Penguin Direct
Penguin Books Ltd
Bath Road
Harmondsworth
West Drayton
Middlesex
UB7 0DA